CHALO! india

Eine neue Ära indischer Kunst | A New Era of Indian Art

PRESTEL
Munich • Berlin • London • New York

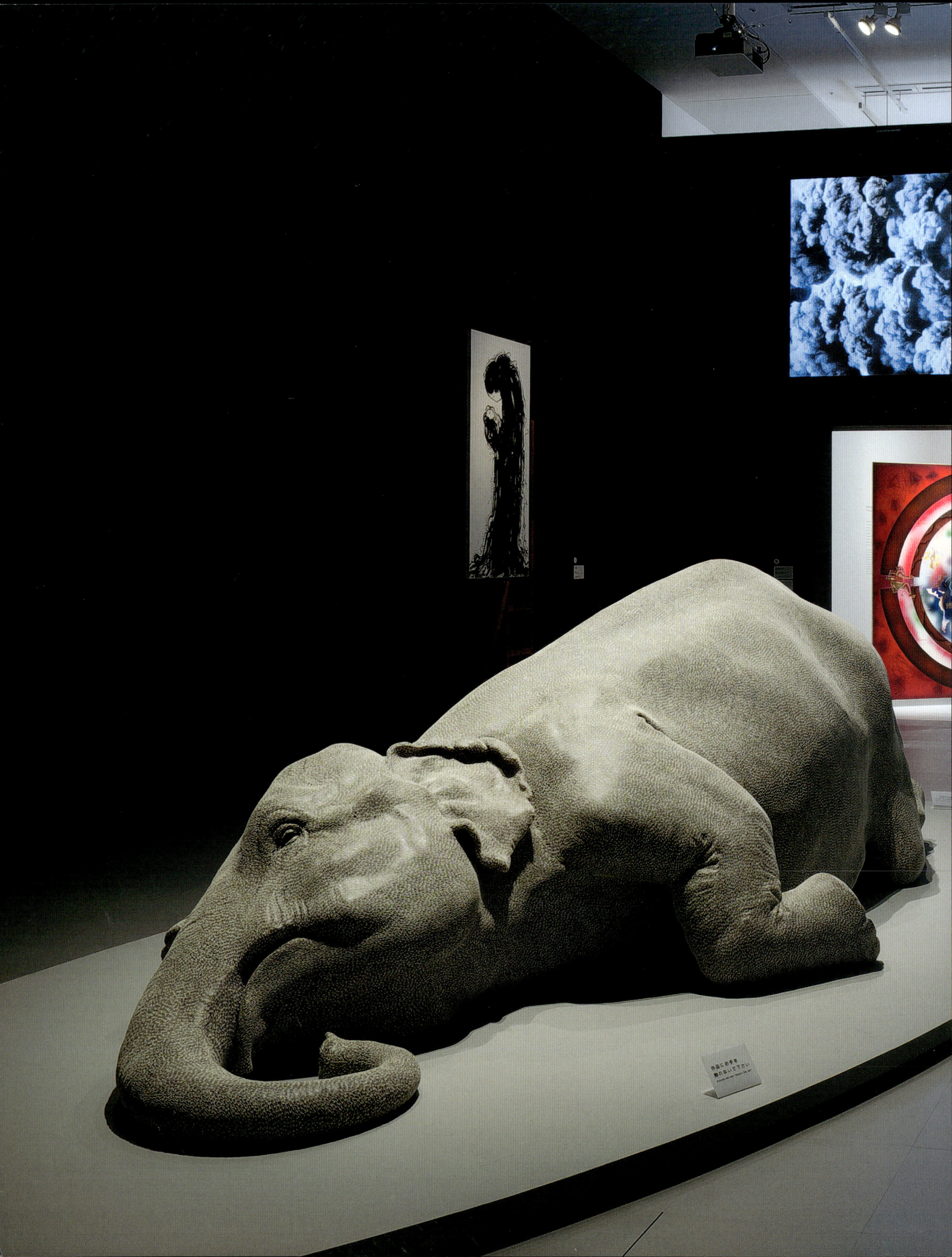

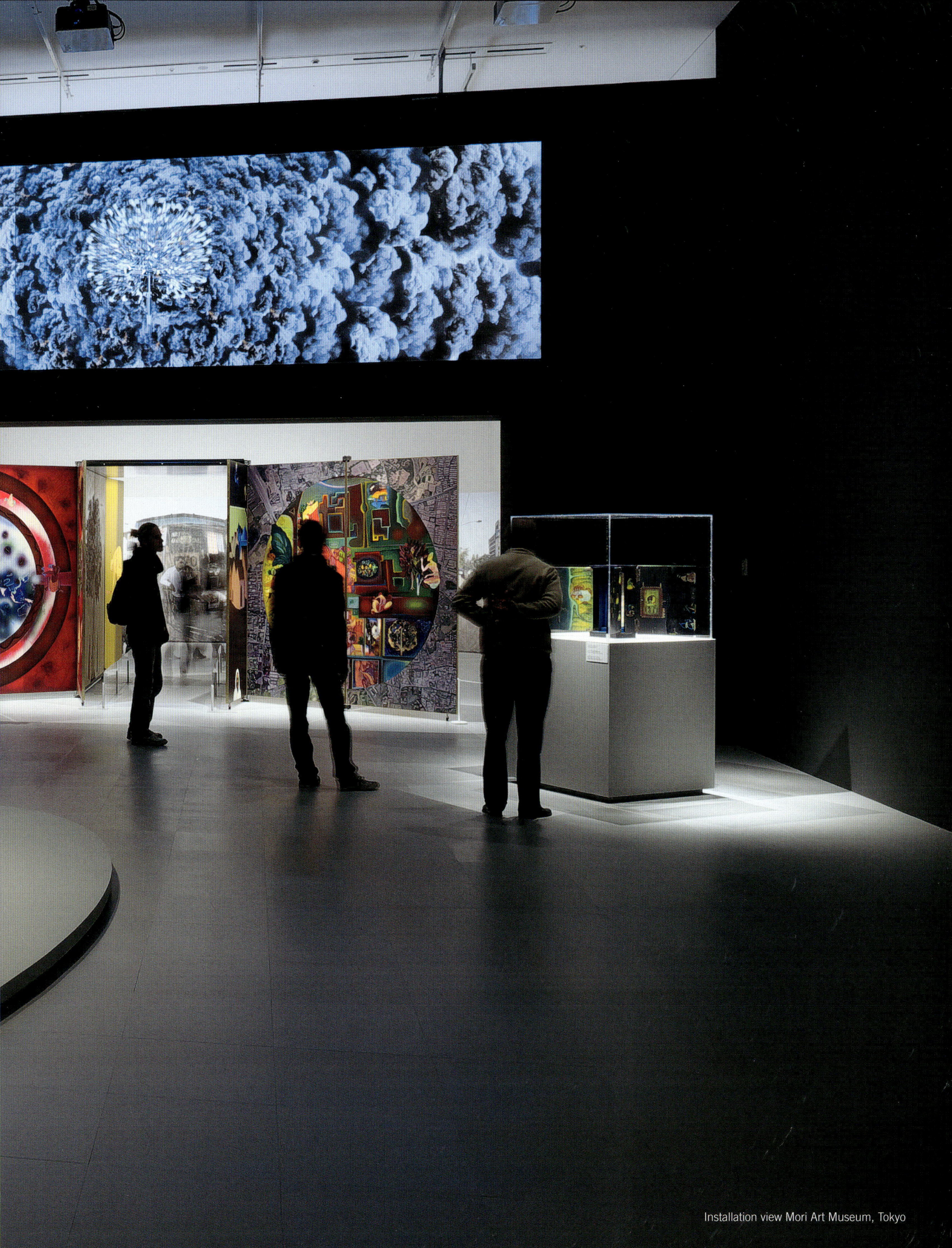

Installation view Mori Art Museum, Tokyo

INHALT | CONTENT

VORWORT

Prof. Karlheinz Essl

Indien zählt neben China zu jenen Regionen der Welt, die in den letzten Dekaden die größten wirtschaftlichen Umbrüche ihrer Geschichte erlebten. Das enorme Wirtschaftswachstum hat die Strukturen dieser Länder tiefgreifend beeinflusst und zu nachhaltigen Veränderungen in der Gesellschaft geführt.

Während das postkommunistische China autokratisch regiert wird, hat sich in Indien der Übergang zu einer demokratischen Staatsform auf beeindruckende Weise vollzogen. China konnte sich als „Werkbank" der Welt etablieren – vor allem im Bereich der Verbrauchsgüterindustrie decken chinesische Produkte einen immer größer werdenden Teil des Weltbedarfs. Indien dagegen hat sich in den letzten Jahren zu einem der Big Player in den Disziplinen IT, Softwareentwicklung, Forschung und Medizin entwickelt. Obwohl sich die Situation der chinesischen in den letzten Jahren zusehends verbessert hat, kann von einer absoluten Freiheit der Kunst nach westlichem Verständnis noch immer keine Rede sein. In Indien dagegen sind die Entfaltungsmöglichkeiten der Künstler in keiner Weise eingeschränkt.

Der beeindruckende wirtschaftliche Fortschritt Indiens hat das Interesse an der künstlerischen Entwicklung des Landes beflügelt: Indische Künstler sind in den letzten Jahren verstärkt in Erscheinung getreten. Sammler aus den USA, Europa und Asien haben die neue indische Kunstszene für sich entdeckt. Werke indischer Künstler erzielen auf Kunstauktionen Höchstpreise.

Meine Kontakte zur indischen Kunstszene reichen bis Anfang der 1990er Jahre zurück. In der National Gallery of Modern Art im Jaipur House, New Dehli, wurde im Jahr 1996 eine Ausstellung mit dem Titel „The Decade of Painting – 1980 to 1990 – Austrian Contemporary Art from the Essl Collection" gezeigt. Mehrfache Reisen nach Indien in den letzten Jahren haben mir die Möglichkeit geboten, die Kunstszene des Landes vertiefend kennen zu lernen.
Angeregt durch deren kraftvolle Vitalität habe ich mich in der Folge entschlossen, im Essl Museum eine Ausstellung zeitgenössischer indischer Kunst auszurichten. Während der Arbeit an diesem Projekt wurden wir auf die Konzeption einer solchen Ausstellung im Mori Art Museum in Tokyo aufmerksam gemacht. Gespräche mit dessen Direktor, Herrn Fumio Nanjo, und der verantwortlichen Kuratorin, Frau Akiko Miki, führten rasch zu der Entscheidung, diese Ausstellung in adaptierter Form zu übernehmen.

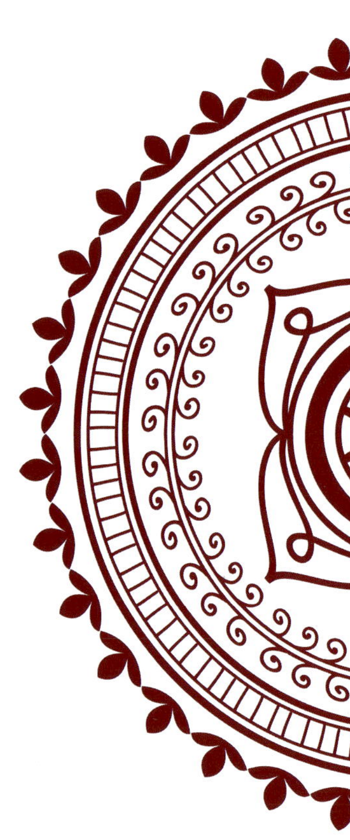

Ich freue mich, diese umfangreiche Schau aktueller indischer Kunst nun im Essl Museum präsentieren zu dürfen und möchte vor allem Herrn Direktor Fumio Nanjo und Frau Akiko Miki für die angenehme Zusammenarbeit sehr herzlich danken. Weiters gilt mein Dank Herrn Günther Oberhollenzer für die kuratorische Begleitung der Ausstellung, Frau Elisabeth Hartmann für die grafische Gestaltung des Kataloges, dem Aufbauteam von Ronald Gollner sowie allen Mitarbeiterinnen und Mitarbeitern des Essl Museums für die erfolgreiche Realisierung dieses ambitionierten Ausstellungsprojektes.

Diese Ausstellung bietet einen umfassenden Einblick in die aktuelle indische Kunstszene, die mit vielfältigen kreativen Konzepten überrascht und weltweit ein immer größer werdendes Publikum in ihren Bann zieht.

PREFACE

Prof. Karlheinz Essl

Like China, India is one of the regions in the world that have lived through the greatest economic transformations in their history in recent decades. The enormous economic growth has had a profound impact on the structures of these countries and resulted in lasting changes in their societies.

While post-communist China has an autocratic system of government, India has impressed the world by its transition to democratic statehood. China has been able to find a place as the "workbench" of the world – particularly in the area of consumer goods; Chinese products are satisfying a growing share of international demand. India, in turn, has developed into one of the big players in the area of IT, software development, research and medicine.
Although the situation of Chinese artists has improved continuously in recent years, they do not really enjoy the kind of absolute freedom of art that is an ideal in the western world. It is different for Indian artists, whose development potential is not restricted in any way.

India's impressive economic progress has spurred interest in the artistic developments of the country. Indian artists have increasingly caught the limelight, and collectors from the USA, Europe and Asia have discovered the new Indian art scene. Works by Indian artists fetch record prices at auctions.

My contacts to the Indian art world go back to the early 1990s. In 1996, an exhibition entitled "The Decade of Painting – 1980 to 1990 – Austrian Contemporary Art from the Essl Collection" was shown at the National Gallery of Modern Art at Jaipur House, New Delhi. Several more recent trips to India have given me the opportunity to gain further insights into the creative scene of the country.

Inspired by the vitality of the contemporary art scene I decided to organise an exhibition of contemporary Indian art at the Essl Museum. During preparations for this project we were made aware of a similar exhibition concept being elaborated at the Mori Art Museum in Tokyo. Talks to the director of the museum, Mr. Fumio Nanjo, and the curator of the show, Ms. Akiko Miki, have soon led us to decide that we would take on this exhibition in an adapted form.

I am very happy to be able to present this comprehensive exhibition of contemporary Indian art at the Essl Museum and would like, first and foremost, to give cordial thanks to Fumio Nanjo and Akiko Miki for the very pleasant co-operation. Furthermore I would like to thank Günther Oberhollenzer for the curatorial support, Elisabeth Hartmann for the graphic design of the catalogue, the installation team of Ronald Gollner, as well as the entire team of the Essl Museum for the successful implementation of this ambitious exhibition project.

This exhibition offers a good impression of the current Indian art scene which surprises by the diversity of its creative concepts and attracts the attention of a growing worldwide audience.

VORWORT

Fumio Nanjo

„Chalo! India. Eine neue Ära indischer Kunst" wurde als Teil der Festivitäten zum fünfjährigen Bestehen unseres Museums erstmals von 22. November 2008 bis 15. März 2009 am Mori Art Museum in Tokio präsentiert. In diesen fünf Jahren war das Mori Art Museum stets bemüht, bei seinen Kunstausstellungen zwei Hauptziele im Auge zu behalten: den Anspruch auf Internationalität einerseits, einen Schwerpunkt auf zeitgenössische Kunst andererseits. Gleichzeitig haben wir der asiatischen Kunst immer einen besonderen Platz eingeräumt, und „Chalo! India", die bisher größte Ausstellung zeitgenössischer indischer Kunst in Japan, ist unser jüngstes Beispiel dafür.

Natürlich machen die gegenwärtigen wirtschaftlichen, kulturellen und städtischen Entwicklungen in Indien dieses Land zu einer der dynamischsten und interessantesten Nationen dieser Erde. Der Ausstellung gingen umfangreiche Recherchen voraus, darunter mehr als 60 Atelierbesuche. Letztendlich wurden 100 Kunstwerke – viele davon gerade erst entstanden – von 27 Künstlerinnen und Künstlern bzw. Künstlergruppen ausgewählt. Die Arbeiten spiegeln die großen Umwälzungen auf allen Ebenen der indischen Gesellschaft wider. Sie geben Einblick in die Lebensgewohnheiten und Hoffnungen der indischen Bevölkerung, eröffnen faszinierende Ausblicke auf die große kulturelle Vielfalt des Landes und setzen sich auch mit aktuellen sozialen Fragen auseinander.

Das Wort „chalo" aus dem Titel der Ausstellung bedeutet auf Hindi so viel wie „Auf geht's, gehen wir" und dient auch als Grußwort. Ich hoffe sehr, dass dieser Gruß – „Auf geht's, Indien" – und die Ausstellung selbst als Einladung wahrgenommen werden, die wunderbare Kulturszene eines unserer größten asiatischen Nachbarländer zu entdecken. Es wäre wünschenswert, wenn dieses Projekt zu weiteren kulturellen Austauschen zwischen Indien, Österreich und Japan führen würde.

Abschließend möchte ich mich sehr herzlich beim Ehepaar Essl und dem Team des Essl Museums für die Realisierung dieser Ausstellung bedanken. Ich hoffe, dass damit der Grundstein für eine möglicherweise noch aktivere künftige Zusammenarbeit zwischen unseren Institutionen gelegt wurde.

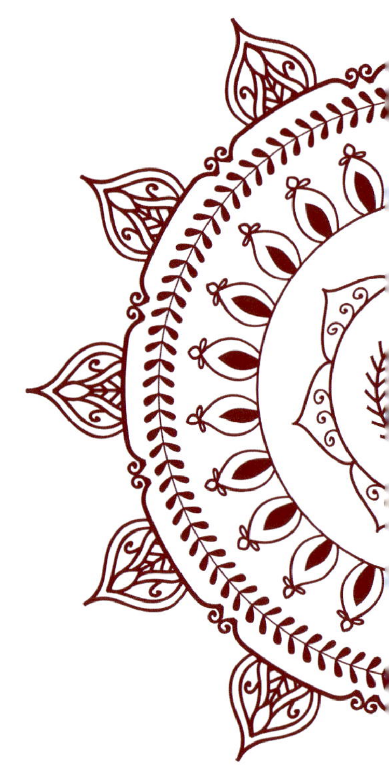

Fumio Nanjo ist Direktor des Mori Art Museums, Tokyo.

PREFACE

Fumio Nanjo

"Chalo! India: A New Era of Indian Art" was first held at the Mori Art Museum, Tokyo, from November 22, 2008, until March 15, 2009, as part of the celebrations of the fifth anniversary of our museum's founding. Over these five years the Mori Art Museum has endeavoured to present exhibitions of art while keeping sight of our two main missions: to always maintain an international outlook and to always remain focused on the contemporary. At the same time we have given particular emphasis to the contemporary art of Asia, and the latest example of this was "Chalo! India" the largest show of contemporary Indian art ever held in Japan.

It goes without saying that the economic, cultural, and urban development occurring in India today make it one of the most dynamic and interesting nations in the world. Much research went into planning this exhibition, including over 60 visits to artists' studios. Ultimately, over 100 artworks – many of them new – by 27 artists and artist groups were selected. The works reflect the transformation that is occurring at all levels of Indian society today. They shed light on the lifestyles and hopes of Indian citizens, provide fascinating indications of the country's diverse popular and urban cultures and also address current social issues.

The word "chalo", used here in the exhibition title, means "let's go" in Hindi, and can be considered as a form of greeting. It is my sincere hope that this greeting – "Let's go India" – and the exhibition itself serve as an invitation to explore the wonderful culture of one of our largest Asian neighbours, and ultimately leads to further cultural exchange between India, Austria and Japan.

Finally, I would like to extend my sincere thanks to Mr. and Mrs. Essl and the staff of the Essl Museum for realizing this exhibition. I hope it becomes a stepping stone towards even more interaction between our two institutions in the future.

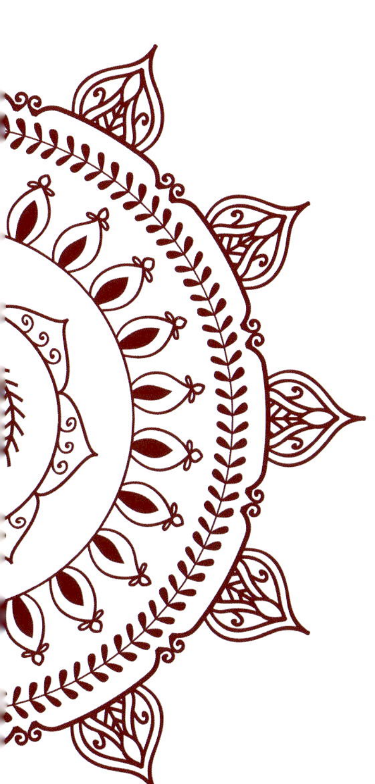

Fumio Nanjo is director of the Mori Art Museum, Tokyo.

CHALO! INDIA.
Eine neue Ära indischer Kunst | A New Era of Indian Art

Akiko Miki

Neue Autos – Toyotas, Fiats, und Mercedes' – sausen mit hoher Geschwindigkeit dahin. Plötzlich taucht ein langsam fahrender, schäbiger, alter und mit Passagieren überladener Bus vor ihnen auf. Die Fahrer geraten in Panik, bremsen und wechseln die Spur, aber schon bald darauf kommen ihnen ein von einem Kamel gezogener Wagen, Fahrräder und ein Minibike entgegen – sie sind ohne Rücksicht auf Verkehrsregeln in der falschen Richtung unterwegs. Während die Fahrer noch mühsam diesen Hindernissen auszuweichen versuchen, tauchen unablässig neue Probleme auf. Schließlich wird die Straße von einer Herde Ziegen komplett blockiert. Edward Luce, ehemaliger Korrespondent für die Financial Times in Delhi, vergleicht den wirtschaftlichen Fortschritt Indiens mit den „Schnellstraßen" des Landes und verwendet dafür Ausdrücke wie „unterschiedliche Geschwindigkeiten" und „schizophren".[1] Dieses Chaos, das die meisten Menschen schockiert, die Indien zum ersten Mal bereisen, kann als symbolisch für viele Aspekte des Lebens im heutigen Indien angesehen werden. Es liegt etwas zutiefst Demokratisches in der bunten Vielfalt von unterschiedlich schnellen Fortbewegungsmitteln und dem Gemisch von Tieren und Menschen, die alle zusammen unterwegs sind. Sich auf diesen Straßen zu behaupten erfordert ein hohes Maß an Wachsamkeit, Navigationsgeschick und Geduld. Das Chaos und der Tumult sind außergewöhnlich eindrucksvoll und vermitteln ein Gefühl großer Vitalität, Energie und Offenheit für neue Möglichkeiten.

„Chalo! India. Eine neue Ära indischer Kunst" präsentiert den gegenwärtigen Stand der indischen zeitgenössischen Kunst und spürt den großen Veränderungen der letzten Jahre nach. Die Ausstellung zeigt die Werke von Künstlern, die sich durch Bearbeitung von Themen aus ihrer Alltagsumgebung mit den Realitäten ihrer Gesellschaft und ihrer Zeit auseinandersetzen und sie durch ihre Kunst in ein Theater des Lebens transformieren. „Chalo!" bedeutet auf Hindi so etwas wie „Gehen wir!" oder „Los geht's!". Diese Ausstellung ist eine Einladung zu einer Begegnung mit der neuen Kreativität und Energie der zeitgenössischen indischen Kunst. Die Kunstwerke vermitteln einen Eindruck von „India now", und jeder Besucher mag bei ihrer Betrachtung unterschiedliche Denkweisen für sich entdecken. Indien ist schon seit alters her eine Quelle der Faszination und motiviert viele Menschen es zu bereisen. Im Laufe der Geschichte sind viele von ihnen mit den unterschiedlichsten Ideen und Motivationen nach Indien aufgebrochen. Alexander der Große, der buddhistische Priester Xuanzang, Christoph Columbus (der aller-

New cars – Toyotas, Fiats, and Mercedes Benzes – breeze along at high speed. Suddenly, a slow, rickety old bus, overloaded with passengers, looms up in the road ahead of them. The drivers panic, braking and changing lanes, but soon are confronted by a wagon pulled by a camel, bicycles, and a mini-bike coming toward them – going the wrong way with no regard for the rules. As the drivers struggle to somehow avoid these obstacles, new problems appear one after the other. Finally, the street is completely blocked by a herd of goats. Edward Luce, former Delhi correspondent for the *Financial Times,* compares Indian economic progress to the country's "expressways," describing it with words like "multi-speed" and "schizophrenic".[1] This chaos, which shocks most people who visit Indian cities for the first time, is symbolic of many aspects of life in today's India. There is something extremely democratic about the wide assortment of vehicles, each moving at a different speed, and the mix of people and animals moving along together. Competing with everyone else on these streets requires a high level of alertness, negotiating skill, and patience. This chaos and commotion is strangely impressive, and it suggests the presence of great vitality, energy and openness to new possibilities.

"Chalo! India. A New Era of Indian Art" explores the present state of Indian contemporary art and the great changes it has gone through in recent years; examining the work of artists who attempt to question the reality of the society and age in which they live, by taking subject matter from their everyday surroundings and transforming them through their art into a theatre of life. "Chalo!" means "Let's go!" in Hindi, and this exhibition is an invitation on a journey to encounter the new creativity and energy of Indian contemporary art. It is a visit to "India now" via these works of art, and an exploration of diverse ways of thinking that each visitor may discover for him or herself. India has been a source of fascination since ancient times, motivating many people to embark on a journey. Throughout history, many have set out for India with different ideas and purposes in mind: Alexander the Great, the Buddhist priest Xuanzhang, Columbus (although he arrived in America, not in India), Vasco da Gama, Rudyard Kipling, the Beatles, *Hotta Yoshie, Yokoo Tadanori,* and, in recent years, businessmen from all over the world. What will visitors discover about India? What journeys of thought will they pursue when they experience this kaleidoscopic and uniquely creative array of art, which reveals many intriguing aspects of India in this post-colonial, global age at the beginning of the 21st century? This friendly "Chalo!" is not an invitation to seek a

„Chalo!" bedeutet auf Hindi so etwas wie „Gehen wir!" oder „Los geht's!". Diese Ausstellung ist eine Einladung zu einer Begegnung mit der neuen Kreativität und Energie der zeitgenössischen indischen Kunst.

"Chalo!" means "Let's go!" in Hindi, and this exhibition is an invitation on a journey to encounter the new creativity and energy of Indian contemporary art.

Das freundliche „Chalo!" ist (...) eine Aufforderung, einen intimen Blick auf die Spuren zu werfen, die das reale Leben mit all seinen Träumen, Hoffnungen, Komplexitäten und Widersprüchlichkeiten hinterlässt.
This friendly "Chalo!" is (...) a call to take an intimate look at traces of real life, with all its dreams and hopes, complexities and contradictions.

dings statt in Indien in Amerika landete), Vasco da Gama, Rudyard Kipling, die Beatles, der Schriftsteller Hotta Yoshie, der Künstler Yokoo Tadanori und in letzter Zeit Geschäftsleute aus aller Welt. Was werden die Besucher der Ausstellung über Indien erfahren? Welche Gedankenreisen werden sie angesichts dieser kaleidoskopisch bunten und einzigartig kreativen Bandbreite an Kunstwerken vollziehen, die so viele faszinierende Aspekte Indiens in diesem post-kolonialen Zeitalter zu Beginn des 21. Jahrhunderts enthüllen? Das freundliche "Chalo!" ist keine Einladung, ein Land der geheimnisvollen Illusionen aufzusuchen, sondern eine Aufforderung, einen intimen Blick auf die Spuren zu werfen, die das reale Leben mit all seinen Träumen, Hoffnungen, Komplexitäten und Widersprüchlichkeiten hinterlässt. Dieses Wort, das die Menschen zum Aufbruch ermuntert, kann auch als Verkörperung der vielschichtigen Dynamik und unglaublichen Veränderungen der indischen Gesellschaft angesehen werden. Der faszinierte Blick der Welt ruht auf Indien. Man erlebt die Wirkung der zeitgenössischen indischen Kunst auf die internationale Kunstszene und Denkweisen, die zu Migrationen, fließenden Veränderungen, amorphen Gebilden und Grenzüberschreitungen führen.[2)]

Hintergrund: Von den 1990er Jahren ins 21. Jahrhundert

In der Meinung von Geeta Kapur, der wichtigsten Kritikerin zeitgenössischer indischer Kunst, stellt die gegenwärtige Situation eine Erweiterung der Trends der 1990er, einer Periode des revolutionären Wandels, dar.[3)] Die Dekade begann mit der Ermordung von Rajiv Gandhi, der schnellen Entscheidung für Narasimha Rao von der nationalen Kongress-Partei als neuen Premierminister und den von Rao unverzüglich umgesetzten marktwirtschaftlichen Reformen. Die Öffnung des Marktes und der Abbau des seit der Unabhängigkeit etablierten sozialistischen Wirtschaftssystems brachten eine Flut von ausländischem Kapital nach Indien. Die Städte wurden mit ausländischen Produkten überschwemmt, was zornige Proteste der lokalen Industrien nach sich zog. Nach der Zerstörung der Babri-Moschee in Ayodhya durch Hindu-Fundamentalisten entzündeten sich schwelende religiöse Ressentiments und es kam zu gewalttätigen Zwischenfällen im ganzen Land. Das gefährdete die Trennung von Politik und Religion, einem Grundprinzip der indischen Nation, sowie die Toleranz für Viel-

land of mysterious illusions, but a call to take an intimate look at traces of real life, with all its dreams and hopes, complexities and contradictions. This word, that encourages people to move forward, can also be perceived as encapsulating the multi-vectored dynamic movement, and tremendous changes, of Indian society; the fascinated gaze of the world focused on India; the impact of contemporary Indian art on the international art scene; and ways of thinking that entail migration, flux, amorphousness and boundary crossing.[2)]

Background: From the 1990s to the 21st Century

Geeta Kapur, the foremost critic of contemporary Indian art, says that the current situation is an extension of the trends of the 1990s, a period of revolutionary change.[3)] The decade began with the assassination of Rajiv Gandhi, the quick selection of Narasimha Rao of the National Congress Party as the new Prime Minister, and the free-market economic reforms that Rao rapidly put into effect. The opening up of the market, and the dismantling of the socialist economic system that had been in place since independence, brought a flood of foreign capital into India. The cities became inundated with foreign products, arousing angry protest from local industry. Beginning with the destruction of the Babri Mosque in Ayodhya by Hindu fundamentalists, smouldering religious resentments surfaced and violent incidents broke out all over the country. This threatened the separation between politics and religion, a founding principle of the Indian nation, and the tolerance for diversity that has characterized India's history and culture. New tensions appeared between India and Pakistan, when the Vajpayee government resumed nuclear testing and Pakistan responded with its own nuclear tests. Around 2003, however, the two countries began to move in the direction of reconciliation, and the peaceful mood was conducive to greater prosperity. The rate of economic growth reached 9 percent in 2007. Ironically, however, this prosperity was accompanied by greater terrorist activity, exemplified by the Mumbai train bombings of 2006 that resulted in more than 200 casualties. At the same time, economic growth transformed the urban landscape of India. The suburbs of large cities like Delhi, Mumbai, Bangalore, and Hyderabad are taking on a new, more artificial look as modern high-rise condominiums and shopping

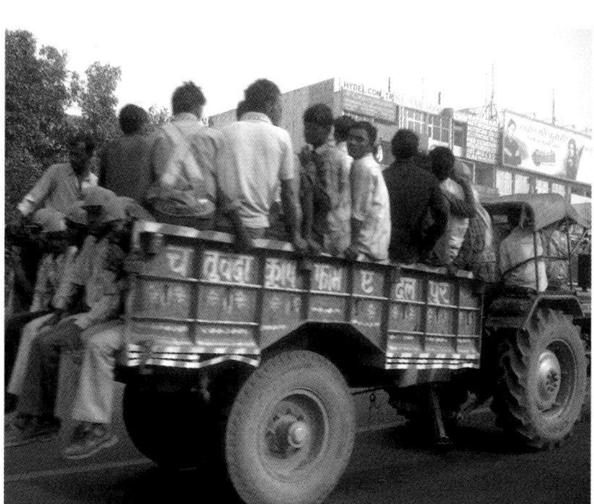
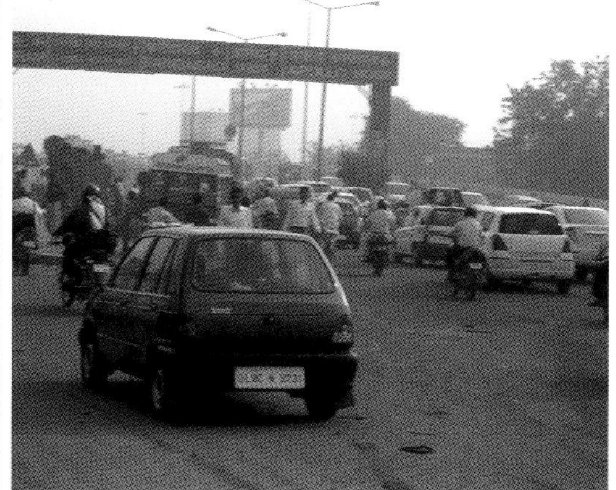
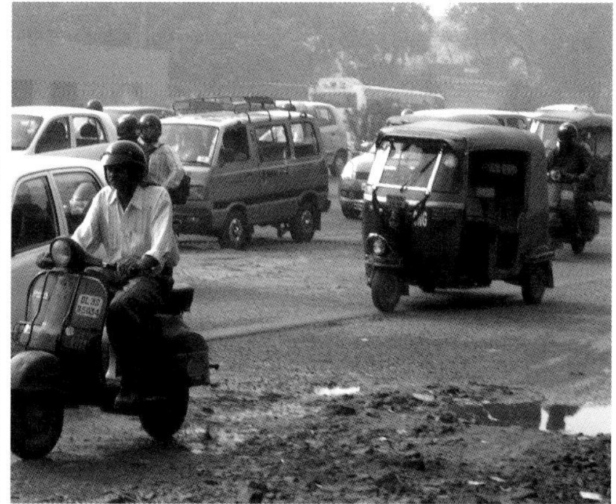

Indische Impressionen / Indian impressions

falt, die Indiens Geschichte und Kultur auszeichnet. Neue Spannungen zwischen Indien und Pakistan entstanden, als die Regierung Vajpayee die Atomtests wieder aufnahm und Pakistan seinerseits mit Atomtests reagierte. Um das Jahr 2003 gingen die beiden Länder jedoch auf Versöhnungskurs, und die friedliche Stimmung förderte auch den wirtschaftlichen Wohlstand. Im Jahr 2007 betrug das Wirtschaftswachstum neun Prozent. Ironischerweise wurde dieser Wohlstand jedoch von stärkeren terroristischen Aktivitäten begleitet, wie zum Beispiel dem Bombenattentat auf einen Zug in Mumbai im Jahr 2006, das mehr als 200 Todesopfer forderte. Gleichzeitig veränderte das Wirtschaftswachstum die urbane Welt Indiens. Die Vororte großer Städte wie Delhi, Mumbai, Bangalore und Hyderabad erhalten durch die überall aus dem Boden schießenden vielgeschossigen Apartmenthäuser und Shopping Center ein neues, künstlicheres Erscheinungsbild. Wie die Massenmedien berichten, träumt der neu entstandene „Mittelstand" von einem luxuriöseren Lebensstil und begehrt mehr materielle Güter. Da Armut immer noch weit verbreitet ist, wird das Einkommensgefälle ständig größer.

Anfang der 90er Jahre begannen einige in den 40ern geborene Künstler, darunter Vivan Sundaram oder Nalini Malani, die bereits höchst eigenständige Stile entwickelt hatten, gleichsam als Reaktion auf diese Veränderungen in der Gesellschaft, mit neuen Medien wie Video und Installationen zu experimentieren. Künstler, die in den späten 50er, 60er oder sogar 70er Jahren des 20. Jahrhunderts geboren wurden, begannen eine wesentlichere Rolle in der Kunstwelt zu spielen oder aktiver die Aufmerksamkeit auf ihre Arbeiten zu lenken. Die jüngere Künstlergeneration widmete sich neuen Techniken, aber auch unterschiedlichen Themen, beispielsweise dem Geschlechterverhältnis oder der Konsumgesellschaft, wodurch die gesamte Kunstszene vielfältiger und vielschichtiger wurde. Die Jüngeren hatten die Kolonialzeit nie persönlich erlebt und begannen ihre Laufbahn inmitten der Strömungen der Postmoderne, der Globalisierung und wirtschaftlichen Liberalisierung. Daher hatten sie auch wenig Interesse an der Betonung ihrer „Indisch-heit" in Bezug auf Geschichte, Kultur und nationales Temperament, die der früheren Generation noch ein wichtiges Anliegen war. Außerdem tendierten sie in ihren Reaktionen auf die Gegebenheiten ihrer Gesellschaft und ihres Alltagslebens ganz eindeutig zu einem internationalen Kunstvokabular. Wie andere nicht-westliche Künstler waren jedoch auch sie mit der paradoxen Situation konfrontiert, nur dann Anerkennung als „echte" indische Künstler zu erhalten, wenn ihre indische Identität in ihren Kunstwerken klar zum Ausdruck kam.[4)]

Diese neuen Entwicklungen standen natürlich in engem Zusammenhang mit Veränderungen in der globalen indischen Kunstwelt. Auch vor den 90ern gab es vor allem in Mumbai viele Gemäldegalerien, aber erst gegen Ende der 90er begannen alternative Kunsträume und neue Galerien, einige davon gänzlich der Medienkunst gewidmet, aufzutauchen. Im Jahr 2008 errichteten die Poddars, Mutter und Sohn, die als private Kunstsammler Berühmtheit errungen hatten, ein privates Museum mit einer riesigen Ausstellungsfläche. Damit stand nun der experimentellen Kunst ein wesentlich

centres sprout up everywhere. As the mass media continues to report, newly emerged "middle-income" earners dream of a more luxurious lifestyle and are anxious to buy more material goods, but many people are still poor and the income gap is expanding.

In art, as soon as entering the 90s, some artists born in the 40s such as Vivan Sundaram or Nalini Malani, who had already been developing highly original styles, started experimenting with new media such as video and installation, as if responding to these changes in society. Younger generation artists, who were born in the late 50s, 60s, and even 70s, began to play a more central role in the art scene or show their work more actively. Different issues, like gender and consumerism, as well as new techniques were further explored by these younger artists, and the overall art scene became more diverse and multifaceted. The younger generation had no experience of the colonial era, and they began their careers surrounded by the currents of postmodernism, globalization, and economic liberalization. As a result, they had little interest in the sort of "Indian-ness" rooted in Indian history, culture, and national temperament that had been a common concern of the previous generation. Moreover, they clearly tended to adopt an international artistic vocabulary for commenting on their own society and everyday reality. Like other non-Western artists, however, they were confronted with the paradoxical situation of receiving international recognition as "genuine" Indian artists only if they inserted codes of Indian identity into their art.[4)]

These new developments were naturally closely related to changes in the overall art environment. There had been many galleries dealing in paintings, especially in Mumbai, before the 90s, but alternative spaces as well as new galleries began to appear in the late 90s, including some devoted entirely to media art. In 2008, a private museum with a huge exhibition space was established by the Poddar's, a mother and son, famous as private collectors. Thus, the number of venues available for experimental art has expanded dramatically. And since the 90s, Indian artists have had many more opportunities to show overseas: both in exhibitions focusing on Asian art, such as the Asia-Pacific Triennial of Contemporary Art and the Fukuoka Asian Art Triennale; and in the growing number of large international events held throughout the world. By participating in such shows, they have obtained a more objective perception of their own activities, as well as seeing much non-Western art for the first time.

In the last few years, there are also some significant exhibitions focusing on contemporary Indian art organized by major foreign art institutions,[5)] but the most remarkable success has been in the market. Auction houses and new corporately-owned commercial galleries opened in the major cities, and Indian art suddenly become an object of speculative investment, reaching a peak in 2006. It is said that things have settled down somewhat recently, but we still hear news of incredible sums being spent on Indian art at auctions in New York and London.

Art critic Ranjit Hoskote points out that Indian artists in the 1990s were engaged in the "de-classicization" of art

Künstler, die in den späten 50er, 60er oder sogar 70er Jahren des 20. Jahrhunderts geboren wurden, begannen eine wesentlichere Rolle in der Kunstwelt zu spielen oder aktiver die Aufmerksamkeit auf ihre Arbeiten zu lenken. (...) Die Jüngeren hatten die Kolonialzeit nie persönlich erlebt und begannen ihre Laufbahn inmitten der Strömungen der Postmoderne, der Globalisierung und wirtschaftlichen Liberalisierung.

Younger generation artists, who were born in the late 50s, 60s, and even 70s, began to play a more central role in the art scene or show their work more actively. (...) The younger generation had no experience of the colonial era, and they began their careers surrounded by the currents of postmodernism, globalization, and economic liberalization.

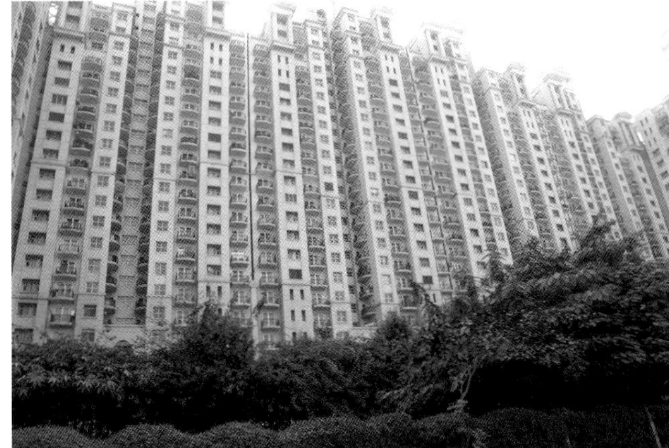

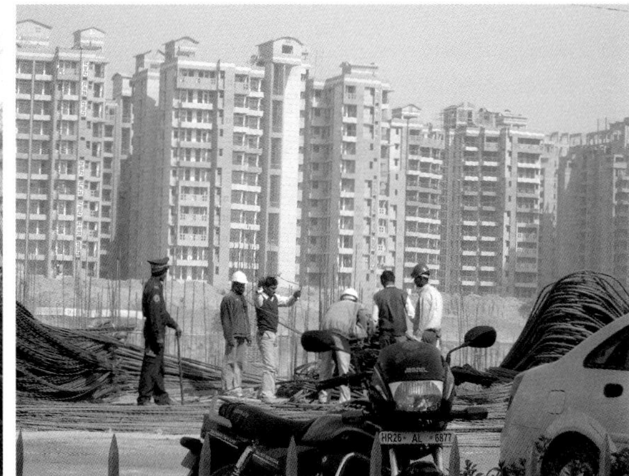

Indische Impressionen / Indian impressions

Seit den 90ern haben indische Künstler auch wesentlich mehr Gelegenheit, im Ausland auszustellen: sowohl in Ausstellungen asiatischer Kunst (...) als auch in einer wachsenden Anzahl von großen internationalen Kunstausstellungen in der ganzen Welt.
And since the 1990s, Indian artists have had many more opportunities to show overseas: both in exhibitions focusing on Asian art (...) and in the growing number of large international events held throughout the world.

Heute, gegen Ende der ersten Dekade des 21. Jahrhunderts, gerät die indische Kunst immer mehr in den Strudel des internationalen Kunstmarktes und der internationalen Kritik, und es ist keine Übertreibung zu sagen, dass sie in ein neues Stadium eingetreten ist.
Today, approaching the end of the 2000s, Indian art is being drawn more and more into the maelstrom of the international art market and critical opinion, so it is no exaggeration to say that it has entered a new stage in its history.

vergrößerter Raum zur Verfügung. Seit den 90ern haben indische Künstler auch wesentlich mehr Gelegenheit, im Ausland auszustellen: Sowohl in Ausstellungen asiatischer Kunst, wie etwa der „Asia-Pacific Triennial of Contemporary Art" und der „Fukuoka Asian Art Triennial", als auch in einer wachsenden Anzahl von großen internationalen Kunstausstellungen in der ganzen Welt. Die Beteiligung an solchen Ausstellungen ermöglicht ihnen eine objektivere Wahrnehmung ihrer eigenen Aktivitäten und eröffnet ihnen auch erstmals die Möglichkeit, eine große Bandbreite an nicht-westlicher Kunst zu sehen.

Auch wenn es in den letzten Jahren einige wichtige von großen ausländischen Kunsteinrichtungen organisierte Ausstellungen zeitgenössischer indischer Kunst gab[5], erlebten die Künstler den durchschlagendsten Erfolg doch am Kunstmarkt. Auktionshäuser und neue kommerziell geführte Galerien eröffneten in den großen Städten, und indische Kunst wurde plötzlich zum begehrten Spekulationsobjekt für Investoren. Den Höhepunkt erreichte diese Entwicklung im Jahr 2006. Man sagt, die Lage hätte sich seither ein wenig beruhigt, aber immer noch hört man, dass bei Auktionen in New York und London unglaubliche Summen für indische Kunst bezahlt werden.

Der Kunstkritiker Ranjit Hoskote erklärt, dass indische Künstler in den 90ern viele der „klassischen" Elemente der indischen Kunstpraxis hinter sich gelassen hätten.[6] Man könnte auch sagen, dass sie mit ihren Reaktionen auf die indische Realität neue Ausdrucksformen geschaffen haben, wobei in einem heiklen Balanceakt die dualistische Gegenüberstellung von „Indien hier – Westen dort" vermieden wird. Heute, gegen Ende der ersten Dekade des 21. Jahrhunderts, gerät die indische Kunst immer mehr in den Strudel des internationalen Kunstmarktes und der internationalen Kritik, und es ist keine Übertreibung zu sagen, dass sie in ein neues Stadium eingetreten ist. Gleichzeitig finden viele Künstler, trotz des vermehrten Zuganges zu Kunsträumen, der Vitalität des Marktes und der größeren internationalen Aufmerksamkeit, die gegenwärtige Situation problematisch. Als ich in Vorbereitung für diese Ausstellung mit Künstlern sprach, fiel oft das Wort „Widerstand". Das liegt daran, dass sie sich ernsthaft fragen, was sie als Künstler tun können, um gesellschaftliche Probleme, wie etwa die Gefahren einer exzessiven Kommerzialisierung sowie die Zwänge der internationalen

practice.[6] It may be also possible to say that they have been able to create new forms of expression, with a delicately balanced approach that avoids the dualistic concept of India versus the West, in the course of responding to Indian reality. Today, approaching the first decade of the 21st century, Indian art is being drawn more and more into the maelstrom of the international art market and critical opinion, so it is no exaggeration to say that it has entered a new stage in its history. At the same time, in spite of the greater availability of art venues, the vitality of the market, and greater world attention, many artists find the present situation problematic. When speaking to artists in preparation for this exhibition, I often heard the word "resistance". This is because artists are sincerely asking what they can do as artists about the problems of contemporary society; such as the dangers of the excesses of commercialization, and the exigencies of international marketing strategies where critical viewpoints may be eliminated. In such a situation, younger artists who are suspicious of the market-oriented art scene are engaging in projects that intervene in the urban system, and developing the interactive media art works that can be shared with a wider public as well as conceptual works that have not often been seen before in India. It is important to note that they are attempting to create a new structure that is not based on the commodification of art. As clamorous voices call out "Chalo!" encouraging artists to strive for national honour, economic success, and international fame, how can they get an accurate idea of the place in which they find themselves and their possible destinations? Our journey into the work of these artists, who are entering a new era, is an exploration into artistic experiment and resistance, entailing both pain and possibility.

Prologue: Journeys

This exhibition presents more than one hundred works of art by 27 artists/artist groups. Most of them are based in the cities of Delhi, Mumbai, Bangalore, and Vadodara. Following Mumbai, the great centre of international commerce, and Delhi, the national capital, the southern city of Bangalore, known for its IT businesses and biotechnology industry, has gained more importance as an art centre in recent years.[7] Vadodara is the city which established the Maharaja Sayajirao (MS) University of Baroda, following

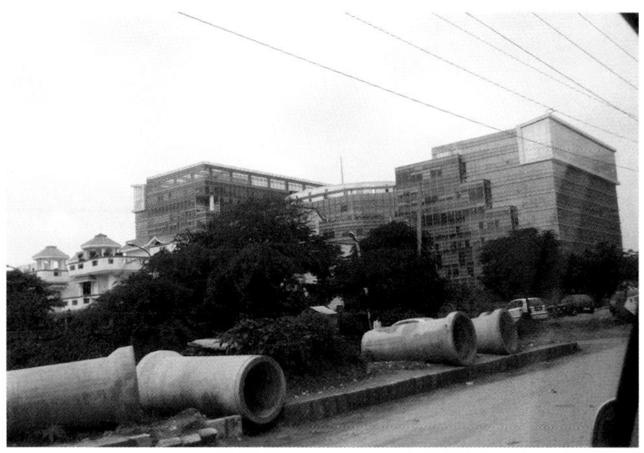

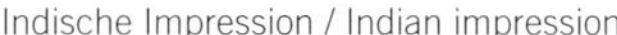
Indische Impression / Indian impression

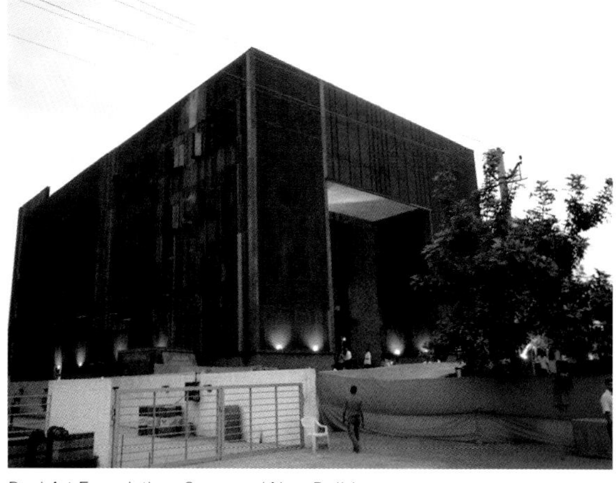

Devi Art Foundation, Gurgaon / New Delhi

Marketingstrategien, unter deren Vorherrschaft kritische Standpunkte oft weichen müssen, zu lindern. In dieser Situation engagieren sich jüngere Künstler, die der marktorientierten Kunstszene mit Misstrauen entgegentreten, in Projekten, die in das urbane System eingreifen und entwickeln jene interaktive Medienkunstwerke, die einem größeren Publikum zugänglich sind, oder auch konzeptuelle Arbeiten, die in Indien noch Seltenheitswert haben. Es muss festgehalten werden, dass sie versuchen, eine neue Struktur zu schaffen, die nicht auf dem Konzept von Kunst als Ware aufbaut. Wenn laute Stimmen „Chalo!" rufen und Künstler ermutigt werden, nationale Ehren, wirtschaftlichen Erfolg und internationale Berühmtheit anzustreben, wie können sie dann eine genaue Vorstellung von ihrem Platz und möglichen Orientierungen bekommen? Unsere Reise zu den Arbeiten dieser Künstler, die in eine neue Ära eintreten, ist eine Entdeckungsreise zu einem künstlerischen Experiment und Widerstandsphänomen, das gleichzeitig Schmerz und Möglichkeit birgt.

Prolog: Reisen

Diese Ausstellung präsentiert mehr als 100 Kunstwerke von 27 Künstlern bzw. Künstlergruppen. Die meisten von ihnen arbeiten in den Städten Delhi, Mumbai, Bangalore und Vadodara. Nach Mumbai, dem großen internationalen Handelszentrum, und Delhi, der nationalen Hauptstadt, hat in den letzten Jahren auch die südindische Stadt Bangalore, die für ihre EDV-Unternehmen und Biotechnologieindustrien bekannt ist, immer mehr Bedeutung als Kunstzentrum gewonnen.[7] In Vadodara hat sich nach der Erlangung der Unabhängigkeit die Maharaja Sayajirao (MS) Universität Baroda etabliert – ihre Kunstfakultät gilt als eine der besten in Indien. Obwohl sie früher einflussreicher war, ist es bemerkenswert, dass viele der an dieser Ausstellung teilnehmenden Künstler Absolventen dieser Universität sind. Die Stadt ist in der Kunstwelt auch für den lose verbundenen Künstlerkreis der „Baroda Schule" bekannt,[8] deren Stil durch eine figurativ-narrative Darstellung „lokaler" Elemente geprägt ist. In der Ausstellung sind Künstler unterschiedlichsten Alters vertreten: Von jenen, die wie Gulammohammed Sheikh und Vivan Sundaram in den 60er und 70er Jahren Teil der Baroda Schule waren, bis zu jungen Künstlern, die in den späten 70ern geboren wurden. Die Ausstellung umfasst eine Vielzahl

independence – its Faculty of Fine Arts became recognized as one of the finest in India. Although less influential than before, it is noteworthy that many of the artists participating in this exhibition graduated from the art department of this school. The city is also known in the art world for its loosely affiliated fraternity of artists, referred to as the "Baroda School"[8] and characterized by a figurative-narrative mode of rendering "local" elements. This exhibition includes artists spanning a wide range of ages: from those like Gulammohammed Sheikh and Vivan Sundaram, who were associated with the Baroda School from the 60s and 70s, to young artists born in the late 70s. The exhibition features a diversity of forms of expression as well as subject matter. The works are predominantly new, made especially for this or other recent exhibitions – and they include some of the artists' chefs-d'oeuvre.

The gallery space is divided into five sections, "Prologue: Journeys", "Creation and Destruction: Urban Landscape", "Reflections: Between Extremes", "Fertile Chaos", and "Epilogue: Individuality and Collectivity/Memory and Future". In this essay, I will introduce the works as they appear in the exhibition. In the prologue section, "Journeys", visitors are greeted by art that suggests to travel to different dimensions and territories. Here, special attention is given to the use of typically Indian motifs, such as elephants and circles, while creating a strong visual sensation.

Bharti Kher shows a great interest in half-human, half-animal creatures, transformation of species, mutations, as well as kitsch consumer society. She is particularly known for the use of *bindis,* usually denoting a third eye, which used to be painted on the forehead of Indian women, but there are now manufactured ones as a decorative item. The skin of a full-sized female elephant is covered with millions of swarming *bindis* in the shape of sperm. The repetition of the motif eliminates the original meaning of the *bindi* as a sign of being married, or of sperm as a symbol of reproduction or fertility, and the elephant is transformed to a somewhat enigmatic being. The newly emerging Indian economy is often described as a giant elephant, waking up or on the move, so this meaning may also be applied to the piece. Whether Kher's elephant is about to wake up, or maybe is wounded, it presents itself as a thought-provoking metaphor for the present and future of Indian society and art. The hybrid visual world created in

Unsere Reise zu den Arbeiten dieser Künstler, die in eine neue Ära eintreten, ist eine Entdeckungsreise zu einem künstlerischen Experiment und Widerstandsphänomen, das gleichzeitig Schmerz und Möglichkeit birgt.
Our journey into the work of these artists, who are entering a new era, is an exploration into artistic experiment and resistance, entailing both pain and possibility.

Diese Ausstellung präsentiert mehr als 100 Kunstwerke von 27 Künstlern bzw. Künstlergruppen. Die meisten von ihnen arbeiten in den Städten Delhi, Mumbai, Bangalore und Vadodara.
This exhibition presents more than one hundred works of art by 27 artists/artist groups. Most of them are based in the cities of Delhi, Mumbai, Bangalore, and Vadodara.

In der Ausstellung sind Künstler unterschiedlichsten Alters vertreten: von jenen, die wie Gulammohammed Sheikh und Vivan Sundaram in den 1960er und 1970er Jahren Teil der Baroda Schule waren, bis zu jungen Künstlern, die in den späten 1970ern geboren wurden.
This exhibition includes artists spanning a wide range of ages: from those like Gulammohammed Sheikh and Vivan Sundaram, who were associated with the Baroda School from the 1960s and 1970s, to young artists born in the late 1970s.

Die Ausstellung umfasst eine Vielzahl von Ausdrucksformen und Themen. Die meisten Arbeiten sind neu und speziell für diese oder andere Ausstellungen der jüngeren Vergangenheit entstanden – unter ihnen finden sich auch einige Hauptwerke dieser Künstler.
The exhibition features a diversity of forms of expression as well as subject matter. The works are predominantly new, made especially for this or other recent exhibitions – and they include some of the artists' chefs-d'oeuvre.

Die Haut eines lebensgroßen weiblichen Elefanten ist mit Schwärmen spermaförmiger Bindis überzogen. (...)
Die aufstrebende indische Wirtschaft wird oft als „erwachender Elefant" beschrieben, und auch diese Bedeutung mag dem Kunstwerk zugrunde liegen. Wie auch immer, ob Barthi Khers Elefant nun gerade erwacht oder vielleicht verwundet ist, er präsentiert sich jedenfalls als nachdenkliche Metapher für die Gegenwart und die Zukunft der indischen Gesellschaft und Kunst.
The skin of a full-sized female elephant is covered with millions of swarming bindis in the shape of sperm. (...) The newly emerging Indian economy is often described as a giant elephant, waking up or on the move, so this meaning may also be applied to the piece. Whether Kher's elephant is about to wake up, or maybe is wounded, it presents itself as a thought-provoking metaphor for the present and future of Indian society and art.

von Ausdrucksformen und Themen. Die meisten Arbeiten sind neu und speziell für diese oder andere Ausstellungen der jüngeren Vergangenheit entstanden – unter ihnen finden sich auch einige Hauptwerke dieser Künstler.
Die Galerieräume sind in fünf Abschnitte unterteilt: „Prolog: Reisen", „Kreation und Destruktion: Stadtlandschaften", „Reflektionen: Zwischen Extremen", „Fruchtbares Chaos" und „Epilog: Individualität und Kollektivität / Gedächtnis und Zukunft". In diesem Aufsatz werde ich die Arbeiten gemäß ihrer Reihenfolge in der Ausstellung beschreiben. In der Prologsektion „Reisen", werden die Besucher von Kunstwerken begrüßt, die Reisen in verschiedene Gebiete und Dimensionen andeuten. Besondere Aufmerksamkeit gilt als typisch indisch geltenden Motiven wie Elefanten und Kreisen mit starker visueller Kraft.
Bharti Khers Interesse gilt Wesen, die halb Mensch halb Tier sind, der Transformation von Arten, Mutationen, sowie dem Kitsch der Konsumgesellschaft. Besonders bekannt ist sie für die Verwendung von Bindis, jene Punkte auf der Stirn indischer Frauen, die das dritte Auge symbolisieren. Früher wurden sie aufgemalt, jetzt gibt es sie auch als dekoratives „Fertigprodukt". Die Haut eines lebensgroßen weiblichen Elefanten ist mit Schwärmen spermaförmiger Bindis überzogen. Die Wiederholung des Motivs eliminiert die ursprüngliche Bedeutung des Bindis als Symbol der verheirateten Frau oder des Spermiums als Symbol der Vermehrung bzw. der Fruchtbarkeit, und der Elefant wird damit in ein rätselhaftes Wesen verwandelt. Die aufstrebende indische Wirtschaft wird oft als „erwachender Elefant" beschrieben, und auch diese Bedeutung mag dem Kunstwerk zugrunde liegen. Wie auch immer, ob Khers Elefant nun gerade erwacht oder vielleicht verwundet ist, er präsentiert sich jedenfalls als nachdenkliche Metapher für die Gegenwart und die Zukunft der indischen Gesellschaft und Kunst. Die visuelle Hybridwelt in den digitalen Bildern, Gemälden und Skulpturen von **Gulammohammed Sheikh** erweckt Assoziationen zu Miniaturschreinen und mittelalterlichen Weltkarten, und einige Bilder erinnern an Mandalas. Diese Fantasiewelt entsteht durch eine Mischung unterschiedlicher kultureller Elemente aus verschiedensten Zeiten und Gegenden. Sie erinnert an Begriffe wie „Entdeckung" und „Kolonisierung" und drückt den Wunsch aus, Grenzen und festgesteckte Rahmen zu überwinden. **A. Balasubramaniam** präsentiert in die Wand

Gulammohammed Sheikh's digital images, paintings, and sculptures are associated with miniature shrines and medieval world maps, and in some images mandalas are called to mind. This fantasy is created by an amalgam of diverse cultural elements from all times and places; bringing to mind concepts of discovery and colonization, as well as expressing a desire to transcend boundaries and frameworks. The work of **A. Balasubramaniam** presents parts of the body integrated with the wall. It deals with the relationship of visibility and invisibility, perceptions of reality and its limits. Reflecting the artist's special eye for grasping the world and things differently, and suggesting the nature of human existence in the midst of a wider universe, his works are also quite appropriate in the context of this introductory section. **N. S. Harsha** frequently intervenes in the exhibition space as a whole, by combining objects and site-specific painting on the walls or floors of the space. Here he makes the chairs sat on by the gallery monitors/invigilators into the art work; reversing the usual arrangement where they watch the exhibition visitors. Examining the concept of "monitoring" or observing, the artist questions the relationship between traditional painting and popular expression, imagination and reality. These chairs are dispersed throughout the gallery space, as if taking on the role of a travel guide who leads us to various encounters and discoveries.

Creation and Destruction: Urban Landscape

After passing through a piece by Sheikh, which is in the form of a tunnel or passage, we are suddenly confronted with a street scene from contemporary India. This section focuses on works that comment on the city or the environment, pondering the contradictions and new possibilities in cycles of creation and destruction.
The panoramic photographic work of **Jitish Kallat** treats the city streets as a theatre of life. When examining the work carefully, we notice that the artist has skilfully manipulated the details, and the image is filled with contradictory elements suggesting changing times and the effects of modernization. Kallat's auto-rickshaw, transformed into a monster's skeleton, arouses memories of terrorist bombings. With his "grotesque, arabesque, burlesque" aesthetic, the artist may have accurately evoked the aggressive atmosphere of the times. **Krishnaraj Chonat** often creates

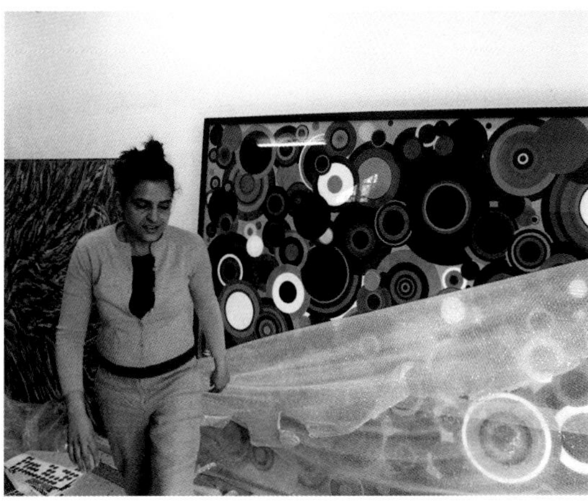
Bharti Kher in ihrem Atelier / at her studio

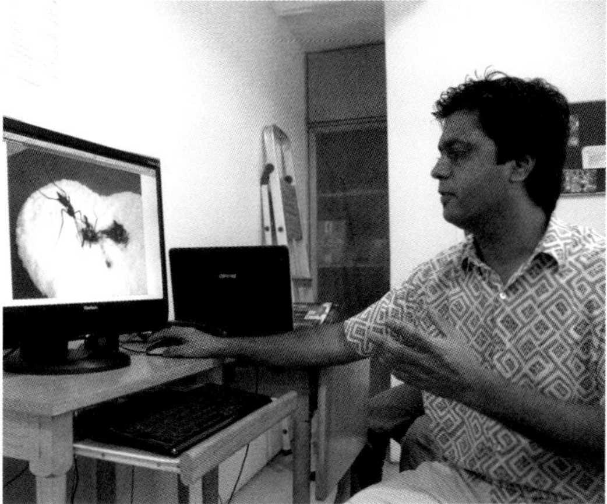
Krishnaraj Chonat at / bei GALLERYSKE

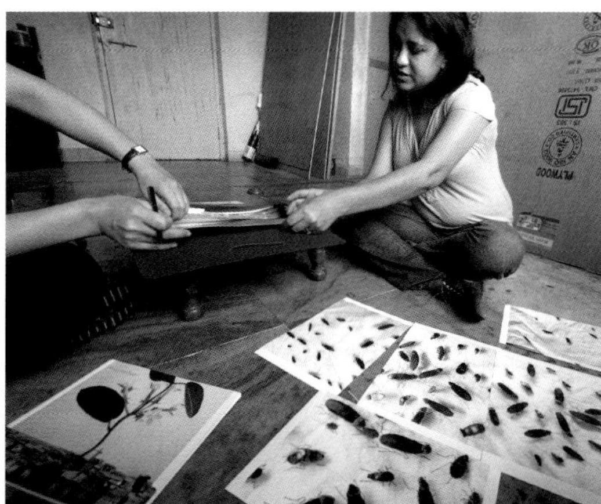
Hema Upadhyay in ihrem Atelier / in her studio

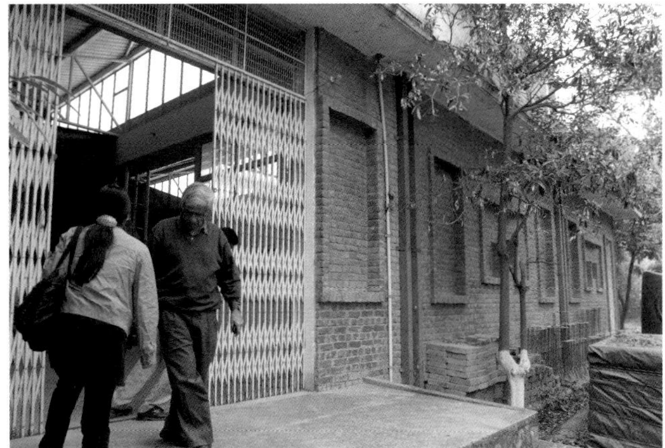

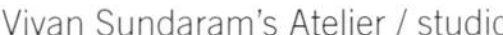
Vivan Sundaram's Atelier / studio

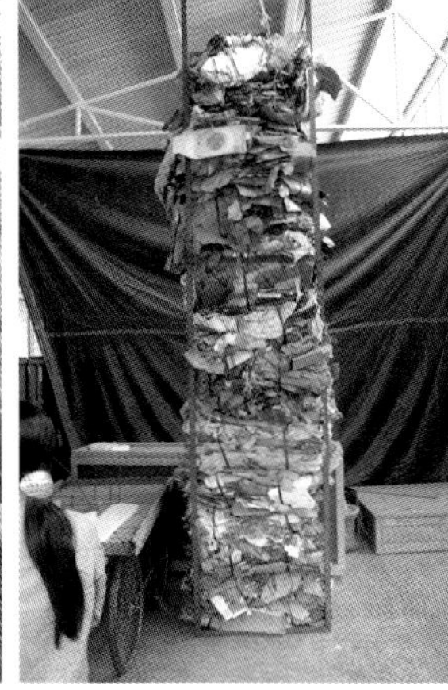
Vivan Sundaram's Atelier (Innenraum) / studio (interior)

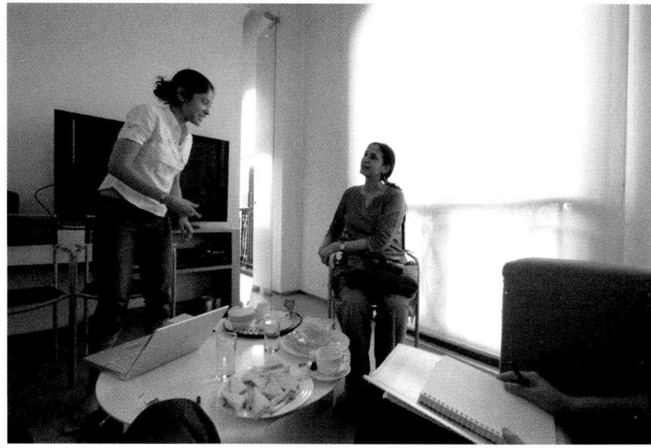
Shilpa Gupta mit der Kunstkritikerin / along with art critic Nancy Adajania

integrierte Teile des Körpers. Hier geht es um die Beziehung von Sichtbarkeit und Unsichtbarkeit, Wahrnehmungen von Realität und deren Grenzen. Die Arbeiten spiegeln den ganz speziellen Blickwinkel des Künstlers auf die Welt und ihre Dinge wider und kommentieren die menschliche Existenz inmitten eines größeren Universums, womit sie gut in diesen einführenden Teil passen. **N. S. Harsha** greift oft in den gesamten Ausstellungsraum ein, indem er Objekte mit ortsspezifischen Malereien auf Wänden oder Fußböden kombiniert. In diesem Fall verwandelt er die für die Museumsaufsichtspersonen vorgesehenen Stühle in Kunstwerke und sorgt so für eine Umkehr der normalen Situation, in der die Aufsichtspersonen die Besucher beobachten. Indem er das Konzept des „Überwachens" oder Beobachtens beleuchtet, hinterfragt der Künstler die Beziehung zwischen traditioneller Malerei und üblichen Ausdrucksformen, Vorstellungen und Realitäten. Die Stühle sind überall in den Galerieräumen verteilt, so als wären sie Reiseleiter, die uns zu verschiedenen Begegnungen und Entdeckungen führen.

Kreation und Destruktion: Stadtlandschaften

Wir durchschreiten eine Arbeit von Sheikh in der Form eines Tunnels und finden uns plötzlich mit einer Straßenszene aus dem heutigen Indien konfrontiert. Dieser Abschnitt enthält Werke, die Städte oder die Umwelt kommentieren und Widersprüche und neue Möglichkeiten in Zyklen der Erschaffung und Zerstörung finden.

Die Panoramafotografien von **Jitish Kallat** setzen die Straßen der Stadt als Theater des Lebens in Szene. Bei sorgfältiger Betrachtung fällt auf, dass der Künstler die Details geschickt manipuliert und das Bild mit widersprüchlichen Elementen gefüllt hat, die den Wandel der Zeiten und die Auswirkungen der Modernisierung andeuten. Die von Kallat in ein Riesenskelett verwandelte Auto-Rikscha erinnert an terroristische Bombenanschläge. Mit seiner Ästhetik der „Groteske, Arabeske und Burleske" hat der Künstler die aggressive Atmosphäre des Zeitgeistes vielleicht sehr präzise wiedergegeben. **Krishnaraj Chonat** erzeugt oft unerwartete Effekte durch die Kombination von Objekten, die nicht in Beziehung zueinander stehen. In dieser neuen Arbeit wird eine Jacuzzi-Badewanne zum Boot, das zwischen den Wünschen und Träumen der „Neureichen" dahinzutreiben scheint und damit die Wellen von auslän-

unexpected effects by combining unrelated objects. In this new work, a Jacuzzi tub becomes a boat, which seems to drift among the diverse desires and dreams of the "new-rich" class; commenting on the waves of foreign capital pouring into India, indiscriminate land development, and growing environmental destruction. It seems that a pair of binoculars set on the top of the sculpture are asking, "What next?". **Gigi Scaria** looks at urban problems, like the horrendous traffic jams of Indian cities and the evictions and demolitions that result from illegal construction. In his paintings, he presents an alternative urban plan for the city of Delhi, marked by irony and humour. **Hema Upadhyay** is also interested in cityscapes, but in a more poetic way. She has made a large sculptural installation that looks like a model of the Mumbai slums, as if seen from above in a dream of flying. The work expresses a sense of free-floating anxiety and uprootedness. **Vivan Sundaram,** on the other hand, creates an imaginary city with all sorts of junk. This work might be described as an archaeological investigation of present times, based on penetrating observation of the social environment. By referring to people who are forced to make a living by picking up garbage and selling it, the problem of public cleaning system, and recycling, the artist makes us think about the fragility of the city and the consumer economy. As Jean-Luc Godard said, "Art is not a reflection of reality but the reality of a reflection." In Sundaram's works, we sense an interest in the relation of a reflection possessing reality to the present age, rather than a simple description of reality. He portrays multiple histories experienced by his own family, or people from the lower classes, rather than the unitary history determined by people in power. A similar interest in fantasy, elevated views, and a moving gaze are found in the large installation, *Air Show,* by **Nataraj Sharma.** At first glance, it looks like an amusement-park attraction, but the heavy, rusted ascending and descending fighter planes could be metaphors for the rise and fall of the economy. This sculpture, with its uncanny atmosphere, may also remind us that war is a kind of spectacle.

Reflections: Between Extremes

The next section features interplays of light and shadow, fluidity and amorphousness, contrasts and gaps. The works of art presented here evoke narratives arising from

Die von Jitish Kallat in ein Riesenskelett verwandelte Auto-Rikscha erinnert an terroristische Bombenanschläge. Mit seiner Ästhetik der „Groteske, Arabeske und Burleske" hat der Künstler die aggressive Atmosphäre des Zeitgeistes vielleicht sehr präzise wiedergegeben.
Kallat's auto-rickshaw, transformed into a monster's skeleton, arouses memories of terrorist bombings. With his "grotesque, arabesque, burlesque" aesthetic, the artist may have accurately evoked the aggressive atmosphere of the times.

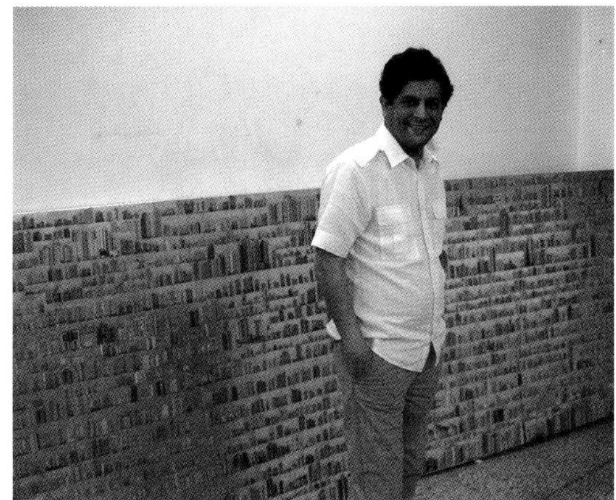

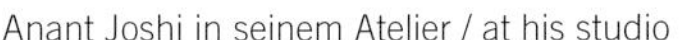
Anant Joshi in seinem Atelier / at his studio

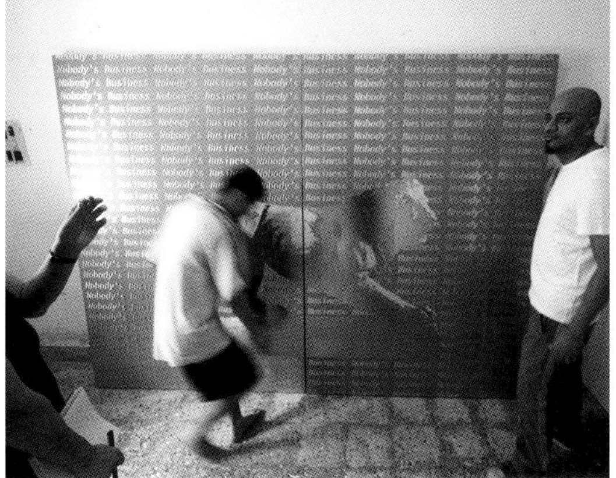

Justin Ponmany in seinem Atelier / bin his studio

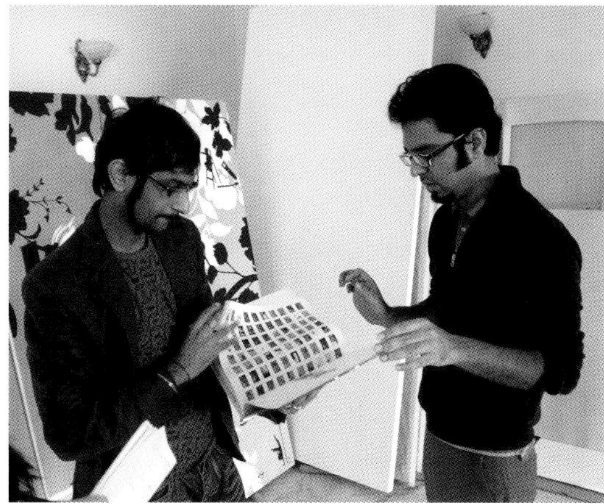

Thukral & Tagra in ihrem Atelier / in their studio

Vivan Sundaram wiederum baut aus Abfällen eine imaginäre Stadt. (...) Mit dem Verweis auf Menschen, die gezwungen sind, ihren Lebensunterhalt durch das Sammeln und Verkaufen von Müll zu verdienen, dem Hinweis auf die Probleme der Straßenreinigung und des Recyclings, macht uns der Künstler auf die Verwundbarkeit der Stadt und der Konsumwirtschaft aufmerksam.

Vivan Sundaram, on the other hand, creates an imaginary city with all sorts of junk. (...) By referring to people who are forced to make a living by picking up garbage and selling it, the problem of public cleaning system, and recycling, the artist makes us think about the fragility of the city and the consumer economy.

dischem Kapital, das nach Indien fließt, sowie die sorglose Landverbauung und die wachsende Umweltzerstörung kommentiert. Ein Fernglas an der Spitze der Skulptur scheint mit der Frage „Wie geht es weiter?" in die Zukunft zu blicken. **Gigi Scaria** behandelt urbane Problemfelder, wie etwa die Verkehrsinfarkte in indischen Städten sowie Zwangsräumungen und den Abriss illegal erbauter Gebäude. In seinen Bildern stellt er mit Humor und Ironie einen alternativen Stadtentwicklungsplan für die Stadt Delhi vor. Auch **Hema Upadhyay** interessiert sich für Stadtlandschaften, wenn auch auf poetischere Weise. Sie zeigt eine große skulpturale Installation, die wie ein Modell der Slums von Mumbai aussieht, wie sie einem Schläfer, der im Traum darüber hinweg fliegt, erscheinen mögen. Die Arbeit ist durchdrungen von Wurzellosigkeit und einem Gefühl unbestimmter Angst. **Vivan Sundaram** wiederum baut aus Abfällen eine imaginäre Stadt. Man könnte seine Arbeit als archäologische Untersuchung der Gegenwart bezeichnen, die auf einer tiefgreifenden Beobachtung des sozialen Umfeldes beruht. Mit dem Verweis auf Menschen, die gezwungen sind, ihren Lebensunterhalt durch das Sammeln und Verkaufen von Müll zu verdienen, dem Hinweis auf die Probleme der Straßenreinigung und des Recyclings, macht uns der Künstler auf die Verwundbarkeit der Stadt und der Konsumwirtschaft aufmerksam. Wie Jean-Luc Godard sagte, „Kunst ist nicht die Reflektion der Realität, sondern die Realität einer Reflektion": In Sundarams Arbeiten spüren wir ein Interesse an der Beziehung zwischen einer Reflektion über die Realität und die Gegenwart, das über eine simple Beschreibung der Realität hinausgeht. In seinen Darstellungen finden wir die vielschichtigen Geschichten seiner eigenen Familie oder der Angehörigen der ärmeren Schichten und nicht nur die Einheitsgeschichte, wie sie von jenen an der Macht bestimmt wird. Ein ähnliches Interesse an Fantasie, einem Blick von oben und einem bewegten Blick findet man in der großen Installation „Air Show" von **Nataraj Sharma.** Auf den ersten Blick sieht sie aus wie eine Attraktion in einem Vergnügungspark, aber die schweren, verrosteten auf- und absteigenden Kampfflugzeuge könnten auch ein Gleichnis für die wechselhafte Entwicklung der Wirtschaft darstellen. Mit ihrer unheimlichen Atmosphäre mag uns diese Skulptur auch daran erinnern, dass der Krieg eine Art von Spektakel darstellt.

interactions between things of different kinds, suggesting multifaceted views or expressing inner thoughts. Conflicts are highlighted, while new circuits are created to bring opposing things together and encourage dialogue between them.

Shilpa Gupta's art reveals harsh social realities, such as the illicit sale of organs and terrorism. She questions the concepts of freedom and safety in contemporary society, as well as exploring themes like ideology and split identity. The "Shadow Piece" series she has been working on in recent years are interactive, participatory, multimedia works that sensitively reflect the surreal conditions produced by the penetration of media into our everyday lives. **Ranbir Kaleka** has been working on a new format of painting combined with video projection. In his chef-d'oeuvre, *Crossings,* independent stories are played out on four different panels/screens simultaneously. They proceed separately but synchronize at certain moments, producing a composite, overlapping narrative. **Anant Joshi** makes effective use of light and shadow to draw the viewer into a world of complex imagery. Using cheap children's toys fabricated in India and razor blades, he refers to an urban symbolism, exposing the amorphous and unstable nature of the city and showing violence hiding behind cute or innocent surfaces. *Navel One and the Many* – a labyrinth of imagery that forces the viewer to see – functions as a metaphor of the city of Mumbai and its overflow of images. **Kiran Subbaiah** makes video works with a conceptual flavour that is uncommon in India. *Suicide Note* is a piece based on the idea of the artist leaving a will on video tape. It appears to be quite simple, but manipulates space-time in complex ways; showing a characteristic black humour and a quirky and interesting sensibility that alternates between joking and seriousness, lightness and heaviness. In **Justin Ponmany's** photographs, a torn-up cricket ball is made to appear as something completely different, by converting it into two dimensions and expanding its size. His works, produced with unusual pigment made from the magnetic substance used in credit cards, take on different appearances depending on how they are struck by light, projecting a feeling of capriciousness and instability. **Jitish Kallat's** enlarged one-rupee coin represents a world that shows two different sides, depending on where the viewer is standing. Kallat has often dealt with the theme of human

Reflektionen: Zwischen Extremen

Im nächsten Teil der Ausstellung geht es um das Wechselspiel von Licht und Schatten, fließende Grenzen und amorphe Formen, Kontraste und Zwischenräume. Die Narrative der hier ausgestellten Werke ergeben sich aus der Interaktion zwischen unterschiedlichen Dingen. Sie deuten vielschichtige Ansichten an oder verleihen inneren Befindlichkeiten Ausdruck. Konflikte werden herausgearbeitet und gleichzeitig werden neue Verbindungen geschaffen, um Gegensätze einander anzunähern und Dialoge in Gang zu setzen.

Shilpa Guptas Kunst enthüllt harte gesellschaftliche Realitäten, wie etwa den illegalen Organhandel oder Terrorismus. Sie hinterfragt die Konzepte von Freiheit und Sicherheit in der heutigen Gesellschaft und untersucht Themen wie Ideologie und gespaltene Identitäten. Bei der Serie „Shadow Piece", an der sie in den letzten Jahren gearbeitet hat, handelt es sich um interaktive partizipatorische Multimediaarbeiten, die auf sensible Weise die surrealen Gegebenheiten widerspiegeln, die sich aus dem Eindringen der Medien in unser Alltagsleben ergeben. **Ranbir Kaleka** arbeitet an einem neuen Format, in dem er Malerei mit Videoprojektionen verbindet. In seinem Hauptwerk „Crossings" werden voneinander unabhängige Geschichten auf vielen unterschiedlichen Bildschirmen gleichzeitig projiziert. Sie laufen getrennt ab, synchronisieren sich aber in gewissen Momenten und erzeugen damit ein größeres Narrativ mit Überschneidungen. **Anant Joshi** nützt auf sehr effektvolle Weise die Wirkung von Licht und Schatten, um den Betrachter in eine Welt der komplexen Bilder hereinzuholen. Billige, in Indien produzierte Kinderspielzeuge und Rasierklingen verweisen auf urbane Symbolik. Sie legen das amorphe und instabile Wesen der Stadt bloß und zeigen die Gewalt unter der hübschen oder unschuldig wirkenden Oberfläche. „Navel One and the Many" – ein Labyrinth von Bildern, das den Betrachtern aufgezwungen wird – dient als Metapher für die Stadt Mumbai mit ihrer Flut an Bildern. **Kiran Subbaiah** hingegen erstellt Arbeiten mit einem für indische Verhältnisse ungewöhnlichen konzeptuellen Anstrich. In „Suicide Note" geht es darum, dass der Künstler ein Testament auf Video hinterlässt. Das scheint ganz einfach zu sein, manipuliert aber Raum und Zeit in komplexer Weise. In der Arbeit schwingt ein charakteristischer schwarzer Humor mit, sowie eine existence and suffering. Here he points out the economic reality of India, like two sides of the same coin, where some Indians have entered the ranks of the ten wealthiest people in the world, while 300 million others live on less than a dollar a day.

Fertile Chaos

In this section, we turn our eyes to art that refers to people and diverse aspects of everyday life. The works shown here deal with people's dreams; they question ideas of nation and history, identity, gender, and tradition; they show an interest in transformation, overturning and abstraction of meaning through eclecticism, repetition and copying.

The activist artist **Tushar Joag** is carrying out a series of projects using the Internet, centred on his establishment of a virtual agency, "UNICELL Public Works Cell," in which he mimics government operations and the activities of the Public Works Agency – pointing out dishonesty and arrogance, and proposing alternative solutions. His suggestions are both absurd and serious. For example, he has invented products and methods for getting on the famously crowded trains of Mumbai, and sent eviction notices to thousands of residents in certain areas, telling them that a new network of canals will be built in their area to alleviate traffic congestion. The youngest participants in this exhibition, **Thukral & Tagra,** also work as graphic designers. They design office interiors and produce all sorts of fashionable products, including men's underwear and accessories. The male figures portrayed in their work are young men they have actually met, and the world of their art reflects the dreams of young people in India today. The Hershey's chocolate syrup bottles they use, for example, are symbols of the "American dream". As young men move to the city from the country, they wear the latest fashions and dream of moving some day to Switzerland or Canada. The colourful, superficial, kitsch style of their paintings make it look as if the graphic images are printed, but many are actually painted by hand. **Pushpamala N.** has compiled a series of photographs in a book called *Native Women of South India: Manners and Customs.* They show the artist in costume, playing the roles of what are considered uniquely Indian types of women, taken from high art, popular media, and documentary images. Her sources include famous nineteenth-century Indian paintings, popular pictures of the

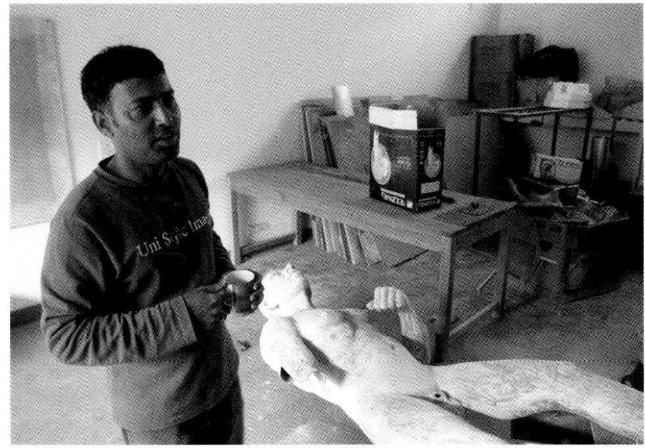

Jagannath Panda in seinem Atelier / in his studio

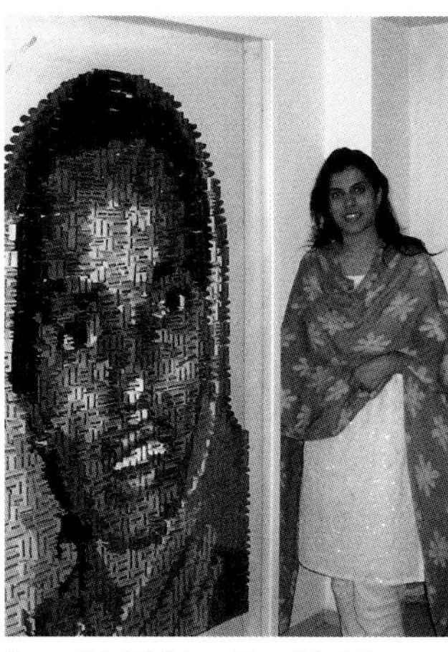

Reena Saini Kallat und ihre Arbeit / and her work

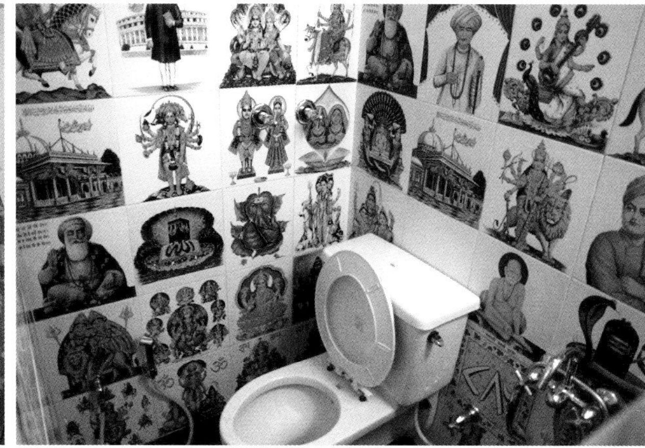

Atul Dodiya's Ateliertoilette / studio toilet

In verschiedenen Kostümen schlüpft die Künstlerin Pushpamala N. in als typisch indisch geltende Frauenrollen, wie man sie aus künstlerischen Darstellungen, populären Medien und Dokumentationen kennt. (...) Die so entstandenen Fotografien beleuchten Stereotype, die für die verschiedensten Zwecke, z. B. für den Kolonialismus und Nationalismus, geschaffen wurden, und sie zeigen, wie Bilder politisch manipuliert werden.

Pushpamala N. has compiled a series of photographs which show the artist in costume, playing the roles of what are considered uniquely Indian types of women, taken from high art, popular media, and documentary images. (...) The resulting photographs shed light on stereotypical ideas created for various purposes, including for colonialism and nationalism, and show how images are politically manipulated.

schräge und reizvolle Sensibilität, die zwischen Scherz und Ernsthaftigkeit, Leichtigkeit und Schwere wechselt. In **Justin Ponmanys** Fotografie verwandelt sich ein zerrissener Cricketball durch die Verlagerung in die Zweidimensionalität und die veränderten Größenverhältnisse in etwas völlig Anderes. Ein ungewöhnliches Pigment, das durch Verwendung einer magnetischen Substanz, wie sie auch in Kreditkarten enthalten ist, je nach Lichteinfall unterschiedlich aussieht, verleiht den Arbeiten ein Gefühl der kapriziösen Instabilität. **Jitish Kallats** vergrößerte 1-Rupie-Münze verkörpert eine Welt die – je nach Betrachterstandpunkt – zwei verschiedene Seiten hat. Kallat hat sich schon oft mit den Themen der menschlichen Existenz und des Leids auseinandergesetzt. In diesem Fall verweist er auf die wirtschaftliche Realität in Indien. Ebenso wie eine Münze hat auch Indien zwei Seiten: einerseits leben dort einige der zehn reichsten Menschen der Welt, während 300 Millionen Menschen mit weniger als einem Dollar pro Tag auskommen müssen.

Fruchtbares Chaos

In diesem Abschnitt begegnen uns Kunstwerke, die auf Menschenbilder und unterschiedliche Aspekte des Alltagslebens verweisen. Die Künstler beschäftigen sich mit den Träumen der Menschen, sie hinterfragen Vorstellungen von Nation und Geschichte, Identität, Geschlecht und Tradition. Hier geht es um Transformation, um die Umkehr und Abstraktion von Bedeutung durch Eklektizismus, Wiederholung und Kopie.

Der Aktivist und Künstler **Tushar Joag** verwendet für seine Projektserie das Internet. Im Mittelpunkt steht die von ihm gegründete virtuelle Organisation mit dem Namen „UNICELL Public Works Cell", in der er Regierungsaktivitäten und die Tätigkeit der Behörde für öffentliche Bauvorhaben imitiert. Er weist nicht nur auf Unaufrichtigkeit und Arroganz hin, sondern bietet auch alternative Lösungsvorschläge, die teils absurd, teils ernst gemeint sind. So hat er beispielsweise Produkte und Verbesserungsvorschläge für die Benutzer der notorisch überfüllten Züge von Mumbai entwickelt, oder Räumungsbescheide an Tausende von Bewohnern in bestimmten Gebieten geschickt, in denen er ihnen mitteilte, dass man in ihrer Gegend ein neues Kanalnetz zur Linderung des Verkehrsproblems errichten würde. Die jüngsten Teilnehmer der Ausstellung, **Thukral & Tagra,** arbeiten auch als Grafiker. Sie entwerfen Büroeinrichtungen und diverse Modeprodukte, wie etwa Unterwäsche oder Accessoires für Männer. Bei den männlichen Figuren in ihrer Arbeit handelt es sich um junge Männer, die sie tatsächlich kennen gelernt haben, und ihre Kunstwelt spiegelt die Träume junger Menschen im heutigen Indien wider. So steht beispielsweise der Schokoladesirup von Hershey's als Symbol für den amerikanischen Traum. Junge Männer, die vom Land in die Stadt ziehen, tragen die neueste Mode und träumen davon, eines Tages in der Schweiz oder in Kanada zu leben. Der bunte, oberflächlich kitschige Stil ihrer Bilder lässt sie wie Drucke aussehen, aber tatsächlich sind viele von ihnen handgemalt. **Pushpamala N.** hat eine Serie von Fotografien in einem Buch mit dem Titel „Native Women of South India:

goddess Lakshmi, movie scenes, and photographs and body measurements used to classify native people by British colonialists. The resulting photographs shed light on stereotypical ideas created for various purposes, including for colonialism and nationalism, and show how images are politically manipulated. **Nikhil Chopra** also masquerades and refers to representational question of portraiture, but his performances are more theatrical or even ritual. Taking on the virtual personae of "Sir Raja" and "Yog Raj Chitrakar", he creates complex situations involving himself, his family history, the country of India, and the history of the place where the performance is carried out. He invites the viewer to experience a unique world that blends fiction and reality, male and female identities, painting, photography and theater.

Ashim Purkayastha creates art by focusing on portraits of Gandhi, the father of modern India, printed on pieces of paper with a public social function like stamps or currency. His family is from Assam, close to the border of India and Bangladesh, and his works question the nature of central government, nationhood, patriarchal and matriarchal societies, and identity, based on his family's experiences. Cutting out parts of the image of Gandhi from stamps is a painstaking process, and the artist seems to find meaning in facing resistance and challenging the limits of patience.

Reena Saini Kallat refers more directly to the problem of national borders. In a series of photographs dealing with the shifting contested border between Pakistan and India, she highlights wounds cut into the body (representing Mother Earth) in its process of transformation. As the viewers actually cross borders placed on the floor, their awareness is raised by the complex flow of people, confluence of crowds, and resulting friction. Her work shows an obvious interest in wounding or imprinting. Her series of portraits, *Synonym,* is made with large numbers of rubber stamps. For this series, she started by depicting the faces of missing persons, but the completed images are anonymous. They could be anyone or no one. The many rubber stamps are carved with names in the number of different languages of India. These portraits symbolically convey the unity in diversity of India, a multilingual world without a single national language.

Perhaps the artist who best represents the method of accumulating many objects is **Subodh Gupta.** He uses large numbers of mass-produced, everyday products, such as stainless steel milk cans and bowls, to effectively enhance the sculptural strength of his work. He also employs such symbolic materials as cow dung and the Ambassador, the national car of India, as material for art, commenting on materialistic consumer culture, the relationship between the city and the rural area where he was born and raised, the vanishing natural paysage, and movements of people.

The three artists, **Atul Dodiya, Prabhavathi Meppayil,** and **Jagannath Panda,** have each developed innovative approaches in the field of painting. Dodiya has experimented with a variety of different methods, painting on shutters and incorporating fragmented shirts as collage elements in his paintings. In this exhibition he is showing a series, mainly portraits of couples, entitled *Saptapadi,* which is a

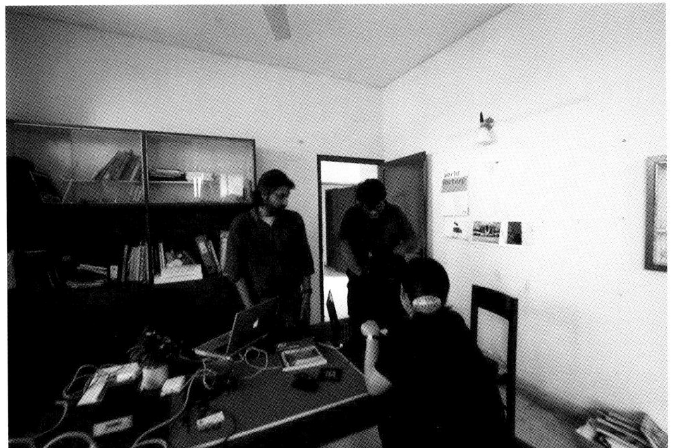

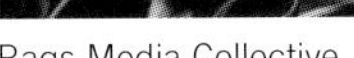
Raqs Media Collective

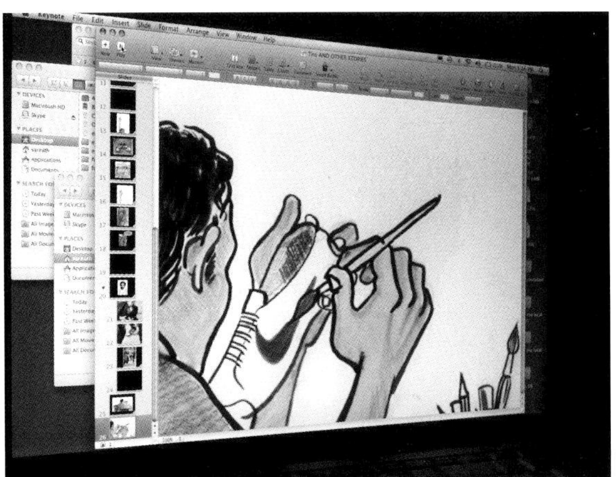

Bei einem Treffen mit / At a meeting with Sarnath Banerjee

Manners and Customs“ zusammengestellt. In verschiedenen Kostümen schlüpft die Künstlerin in als typisch indisch geltende Frauenrollen, wie man sie aus künstlerischen Darstellungen, populären Medien und Dokumentationen kennt. Unter ihren Quellen finden sich berühmte indische Gemälde aus dem 19. Jahrhundert, gängige Bilder der Göttin Lakshmi, Filmszenen, sowie Fotografien und Körpervermessungen, wie sie von den britischen Kolonialherren zur Klassifizierung der Einheimischen angefertigt wurden. Die so entstandenen Fotografien beleuchten Stereotype, die für die verschiedensten Zwecke, z. B. für den Kolonialismus und Nationalismus, geschaffen wurden, und sie zeigen, wie Bilder politisch manipuliert werden. Auch **Nikhil Chopra** verkleidet sich und verweist auf Themen der Darstellung in Porträts, aber seine Performances haben einen mehr theatralischen oder sogar rituellen Charakter. Er schlüpft in die erfundenen Charaktere „Sir Raja“ und „Yog Raj Chitrakar“ und erschafft komplexe Situationen, in denen er sich selbst, seine Familiengeschichte, das Land Indien und die Geschichte des Ortes, an dem die Performance durchgeführt wird, einbringt. Er lädt den Betrachter ein, eine einzigartige Welt zu betreten, in der Fiktion und Realität, männliche und weibliche Identitäten, Malerei, Fotografie und Theater ineinander übergehen.

Ashim Purkayastha konzentriert sich in seiner Arbeit auf Porträts von Gandhi, den Vater des modernen Indien, auf Wertzeichen wie etwa Briefmarken oder Banknoten. Seine Familie stammt aus Assam, in der Nähe der Grenze zwischen Indien und Bangladesch. Aufbauend auf die Erfahrungen seiner Familie hinterfragt seine Arbeit das Wesen von Zentralregierung, Nationalstaat, patriarchalischen und matriarchalischen Gesellschaften sowie das Konzept der Identität. Die Bilder von Gandhi aus Briefmarken auszuschneiden ist ein mühsamer Prozess, und der Künstler scheint im Überwinden und Ausloten der Grenzen seiner Geduld eine gewisse Bedeutung zu finden. **Reena Saini Kallat** verweist in ihrer Arbeit unmittelbarer auf das Problem von nationalen Grenzen. In eine Serie von Fotografien zum Thema der umstrittenen Grenze zwischen Pakistan und Indien akzentuiert sie Wunden in einem sich transformierenden Körper (symbolisch für Mutter Erde). Die Besucher müssen tatsächlich auf dem Boden platzierte Grenzen überschreiten und der komplexe Menschenfluss, das Zusammentreffen von Menschenmengen und die

part of the traditional Hindu wedding ceremony. Unrelated images are juxtaposed on the canvas to create a strong visual impact. This style pays homage to the kitsch, hand-painted Bollywood movie posters that used to be a common sight in Indian cities. While Dodiya is following a tradition of popular art, Meppayil uses traditional metalwork and painting techniques. In contrast with Dodiya's splashy images, Meppayil's art is very minimal and delicate. She applies gold leaf to a white surface with the tools used by her father, a fine metal craftsman, and paints dotted lines with pigment made from malachite. Through this micro-world, created with the beauty of handmade crafts, she poses larger questions about an industry that is disappearing because of mechanization. Panda, who was originally a sculptor, treats two-dimensional art as an extension of his sculptural experiments. His works are characterized by mixing pieces of fine fabric with a variety of other elements, presenting contrasting viewpoints and senses of scale on the same plane, and the frequent use of animal motifs. These works call attention to the tension between progress and tradition, and the relationship between human beings and animals.

Epilogue: Individuality and Collectivity / Memory and Future

The epilogue section is a space of intersection between individual and collective experience, where thoughts are extended from past memories to the future. A singing voice pervaded by nostalgia issues from an old-fashioned microphone. It is the voice of **Shilpa Gupta,** singing the text of the famous "Tryst with Destiny" speech given by Jawaharlal Nehru, India's first Prime Minister, to the Constituent Assembly on the eve of independence. The function of the speaker and microphone are reversed, making an official event into a very private experience, and creating awareness of the 60 years that has passed since Indian independence. The related, but different, images of maps of India drawn by 100 people from memory, suggest an intimate relationship between memory and imagination – as if recalling the words of Agnès Varda, "If you cannot remember something, imagine it." The work also reveals awkwardness, and slight discrepancies, that cannot be expressed in words or pictures, asking universal questions about memory and experiences in a global age overflowing with information. **Sarnath Banerjee** has participated in the development

Subodh Gupta verwendet große Mengen von massenproduzierten Alltagsprodukten, etwa Milchkrüge und Schüsseln aus rostfreiem Stahl (...), er kommentiert damit die materialistische Konsumkultur, die Beziehung zwischen Ballungsräumen und den ländlichen Gebieten in denen er aufwuchs, die verschwindende natürliche Landschaft und die Menschenströme.

Subodh Gupta uses large numbers of mass-produced, everyday products, such as stainless steel milk cans and bowls (...), commenting on materialistic consumer culture, the relationship between the city and the rural area where he was born and raised, the vanishing natural paysage, and movements of people.

sich daraus ergebenden Spannungen erhöhen das Bewusstsein für dieses Thema. In ihrer Arbeit zeigt sich immer wieder das Interesse für Verwundungen oder Prägungen. Die Porträtserie „Synonym" besteht aus einer großen Anzahl von Gummistempeln. Sie bildete dafür die Gesichter von vermissten Personen ab – die fertigen Bilder bleiben jedoch anonym und könnten jede beliebige Person darstellen. In die vielen Gummistempel sind Namen in den verschiedenen Sprachen Indiens eingeschnitten. So symbolisieren diese Porträts die Einheit in der Vielfalt Indiens, eine vielsprachige Welt ohne eine einzige nationale Sprache.

Subodh Gupta ist wahrscheinlich der repräsentativste Vertreter der Methode, eine Vielzahl von Objekten anzuhäufen. Er verwendet große Mengen von massenproduzierten Alltagsprodukten, etwa Milchkrüge und Schüsseln aus rostfreiem Stahl, um die skulpturale Ausdruckskraft seiner Arbeiten sehr effizient zu verstärken. Auch symbolische Materialien wie Kuhdung oder den Ambassador, Indiens Nationalauto, setzt er für seine Arbeiten ein und kommentiert damit die materialistische Konsumkultur, die Beziehung zwischen Ballungsräumen und den ländlichen Gebieten in denen er aufwuchs, die verschwindende natürliche Landschaft und die Menschenströme.

Jeder der drei Künstler **Atul Dodiya, Prabhavathi Meppayil,** und **Jagannath Panda** hat innovative Ansätze auf dem Gebiet der Malerei entwickelt. Dodiya hat mit einer ganzen Reihe von unterschiedlichen Methoden experimentiert, Fensterläden als Malgrund verwendet und zerschnittene Hemden als Collageelemente in seine Bilder eingebaut. In dieser Ausstellung zeigt er eine Serie von Porträts, hauptsächlich von Paaren, mit dem Titel „Saptapadi", ein Begriff im Zusammenhang mit der traditionellen Hinduhochzeitszeremonie. Durch die Gegenüberstellung auf der Bildfläche erzeugen zusammenhanglose Bilder einen starken visuellen Effekt. Dieser Stil nimmt Anleihen von kitschigen handgemalten Bollywood-Filmplakaten, wie sie überall in indischen Städten zu sehen waren. Während Dodiya hier eine Tradition der Populärkunst aufnimmt, setzt Meppayil traditionelle Metallverarbeitungs- und Maltechniken ein. Im Unterschied zu Dodiyas protzigen Bildern sind die Arbeiten von Meppayil sehr minimalistisch und zart. Sie appliziert Blattgold auf einer weißen Oberfläche mit Hilfe der Werkzeuge ihres Vaters, der ein Meister der Metallbearbeitung war, und malt gepunktete Linien aus Malachitpigment. In dieser Mikrowelt, die aus der Schönheit großer Handwerkskunst entsteht, hinterfragt sie das Verschwinden eines ganzen Industriezweigs, der von der Mechanisierung verdrängt wird. Panda war ursprünglich Bildhauer und verwendet die zweidimensionale Kunst als Erweiterung seiner bildhauerischen Experimente. Typisch für seine Arbeiten sind die Kombination von feinen Stoffstücken mit anderen Elementen, kontrastierende Standpunkte und Größenordnungen auf derselben Ebene sowie die häufige Verwendung von Tiermotiven. Mit seinen Arbeiten lenkt er die Aufmerksamkeit auf das Spannungsfeld von Fortschritt und Tradition und das Verhältnis zwischen Mensch und Tier.

of the new genre of the "graphic novel" in India, mixing texts and graphic images to produce a new form of satirical art. His work portrays his private experiences and memories of different periods of his life, particularly growing up in the 80s and 90s, set against the backdrop of the changing tenor of these times in India itself. He portrays himself in various life stages: such as when he was a child, wishing for Nike shoes and receiving a used pair from his cousin in America; and when he worked in television and interviewed a forensic doctor 12 years after the Bhopal gas tragedy which killed thousands. The images range from his own memories of the 80s to recent incidents in the city of Delhi, raising many questions and quandaries: Has greater material prosperity made life better? Did people have more confidence in the past? Banerjee originally studied biochemistry in college, and the new forms of expression that he is exploring suggest new directions and open up new territories in art. Like Banerjee, the **Raqs Media Collective** is not limited by the ordinary framework of art. The group is composed of three members, Jeebesh Bagchi, Monica Narula, and Shuddhabrata Sengupta, who were previously working on documentary films. They also co-founded the *Sarai* research unit in Delhi, coordinating media productions, pursuing independent research, and carrying out interdisciplinary projects, etc. with experts in various fields, including architects, philosophers, and poets. Their wide range of activities also extends to curation, so it may be more accurate to call them "cultural process catalysts" rather than artists. Their work for this exhibition, which can be described as "thinking architecture", is based on data and archival material related to contemporary India. It is an "open work" that encourages participation, and is, according to the artists, "a machine that speculates about the future".

Chalo! Where Are We Going?

"The image, the imagined, the imaginary – these are all terms that direct us to something critical and new in global cultural processes: the imagination as a social practice. No longer mere fantasy (opium for the masses whose real work is elsewhere), no longer simple escape (from a world defined principally by more concrete purposes and structures), no longer elite pastime (thus not relevant to the lives of ordinary people), and no longer mere contemplation

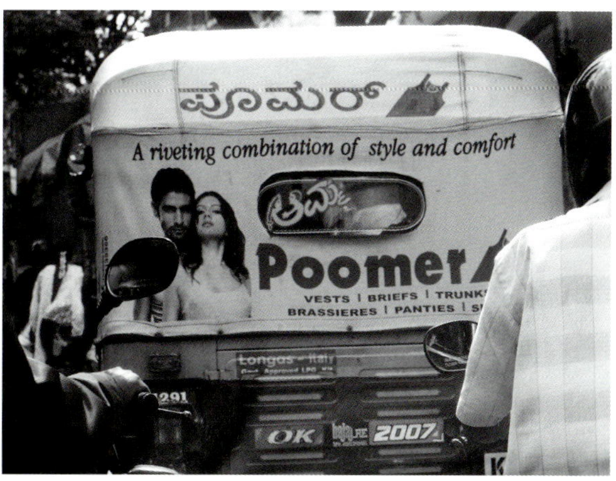

Indische Impression / Indian impression

Epilog: Individualität und Kollektivität / Erinnerung und Zukunft

Der Epilog ist am Schnittpunkt zwischen individueller und kollektiver Erfahrung angesiedelt, wo Gedanken, die sich aus Erinnerungen an die Vergangenheit ergeben, in die Zukunft weiter gesponnen werden. Die nostalgisch klingende Singstimme ertönt aus einem altmodischen Mikrofon. Es ist die Stimme von **Shilpa Gupta,** und sie singt den Text der berühmten Ansprache „Tryst with Destiny" (Verabredung mit dem Schicksal) die Jawaharlal Nehru, der erste Premierminister Indiens, am Vorabend der Unabhängigkeit vor dem indischen Parlament hielt. Die Funktion von Redner und Mikrofon sind ins Gegenteil verkehrt, verwandeln einen offiziellen Anlass in eine sehr private Erfahrung und machen den Zuhörern bewusst, dass 60 Jahre vergangen sind seit Indien seine Unabhängigkeit erlangte. Verwandt aber doch unterschiedlich sind die Bilder der Landkarte Indiens, die 100 Menschen aus dem Gedächtnis zeichneten. Sie zeugen von einer engen Beziehung zwischen Gedächtnis und Vorstellungskraft – als würde man sich die Worte von Agnès Varda vergewärtigen, „Wenn du dich an etwas nicht erinnern kannst, dann male es dir aus." In der Arbeit kommen auch eine gewisse Unbeholfenheit und kleine Diskrepanzen zum Vorschein, die man nicht in Worten oder Bildern ausdrücken kann. Hier stellen sich universelle Fragen über Gedächtnis und Erfahrungen in einem globalen Zeitalter, das von Informationen überflutet wird. **Sarnath Banerjee** war an der Entwicklung des neuen Genres des „grafischen Romans" in Indien beteiligt, worin Texte und Grafiken zu einer neuen Form von satirischer Kunst verbunden werden. Sein Werk spiegelt seine privaten Erfahrungen und Erinnerungen unterschiedlicher Perioden seines Lebens wider, besonders seine Jugend in den 80er und 90er Jahren vor dem Hintergrund der großen Veränderungen, die im Land vor sich gingen. Er porträtiert sich in verschiedenen Lebensstadien: als Kind, das sich Nike Schuhe wünschte und ein gebrauchtes Paar von seinem Cousin aus Amerika erhielt; als Reporter im Fernsehen, der zwölf Jahre nach der Gastragödie von Bhopal, bei der Tausende Menschen getötet wurden, einen Gerichtsmediziner interviewte. Die Bilder spannen einen breiten Bogen von seinen eigenen Erinnerungen in den 80er Jahren bis zu jüngsten Vorfällen in der Stadt Delhi und werfen viele Fragen auf: hat der größere materielle Wohlstand das Leben verbessert? Waren die Menschen in der Vergangenheit zuversichtlicher? Banerjee, der ursprünglich Biochemie studierte, eröffnete mit den neuen Ausdrucksformen, die er entwickelte, neue Bereiche in der Kunst. Ebenso wie Banerjee lässt sich auch das Künstlerkollektiv **Raqs Media Collective** nicht in den üblichen Kunstrahmen einordnen. Die Gruppe besteht aus drei Mitgliedern, Jeebesh Bagchi, Monica Narula und Shuddhabrata Sengupta, die ursprünglich Dokumentarfilme machten. Sie gründeten auch gemeinsam in Delhi die Forschungsstelle „Sarai", die Medienproduktionen koordiniert, unabhängige Forschungsarbeiten verfolgt und interdisziplinäre Projekte mit Experten aus den verschiedensten Gebieten, darunter Architekten, Philosophen und Dichtern, durchführt. Zum breit gespannten Bogen ihrer

(irrelevant for new forms of desire and subjectivity), the imagination has become an organized field of social practices, a form of work (in the sense of both labor and culturally organized practice), and a form of negotiation between sites of agency (individuals) and globally defined fields of possibility. This unleashing of the imagination links the play of pastiche (in some settings) to the terror and coercion of states and their competitors. The imagination is now central to all forms of agency, is itself a social fact, and is the key component of the new global order."

Arjun Appadurai [9)]

This exhibition does not claim to present all the historical trends of Indian art since the 1990s or to be a comprehensive introduction to today's art scene. Neither is it organized around a single theme. As a foreign curator, I approached this art scene, which is like a sea of diversity, by visiting India (and other relevant cities outside India), listening to the opinions of Indian art critics, visiting galleries, meeting artists, observing lots of works in their studios, and discussing it. I based my understanding of what is happening today on this experience, looking for the factors that characterize this new age, as well as social and artistic changes. As a result, this exhibition might be described as a travelogue. There are cities like Kolkata, however, which I did not visit this time; and many artists who could not be introduced within the framework of this exhibition. So I hope that there will be further exhibitions organized in the future; solo shows analyzing the work of individual artists and group shows with new themes, in addition to those frequently discussed, such as narrative and the relationship with the city, and based on broader-ranging and more extensive research. We hope that it will provide basic knowledge for people who want to learn more about Indian art, as well as scholars and experts.

Thus, as mentioned, I have chosen to briefly point out trends exemplified by the works on display rather than making a more thorough analysis of the landscape. When I think, however, about the overall atmosphere of Indian art today, I recall the words quoted at the beginning of this section, of sociologist Arjun Appadurai who analyzed the phenomenon of globalization from different angles and delineated the nature of a world going through endless changes. If we substitute "art" for his concept of "imagi-

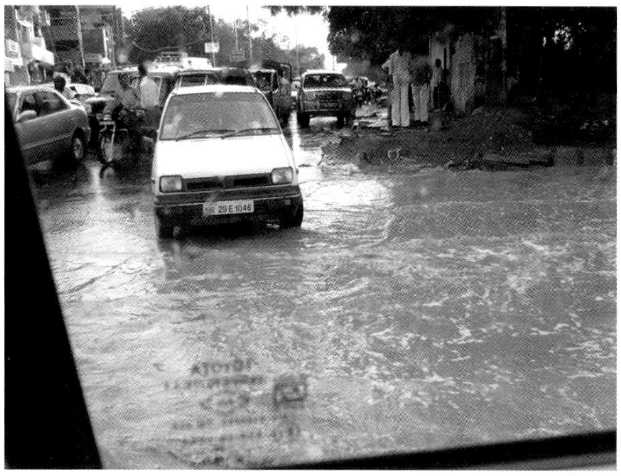

Indische Impression / Indian impression

Es ist die Stimme von Shilpa Gupta, und sie singt den Text der berühmten Ansprache „Tryst with Destiny" (Verabredung mit dem Schicksal) die Jawaharlal Nehru, der erste Premierminister Indiens, am Vorabend der Unabhängigkeit vor dem indischen Parlament hielt. Die Funktion von Redner und Mikrofon sind ins Gegenteil verkehrt, verwandeln einen offiziellen Anlass in eine sehr private Erfahrung und machen den Zuhörern bewusst, dass 60 Jahre vergangen sind seit Indien seine Unabhängigkeit erlangte.

It is the voice of Shilpa Gupta, singing the text of the famous "Tryst with Destiny" speech given by Jawaharlal Nehru, India's first Prime Minister, to the Constituent Assembly on the eve of independence. The function of the speaker and microphone are reversed, making an official event into a very private experience, and creating awareness of the 60 years that has passed since Indian independence.

Viele Künstler, mit denen ich zusammentraf, sprachen von der Notwendigkeit des Widerstands, und ich war beeindruckt von ihrem Glauben an die Möglichkeit, die Gesellschaft mit Ansätzen zu verändern, die nichts mit Fundamentalismus, Konsumwahn oder bloßem Internationalismus zu tun haben.
Listening to the artists I met speaking frequently about the need for resistance, I was impressed with their belief in the possibility of changing society with approaches that differ from fundamentalism, consumerism or mere internationalism.

Aktivitäten zählt auch kuratorische Betreuung, und es wäre vielleicht präziser, sie nicht als Künstler sondern als „kulturelle Prozesskatalysatoren“ zu bezeichnen. Ihre Arbeit für diese Ausstellung, die man als „denkende Architektur“ beschreiben könnte, basiert auf Daten und Archivmaterial aus dem zeitgenössischen Indien. Es ist ein offenes Werk, das zur Teilnahme ermuntert, oder, in den Worten der Künstler, „eine Maschine, die Spekulationen über die Zukunft anstellt“.

Chalo! Wohin gehen wir?

„Das Bild, die bildhafte Vorstellung, das Imaginäre – all das sind Ausdrücke, die uns auf einen kritischen und neuen Aspekt in globalen Kulturprozessen hinführen: die Imagination als soziale Praxis. Nicht länger bloße Fantasie (Opium für die Massen, deren reale Arbeit anderswo liegt), nicht länger bloße Flucht (vor einer Welt die prinzipiell über konkretere Zwecke und Strukturen definiert ist), nicht länger Freizeitvergnügen der Elite (und damit nicht relevant für das Leben der normalen Menschen), und nicht länger bloße Gedankenspielerei (irrelevant für neue Formen von Begehrlichkeit und Subjektivität); somit ist die Imagination zu einem organisierten Feld der Sozialpraxis geworden, einer Form von Arbeit (i. S. von Beschäftigung und kulturell organisierte Praxis), und einer Form von Verhandlung zwischen Orten der Aktion (Individuen) und global definierten Feldern der Möglichkeit. Diese Entfesselung der Imagination verbindet das Spielerische des Pastiche (in manchen Kontexten) mit dem Terror und Zwang von Staaten und ihren Konkurrenten. Die Imagination ist jetzt von zentraler Bedeutung für alle Formen der Aktion, ist selbst soziales Faktum und Schlüsselkomponente der neuen globalen Ordnung.“

Arjun Appadurai [9)]

Diese Ausstellung erhebt nicht den Anspruch, alle historischen Trends in der indischen Kunst seit den 90er Jahren zu präsentieren oder eine umfassende Einführung in die heutige Kunstszene zu bieten. Sie baut auch nicht auf einem einzigen Thema auf. Als ausländische Kuratorin näherte ich mich dieser Kunstszene, die wie ein Meer der Vielfalt erscheint, indem ich Indien besuchte (und auch andere relevante Städte außerhalb von Indien), mir die Meinungen indischer Kunstkritiker anhörte, Galerien besuchte, Künstler traf, in ihren Ateliers viele Werke betrachtete und diskutierte. Mein Verständnis dessen, was heute passiert, gründet sich auf diese Erfahrung. Ich suchte nach den Faktoren, die für dieses neue Zeitalter sowie für die sozialen und künstlerischen Veränderungen charakteristisch sind. Man könnte diese Ausstellung als Reisebeschreibung betrachten. Es gibt jedoch auch Städte wie Kolkata, die ich diesmal nicht besuchte, und viele Künstler, die nicht in den Rahmen dieser Ausstellung aufgenommen werden konnten. Ich hoffe also, dass es weitere Ausstellungen geben wird: Solo-Ausstellungen, die auf das Werk einzelner Künstler eingehen, sowie Gruppenausstellungen mit neuen Themen, zusätzlich zu den oft diskutierten Themen, aufbauend auf umfassenderen, weiter reichenden Recherchen. Wir hoffen, dass wir damit

nation”, his statement may suggest an effective way of looking at the present and future of contemporary Indian art. That is, it now seems possible to see art as something different from “mere fantasy”, “simple escape”, “mere contemplation”, or “an elite pastime”. It has begun to have an important effect on social agency and has potential as a tool for stimulating dialogue and action. Today, most artists are seriously considering the questions of how to engage and negotiate with the world, approach problems, survive, and create the future. Most of them are directing a critical gaze at the reality of their time and society, exercising incisive powers of observation, freedom of spirit, and imagination. At the same time, they are attempting to create new spaces and platforms for debate. To return to the metaphor of the expressway, many artists may have learned through the experience of everyday life to accept unavoidable paradoxes and contradictions in order to survive and keep moving forward with patience and tenacity.[10)] Listening to the artists I met speaking frequently about the need for resistance, I was impressed with their belief in the possibility of changing society with approaches that differ from fundamentalism, consumerism or mere internationalism.
At the end of the exhibition, we come to Subodh Gupta’s golden door, leading to a way out, or to the future. Standing next to it we hear Nehru’s words sung by Shilpa Gupta: “The future beckons to us. Whither do we go and what shall be our endeavour?” These questions, which link past, present, and future, are meant for all of us.

Akiko Miki
“Chalo! India” Curator / Chief Curator, Palais de Tokyo, Paris
Miki studied art history at the University of Washington and completed MA at Université de Paris IV, Sorbonne. After working as Independent curator, as Co-director of Dentsu Art Project and amongst others, She has been at the Palais de Tokyo since 2000 (On sabbatical leave in 2008). Major exhibitions curated/co-curated include: “The 46th Venice Biennial: TransCulture” (1995); “Immutability and Fashion: Contemporary Chinese Art in the Midst of Changing Surroundings” (1997), “1998 Taipei Biennial: Site of Desire”(1998), “SPIRAL TV” (1999), “Twilight Sleep: Japanese Video Art” (2000), “Nobuyoshi Araki: Self, Life, Death” (2005), and “Programme Tropico-Vegetal” (2006). She has written extensively for a number of international exhibition catalogues’ such as the Sharjah Biennial and for both Japanese and foreign magazines. She has also co-authored many books including Hanayo (agnès b, 2003) and Nobuyoshi Araki: Self, Life, Death (Phaidon Press, 2005).

1) Edward Luce has written many articles about India, but his views are summarized in his book, In Spite of the Gods: The Strange Rise of Modern India, Little, Brown, 2006.
2) This title also owes something to the film, Chak De India, which became a hit when it was released last year. This was a sports movie depicting the process of a once-weakly women’s national hockey team, in danger of being disbanded, moving up the ladder to finally win the World Cup victory. It was rather nationalistic, but I felt that it was new and fresh in many ways because it contained no dancing and singing and expressed a kind of confidence. Some Indian artists and critics noted that it was similar to the independence slogan of Subhash Chandra Bose, “Chalo Delhi!” and worried that it might be reminiscent of Japanese militarism. This was something that was not at all intended in this exhibition, but it might be meaningful if it leads to greater interest and further study into the history of relations between Japan and India.
3) Interview with the author in Delhi, November 2007.
4) Chaitanya Sambrani, art critic and curator of “Edge of Desire: Recent Art in India,” The Art Gallery of Western Australia, and other venues, 2005; wrote in detail about the problem of “native” flavor and escaping from the burden of history in his article, “Contemporary Art of India: Turbulent Belonging”, Art It, Winter-Spring, 2007.
5) Some of the most important recent exhibitions include “Edge of Desire: Recent Art in India”, “Indian Summer: La Jeune Scene Artistique Indienne”, École Nationale Supérieure des Beaux-Arts, Paris, 2005; “SUBCONTINGENT: The Indian Subcontinent in Contemporary Art”, Fondazione Sandretto Re Rebaudengo, Turin, Italia, 2006; “Horn Please: Narratives in Contemporary Indian Art”, Kunstmuseum Bern, Switzerland, 2007.
6) Ranjit Hoskote, “Contemporary Indian Art: A Brief Survey”, Private Mythology: Contemporary Art from India, exhibition catalogue, Japan Foundation Asia Center, 1998.
7) Kolkata, Chennai, and Shantiniketan are also important.
8) Baroda is the old British word for Vadodara. The Baroda School refers to artists who have been active around the Faculty of Fine Arts at Maharaja Sayajirao (MS) University from the 1960s. K.G. Subramanyan is a mentor-figure. A closely associated group including Bhupen Khakhar, Gulammohammed Sheikh and Vivan Sundaram, along with Mumbai associates, Nalini Mala-

nicht nur jenen Menschen grundlegendes Wissen vermitteln können, die mehr über die indische Kunst erfahren wollen, sondern auch Wissenschaftlern und Experten.
Wie bereits erwähnt, habe ich mich entschlossen, einige Trendlinien herauszuarbeiten, die von den gezeigten Werken angedeutet werden und keine tiefgehende Analyse der gesamten Landschaft anzubieten. Wenn ich jedoch an die generelle Atmosphäre der indischen Kunst heute denke, erinnere ich mich an die Worte, die am Beginn dieses Abschnitts zitiert werden. Sie stammen vom Soziologen Arjun Appadurai, der das Phänomen der Globalisierung aus verschiedenen Blickwinkeln analysierte und das Wesen einer Welt absteckte, die sich in einem endlosen Prozess des Wandels befindet. Wenn wir an Stelle seines Konzepts der „Imagination" das Wort „Kunst" einsetzen, könnte sein Statement gut als Perspektive auf die Gegenwart und Zukunft der zeitgenössischen indischen Kunst dienen. Das heißt es scheint jetzt möglich, die Kunst als etwas anderes anzusehen als „bloße Fantasie", „bloße Flucht", „bloße Gedankenspielerei" oder ein „Freizeitvergnügen für die Elite". Sie hat begonnen, auch einen wichtigen Effekt auf das soziale Handeln zu haben, und sie hat Potenzial als Werkzeug zur Anregung von Dialog und Aktion. Heute denken die meisten Künstler ernsthaft über die Frage nach, wie sie sich in die Welt einbringen, Problemansätze liefern, überleben und eine Zukunft schaffen können. Die meisten von ihnen werfen einen kritischen Blick auf die Realität ihrer Zeit und der Gesellschaft. Sie beweisen scharfen Beobachtungssinn, geistige Freiheit und Vorstellungskraft. Gleichzeitig versuchen sie, neue Räume und Plattformen für Diskussionen zu schaffen. Um auf die Metapher der Schnellstraße zurückzukommen: die meisten Künstler haben aus der Erfahrung des Alltagslebens gelernt, als Überlebensstrategie unvermeidbare Paradoxa und Widersprüche zu akzeptieren und mit Geduld und Zähigkeit immer weiter vorwärts zu gehen.[10] Viele Künstler, mit denen ich zusammentraf, sprachen von der Notwendigkeit des Widerstands, und ich war beeindruckt von ihrem Glauben an die Möglichkeit, die Gesellschaft mit Ansätzen zu verändern, die nichts mit Fundamentalismus, Konsumwahn oder bloßem Internationalismus zu tun haben.
Am Ende der Ausstellung erreichen wir das goldene Tor von Subodh Gupta, das uns den Weg nach draußen oder in die Zukunft weist. Dort erklingen auch die Worte von Nehru, gesungen von Shilpa Gupta: „Die Zukunft winkt uns zu. Wohin wenden wir uns, und was sollen wir anstreben?" Diese Fragen, die Vergangenheit, Gegenwart und Zukunft verbinden, sind an uns alle gerichtet.

Akiko Miki
„Chalo! India" Kuratorin / Chefkuratorin, Palais de Tokyo, Paris
Miki studierte Kunstgeschichte an der University of Washington und erwarb ihr Masterdiplom an der Université de Paris IV, Sorbonne. Sie war zunächst als freiberufliche Kuratorin tätig, unter anderem als Kodirektorin des Dentsu Art Project. Seit dem Jahr 2000 arbeitet sie im Palais de Tokyo in Paris (2008 auf Studienurlaub). Bedeutende von ihr kuratierte oder ko-kuratierte Ausstellungen: „The 46th Venice Biennial: TransCulture" (1995); „Immutability and Fashion: Contemporary Chinese Art in the Midst of Changing Surroundings" (1997), „1998 Taipei Biennial: Site of Desire"(1998), „SPIRAL TV" (1999), „Twilight Sleep: Japanese Video Art" (2000), „Nobuyoshi Araki: Self, Life, Death" (2005) und „Programme Tropico-Vegetal" (2006). Sie hat umfangreiche Beiträge für eine Reihe internationaler Kataloge, u.a. für die Sharjah Biennial, und für japanische und ausländische Fachzeitschriften verfasst. Außerdem ist sie Koautorin zahlreicher Bücher, darunter „Hanayo" (agnès b, 2003) und „Nobuyoshi Araki: Self, Life, Death" (Phaidon Press, 2005).

ni, and Sudhir Patwardhan, launched a movement of figurative-narrative painting with an emphasis on locality and mounted the exhibition, Place for People, in 1981. A very large number of artists continue to live and work in Vadodara and show broad artistic affinities.

9) Arjun Appadurai, Modernity at Large: Cultural Dimension of Globalization, University of Minnesota Press, Minneapolis (MN), U.S.A, 1996, p. 31.

10) Japanese artist, Koganezawa Takehito resided and worked in New Delhi last year and rode in an auto-rickshaw every day. He noticed that the speedometer and rearview mirror were broken and could not tell whether the driver was looking at the road or not since he was talking to someone riding a motorcycle to one side. Because of his experience of physical or tactile sensations, he suggested that the sense of sight does not occupy a special position and the concept of plural numbers has little meaning in India. Comment in Vanishing Points: Japanese Contemporary Art (exhibition catalogue), Delhi and Mumbai, 2007.

[1] Edward Luce hat viele Artikel über Indien geschrieben, aber eine Zusammenfassung seiner Ansichten findet sich in seinem Buch, „In Spite of the Gods: The Strange Rise of Modern India“, Little, Brown, 2006.

[2] Der Titel verdankt sich auch in gewisser Weise dem Film „Chak De India“, der sofort zum Hit wurde, als er letztes Jahr heraus kam. Es handelt sich um einen Sportfilm, der die Geschichte einer einstmals schwachen Frauen-Hockeynationalmannschaft beschreibt, die eigentlich aufgelöst werden sollte, dann aber immer besser wurde und letztendlich den World Cup gewann. Der Film ist zwar ziemlich nationalistisch, fühlte sich für mich aber doch in gewisser Weise neu und frisch an, weil er keine Tanz- und Gesangsszenen enthielt und Selbstvertrauen ausstrahlte. Einige indische Künstler und Kritiker merkten an, dass es Ähnlichkeiten mit dem Unabhängigkeitsslogan von Subhash Chandra Bose gäbe- "Chalo Delhi!" - und waren besorgt, dass hier Anklänge an japanischen Militarismus aufkommen könnten. Das war zwar in dieser Ausstellung überhaupt kein Thema, könnte sich aber als bedeutungsvoll erweisen, wenn es zu größerem Interesse und einer weiteren historischen Aufarbeitung der Beziehungen zwischen Japan und Indien führt.

[3] Interview mit der Verfasserin in Delhi, November 2007.

[4] Chaitanya Sambrani, Kunstkritiker und Kurator von „Edge of Desire: Recent Art in India“ (2005) in The Art Gallery of Western Australia und andernorts, schrieb detailliert über das Problem der „einheimischen“ Färbung und die Last der Geschichte in seinem Artikel „Contemporary Art of India: Turbulent Belonging“, Art It, Winter-Spring, 2007.

[5] Zu den wichtigsten Ausstellungen der jüngsten Zeit gehörten „Edge of Desire: Recent Art in India“, „Indian Summer: La Jeune Scène Artistique Indienne“, École Nationale Supérieure des Beaux-Arts, Paris, 2005; „SUBCONTINGENT: The Indian Subcontinent in Contemporary Art“, Fondazione Sandretto Re Rebaudengo, Turin, Italien, 2006; „Horn Please: Narratives in Contemporary Indian Art“, Kunstmuseum Bern, Schweiz, 2007.

[6] Ranjit Hoskote, „Contemporary Indian Art: A Brief Survey“, Private Mythology: Contemporary Art from India, Ausstellungskatalog, Japan Foundation Asia Center, 1998.

[7] Ebenso bedeutsam sind Kolkata, Chennai und Shantiniketan.

[8] Baroda ist die alte britische Bezeichnung für Vadodara. Als „Baroda Schule“ wird der Künstlerkreis um die Kunstfakultät der Maharaja Sayajirao (MS) Universität in den 1960er Jahren bezeichnet. K.G. Subramanyan spielte eine wichtige Rolle als Mentor. Eine eng verbundene Gruppe, zu der auch Bhupen Khakhar, Gulammohammed Sheikh und Vivan Sundaram, gemeinsam mit den Kollegen aus Mumbai, Nalini Malani und Sudhir Patwardhan, zählten, gründete eine Bewegung der figurativ-narrativen Malerei mit einem Schwerpunkt auf Lokalität und organisierte 1981 die Ausstellung „Place for People“. Auch heute lebt und arbeitet eine große Zahl von Künstlern mit breiter künstlerischer Ausrichtung in Vadodara.

[9] Arjun Appadurai, „Modernity at Large: Cultural Dimension of Globalization“, University of Minnesota Press, Minneapolis (MN), U.S.A, 1996, S. 31.

[10] Der japanischer Künstler Koganezawa Takehito lebte und arbeitete letztes Jahr in New Delhi und fuhr jeden Tag mit einer Auto-Rikscha. Er bemerkte, dass der Tachometer und der Rückspiegel kaputt waren und konnte auch nicht sagen, ob der Fahrer, der mit einem nebenan fahrenden Motorradfahrer in ein Gespräch verwickelt war, auf die Straße achtete. Aufgrund seiner Erfahrung physischer oder taktiler Sinnesempfindungen ist er der Ansicht, dass der Sehsinn in Indien keine besondere Stellung einnimmt und auch das Konzept der größeren Zahlen wenig Bedeutung hat. Kommentar in „Vanishing Points: Japanese Contemporary Art“ (Ausstellungskatalog), Delhi und Mumbai, 2007.

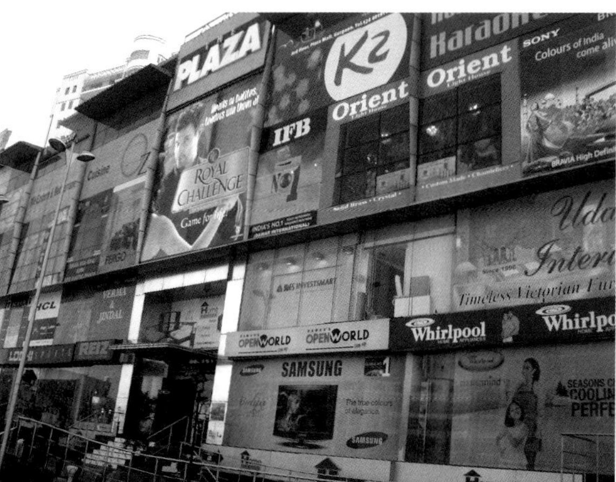

Indische Impressionen / Indian impressions

FREMDE BILDER GANZ VERTRAUT I STRANGE AND FAMILIAR IMAGES

Eine Annäherung an die zeitgenössische indische Kunst I Getting acquainted with contemporary Indian art

Sabine B. Vogel

I. Befremden oder Vertrautheit?

Kunst ist tief in der nationalen Kultur eines Landes verankert. Wer in ein anderes Land kommt, ist oft verblüfft ob der in Museen und Nationalgalerien zu entdeckenden lokalen Vielfalt und historischen Querverbindungen. Auch Kunstzeitschriften und Kunstmessen vermitteln oft eine regionale Kultur, flankiert von wenigen internationalen Positionen. Wenn diese Erfahrung bereits für den Schritt von Deutschland nach Österreich, von der Schweiz nach Italien gilt, wie groß ist dann die Wissenslücke über die in der westlichen Kunstgeschichte nahezu unbekannte indische Kunst?

Zum Verständnis jeder Kunstszene bedarf es eines zumindest rudimentären Wissens um Kontexte und Traditionen, damit Befremden in Wiedererkennen übergehen kann. Denn in jeder Wahrnehmung suchen wir im Gedächtnis nach Vertrautem. „Mit zunehmender Vertrautheit steigt das Gefallen für weniger eingängige Stile, die dann vermutlich interessanter und anregender sind. In einer weiteren Verarbeitungsstufe kommt das Verstehen, das in einem ständigen Austausch von kognitiven Erklärungen und gefühlsmäßigen Bewertungen steht. Hat der Betrachter das Gefühl, die Herausforderung des Kunstwerkes gemeistert zu haben, kommt es zu einem ästhetischen Urteil (‚Dies gefällt mir!') und einer so genannten ästhetischen Emotion, die im günstigen Fall ein Genuss, ein Wohlgefühl ist", erklärt Helmut Leder[1] den Prozess der ästhetischen Wahrnehmung. Für eine erste Annäherung an die indische Kunst wird daher im Folgenden der Blick auf einige gesellschaftliche Voraussetzungen und (Bild-)Traditionen gerichtet.

II. Wirtschaftliche Umbruchsituation

Lange Zeit war Indien im Westen vor allem eine Projektionsfläche spiritueller Erwartungen. Dabei beteiligt sich Indien bereits 1959 an der 5. „Bienal de São Paulo" in Brasilien und ist dort immer wieder mit umfassenden Präsentationen vertreten. Seit 1968 findet in New Delhi die „India Triennale" statt, zu der bis heute europäische Länder bzw. KünstlerInnen eingeladen sind. In Indien berühmte Künstler wie Francis Newton Souza[2], S. H. Raza[3] und M. F. Husain[4], die 1947 die einflussreiche „Progressive Artists Group"[5] gründeten, auch K. G. Subramanyan[6] und Bhupen Khakhar[7], lebten zwar zeitweilig in Paris, London oder New York und stellten dort aus, sind im westlichen Kunstkontext aber ebenso unbekannt geblieben wie uns kunsthistorische Einflüsse wie die Pahari Miniaturmalereien und die Kalighat Malerei unvertraut sind.

I. Strange or familiar?

Art is deeply rooted in a country's national culture. When one goes to another country one is often amazed at how much local variety and historical interconnections can be found in museums and national galleries. Art journals and art fairs often concentrate on regional culture, merely flanked by a few international aspects. If that holds true between Germany and Austria or Switzerland and Italy, how huge must the information gap be in the case of Indian art, which is almost unknown in western art history?

In order to understand a given art scene one needs at least a rudimentary awareness of contexts and traditions, so that strangeness can be transformed into recognition. Whenever we perceive anything we search our memory for something familiar. "As familiarity increases so does enjoyment of less catchy styles, which then presumably are the ones that are more interesting and stimulating. Another step in the chain of processing is understanding, which happens in a constant exchange of cognitive explanations and emotional assessments. When the viewer feels that he has mastered the challenges of a work of art, he will make an aesthetic judgment ('I like that!') and feel a so-called aesthetic emotion which, in the favourable case, is a feeling of enjoyment, of pleasure", is how Helmut Leder[1] explains the process of aesthetic perception. That is why this essay will first look at some social conditions and traditions (of imagery) in attempting to become familiar with Indian art.

II. Profound economic change

For a long time, India was mainly a projection screen for spiritual expectations harboured by the West, although the country was represented in the 5th *Bienal de São Paulo* in Brazil as early as 1959 and has continued to put comprehensive presentations on show there ever since. The *India Triennial,* where European countries and/or artists have always been invited, has been taking place in New Delhi since 1968. Even though artists who are famous within India – such as Francis Newton Souza[2], S. H. Raza[3] and M. F. Husain[4], who founded the influential "Progressive Artists Group" in 1947[5], as well as K. G. Subramanyan[6] and Bhupen Khakhar[7] – spent some time in Paris, London or New York and exhibited there, they have remained as unfamiliar in the western art context as art-historical influences such as Pahari miniature paintings and Kalighat painting. And while modern art developments within the subcontinent were highly interesting, the study of contemporary Indian art only started around the turn of the millennium.

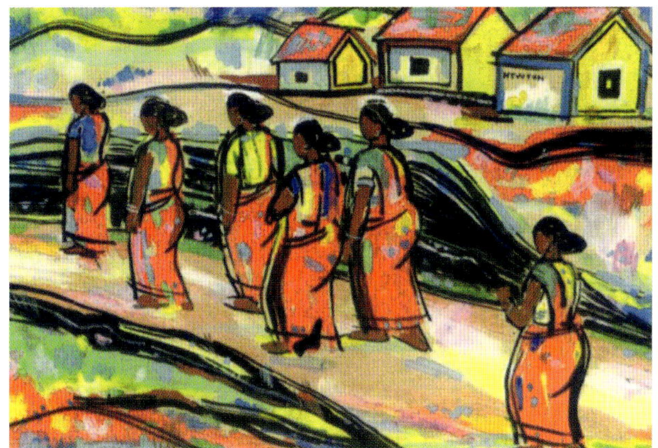

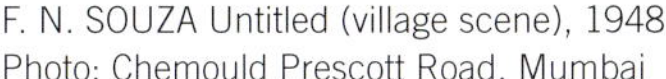

F. N. SOUZA Untitled (village scene), 1948
Photo: Chemould Prescott Road, Mumbai

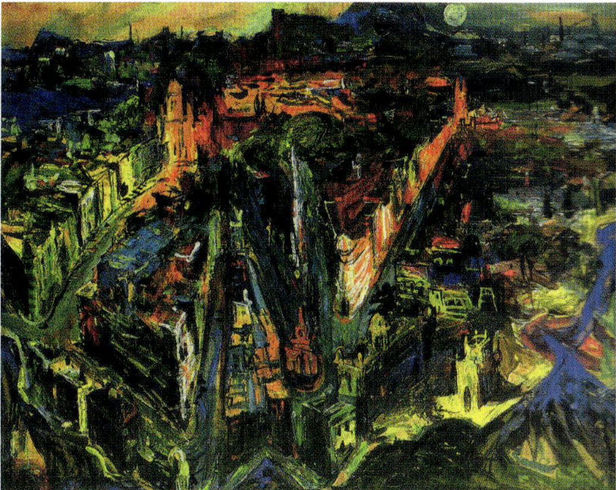

S. H. RAZA Earth, 1978
Photo: Estate of Jehangir Nicholson, Mumbai

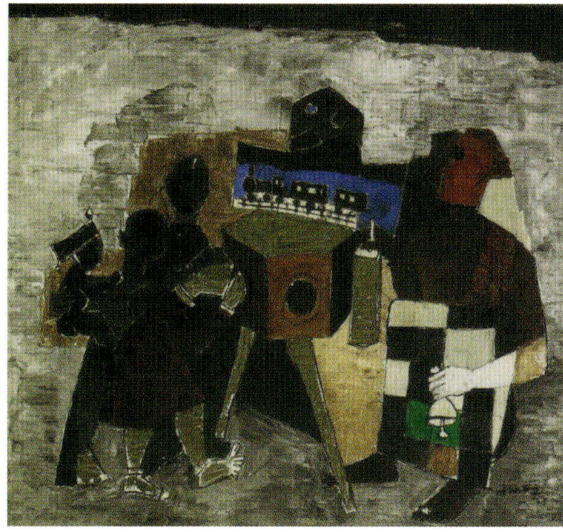

M. F. HUSAIN Amusement in the street
Photo: Chemould Prescott Road, Mumbai

Obwohl sich auf dem Subkontinent eine hochinteressante Kunst der Moderne entwickelte, setzt die Beschäftigung mit zeitgenössischer indischer Kunst erst um die letzte Jahrtausendwende ein.

Das heutige Indien beginnt Anfang der 1990er Jahre. Ein Sozialismus nach dem Vorbild der Sowjetunion und der wirtschaftliche Autarkie-Anspruch seit der Unabhängigkeit am 15. August 1947 hatten Indien in eine verheerende Finanzkrise schlittern lassen. Dem viertgrößten Schuldner der Welt lieh nur noch der Internationale Währungsfond weitere Gelder – und verlangte dafür die Globalisierung der indischen Wirtschaft. 1991 beschließt Indien einen Fünf-Jahresplan mit der Liberalisierung des Marktes und Privatisierungen im Binnenmarkt. Mit seinen starken wirtschaftlichen Wachstumsraten gilt das Land heute als Zukunftsmarkt mit höchstem Potential – und das spiegelt sich auch in der zeitgenössischen Kunst wider. Bereits Mitte der 1990er Jahre starten erste, erfolgreiche Auktionen mit indischer Kunst der Moderne in London und New York. Die Preise für Werke der „Progressive Artists Group" überschreiten 2003 erstmals die $ 100.000,– Marke. Anfangs ist es ein ausschließlicher Binnenmarkt, auf dem vor allem die „Non Residential Indians" (NRI) in London und New York die Preise auf Online-Auktionen in die Höhe treiben. „(Sie) sehen die neue Kunst als einen Weg, ihre ethnische Identität zu bekräftigen", beschreibt Randeep Ramesh das Phänomen im britischen „Guardian"[8]. Gehandelt wird vor allem eine deutliche „indishness" Kunst: Werke, die deutlich im kulturellen Kontext Indiens verwurzelt sind, indem religiöse Figuren, ethnische Objekte, kunsthistorische Traditionen zitiert und variiert werden.

Bald setzt das Interesse westeuropäischer Kunsthäuser an der indischen Kunst ein. Ob „Century City" 2000 in der Tate London, „Kapital & Karma" 2002 in der Kunsthalle Wien, „Body. City. Siting contemporary culture in India" im Haus der Kulturen der Welt in Berlin 2003, „Urban Manners" 2004 im Hangar Bicocca in Mailand, „Indian Summer" in der École Nationale Supérieure des Beaux-Arts in Paris 2005, „Horn Please" in der Kunsthalle Bern 2007 oder 2009 „Indian Highway" in der Serpentine Gallery, London: Am Beginn des neuen Jahrtausends rückt die indische Gegenwartskunst in den Fokus.

Modern-day India emerged only in the early 1990s. After independence on 15 August 1947, the Socialist-style government modelled on the Soviet Union and the claim for economic autarchy drove the country into a disastrous financial crisis. The International Monetary Fund was the only lender willing to grant further loans to the fourth-largest debtor in the world – and in exchange it demanded the globalisation of the Indian economy. In 1991, India adopted a five-year plan involving the liberalisation of the market and privatisation projects in the domestic market. With its strong economic growth the country is now considered as a market with great potential for the future – a fact that is also reflected in contemporary art. As early as the mid-1990s, the first successful auctions of Indian contemporary art were held in London and New York. 2003 was the first year when prices achieved for works of the "Progressive Artists Group" exceeded the USD 100.000 mark. It started out as a domestic market, in which mainly the "Non Residential Indians" (NRI) in London and New York drove up prices in online auctions. "(They) see the new art as a way of reconfirming their ethnic identity", is how Randeep Ramesh described the phenomenon in the British newspaper The Guardian[8]. The interest of buyers lies particularly in art with a marked "Indian-ness": works that are clearly rooted in the cultural context of India and which quote and show variations of religious figures, ethnic objects and art-historical traditions.

Soon western European art institutions started to develop an interest in Indian art. *Century City* at the Tate London in 2000, *Kapital & Karma* at Kunsthalle Vienna in 2002, *Body. City. Siting contemporary culture in India* at the Haus der Kulturen der Welt in Berlin in 2003, *Urban Manners* at Hangar Bicocca in Milan in 2004, *Indian Summer* at the École Nationale Supérieure des Beaux-Arts in Paris in 2005, *Horn Please* at Kunsthalle Bern in 2007 or *Indian Highway* at the Serpentine Gallery, London in 2009: at the dawn of the new millennium, Indian contemporary art is at the centre of attention.

III. The Babri Mosque

On 6 December 1992, militant Hindu groups destroyed the Babri Mosque in Ayodhya, the religious site which had been built in 1528 on the foundations of a Hindu temple destroyed by Muslim conquerors. According to legend it

III. Babri-Moschee

Am 6. Dezember 1992 zerstören parteinahe, militante Hindu-Gruppen die Babri-Moschee in Ayodhya, jene religiöse Stätte, die 1528 auf den Grundfesten eines von muslimischen Eroberern zerstörten Hindu-Tempels errichtet wurde. Einer Legende nach soll hier der Gott Rama geboren worden sein. Auf den Anschlag folgen landesweite Ausschreitungen und Unruhen. Diese Tat gilt als Angriff auf den grundlegenden Säkularismus Indiens, auf das Ideal von Toleranz, das Indiens erster Premierminister Jawarharlal Nehru als „unity in diversity" (Einheit in der Vielfalt) formulierte. Der Säkularismus Indiens bedeutet dabei nicht nur eine klare Trennung zwischen Religion und Politik wie im Westen, sondern auch eine Überfülle und Gleichwertigkeit verschiedenster Religionen. Doch diese Säkularismus ist gefährdet, seit die hinduistische Volkspartei BJP (Bharatiya Janata Party) jenen Anschlag von 1992 gezielt organisierte und die Religion für nationalistische Anliegen benutzt.

Der Künstler **Jitish Kallat** fasst die gesellschaftliche Bedeutung des Ereignisses zusammen: „Die im Jahr 1992 auf die Zerstörung der Babri Masjid folgenden Aufstände zeigten erstmals, wie sehr gesteuerte Spannungen in der Bevölkerung polarisieren können und welche Gefahr sie für die säkulare Struktur der Verfassung und des Landes darstellen. Sie zeigten auch, wie unliberale und fundamentalistische Strömungen einen neo-faschistischen ‚Schlagarm' nach sich ziehen, der sich sehr leicht im Namen der Religion zu destruktiven Aktionen mobilisieren lässt. Das läutete die rechtsgerichtete Aufruhrpolitik ein, deren Höhepunkt wir im Pogrom nach dem Anschlag von Godhra sehen können. Man kann dies vielleicht als die extremste Form der Endo-Kolonisierung bezeichnen, die dieses Land je erlebte. Die Wahlstrategie war es einfach, mögliche Gegenstimmen zu eliminieren. Und schließlich erleben wir wie Hass-Propaganda die üblichen ‚Brot-und-Butter' Versprechen ablösen, die wir traditionell aus den Wahlkämpfen in Indien kennen."[9]

„Diese Bewegung hat viele Künstler angeregt, ihre Praktiken zu überdenken. Viele hatten das Gefühl, die Anschläge stellten einen Bruch dar und einen Anlass, ihre Themen und Werkzeuge neu zu gestalten",[10] erklärt Jitish Kallat die Bedeutung dieses Ereignisses für die Künstler. Mit Werken wie „Public Notice" (2003) und „Public Notice - 2" (2007)

was the birthplace of the god Rama. Following the attack, violence and unrest erupted all over the country. The incident was seen as an attack on the fundamental secularism of the India, on the ideal of tolerance which India's first prime minister, Jawarharlal Nehru, described as "unity in diversity". Indian secularism not only means a clear separation between religion and politics, as it does in the West, but also a plethora of different religions and equality between them. And this principle has been threatened ever since the Bharatiya Janata Party (BJP), the Hindu nationalist party, masterminded the attack in 1992 and instrumentalised religion for nationalist ends.

The artist **Jitish Kallat** summarises the social impact of this incident: "The 1992 riots following the destruction of the Babri Masjid first revealed the extent to which choreographed, communal tensions can polarise people and play havoc with the secular fabric of the constitution and the country. It was also a demonstration of how illiberal and fundamentalist outfits breed a neo-fascist 'hit' brigade that can be easily mobilised into destructive actions in the name of religion. It marshalled the beginning of right-wing 'rioting' politics whose culmination we saw in the post-Godhra pogrom, which can perhaps be described as the most extreme form of endo-colonisation this country has ever seen. The election strategy laid out was simply to eliminate the constituency that may vote against you. Finally we have ‚hate-based' propaganda taking over 'bread-and-butter' promises that have traditionally been the leitmotifs of Indian election campaigns."[9]

"This movement did drive many artists to rethink their practice, many felt that the attacks were a moment of rupture that made them re-evaluate the themes of their work and the tools they used to engage with them",[10] is how Jitish Kallat explains the significance of this event for artists. With works such as *Public Notice* (2003) and *Public Notice - 2* (2007) Kallat responded directly to the "climate of threat and intolerance that threatens a country that has just woken up to its full potential in the last few years". In an earlier work, Kallat wrote the independence speech delivered by India's first prime minister, Jawarharlal Nehru, on to a mirror – a speech full of hope for tolerance and peace. In *Public Notice - 2,* Kallat uses Gandhi's speech at the beginning of his 24-day Salt March in 1930 during the struggle for independence, in which Gandhi postulated

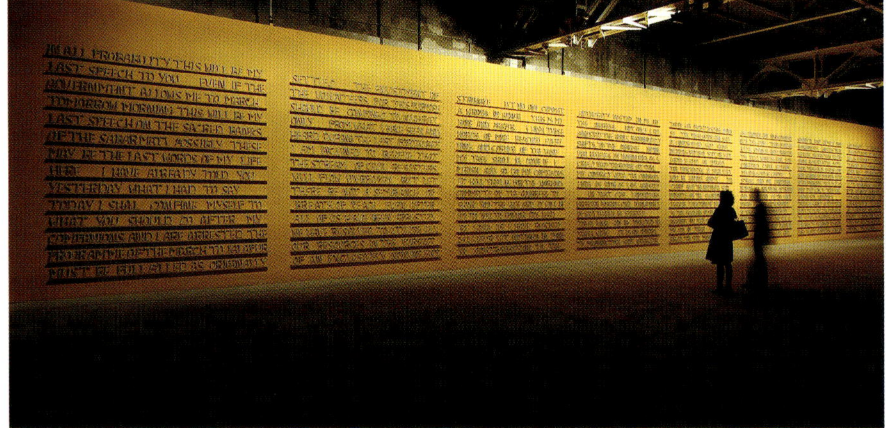

JITISH KALLAT Public Notice - 2, 2007
Photo: Hangar Bicocca © Jitish Kallat

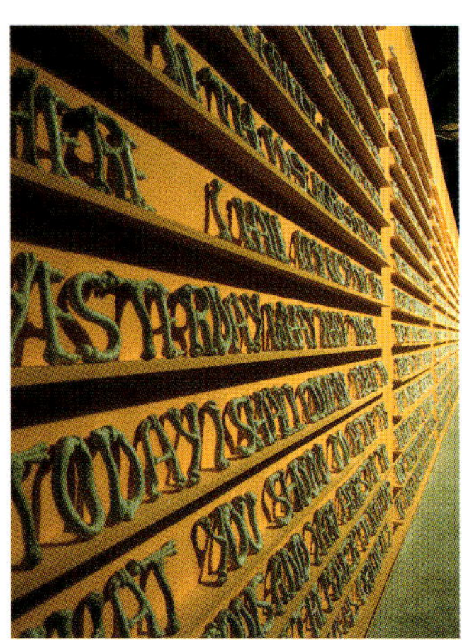

JITISH KALLAT Public Notice - 2, 2007
(Detail) Photo: Jitish Kallat © Jitish Kallat

reagiert Kallat direkt auf das „Klima von Bedrohung und Intoleranz in einem Land, das gerade erst in den letzten Jahren seines vollen Potenzials gewahr wurde". In der früheren Arbeit schreibt Kallat die Rede von Indiens erstem Premierminister Jawarharlal Nehru anlässlich der Unabhängigkeit auf Spiegel – eine Rede voller Hoffnung auf Toleranz und Frieden. In „Public Note - 2" greift Kallat Gandhis Rede zu Beginn seines 24-tägigen Salz-Marsches 1930 während des Unabhängigkeitskampfes auf, in der Gandhi absoluten Frieden und Gewaltfreiheit postuliert. Die Buchstaben der Worte sind aus Knochen gebaut und bedecken mächtig die Wände des Raumes. Nur das Skelett scheint übriggeblieben zu sein, ein Bild voller Gewalt und Eindringlichkeit, zugleich eine Warnung und eine Erinnerung.

Bezieht sich Kallat vor allem inhaltlich auf zentrale indische Werte, die von der Radikalisierung des Hinduismus bedroht werden, so greifen andere KünstlerInnen auch deutlich religiöse Motive und Traditionen auf, um etwa an die „Verspieltheit der Hindu-Epik" zu erinnern, wie es Nalini Malani[11] formuliert. Wie in ihrer Malerei dienen dazu immer wieder formale Anspielungen an die Kalighat-Malerei. Im 19. Jahrhundert verkauften Autodidakten nahe des hinduistischen Tempels in Kalighat im Süden Kolkattas (ehemals Kalkutta) ihre hoch stilisierten Aquarelle auf der Straße. Es ist eine urban-säkulare Malerei, die sowohl hinduistische Gottheiten als auch humorvolle alltägliche Szenen darstellt. Transparente Farben, dünne Konturlinien, flache Schatten der Figuren und ein heller, fast farbloser Hintergrund gehören zu den formalen Merkmalen, die Rolle des Künstlers als sozialer Kommentator zu den einflussreichen inhaltlichen Innovationen, die in der zeitgenössischen indischen Kunst immer wieder zitiert werden.

IV. Traditionen

Diese Kombination eines säkularisierten Umgangs mit Religion, der Integration von Traditionen und des thematischen Fokus auf das urbane Leben lassen sich in der indischen Gegenwartskunst immer wieder feststellen. Anders als in der westlichen Moderne antworten die KünstlerInnen nicht mit der Tabula-rasa-Methode und erfinden Formensprache und Themenwahl jeweils radikal neu, sondern greifen dazu Elemente der Mythologie und Ikonographie auf. Dem Subkontinent mit einer viertausend Jahre alten Kulturgeschichte und einer Bevölkerung von heute eineinhalb Milliarden Bewohnern (die laut einer Studie von 2001 122 Sprachen sprechen, von denen 22 als offizielle Sprachen in der Verfassung aufgenommen sind), und vier großen Religionen steht ein reichhaltiger Fundus an Bildern und Geschichten zur Verfügung.

„Ich versuche, mich mit dem Erbe der religiösen und geistigen Ikonographie auseinanderzusetzen", erklärt **Jagannath Panda** zur Frage, wie seine sozialkritischen Bildinhalte mit der Skulptur eines Pfaus – dem Nationaltier Indiens – zusammenkommen. „In der indischen Mythologie verkörpert der Pfau den Geist der Jugendlichkeit, und mir gefällt der Gedanke des unschuldigen Staunens, den er vermittelt, und auch seine magischen Kräfte. Leider verschwindet

absolute peace and nonviolence. The letters in the words are built from bones and cover the walls of the room. Only the skeleton seems to have remained, a violent and forceful image, warning and remembrance combined.

If the content of Kallat's work refers mainly to central Indian values threatened by the radicalisation of Hinduism, other artists include clearly religious motifs and traditions, for instance to recall the "playful nature of Hindu epics", as Nalini Malani[11] puts it. To do this she includes formal references to Kalighat painting. In the 19th century, self-taught painters sold their highly stylised watercolours on the road near the Hindu temples of Kalighat, south of Kolkata (formerly Calcutta). It was an urban, secular painting style which depicts Hindu divinities and humorous scenes from everyday life. Transparent colours, thin contour lines, flat shadows cast by the figures and a light, almost colourless, background are amongst the formal characteristics. The artist's role as a social commentator introduced by this style is among the influential substantial innovations which continue to be quoted in contemporary Indian art.

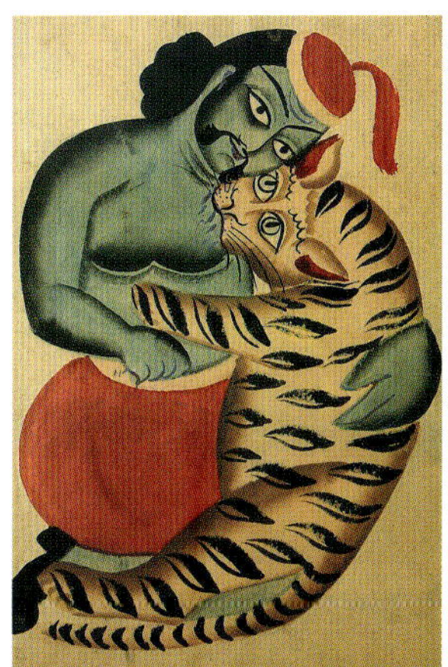
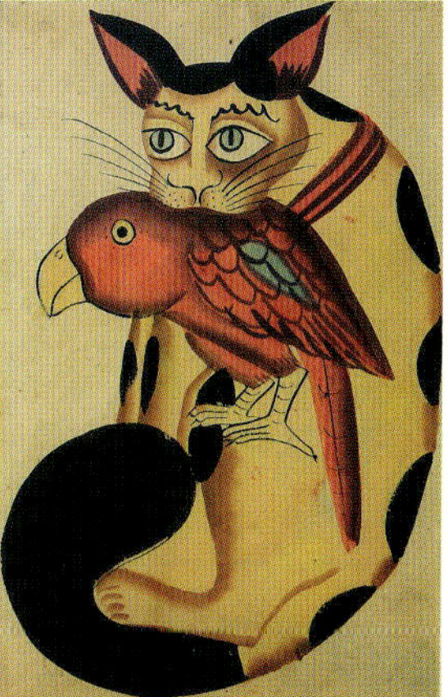

KALIGHAT Untitled (Man with Tiger), Untitled (Cat with bird), undat.
Photo: Chemould Prescott Road, Mumbai

IV. Traditions

This combination of a secularised approach to religion, the integration of traditions and the thematic focus on urban life, is frequently found in Indian contemporary art. In contrast to western Modernism, artists do not respond by eradicating everything and radically reinventing formal languages and themes, but integrate elements of mythology and iconography. The subcontinent, with its 4000 years of cultural history, a current population of 1.5 billion people (according to a study in 2001 they speak 122 languages, of which 22 have been enshrined in the constitution as official languages) and four major religions, has a great wealth of images and stories at its disposal.

"I am trying to engage myself with the heritage of religious and spiritual iconography", declares **Jagannath Panda** when asked how he combines his criticism of social conditions with the sculpture of a peacock – the national animal of India. "In Indian mythology the peacock represents youthful spirit, and I like the idea of innocent wonder it seems to convey and also its magical powers. Unfortunately, this beautiful proud bird is gradually disappearing from

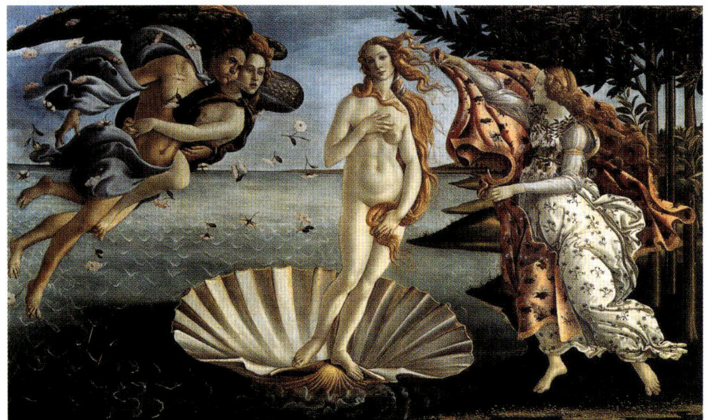

SANDRO BOTTICELLI La nascita de Venere, 1486
Photo: http://wikimedia.org/

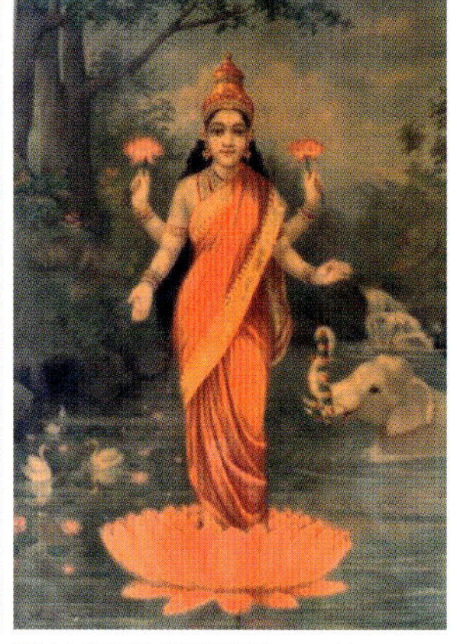

RAJA RAVI VARMA The goddess Lakshmi, undat.
Photo: http://wikimedia.org/

dieser schöne stolze Vogel immer mehr aus unseren Städten, und das führt uns zum Thema der paradigmatischen Spannung und seiner Funktion als Erinnerung und Spiegel in einer kontradiktorischen Realität." Der Pfau ist ein Sinnbild für Gegensätze: „Meine Arbeit verweist auf die grundlegenden Widersprüche und Dichotomien zwischen Natur und Kultur, Urbanität und Ruralität, Lokalität und Globalität. Die Verwendung von Tieren, Vögeln und Pflanzen spricht auch Umweltbelange an; es geht darum, den Zusammenprall der Natur mit der Kultur zu untersuchen, der unser Leben so sehr bestimmt. Es geht auch darum, die Entwicklungsbedürfnisse einer immer habsüchtigeren urbanen Gesellschaft zu hinterfragen. Ich würde diese Probleme gerne gelöst sehen und erleben, dass wir als Gemeinschaft den Lebensraum der Tiere schützen und die Werte der indigenen Bevölkerung respektieren."[12]

Deutlich geprägt von ikonographischen Anspielungen sind auch die Fotografien von **Pushpamala N.** In ihrer Foto-Serie „The Native Types" nennt sie immer wieder Ravi Varma als Vorbild. Raja Ravi Varma[13], geboren als Prinz im Kilimanoor Palast, wurde gleichermaßen in indischer und europäischer Maltechnik unterrichtet. Er war der erste indische Maler, der Geschichten und Figuren der Hindu-Epen im Stile des europäischen Realismus darstellte und der 1873 einen Preis für seine Malerei auf der Weltausstellung in Wien erhielt. Seine Werke waren so gefragt, dass er eine eigene Druckerei für seine Farblithographien gründete, die zum Vorbild der „calendar art" wurden und bis heute die Kunst, Literatur und Filmindustrie Indiens beeinflussen. Pushpamalas Fotografie „Lakshmi" ist in engster Anlehnung an Ravi Varmas gleichnamiges Bild inszeniert – das übrigens durchaus an Sandro Botticellis „Geburt der Venus" (1485/86) erinnert. Während die Venus einer Muschel entsteigt, steht die Göttin Lakshmi allerdings in einer Lotusblüte und ist nicht umgeben von Göttern, sondern von Schwänen und einem Elefanten. Vergleichbar ist zwar der vereinfachte und idealisierte Umraum, allerdings ist die Venus nackt und Lakshmi mit einem Sari bekleidet – womit der kulturelle Kontext in den zentralen Details unübersehbar ist.

Varmas Drucke und Bilder sind in Indien allgegenwärtig, gerade „Lakshmi" ist eine weltweite Ikone für „indishness" geworden. Mit diesem Bild wie auch ihrer gesamten „Native

urban space and this leads us to the issue of the paradigmatic tension and function as both memory and mirror, it is contradictory reality." The peacock is a symbol of opposites: "My work addresses the vital fundamental contradictions and the dichotomies that exist between nature and culture, urban and rural, the local and the global communities. The use of animals, birds and plants expresses environmental concern; examining at length the collision of nature with culture which has come to dominate our lives. It also questions the developmental needs of an increasingly avaricious urban society. I would like to see such issues resolved and that we as a community protect wild life habitat and respect the value of indigenous people."[12]

Iconographic references have also clearly marked the photographs of **Pushpamala N.** In her photo series *The Native Types* she frequently mentions Ravi Varma as a model. Raja Ravi Varma[13], born a prince at the Kilimanoor Palace, received instruction in both Indian and European painting techniques. He was the first Indian painter to describe stories and figures of Hindu epics in the style of European realism, and in 1873 he received an award for his paintings at the World Expo in Vienna. His paintings were so much in demand that he founded his own printing shop for colour lithographs which became the models for "calendar art" and have gone on exerting an influence on India's art, literature and movie industry to this day. Pushpamala's photograph *Lakshmi* is staged very much along the lines of Ravi Varma's homonymous painting – which, by the way, bears reminiscences of Sandro Botticelli's *Birth of Venus* (1485/86). Whereas Venus alights from a shell, the goddess Lakshmi stands in a lotus flower, and she is not surrounded by gods, but by swans and an elephant. Although the simplified and idealised surroundings are comparable, Venus is naked while Lakshmi is dressed in a sari – making the cultural context very obvious in the central details.

In India, Varma's prints and paintings are omnipresent and particularly *Lakshmi* has become a worldwide icon of "Indian-ness". With this image, as with her entire *Native Types* series, Pushpamala makes reference to the foreign (colonialist) and to her own perspectives. She links ethnographic images with pictures from daily life and thus opens up a discussion on clichés about India. Two further artists

Types"-Serie spielt Pushpamala sowohl auf den fremden (kolonialistischen) als auch den eigenen Blick an, verbindet ethnographische mit alltagstypischen Bildern und stellt so die Klischees über Indien zur Diskussion. Zwei weitere, heute noch arbeitende Künstler sind dabei ebenfalls von bedeutendem Einfluss für ihr Werk: Bhupen Khakhar und K. G. Subramanyan. Der Autodidakt Bhupen Khakhar ist auch im westlichen Kontext kein Unbekannter, stellte er doch 1992 auf der IX. documenta in Kassel aus. Sein Werk hing in den temporären Bauten in der Karlsaue zwischen Thomas Struth und Eran Scharf und bot eine spannende Alternative zu den westlichen Narrationen. Khakhars figurative Szenen erzählen vom Alltag, bewegen sich dabei allerdings formal zwischen der Flächigkeit der Miniaturmalerei und dem westlichen Illusionismus. Auch K. G. Subramanyan greift Momente des Alltags auf, aber eher als Rückgriff auf angewandte Traditionen wie Glasmalerei und auf Themen aus dem Reich der Mythen, Erinnerungen. „KGS sprach in gewisser Weise über die Schaffung einer zeitgenössischen indigenen Sprache mit seinen Verweisen auf Volkskunst und die Verwendung von billigen Materialien aus der Volkskunst", erklärt die Künstlerin[14]. „Bhupens Arbeit ist ein viel älterer und stärkerer Einfluss. Ich dachte an seine frühen Kataloge, als ich meine erste Fotoromanze, Phantom Lady, begann. ... Bhupen war der Guru des Indian Pop, seine Vision der indischen Gesellschaft. Die von ihm verwendeten Quellen – Kalenderkunst, Kramläden, Schilder, billige Magazine, banales Alltagsleben, etc. – verwende auch ich immer noch in meiner Arbeit."

V. Alltag

Die junge Generation indischer Kunst bezieht sich selbstverständlich und stolz auf Traditionen, etwa **N.S. Harsha** auf die Miniaturmalerei in der Gleichzeitigkeit vieler kleiner Geschichten auf einem Blatt; **Bharti Kher** mit ihren Elefanten auf die Mythen- und Tierwelt Indiens. In den Werken vieler MalerInnen wird auf Farben und Details wie etwa die fischförmigen Augen und pointierten Nasen mit monographischen Hintergründen, die in der Pahari Malerei (17.-19. Jahrhundert) entwickelt wurden, zurück gegriffen. Immer wiederkehrendes Thema vieler Werke ist dabei der urbane Alltag mit den Subthemen Migration und Globalisierung.

Ein Großteil der jungen indischen KünstlerInnen lebt in den beiden Metropolen New Dehli und Mumbai (ehemals Bombay) und verarbeitet ihre Erfahrungen mit dem kontrastreichen Alltag in ihren Werken. Während New Delhi als Kunstmetropole bereits durch alteingesessene Galerien und die „India Triennale" etabliert ist, entwickelte sich Mumbai erst in den letzten Jahren in einem atemberaubenden Tempo von der Filmmetropole „Bollywood" zum Mittelpunkt der indischen Kunstszene. Es herrscht eine enorme Aufbruchstimmung. Im südlichen Viertel am „Gate of India" eröffnen mehr und mehr Clubs, Modegeschäfte und Galerien. Ob als Loft-ähnlich umgebaute Wohnung wie die Chemould Gallery, ob in Hinterhöfen wie „Project 88", in ehemaligen Lagerräumen wie Gallery Chatterjee & Lal, in einer kleinen Wohnung direkt neben

still active today have also been very influential for her work: Bhupen Khakhar and K. G. Subramanyan. The self-taught Bhupen Khakhar is not entirely unknown in the west since he took part in the 9th *documenta* in Kassel in 1992. Displayed at the temporary buildings in Karlsaue between Thomas Struth and Eran Scharf, his work offered an exciting alternative to western narratives. While Khakhar's figurative scenes tell stories from everyday life, formally speaking they move between the two-dimensional quality of miniature painting and western illusionism. K. G. Subramanyan, too, uses incidents from daily life, but more as a fallback to traditions in applied art such as glass painting and themes from the realm of myths and memories. "KGS was in a way talking about creating an indigenous contemporary language referring to the popular and the folk which interested me, using low cost folk/popular materials", explains the artist[14]. "Bhupen's work has been a much longer and stronger influence. I had his early catalogues in mind when I started off with my first photo-romance, Phantom Lady. ... Bhupen was the guru of Indian Pop, his kind of vision of Indian society. The sources he used – calendar art, petty shops /signs, cheap magazines, banal daily life etc. – I still use in my work."

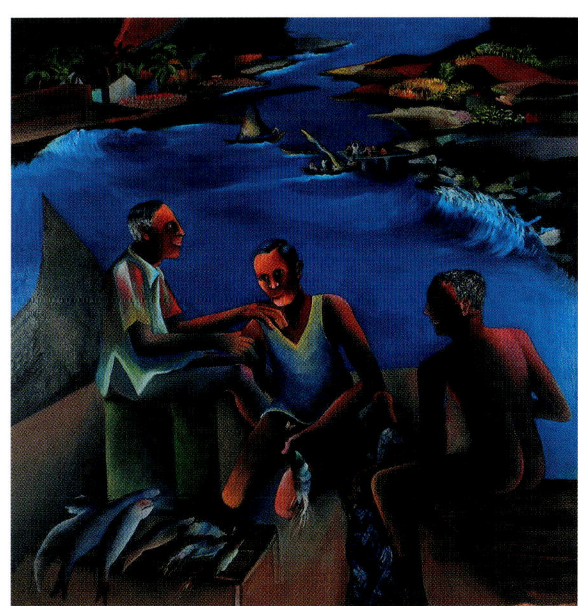

BHUPEN KHAKHAR Fishermen in Goa, 1985
Photo: Chemould Prescott Road, Mumbai

V. Everyday life

The young generation of Indian artists makes very natural and proud use of traditions. **N.S. Harsha,** for instance, makes reference to miniature painting with the simultaneity of many small stories on one sheet; **Bharti Kher** uses elephants to refer to the myths and animal life of India. In the work of many painters, one finds colours and details, such as the fish-shaped eyes and pointed noses with monographic backgrounds that were developed in Pahari painting (17th-19th centuries). A recurring theme is urban everyday life with the sub-themes of migration and globalisation.

A majority of young Indian artists live in the two metropolises New Dehli and Mumbai (the former Bombay) and in their work they engage with their experiences in a richly

dem Eingang eines preisgünstigen Hotels wie The Bombay Art Gallery oder zugleich prominent und versteckt wie die Galerie Mirchandani + Steinruecke auf der Rückseite des glamourösen Hotels „Taj Mahal" – die Galerien für zeitgenössische Kunst nehmen ihren festen Platz ein in Mumbai.

Dieser partyfröhlichen Welt steht die andere Realität Mumbais gegenüber: 60% der mehr als 20 Millionen Einwohner Mumbais leben in Slums, die überall angesiedelt sind und jederzeit abgerissen werden können. Der Blick aus den Redaktionsräumen der namhaften indischen Kunstzeitschrift „Art India" fällt auf einen vergleichsweise kleinen Slum, der allzu nah an eine Baustelle modernster Architektur grenzt – wer weiß, worauf der Blick beim nächsten Besuch fallen wird.

Mumbai ist die Stadt der Hoffnung, eine multikulturelle, multisprachliche und multireligiöse Gemeinschaft[15], in der die Schulbildung allen kostenlos zur Verfügung steht – und damit die Chance zum sozialen Aufstieg. Ob die autobiographischen Comic-Erzählungen von **Sarnath Banerjee, Krishnaraj Chonats** Werke rund um „ideal lifestyles", **Subodh Guptas** Skulpturen aus Blechgeschirr als Sinnbild für Urbanisierung, **Tushar Joags** Verbesserungsvorschläge für urbane Probleme, **Gigi Scarias** humorvolle Stadtentwürfe und **Hema Upadhyays** collagenhafte Bilder, die immer wieder Mumbais größten Slum namens „Dharavi" thematisieren – immer steht das Leben der Menschen im Mittelpunkt. „Migration, Bewegung, Urbanisierung, Trauma sind die Hauptthemen meiner Arbeit, die ich oft aus eigener Erfahrung kenne", erklärt Upadhyay. In „Urban Dance" wird das Labyrinth zur Metapher für das urbane Leben: „Urban Dance ist stellvertretend für die Wiederholung/Routine, die Endlosschleifen des Lebens der arbeitenden Bevölkerung in einer Großstadt. Die schwarzen geometrischen Formen stehen für Häuser (oft billigster Art) und die weißen Punkte sind die Lichter der U-Bahn. Routine wird selbst zum Muster."[16] In „Mute Migration" konfrontiert uns Upadhyay direkt mit der Welt des Slums, nicht als Modell, sondern als Ergebnis sozialpolitischer Probleme und als Teil unserer Kultur: „Man steht Auge in Auge mit diesen Bildern/Objekten, die den Betrachter aus seiner Wohlfühlzone herausholen und versucht gleichzeitig, die gelebten und ungelebten

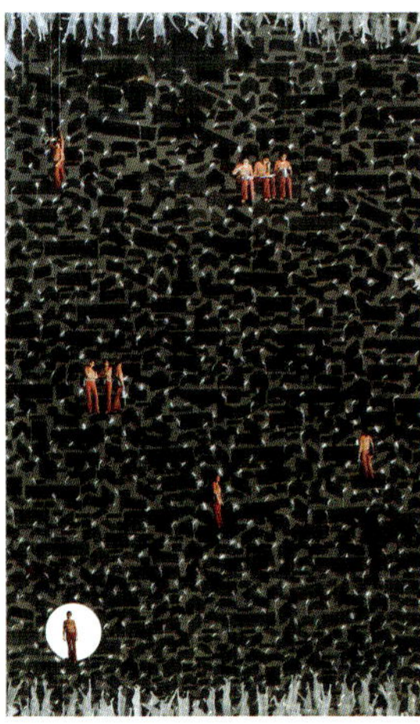

HEMA UPADHYAY Urban Dance, 2004
Photo: Prakash Rao (Mumbai)
© Hema Upadhyay

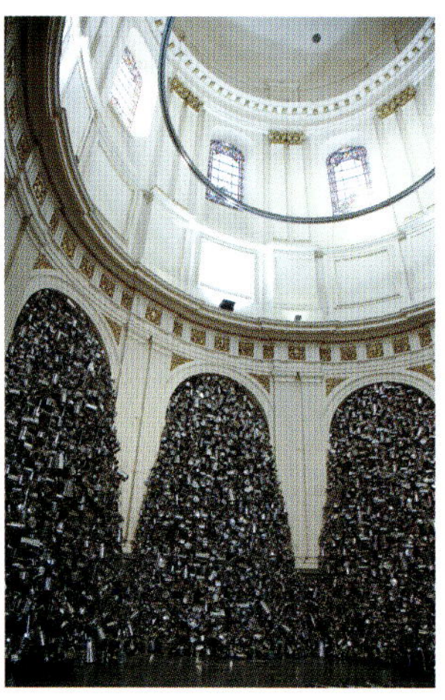

SUBODH GUPTA God Hungry, 2006
Photo: Marc Domage
© Subodh Gupta

contrasted urban context. Whereas New Delhi has already become recognised as an art metropolis due to many old-established galleries and the *India Triennal,* it was only within the last ten years that Mumbai has developed at a breathtaking pace from the Bollywood capital to the centre of the Indian art scene. The city is characterised by an enormous trailblazing spirit. More and more clubs, fashion shops and galleries open their doors in the southern quarter at the "Gate of India". Whether housed in apartments turned into lofts such as the Chemould Gallery, in backyards such as "Project 88", in former warehouses, such as Gallery Chatterjee & Lal, a small apartment next to the entrance of a low-cost hotel, such as The Bombay Art Gallery or at a both prominent and hidden site, such as Mirchandani + Steinruecke at the back of the glamorous Taj Mahal Hotel – contemporary art galleries have come to stay in Mumbai.

This world of cheerful partying is contrasted by the other reality of Mumbai: 60% of the more than 20 million inhabitants of Mumbai live in slums, which can spring up everywhere and run the risk of being demolished anytime. From the offices of the renowned Indian art journal *Art India* one has a view of a comparatively small slum area which seems a bit too close for comfort to a building site of modern architecture – who knows what the view will reveal on the next visit.

Mumbai is the city of hope, a multicultural, multilingual, and multi-religious community[15], where school - and thus the opportunity for upward social mobility - is open free of cost to everyone. Whether it's the autobiographical comic-strip stories of **Sarnath Banerjee, Krishnaraj Chonat's** works centring around "ideal lifestyles", **Subodh Gupta's** sculptures made of metal kitchen utensils as a the symbol of urbanisation, **Tushar Joag's** proposals for easing urban problems, **Gigi Scaria's** humorous urban designs or **Hema Upadhyay's** collage-like images which frequently comment on Mumbai's largest slum by the name of *Dharavi* – it is always the life of people that is at the centre. "Migration, movement, urbanization, trauma are main themes of my work, often drawn from personal experiences," explains Upadhyay. In *Urban Dance* the labyrinth turns into a metaphor for urban life: "Urban Dance represents the repeated/routine or in-loop lifestyle a metropolitan city offers to a working class. The black geometrical forms are the shapes of homes (sometimes low-cost housing) and the white dots are tube lights. Routine becomes a pattern itself."[16] In *Mute Migration* Upadhyay confronts us directly with the slums, not as a model but as the result of socio-political problems and as part of our culture: "One comes face to face with these visuals / objects that tease the viewer out of his comfortable space and at the same time attempt to commemorate the wishes, dreams and aspirations lived and unlived in these small cities within a city."[17]

Contemporary Indian art is a meeting of religious references and national symbols, tradition and the present. Socio-political issues are handled with particularly folkloristic materials and techniques, such as in the sculptures of Hema Upadhyay or the interactive installations of Shilpa Gupta's work. "The main influence in my work is the space

Wünsche, Träume und Ziele dieser kleinen Stadt in der Stadt zu würdigen."[17]

In der zeitgenössischen indischen Kunst treffen religiöse Verweise und nationale Symbolik, Tradition und Jetztzeit aufeinander, werden soziopolitische Themen mit betont folkloristischen Materialien und Techniken umgesetzt wie in Hema Upadhyays Skulpturen oder in interaktiven Installationen in Shilpa Guptas Werk. „Der Haupteinfluss auf meine Arbeit kommt aus meiner täglichen Umgebung," erklärt Shilpa Gupta – und das ist die Stadt Mumbai, „in die Migranten aus dem ganzen Land geströmt sind" bis zur Zerstörung der Babri Moschee 1992 und der seither zunehmenden Macht der rechtsgerichteten Partei BJP. „Gujarat wählte seinen Premierminister, den Mann der hinter dem Genozid an den Moslems im Staat Gujarat stand. Es ist dieser langsame Wandel in den Denkweisen über mehrere Jahre, die Blindheit der Menschen, die Rolle der Medien in diesem Prozess, die mich zu einigen meiner Arbeiten inspiriert haben – ich interessiere mich für ‚Unterschied' und seine Wahrnehmung, sowie für die Vorurteile, die über Geographie, Rasse, Religion, Geschlecht und Klasse hinweg ausgespielt werden, und den Anstieg absurder Sicherheit in diesem Bereich."[18] Es ist das Nebeneinander von nationalen Bezügen und globalen Themen, von Tradition und Heute, von Kritik und Hoffnung, das die indische Kunst zugleich so fremd und vertraut erscheinen lässt – und uns so fasziniert.

Sabine B. Vogel
Freie Kuratorin und Kunstkritikerin in Wien
Sabine B. Vogel lebt seit 1995 in Wien; Magister-Abschluss des Kunstgeschichtsstudiums an der Ruhr-Universität-Bochum 1987; seit 1987 freie Kuratorin (u.a. Wiener Secession 1992, Kunsthalle Düsseldorf 1994, Wiener Kunstverein 1997-99, Belvedere 2009) und Kunstkritikerin (u.a. Die Presse, Wien; NZZ/Zürich, Artforum/New York; zahlr. Katalogtexte und Publikationen, zuletzt „Die Macht des Ornaments", Hg. SBV und Agnes Husslein-Arco); seit 1997 korrespondierendes Mitglied der Wiener Secession; seit 2003 Lektorin an der Universität für Angewandte Kunst, Wien; seit 2004 Vorstandsmitglied, seit 2009 Präsidentin der AICA AUSTRIA (internationale Kunstkritiker Vereinigung).

1 Helmut Leder, Wem Schönheit nützt. Psychologische Ansätze zur Ästhetik. Antrittsvorlesung am 18.3.2005 an der Universität Wien, www.dieuniversitaet-online.at/pdf/2005/AntrittsVO_Leder.pdf (zuletzt besucht am 20. Februar 2009).
2 Francis Newton Souza, 1924-2002.
3 Syed Haider Raza, geboren 1922 in Babaria, Indien; lebt seit 1950 in Paris und Gorbio, Südfrankreich.
4 Maqbul Fida Husain, geboren 1915 in Pandharpur, Indien; lebt hauptsächlich in Mumbai.
5 „Wir haben damals gegen zwei vorherrschende Denkarten angekämpft. Einerseits die Royal Academy, die britisch orientiert war, und andererseits die traditionelle Schule in Mumbai, die gar nicht fortschrittlich war. Wir haben gegen beide gekämpft und sie erledigt. Die Bewegung die darauf abzielte, diese Einflüsse loszuwerden und eine Sprache zu entwickeln die in unserer eigenen Kultur verwurzelt ist, war großartig, aber von den Historikern wurde sie nicht gewürdigt ", schreibt M. F. Husain in „Frontline" 1997 (M. F. Hussain, „An Artist and a Movement", in: Frontline. India´s National Magazine, Vol 14, No. 16, August 09-22, 1997).
6 Bhupen Khakhar, geboren 1934 in Bombay, lebt in Baroda.
7 K. G. Subramanyan, geboren 1924 in Nord-Kerala, lebt in Baroda.
8 Randeep Ramesh, in: The Guardian, 20. Februar 2007.
9, 10 Jitish Kallat in einer email-Korrespondenz vom 18. Februar 2009.
11 Nalini Malani, geboren 1946 in Karachi, lebt in Mumbai. Stipendien und Ausstellungen seit den 80er Jahren weltweit.
12 Jagannath Panda in einer email-Korrespondenz mit der Autorin vom 28. Februar 2009.
13 Ravi Varma, 1846-1906 in Kerala.
14 Pushpumala N. in einer email-Korrespondenz mit der Autorin vom 17. Februar 2009
15 Der Schriftsteller Dilip Chitre erzählt in einem Gespräch mit Henning Stegmüller: „Ursprünglich war Bombay nur ein Häufchen von sieben kleinen Inseln nahe der Westküste Indiens. ... (Die Engländer) ließen sich dort nieder und gründeten eine Handelsniederlassung, die East India Company. Sie garantierten die Freiheit des Handels und priesen den Wettbewerb. Ein Eisenbahnnetz für die Halbinsel wurde geplant und die ersten zwanzig Meilen 1815 dem Verkehr übergeben. Textilfabriken öffneten ihre Tore; Bombay wurde zum Brückenkopf der industriellen Revolution in Indien. ... Für die Armen und Besitzlosen aus anderen Teilen Indiens wurde Bombay zur sagenumwobenen Hoffnung, zum magischen Fixpunkt. ... Ob Muslime, Hindus oder Parsis, jeder war willkommen. Die Dalits aus ganz Indien strömten nach Bombay, weil sie an diesem säkularen Ort frei leben konnten. Überall sonst in Indien wurden sie als Unberührbare unterdrückt, auch physisch." In: Bombay, Mumbai. Bilder einer Mega-Stadt, Hg. Stegmüller, Chitre, Dhasal, A1 Verlag München 1996.
16, 17 Hema Upadhyay in einer email-Korrespondenz mit der Autorin am 17. August 2008 und 02. März 2009.
18 Shilpa Gupta in einer email-Korrespondenz mit der Autorin am 07. März 2009.

I live in", notes Shilpa Gupta – and that is the city of Mumbai, "in which migrants have flowed in from all over the country" until the destruction of the Babri Mosque in 1992, when the right-wing BJP party started to rise in power. "Gujarat elected its Chief Minister, the man who stood behind the genocide of Muslims in the state of Gujarat. It is this slow change of peoples' attitudes over several years, their blindness, the role of the media in this process, that has spurred several of my works – I am interested in 'difference' and its perception, and the prejudice that is played out across the geography, race, religion, gender and class, and the increase of absurd security around these."[18] It is this side-by-side existence of national references and global issues, of tradition and the present, of criticism and hope, which makes Indian art appear so strange and yet familiar at one and the same time – and which thus holds such great fascination for us.

Sabine B. Vogel
Vienna-based independent curator and art critic
Sabine B. Vogel took up residence in Vienna in 1995; she graduated in art history at Ruhr-Universitat-Bochum in 1987; as of 1987 independent curator (i.a. at Wiener Secession 1992, Kunsthalle Düsseldorf 1994, Wiener Kunstverein 1997-99, Belvedere 2009) and art critic (i.a. for Die Presse, Wien; NZZ/Zürich, Artforum/New York; numerous essays in catalogues and publications, most recently „Die Macht des Ornaments", ed.by SBV and Agnes Husslein-Arco); as of 1997 corresponding member of Wiener Secession; as of 2003 lecturer at the Vienna University of Applied Arts; as of 2004 member of the board, as of 2009 president of AICA AUSTRIA (International Association of Art Critics).

1 Helmut Leder, Wem Schönheit nützt. Psychologische Ansätze zur Ästhetik. Antrittsvorlesung am 18.3.2005 an der Universität Wien, www.dieuniversitaet-online.at/pdf/2005/AntrittsVO_Leder.pdf (last visited on 20 Feb 2009).
2 Francis Newton Souza, 1924-2002.
3 Syed Haider Raza, born 1922 in Babaria, India; has been living in Paris and Gorbio, southern France since 1957.
4 Maqbul Fida Husain, born 1915 in Pandharpur, India, lives mainly in Mumbai.
5 "We came out to fight against two prevalent schools of thought in those days, the Royal Academy, which was British-oriented, and the revivalist school in Mumbai, which was not a progressive movement. These two we decided to fight, and we demolished them. The movement to get rid of these influences and to evolve a language that is rooted in our own culture was a great movement, and one that historians have not taken note of", wrote M. F. Husain in "Frontline" 1997 (M. F. Hussain, "An Artist and a Movement", in: Frontline. India´s National Magazine, Vol 14, No. 16, August 09-22, 1997).
6 Bhupen Khakhar, born 1934 in Bombay, lives in Baroda.
7 K. G. Subramanyan, born 1924 in North-Kerala, lives in Baroda.
8 Randeep Ramesh, in: The Guardian, 20 February 2007.
9, 10 Jitish Kallat in an email of 18 February 2009.
11 Nalini Malani, geboren 1946 in Karachi, lebt in Mumbai. Stipendien und Ausstellungen seit den 80er Jahren weltweit.
12 Jagannath Panda in an email to the author, 28 February 2009.
13 Ravi Varma, 1846-1906 in Kerala.
14 Pushpumala N. in an email to the author on 17 February 2009.
15 in a conversation with Henning Stegmüller, the writer Dilip Chitre said the following: "originally, Bombay was just a group of seven small island near India's western coast.... (the British) settled there and founded a trading company, the East India Company. The guaranteed the freedom of trade and glorified competition. A railway network was planned for the peninsula, and the first 20 miles were opened for transport in 1815. Textile factories opened the doors; Bombay became the bridgehead of industrial revolution in India.... for the poor and disinherited from other parts of India and disappeared from other parting of Bombay became the legendary city of hope, a magical pole star.... Muslims, Hindus or Parsis, everyone was welcome. Dalits from all over Indian streamed to Bombay because they could live freely in this secular place. Everywhere else in India they were suppressed as Untouchables, also in physical terms." (Translated from the German) In: Bombay, Mumbai. Bilder einer Mega-Stadt, Ed. by Stegmüller, Chitre, Dhasal, A1 Verlag Munich 1996.
16, 17 Hema Upadhyay in an email to the author on 17 August 2008 and on 02 March 2009.
18 Shilpa Gupta in an email to the author on 07 March 2009.

DIE BALLADE VOM KULTURELLEN RELATIVISMUS

(oder wie ich aufhörte, mir Sorgen zu machen und lernte, die Launen der indischen Kunstszene zu lieben)

THE BALLAD OF CULTURAL RELATIVISM

(or how I stopped worrying and learned to love the vicissitudes of the Indian art scene)

Peter Nagy

Als ich 1997 meine Galerie in New Delhi eröffnete, gewöhnte ich mich schnell an zwei Wörter, die oft verwendet wurden, wenn jemand sich von den bei uns ausgestellten Kunstwerken wahrhaft unbeeindruckt zeigen wollte. Das erste, besonders beliebte, war „Gimmick", und wurde gewöhnlich auf Arbeiten angewandt, die keine Malerei waren und Fundstücke oder unkonventionelle Materialien beinhalteten. Diesen Kommentar äußerten meist Personen, die sich für kunstkundig hielten und sich bei der Beurteilung solcher Arbeiten fragten, ob das gewählte Material oder die gewählte Darstellungsweise nur ein „Gimmick" sei. Das zweite beliebte abschätzige Wort, naserümpfend und mit säuerlicher Miene dargebracht, war „derivativ".

Laut Wörterbuchdefinition ist ein Gimmick ein Kunstgriff oder Taschenspielertrick, der Aufmerksamkeit erregen oder den Reiz einer Sache erhöhen soll, wobei oft impliziert wird, dass es sich um eine verstohlene oder leicht unlautere Vorgangsweise handelt. Derivativ bedeutet „unoriginell" oder „abgeleitet". Diese beiden Ausdrücke und die Häufigkeit, mit der sie von Menschen verwendet wurden, die meiner Meinung nach der zeitgenössischen Kunst entweder ängstlich oder feindselig begegneten, erschienen mir exemplarisch für die sehr unterschiedlichen Kontexte der zeitgenössischen Kunst an meinem neuen Arbeitsort (Indien) und jenem davor (New York).

Die künstlerische Moderne hatte in Indien eine sehr lange Inkubationszeit, da sie zu einer Zeit entstand, als das Land versuchte, das lange Kolonialerbe abzuschütteln und mit seiner eigenen nationalen Identität zu Rande zu kommen. Der Künstler Rabindranath Tagore und sein Kreis entschlossen sich (wann?), die Moderne als eine Gelegenheit anzusehen, internationale Trends mit traditionellen Verweisen zu kombinieren. Inspirationen suchten sie eher in anderen Teilen Asiens als in Europa und Amerika. Nach der Unabhängigkeit im Jahr 1947 etablierte sich in Bombay eine kosmopolitische Moderne, als eine Gruppe von Malern begann, mit figurativer Abstraktion zu experimentieren. Ihnen folgten andere Maler (hauptsächlich in New Delhi) die versuchten, eine Synthese zwischen indigenen Abstraktionsidiomen und westlichen Trends herzustellen. In allen Fällen jedoch war das angestrebte Ergebnis eine Moderne, die stets in indischen Themen und Idiomen verwurzelt war und sich keinesfalls in jenen patriziden oder adoleszenten Formen der Rebellion erging, die wir mit vielen Schulen der europäischen und amerikanischen Moderne des 20. Jahrhunderts assoziieren.

Erst mit dem Beginn der Postmoderne in den 1970er Jahren, besonders mit jenem Künstlerkreis, der als „Baroda

When I started my gallery in New Delhi in 1997 I soon became accustomed to two words that were frequently used when someone wanted to act duly unimpressed by something we had on show. The first, and most popular, was "gimmick", usually applied to an art work that was not a painting and might employ found objects or unconventional materials. The commentator was most likely someone who believed him or herself to be knowledgeable about art and when judging such an art work would question if the chosen material or imagery was "just a gimmick". The second most popular term of derision was "derivative," sniffed in a surly sort of way.

The dictionary defines a gimmick as an ingenious or novel device designed to attract attention or increase appeal, with an element of something devious or hidden often implied. Derivative is defined as not original or secondary. Both terms, along with the frequency of their use by people who, it seemed to me, were either intimidated by or hostile towards contemporary art, seemed to act as beacons illuminating the very different contexts for contemporary art within my new arena (India) and my previous one (New York).

Artistic Modernism had a very long gestation period within India, arriving at a time when India was attempting to shake off the long legacy of colonization and grappling with its own national identity. Rabindranath Tagore and his circle chose to see Modernism as an opportunity to meld international trends with traditional references, chose to look towards other parts of Asia rather than Europe or America for inspiration. After Independence in 1947, a cosmopolitan Modernism took hold in Bombay as a group of painters began to experiment with figurative abstraction, followed by other painters (mainly in New Delhi) who attempted a synthesis with indigenous languages of abstraction and Western trends. But in all cases, the desired outcome was to craft a Modernism that was always rooted in Indian subjects and idioms, certainly never indulging in the patricidal or adolescent forms of rebellion we associate with many schools of European and American Modernism of the 20th Century.

It is only with the advent of Post-Modernism in the 1970s, and specifically with the group of artists known as the Baroda School, that Indian art achieves a successful integration of the local with the global. These painters were able to address their own cultural hybridity with an appropriately international painterly language, while actually advancing that language from its Western parameters instead of simply grafting one type of imagery with another. By the

Schule" bekannt wurde, gelang der indischen Kunst eine erfolgreiche Integration von lokalen und globalen Elementen. Diese Maler waren in der Lage, ihre eigene kulturelle Hybridnatur mit einer angemessen internationalen malerischen Sprache zu erörtern, wobei sie diese Sprache aus ihren westlichen Parametern weiterentwickelten und nicht nur zwei unterschiedliche Arten der Bildhaftigkeit zusammenfügten. Als ich in den frühen 1990er Jahren die indische Kunstwelt betrat, umfasste die Szene eine Fülle von Kitschpotenzialen (kubistische Ganeshas, pseudo-impressionistische rajasthanische Dorfmädchen, Rembrandtsche Bettler und Cartoon-Krishnas), aber auch eine Generation von Künstlern, die ernsthaft bemüht waren, das formale Vokabular einer indigenen Postmoderne in Fotografie, Skulptur und Installation weiterzuentwickeln.

Daher also der Aufstieg der „Gimmicks". Wiewohl die Malerei sicherlich relevant blieb, orientierten sich die smartesten Künstler nun an Dada, Pop Art, Arte Povera und Konzeptkunst und fanden diese Genres unglaublich relevant für ihren unmittelbaren indischen Kontext (das Land, das sich nun ausländischen Medien öffnete, begann einem internationalen Konsumbewusstsein nachzueifern). Da der Unterricht in den Kunsthochschulen des Landes hauptsächlich auf Englisch erfolgt, hatten die Künstler auch Zugang zu den theoretischen Kanons der marxistischen, feministischen und post-strukturellen Kritik, und natürlich zum Zweig der postkolonialen Studien, die im Zuge der Globalisierung der internationalen Kunstwelt durch Biennalen und Kunstmessen immer größere Bedeutung erlangten. Wie viel Inspiration und Kraft die indischen Künstler daraus zogen, lässt sich an den ausgereiften Ergebnissen ihrer Bemühungen heute ablesen.

Die überwiegende Mehrzahl des indischen Publikums (und dazu gehören auch einige „Kunstprofis" wie etwa Kuratoren, Händler und Kritiker) war nicht an Provokation oder Konfrontation interessiert, sondern zog für die Kulturproduktion eine vertraute Wohlfühlzone vor. Damit war sichergestellt, so dachten sie, dass Indien die notwendige Vorsicht gegenüber dem westlichen Kulturimperialismus walten ließ. Ihre Skepsis wurde von der Tatsache weiter verstärkt, dass die Arbeiten von Marcel Duchamp oder Andy Warhol vielerorts unbekannt waren, von Künstlern wie Jeff Koons oder Damien Hirst ganz zu schweigen. Dieses Segment des Kunstpublikums ignorierte damit nicht nur die tiefgreifenden Veränderungen in der indischen Gesellschaft, sondern vernachlässigte auch das Potenzial der indischen Kultur, den postmodernen Diskurs auf globaler Ebene mitzugestalten. Allen neuen Ansätzen in Bezug auf Materialien und Techniken (unter der Überschrift „Installationskunst" zusammengefasst) begegnete man mit Zynismus und Verachtung. Vielleicht trug ich selbst, ein amerikanischer Unternehmer, der diese neuen Kunstformen in seiner Galerie in New Delhi ausstellte und förderte, mein Scherflein zu dieser feindseligen Haltung bei. Erst heute, und sehr zögerlich, beginnen die höheren Mächte im indischen Kulturmilieu die Bedeutung dieser neuen Kunstformen anzuerkennen, weil sie auf der internationalen Kunstszene so prominent vertreten sind (wie beispielsweise in dieser Ausstellung).

time I entered the Indian art world in the early 1990s the scenario accommodated a plethora of kitsch possibilities (Cubistic Ganeshas, pseudo-Impressionist Rajasthani village girls, Rembrandtesque beggars and cartoon Krishnas) but also a generation of artists who were eager to advance the formal languages of an indigenous Post-Modernism into photography, sculpture and installation.

Hence the rise of the "gimmicks". Painting certainly remained relevant, but the smartest artists now looked towards Dada, Pop, Arte Povera and Conceptual Art and found these genres exceedingly relevant to their immediate Indian context (as the country opened itself up to foreign media and began to emulate an international consumer consciousness). As the country's art colleges are conducted primarily in English, the artists also had access to the theoretical canons of Marxist, Feminist and Post-Structural Critique and, of course, to the field of Post-Colonial Studies, which gained an even greater sense of urgency as the international art world became increasingly globalized through biennials and art fairs. The Indian artists were both inspired and emboldened, the mature results of which we are witnessing today.

The majority of the audience in India (and this would also include some "art professionals" such as curators, dealers and critics) didn't want art to be confrontational, preferring a well-known comfort zone for cultural production. This they felt retained a necessary Indian suspicion of Western cultural imperialism. Their scepticism was further compounded by the fact that many did not know the work of Marcel Duchamp or Andy Warhol, let alone Jeff Koons or Damien Hirst. What this segment of the art audience chose not to acknowledge was not only the profound changes taking place in Indian society but also the potential that Indian culture now had to reinvigorate the Post-Modern dialogue on the world stage. Any new strategies of materials and techniques (the catch-all term being "installation art") were greeted with cynicism and derision. Perhaps my own persona, that of an American entrepreneur exhibiting and promoting these new art forms in my gallery in New Delhi, instigated an increased hostility. Only today, very hesitantly, are the larger powers-that-be in the Indian cultural milieu beginning to recognize the importance of these new art forms, goaded by their prominent display on the international art world's stage (such as our present exhibition).

On the one hand an animosity towards radical expressions, yet on the other the old expectations of originality. Derivation itself is a difficult subject to address. All cultural products, of course, come somehow from other cultural products, yet one is expected to either mask or deny one's sources or mine from particularly distant ones. India's artistic traditions advocated an almost anonymous inheritance of artistic license and technique, propagating celebrated artists only with the involuted introduction of Modernism. In the Indian art world of the 90s, gallerists and collectors wanted experimentation only within the proscribed limits of painting (unique, handmade, oil on canvas, with an Indian identity). This constriction corresponded to the general desire to keep art and art spaces

Einerseits gab es eine Ablehnung radikaler Ausdrucksformen, andererseits aber auch die alte Erwartungshaltung, Originalität zu erleben. Derivate sind ein schwieriges Thema. Natürlich ergeben sich alle Kulturprodukte in gewisser Weise aus anderen Kulturprodukten, aber es wird erwartet, dass man seine Quellen entweder verschleiert oder sich aus besonders weit entfernten Quellen bedient. Die künstlerischen Traditionen Indiens plädierten für ein fast anonymes Erbe von künstlerischer Freiheit und Technik, und gefeierte Künstler wurden nur durch die komplizierte Einführung der Moderne propagiert. In der indischen Kunstwelt der 90er wollten Galeristen und Sammler Experimente nur innerhalb der festgesteckten Grenzen der Malerei (Unikat, handgemalt, Öl auf Leinwand, mit einer indischen Identität) zulassen. Diese Zwänge entsprachen dem allgemeinen Wunsch, die Kunst und ihre Räume als kontrolliert-dekorative Orte zu bewahren und sie so weit wie möglich vom unkontrollierbaren öffentlichen Leben der Straße und der Politik fern zu halten. Auch das Eindringen der Fotografie (und ihrer Abkömmlinge) in die Räume der bildenden Kunst stieß auf Widerstand, ebenso wie frühere Generationen strikte Trennlinien zwischen „urbanen" und „ruralen" (Tribal Art, Volkskunst und Kunsthandwerk) Kunstzweigen gezogen hatten. Selbst als die Tatsache Anerkennung fand, dass Künstler in ihren Arbeiten Anleihen nehmen, wollten viele Kritiker nur indische Quellen akzeptieren, da es ihnen peinlich war zuzugeben, dass besagte Künstler auf Reisen oder Studienaufenthalten im Ausland auch internationale Einflüsse aufnahmen.

Ich bin von der New Yorker Kunstwelt der 80er geprägt, wo man Themen wie Autorschaft, Aneignung und künstlerische Einflüsse auf radikale Weise neu ausverhandelte. Zu dieser Zeit hinterfragten Künstler die Parameter der künstlerischen Produktion, und die Kunst wurde angereichert durch Theorie und Politik sowie eine ehrliche Würdigung des derivativen Sumpfes, in dem alle Bilder notwendigerweise ihren Ursprung nehmen. Das führte mich zu einer ökumenischen Sichtweise in Bezug auf den Kreislauf von künstlerischen Ideen und Strategien, die rund um die Welt reisen. Die zeitgenössische Kunstszene Indiens in den 90ern erschien mir tröstlich. Ich freute mich zu sehen, wie Ideen und Standpunkte auf einen neuen Kontext angewandt wurden und fand es spannend, einer Künstlergeneration dabei zuzusehen, wie sie aus einer Vielfalt von Einflüssen ihre Identität schmiedete.

Während die einheimische Kunstszene in Indien heute in eine Reihe von Richtungen expandiert, ist der Kunstmarkt des Landes immer noch konservativ und auf Malerei fixiert. Sammler beginnen aufgrund der steigenden Preise und des Konkurrenzdrucks für Malerei auch Fotografie als Option wahrzunehmen, aber Skulpturen oder Installationen werden oft nur dann gewürdigt, wenn der Künstler bereits Lorbeeren als Maler verdient hat. Kritiker und Kuratoren zögern immer noch, indische zeitgenössische Kunst in einem internationalen Trendkontext zu sehen und schnüren lieber hermetisch abgeschlossene „indische" Pakete. Auf diese Weise lassen sich Themen wie Anleihen und Einflüsse vermeiden, und der kastrierte „Genius" kann in uneingeschränktem Glanz präsentiert werden.

as sites of control and decorum, as far as possible from the unwieldy public life of the streets and politics. Opposition also greeted the introduction of photography (and its off-shoots) into the spaces of Fine Art, just as strong lines had been drawn between the "urban" and "rural" (read: tribal, folk, and craft) arts by previous generations. When derivation in an artist's work was acknowledged, many critics allowed only the Indian sources to be cited, embarrassed to admit the international influences said artist would certainly have absorbed while travelling or studying abroad.

I came of age in the New York art world of the 80s, when issues of authorship, appropriation and artistic influence were radically renegotiated. At that time, artists questioned the parameters of artistic production, invigorating art with theory and politics and an honest regard for the quagmire of derivation that all images necessarily reside within. This led me to an ecumenical outlook towards the circulation of artistic ideas and strategies as they travelled around the world. I found a sense of comfort in the contemporary art scene of India in the 90s, pleased to see ideas and attitudes applied to a new context, excited to witness a generation shape their identity from a variety of influences.

Today, while the home-grown art scene of India continues to expand in a number of directions, the country's art market remains conservative and fixated on painting. Collectors have begun to consider photography as an option due to the increasing cost and competition for paintings, while artists' sculptures or installations are deemed worthy of attention only after they have proven their mettle as painters. Critics and curators continue to shy away from contextualizing Indian contemporary art with international trends, preferring hermetically sealed packages of the "Indian." Thus, the subjects of derivation and influence can be avoided, the better to present neutered "genius" whole and uncompromised.

As the spot-lights of the international art world begin to focus on them, the Indian artists who find themselves most in demand globally are often those with scant possibilities at home. The world wants hard-hitting art from India that speaks of its anxieties and traumas, psychological density and political complexity. India, however, is a difficult place to live and its multiple internal cultures and cacophony of voices are confusing to negotiate. This often results in the desire for art to be escapist, comforting and non-confrontational. Many of the most talented artists working in India today have almost engineered their works so as to appeal to both contexts, operating simultaneously on a number of different levels. In the immediate future we will see how these different attitudes towards contemporary art are resolved (or not) through the practices of artists themselves, the vagaries of the art market, the formation of institutions and an introspective assessment (or lack thereof) of contemporary art from India and its place in the world.

In dem Maß, als die internationale Kunstwelt auf sie aufmerksam wird, finden jene Künstler, die global am begehrtesten sind, zu Hause die spärlichsten Möglichkeiten. Die Welt möchte knallharte Kunst aus Indien, die Ängste und Traumata, psychologische Dichte und politische Komplexität erahnen lässt. Indien ist allerdings ein schwieriger Ort, um dort zu leben und verwirrt mit seinen vielfältigen internen Kulturen und der Kakophonie seiner Stimmen. Daher erlebt man oft, dass von der Kunst verlangt wird, eskapistisch, tröstlich und unprovokant zu sein. Viele der talentiertesten Künstler, die heute in Indien arbeiten, haben ihre Arbeiten nahezu darauf getrimmt, in beiden Kontexten zu gefallen und gleichzeitig auf einer ganzen Reihe von Ebenen zu wirken. In naher Zukunft werden wir sehen, wie sich diese unterschiedlichen Einstellungen zur Gegenwartskunst auflösen (oder auch nicht auflösen). Einflussfaktoren in diesem Zusammenhang sind die Praktiken der Künstler selbst, die Unwägbarkeiten des Kunstmarkts, die Bildung von Institutionen und eine introspektive Bewertung (oder deren Fehlen) zeitgenössischer Kunst aus Indien und ihres Platzes in der Welt.

Peter Nagy
Direktor der Gallery Nature Morte, New Delhi

Nagy wuchs in einem Vorort von New York City auf und studierte von 1977-1981 Kommunikations-Design an der Parsons School of Design, New York. 1982 war er Mitbegründer von Nature Morte, einer kommerziellen Galerie im New Yorker East Village. Dort wurde eine breite Palette an Arbeiten ausgestellt, die in ihrer Mehrzahl von New Yorker Künstlern seiner eigenen oder der Generation davor stammten. 1988 schloss er die Galerie, um sich seiner eigenen künstlerischen Arbeit zu widmen, und 1990 besuchte er zum ersten Mal Indien als Tourist. 1992 kam er ein weiteres Mal nach Indien, lebte ein Jahr in Delhi und folgte den Einladungen als „Artist in Residence" nach Vadodara und Ahmedabad. Im Jahr 1994 ließ er sich in Delhi nieder, wo er 1997 die Galerie Nature Morte wiedereröffnete, in der bis heute vor allem indische Kunst unterschiedlicher Medien präsentiert wird.

Peter Nagy
Director of Gallery Nature Morte, New Delhi

Nagy grew up in the suburbs of New York City and studied Communication Design at Parsons School of Design, New York from 1977–1981. In 1982, he co-founded Nature Morte, a commercial gallery in New York's East Village, where he exhibited a wide range of works, mostly by New York artists, both from his own generation and those senior to him. He closed Nature Morte in 1988 to pursue his own work as an artist and first visited India in 1990 as a tourist. In 1992 he returned to live in India for one year, based in Delhi and with artist residencies in Vadodara and Ahmedabad. Returning in 1994, he settled in Delhi and re-opened Nature Morte there in 1997, which continues today, exhibiting the work of primarily Indian artists in a wide variety of media.

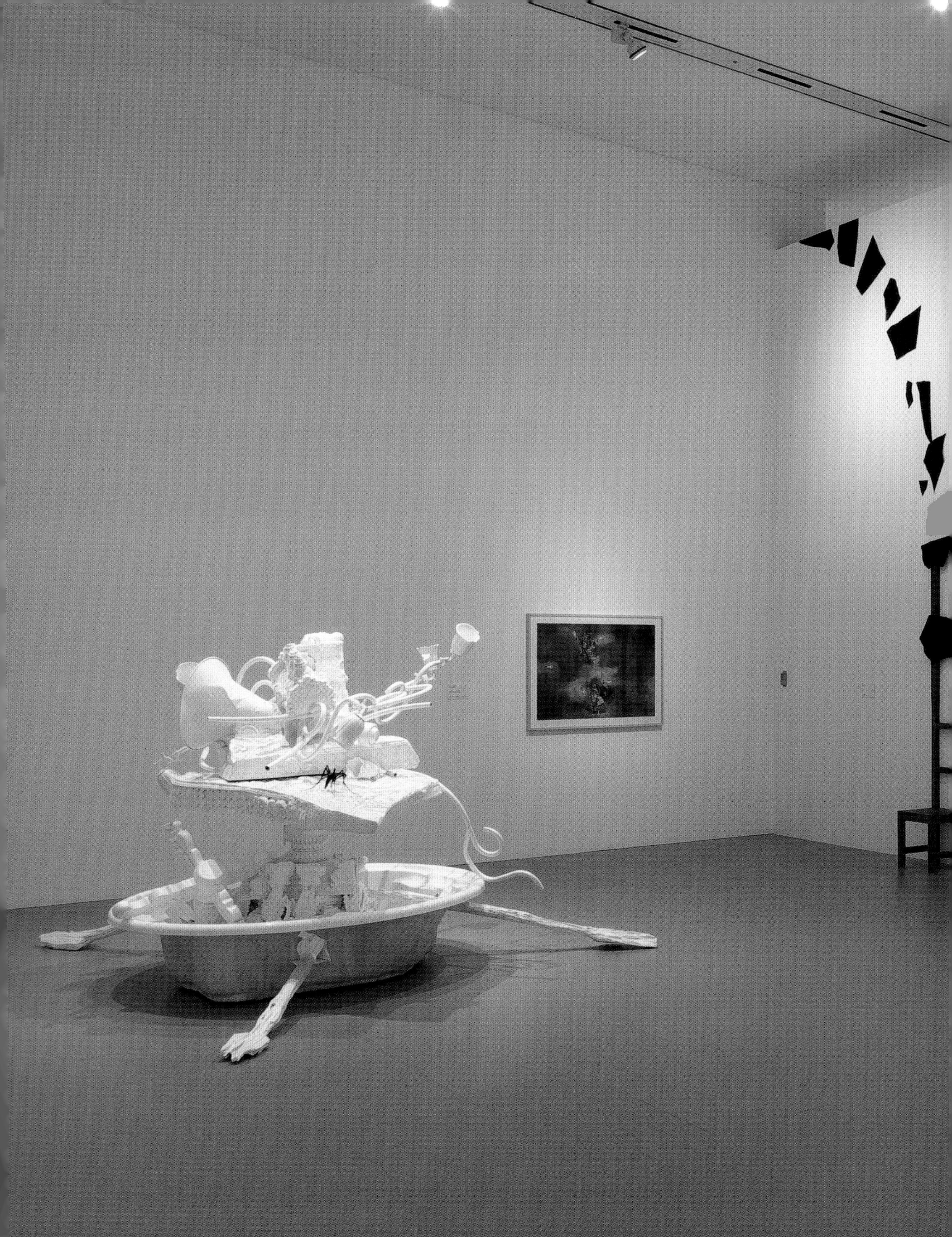

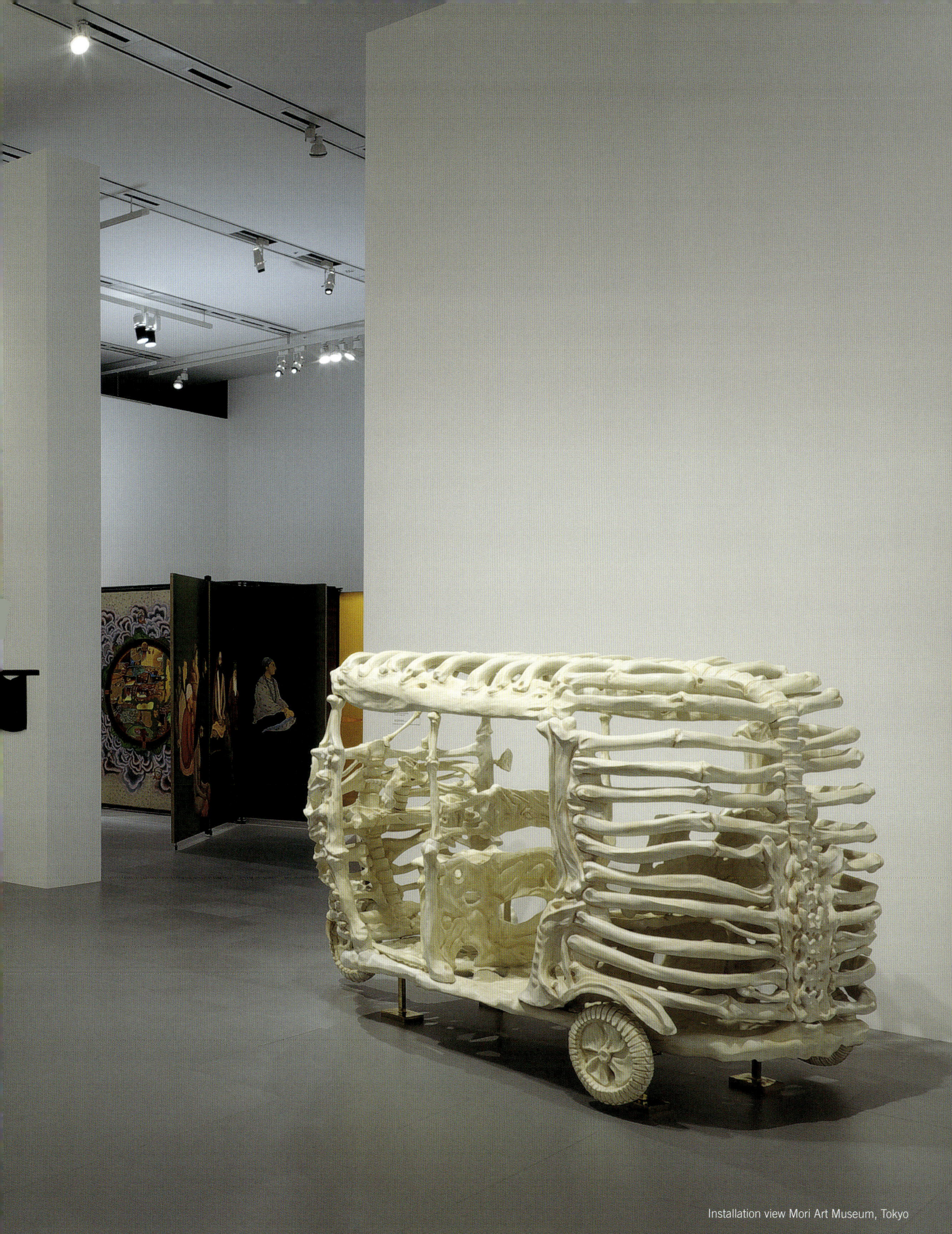

Installation view Mori Art Museum, Tokyo

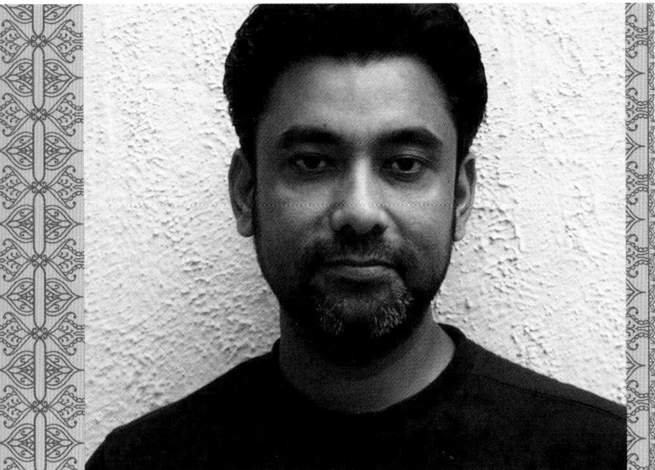

a. balasubramaniam

A. BALASUBRAMANIAM Geboren 1971 in Chennai / Lebt in Bangalore
Born 1971 in Chennai / Lives in Bangalore

Nach seinem Studium am Government College of Arts, Madras (Chennai), studierte A. Balasubramaniam Druckgrafik an der Universität in Edinburgh und in Wien. Seit 2000 hat er seinen Arbeitsschwerpunkt allerdings auf die Bildhauerei verlegt, wobei er ganz unterschiedliche Materialien (Fiberglas, Holz, Plastik, PVC) und Formen verwendet. Typisch für das Frühwerk von A. Balasubramaniam ist eine Methode der Formgebung, für die er Abdrücke seines eigenen Körpers oder eigener Körperteile benutzt, sowie sein Interesse an der Schwerkraft, an der Spannung zwischen Objekten und der Beziehung zwischen dem Objekt und seinem Schatten. In letzter Zeit beschäftigen sich seine Arbeiten mit der Beziehung zwischen dem Sichtbaren und dem Unsichtbaren, dem Schein und der Wirklichkeit sowie mit Grenzen unterschiedlicher Art. „Emerging Angels" (2004), eines seiner maßgeblichen Werke, die er bei der 1. Singapur Biennale ausstellte, zeigt die Skulptur eines schlafenden Engels in einer versiegelten Vitrine. Auf den ersten Blick wirkt das Material wie Marmor, tatsächlich aber verdampft es, wenn es mit Luft in Kontakt kommt. Das Werk „Container as Content" (2006), das sich mit der Grenzlinie zwischen Behälter und Inhalt auseinandersetzt, ist ein weiteres Beispiel für die Auseinandersetzung des Künstlers mit den Themen Schein und Wirklichkeit und Ungewissheit des Daseins. Skulpturen aus Abdrücken des Körpers bzw. von Körperteilen des Künstlers, wie z.B. von seinem Ohr, werden an verschiedenen Wänden des Ausstellungsraums gezeigt. „Kaayam" (2008) ist ein neues Werk, mit einem vieldeutigen tamilischen Wort als Titel, das unter anderem „Körper", „das könnte passen" und „Wunde" bedeuten kann. Diese in die Wand integrierten Skulpturen stellen daher im wahrsten Sinn des Wortes eine „Wand der Wunden" dar.

A. Balasubramaniam ist in seinem Ansatz immer zurückhaltend und doch gelingt es ihm durch seine tiefgründige Betrachtung der menschlichen Existenz, eindrucksvoll in bestehende Räume einzugreifen. So erscheint eine kompakte Wand wie weiche Haut, die uns die unsichtbare Präsenz bewusst macht, die sich hinter der Membran befinden könnte. A. Balasubramaniam versucht in seinem Werk die Welt von zwei Seiten zu erfassen – aus einer positiven und einer negativen Perspektive. Auch der Einfluss

After studying at the Government College of Arts, Madras (Chennai), A. Balasubramaniam went on to study printmaking at universities in Edinburgh and in Vienna. Since 2000, however, his focus has shifted to sculpture created with diverse materials – fibreglass, timber, plastic and PVC, amongst others – and in diverse shapes. A. Balasubramaniam's early work was characterized by the application of a moulding method, in which he took moulds of his own body or body parts, and an interest in gravity, the tension between two objects, and the relationship between the object and its shadow. In recent years, his work has been underpinned by themes such as the relationship between the visible and the invisible, appearance and reality and various kinds of boundaries. For example, *Emerging Angels* (2004), one of his representative works exhibited in the 1st Singapore Biennale, is a sculpture of a sleeping angel inside a sealed display cabinet. At first glance it appears to be made of marble, but it is in fact made of a material that evaporates when it comes into contact with the atmosphere. It is an outstanding work concerned with appearance and reality, and the uncertainty of existence. *Container as Content* (2006), which refers to the boundary that lies between the container and its content, is another example that conveys the concerns of this artist.
Sculptures that represent the artist's body and body parts, such as his ear, will be shown on several walls inside the exhibition space. *Kaayam* (2008) is a new work named with a Tamil word that has multiple meanings that include body, this would go, and wound. These sculptures, integrated into the wall, represent "a wall of wounds" in every way. A. Balasubramaniam is always extremely low-key in his approach and yet succeeds in intervening in existing spaces as a result of his deep contemplation of human existence. A solid wall therefore appears like soft skin, prompting our awareness of the invisible presence that could lie behind the membrane. There are often comments that A. Balasubramaniam appears to be attempting to capture the world from the front and from the back, from a positive and negative perspective. His early experience as a printmaker arguably also informs his work.

Major exhibitions include "Indian Summer: la Jeune Scène Artistique Indienne" (École Nationale Supérieuredes Beaux-

seiner Erfahrungen mit der Druckgrafik am Anfang seiner künstlerischen Laufbahn ist nicht von der Hand zu weisen.

Wichtige Ausstellungen: „Indian Summer: La Jeune Scène Artistique Indienne“ (École Nationale Supérieure des Beaux-Arts, Paris, 2005), „Die erste Singapur Biennale: Glaube“ (2006), und eine Einzelausstellung unter dem Titel „(in) visible“ (Talwar Gallery, New Delhi, 2007). (AM)

Arts, Paris, 2005), “The 1st Singapore Biennale: Belief” (2006), and a solo exhibition titled “(in)visible” (Talwar Gallery, New Delhi, 2007). (AM)

A. BALASUBRAMANIAM
Shell As Body, 2007

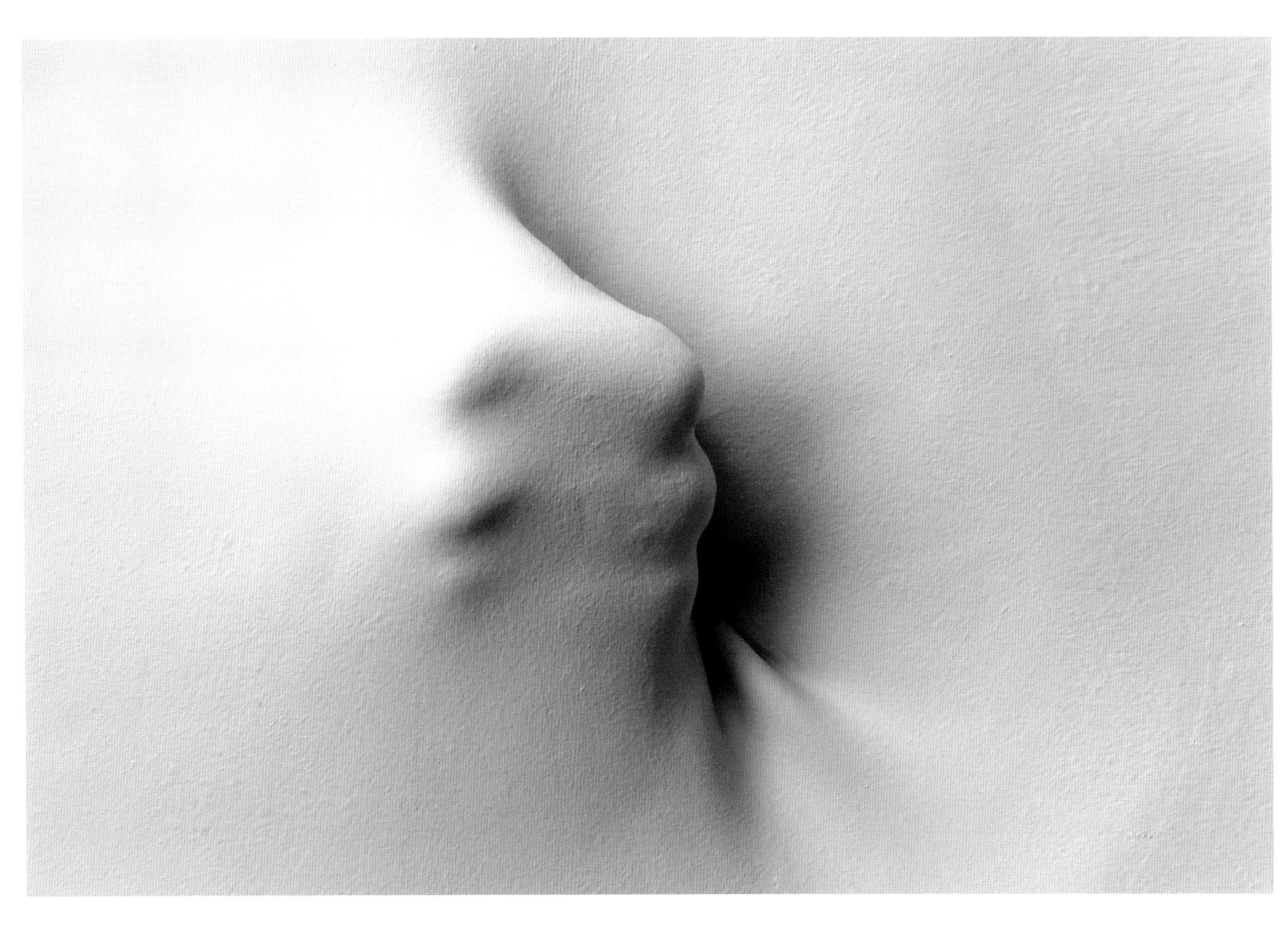

A. BALASUBRAMANIAM
Hidden Sight, 2007

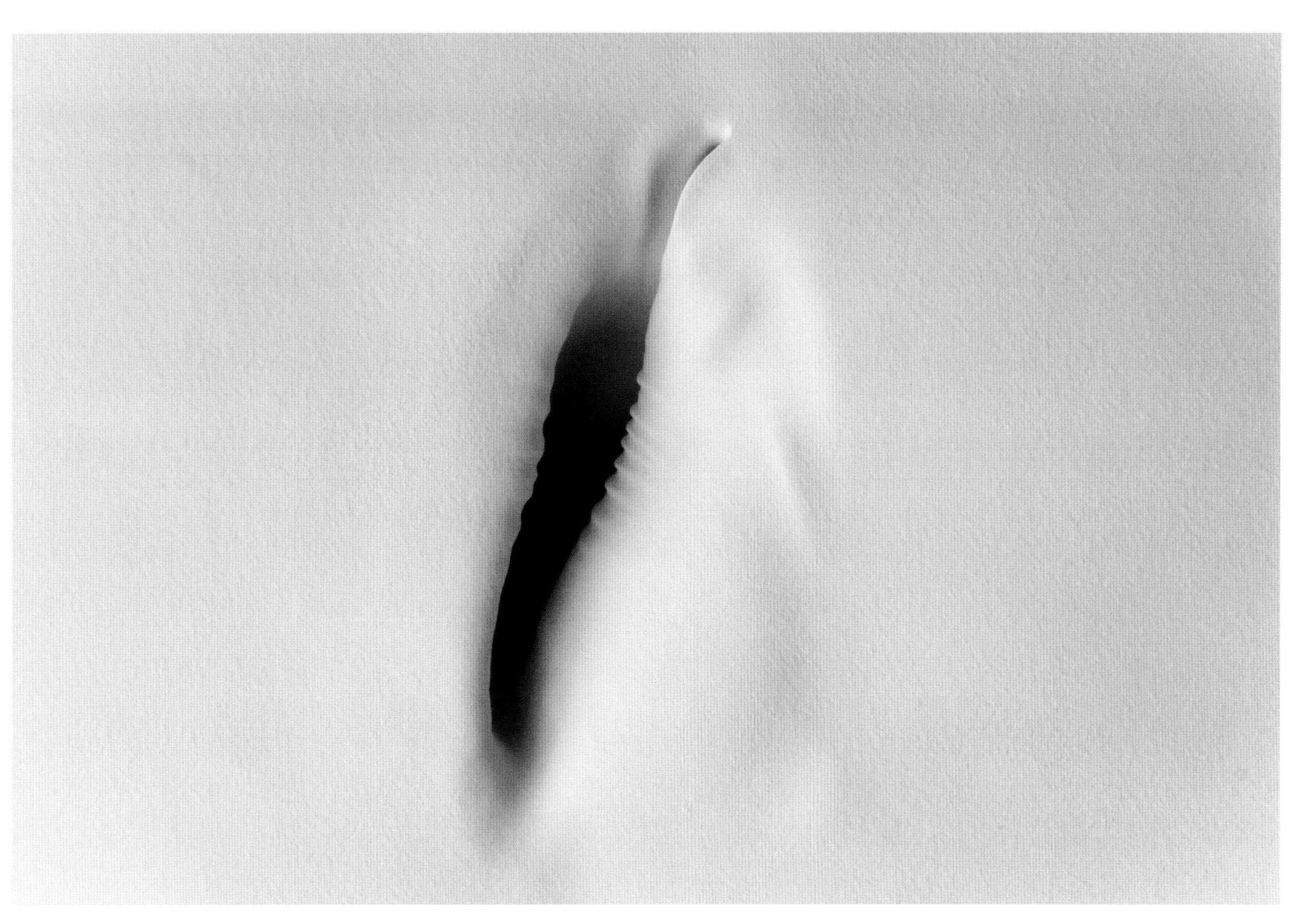

A. BALASUBRAMANIAM
Shell As Body, 2007 (Detail)

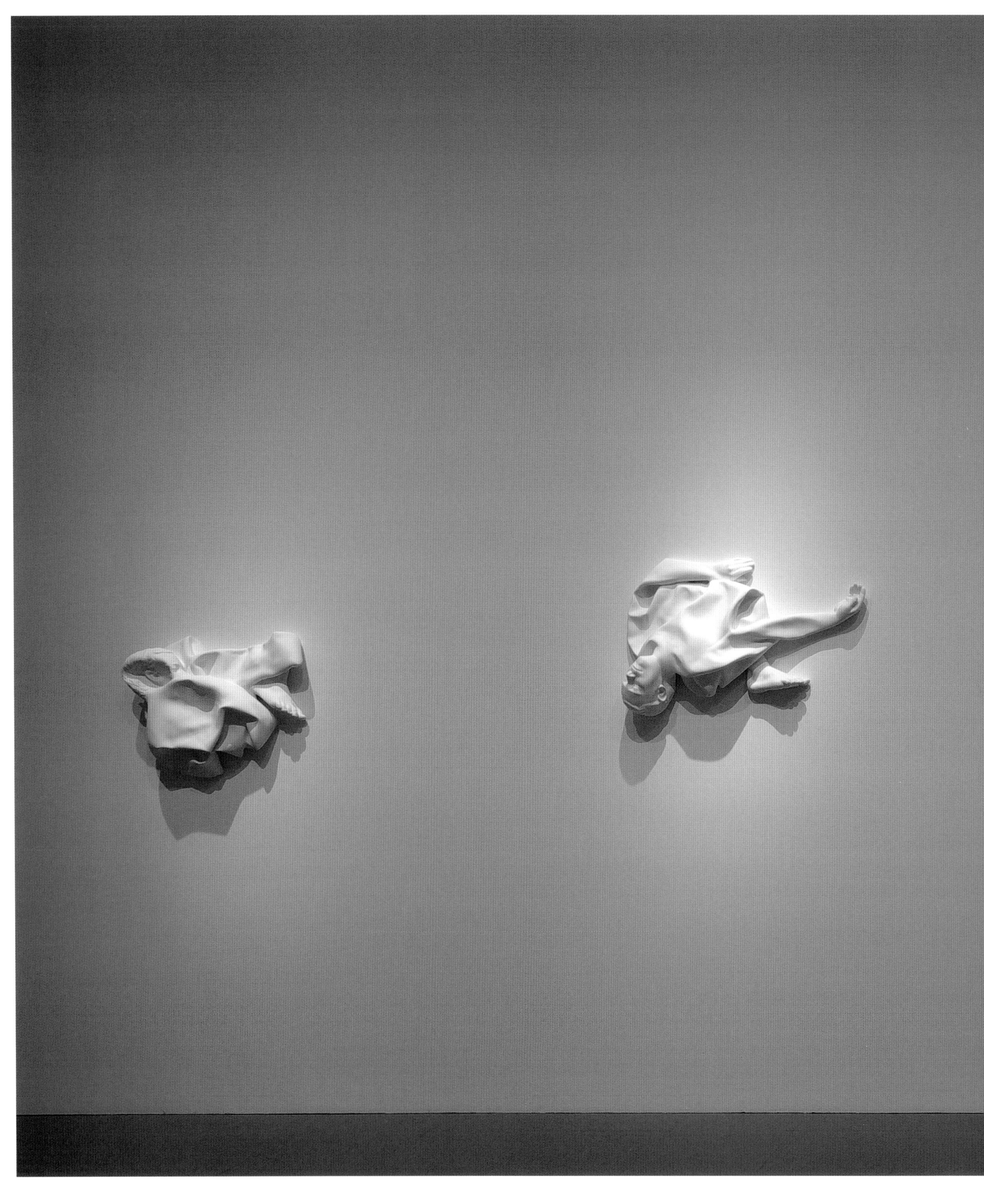

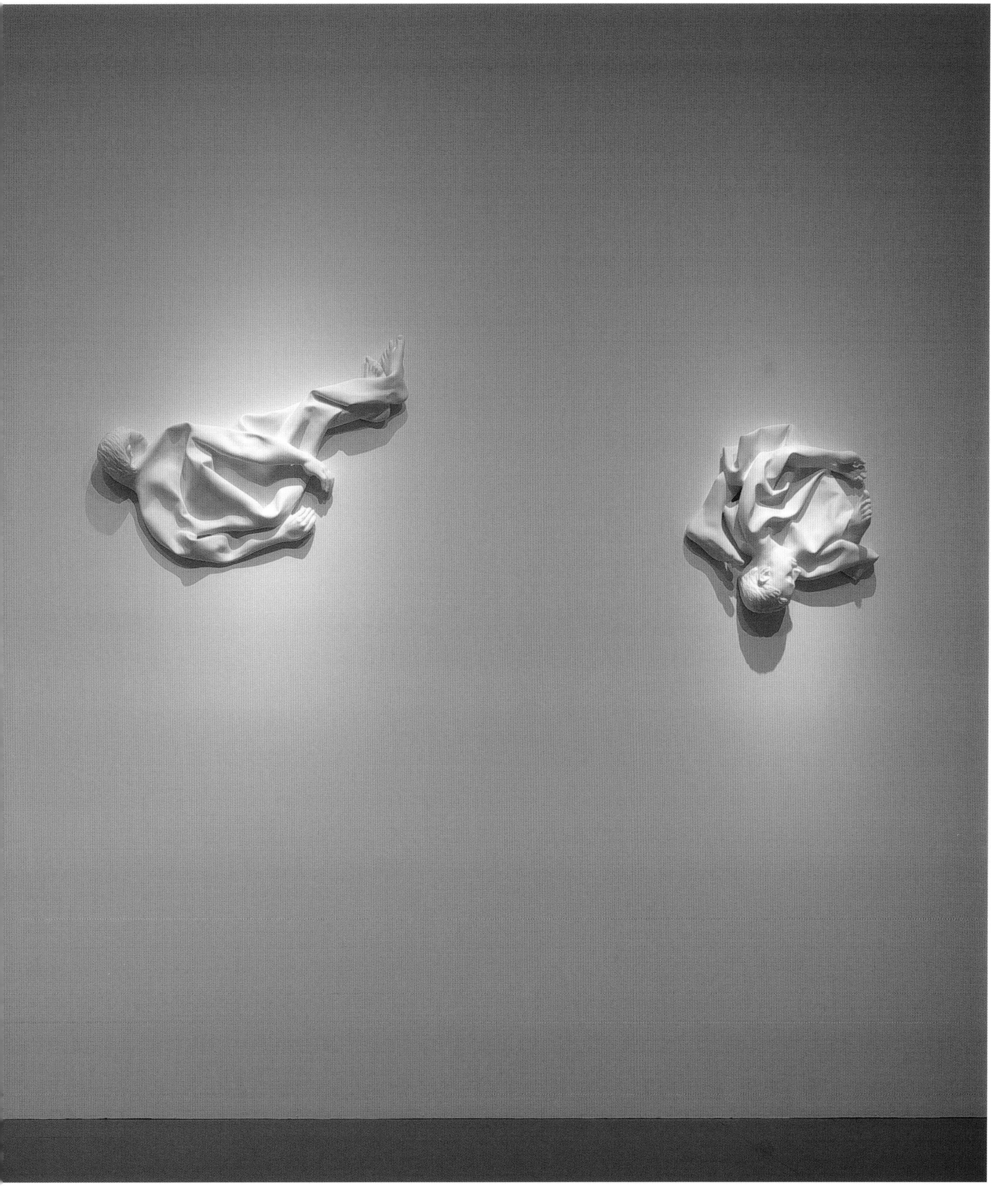

A. BALASUBRAMANIAM
Kaayam, 2008

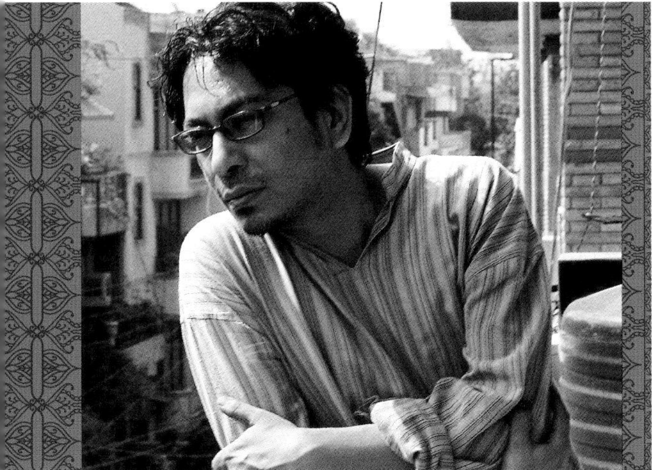

sarnath banerjee

SARNATH BANERJEE Geboren 1972 in Kolkata / Lebt in Delhi
Born 1972 in Kolkata / Lives in Delhi

Banerjee studierte zunächst Biochemie an der Delhi University und arbeitete dann bei einer Fernsehstation. Anschließend erwarb er einen Master in Bild und Kommunikation (MA Image and Communications) am Goldsmiths College an der University of London. Im Jahr 2004 brachte Banerjee einen illustrierten Roman unter dem Titel „Corridor" heraus – Banerjees Debut als Verfasser illustrierter Romane, die das Leben der Jugend im heutigen Indien beschreiben. Ausgangspunkt der Geschichte sind drei Personen, die in den Kolonnaden von Connaught Place – einer ringförmigen Promenade mit Einkaufsviertel im Zentrum von Delhi – eine antiquarische Buchhandlung besuchen. Banerjees illustrierte Romane verdanken ihren Erfolg den teilweise autobiografischen, an realen Orten spielenden Erzählungen, ebenso wie seinem eigenwilligen Stil und Illustrationen, in denen Geschichte, Naturwissenschaft und Volkskultur miteinander verschmelzen. Sein zweiter Roman, „The Barn Owl's Wondrous Capers" (Der Schleiereule lustige Streiche) von 2007, ist ein historischer Kriminalroman, dessen Handlung sich im Deutschland des 17. Jahrhunderts, im Kolkata des 18. Jahrhunderts und im heutigen Paris und London abspielt. In den letzten Jahren hat Banerjee seine Tätigkeit auf die Teilnahme an Kunstausstellungen, auf Animation, das Schreiben von Libretti für Taschenopern und auf ein Projekt für ein fiktives Café ausgeweitet.

Banerjee zeigt in dieser Ausstellung drei Werke, die auf Ereignisse aus seiner Kindheit, seiner Jugend und seinem heutigen Leben Bezug nehmen. „Tito Years" (2008) ist eine Geschichte aus dem Kolkate der 1980er Jahre, vor der Liberalisierung der indischen Wirtschaft, und erzählt vom damals sehnlichen Wunsch des Künstlers, ein Paar amerikanischer Nike Schuhe zu besitzen. Banerjee schildert seine kultische Begeisterung für Nike, erzählt von den Olympischen Spielen in Los Angeles, von populären indischen Filmen und amerikanischen Seifenopern, die man damals von Sendern aus Bangladesch empfangen konnte, von seinen in Übersee lebenden indischen Verwandten und der Beziehung zu seinem Vater. „Colonel's Brain" (2008) handelt von Banerjees Erfahrungen bei der Fernsehstation, unter anderem als Mitarbeiter an einer Dokumentation, die den Giftgasunfall in Bophal

Banerjee majored in biochemistry at Delhi University, and after working for a television broadcaster, obtained an MA in image and communication at Goldsmiths College, University of London. Banerjee released a graphic novel in 2004 titled *Corridor,* set in the colonnaded corridors of Connaught Place, the donut-shaped promenade and shopping area of central Delhi. The story develops around three characters that visit a second-hand bookshop, and marks Banerjee's debut as a graphic novelist who depicts the lives of contemporary Indian youth. His semi-autobiographical stories set in real locations combined with his unique style and illustrations that incorporate history, natural science, and popular culture have established Banerjee's reputation as the standard-bearer of the graphic novel. His second novel, *The Barn Owl's Wondrous Capers* (2007) is a historical mystery story surrounding events that took place in 17th century Germany, 18th century Kolkata, and Paris and London today. In recent years, Banerjee's activities have expanded to include participation in art exhibitions, animation, writing a pocket opera script, and a fictional café project.

Banerjee is showing three works in this exhibition, based on events from his childhood, adolescence, and his life today. *Tito Years* (2008) is a story about the artist, set in Kolkata during the 80s, before the deregulation of the Indian economy, and how much he wants a pair of American Nike shoes. He depicts his life at the time by describing his worship of Nike as well as the Los Angeles Olympics, popular Indian movies and American soap operas that could be seen through signal from Bangladesh, his Indian relatives living overseas and the relationship with his father. *Colonel's Brain* (2008) is about Banerjee's experiences while he was working in television, involved in making a program that reexamined the poison gas leak incident that took place in Bophal in 1983. He visited the basement morgue of the hospital with a doctor of forensic medicine who had been involved in the aftermath of what was the worst industrial accident in history, and depicts his own experiences through an anecdotal description that is part-truth, part-fiction. *Nano* (2008) takes its title from the name given to the *One Lakh Car* (100,000 rupee car), an ultra-affordable car to be produced in India, announced

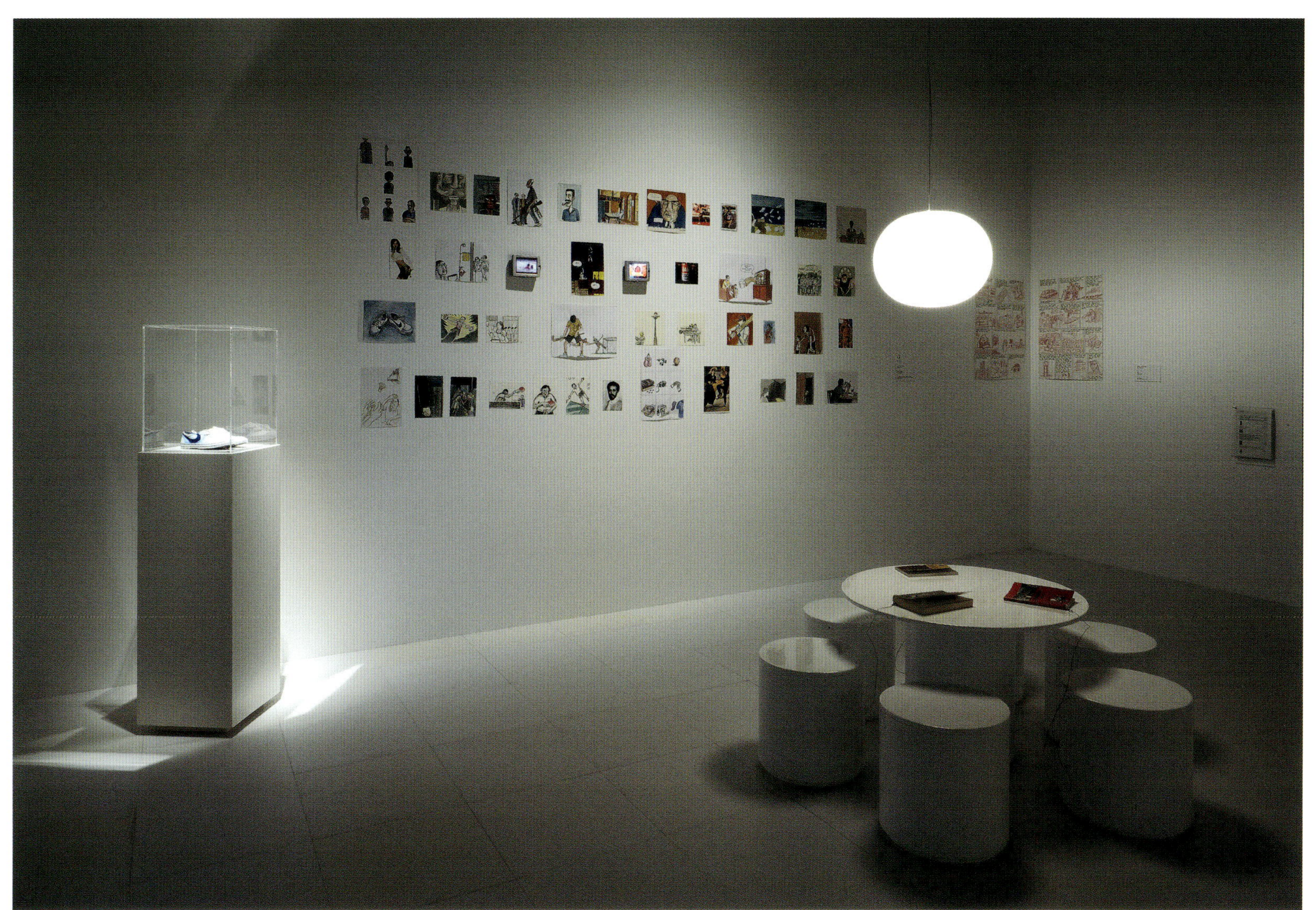

SARNATH BANERJEE
Installation view

1983 nochmals aufrollte. Er besuchte die unterirdische Leichenhalle des Krankenhauses mit einem Arzt, der die Folgen des schlimmsten Betriebsunfalls der Geschichte miterlebte und beschreibt seine eigenen Erlebnisse in einer anekdotenhaften, teils auf Realität und teils auf Fiktion beruhenden Darstellung. „Nano" (2008) leitet seinen Titel von der Bezeichnung des „One Lakh Car" („100,000 Rupien-Auto") her; der Bau dieses supergünstigen Autos in Indien wurde im Jänner 2008 angekündigt. Der Protagonist behauptet, er sei der letzte Fußgänger auf den Straßen von Delhi und erklärt, dass der Nano helfen wird, die Verkehrsstaus in Delhi zu reduzieren. In Banerjees illustrierten Romanen vereinigen sich Kunst und Geschichte zu einem dichten Lokalkolorit und thematisieren gleichzeitig globale Fragen und Probleme.

Wichtige Ausstellungen: „SUBCONTINGENT: The Indian Subcontinent in Contemporary Art / Il Subcontinente Indiano nell'Arte Contemporanea" (Fondazione Sandretto Re Rebaudengo, Turin, Italia, 2006), „Horn Please: Narratives in Contemporary Indian art" (Kunstmuseum Bern, 2007), und „28th São Paulo Biennial" (2008). (TK)

in January 2008. The central character claims that he is the last person to walk the streets of Delhi, asserting that the Nano will assist in improving traffic congestion in Delhi. Banerjee's graphic novels incorporate not only art and history but a range of diverse elements which combine to create a local flavour, while at the same time presenting the ubiquitous contemporary issues faced by the world today.

Major exhibitions include "SUBCONTINGENT: The Indian Subcontinent in Contemporary Art / Il Subcontinente Indiano nell'Arte Contemporanea" (Fondazione Sandretto Re Rebaudengo, Turin, Italia, 2006), "Horn Please: Narratives in Contemporary Indian art" (Kunstmuseum Bern, 2007), and "28th São Paulo Biennial" (2008). (TK)

Ich saß und legte Solitaire. Das einsame Leben eines Videoeditors.
Ich dachte, ich wäre mutterseelenallein in dem riesigen Büro.

I sat playing solitaire. The lonely life of a video editor.
Alone in the vast office or so I thought.

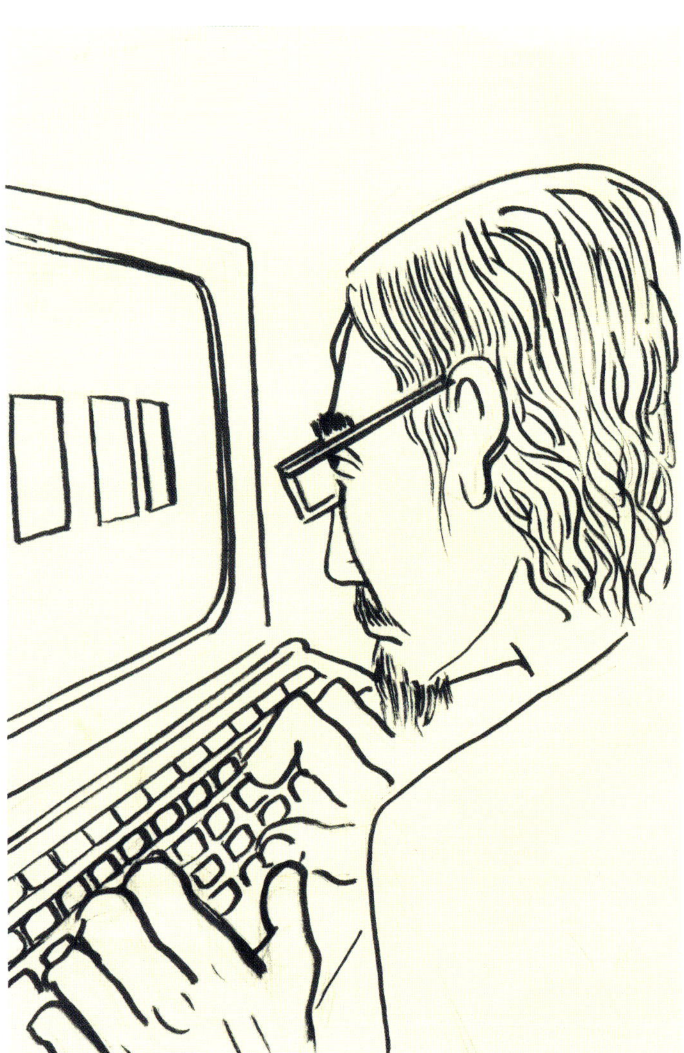

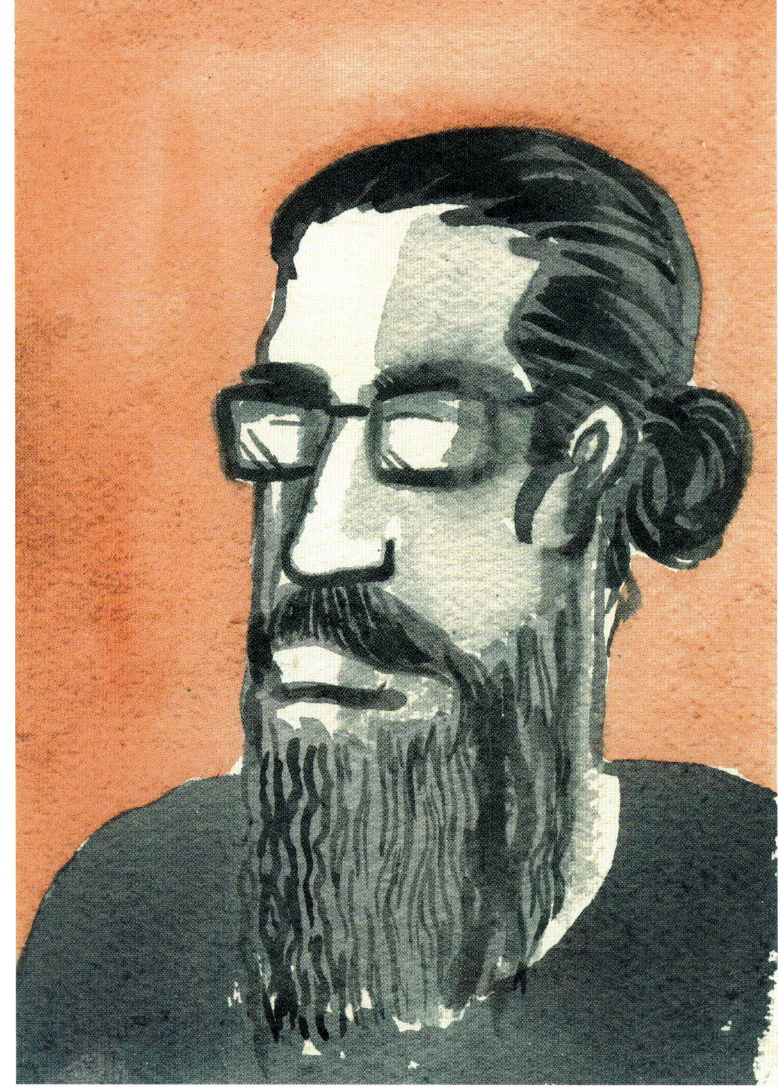

„Sarnath“
Bhasker Bhattacharya, Programmchef, Impresario, Epikuräer und eine Kombination aus Jerry Garcia und Alan Ginsberg. Seine Rekrutierungs- und Beförderungspolitik orientierte sich an der Zahl der Charas (indische Bezeichnung für Haschisch), die seine Angestellten zu rauchen imstande waren. Ich glaube, er hätte gern einen Joint gehabt.

"Sarnath"
Bhasker Bhattacharya, Head of programming, impresario, epicurean, a combination of Jerry Garcia and Alan Ginsberg. His employment and promotion policies were based upon the amount of charas his employees could smoke. I thought he wanted a joint.

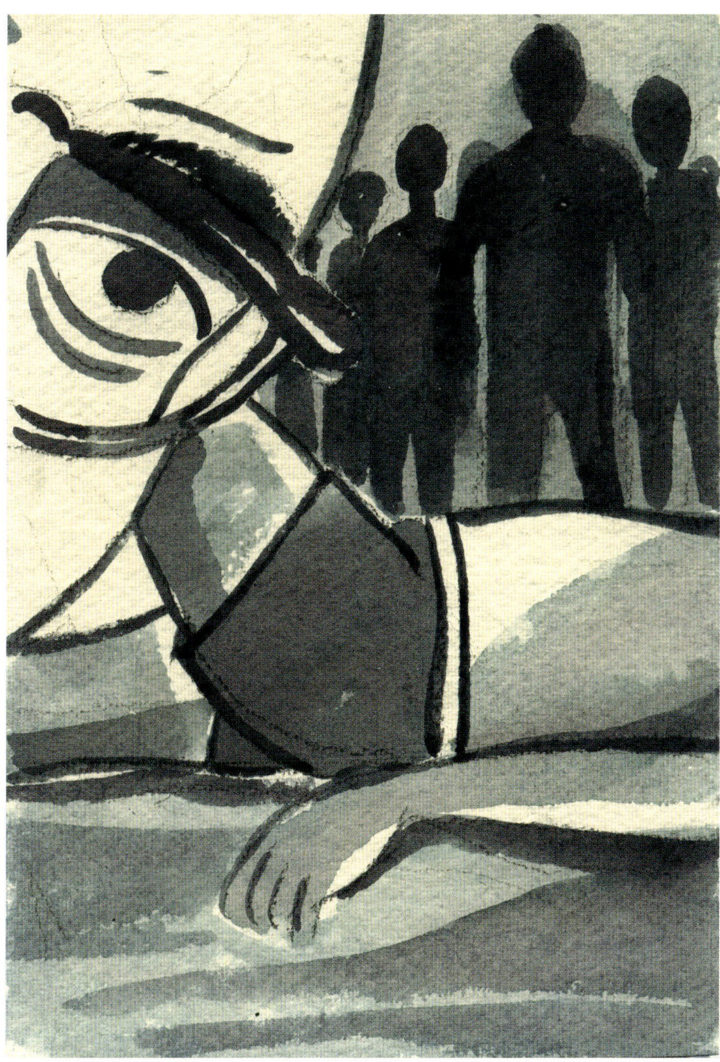

Aber an diesem Samstag Abend erteilte er Anweisungen.
„Ich habe dich dazu bestimmt, nach Bhopal zu fahren und einen Dokumentarfilm zum zwölften Jahrestag der Gaskatastrophe zu drehen – ob zur Feier, zur Trauer oder was immer sonst, bleibt dir überlassen."
„Ich habe dich dazu bestimmt ..." „Ich habe dich dazu bestimmt", was für ein Scheiß; ich war das einzige Arschloch, das an diesem Abend in der Programmabteilung herumgammelte. Er hat mich einfach nur im richtigen Augenblick erwischt.
Damals musste jeder Filmemacher, der etwas auf sich hielt, einen Film über die Gastragödie von Bhopal, Aids, die Tötung weiblicher Kinder drehen.

But that Saturday night he was giving instructions.
"I have chosen you to go to Bhopal and make a documentary, celebrating or lamenting or whatever you might want, the 12th anniversary of the gas tragedy."
"I have chosen you..." "I have chosen you" what a load of bollocks, I was the only bugger mucking about at the programme floor that evening. He just happened to catch me at the right time.
Every self-respecting documentary filmmaker of that era had to make a film on the Bhopal gas tragedy, Aids, female infanticide.

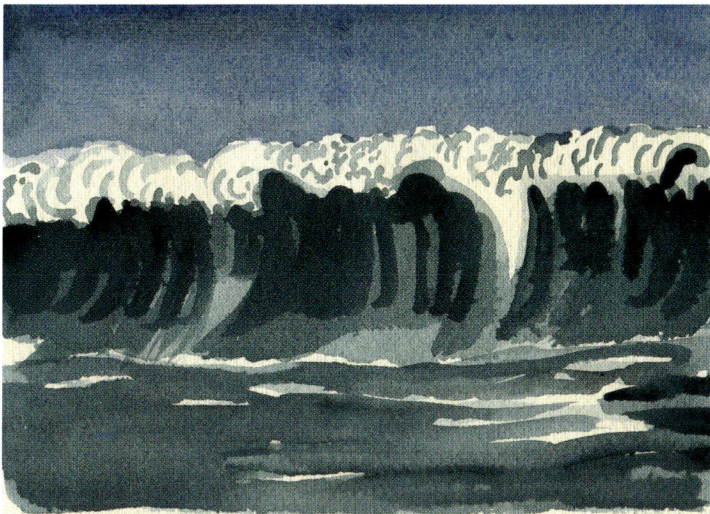

11 Jahre danach ging er in Madras nachts im Meer schwimmen und kam nicht mehr lebend zurück.
Die Gewässer in dieser Gegend sind unberechenbar.

11 years later, he would go for a swim at night into the sea in madras.
And wouldn't return alive.
Waters in these parts can be unpredictable.

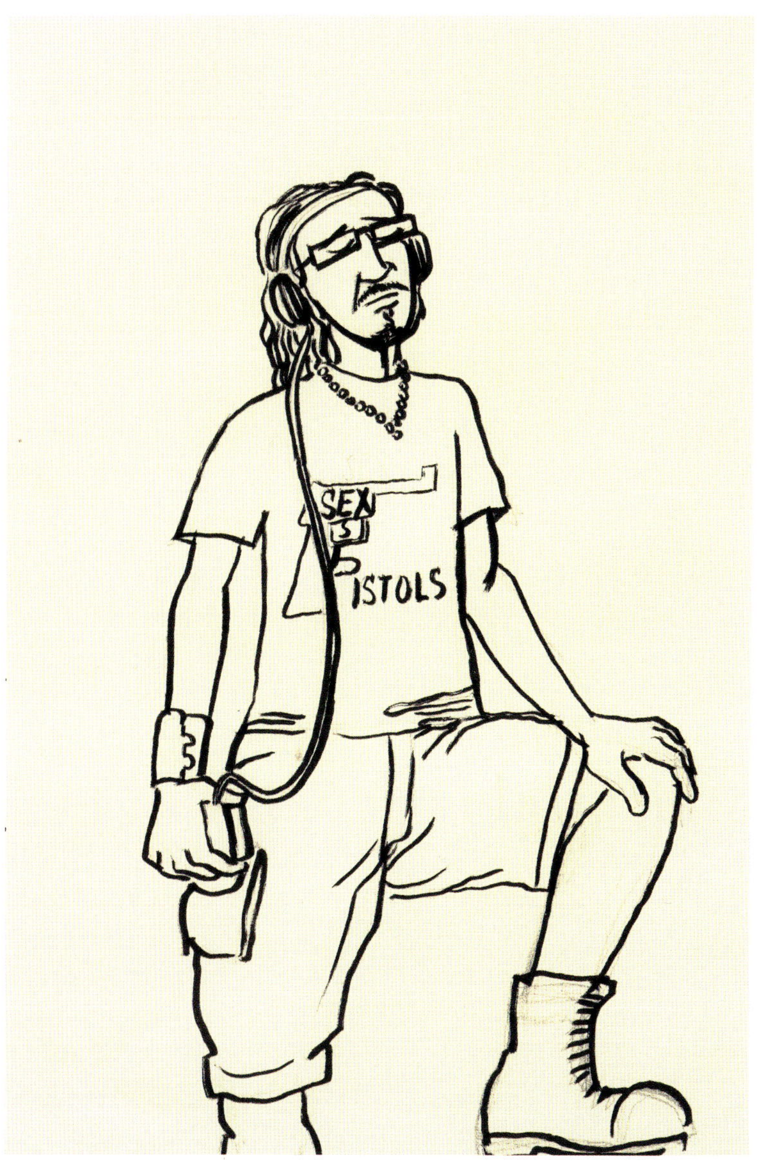

SARNATH BANERJEE
Coronel's Brain, 2008

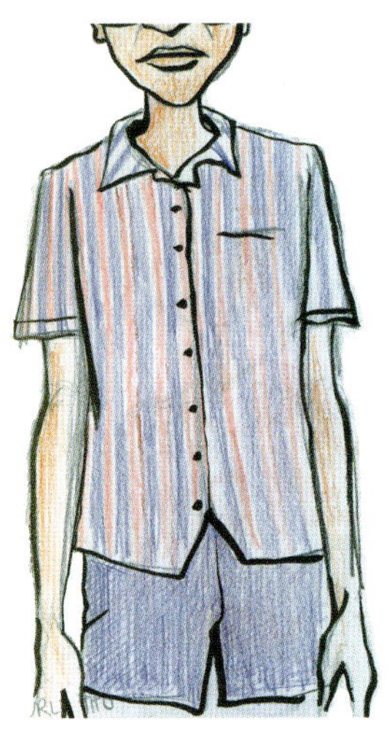

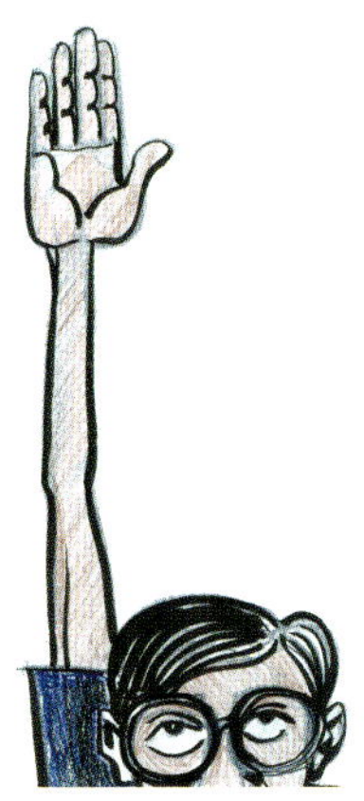

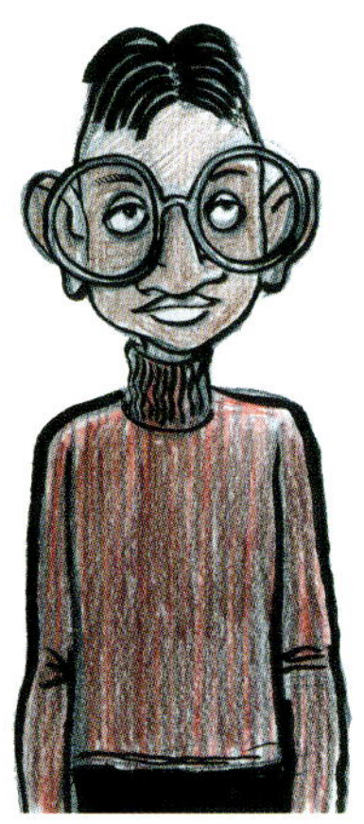

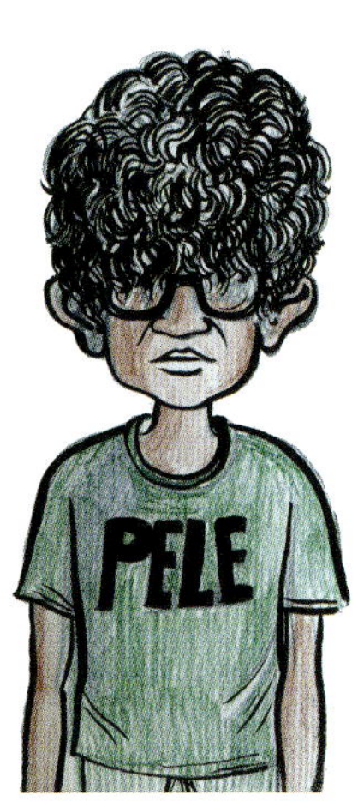

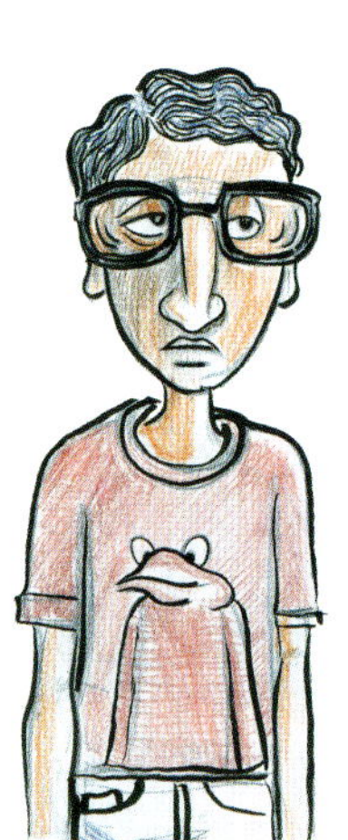

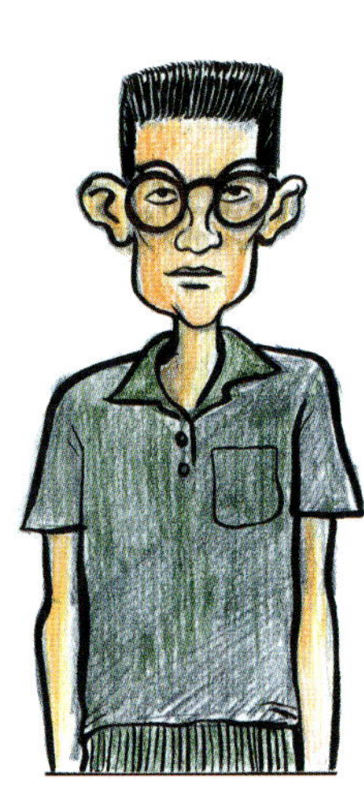

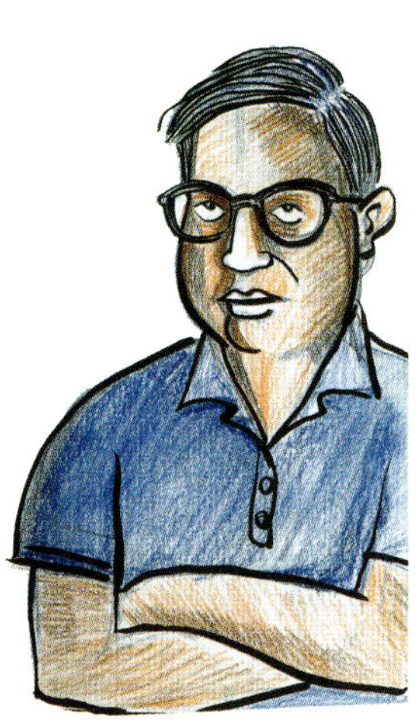

Das war die Zeit, als Kinder noch Hockey spielten (inzwischen ein obskures Spiel, dessen Regeln keiner mehr kennt); ihre Spitznahmen leiteten die Buben von Marschall Tito her, und ein Paar Nikes stellten den Gipfelpunkt ihrer Sehnsüchte dar.
Es war unmöglich, sie käuflich zu erwerben.

This was the time when children still played hockey (now an obscure game whose rules no one remembers), the boys were all nicknamed after Marshal Tito and a pair of nikes were the pinnacle of aspiration.
It was impossible to acquire.

Für uns waren ein Paar Nikes in etwa das, was eine Ak 47 für KedarNath Tiwari wäre // den achtzigjährigen Wachmann der Canara Bank, West Patel Nagar, der 60 Jahre lang bei seiner eher theatralisch wirkenden, doppelläufigen Flinte geblieben ist.

A pair of nikes for us was similar to what an Ak 47 would be for KedarNath Tiwari // the octogenarian guard at Canara Bank, West Patel Nagar, who for the last 60 years has been holding on to a rather theatrical looking double barrel.

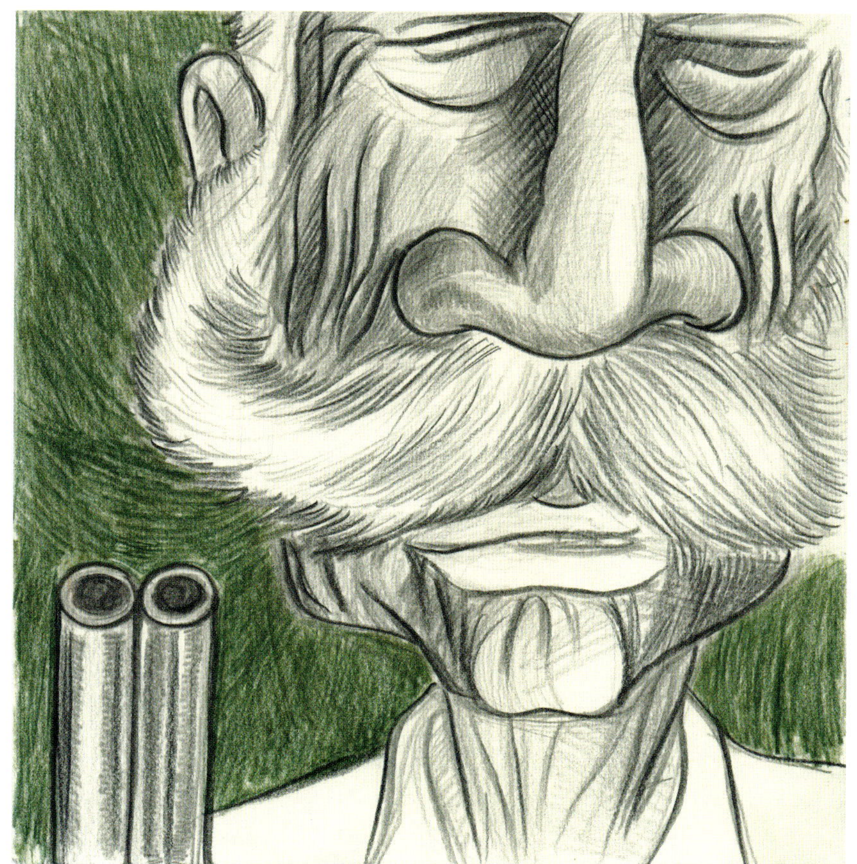

Bei den Olympischen Spielen in LA 1984 erlebten wir alle, wie Carl Lewis // der Brand Ambassador von Nike, den Rekord von Jesse Owen im 100-Meter-Sprint unterbot; wie Edwin Moses // die 400 Meter Hürden im Flug hinter sich brachte; wie Mary Decker // beim 3000-Meter-Lauf tragisch aus dem Rennen ausschied; wie Daley Thompson // im Stabhochsprung ebenso souverän punktete wie im Kugelstoßen; wie Nawal El Moutawakil // als erste muslimische Araberin Gold gewann.

In the '84 LA Olympics we all saw Nike's brand ambassador Carl Lewis // break Jesse Owens' record in 100 meter dash, Edwin Moses // fly through 400 meter hurdles, Mary Decker // tragically pull out of 3000metres, Daley Thompson // pole-vault and shot put with equal ease, Nawal El Moutawakil // become the first Arab-Muslim woman to win a gold.

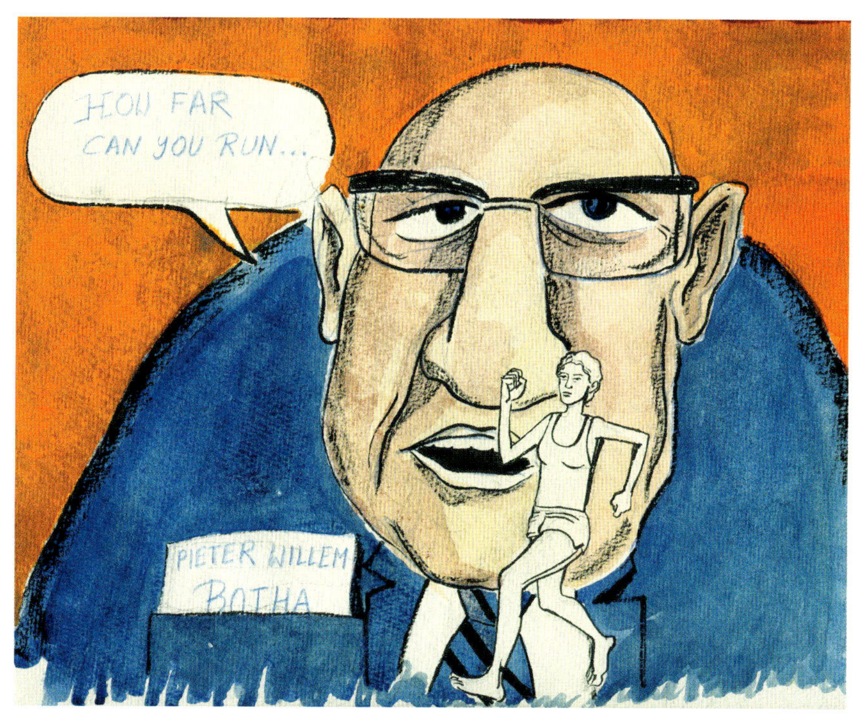

SARNATH BANERJEE
Tito Years, 2008

SARNATH BANERJEE
NANO, 2008

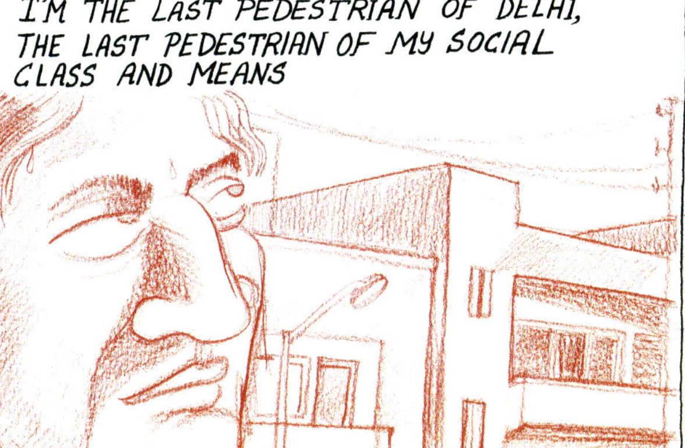

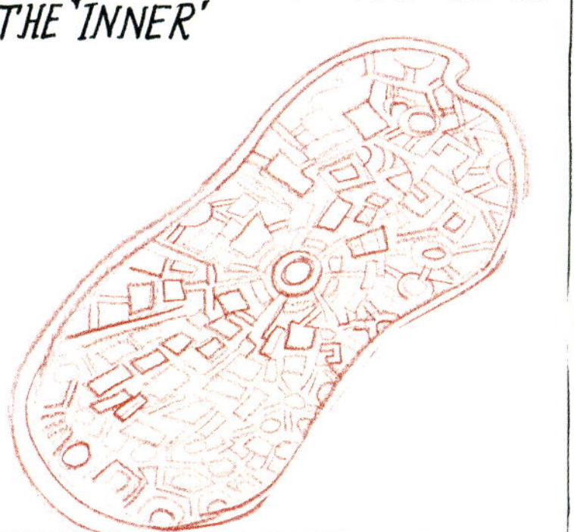

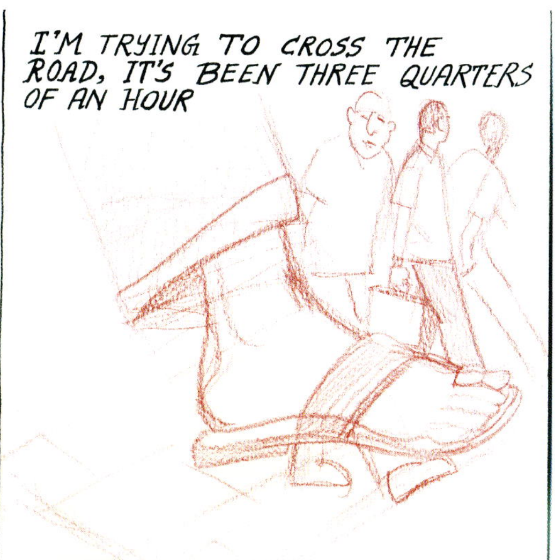

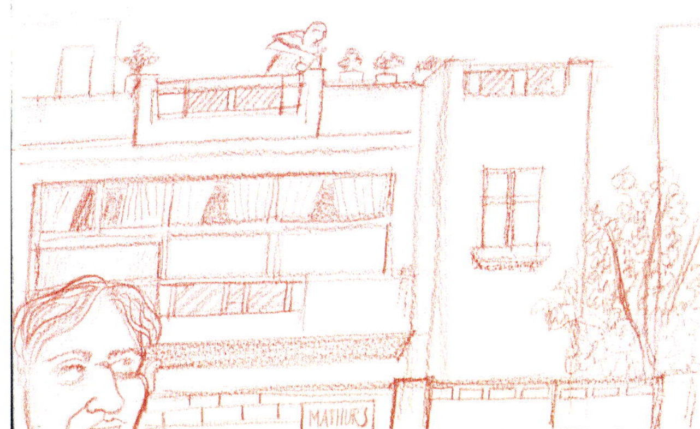

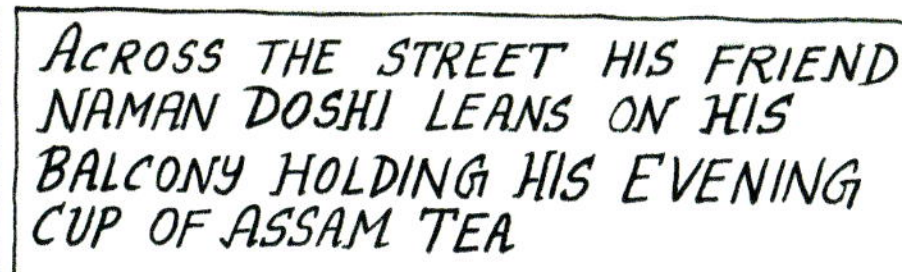
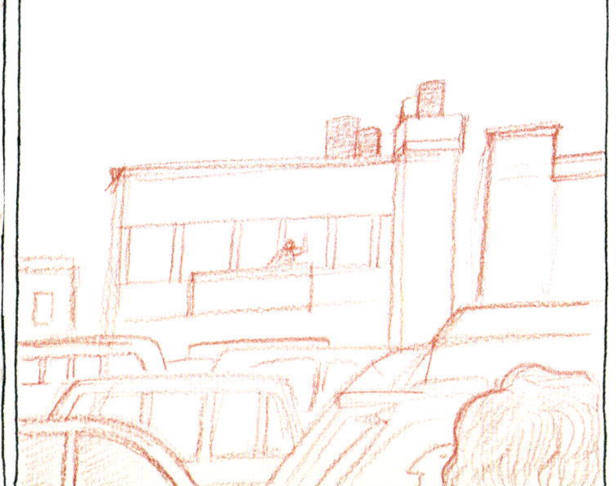

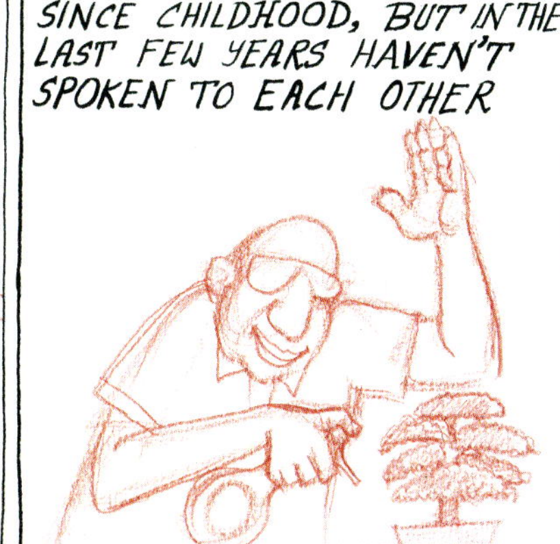

BECAUSE NEITHER OF THEM COULD DARE TO CROSS THE ROAD

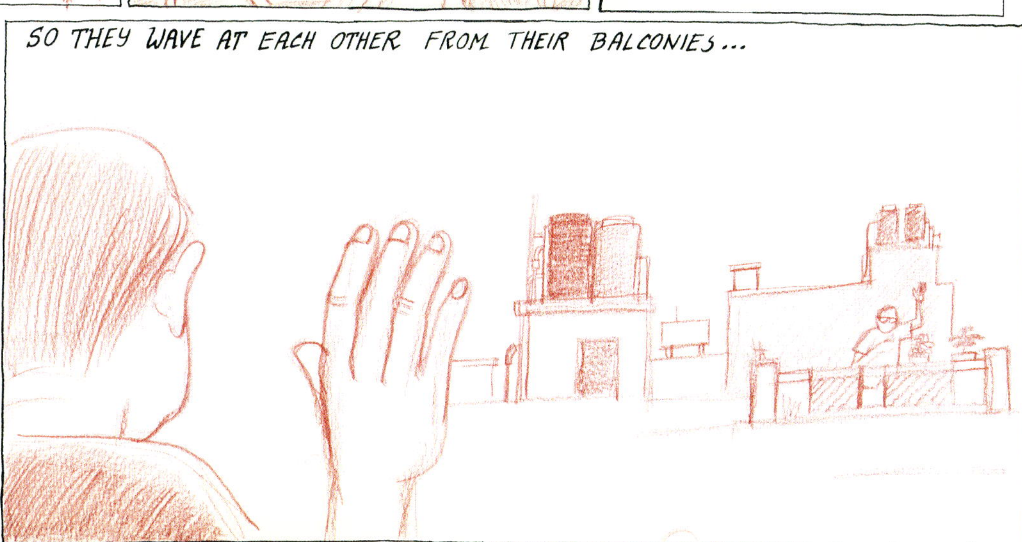

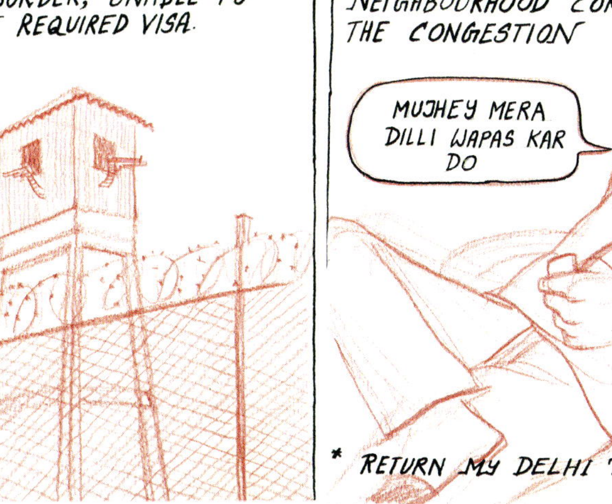

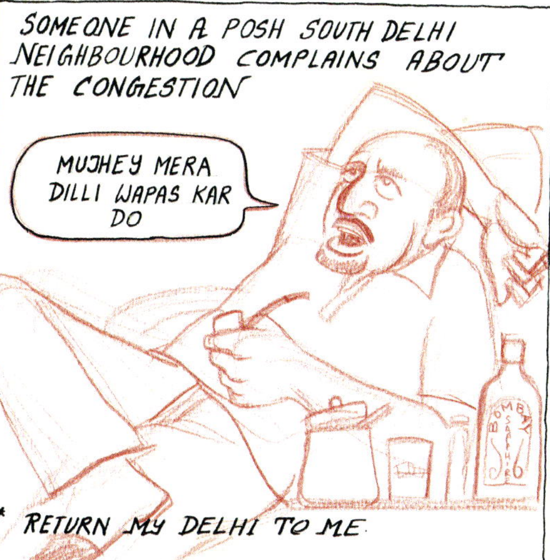

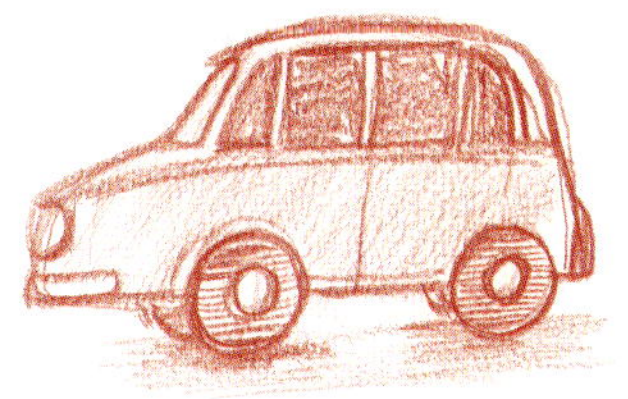

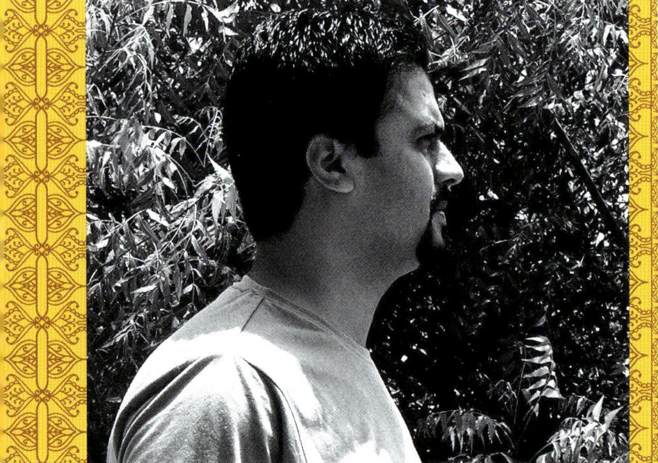

krishnaraj chonat

KRISHNARAJ CHONAT Geboren 1973 in Chennai / Lebt in Bangalore
Born 1973 in Chennai / Lives in Bangalore

Nach Abschluss seines Studiums am Karnataka Chitrakala Parishad College in Bangalore mit einem Bachelor of Fine Arts im Jahr 1994 erwarb Chonat 1996 ein Post-Graduate Diplom in Druckgrafik an der Maharaja Sayajirao University in Baroda (Vadodara). Chonat verbindet Bilder aus der Massenkultur mit ganz persönlichen Darstellungen und kreiert so Arbeiten, die sich durch ihre optisch beeindruckenden und dramatischen Szenen auszeichnen, ähnlich den Szenerien von Kostümfilmen. Nachdem er sich zu Beginn seiner Karriere vor allem auf die Malerei konzentriert hatte, schaffte er in den letzten Jahren zunehmend dreidimensionale Arbeiten wie Skulpturen und Installationen. Unabhängig von der gewählten Ausdrucksform ist Chonats Interesse am sozialen Umfeld einzelner Personen und am Leben der Menschen in der heutigen Konsumgesellschaft ein immer wiederkehrendes Thema in seinen Arbeiten.

Gängige Themen in Chonats jüngsten Arbeiten sind das Aufkommen der Neureichen in Indien und insbesondere die Darstellung der von der großstädtischen Konsumkultur hervorgebrachten Formen „idealen Lebensstils". „Ideal Living" (2004) ist eine Installation nach dem Vorbild eines Wohnzimmers in einer der zunehmend populären städtischen Eigentumswohnungen, komplett mit verschnörkeltem Luster, der mitten im Raum von der Decke hängt, als wäre er ein absolutes „Must-Have" in jeder neuen Wohnung, mit dem „Bild" an der Wand, das rein dekorativen Charakter hat und mit der Grünpflanze als Teil der Innendekoration. Mit Kunstperlen überzogen sind diese Objekte eine satirische Fußnote zur Mittelklasse und zur menschlichen Oberflächlichkeit und Gier. „The Coracle" (Das Curach, Boot), ein neues, hier gezeigtes Werk, stellt zum Einen die ausufernde städtische Entwicklung in Indien in Frage, die trotz der vielen negativen Nebenwirkungen immer rascher um sich greift, und zum Anderen die Zukunftsaussichten der Städter. „The Coracle" ist ein Modell für ein „Mobiles Heim" als Alternative zu einem Grundbesitz und die Chance, einer unerträglichen Wirklichkeit zu entfliehen, aber auch ein Gefährt als Hilfsmittel, in der unbekannten offenen See, Zukunft genannt, zu überleben. Auf dem Boot – geschaffen aus dem Schutt des Lebens und den Fragmenten traditioneller indischer Architektur –

After obtaining a Bachelor of Fine Arts at Karnataka Chitrakala Parishad in Bangalore in 1994, Chonat went on to complete a post-graduate diploma in printmaking at the Maharaja Sayajirao University of Baroda (Vadodara) in 1996. Chonat combines images from mass culture with extremely personal images to create work featuring highly visual and dramatic scenes that resemble the stage sets of a period film. Although focusing on painting in his early career, in recent years there has been a gradual shift towards three-dimensional works such as sculptures and installations. Regardless of the avenue of expression, however, a constant theme in Chonat's work is his interest in the social environment that surrounds the individual and in the consumer culture-dominated lives of people today.

Common themes in his recent work are the emergence of India's new rich and, in particular, the images of "ideal lifestyles" that have been generated by consumer culture in urban centres. *Ideal Living* (2004) is an installation modelled on the living room of the increasingly popular urban condominium, including the ornate chandelier hanging in the centre of the room as if it were a must-have item in any new home, the "picture" hanging on the wall that has no function other than to be decorative, and the indoor plant that is also part of the interior. These have been covered in fake pearls, a satirical comment on the middle classes and people's shallowness and greed. *The Coracle,* a new work being presented in this exhibition, questions the outcome of the extensive urban development that is taking place in India and which, despite the many negative side effects, continues to accelerate, and what the future might hold for people living in urban areas. *The Coracle* is a "model for a mobile home" so to say, as an alternative to real estate, or an opportunity to escape from a reality that makes one wants to avert one's eyes, or to survive the unknown open sea that we call the future. Attached to the top of the boat – created with the debris of life and the fragments of traditional Indian architecture – is a pair of binoculars to perhaps enable the observer to work out which direction s/he is travelling in. The entire work is shrouded in milky white, as though only God knows what lies ahead and which is contrasted by an enormous black mosquito, perhaps suggesting that Southern India

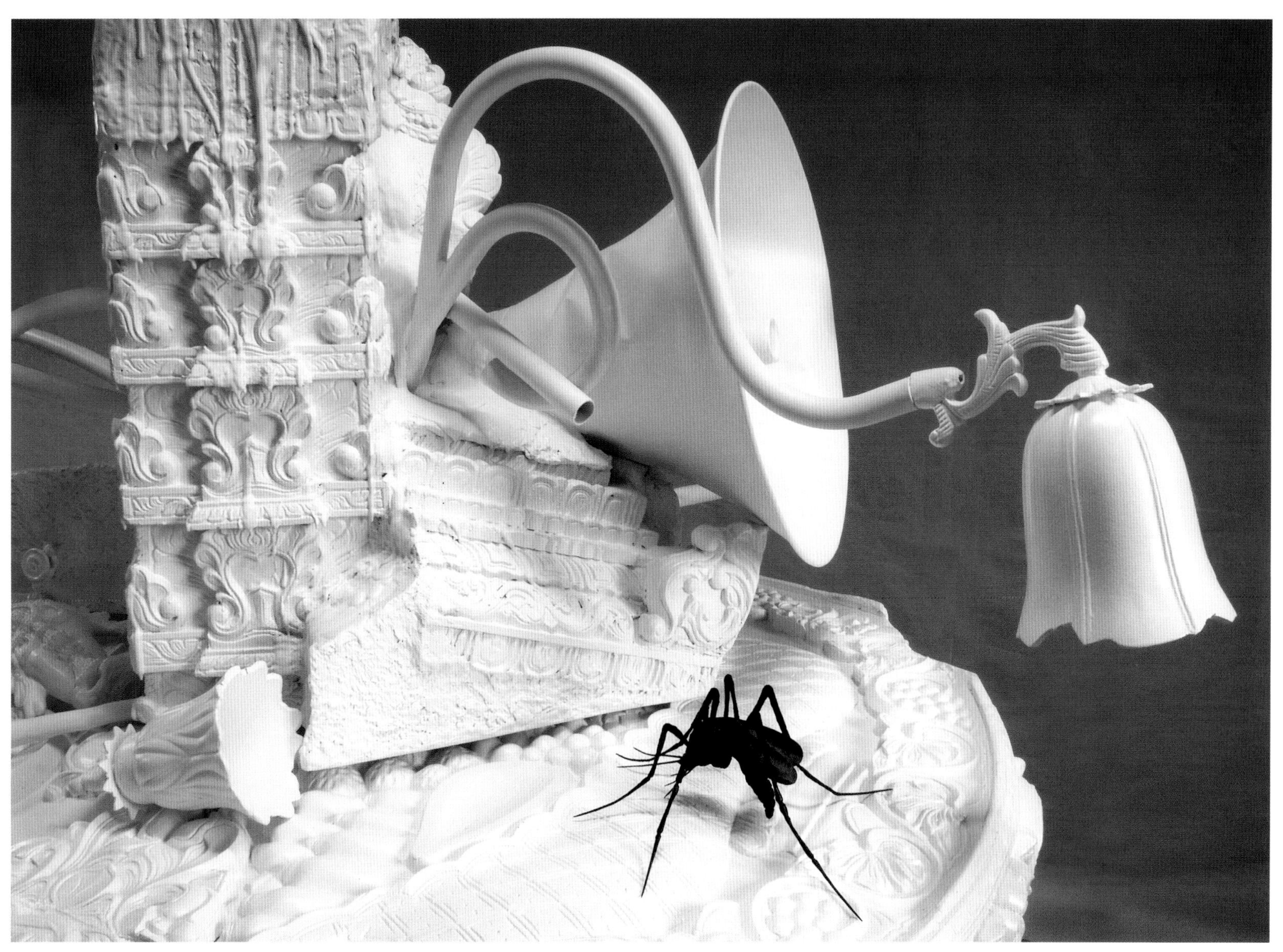

KRISHNARAJ CHONAT
The Coracle, 2008 (Detail)

befindet sich ein Fernglas, das möglicherweise dazu dienen könnte festzustellen, wohin die Reise geht. Das ganze Werk ist in milchiges Weiß gehüllt, als wüsste Gott allein, was die Zukunft bringt. Dieses Weiß kontrastiert mit dem Schwarz eines riesigen Moskitos, der vielleicht darauf hinweisen soll, dass Südindien bis heute ein extremes Feuchtgebiet ist und immer bleiben wird – egal was die Zukunft bringt.

Wichtige Ausstellungen: „Have We Met?" (The Japan Foundation, Tokyo, 2004), „Indian Summer: la Jeune Scène Artistique Indienne" (École Nationale Supérieure des Beaux-Arts, Paris, 2005), und eine Ausstellung neuer Arbeiten im The Mattress Factory Art Museum in Pittsburgh, Pennsylvania (2007). (KM)

remains, and will always be extremely humid no matter what lies in the future.

Major exhibitions include "Have We Met?" (The Japan Foundation, Tokyo, 2004), "Indian Summer: la Jeune Scène Artistique Indienne" (École Nationale Supérieure des Beaux-Arts, Paris, 2005), and an exhibition of new works at The Mattress Factory Art Museum in Pittsburgh, Pennsylvania (2007). (KM)

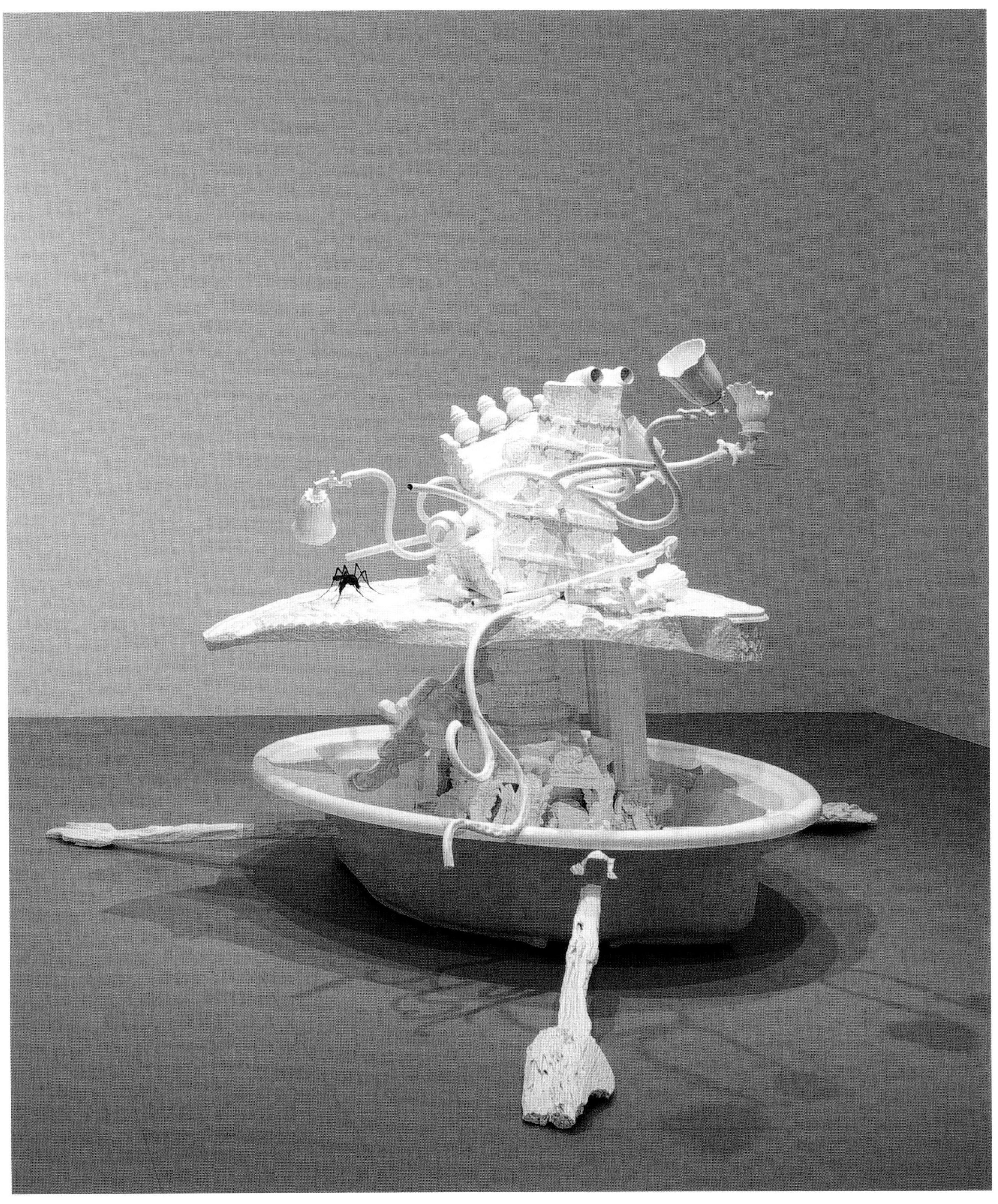

KRISHNARAJ CHONAT
The Coracle, 2008

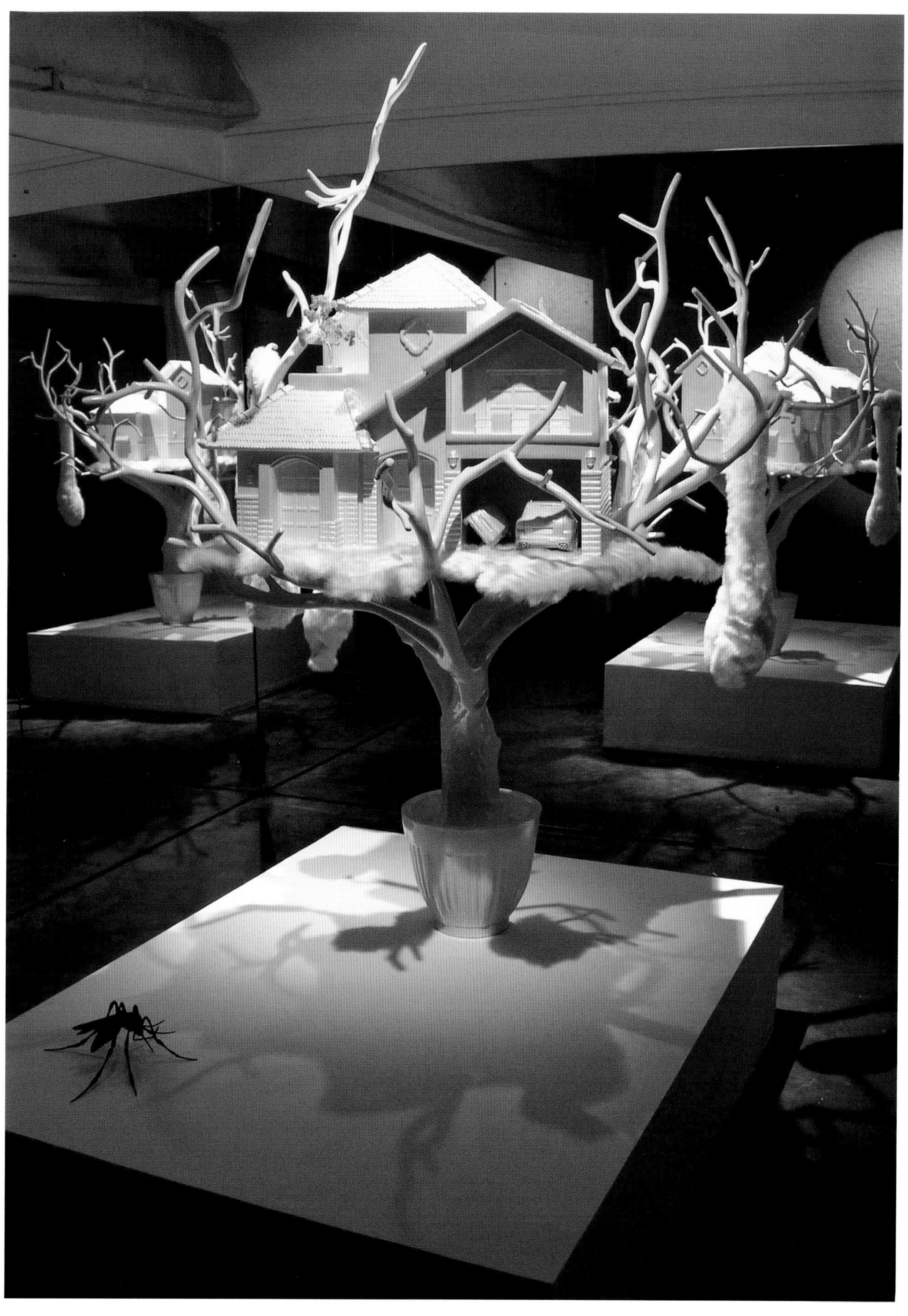

KRISHNARAJ CHONAT
Private Sky, 2007

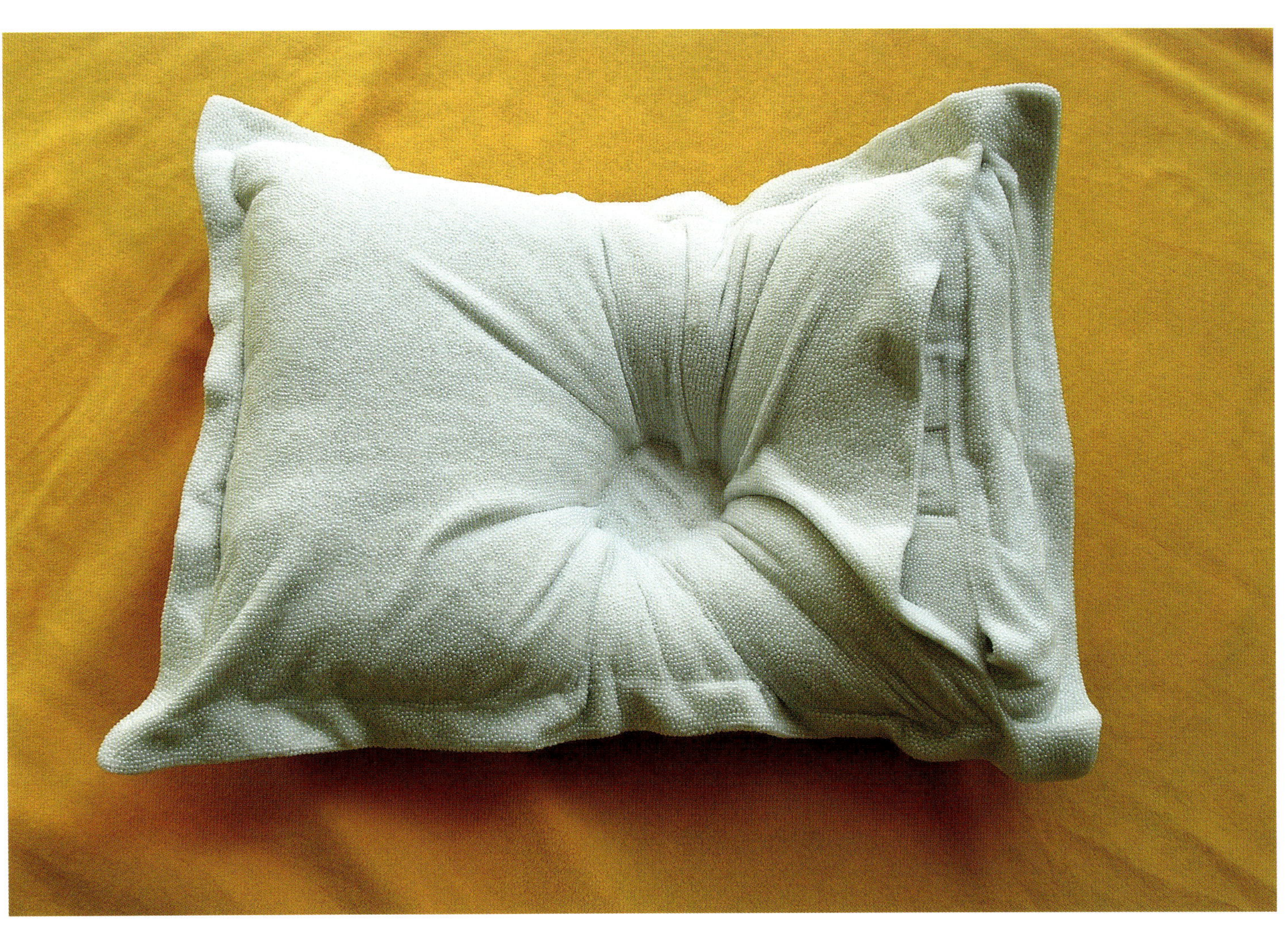

KRISHNARAJ CHONAT
Untitled, 2007

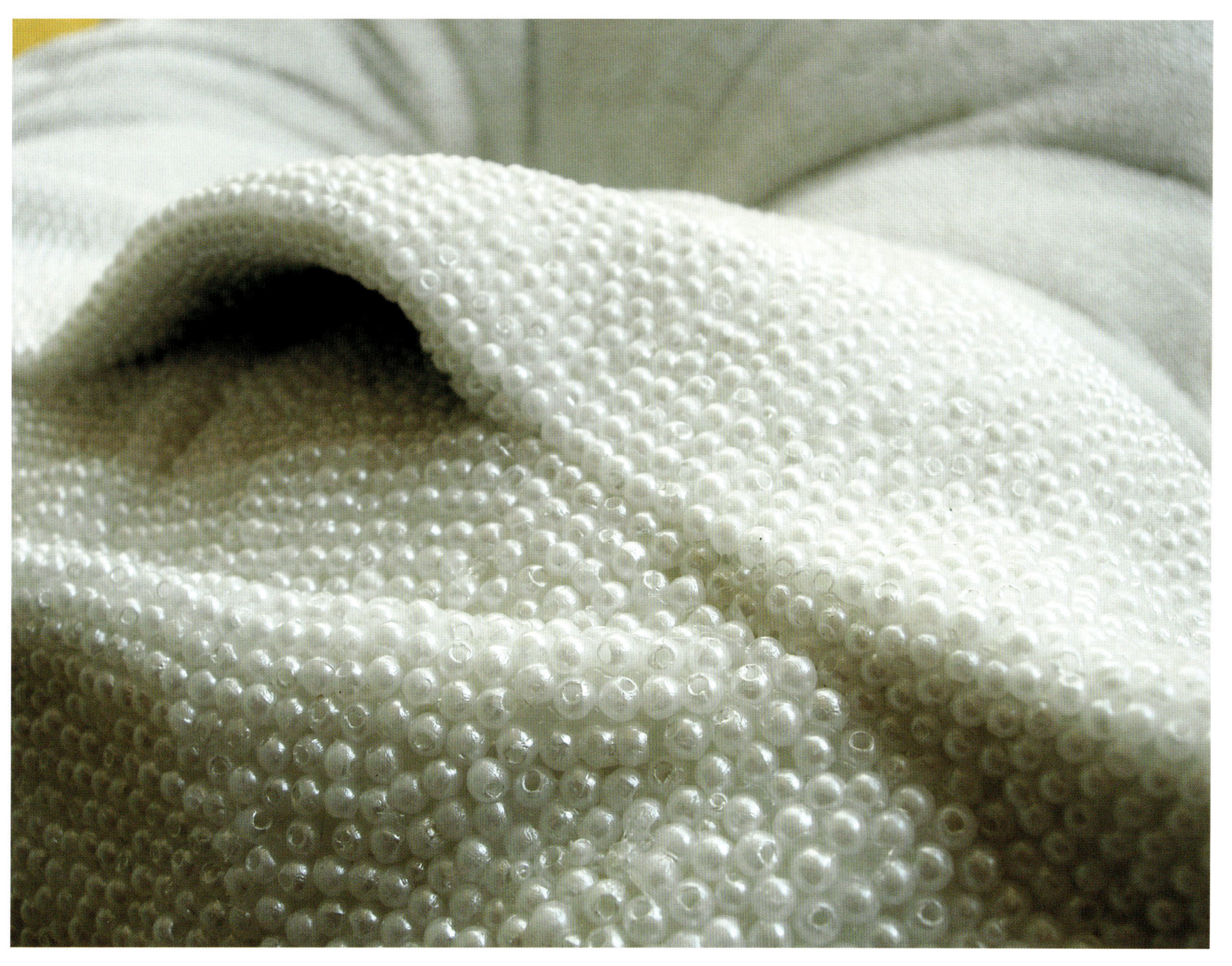

KRISHNARAJ CHONAT
Untitled, 2007 (Detail)

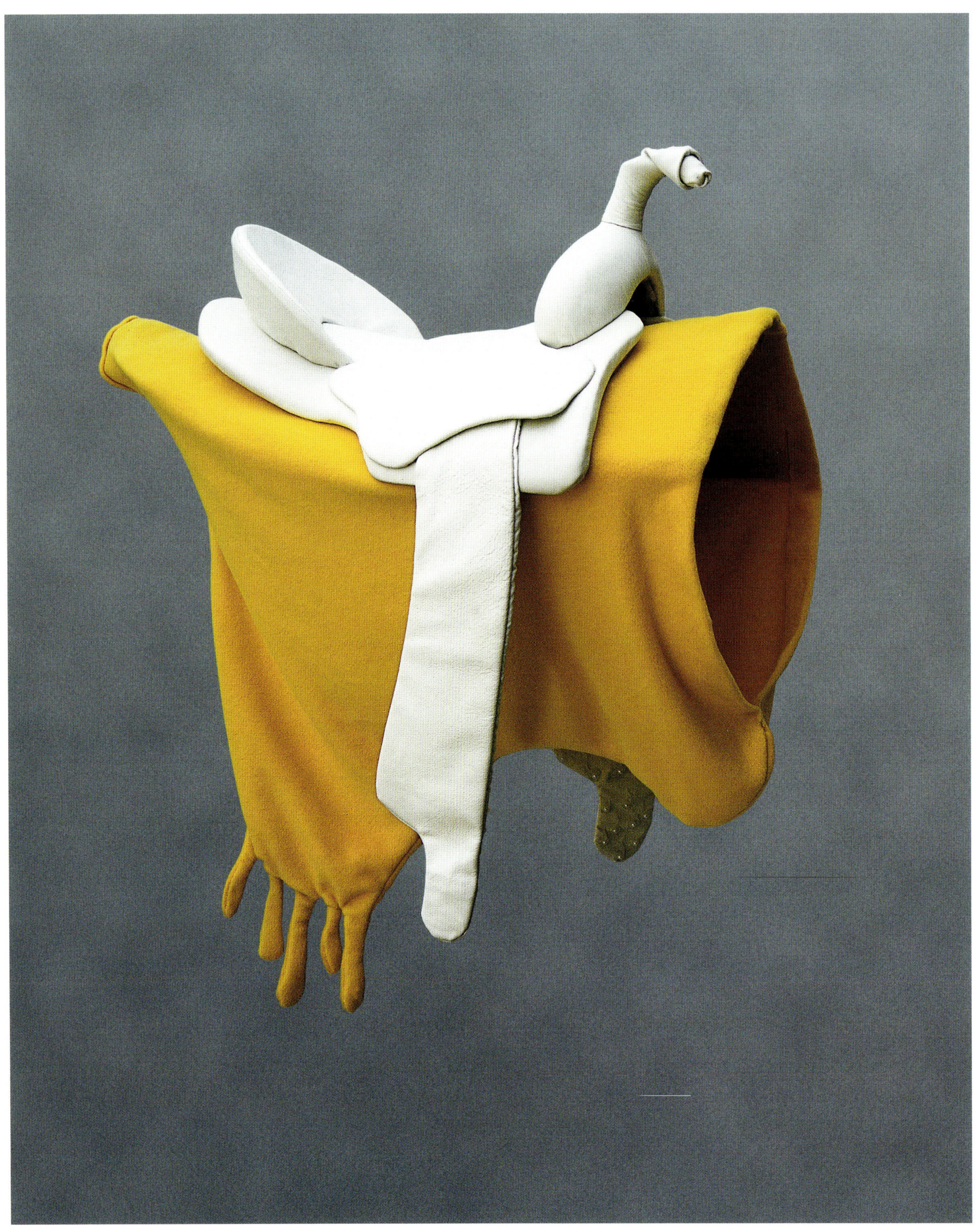

KRISHNARAJ CHONAT
Milk and Skin, 2002

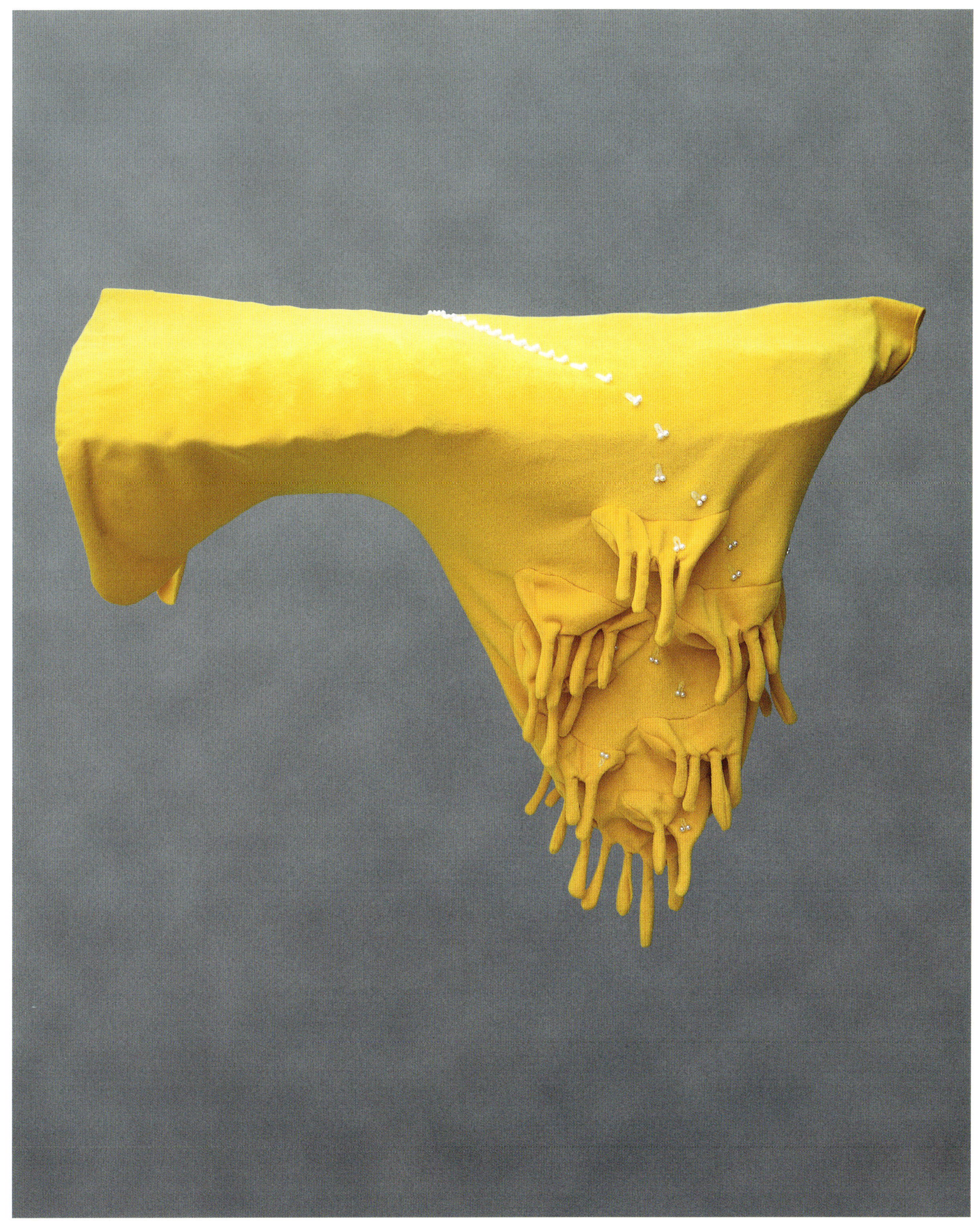

KRISHNARAJ CHONAT
Milk and Skin, 2002

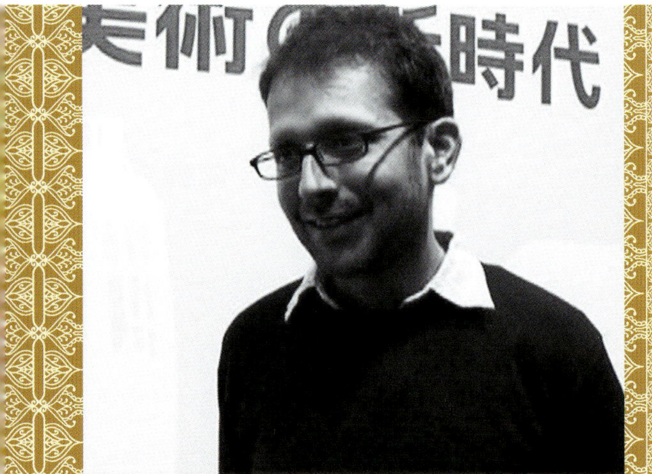

nikhil chopra

NIKHIL CHOPRA Geboren 1974 in Kolkata / Lebt in Mumbai
Born 1974 in Kolkata / Lives in Mumbai

Nikhil Chopra studierte zunächst an der Maharaja Sayajirao University in Vadodara und absolvierte anschließend ein Kunststudium am Maryland Institute College of Art (MICA) bzw. an der Ohio State University. Schon als Student zeigte er aktives Interesse am Theater, und so entwickelten sich seine Arbeiten mehr und mehr zu Live-Performances mit szenischen Elementen. Chopra präsentiert seine Performances häufig als Serien, in denen er die Rolle einer Kunstfigur einnimmt, die man als sein Alter Ego bezeichnen könnte. Seine erste „Rolle" war Sir Raja, den er im Jahr 2002 kreierte. Diese Serie, die in London, den USA, in Indien und Pakistan gezeigt wurde, zeigt klischeehafte Darstellungen Rajas in der Kolonialzeit und enthält szenische Elemente wie z.B. Porträts und Porträtaufnahmen. Sie steht bei Chopra für die Entwicklung einer Kunstform, die zwischen Malerei, Photographie und Theater angesiedelt ist.

„Yog Raj Chitrakar and Tokyo", eine Neuheit bei dieser Ausstellung, stammt aus Chopras zweiter Performance-Serie, in deren Mittelpunkt wieder eine Kunstfigur steht, die während einer Performance in einem historischen Gebäude aus der Kolonialzeit im Bereich des Forts von Mumbai, entstand. Typisch für Chopras Schaffen ist eine enge Beziehung zum Aufführungsort der Performances. In Mumbai ersann der Künstler eine verschlungene Geschichte, in die er das Gebäude – das oberste Stockwerk, von wo der Blick über das „Gate of India" reicht – sowie das historische Kolorit der Region, seine Erinnerungen an seinen Großvater und an Familienmitglieder in Kaschmir mit einbezog. Der Künstler hielt sich drei Tage lang ununterbrochen in diesem Gebäude auf. Er durchlebte in dieser Zeit verschiedene Transformationen und schuf Zeichnungen an den Wänden. Inspiriert von einem gänzlich andersartigen Schauplatz bekommt die Performance in Tokyo zweifellos einen völlig anderen Wahrnehmungscharakter.

Die Grenze zwischen Darsteller und Publikum ist in Chopras Arbeiten äußerst fließend; Performances finden im Inneren des Ausstellungsortes oder auf der Straße statt und beziehen so erfolgreich fremde Elemente in einen vertrauten Schauplatz mit ein. Gleichzeitig vermitteln Chopras

After studying at Maharaja Sayajirao University in Vadodara, Nikhil Chopra went on to study fine arts at Maryland Institute College of Art (MICA) and Ohio State University. He became involved in theatre while a student, and his work gradually developed into live performances incorporating theatrical elements. Chopra's performances are often carried out in a series format in which he takes on an imaginary persona that could be called an alter ego. His first persona was Sir Raja, which he created in 2002. This series, which has been shown in London, the US, India, and Pakistan, refers to stereotypical images of rajas during the colonialist era and incorporates theatrical elements such as old portraits and portrait photographs. It marked the development, by Chopra, of a unique avenue of expression that is positioned somewhere between painting, photography and theatre.

Yog Raj Chitrakar and Tokyo, new for this exhibition, is part of Chopra's second series of performances based on an imaginary persona. The Yog Raj Chitrakar persona developed through a performance held in a historical building in the Fort area of Mumbai that still retains a strong colonialist flavour. The artist stayed in the building for three whole days, during which he underwent various transformations as well as executing drawings on the walls. Chopra's work is characterized by a close relationship with the location where the performances are carried out. In Mumbai, the artist wove a complex story by incorporating the building, the top floor from which one can look out over India Gate, as well as the historical flavour of this region, the artist's memories of his grandfather and other family members in Kashmir, and the memories of his childhood. The performance in Tokyo is sure to reveal other and different elements inspired by the completely different location. The boundary between performer and the audience is extremely ambiguous in Chopra's work; performances are held inside the exhibition venue or on the street, effectively introducing something alien into a familiar setting. At the same time, Chopra's work has the effect of triggering a strange sensibility on the part of the observer, so that it feels as though s/he was crossing the boundaries between performer and audience, the private and the public, between different times in history, between different locations and genders.

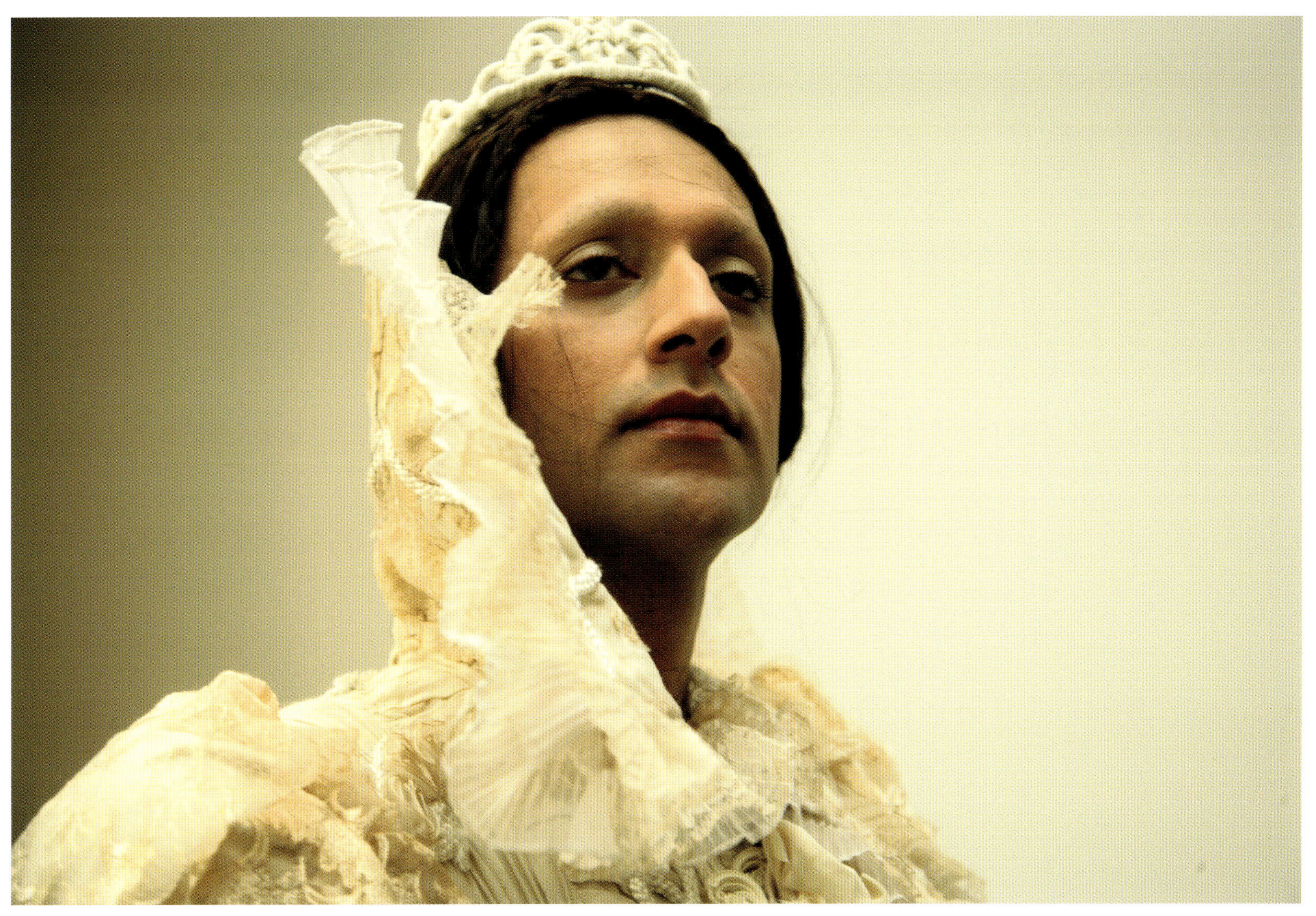

NIKHIL CHOPRA
Yog Raj Chitrakar and Tokyo, 2008
Live performance at Mori Art Museum, Tokyo

Arbeiten den Zusehern das Gefühl, die Grenzen zwischen Darsteller und Publikum, zwischen privat und öffentlich, zwischen unterschiedlichen Geschichtsperioden, Schauplätzen und Geschlechtern zu überschreiten.
Wichtige Ausstellungen: „Asia Contemporary Art Week" (Brooklyn Museum of Art, New York, 2006), „Yog Raj Chitrakar: Memory Drawing II – a Live Performance" (Chatterjee & Lal, Mumbai, 2007), und „The 3rd Yokohama Triennale" (2008). (AM)

Major exhibitions include "Asia Contemporary Art Week" (Brooklyn Museum of Art, New York, 2006), "Yog Raj Chitrakar: Memory Drawing II – a Live Performance" (Chatterjee & Lal, Mumbai, 2007), and "The 3rd Yokohama Triennale" (2008). (AM)

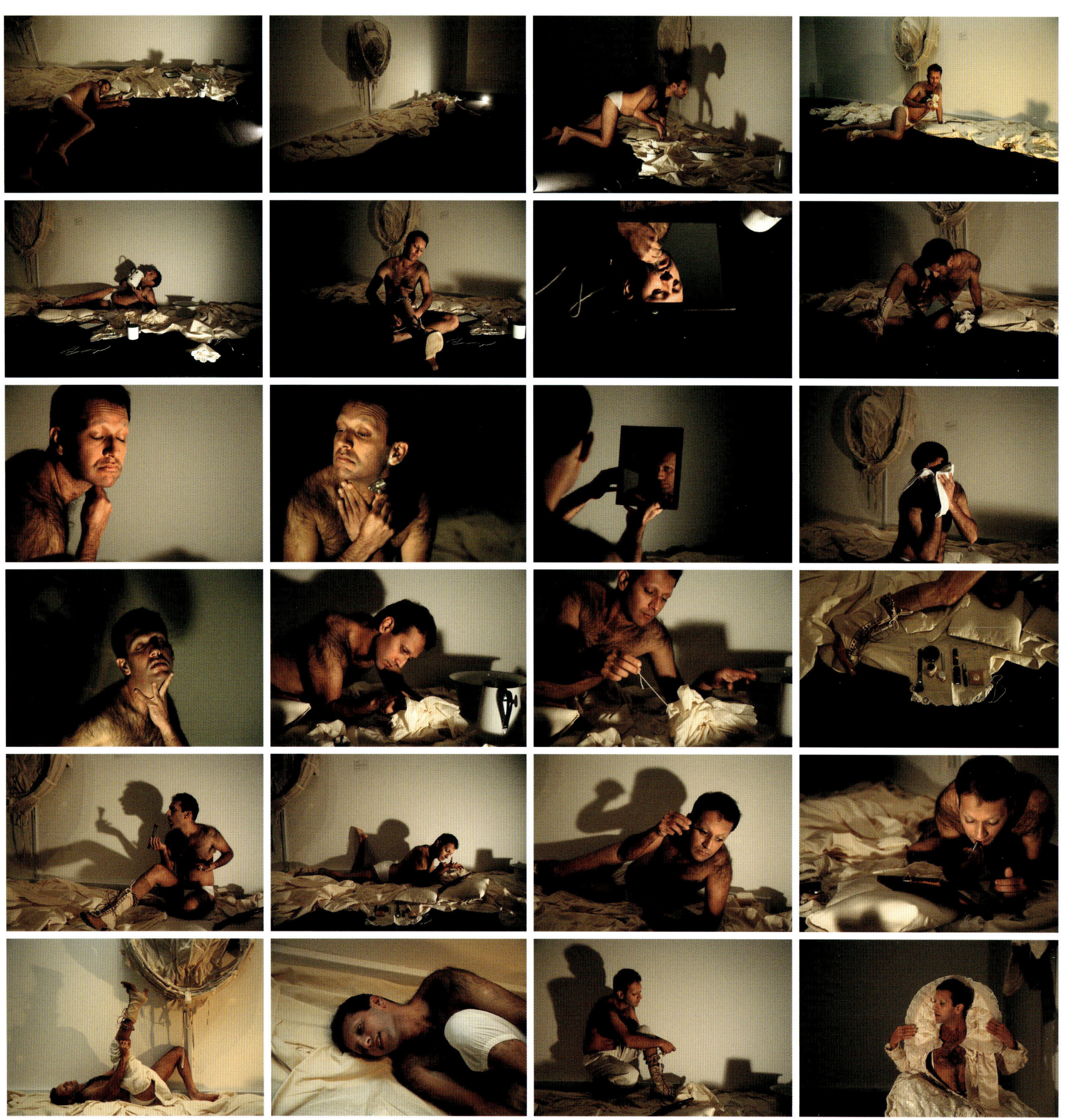

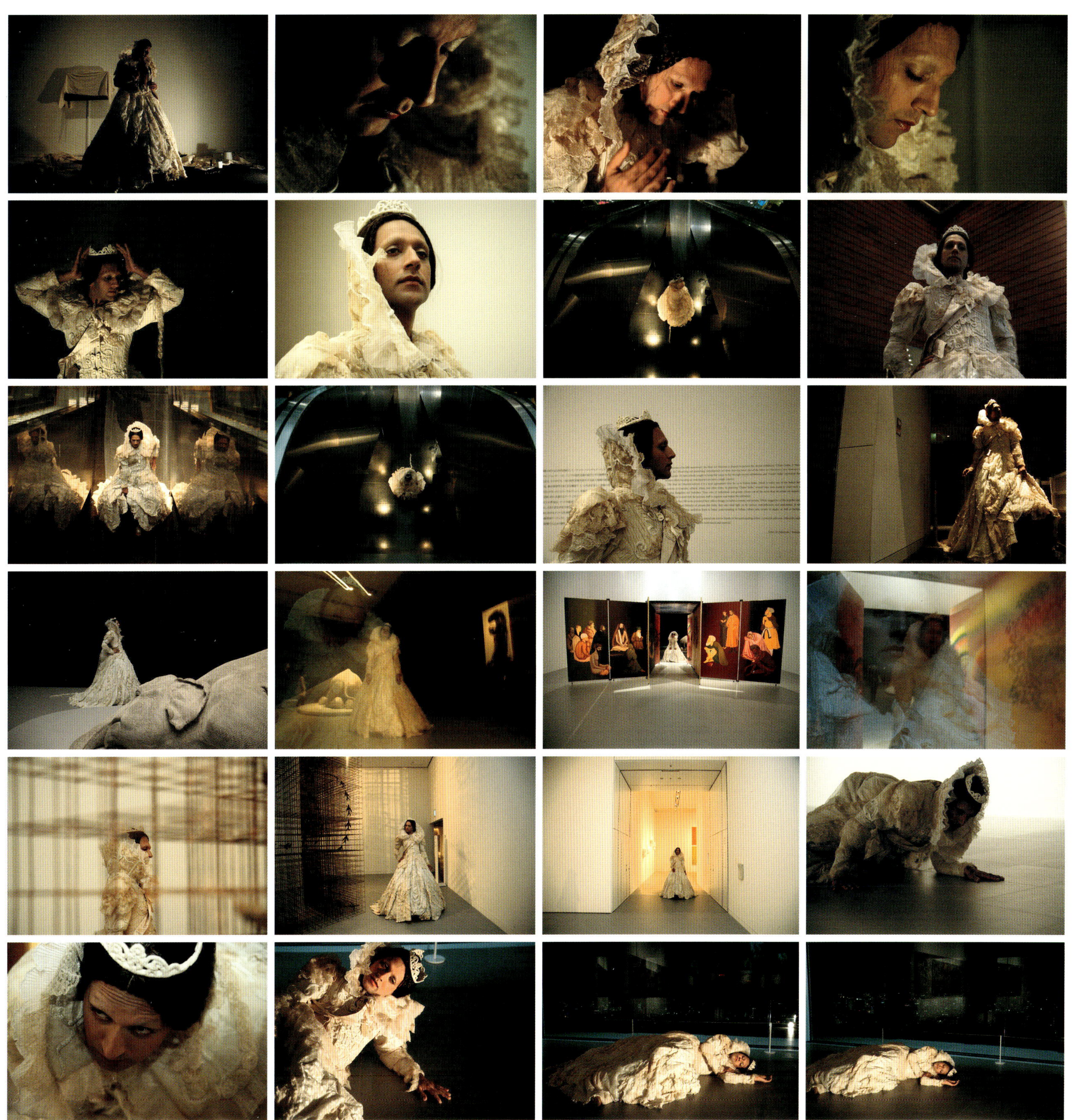

NIKHIL CHOPRA
Yog Raj Chitrakar and Tokyo, 2008
Live performance at Mori Art Museum, Tokyo

What will I do with all this land?, 2005 (S./p. 66)

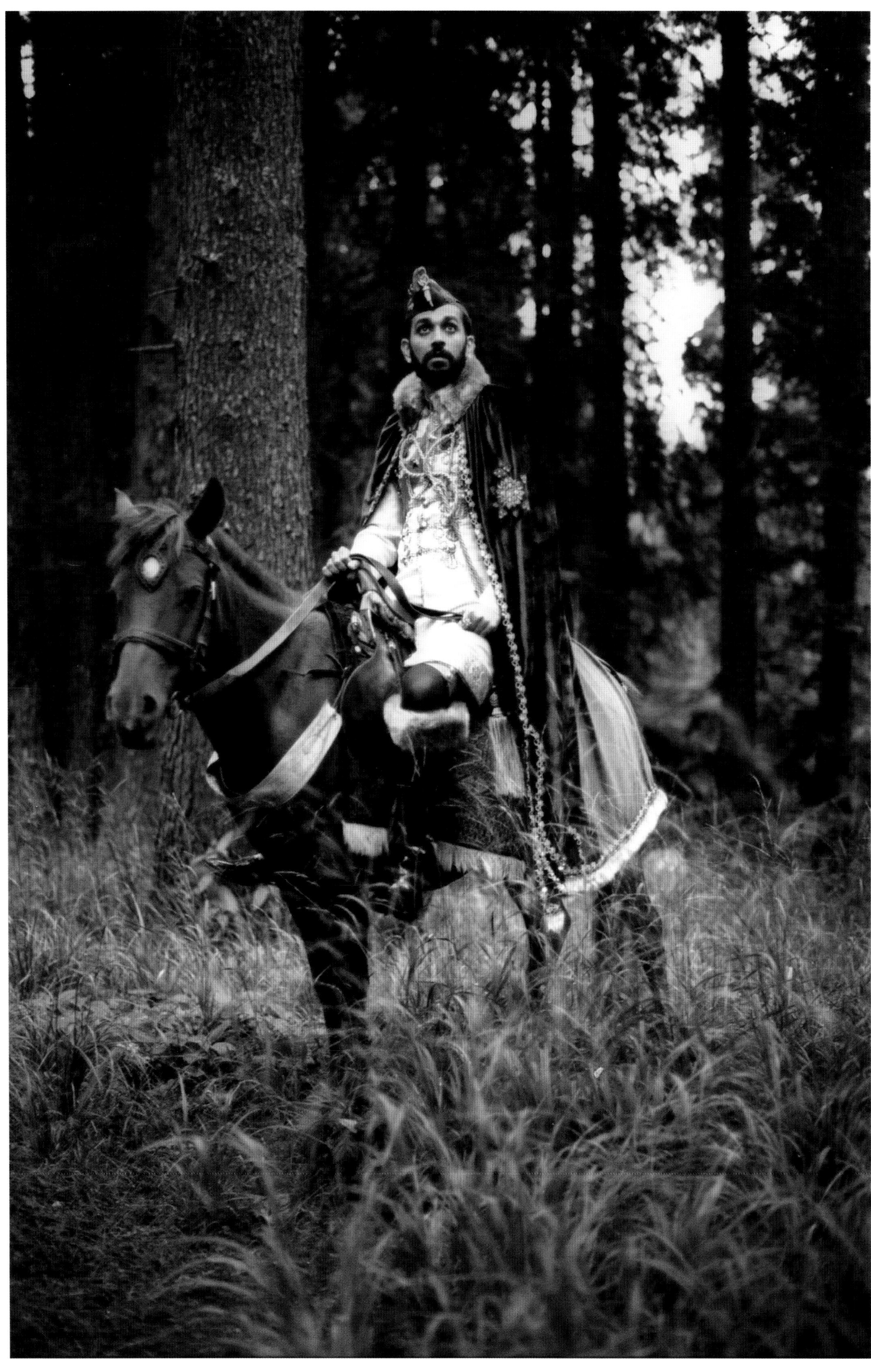

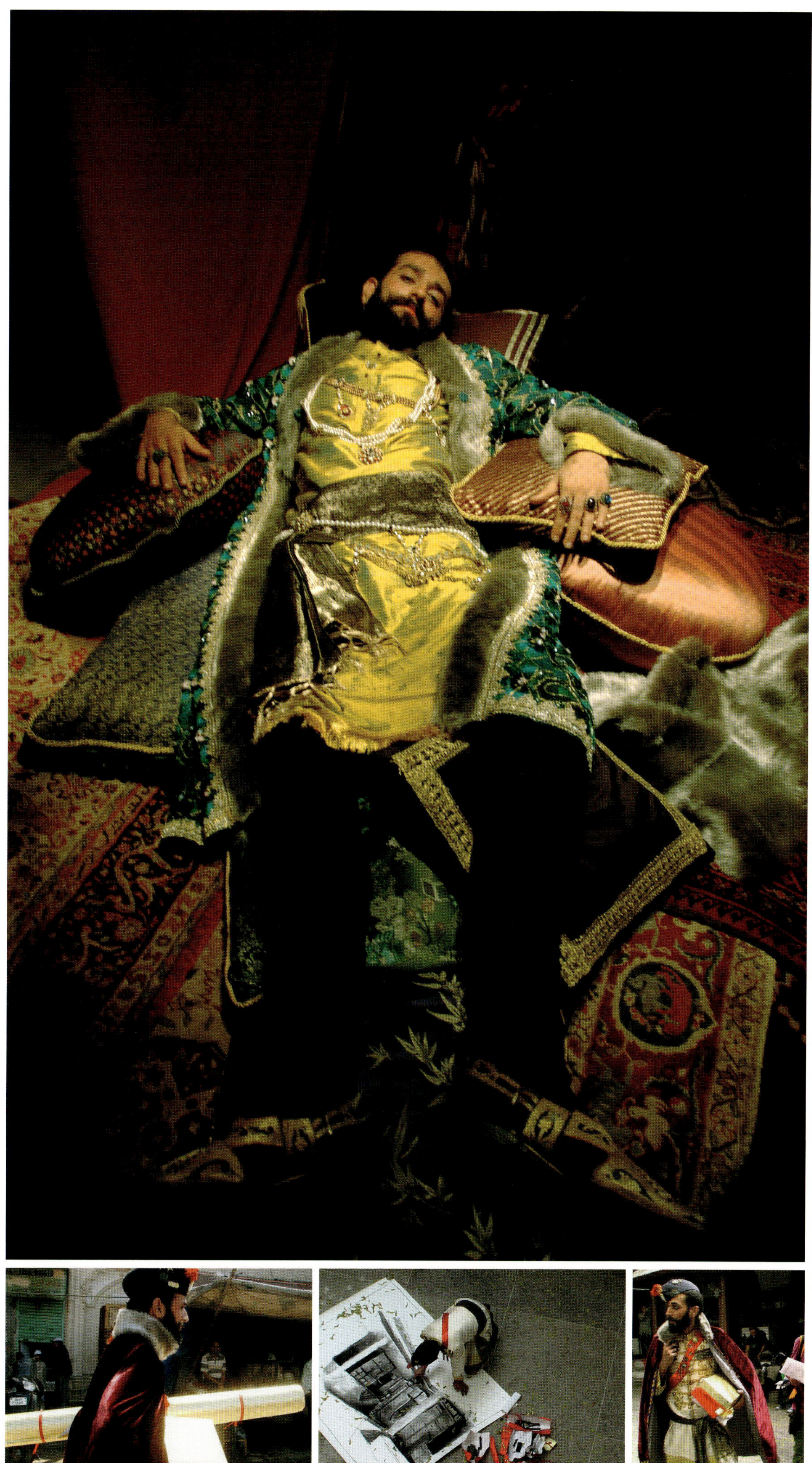

NIKHIL CHOPRA
The Death of Sir Raja III, 2005
Live performance at Kitab Mahal, Mumbai (S./p. 67 oben/top)

Sir Raja III Visits Khowaja Press, 2007
Live performance at Khoj International Artists Association, New Delhi (S./p. 67 unten/bottom)

Yog Raj Chitrakar: Memory Drawing II, 2008
Live performance at Chatterjee & Lal Gallery, Mumbai

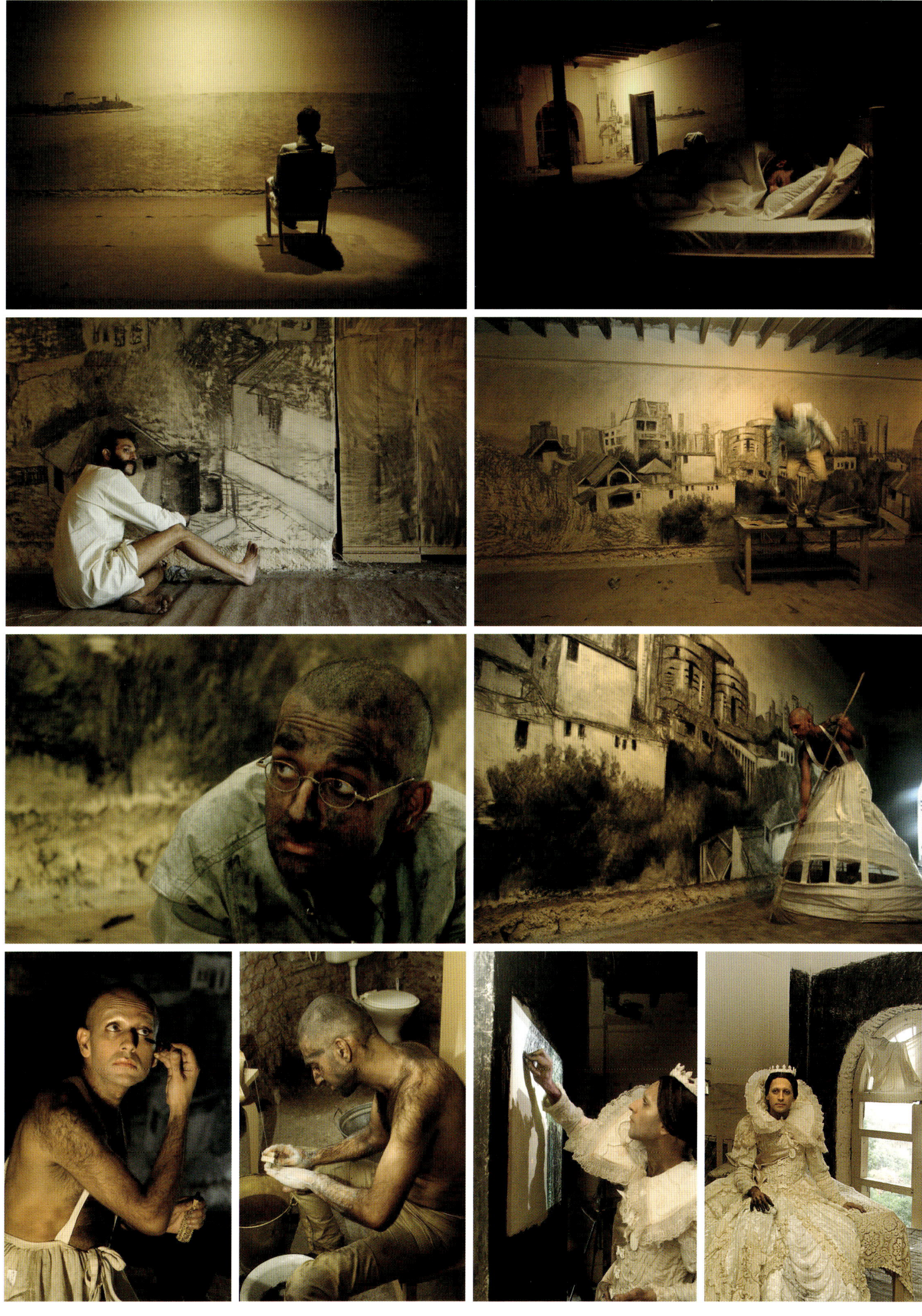

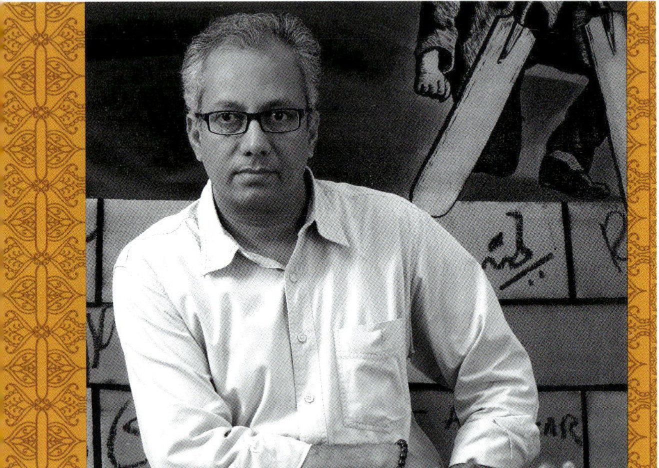

atul dodiya

ATUL DODIYA Geboren 1959 in Mumbai / Lebt in Mumbai
Born 1959 in Mumbai / Lives in Mumbai

Dodiya studierte Malerei an der Sir J.J. School of Fine Arts, Mumbai, wo er 1982 seinen Abschluss machte und eine Malerkarriere begann. Er vereint in seiner Kunst unterschiedliche Elemente des indischen Lebens wie Familie, Tradition, Mythologie, Politik und Kultur und bringt so das Alltagsleben Indiens zum Ausdruck. Seit den 1990er Jahren widmet sich Dodiya auch verstärkt der Fotografie, Collage und Druckgraphik.

Basis der repräsentativen Serie von „Shutter Paintings" sind Rolljalousien, wie sie im Zentrum Mumbais verwendet werden. Dodiyas Malereien auf den Jalousien lassen sich aufrollen und geben darunter liegende neue Bilder frei. Als die Spannungen zwischen Hindus und Muslimen ihren Höhepunkt erreichten, blieben in Mumbai die Jalousien zum Schutz der Bewohner geschlossen; gleichzeitig verhinderten sie das Eindringen von Informationen von außen. Dodiya nutzt diese Doppelfunktion der Jalousien in seinen Arbeiten, um die Vergangenheit und die Gegenwart Indiens symbolisch miteinander zu verbinden.

„Saptapadi: Scenes from Marriage (Regard-less)" ist Teil der aktuellen Ausstellung und besteht aus einer Serie von 24 Gemälden, die Dodiya im Jahr 2003 begann und an der er mehrere Jahre arbeitete. Das im Titel verwendete Wort „Saptapadi" bezeichnet eine traditionelle Hindu-Hochzeitszeremonie und in der Kannada-Sprache ein Liebesgedicht. Ein Mann und eine Frau sind ebenfalls Gegenstand dieser Serie. Scheinbar zusammenhanglose Motive stehen auf der Leinwand nebeneinander – persönliche Motive, wie ein Portrait von Dodiyas Frau, aber auch Bilder von Werbeplakaten (wie etwa Bollywood Filmposter) und berühmte Kunstwerke aus der Vergangenheit (wie Gemälde von Picasso oder Matisse). Jedes Bild für sich hat eine enorme Wirkung, aber gemeinsam erzeugen sie eine ganz eigene Welt.

Wichtige Ausstellungen: „Century City: Art and Culture in the Modern Metropolis" (Tate Modern, London, 2001), „Atul Dodiya Bombay: Labyrinth / Laboratory" (The Japan Foundation Asia Center, Tokyo, 2001), „iCon: India Contemporary" (The 51st Venice Biennale, 2005), und „The 7th Gwangju Biennale" (2008). (SN)

Dodiya studied painting at the Sir J.J. School of Fine Arts, Mumbai, graduating in 1982 and embarked on a career in painting in the early 1980s. He is known for his technique that incorporates diverse Indian elements such as the family, tradition, mythology, politics and culture, and for his style that reflects everyday life in India. Since the 90s, Dodiya has incorporated photography, collage and printmaking into his body of work.

His representative series of "Shutter Paintings" features roller shutters of the type commonly seen in central Mumbai. Dodiya's paintings on the shutters can be rolled up to reveal a different image inside. The Mumbai shutters remained closed during the peak of tension between Hindus and Muslims, protecting those inside from both intruders and the elements. At the same time, they also effectively shut out information from outside. That dual function of the shutters is used symbolically in Dodiya's work to convey India's past and present.

Saptapadi: Scenes from Marriage (Regard-less), part of this exhibition, is a series of 24 paintings that Dodiya embarked on in 2003 and which took several years to complete. The "Saptapadi" in the title refers to a traditional Hindu wedding ceremony or a love poem in the Kannada language. A man and woman are also the subject of this series. Seemingly unrelated motifs coexist on the canvas – personal motifs such as a portrait of Dodiya's wife, images from ads (such as Bollywood movie posters), and images from famous art works from the past (such as paintings by Picasso or Matisse). Each individual motif has an enormous impact on its own, but when combined, they are strangely harmonious and succeed in creating a unique world.

Major exhibitions include "Century City: Art and Culture in the Modern Metropolis" (Tate Modern, London, 2001), "Atul Dodiya Bombay: Labyrinth / Laboratory" (The Japan Foundation Asia Centre, Tokyo, 2001), "iCon: India Contemporary" (The 51st Venice Biennale, 2005), and "The 7th Gwangju Biennale" (2008). (SN)

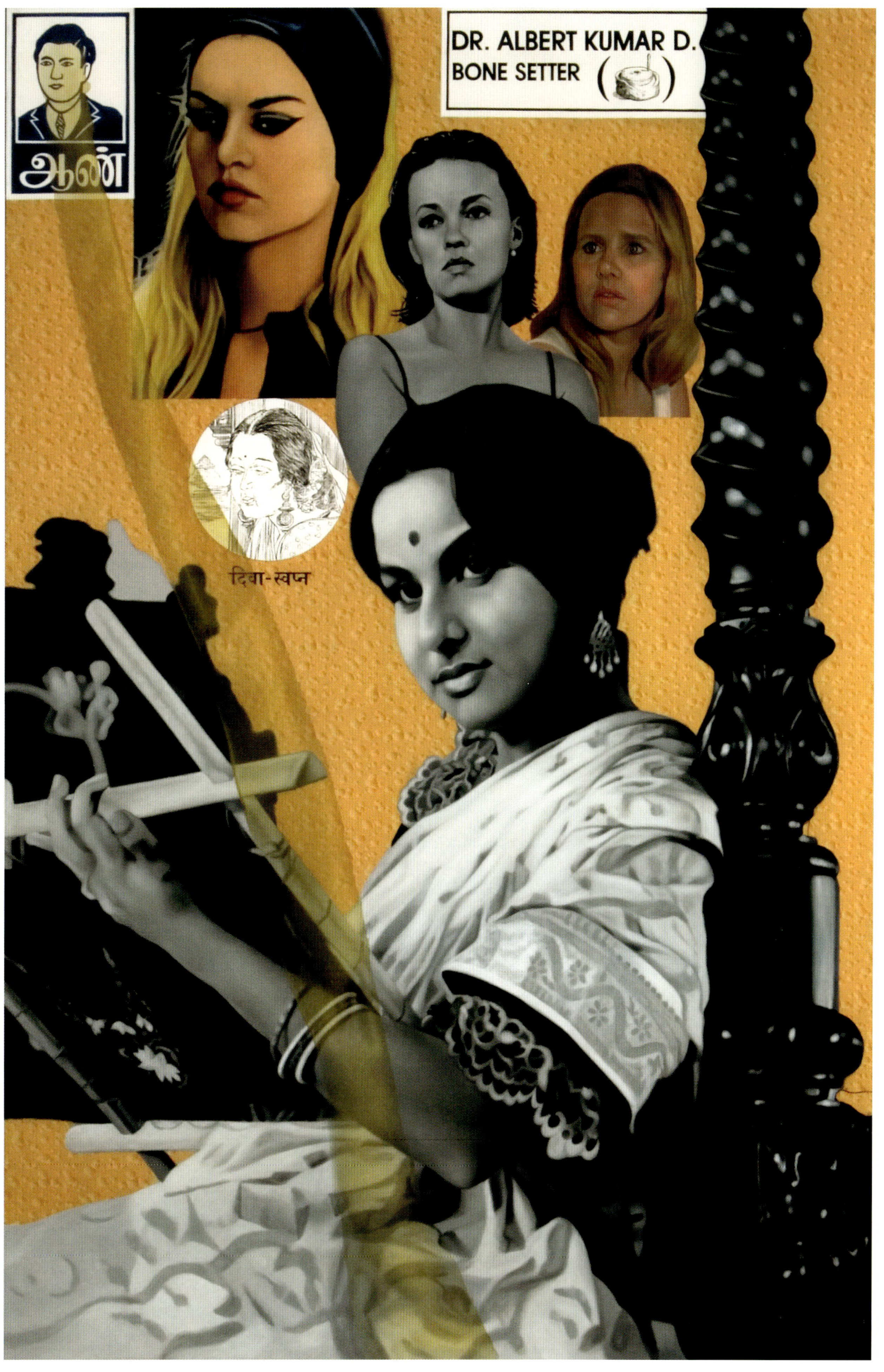

ATUL DODIYA
Charu from Saptapadi: Scenes from Marriage (Regardless), 2004–06

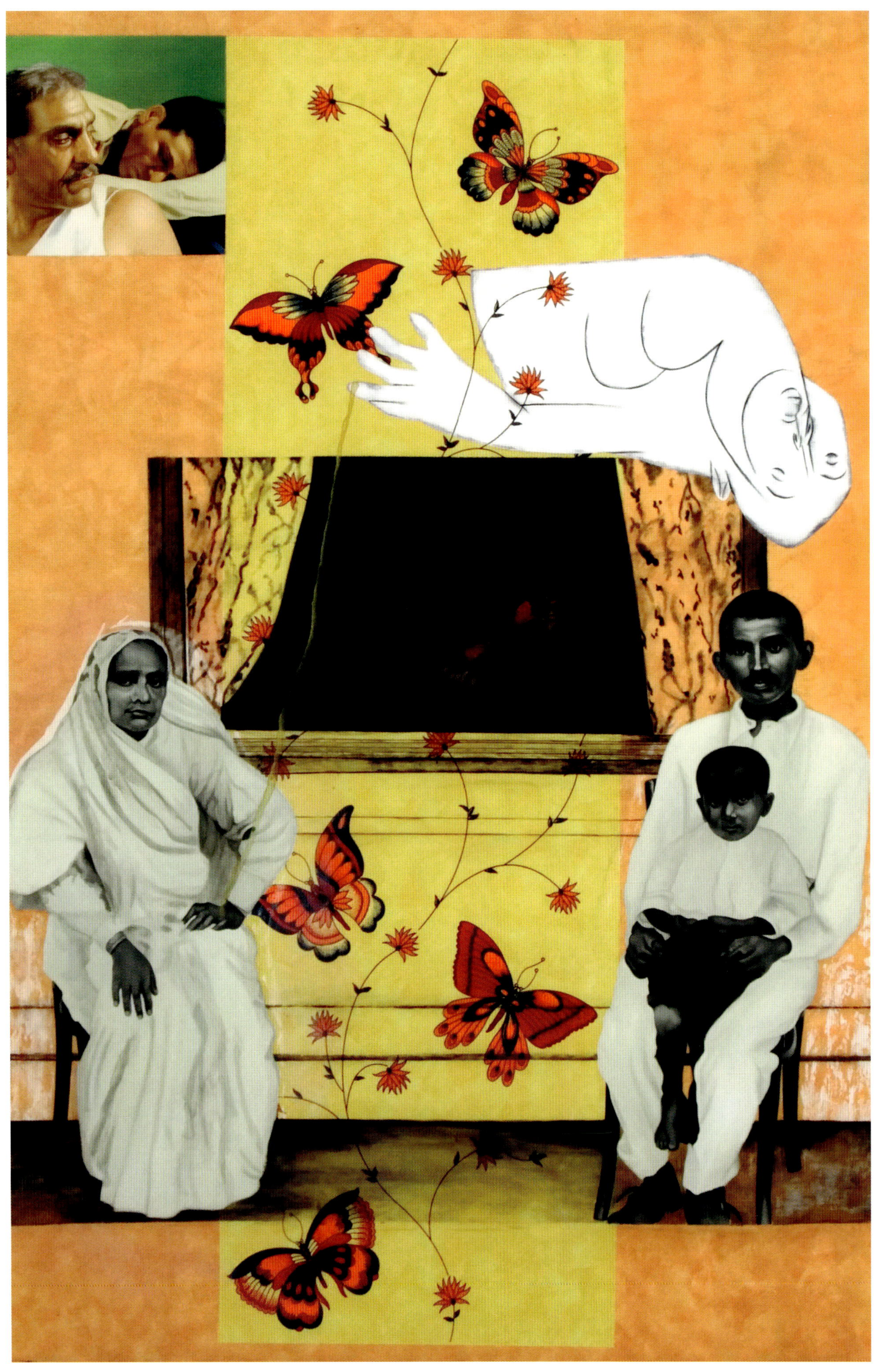

ATUL DODIYA
Bloodline from Saptapadi: Scenes from Marriage (Regardless), 2004–06

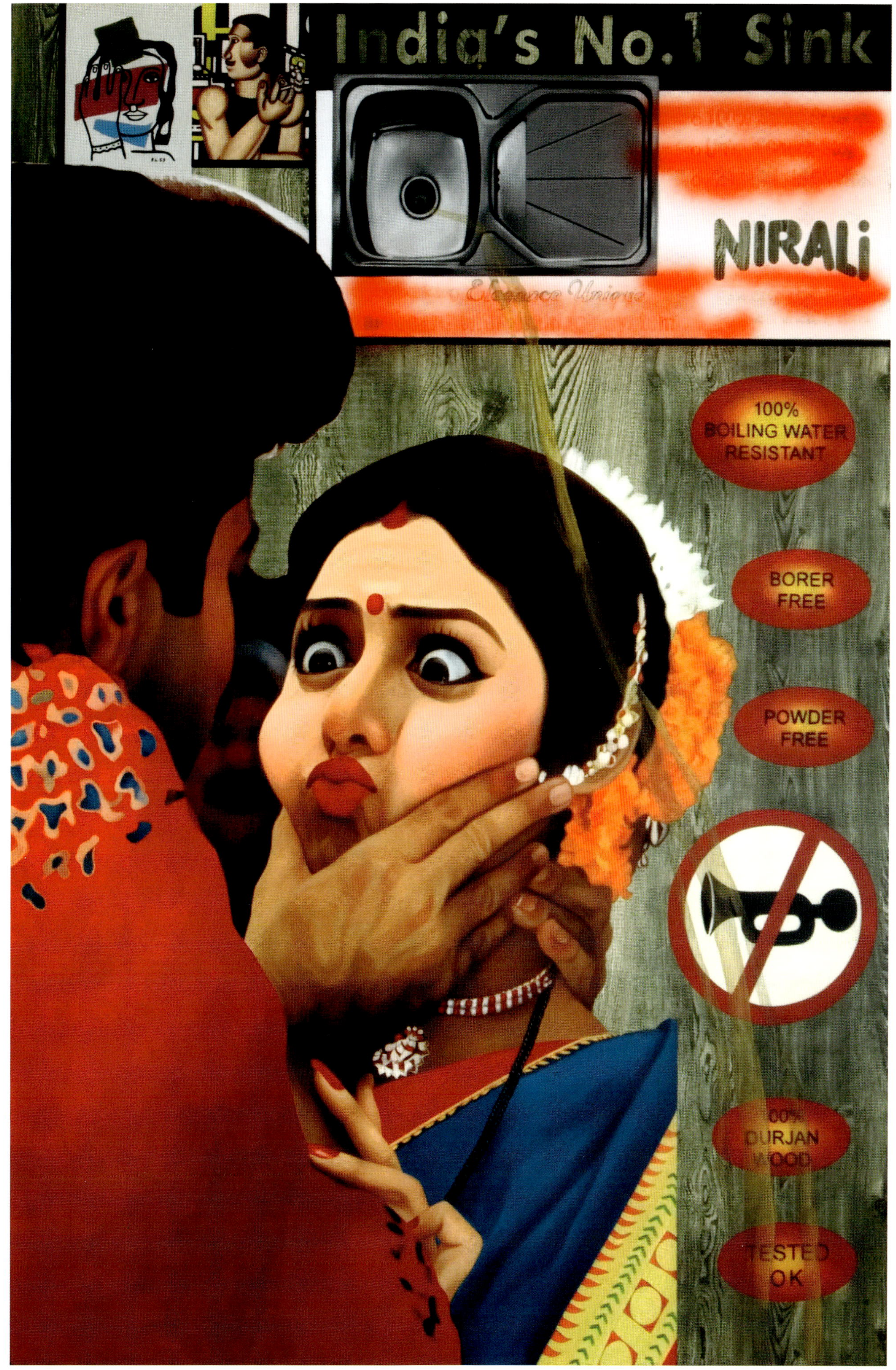

ATUL DODIYA
Devi and Sink from Saptapadi: Scenes from Marriage (Regardless), 2004–06

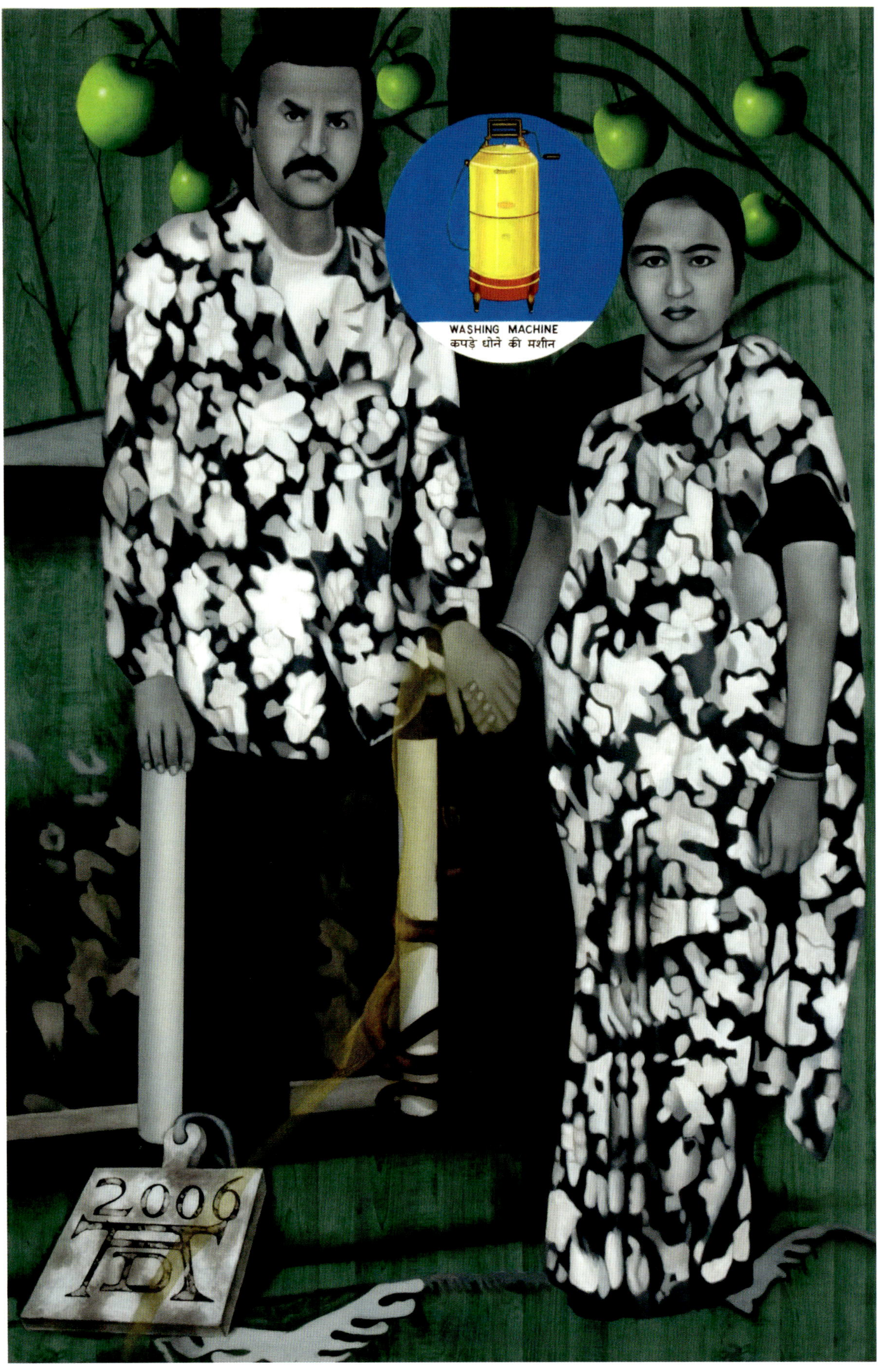

ATUL DODIYA
Adam and Eve from Saptapadi: Scenes from Marriage (Regardless), 2004–06
Pringle Mala from Saptapadi: Scenes from Marriage (Regardless), 2003–06

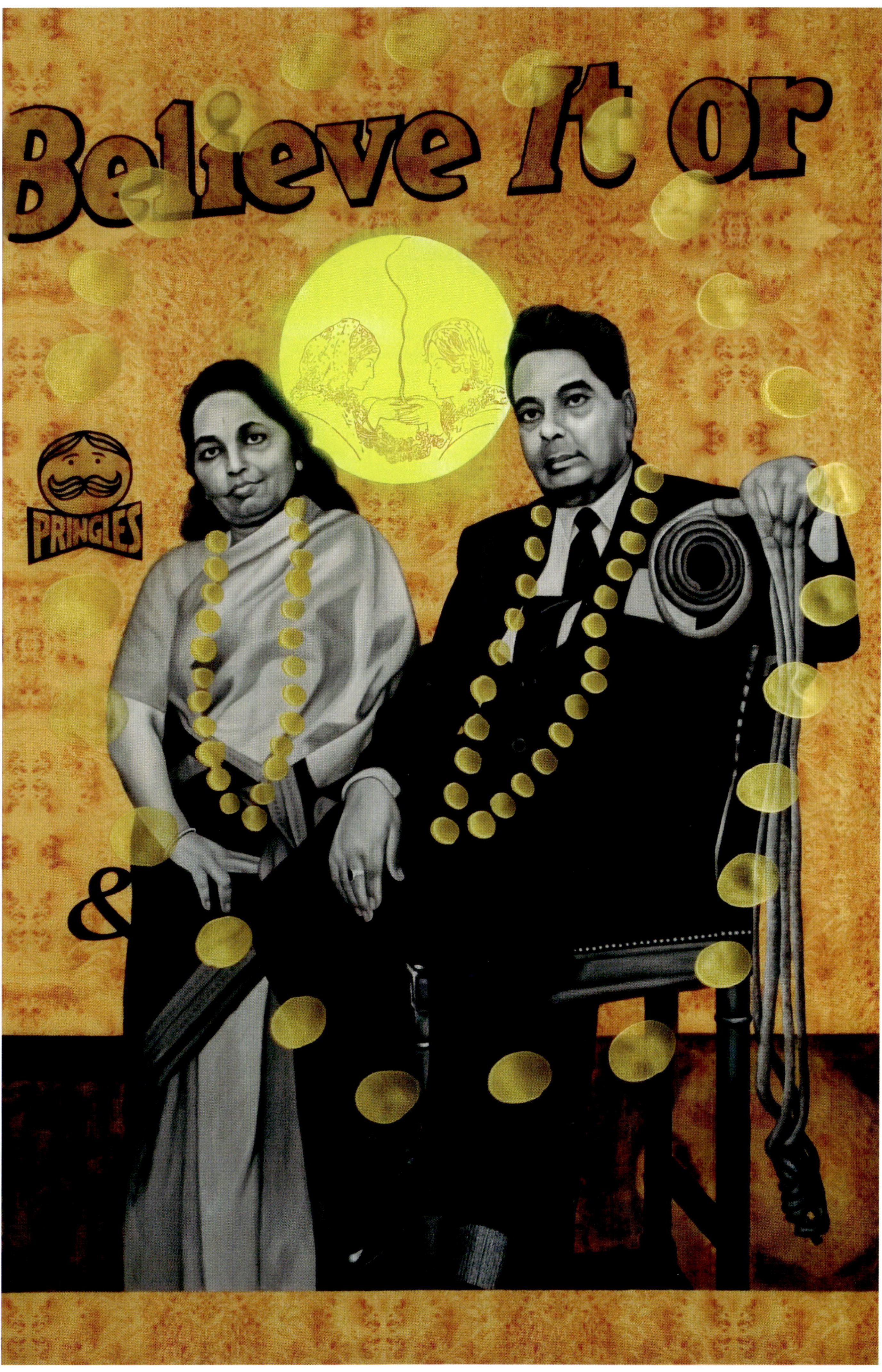
Believe It or
PRINGLES
&

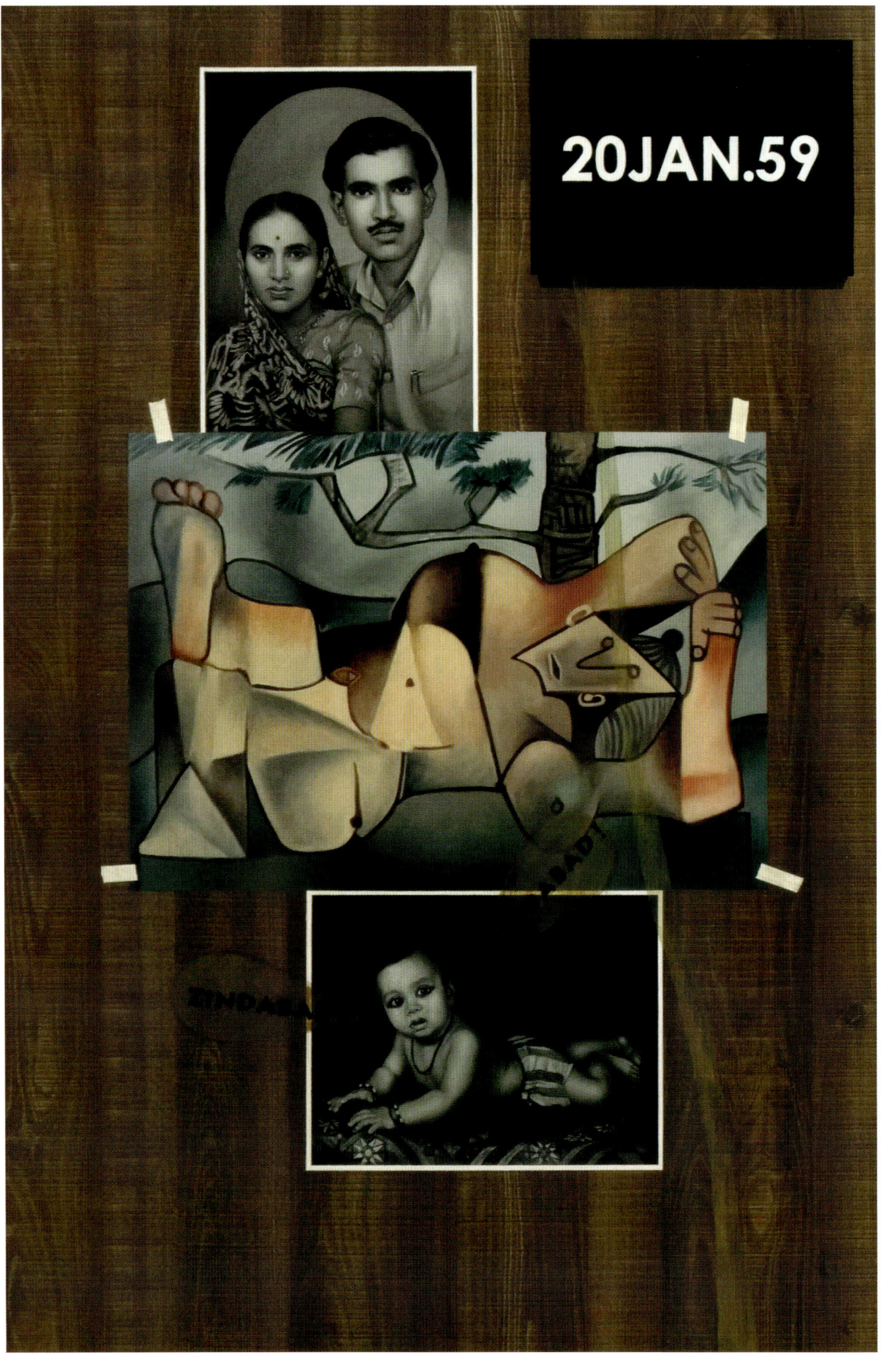

ATUL DODIYA
Family Tree from Saptapadi: Scenes from Marriage (Regardless), 2006
Shri Jivan Chaya of Gandhi Nagar from Saptapadi: Scenes from Marriage (Regardless), 2003–06

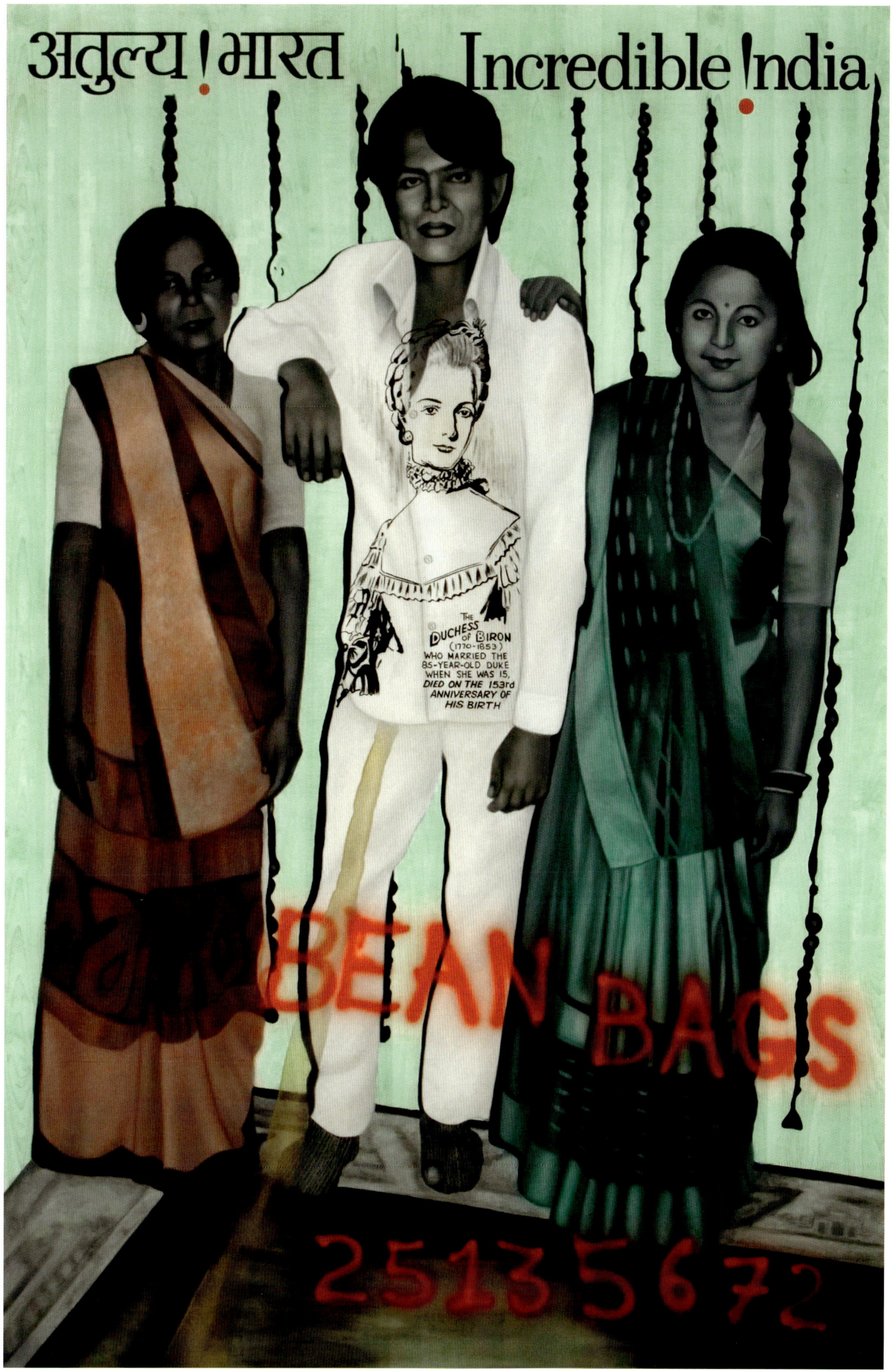
अतुल्य ! भारत
Incredible !ndia
THE
DUCHESS
OF BIRON
(1770-1853)
WHO MARRIED THE
85-YEAR-OLD DUKE
WHEN SHE WAS 15,
DIED ON THE 153rd
ANNIVERSARY OF
HIS BIRTH
BEAN BAGS
25135672

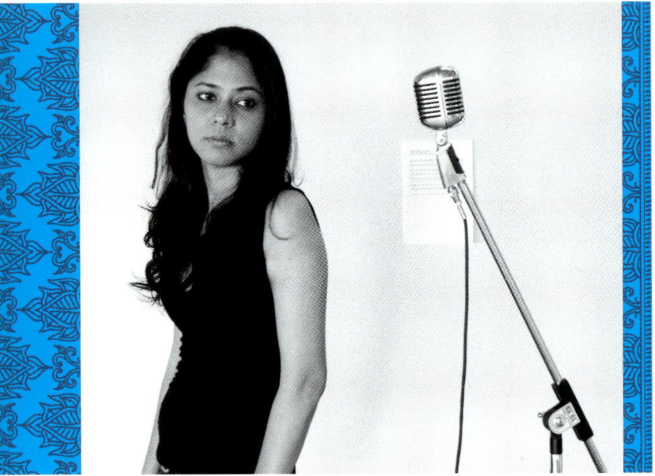

shilpa gupta

SHILPA GUPTA Geboren 1976 in Mumbai / Lebt in Mumbai
Born 1976 in Mumbai / Lives in Mumbai

Shilpa Gupta schloss 1997 ihr Studium der Bildhauerei an der Sir J.J. School of Fine Arts, Mumbai, mit dem „Master of Fine Arts" ab. Mit dem Ziel, „Kunst für die Massen" zu schaffen, entschied sich Gupta für die neuen Medien als künstlerisches Ausdrucksmittel. Gupta ist sich der vielen sozialen Probleme, die unsere zunehmend globalisierte Welt mit sich bringt, voll bewusst. Ihr vordringliches Interesse gilt der Funktion und der Rolle der Kunst in der Gesellschaft und der Beziehung zwischen der Kunst und ihrem Betrachter (Gesellschaft); sie analysiert aber auch Konzepte und Vorstellungen der Konsumgesellschaft – als Schlagworte seien genannt: Erinnerung, Begierde, Glaube, Kreativität und Fantasie, Missachtung von Menschenrechten, Sicherheit und die Universalität der Menschheit. Das Konzept der Interaktivität, demzufolge ein Werk erst durch die aktive Einbindung des Betrachters vollständig ist, ist integraler Bestandteil vieler ihrer jüngsten Arbeiten, darunter „Blessed-bandwidth. net", ein Auftragswerk der Tate Modern (Internet application, 2003). Guptas aktivistische Perspektive einer strategisch sozialen Intervention reflektiert durchaus die Aktivitäten und die Arbeit von Künstlern weltweit seit den 1990er Jahren.

„Untitled (Shadow)" (2006–07) ist eine Serie interaktiver Video-Installationen, bei denen Gupta eine Technik einsetzt, mit deren Hilfe sie Schatten in Echtzeit simuliert. Ausstellungsbesucher werden unweigerlich in Guptas Installationen einbezogen, ganz so wie Menschen in einen religiösen Konflikt hineingezogen werden, der in ihrem Umfeld stattfindet. In „100 Hand Drawn Maps of India" (2007–08), „Memory" (2007–08) und „Tryst with Destiny" (Ansprache von Jawaharlal Nehru anlässlich der Unabhängigkeit Indiens, 2007–08) kommen jeweils andere Techniken zum Einsatz, immer aber geht es um das individuelle oder kollektive Gedächtnis.

Obwohl Gupta keines der einflussreichen Systeme in Anspruch nimmt, die den indischen Kunstmarkt heute unterstützen, schafft sie einzigartige konzeptionelle Arbeiten und zählt zu den bekanntesten Vertretern einer neuen Generation indischer Künstler. Gupta ist Preisträgerin des Berliner Transmediale 2004 Award und nimmt nicht nur

Shilpa Gupta, who obtained a Master of Fine Arts in sculpture at Sir J.J. School of Fine Arts, Mumbai, in 1997, is committed to creating "art meant for the masses," focusing on the great affinity between the media and the general public. Because Gupta's art is aimed at as broad a cross-section of the population as possible, she decided to adopt new media, which so clearly reflects contemporary society, as the most appropriate way of visually conveying her concerns and interests. Gupta remains highly conscious of the many social problems being generated in our increasingly globalizing and diversifying world. She is primarily interested in the function and role of art in society and the relationship between art and observer (society), but also analyzes concepts and notions of consumer society, memory, desire, belief, possibilities of creativity and imagination, human rights abuse, human security and finally, the universality of the human race. Many of her recent works including *Blessed-bandwidth.net* commissioned by Tate Modern (Internet application, 2003), incorporate the concept of interactivity, in which a work only comes into its own with the observer's participation and involvement. Gupta's activist perspective of strategic social intervention arguably reflects the activities and work of artists the world over since the 1990s.

Untitled (Shadow) (2006–07) is a series of interactive video installations in which Gupta utilizes technology that enables her to incorporate simulated shadows into live footage in real time. Exhibition visitors are drawn into participating in the installations, much like people are compelled into involvement in religious conflict taking place around them. *100 Hand Drawn Maps of India* (2007–08), *Memory* (2007–08), and *Tryst with Destiny* (Speech by Jawaharlal Nehru upon the granting of Indian independence, 2007–08) each use different techniques, but they all share the common theme of individual or collective memories.

Despite the fact that Gupta does not rely on the powerful systems that underpin the art market in India today, she is a prolific artist producing unique conceptual work and has become one of the best known representatives of a new generation of Indian artists. Awarded the Transmediale 2004 Award in Berlin in 2004, Gupta not only participates

an Festivals für Medienkunst, sondern auch an vielen internationalen Kunstausstellungen teil.

Wichtige Gruppenausstellungen: „The 3rd Fukuoka Asian Art Triennale“ (Fukuoka Asian Art Museum, 2005), „The 9th Lyon Biennale“ (2006), „The 7th Gwangju Biennale“ (2008), und „The 3rd Yokohama Triennale“ (2008). (KM)

in media art festivals, but also in many international art exhibitions.

Major group exhibitions include “The 3rd Fukuoka Asian Art Triennale” (Fukuoka Asian Art Museum, 2005), “The 9th Lyon Biennale” (2006), “The 7th Gwangju Biennale” (2008), and “The 3rd Yokohama Triennale” (2008). (KM)

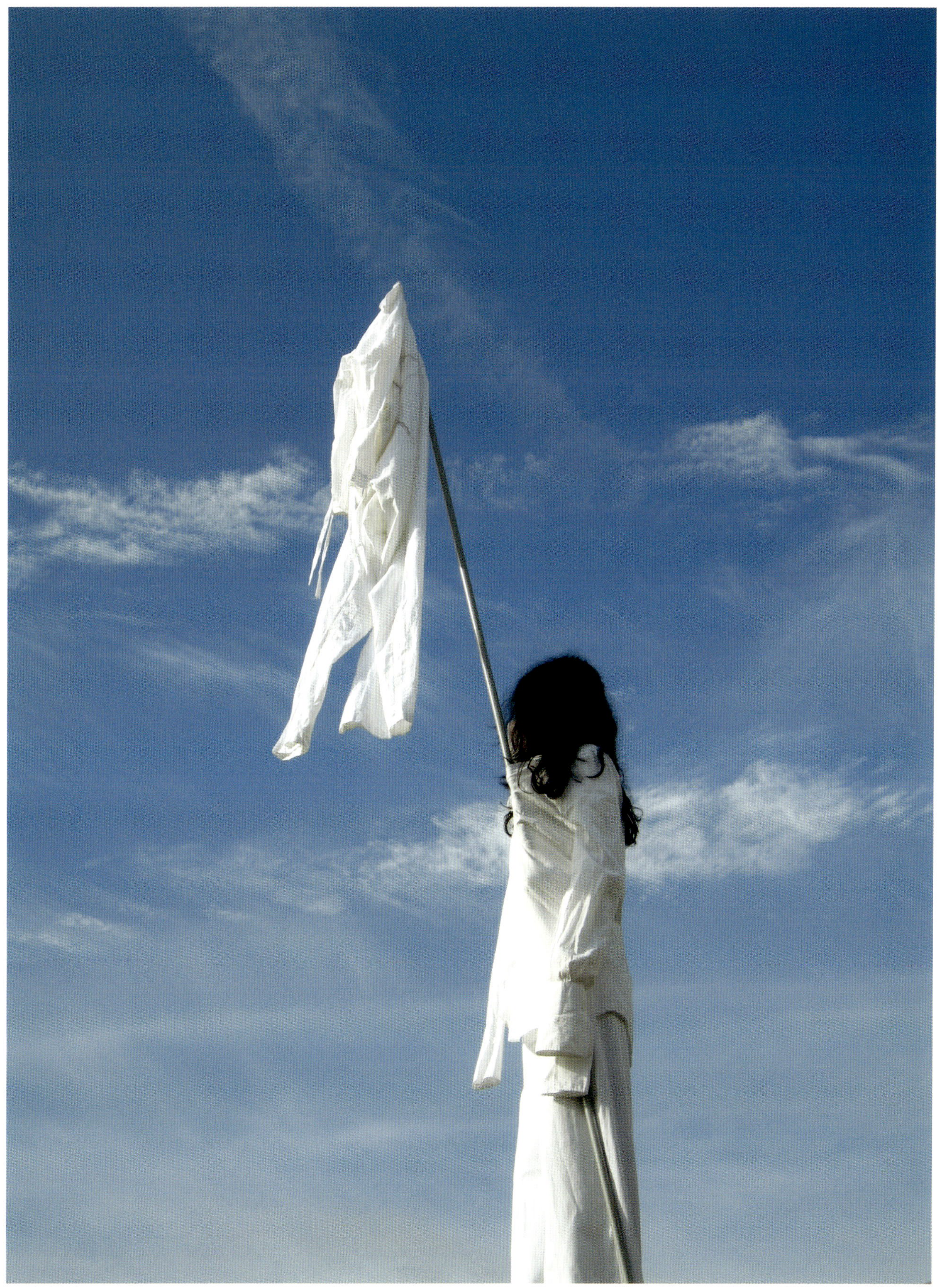

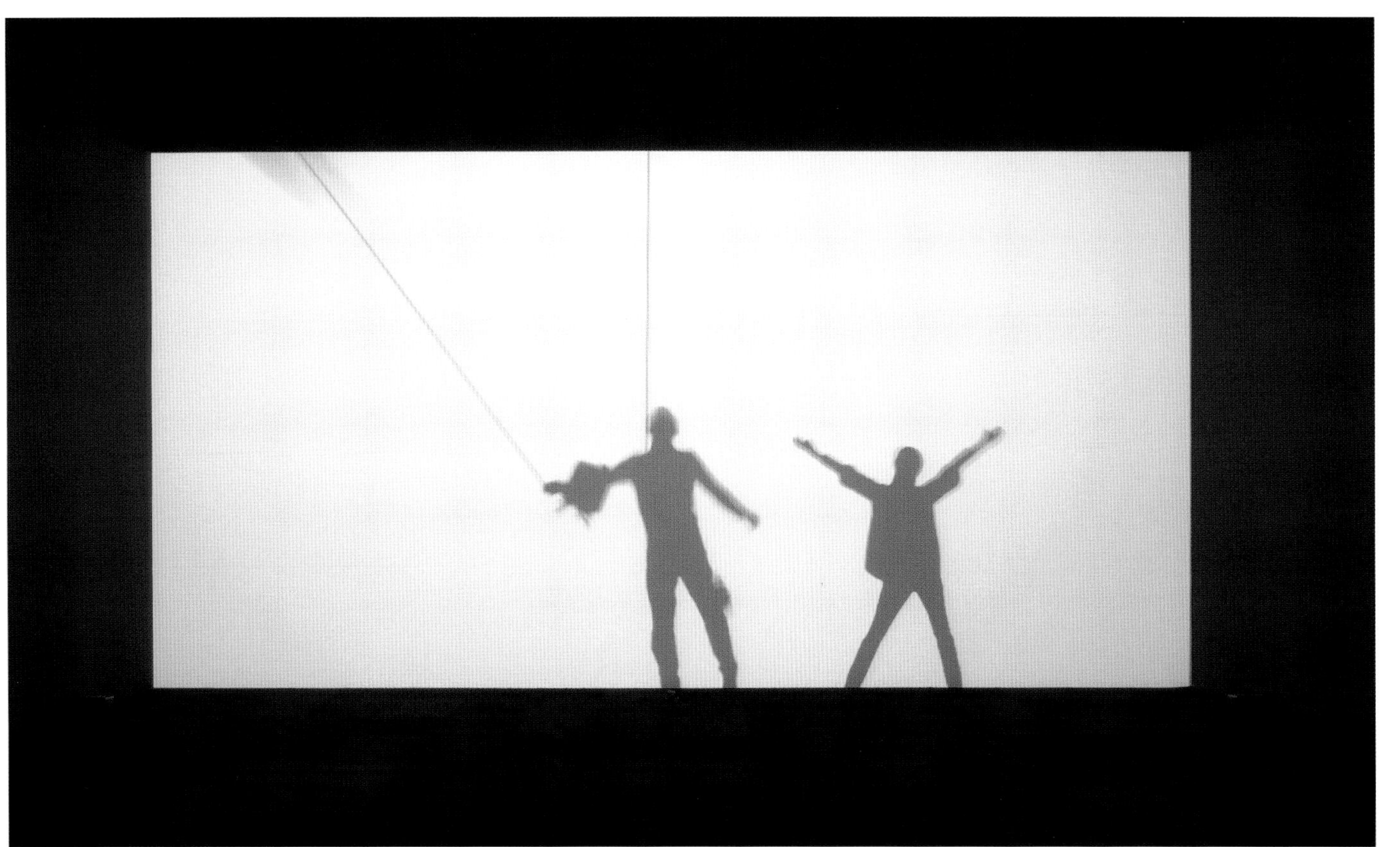

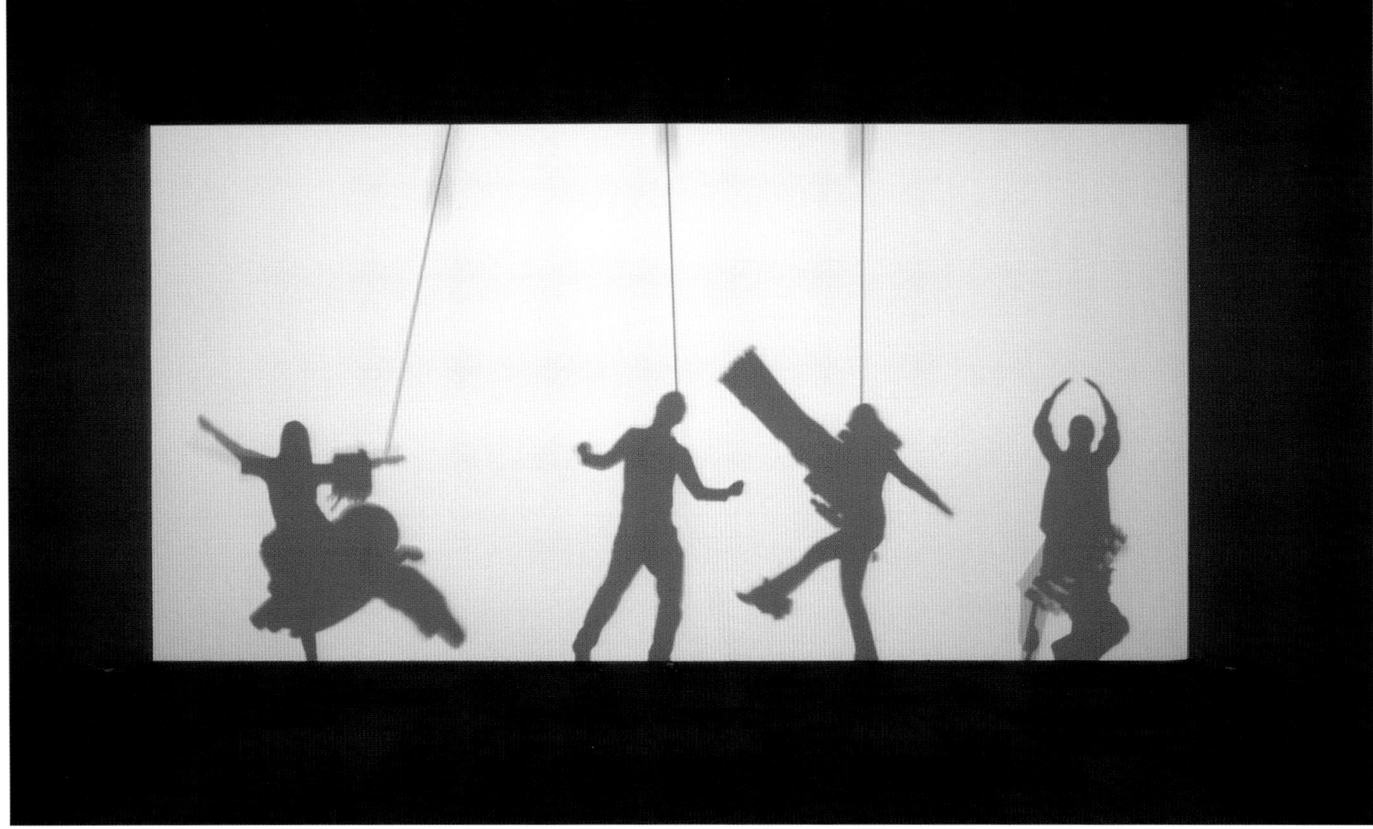

SHILPA GUPTA
Half Windows, 2008 (S./p. 79)

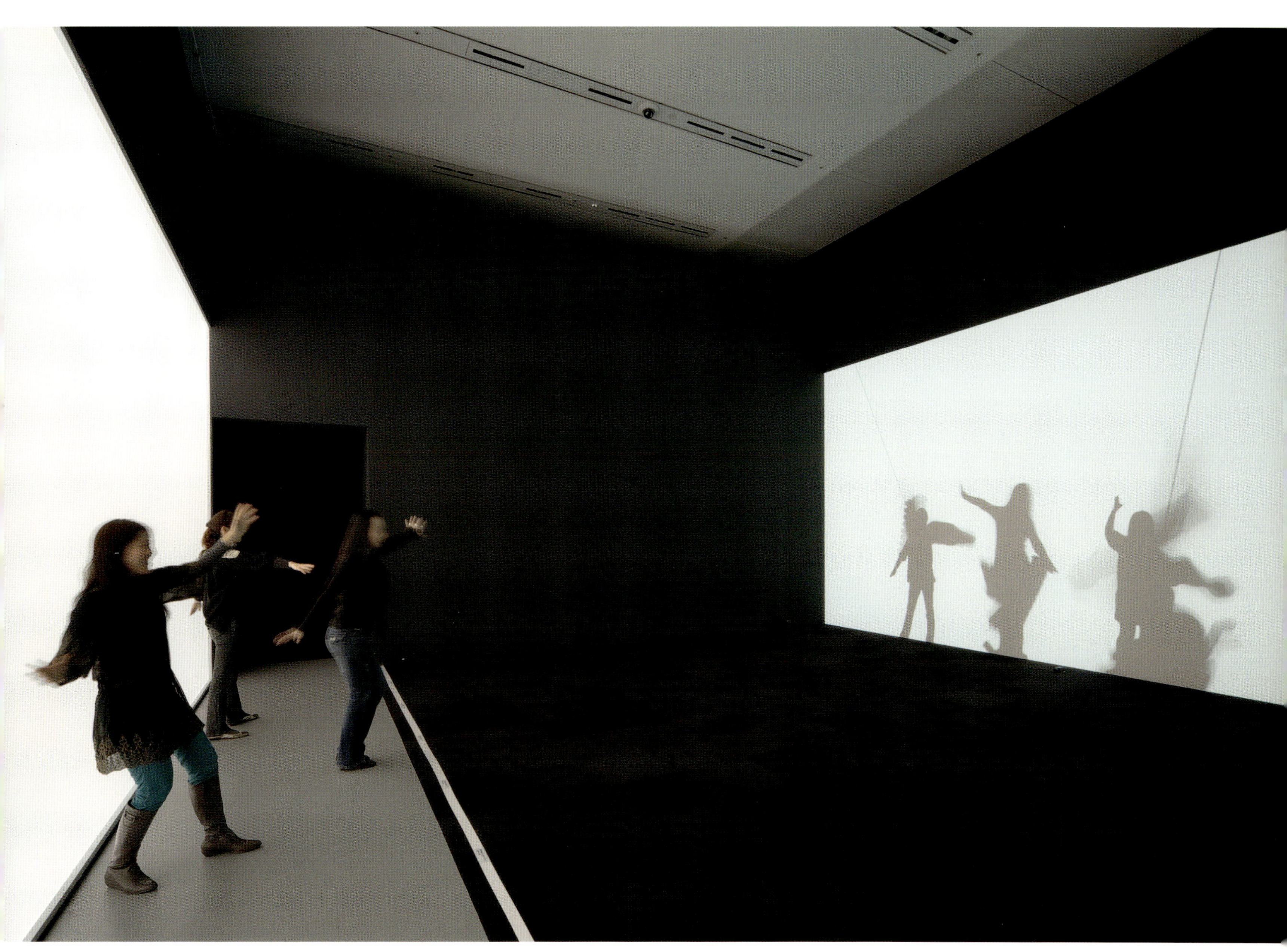

SHILPA GUPTA
Untitled (Shadow #3), 2007

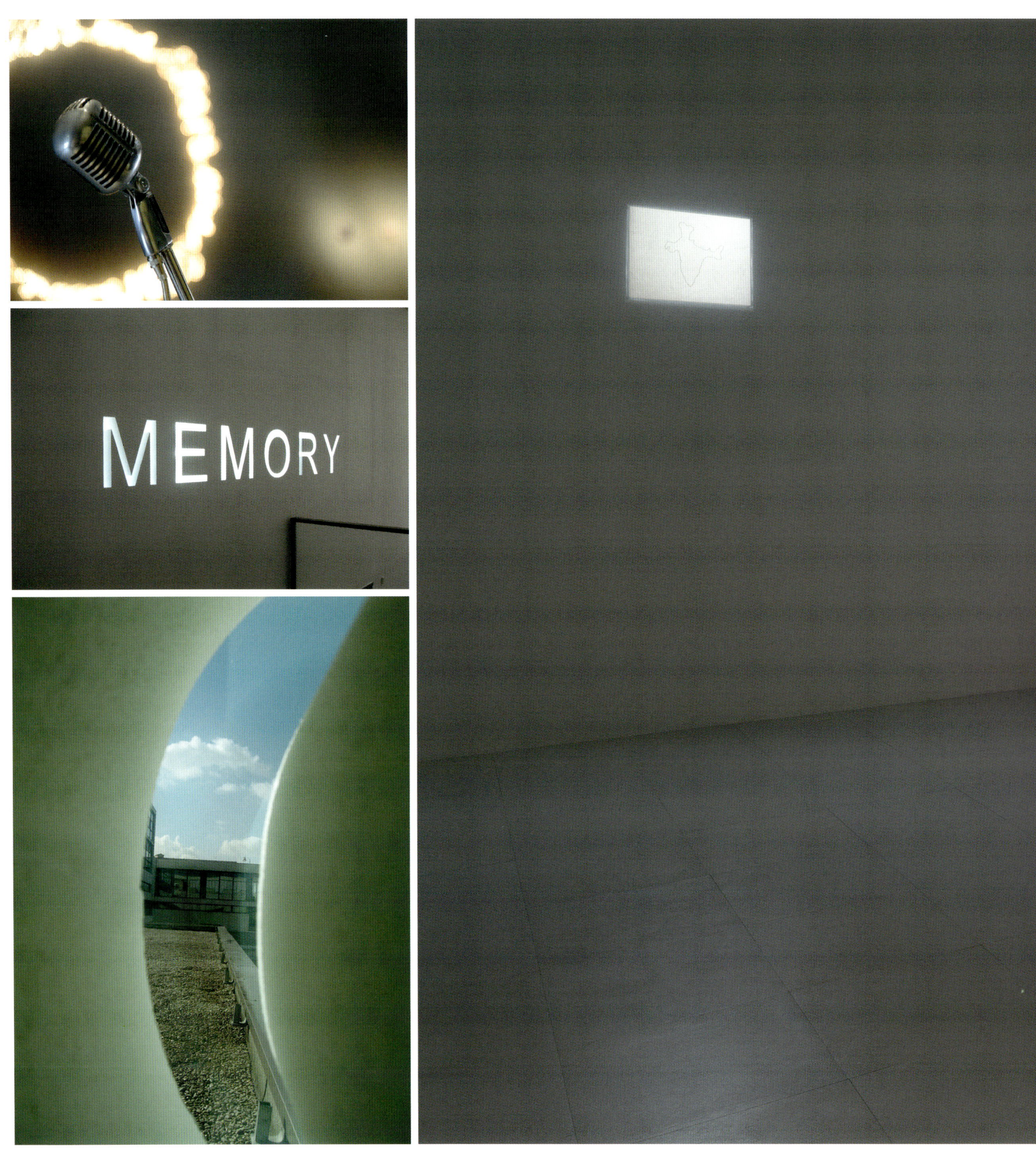
MEMORY

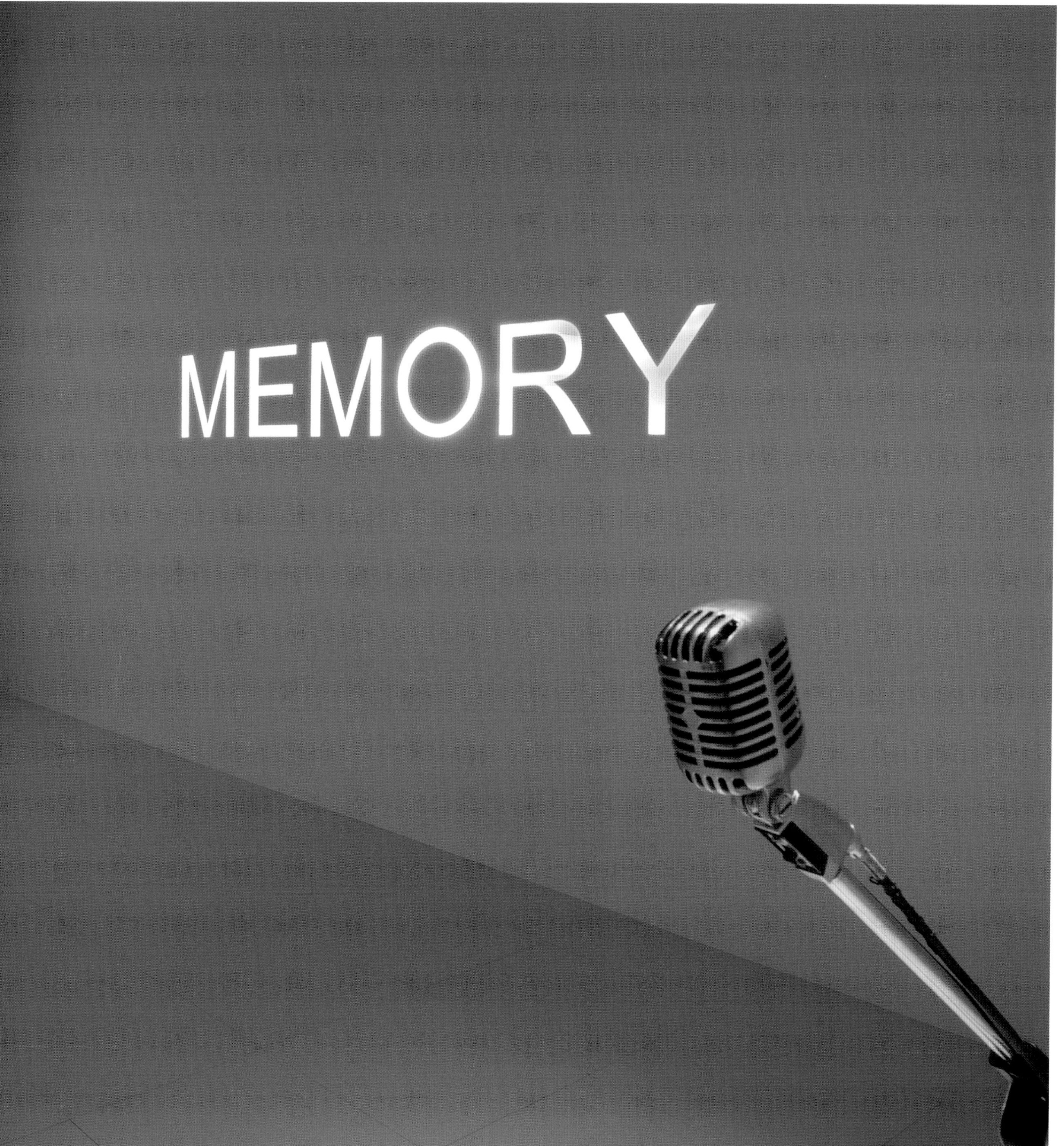

SHILPA GUPTA
100 Hand Drawn Maps of India, 2007–08, Memory, 2008–09, Tryst with Destiny, 2007–08
Installation view

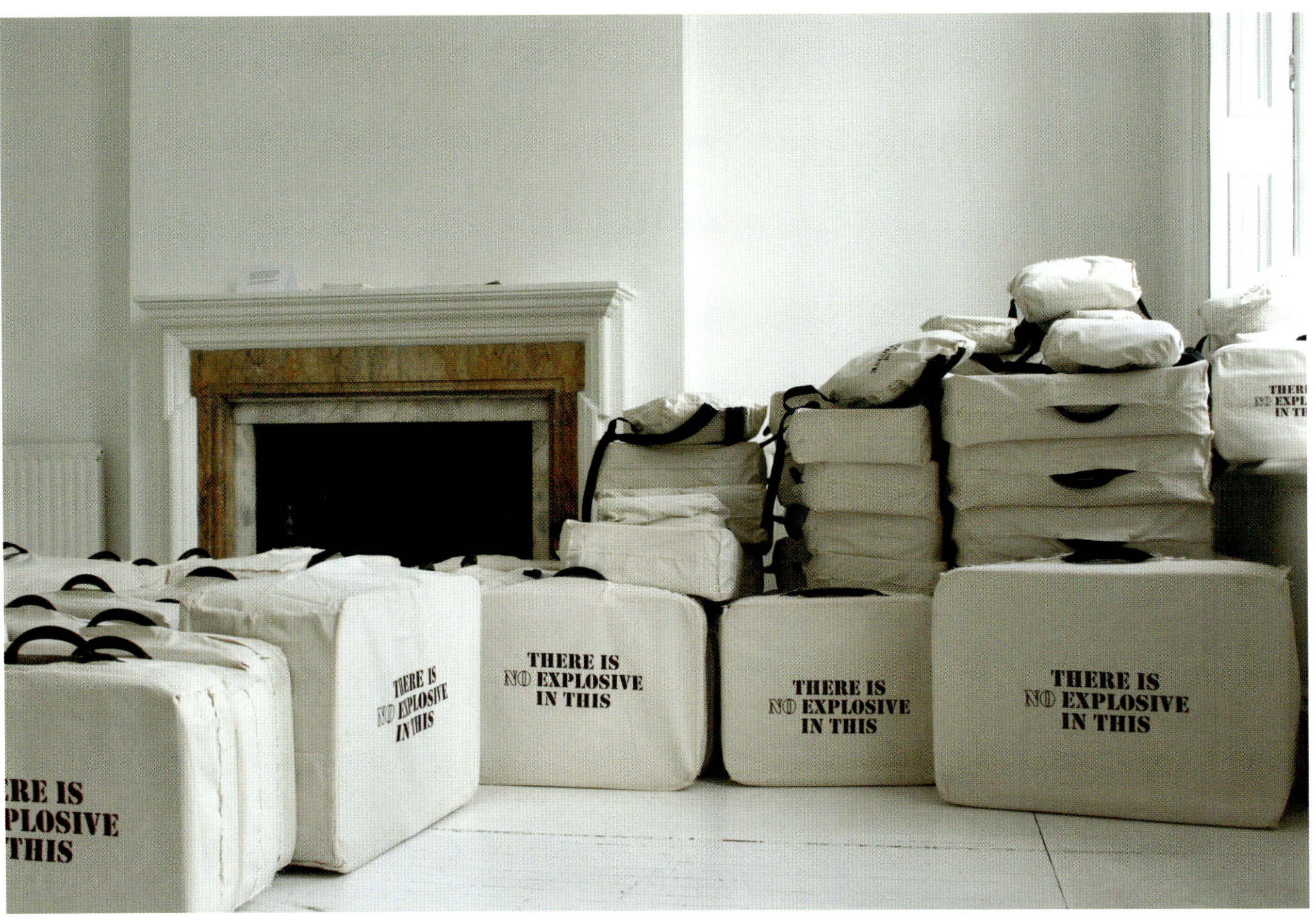

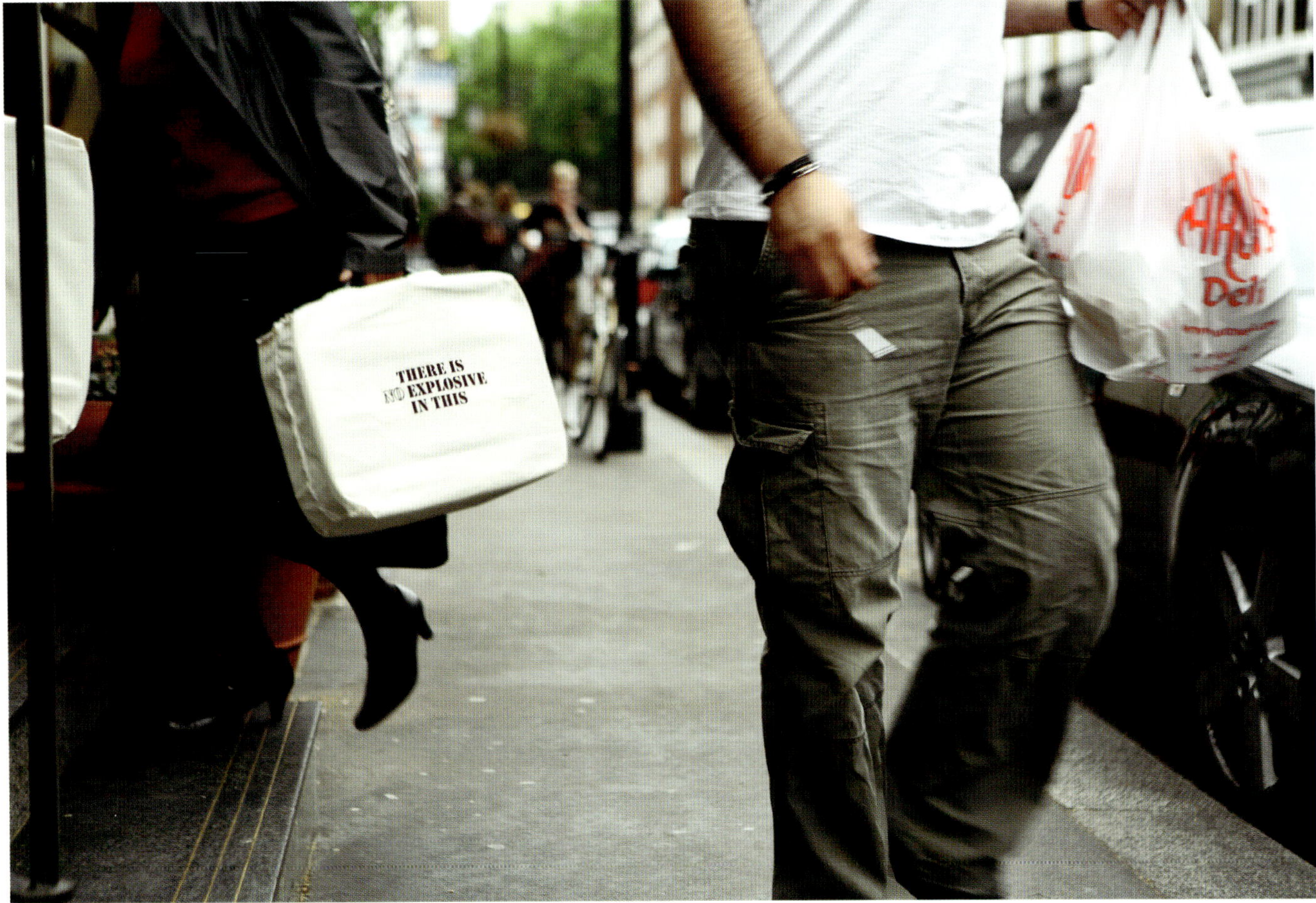

SHILPA GUPTA
There is no explosive in this – III, 2007
There is no explosive in this – II, 2007

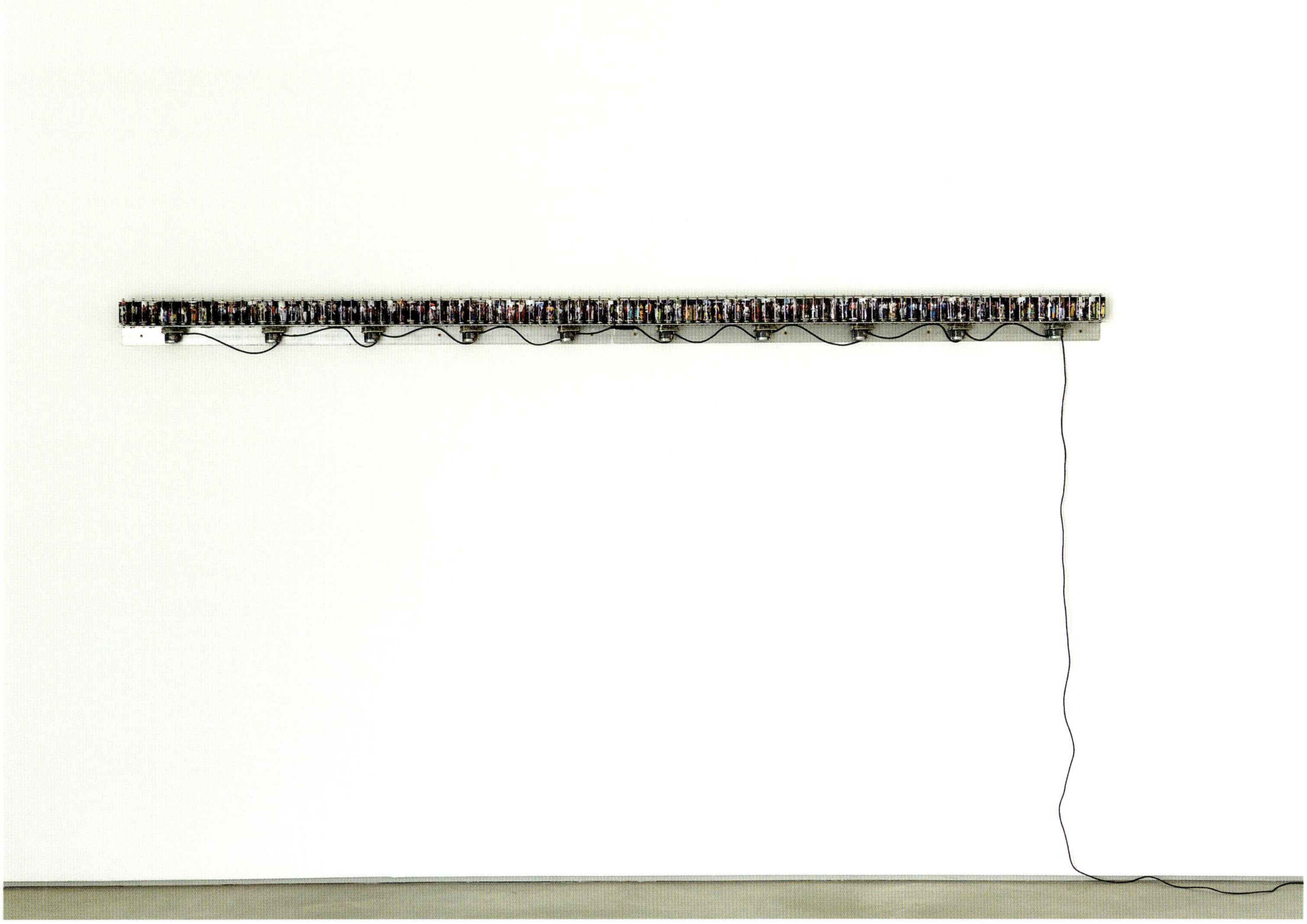

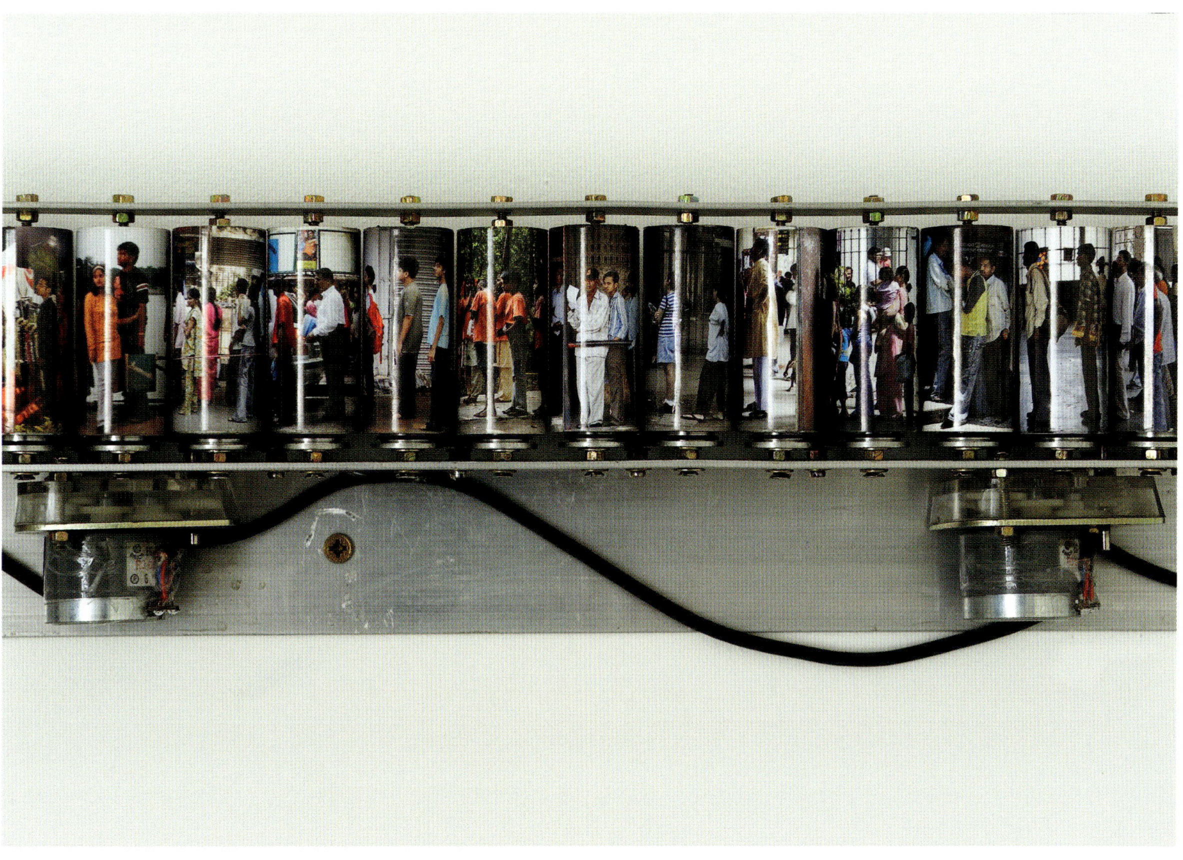

SHILPA GUPTA
100 Queues, 2007–08

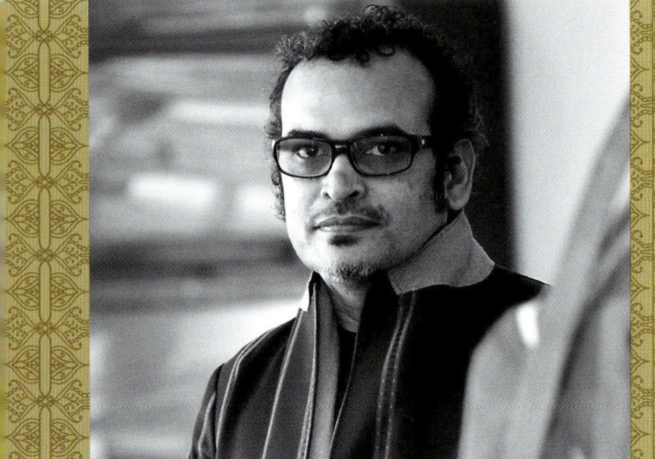

subodh gupta

SUBODH GUPTA Geboren 1964 in Khagaul, Bihar / Lebt in Gurgaon, Haryana
Born 1964 in Khagaul, Bihar / Lives in Gurgaon, Haryana

Subodh Gupta wuchs in einer kleinen Stadt in Bihar, Indien, auf und machte 1988 seinen Abschluss an der Kunsthochschule in Patna. Nachdem er einige Zeit am Theater gearbeitet hatte, verlagerte er seinen Schwerpunkt auf das Kunstschaffen. Seinen Stellenwert als Künstler erwarb Gupta in den Disziplinen Installation, Performance und Videokunst. Mitte der 1990er Jahre begann er, sowohl Alltagsgegenstände mit Objekten zu verbinden, die bei den Feierlichkeiten in seinem Heimatdorf verwendet wurden, als auch Kuhmist-Performances zu veranstalten, in denen das Heilige und das Unheilige dargestellt werden. Guptas Werk ist außerdem geprägt durch die Neudeutung seines eigenen Körpers und seiner persönlichen Erinnerungen im Zusammenhang mit den ländlichen Bräuchen seines Geburtsorts. Im Jahr 2000 verlegte sich Gupta auf die Darstellung der Mobilität und des Konsums als Begleiterscheinungen der rasanten Urbanisierung, wozu er verschiedenste Objekte wie indische Kochutensilien und Essgeräte, Kübel und indische Fahrzeuge verwendete. Besonders bekannt sind Guptas Arbeiten, in denen Symbole der Modernisierung, wie etwa Edelstahlgeräte, zum Einsatz kommen, die statt den Messing-, Kupfer- und Bronzegeräten vergangener Zeiten verwendet werden. Als wollte er das rasante Wachstum der indischen Wirtschaft zum Ausdruck bringen, hat Gupta in den letzten Jahren sowohl Großinstallationen, als auch Skulpturen geschaffen, die wesentlich größer sind als ihre realen Vorbilder.

Bei der aktuellen Ausstellung zeigt Gupta ein neues Gemälde sowie neue Skulpturen und Installationen. „OK Mili“ (2005), besteht aus dutzenden Edelstahlgeräten, die wie ein Kronleuchter von der Decke hängen. Der Klang, den diese Schwärme von Metallgefäßen hervorbringen, wenn sie aneinander stoßen, und die blanken Edelstahloberflächen sind Ausdruck des glänzenden, dynamischen Indien, das im Zeichen der Modernisierung steht. „Bullet“ (2007) stellt das „Bullet“ Motorrad in Kupfer dar: Ursprünglich von Royal Enfield in Großbritannien gebaut, entwickelte sich das Motorrad zum Dauerbrenner und wird heute in Indien hergestellt. Zunächst reisten Techniker aus Indien nach Großbritannien, um sich mit der Fahrzeugtechnik des Bullet vertraut zu machen, das kontinuierlich seit 1955 hergestellt wird. Seit dem Konkurs des

Subodh Gupta was raised in a small town in Bihar, India, and graduated from the School of Painting at the College of Arts and Craft, Patna in 1988. He was involved in theatre before focusing on art. Gupta emerged as an artist with his installations that he embarked on in the mid-90s combining items used in everyday life with items used in the ceremonies held in the village where he was born and raised, and his performances featuring cow dung, representing the sacred and the unsacred, and his video art. Gupta's work is also informed by the reinterpretation of his own body and memories within the context of the traditions of his rural birthplace. Since 2000, however, Gupta has been depicting the mobility and consumption that has accompanied rapid urbanization by featuring everyday items such as Indian cooking and eating utensils, buckets and Indian vehicles. Gupta is particularly well known for his work featuring symbols of modernization such as the stainless steel utensils that have replaced the brass, copper and bronze utensils used in the past. In recent years Gupta has been creating sculptures that are significantly larger in scale than the actual objects they represent, as well as large-scale installations, as though reflecting the rapid growth of the Indian economy.

In this exhibition, Gupta is showing a new painting and recent sculptures and installations. In *OK Mili* (2005), Gupta has suspended dozens of stainless steel utensils from the ceiling like a chandelier. The sound produced by the clusters of metal boxes as they come into contact with each other, and the shiny stainless steel surfaces of the containers convey the gleaming, energetic India as it undergoes modernization. *Bullet* (2007) represents, in brass, the long-selling Bullet motorbike originally manufactured by Royal Enfield in the U.K., and now made in India. Indian technicians initially travelled to the U.K. to learn the technology behind the Bullet, which has remained in production since 1955. After the British parent company collapsed, the Bullet continued to be produced in India by the nationalized local company, and this famous motorbike was even re-exported to England at one stage. In *Still Steal Steel # 11* (2008), Gupta has depicted stainless cooking utensils that are as glossy as a mirrored surface. As conveyed by the title, Gupta has depicted stainless steel

britischen Mutterunternehmens wird dieses berühmte Motorrad in Indien von einem verstaatlichten inländischen Betrieb gefertigt und zwischendurch sogar nach England re-exportiert. In „Still Steal Steel # 11" (2008) hat Gupta erneut spiegelglänzende Kochutensilien aus Edelstahl dargestellt. Wie der Titel besagt, hat Gupta Edel„stahl" abgebildet, der die „Stille" „stiehlt", indem er zu Boden fällt und einen Missklang erzeugt, in der Absicht – umgeben von verstreuten Farbflecken – die heitere Stille des Stilllebens zu zerstören. „Door" (2007) ist der Messingabguss einer Haustür, den Gupta im Ausstellungsraum installiert hat. Was liegt nun hinter dieser alten, schweren Tür – eine glänzende Zukunft oder der Verdrängungswettbewerb auf dem Weg zur Modernisierung? Die Antwort bleibt der Phantasie der Betrachter überlassen, die vor einer verschlossenen Tür stehen.

Wichtige Ausstellungen: „The 1st Fukuoka Asian Art Triennale" (Fukuoka Asian Art Museum, 1999), „Sequence 1, Painting and Sculpture from the François Pinault Collection" (Palazzo Grassi, Venezia, 2007), und eine Einzelausstellung „Silk Route" (BALTIC Centre for Contemporary Arts, Newcastle, U.K., 2007). (TK)

that steals the stillness as it falls down creating a cacophony, around which is scattered pigment to shatter the serene silence represented by still life. In *Door* (2007), Gupta has installed a brass casting of the door of a house inside the gallery space. What lies behind the old, heavy door – a glittering future or the intense competition that takes place in the path to modernization? The answer is left up to the imagination of the audience standing in front of a door that does not open.

Major exhibitions include the "The 1st Fukuoka Asian Art Triennale" (Fukuoka Asian Art Museum, 1999), "Sequence 1, Painting and Sculpture from the François Pinault Collection" (Palazzo Grassi, Venezia, 2007), and a solo exhibition "Silk Route" (BALTIC Centre for Contemporary Arts, Newcastle, U.K., 2007). (TK)

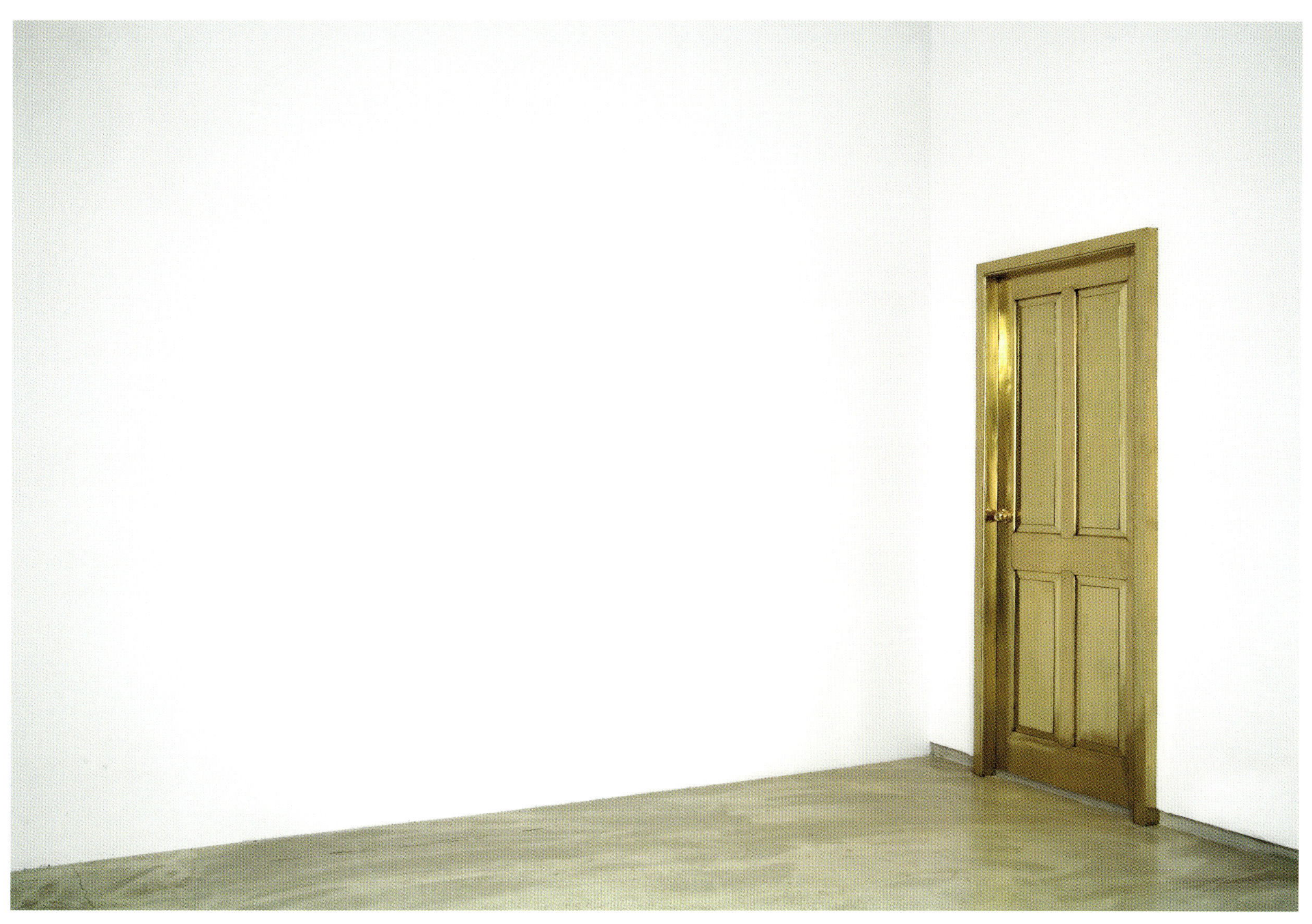

SUBODH GUPTA
Door, 2007

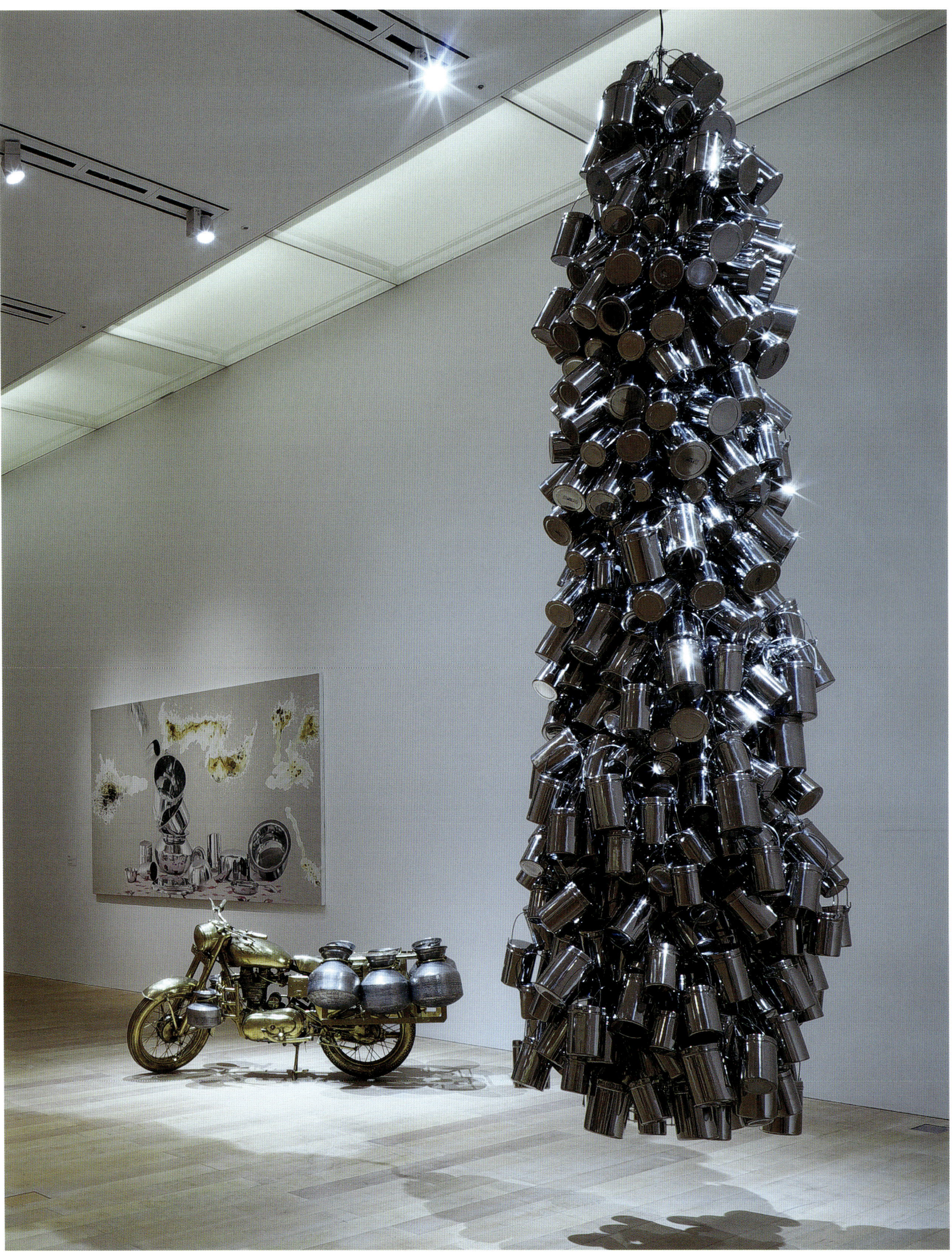

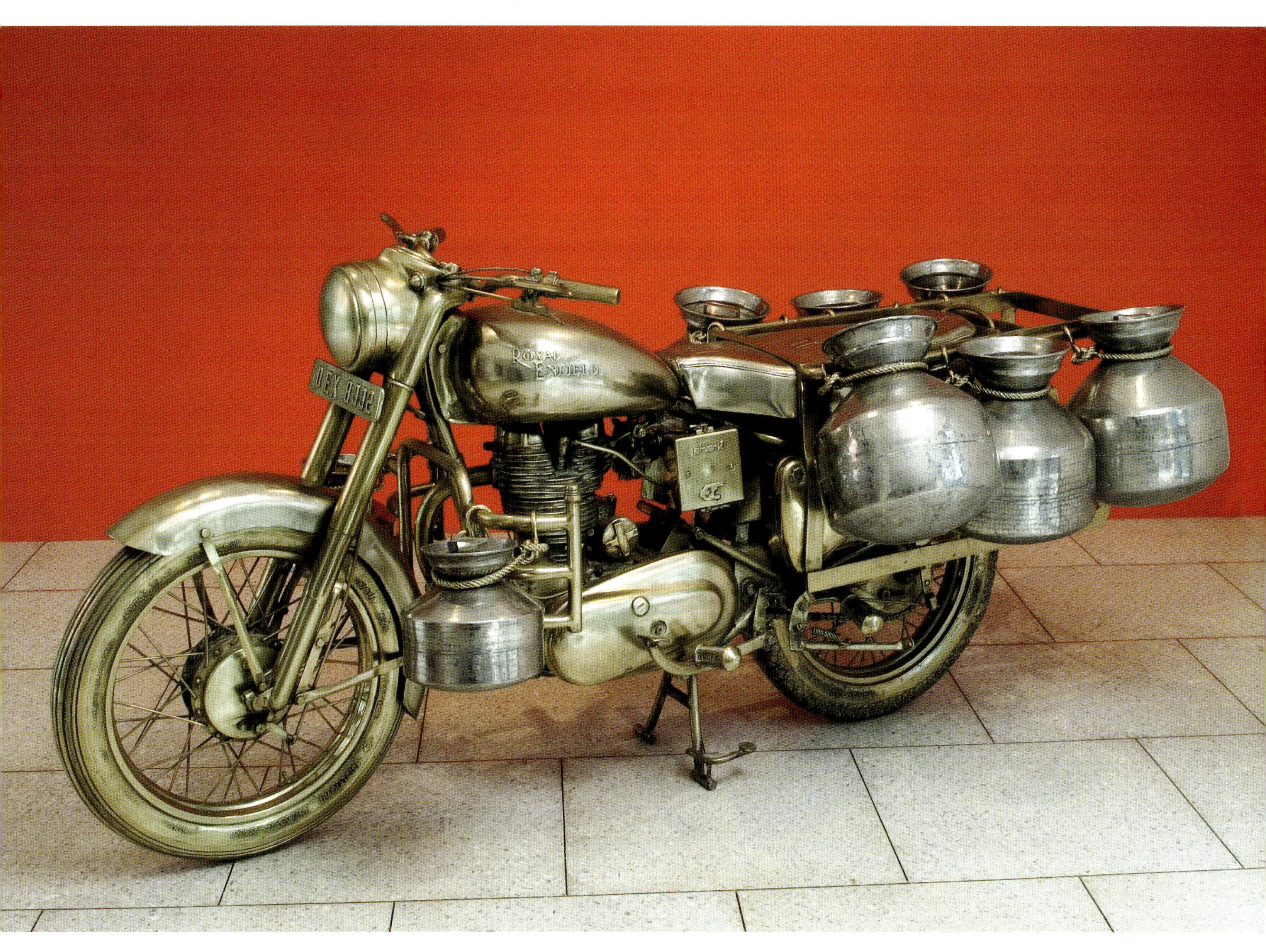

SUBODH GUPTA
OK Mili, 2005
Bullet, 2007

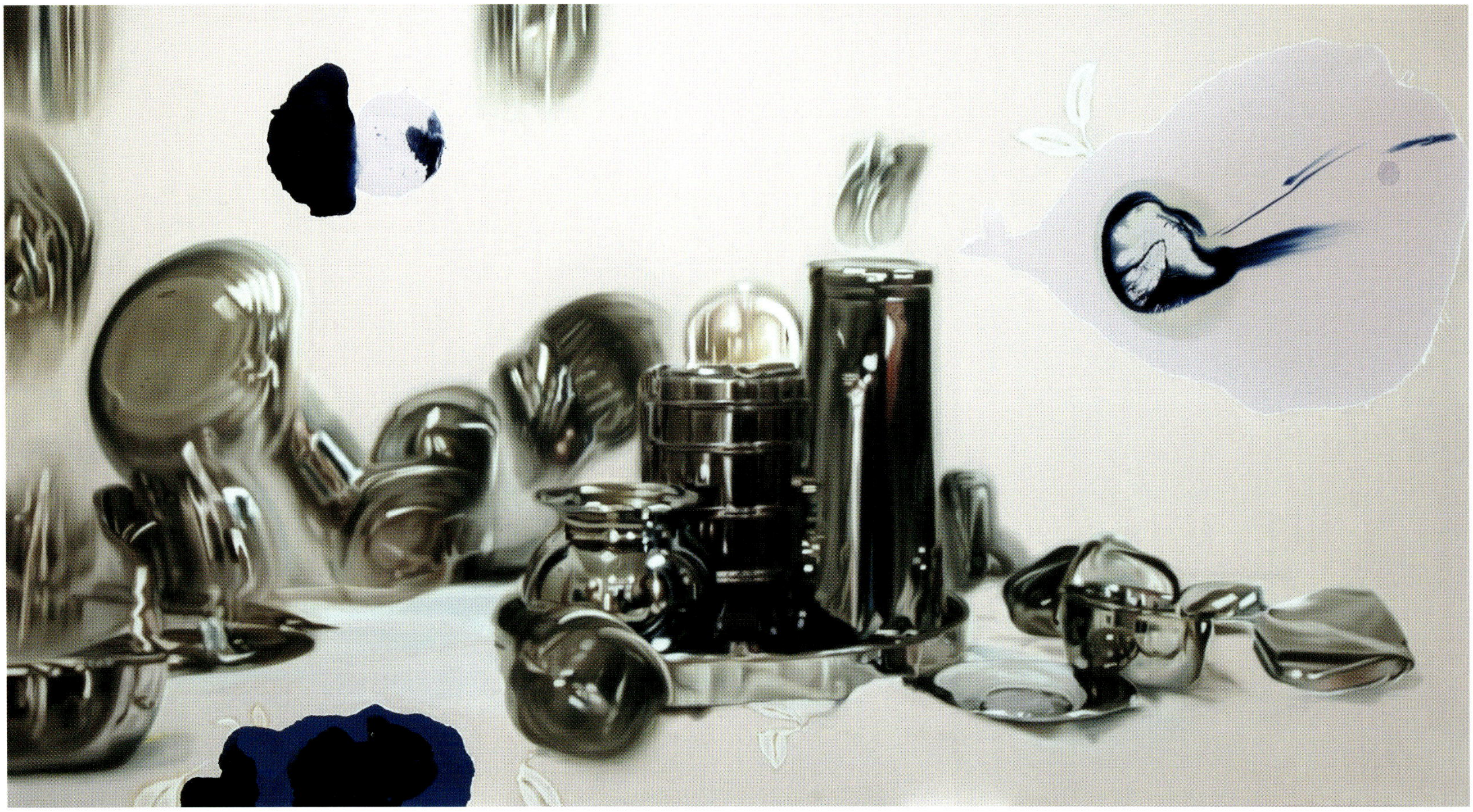

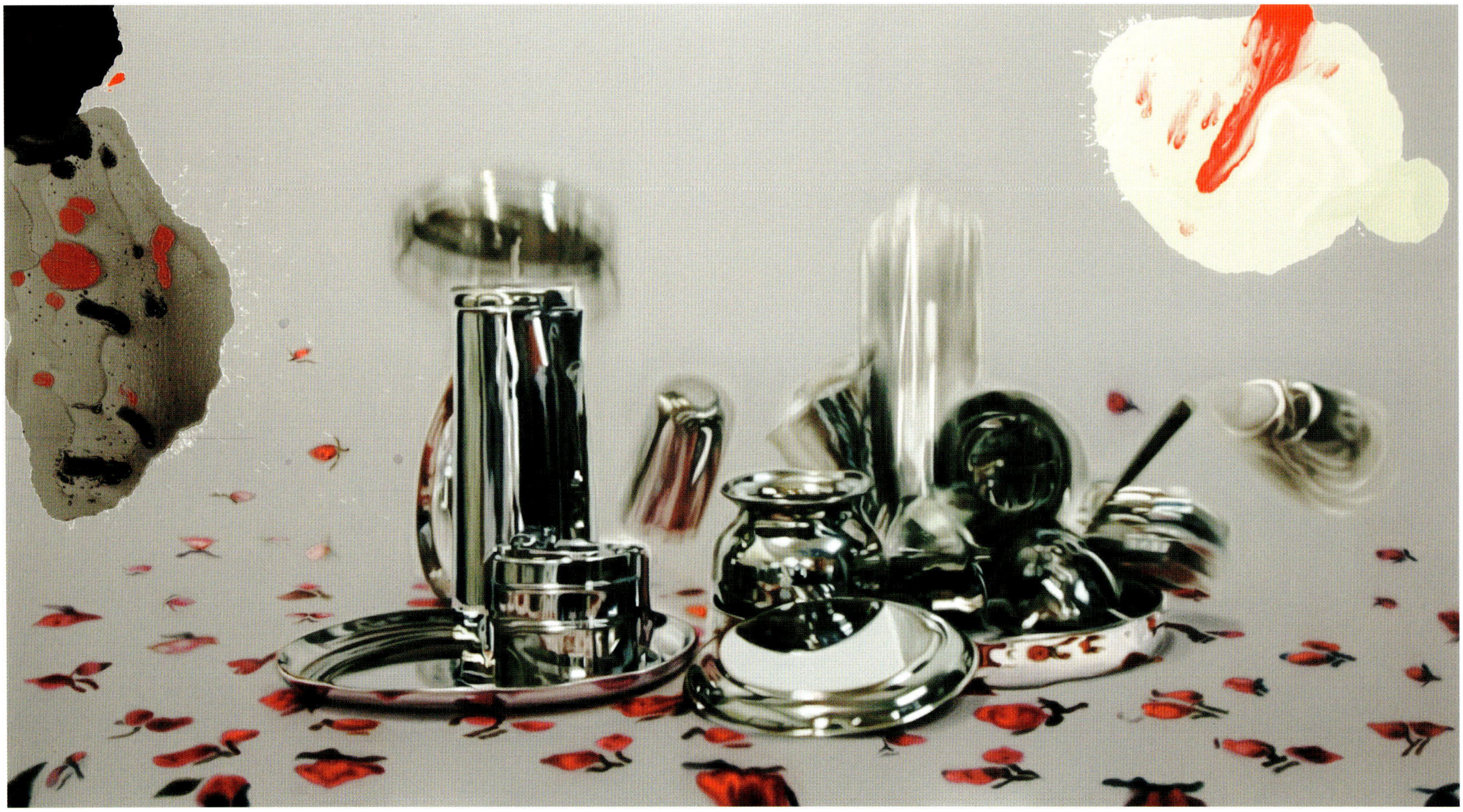

SUBODH GUPTA
Still Steal Steel # 2, 2008
Still Steal Steel # 3, 2008

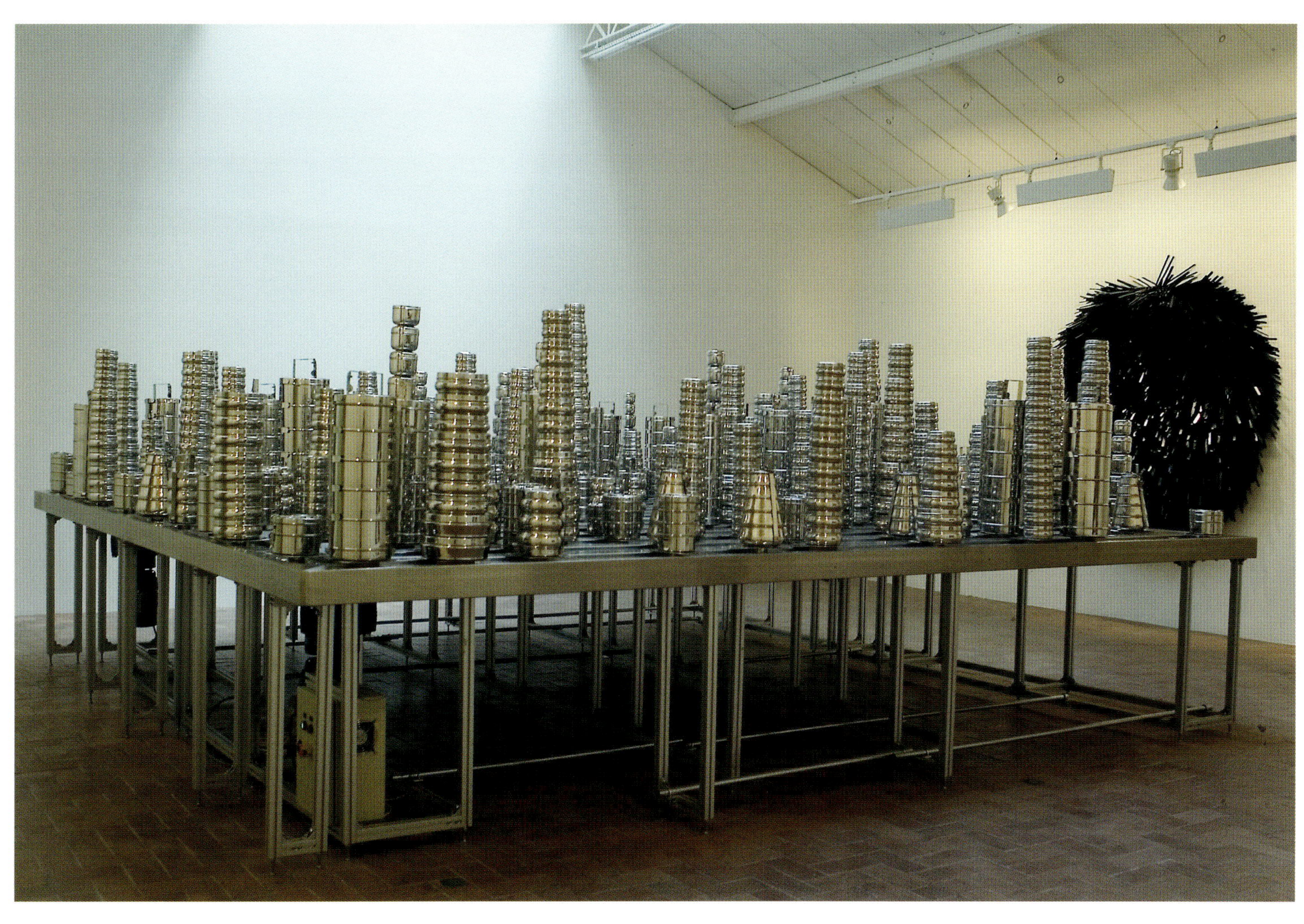

SUBODH GUPTA
Silk Road, 2007

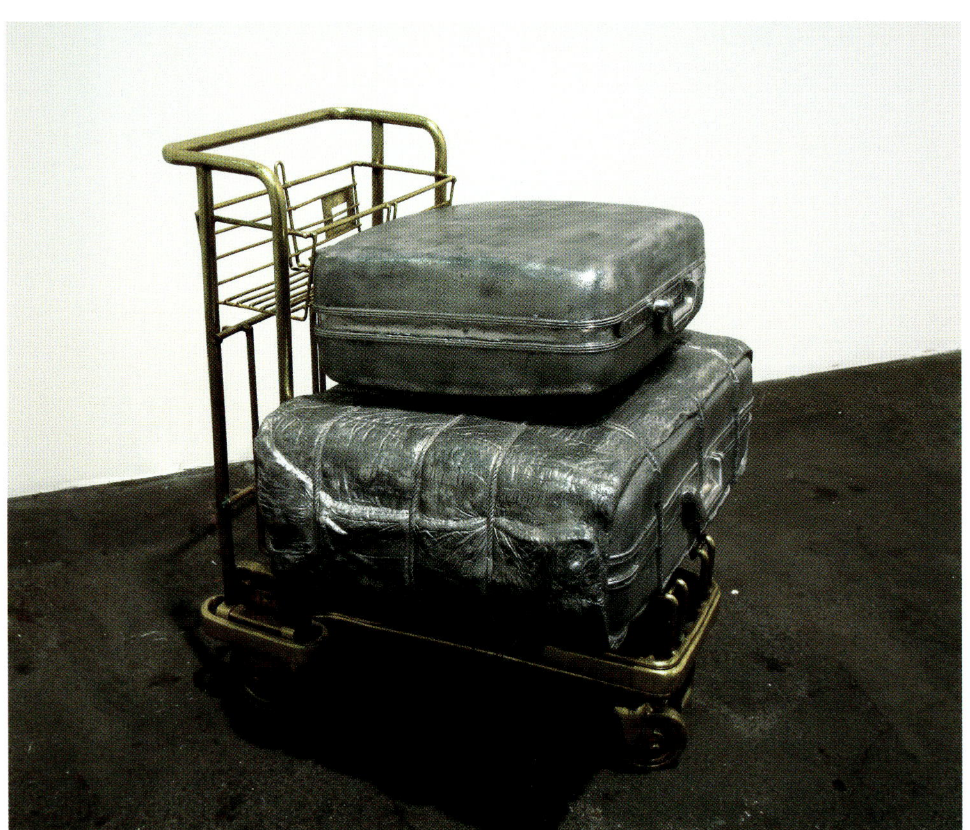

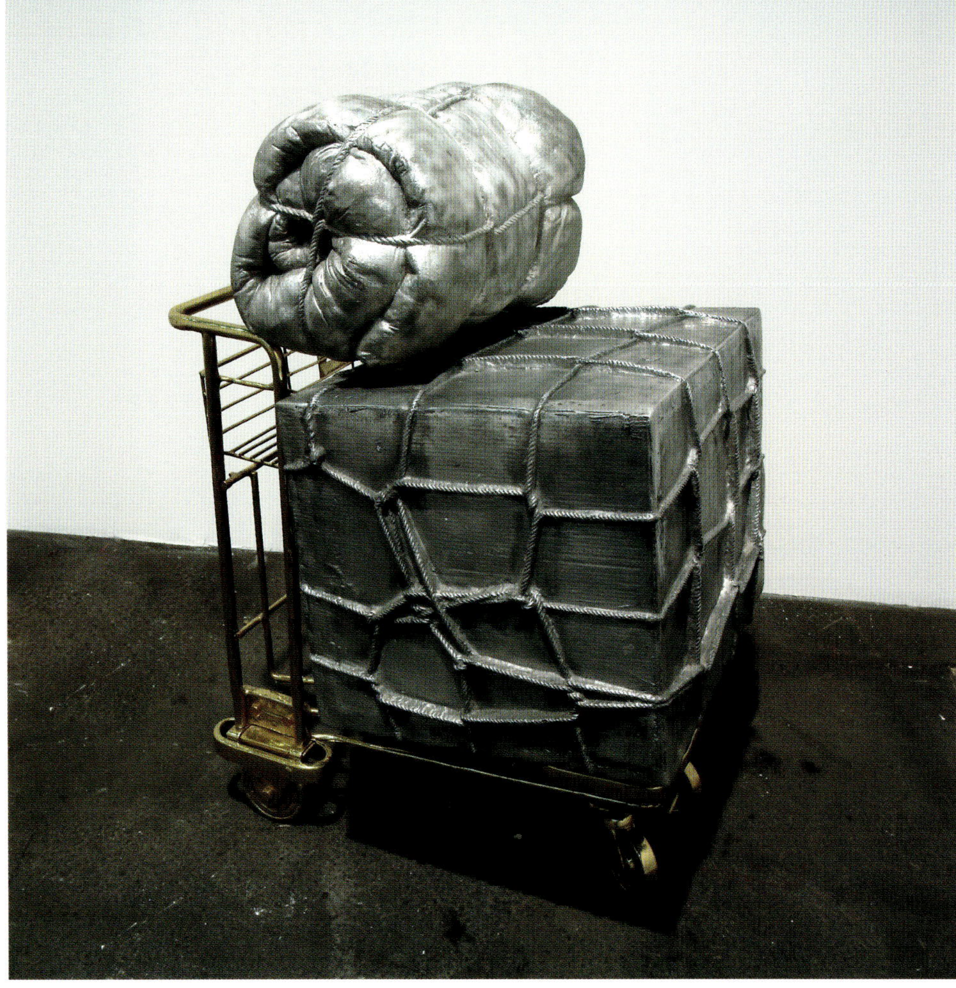

SUBODH GUPTA
Kuwait to Delhi, 2006
Dubai to Calcutta, 2006
God Hungry, 2006

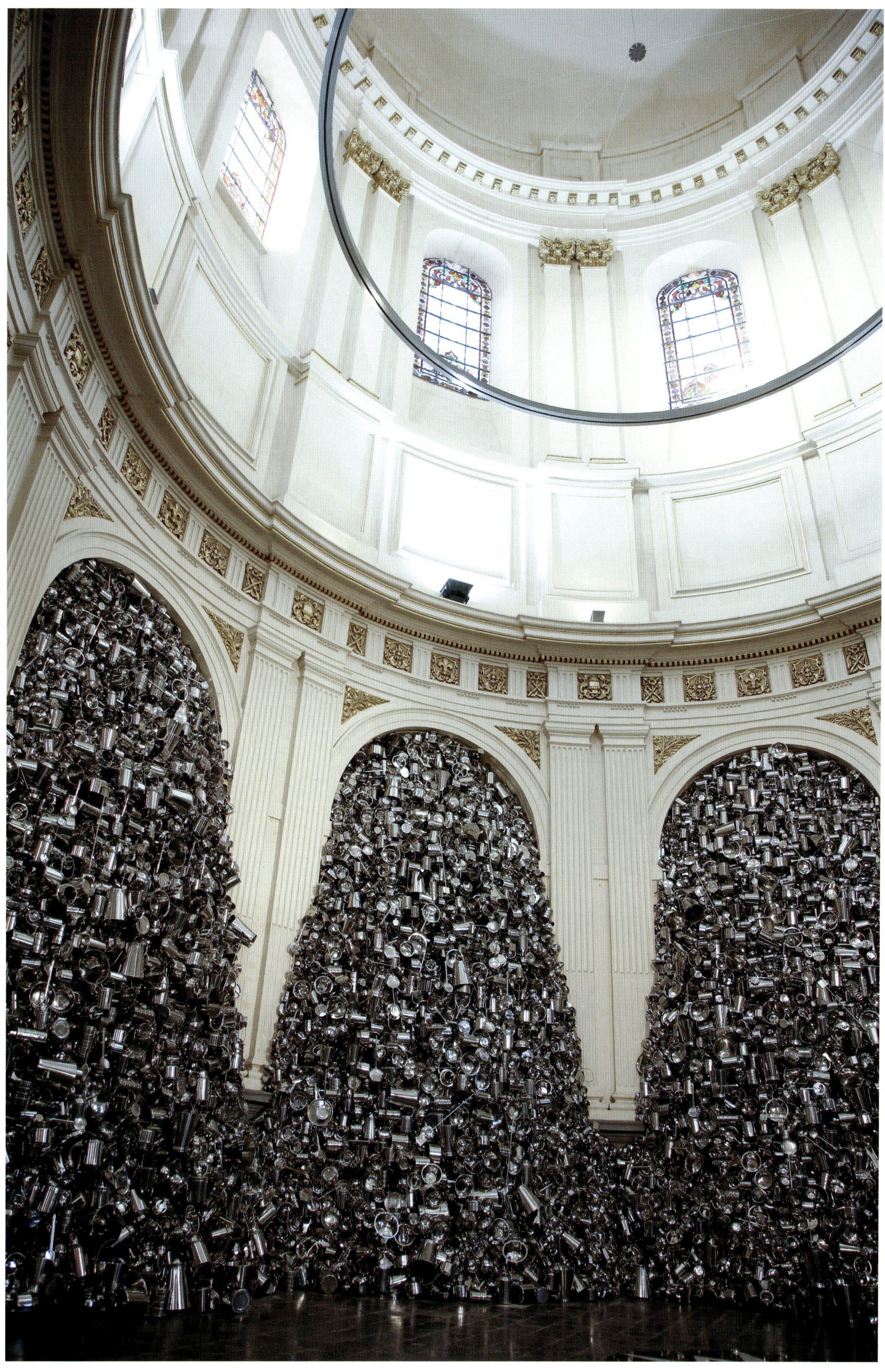

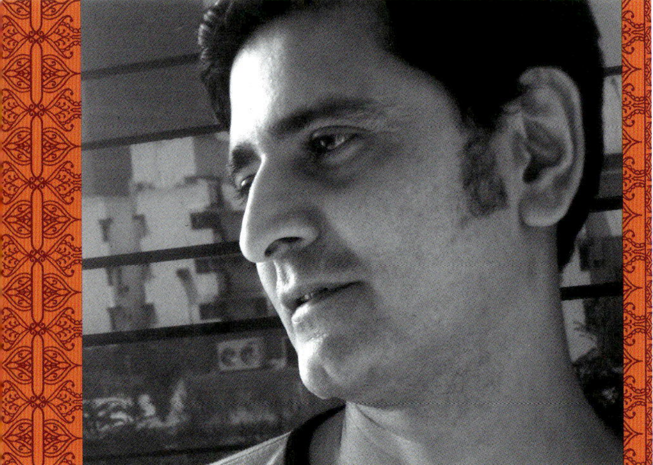

tushar joag

TUSHAR JOAG Geboren 1966 in Mumbai / Lebt in Mumbai
Born 1966 in Mumbai / Lives in Mumbai

Nach Abschluss seines Studiums an der Sir J.J. School of Fine Arts in Mumbai mit einem BA im Jahr 1988, machte Joag 1989 seinen Master an der Maharaja Sayajirao University of Baroda (Vadodara). Joag war Gründungsmitglied der „Open Circle" Künstlerinitiative, die 1999 in Mumbai gegründet wurde und die Homogenisierung der Gesellschaft sowie die wachsende Ablehnung des Nicht-Mainstream als Nebenprodukte der Globalisierung aus unterschiedlichen Gesichtspunkten kritisch kommentierte. Open Circle nahm sich sozialer Fragen an und veranstaltete dazu Diskussionsforen und Workshops. Joags ästhetische Konzepte und Vorstellungen finden ihren Niederschlag in seinem künstlerischen Werk, in dem allerdings auch ein betont aktivistisches Element zum Ausdruck kommt, das sich in der Förderung von sozialem Engagement und sozialer Intervention durch das Ansprechen und die Analyse von gesellschaftspolitischen Geschehnissen und Problemen äußert.

Im Jahr 2004 gründete Joag eine virtuelle Online-Organisation „UNICELL Public Works Cell" (www.unicellpwc.org). Theoretisch handelt es sich um eine Regierungsstelle mit Sitz in Mumbai – dem Wohnort Joags –, die auf regionaler Ebene staatliche Projekte abwickelt. Auf der Website werden Strategien zur Lösung sozialer Probleme mit dem Schwerpunkt auf den städtischen Bereich skizziert. In Wahrheit handelt es sich um eine fiktive Organisation, in der Joag als Einziger sämtliche Positionen ausfüllt (Chief Executive Officer, Creative Divisional Manager, Production Cell-in-charge und Installations Supervisor). „UNICELL Public Works Cell" ist eine satirische Nachbildung von Regierungsstellen und staatlichen Projektagenturen. Als Antwort auf die wachsenden Sorgen der Bürger über eine Reihe ganz unterschiedlicher sozialer Probleme schlägt UNICELL Lösungen vor, die in ihrem Ansatz meilenweit von der gängigen Regierungspolitik abweichen. Die Aktionen fallen in den Bereich des „Social Engineering" und könnten wohl als utopisch und grotesk bezeichnet werden. Sechs der bisher von Joag umgesetzten UNICELL-Projekte sind Teil der Ausstellung. Es handelt sich um unterschiedliche Ideen, z.B. zur Senkung des Stress-Levels von Pendlern in überfüllten Zügen oder eine Anregung für die Eigner von Straßenbuden, die als Unterbau der indischen Wirtschaft fungieren, sowie eine Idee, wie man sich Razzien entziehen kann.

After graduating with a BA from Sir J.J. School of Fine Arts in 1988, Joag went on to obtain an MA from the Maharaja Sayajirao University of Baroda (Vadodara) in 1989. Joag was a founding member of the Open Circle artists' initiative formed in Mumbai in 1999, which adopted a critical and multi-dimensional approach to comment on the homogenization of society and the growing tendency to reject the non-mainstream, which are arguably by-products of globalization. Open Circle addressed social issues by organizing forums and workshops. Joag's art reflects his aesthetic concepts and ideas, but there is also a strong element of activism; of promoting social involvement and intervention by referring to and analyzing socio-political incidents and issues.

In 2004, Joag established an imaginary, online organization that he named "UNICELL Public Works Cell" (http://www.unicellpwc.org). It is, in theory, a government agency carrying out regional public projects, and is based in Mumbai where Joag lives. The website outlines strategic solutions for tackling a range of social issues, with a particular focus on urban areas. It is in actual fact a fictitious organization in which each of the four individuals who make up the organization (Chief Executive Officer, Creative Divisional Manager, Production Cell-in-charge, and Installations Supervisor) is actually played by Joag alone. "UNICELL Public Works Cell" is a satirical imitation of government bureaus and public projects agencies. With citizens increasingly concerned by a range of different social issues, UNICELL proposes solutions by taking an approach that is completely different from existing government policy. Its activities play a social engineering role and could arguably be described as both Utopian and preposterous. Six UNICELL Projects that have been carried out by Joag to date are included in this exhibition. The Projects represent different proposals, such as a solution for reducing the stress levels of commuters travelling on packed trains, another targeted at individual stall holders on the streets who support the Indian economy, and a proposal for ways to avoid the crackdowns.

Aside from a couple of solo exhibitions featuring the ongoing UNICELL Project; "Willing Suspension" (Gallery Che-

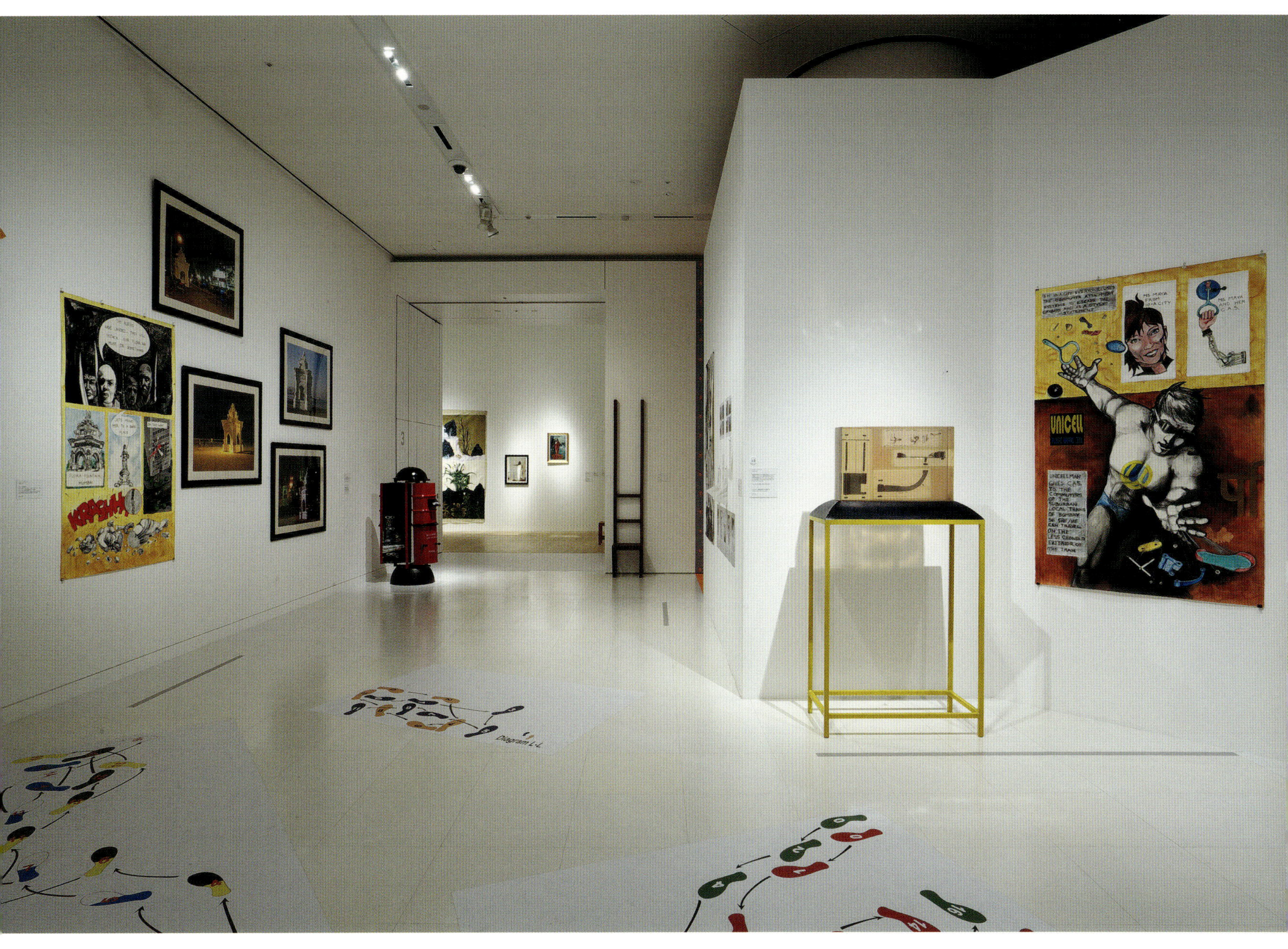

TUSHAR JOAG
Installation view

Einige Einzelausstellung zum laufenden UNICELL Projekt; „Willing Suspension“ (Gallery Chemould, Mumbai, 2005) und „Reconciliation & Truth“ (Chemould Prescott Road, Mumbai, 2008); Joag war auch bei „SUBCONTINGENT: The Indian Subcontinent in Contemporary Art / Il Subcontinente Indiano nell'Arte“ (Fondazione Sandretto Re Rebaudengo, Turin, Italia, 2006), „New Narratives: Contemporary Art from India“ (Chicago Cultural Center, 2007) und anderen vertreten. (KM)

mould, Mumbai, 2005) and “Reconciliation & Truth” (Chemould Prescott Road, Mumbai, 2008), Joag has also participated in “SUBCONTINGENT: The Indian Subcontinent in Contemporary Art / Il Subcontinente Indiano nell'Arte” (Fondazione Sandretto Re Rebaudengo, Turin, Italia, 2006), “New Narratives: Contemporary Art from India” (Chicago Cultural Center, 2007), and others. (KM)

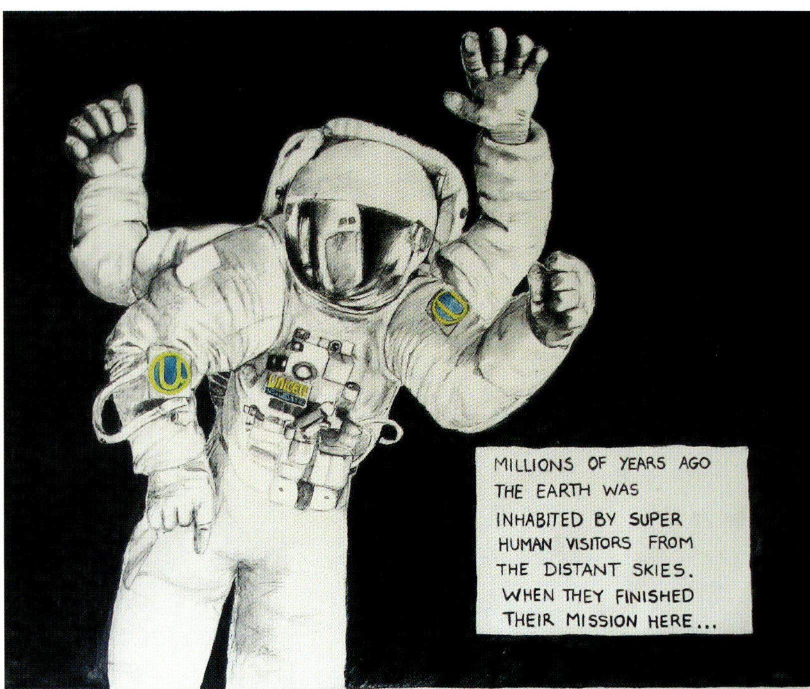

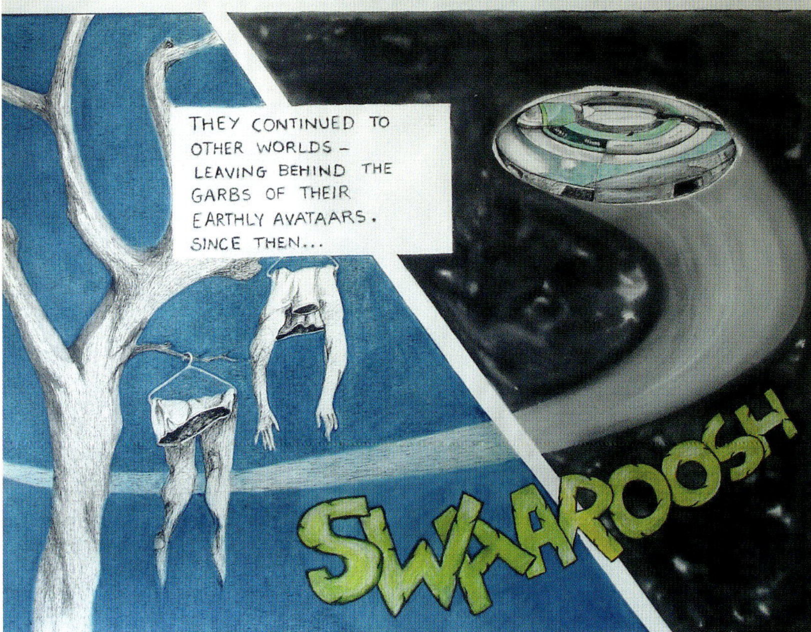

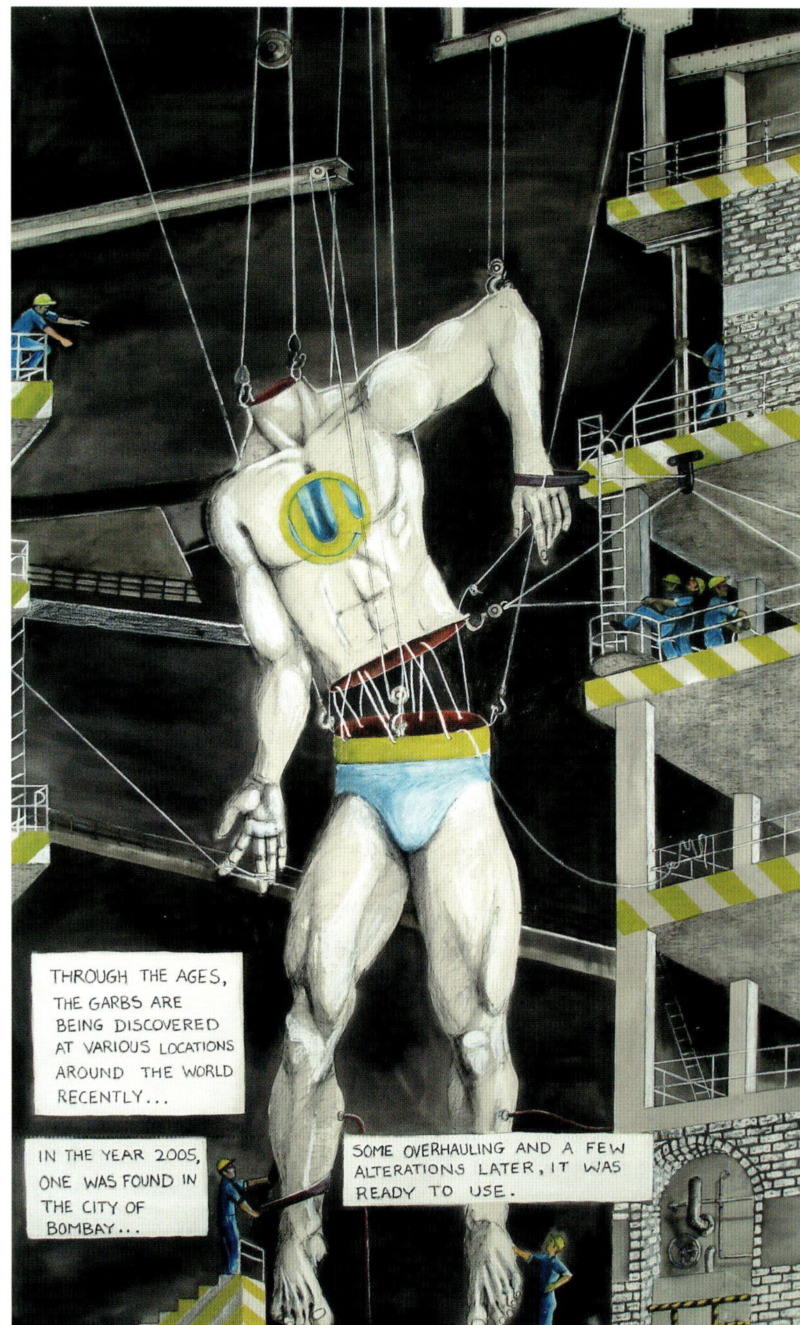

UNICELL

PUBLIC WORKS CELL

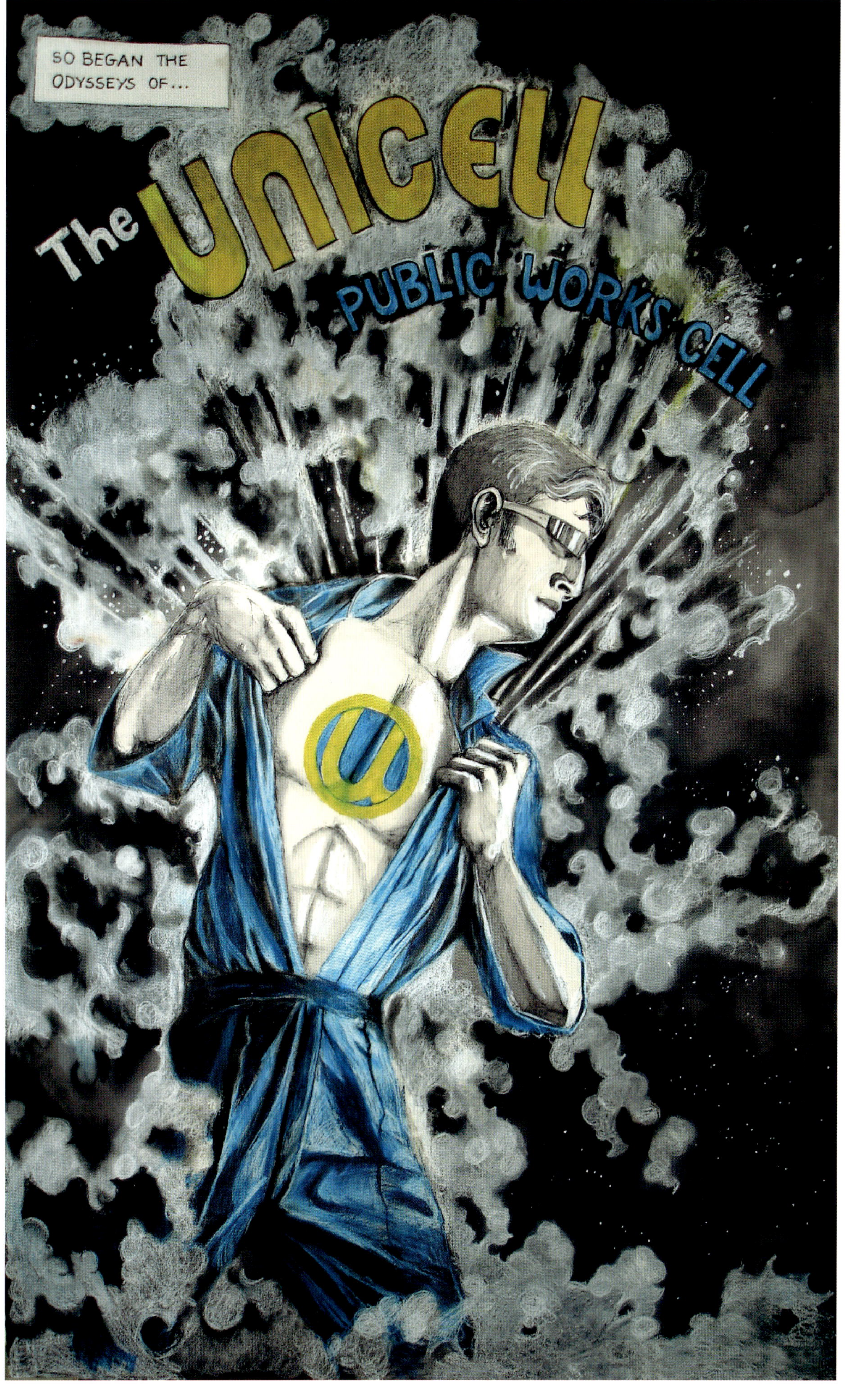

TUSHAR JOAG
Chronicles of UNICELL (Triptych), 2008

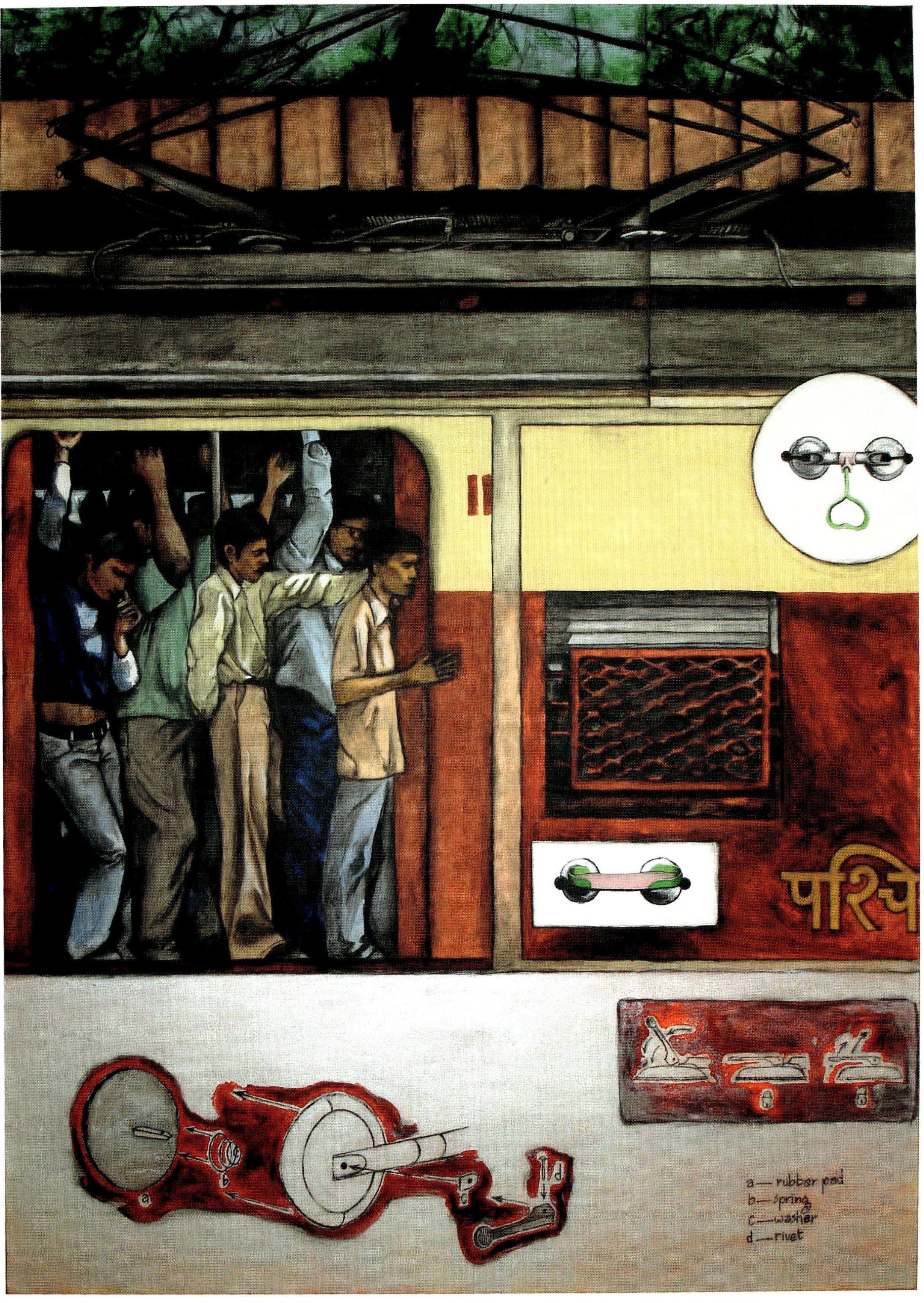
परिचे
a— rubber pad
b— spring
c— washer
d— rivet

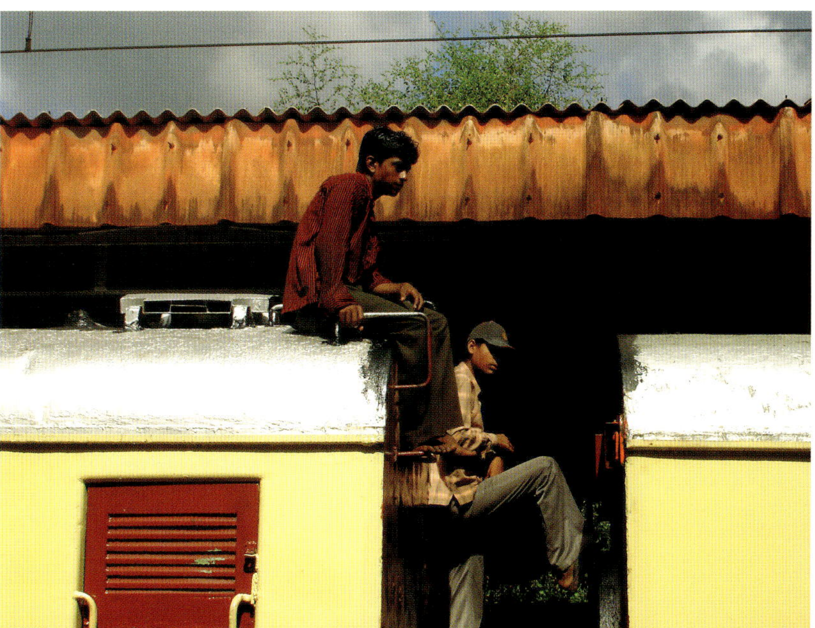

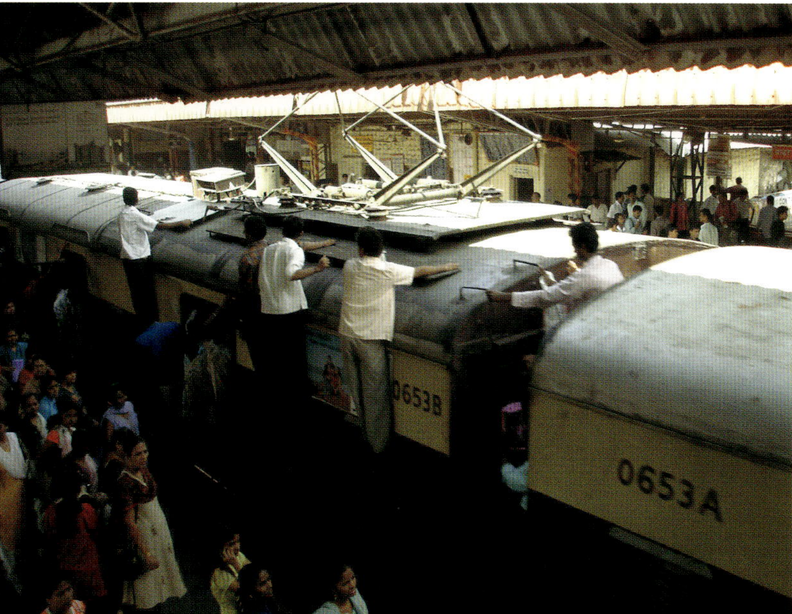

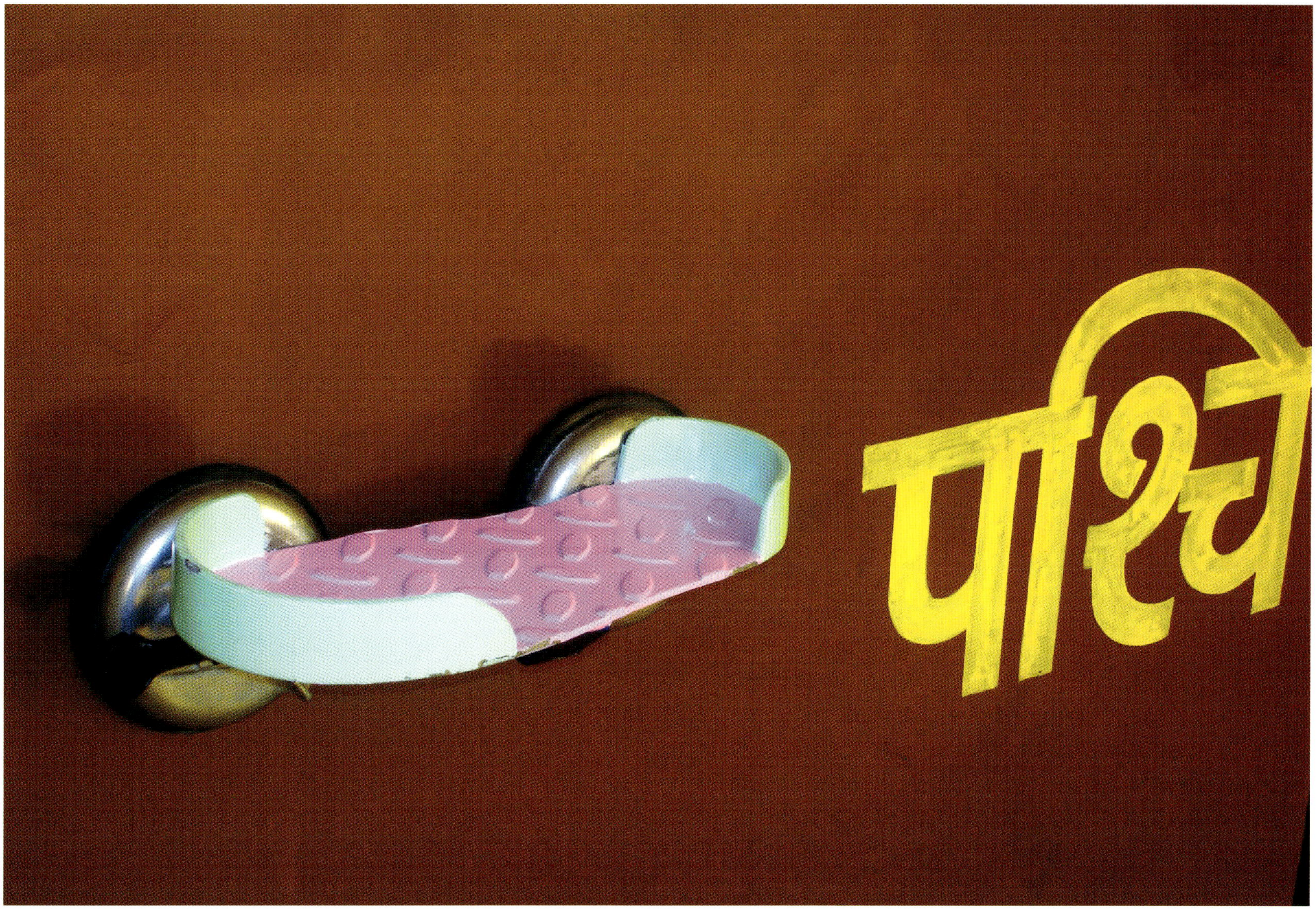

TUSHAR JOAG
UNICELL: Commuter Attachment Systems (C.A.S.) for Local Trains Series, 2005

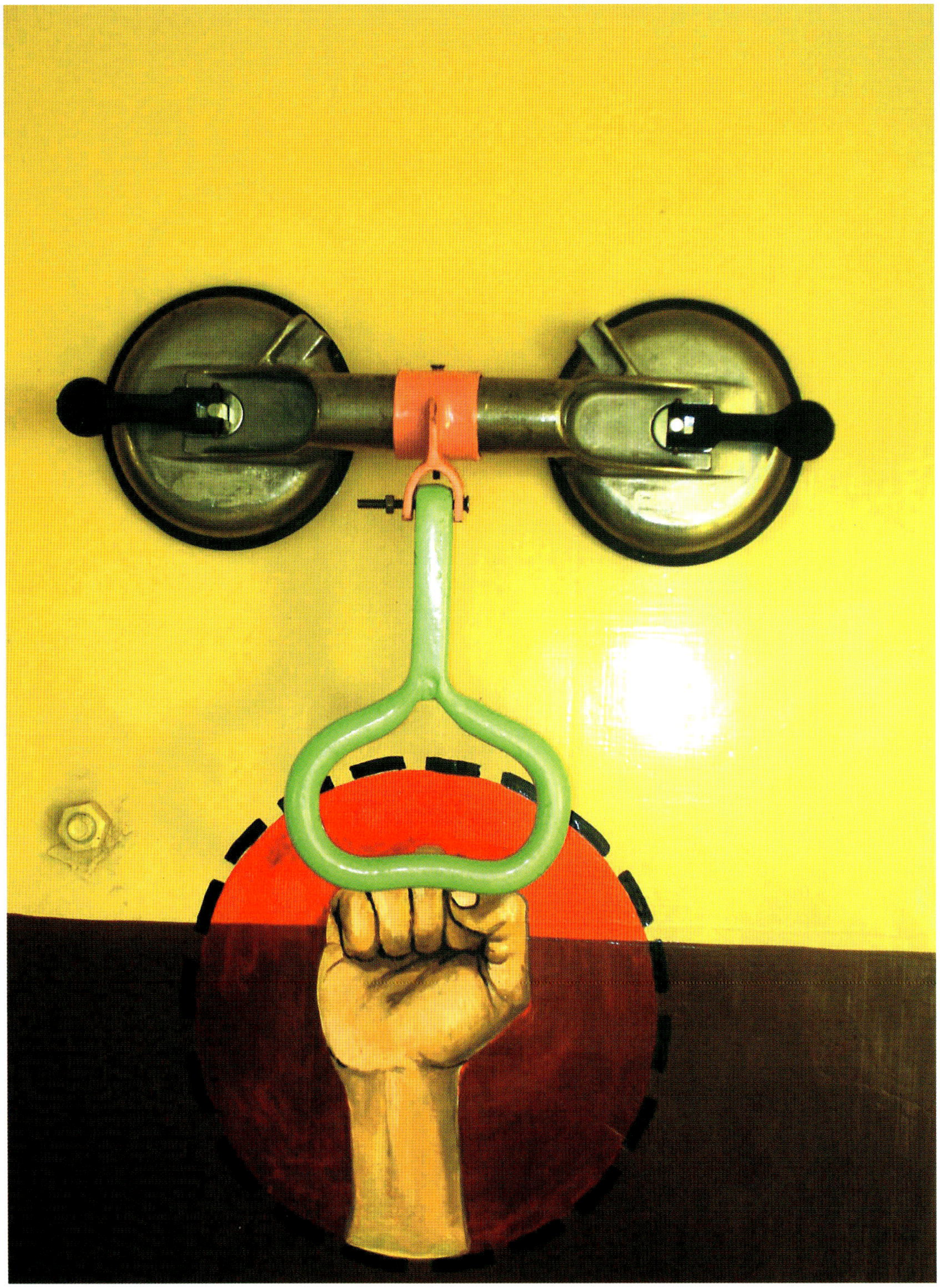

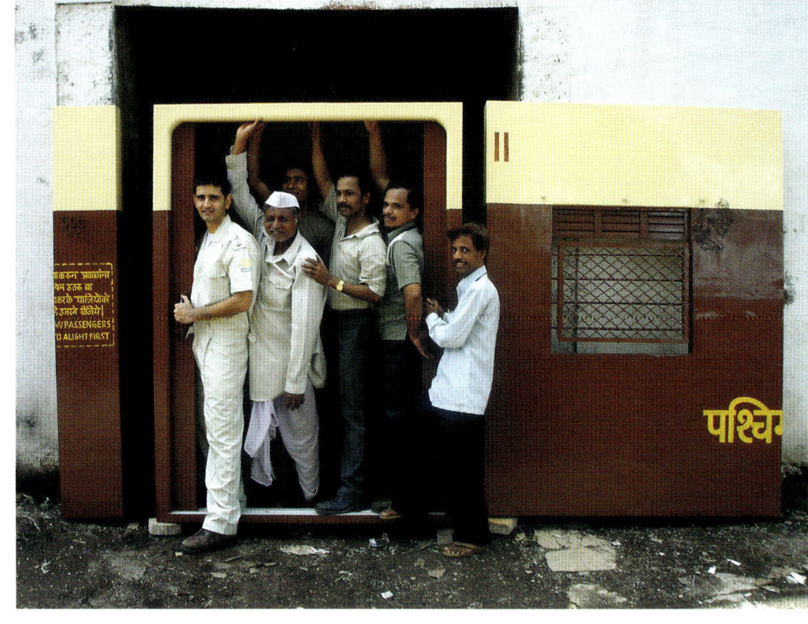

TUSHAR JOAG
UNICELL: Commuter Attachment Systems (C.A.S.) for Local Trains Series, 2005

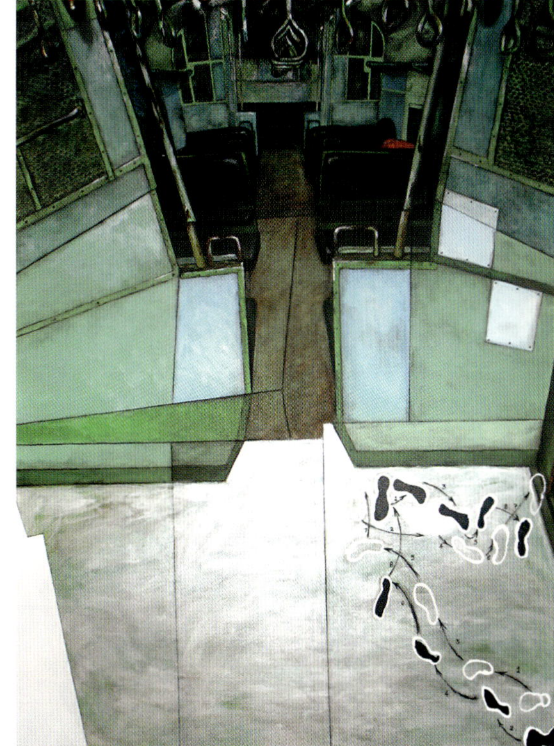

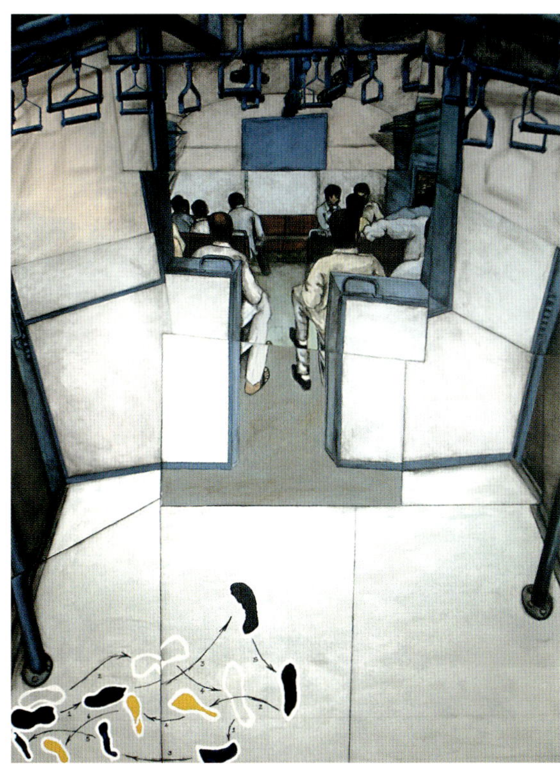

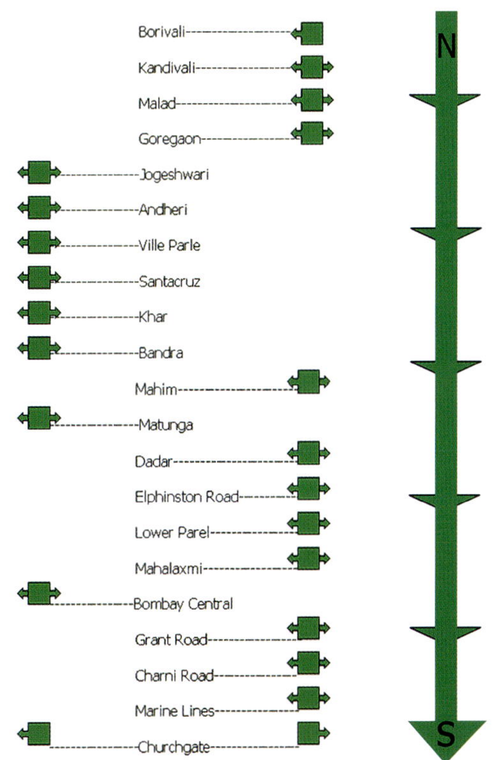

TUSHAR JOAG
UNICELL: Locomotion Course Series, 2008

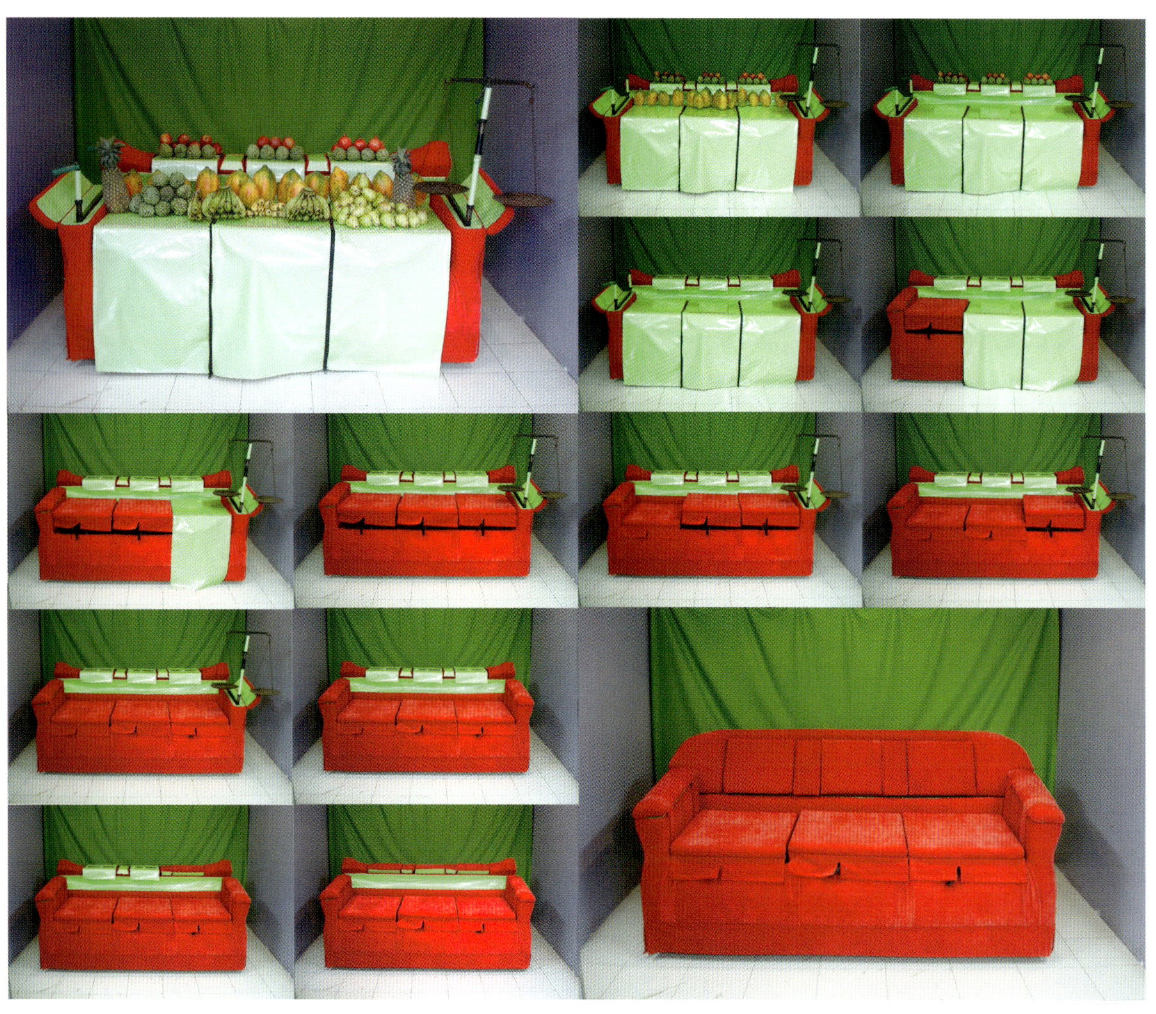

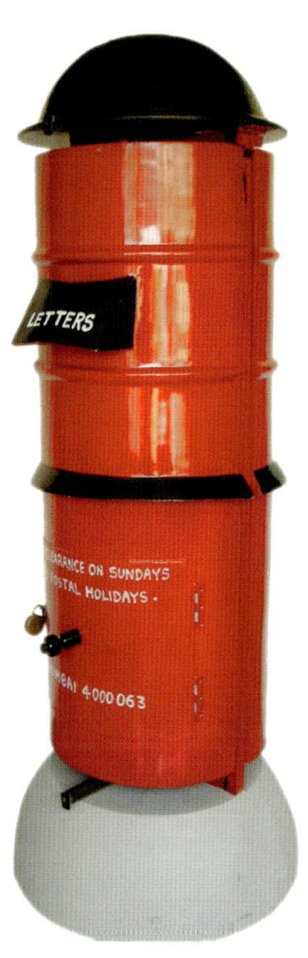

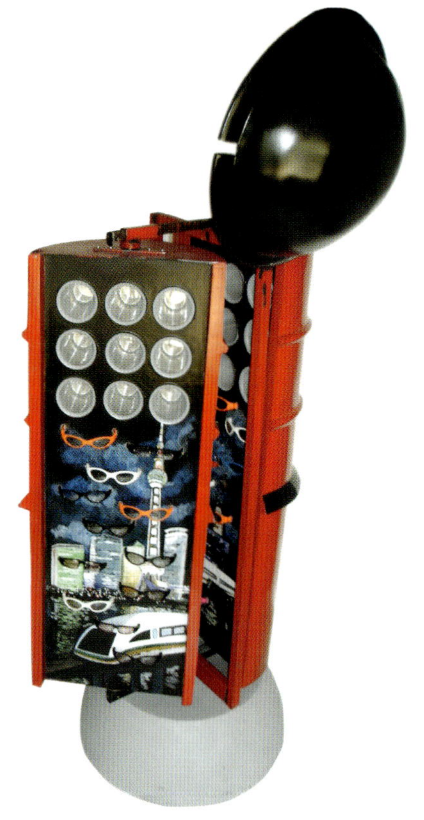

TUSHAR JOAG
UNICELL: Street Vendors Mimetic Scheme (S.V.M.S.) Series:
Shanghai Couch, 2006
Mumbai to Shanghai Post Box 1, 2007

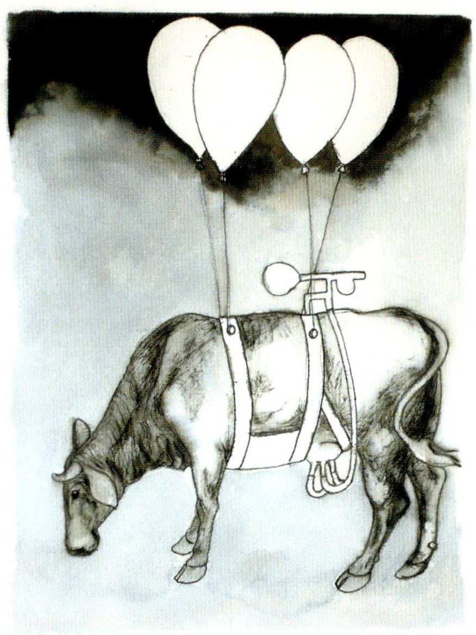

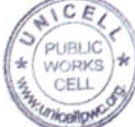

The clearance to increase the dam height to 121.92 M will affect 35,000 families by submerging their houses and lands. The rehabilitation is yet to be completed but the work on the dam though has begun full swing and submergence is expected by June.
UNICELL has designed inflatable apparatus to keep the cattle, humans and even their cultivations afloat.
APRIL 2006

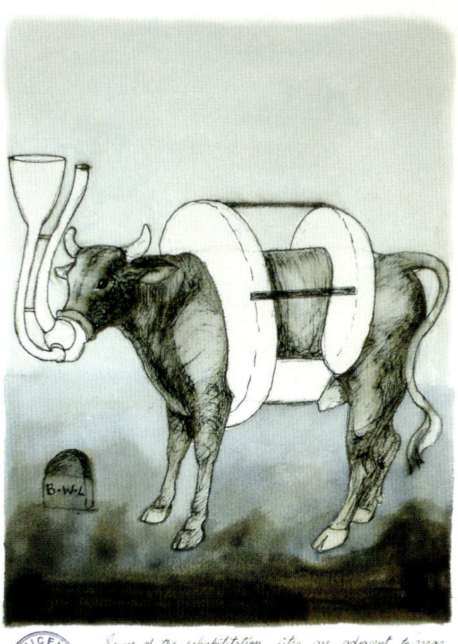

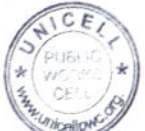

Some of the rehabilitation sites are adjacent to areas having Back Water level markers. It is possible that even the rehabilitation sites will be submerged (as has happened in the case of Bargi dam in the villages of Bijasen, Sarangpur, Larra, Anakwada, Padmi, Sahajpuri, Maili, Gumti etc.). Thus increasing the significance of the UNICELL floatation equipment.
APRIL 2006

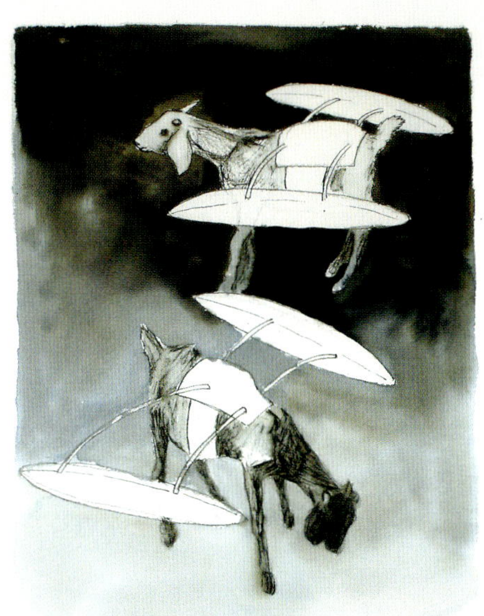

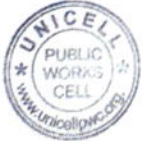

The Madhya Pradesh Government does not have cultivable land to offer to the ousted. In Maharashtra the rehabilitation is yet to be completed. The work on the dam though has begun full swing and submergence is expected by June. Since the State Governments have failed to resettle 35,000 families UNICELL has designed inflatable apparatus to keep the cattle, humans and even their cultivations afloat.
APRIL 2006

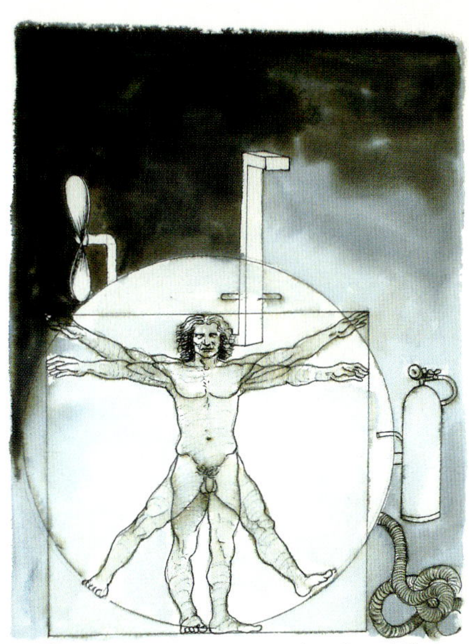

UNICELL PUBLIC WORKS CELL www.unicellpwc.org

UNICELL public works cell opens a rehabilitation and aid office: This office has been set up to facilitate the rehabilitation process of the dam affected Adivasis and farmer families in the Narmada valley. There is a danger that these project affected people might move into our cities and add to our misery (as it is we don't have enough space to park our cars)
Since the state governments have failed to rehabilitate them, UNICELL has designed flotation apparatus to ensure that they remain where they are.

TUSHAR JOAG
UNICELL: Flotaion Devices for the Narmada Dam Affected People, 2005–08

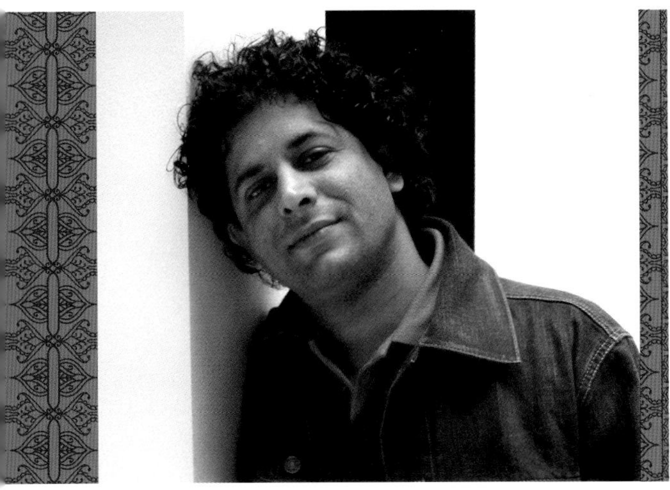

anant joshi

ANANT JOSHI Geboren 1969 in Nagpur, Maharashtra / Lebt in Mumbai
Born 1969 in Nagpur, Maharashtra / Lives in Mumbai

Nachdem Joshi 1994 die Sir J.J. School of Fine Arts, Mumbai, mit dem Bachelor of Arts abgeschlossen hatte, erwarb er 1996 noch den Master of Fine Arts. Während seines Studienaufenthalts an der Rijksakademie van Beeldende Kunsten, Amsterdam (2002–03), schuf Joshi vor allem dreidimensionale Keramikarbeiten. Er begann sich für die Eigenschaften von Schatten und die Reflektion und Brechung des Lichts beim Auftreffen auf diese Keramikarbeiten zu interessieren. Obwohl Joshi zur Zeit vor allem an Bildern und Installationen arbeitet, die er mit komischen Elementen versieht, sind seine Themen von der zunehmenden Verstädterung und Komplexität der modernen Gesellschaft geprägt, von den Aspekten, die in diesem Zusammenhang vernachlässigt werden und den nachteiligen Folgen, die daraus entstehen könnten. Joshis jüngste Installationen haben auch einen szenischen Anstrich, woraus sich räumliche Beziehungen zwischen den einzelnen Komponenten ergeben.

Joshis Beitrag für die Ausstellung, die Arbeit „Navel One and the Many“ (2007), ist ein für den Künstler charakteristisches Werk. Auf beiden Seiten eines Maschinenraums wurde Platz für die Betrachter geschaffen. An den Wänden der einen Seite des Maschinenraums befinden sich riesige „Rahmen“, die wie Schaufenster wirken. Durch ein Fenster sieht man Reihen rotierender, bunter Superhero-Figuren, die auf indischen Märkten billig zu haben sind. Ein Lichtstrahl aus einer Quelle jenseits der Figuren projektiert die Schatten der Betrachter wirkungsvoll auf die dahinter liegende Wand. In der Aussparung auf der anderen Seite des Raums bieten sich den Betrachtern Reihen rotierender Rasierklingen, die an Jalousien erinnern. Die an die Wand projizierten Schatten verändern ihre Form mit den Bewegungen der sich beteiligenden Betrachter und der Richtung des Lichtstrahls. In beiden Räumen werden die ineinander fließenden Bilder zerstückelt, vervielfacht und verwandelt. Ihre Komplexität ist ein Hinweis auf das Gewaltpotenzial und die Widersprüchlichkeit des modernen städtischen Lebens, das gekennzeichnet ist vom Wohnen auf engem Raum und von einer Sintflut an Informationen. In diesen unsicheren Zeiten, in denen man besorgt in die Zukunft blickt, entsteht ein wachsender Trend zum Individualismus. Das Werk könnte eine

After graduating from Sir J.J. School of Fine Arts in 1994 with a BFA, Joshi went on to obtain an MFA in 1996. During his residency at Rijksakademie van Beeldende Kunsten, Amsterdam (2002–03), Joshi focused on creating three-dimensional ceramic works. He began to develop an interest in the characteristics of shadows and the reflection and refraction of light when light is directed at these ceramic works. Although Joshi's current focus is on creating paintings and installations containing a comical element, his subject matter is informed by growing urbanization and the complexity of modern society, the elements that are overlooked during this process, and the harmful consequences possibly caused. Joshi's recent installations also feature a sense of spectacle that conveys the correlation between the various components in that space.

Joshi's submission for this exhibition is *Navel One and the Many* (2007), one of his representative works. Viewers' spaces have been created on either side of a machine room. On the walls of one side of the machine room are enormous "frames" that resemble display windows. Through one window, one can see rotating, rows of the sort of colourful superhero figurines sold cheaply at Indian markets. A beam of light from a source beyond the figures effectively projects the shadows of the observers onto the wall behind. In the space on the other side of the room, the viewer can see rotating rows of razorblades that look like blinds. The shadows projected onto the wall change shape with the movement of the involuntarily participating viewer, the components of the work and the direction of the beam. In both spaces, the blending images become fragmented, multiply, and are transformed. Their complexity hints at the violence and contradiction of modern urban life, marked by high density living and a deluge of information. There is a growing move towards individualism during these unstable times when the future remains unclear. This could be Joshi's warning to the viewer, who is also part of the space, of the dangers of unquestioningly accepting urban life and its almost schizophrenic nature.

Major exhibitions include "Body.City: Siting Contemporary Culture in India" (Haus der Kulturen der Welt [House of the World Cultures], Berlin, 2003), "Have We Met?" (The

Warnung vor den Gefahren einer unkritischen Akzeptanz des fast schizophrenen urbanen Lebens sein, die Joshi an die Betrachter richtet, welche ebenfalls Teil des Raumes sind.

Wichtige Ausstellungen: „Body.City: Siting Contemporary Culture in India" (Haus der Kulturen der Welt [House of the World Cultures], Berlin, 2003), „Have We Met?" (The Japan Foundation, Tokyo, 2004), und „Indian Summer: la Jeune Scène Artistique Indienne" (École Nationale Supérieure des Beaux-Arts, Paris, 2005). (KM)

Japan Foundation, Tokyo, 2004), and "Indian Summer: la Jeune Scène Artistique Indienne" (École Nationale Supérieure des Beaux-Arts, Paris, 2005). (KM)

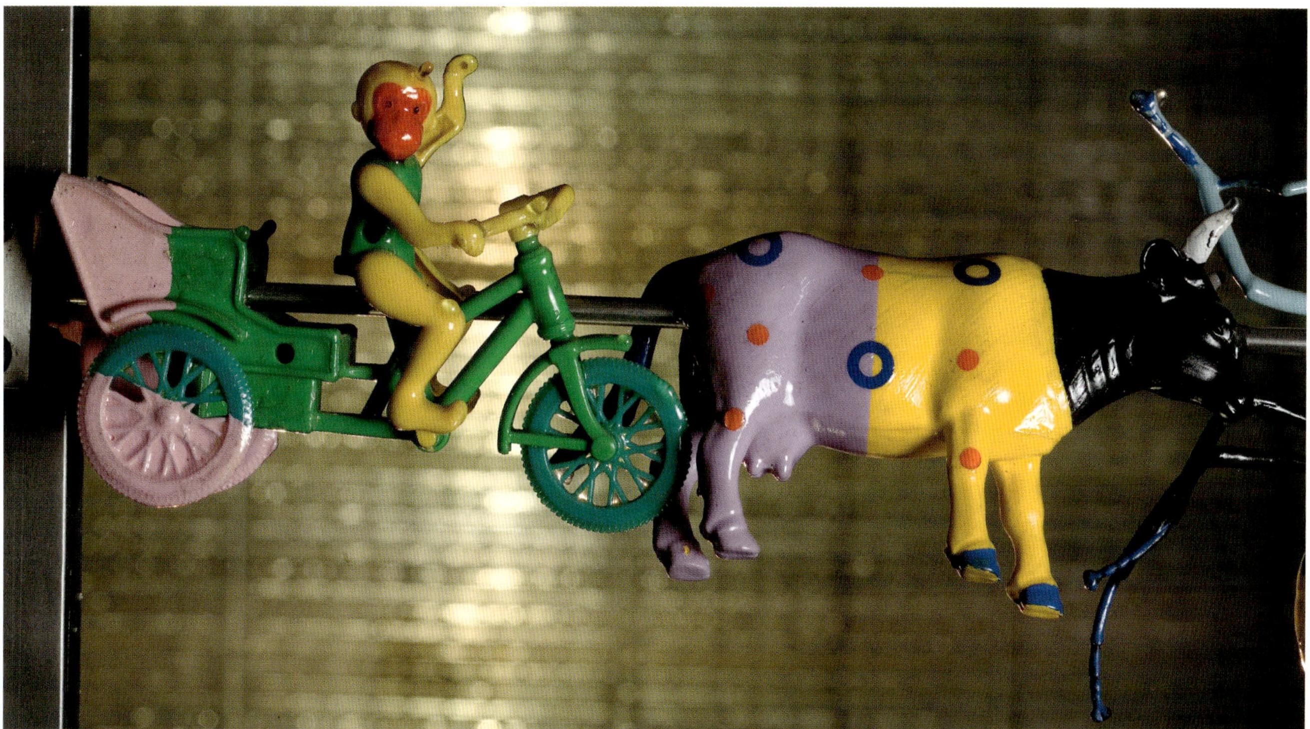

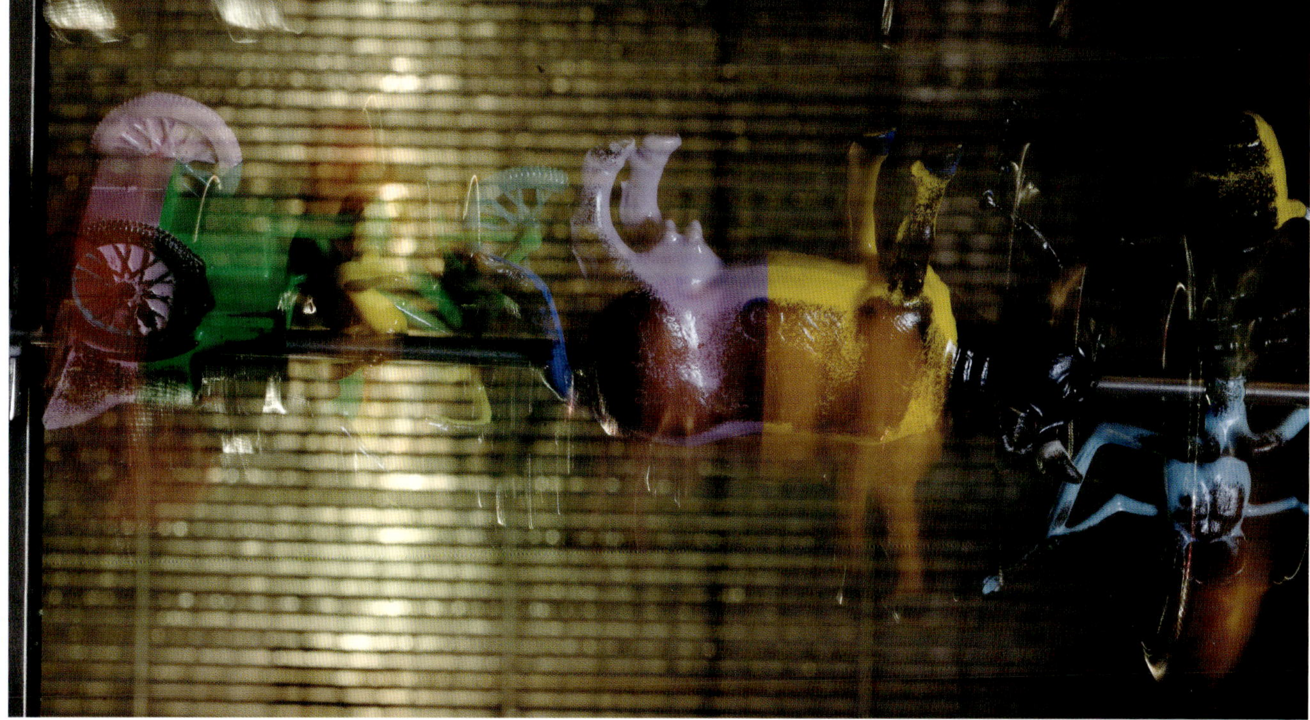

ANANT JOSHI
Navel One and the Many, 2007 (Detail)

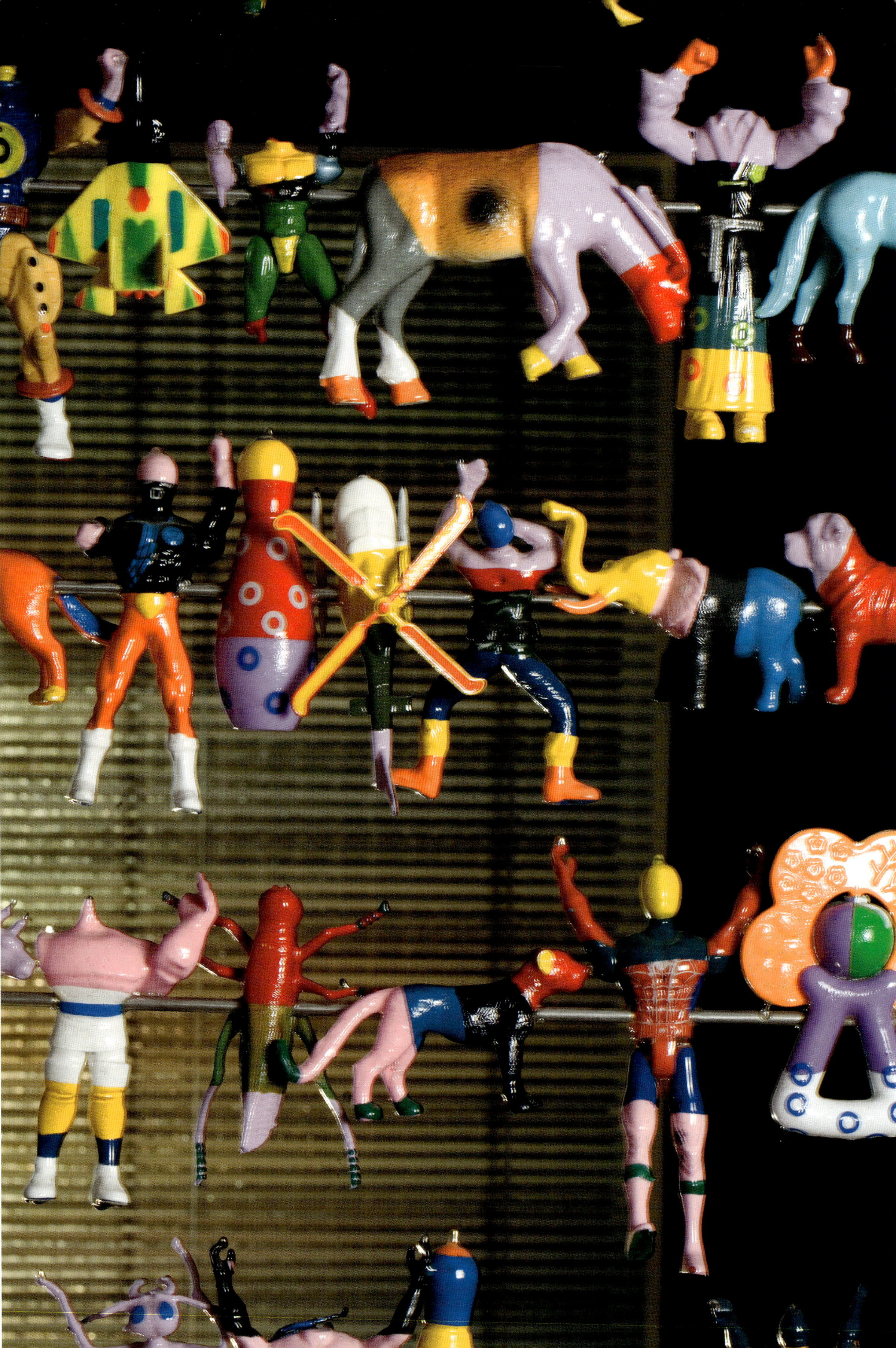

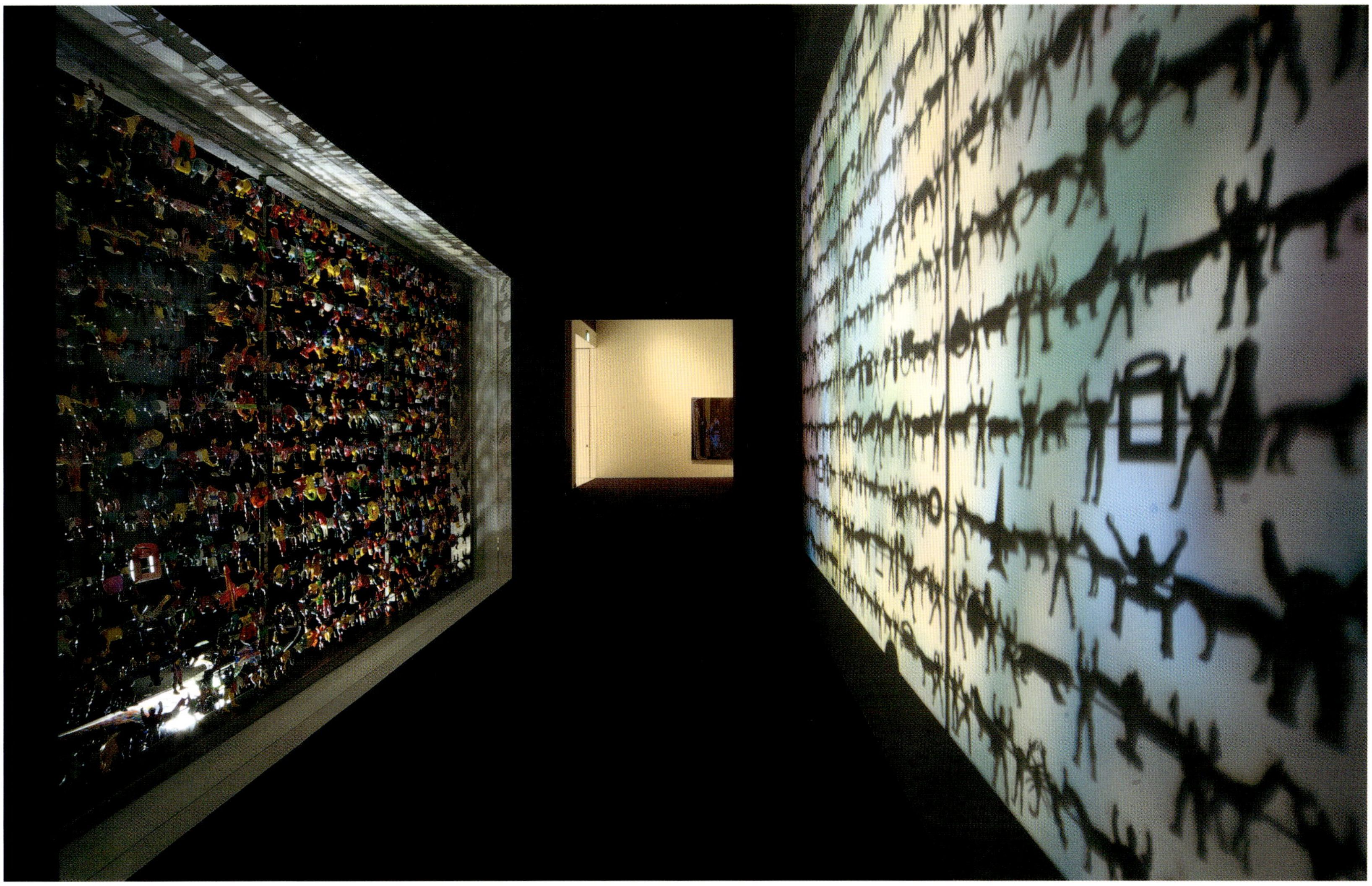

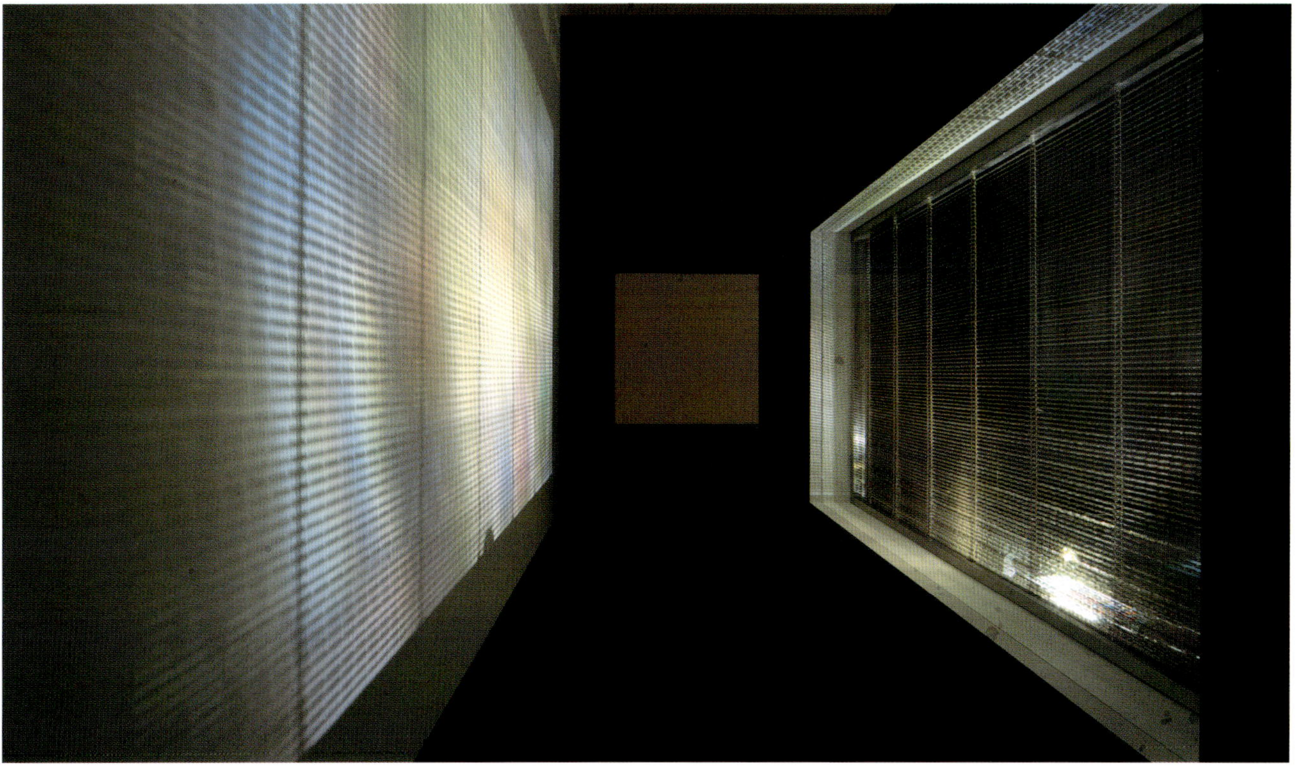

ANANT JOSHI
Navel One and the Many, 2007

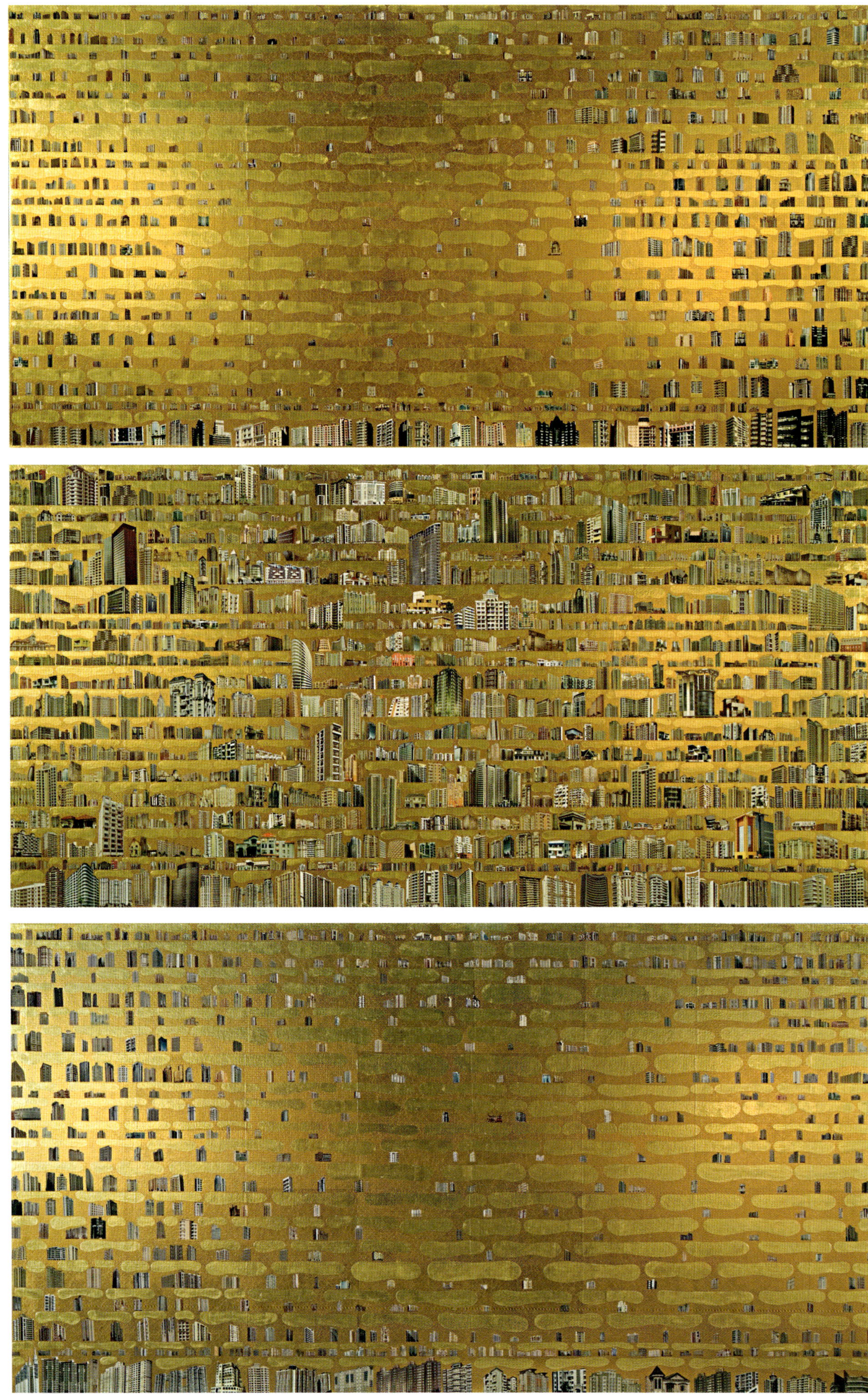

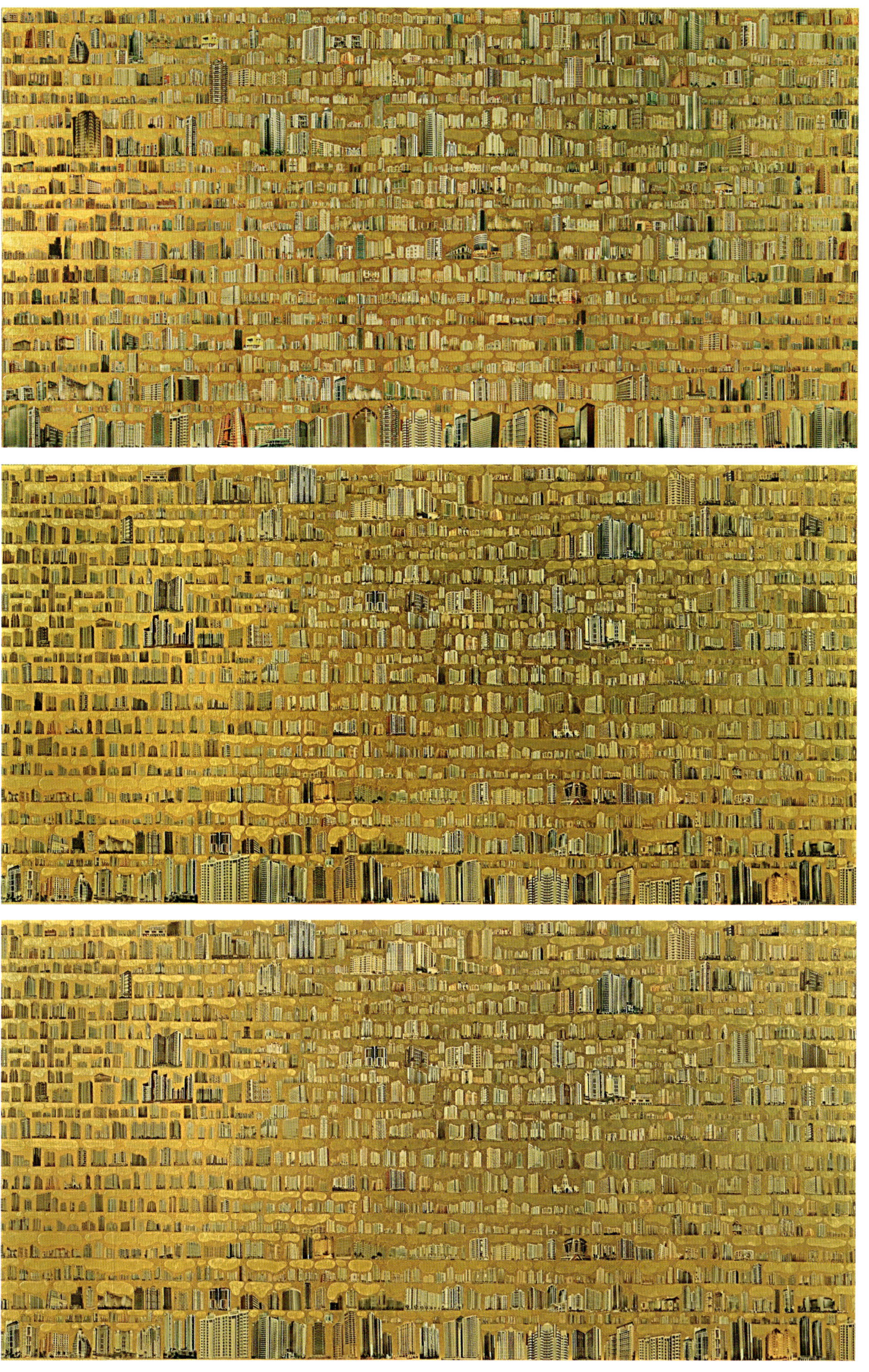

ANANT JOSHI
May Look Closer Than They Appear, 2008

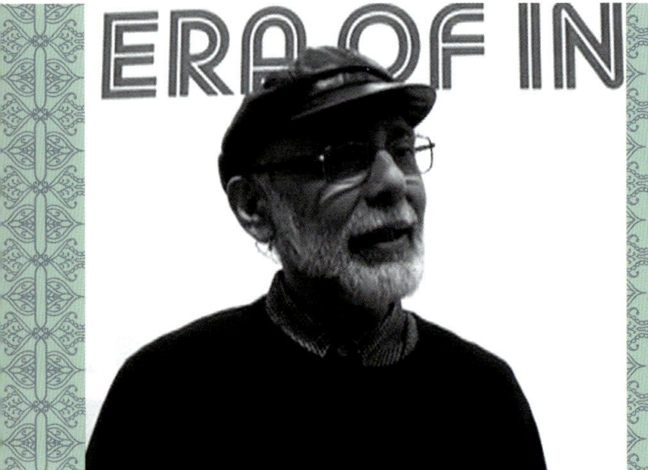

ranbir kaleka

RANBIR KALEKA Geboren 1953 in Patiala, Punjab / Lebt in Delhi
Born 1953 in Patiala, Punjab / Lives in Delhi

Nach Abschluss seines Studiums am College of Art an der Punjab University und seiner Lehrtätigkeit an der Kunstfakultät einer indischen Universität ging Kaleka nach England und erwarb 1987 einen Master in Malerei am Royal College of Art. Kaleka gilt als neoexpressionistischer Maler, der mit kräftiger Palette eine Welt voller Geschichten darstellt. Nachdem er sich in London als Künstler etabliert hatte, kehrte er Mitte der 1990er Jahre nach Indien zurück, wo er begann, die Malerei mit Video zu verbinden und mit dieser neuen Technik Installationen entwickelte. Bis heute kombiniert er in seinen Arbeiten beide Genres.

„Man Threading a Needle" (1999) ist Kalekas erstes Werk, in dem Malerei und Video gepaart sind. Videobilder werden auf eine Leinwand projiziert, auf der Kaleka einen Mann darstellt, der eine Nadel einzufädeln versucht, das leichte Zittern seiner Hände und das Blinzeln der Augen wiedergebend. Kaleka lässt Videoelemente – Licht und Zeit – in das unbewegliche Medium des zweidimensionalen Bildes einfließen. Dadurch werden die Grenzen zwischen Vorstellung und sichtbarer Wirklichkeit verwischt. „Man with Cockerel" (2002) ist ein Video in Endlosschleife, auf dem ein Mann, mit einem Hahn in der Hand, bis zum Bauch im Wasser steht und immer wieder erscheint und verschwindet, womit die Unbeständigkeit und Ungewissheit des Daseins versinnbildlicht wird. In „Crossings" (2005), die hier gezeigte Arbeit Kalekas, entfalten sich auf vier bemalten Projektionsflächen die „Geschichten" eines Mannes, der einen Turban färbt oder von einem Vogelverkäufer, um uns etwas von der Welt zu vermitteln, in der wir leben. Der Turban symbolisiert die Religion und die Gemeinschaft der Sikh. Das Video zeigt den Transport der bunt gefärbten Turbane in einem Koffer, auf dem immer wieder Aufnahmen von Kaleka – der selbst ein Sikh ist – beim Überschreiten der Grenze von Punjab nach England und zurück in den Punjab eingeblendet werden. Wahrscheinlich soll damit auf die soziale Identität der Sikhs angespielt werden. Durch die Verflechtung unterschiedlicher Elemente mit dem Faktor Zeit schafft Kaleka eine fantastische Welt, die allerdings mit Darstellungen der Lebensrealität Indiens und der indischen Gesellschaft unterlegt wird.

After graduating from the College of Art, Punjab University and teaching Art at an Indian university, Kaleka moved to England where he obtained an MA in Painting at the Royal College of Art in 1987. Kaleka can arguably be considered as a neo-expressionist painter who uses a powerful palette to depict a world rich in narrative. After establishing a career as an artist in London, he returned to India in the mid-90s, during which time he began creating installations featuring a new technique of integrating painting and video. He continues to create work incorporating both genres.

Man Threading a Needle (1999) is Kaleka's first work integrating painting and video. Video images were projected onto the canvas, onto which Kaleka has depicted a man attempting to thread a needle, recreating his slightly trembling hands and blinking eyes. He incorporates the elements of video – light and time – onto the stationary medium of a two-dimensional painting. The result is the blurring of the boundaries between illusion and what one is actually seeing. *Man with Cockerel* (2002) is a looped video of a man holding a cockerel and standing up to his waist in water, appearing and disappearing, depicting the impermanence and uncertainty of existence. In *Crossings* (2005), Kaleka's representative work, the "stories" of a man dyeing a turban, or of a bird seller, unfold on four painted screens to convey the world surrounding us. The turban is symbol of the Sikh religion and community, and the video features the turbans dyed in a variety of colours and being transported in a suitcase, onto which the repeated images of Kaleka, himself a Sikh, crossing the border from the Punjab to England and back to the Punjab, are superimposed. It arguably alludes to the social identity of Sikhs. In this way, Kaleka interweaves diverse elements and time to create a fantastical world. Underpinning this, however, are visual representations of the reality of life in India and Indian society.

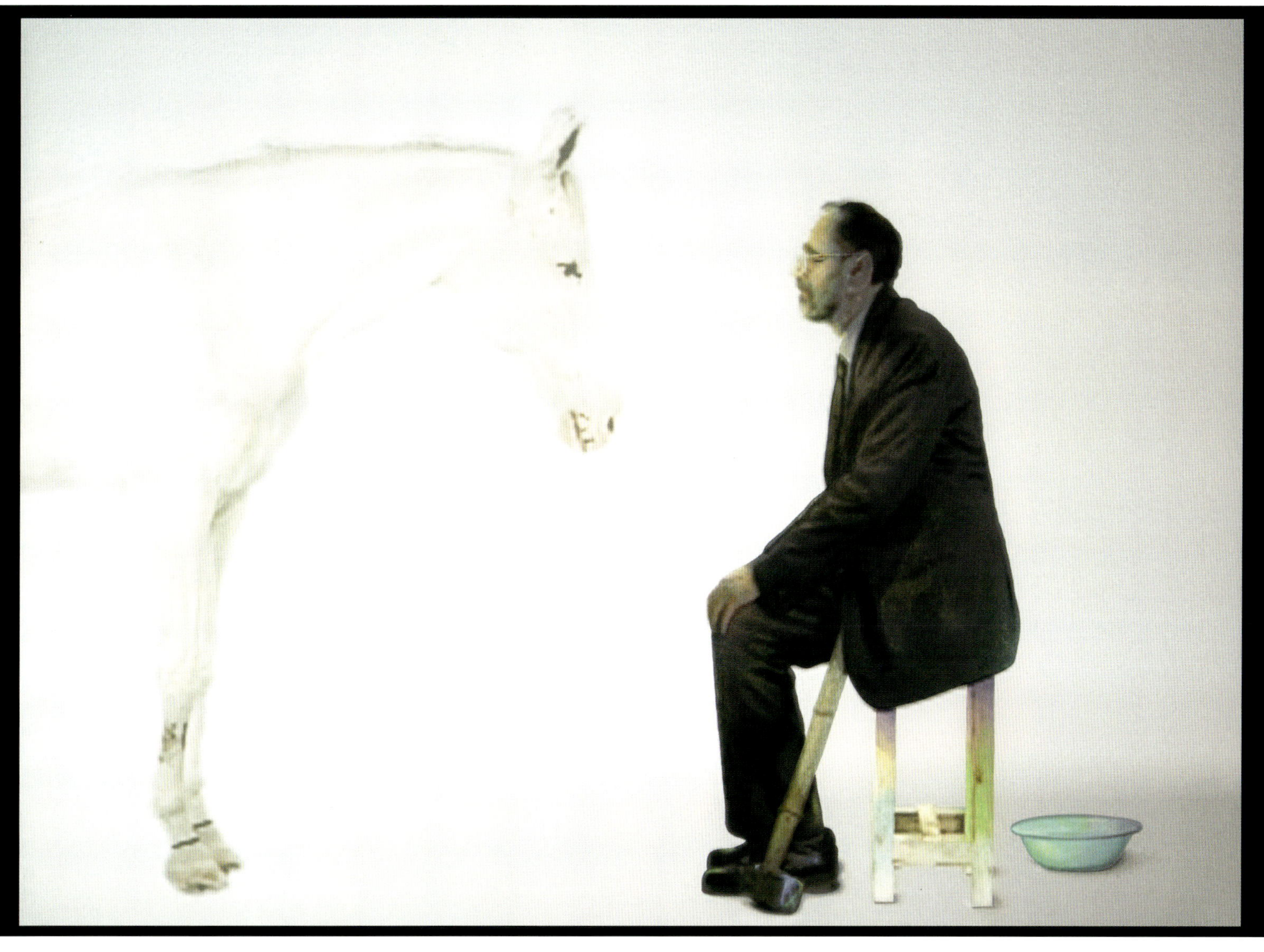

RANBIR KALEKA
Crossings, 2005

Wichtige Ausstellungen: „Body.City: Siting Contemporary Culture in India“ (Haus der Kulturen der Welt [House of the World Cultures], Berlin, 2003), „New Narratives: Contemporary Art from India“ (Chicago Cultural Center, 2007), und „Biennale of Sydney“ (Australia, 2008). (MT)

Major exhibitions include "Body.City: Siting Contemporary Culture in India" (Haus der Kulturen der Welt [House of the World Cultures], Berlin, 2003), "New Narratives: Contemporary Art from India" (Chicago Cultural Center, 2007), and "Biennale of Sydney" (Australia, 2008). (MT)

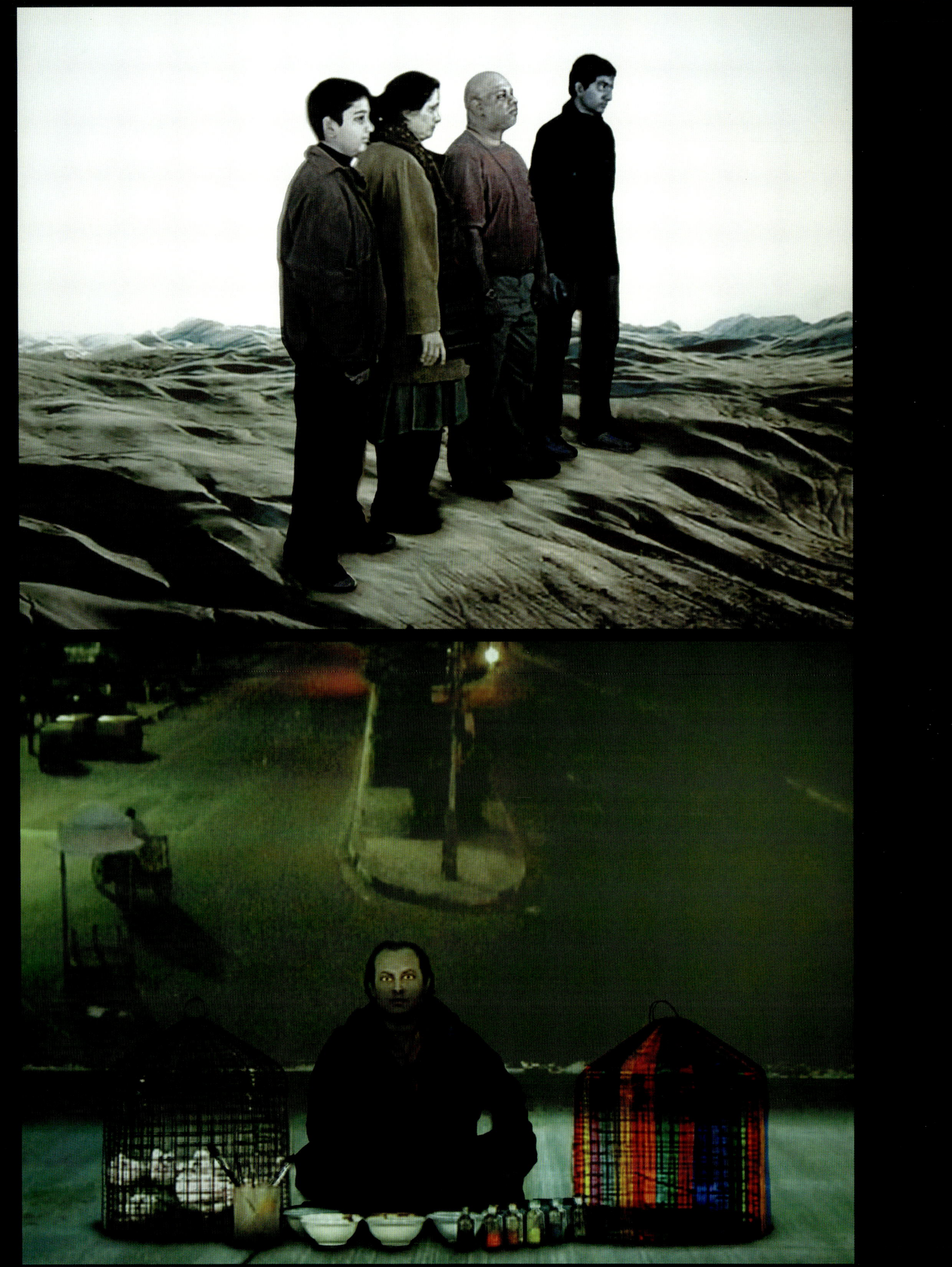

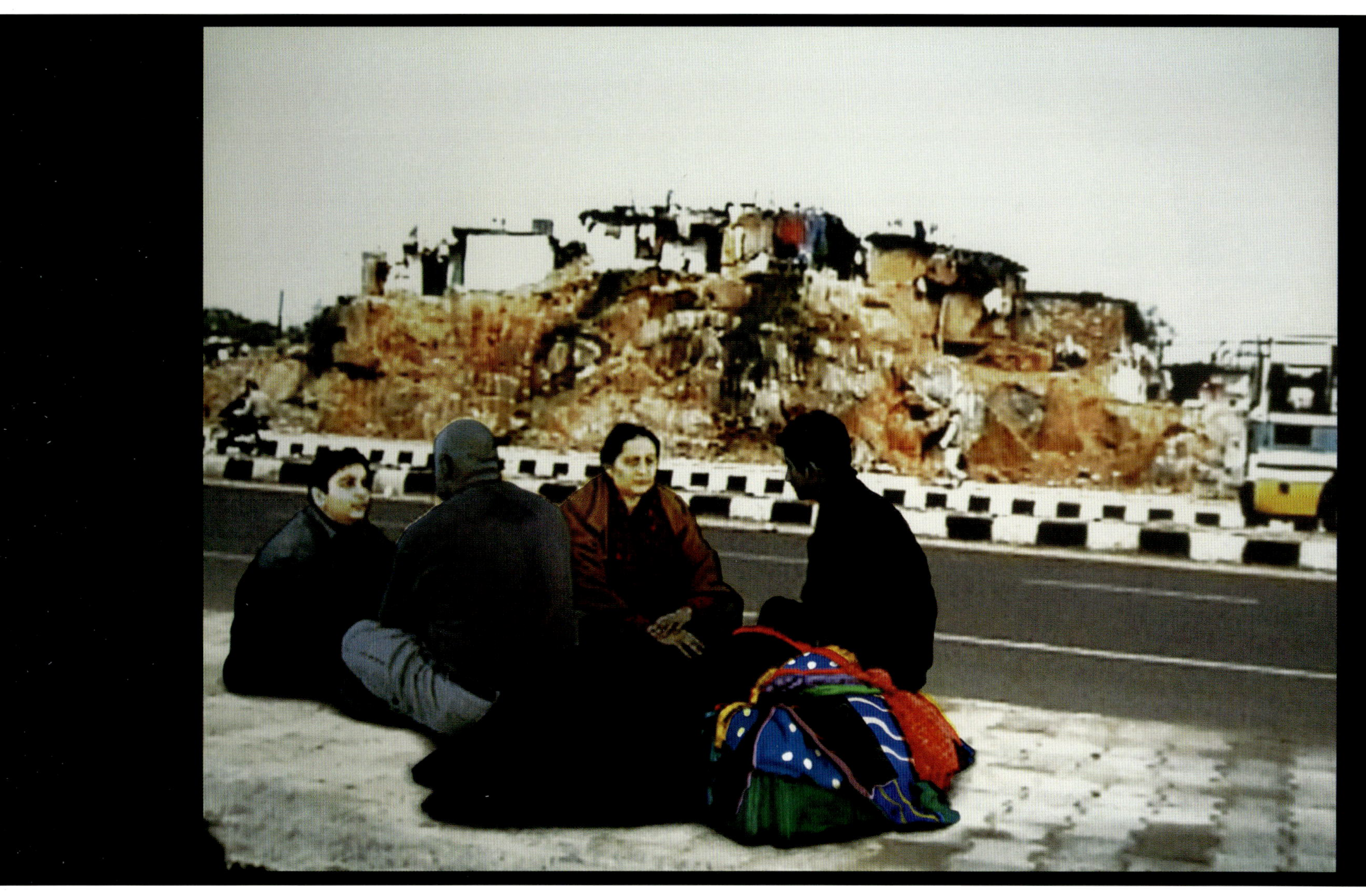

RANBIR KALEKA
Crossings, 2005

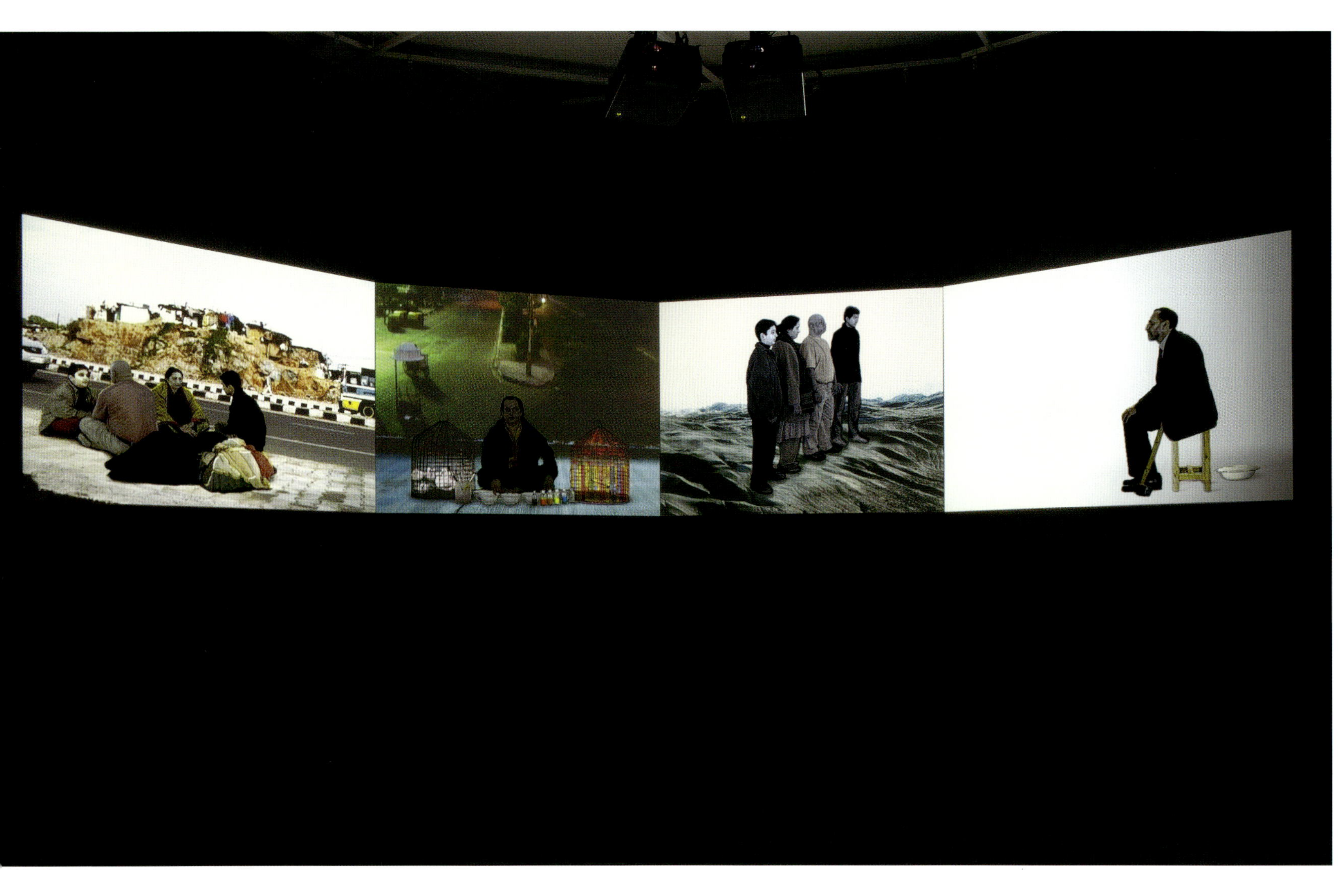

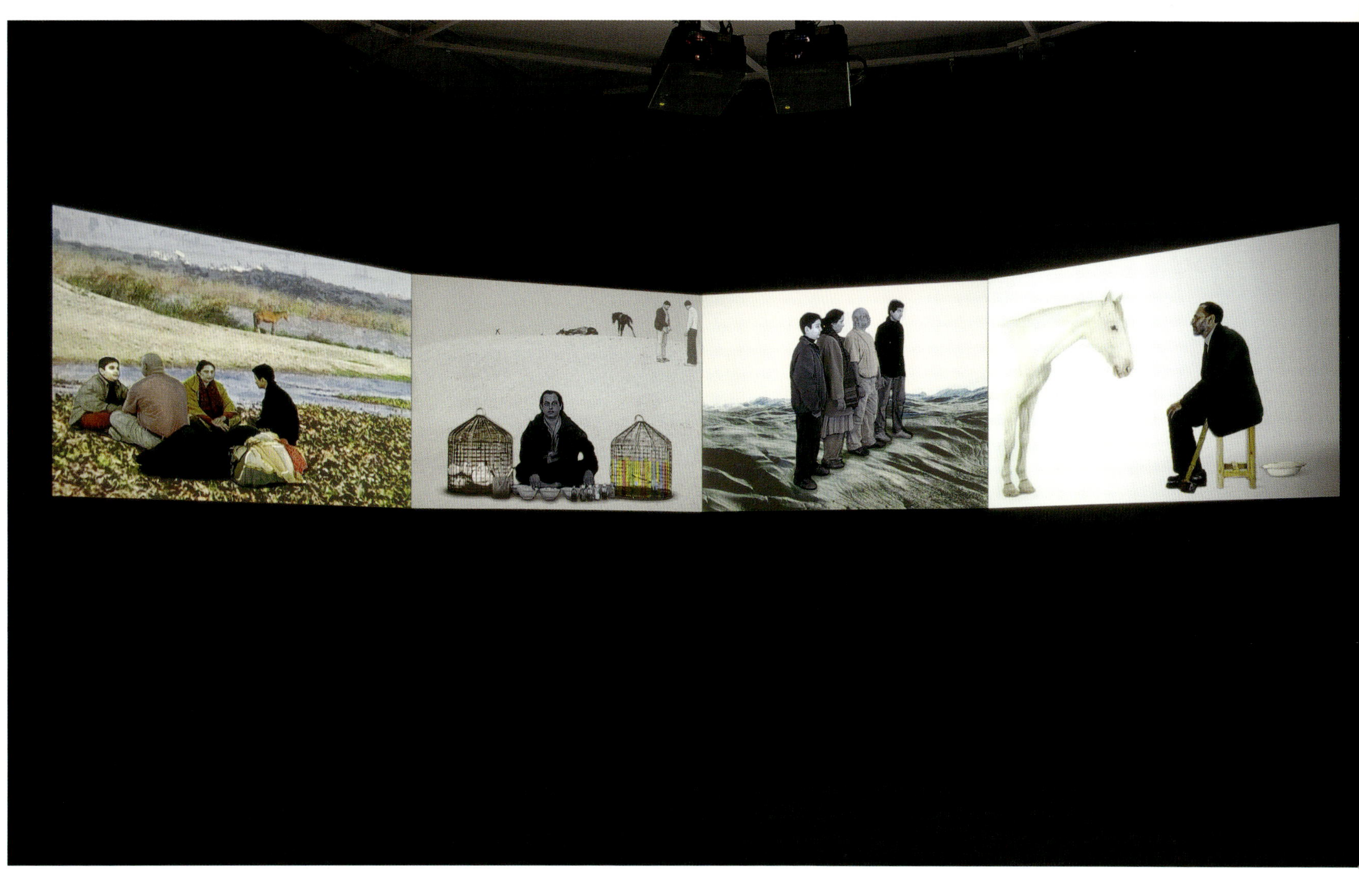

RANBIR KALEKA
Crossings, 2005

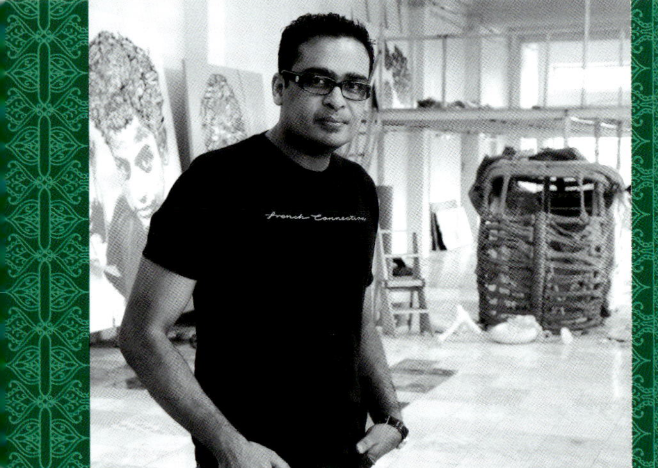

jitish kallat

JITISH KALLAT Geboren 1974 in Mumbai / Lebt in Mumbai
Born 1974 in Mumbai / Lives in Mumbai

Kallat studierte als Hauptfach Malerei an der Sir J.J. School of Fine Arts in Mumbai; nach Abschluss des Studiums mit einem BFA im Jahr 1996 schloss er ein Jahr an der Sir J.J. School of Fine Arts Post-Graduate School an. Kallat schuf zunächst Bilder unter Verwendung von glyzerin-, klebstoff- und metallpulverhaltigem Pigment. In die entstandene Schicht ritzte er mit Hilfe einer speziellen Technik Linien, so dass eine wellige Oberfläche entstand. Er verwendete diese Technik, um den Wandel zu vermitteln, den Mumbai durchgemacht hat – das von der Liberalisierung der indischen Wirtschaft in den 1990er Jahren und dem aufkommenden religiösen Fundamentalismus sehr stark betroffen war – und um sich selbst vor dem Hintergrund dieses Wandels darzustellen. Kallat verwendet Motive wie von Autos wimmelnde Straßen, von Kindern als Straßenhändler, Filmplakate, von Grafitti bedeckte Wände und das Internet, um die urbane Dynamik darzustellen. Gleichzeitig möchte er auf den Tod durch Terrorismus oder Armut und auf das Leid hinweisen, das eine Wettbewerbsgesellschaft mit sich bringt. In seinem Bemühen, den durch die rasante gesellschaftliche Entwicklung ausgelösten Wandel möglichst eindrucksvoll darzustellen, beschäftigt sich Kallat seit 2003 auch eingehend mit Medien wie Fotografie, Bildhauerei und Installation.

Kallat zeigt in der Ausstellung drei Werke: „Autosaurus Tripous“ (2007) ist die Glasfaserskulptur einer Auto-Rikscha, die aussieht, als hätte man sie aus Tier- oder Menschenknochen zusammengebaut. Die Oberfläche der Rikscha wirkt rau, als wäre sie durch lodernde Flammen gefahren. Diese Arbeit wurde von einem Konflikt zwischen Hindu- und Muslimfundamentalisten in Mumbai inspiriert und verweist auf die Gefahren, die von einzelnen ethnischen oder religiösen Gruppen ausgehen, die sich zusammenschließen, um in Mumbai – einer Stadt, die sich zu einem multiethnischen und multikulturellen Ballungsgebiet entwickelt hat – die Vormachtstellung zu erlangen. In „Death of Distance“ (2006) hängt eine Reihe von 5 gerahmten Linsenrasterbildern hinter der Skulptur einer 1-Rupie-Münze. Die holografischen Linsen enthalten zwei Artikel, die aus unterschiedlichen Blickwinkeln sichtbar werden: der eine berichtet davon, dass für nicht mehr als eine Rupie pro Minute von einem Ende Indiens zum

Kallat majored in painting at Sir J.J. School of Fine Arts, and after graduating in 1996 with a BFA, spent the following year at the Sir J.J. School of Fine Arts Post-Graduate School. Kallat initially produced paintings using pigment containing glycerine, glue and powdered metal. He used a unique technique of scratching lines onto the surface to create an undulating surface. He used this technique to convey the transformation undergone by Mumbai – which has been so affected by the deregulation of the Indian economy during the 1990s and the emergence of religious fundamentalism – as well as the artist himself against the background of this transformation. By employing motifs such as roads teeming with cars, child vendors, movie billboards, graffittied walls, and the Internet, Kallat depicts urban dynamism, while also referring to death as a result of terrorism or poverty, and the suffering created by a competitive society. Since 2003, Kallat has also explored media such as photography, sculptures, and installations to convey the changes of rapidly developing society most effectively.

Kallat has submitted three works in this exhibition. *Autosaurus Tripous* (2007) is a fibreglass sculpture of an auto rickshaw that appears to be assembled with animal or human bones. The surface of the rickshaw has a rough quality, as though it has travelled through a ferocious fire. This work, which was inspired by a conflict between Hindu Islamic and fundamentalists that took place in Mumbai, points out the sense of danger surrounding the existence of a movement by specific ethnic groups or religions to achieve supremacy in Mumbai, a city that has developed into a multi-ethnic and multi-cultural city. In *Death of Distance* (2006), a row of five framed lenticulars hang behind a sculpture of a 1 rupee coin. The holographic lenticulars, contain two articles visible from different angles: one about ultra-cheap telephone calls that can be made from one side of India to the other for only a rupee per minute, and another about a young girl who killed herself because she couldn't afford the 1 rupee school lunch. Which story is visible depends on where the observer is standing, effectively revealing the disparity in wealth between the cities and the regional areas. In *Artist Making Local Call* (2005), photographs were taken every two mi-

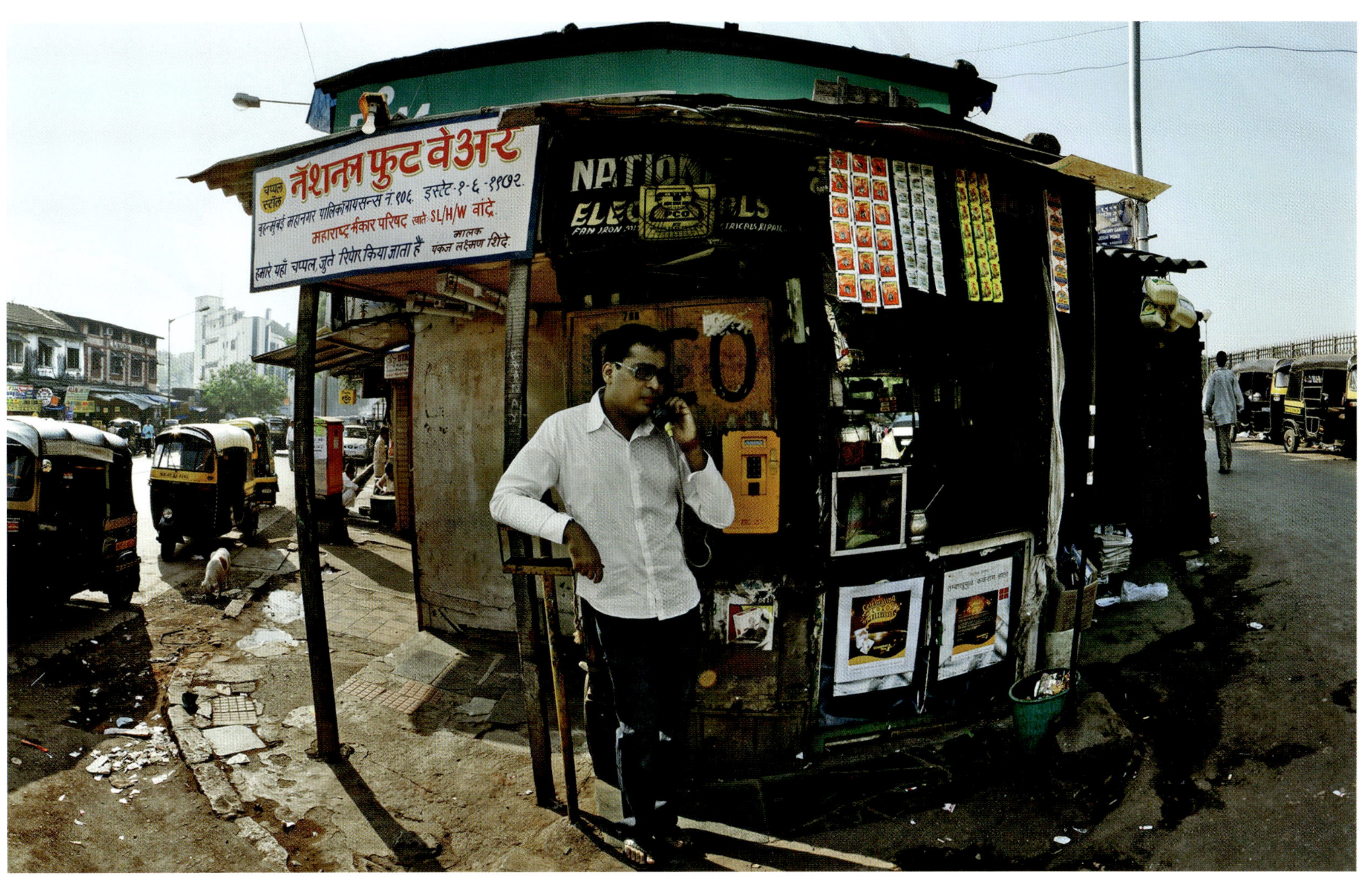

anderen telefoniert werden kann, der andere über ein junges Mädchen, das Selbstmord begangen hat, weil es sich die Schulspeisung zum Preis von 1 Rupie nicht leisten konnte. Es hängt von der Position des Betrachters ab, welcher Artikel sichtbar wird, womit das Wohlstandsgefälle zwischen Stadt und Land verdeutlicht wird. Für „Artist Making Local Call“ (2005) wurden in 2-Minuten-Intervallen Fotos gemacht. Die verschiedenen Zeitachsen wurden digital bearbeitet und so miteinander verlinkt, dass der Zeitablauf als Panoramalandschaft abgebildet wird. Die Stadtlandschaft erinnert an eine Szene auf einem Filmplakat und zeigt ein Taxi, das von einer Auto-Rikscha fotografisch überlagert wird sowie den Künstler beim Telefonieren in einer öffentlichen Telefonzelle in einer Straße von Mumbai. Das Werk ist ein Digitaldruck auf Netz-Vynil mit dem Effekt, dass ein wie von Hand gezeichnetes Plakat zu einem Leuchtschild wird, eine Fahrrad-Rikscha zu einem vierrädrigen Fahrzeug und ein Festnetztelefon zu einem Mobiltelefon, womit der Werdegang der Stadt in die Gegenwart symbolisiert wird.

Wichtige Ausstellungen: „The 1st Fukuoka Asian Art Triennale“ (Fukuoka Asian Art Museum, 1999), „Century City: Art and Culture in the Modern Metropolis“ (Tate Modern, London, 2001), und „Hungry God: Indian Contemporary Art“ (Wanderausstellung, ARARIO Peking etc., 2006–07). (TK)

nutes, and digital processing used to link the different time axes, so that the passing of time is depicted as a panoramic landscape. The urban landscape is reminiscent of a scene from a movie billboard and features an image of a taxi superimposed onto the afterimage of an auto rickshaw, as well as the artist himself depicted making a telephone call from a public phone booth on a Mumbai street. The work is a digital print on vinyl mesh so that the effect is of a hand-drawn billboard being transformed into light material, a trishaw being transformed into a four-wheeled vehicle, and a fixed phone transformed into a cell phone to depict this city as it moves towards a contemporary age.

Major exhibitions include “The 1st Fukuoka Asian Art Triennale” (Fukuoka Asian Art Museum, 1999), “Century City: Art and Culture in the Modern Metropolis” (Tate Modern, London, 2001), and “Hungry God: Indian Contemporary Art” (travelling exhibition, ARARIO Beijing and others, 2006–07). (TK)

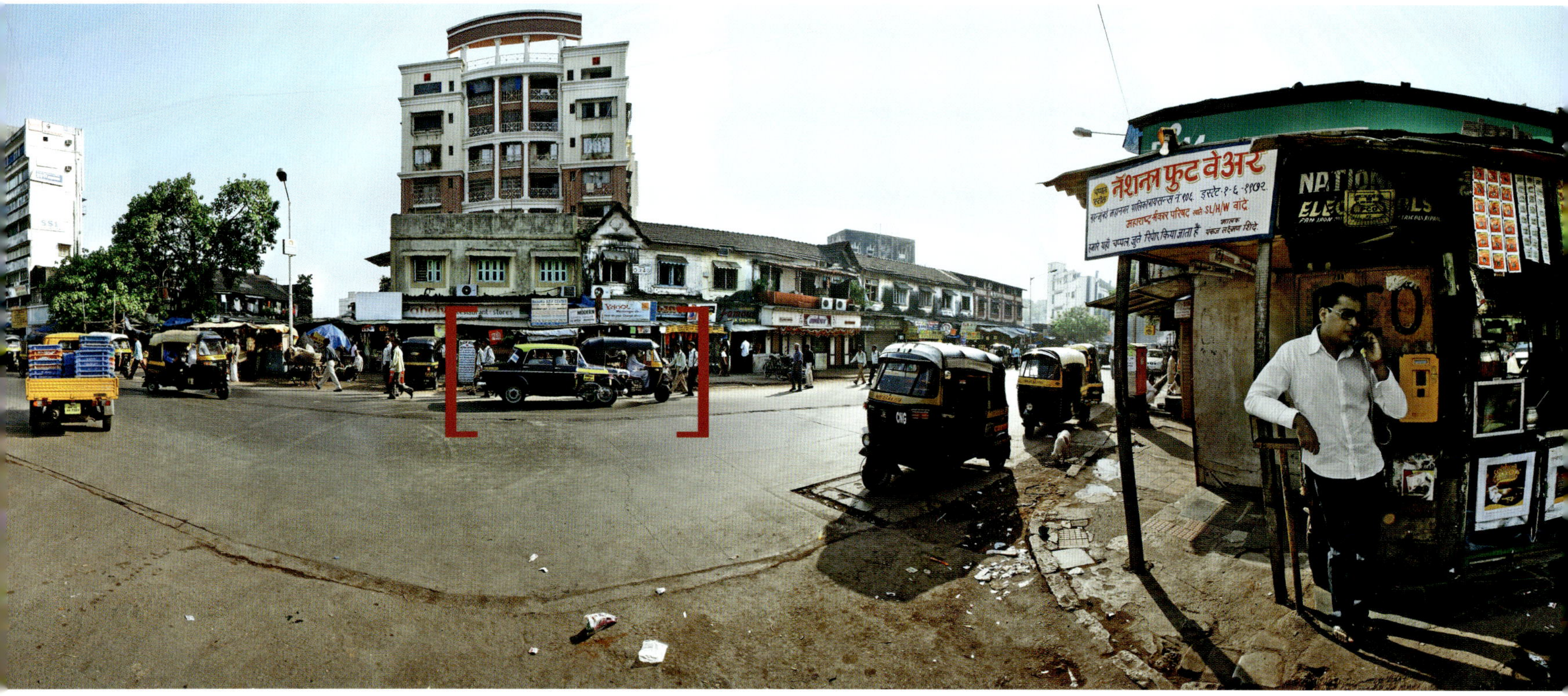

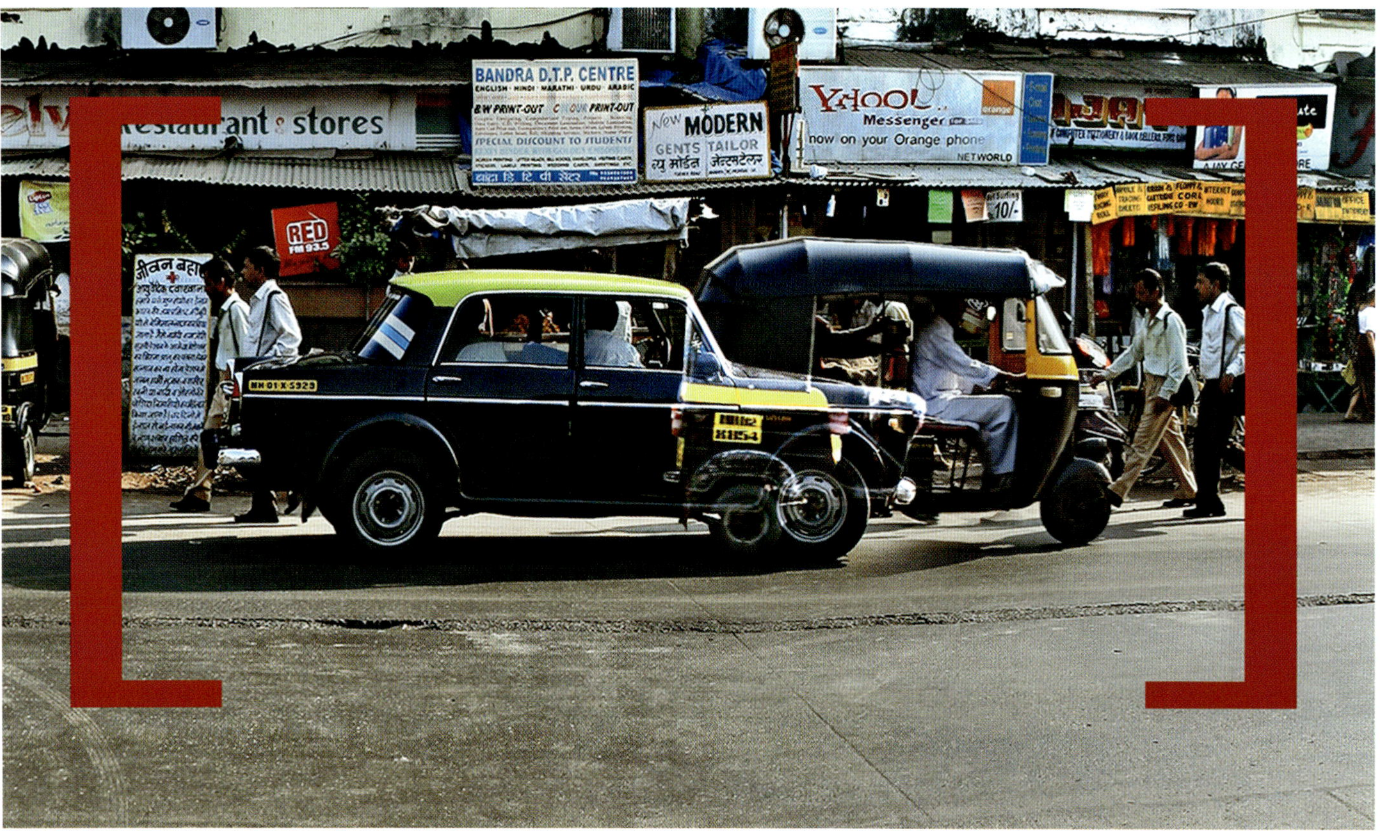
Restaurant & stores
BANDRA D.T.P. CENTRE
ENGLISH · HINDI · MARATHI · URDU · ARABIC
SPECIAL DISCOUNT TO STUDENTS
New MODERN
GENTS TAILOR
Messenger
now on your Orange phone
orange
NETWORLD
RED
FM 93.5
10/-

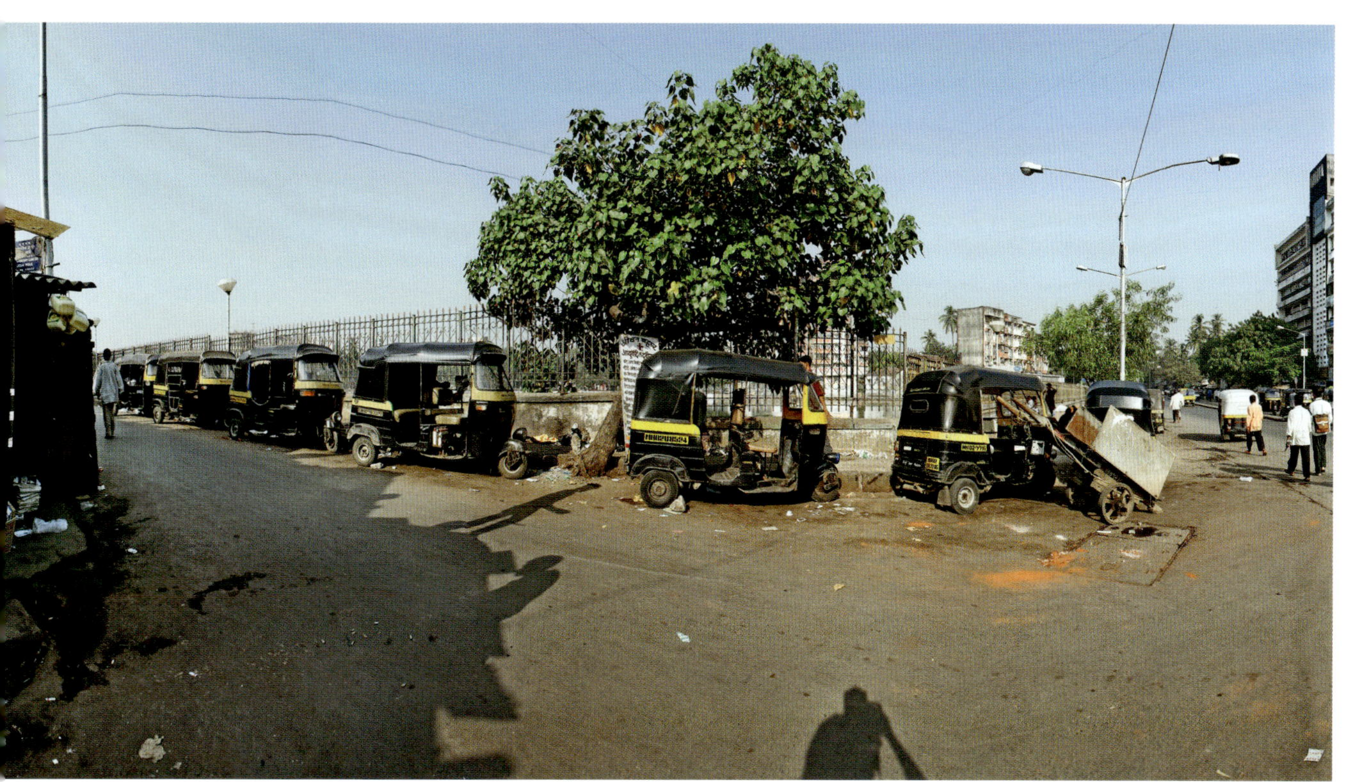

JITISH KALLAT
Artist Making Local Call, 2005
(Detail S./p. 117)

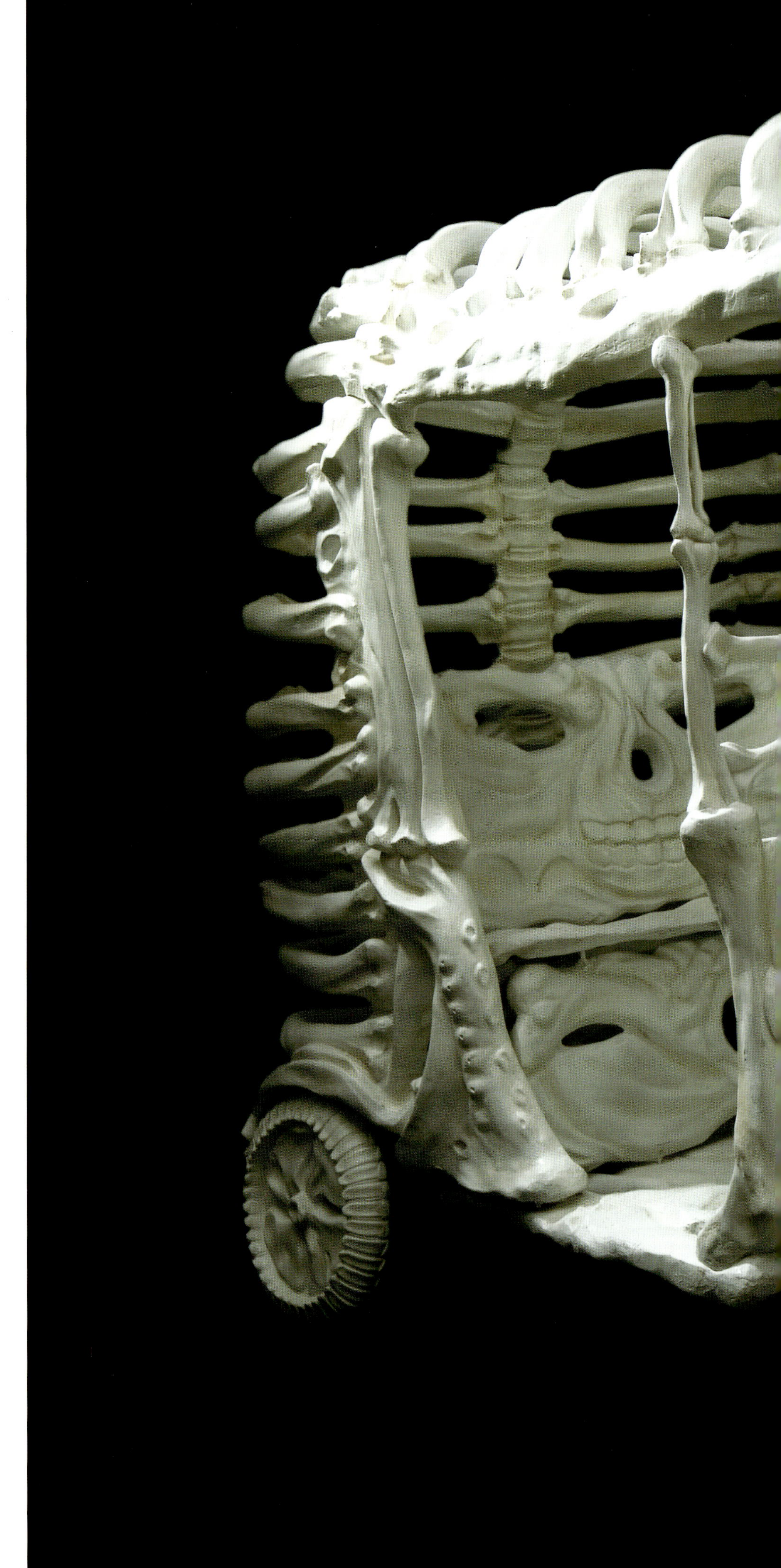

JITISH KALLAT
Autosaurus Tripous, 2007

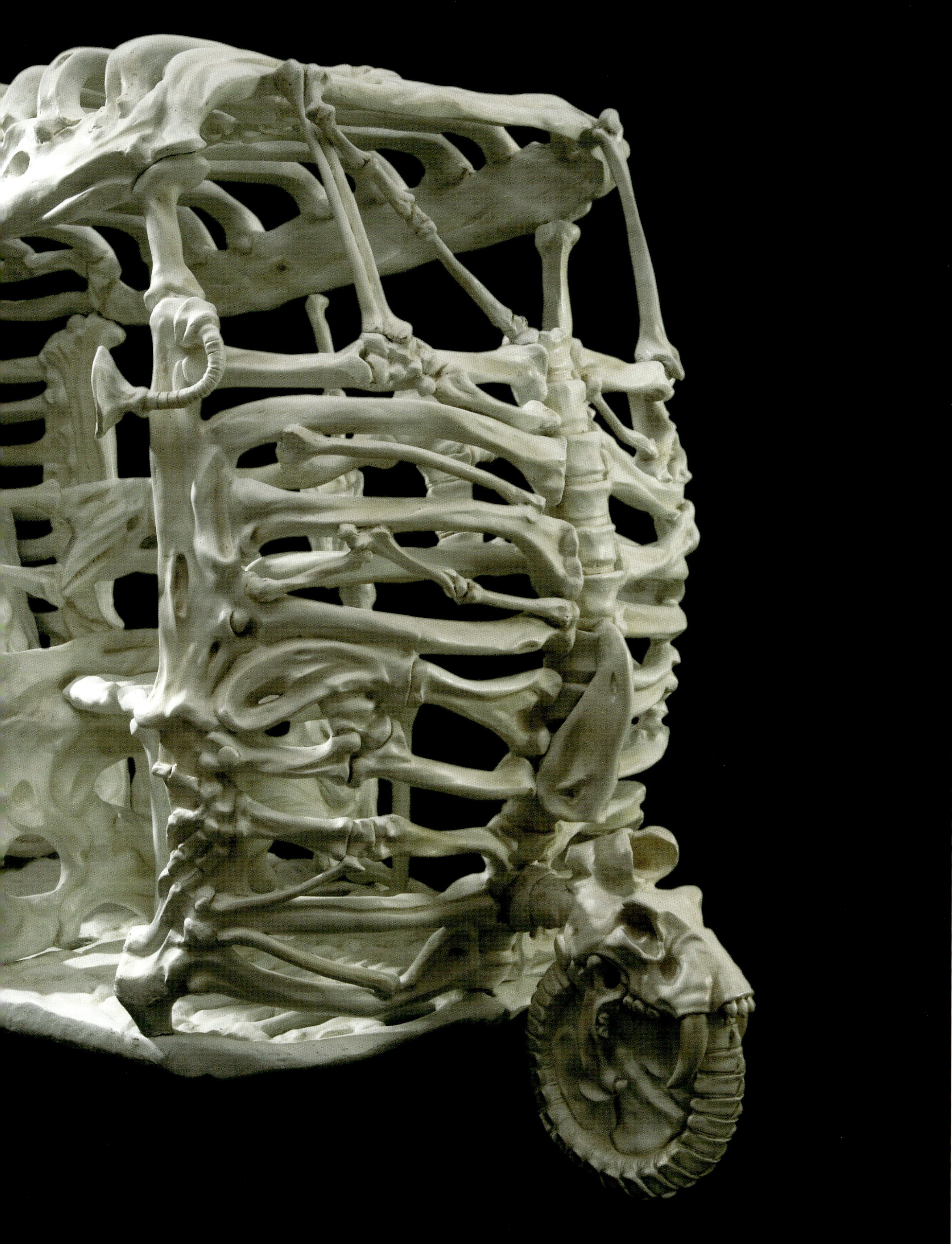

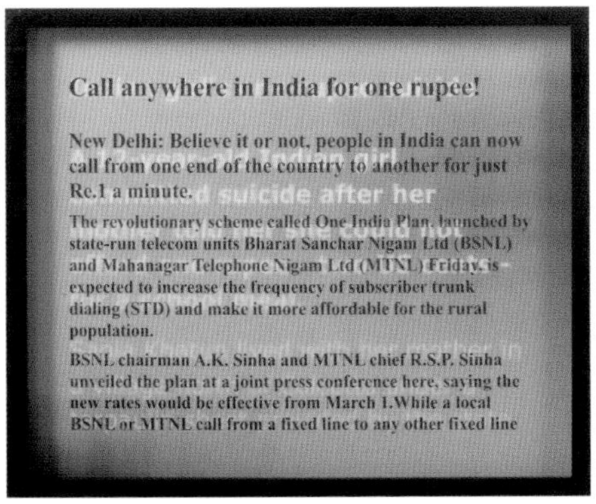

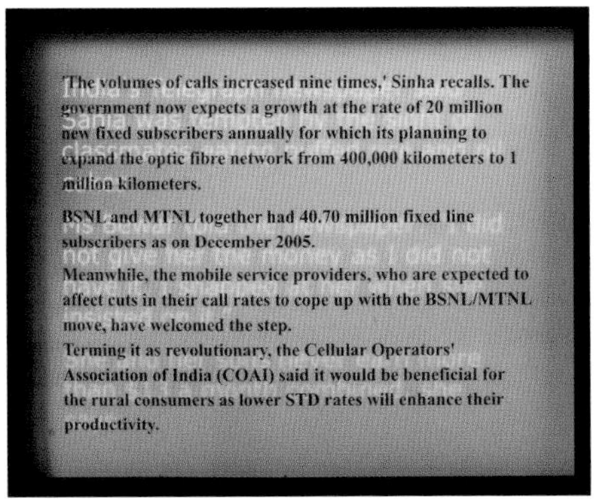

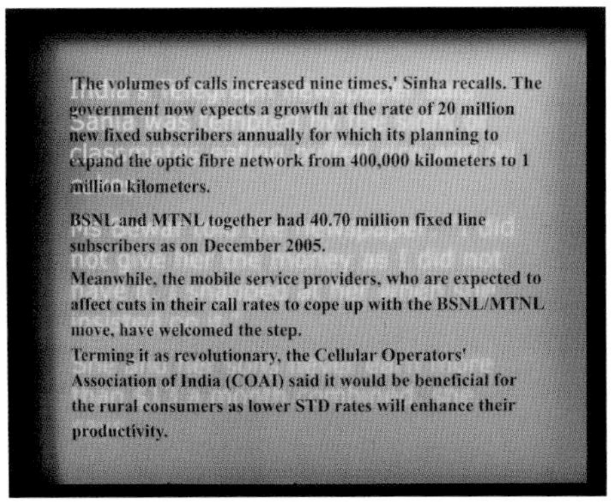

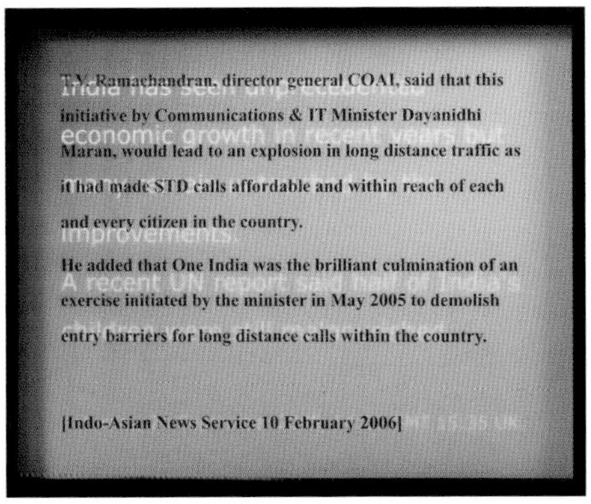

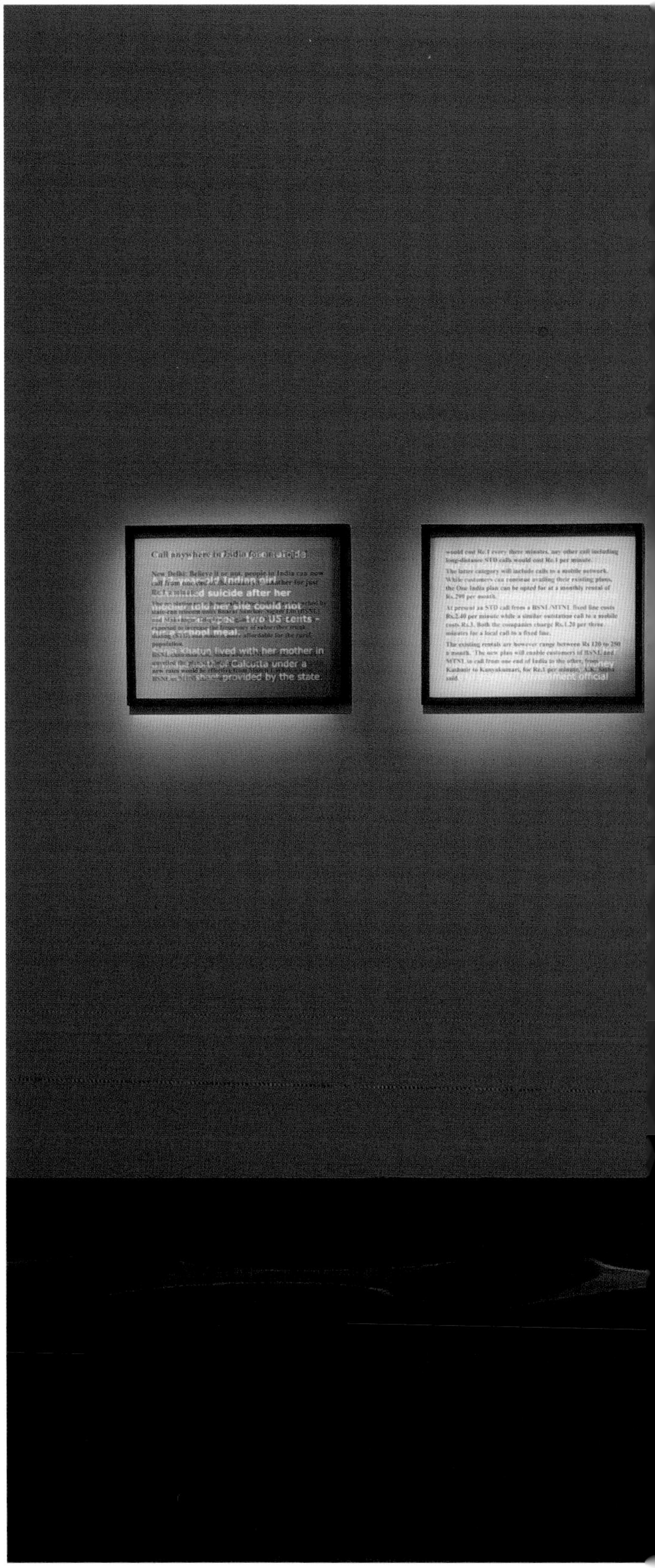

Call anywhere in India for one rupee!

New Delhi: Believe it or not, people in India can now call from one end of the country to another for just Re.1 a minute.

The revolutionary scheme called One India Plan, launched by state-run telecom units Bharat Sanchar Nigam Ltd (BSNL) and Mahanagar Telephone Nigam Ltd (MTNL) Friday, is expected to increase the frequency of subscriber trunk dialing (STD) and make it more affordable for the rural population.

BSNL chairman A.K. Sinha and MTNL chief R.S.P. Sinha unveiled the plan at a joint press conference here, saying the new rates would be effective from March 1.While a local BSNL or MTNL call from a fixed line to any other fixed line

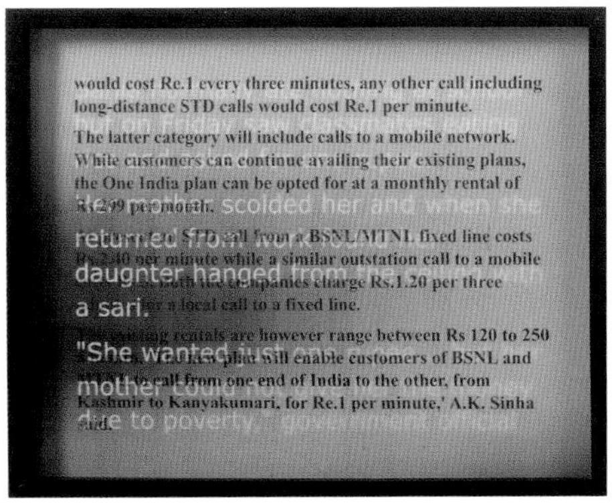

would cost Re.1 every three minutes, any other call including long-distance STD calls would cost Re.1 per minute.
The latter category will include calls to a mobile network.
While customers can continue availing their existing plans, the One India plan can be opted for at a monthly rental of Rs.299 per month.

At present an STD call from a BSNL/MTNL fixed line costs Rs.2.40 per minute while a similar outstation call to a mobile costs Rs.3. Both the companies charge Rs.1.20 per three minutes for a local call to a fixed line.

The existing rentals are however range between Rs 120 to 250 a month. The new plan will enable customers of BSNL and MTNL to call from one end of India to the other, from Kashmir to Kanyakumari, for Re.1 per minute,' A.K. Sinha said.

'The volumes of calls increased nine times,' Sinha recalls. The government now expects a growth at the rate of 20 million new fixed subscribers annually for which its planning to expand the optic fibre network from 400,000 kilometers to 1 million kilometers.

BSNL and MTNL together had 40.70 million fixed line subscribers as on December 2005.
Meanwhile, the mobile service providers, who are expected to affect cuts in their call rates to cope up with the BSNL/MTNL move, have welcomed the step.
Terming it as revolutionary, the Cellular Operators' Association of India (COAI) said it would be beneficial for the rural consumers as lower STD rates will enhance their productivity.

'The volumes of calls increased nine times,' Sinha recalls. The government now expects a growth at the rate of 20 million new fixed subscribers annually for which its planning to expand the optic fibre network from 400,000 kilometers to 1 million kilometers.

BSNL and MTNL together had 40.70 million fixed line subscribers as on December 2005.
Meanwhile, the mobile service providers, who are expected to affect cuts in their call rates to cope up with the BSNL/MTNL move, have welcomed the step.
Terming it as revolutionary, the Cellular Operators' Association of India (COAI) said it would be beneficial for the rural consumers as lower STD rates will enhance their productivity.

T.V. Ramachandran, director general COAI, said that this initiative by Communications & IT Minister Dayanidhi Maran, would lead to an explosion in long distance traffic as it had made STD calls affordable and within reach of each and every citizen in the country.

He added that One India was the brilliant culmination of an exercise initiated by the minister in May 2005 to demolish entry barriers for long distance calls within the country.

[Indo-Asian News Service 10 February 2006]

JITISH KALLAT
Death of Distance, 2006

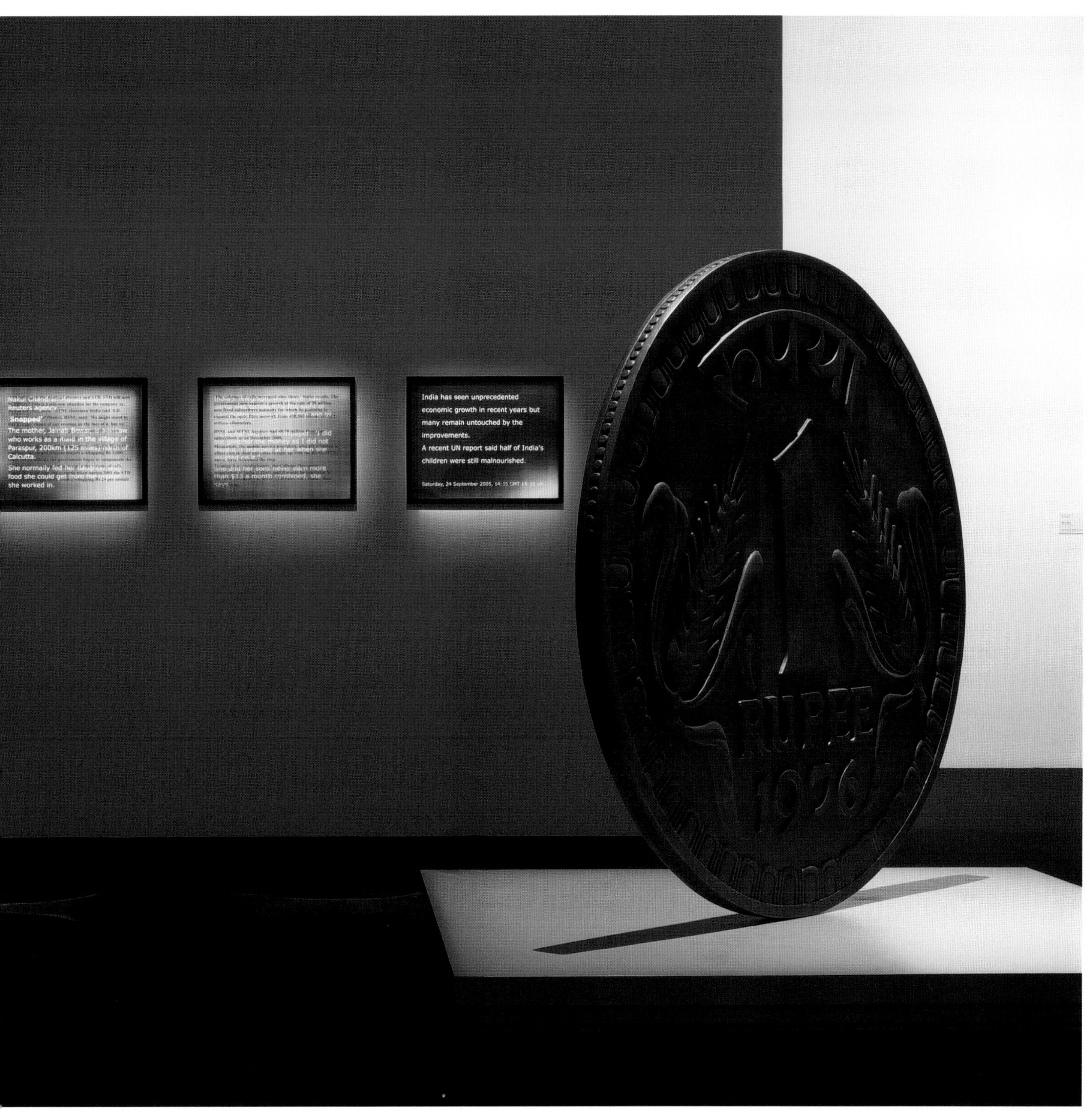
Reuters agency.
'Snapped'
who works as a maid in the village of
Calcutta.
she worked in.
India has seen unprecedented
economic growth in recent years but
many remain untouched by the
improvements.
A recent UN report said half of India's
children were still malnourished.
Saturday, 24 September 2005, 14:35 GMT
1
RUPEE

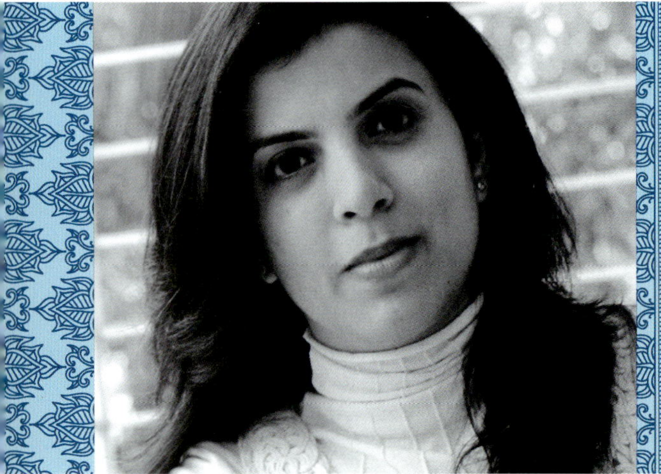

reena saini kallat

REENA SAINI KALLAT Geboren 1973 in Delhi / Lebt in Mumbai
Born 1973 in Delhi / Lives in Mumbai

Kallat, die 1996 ein BFA (Malerei) an der Sir J.J. School of Fine Arts, Mumbai, erwarb, ist eine Malerin, die in ihren Arbeiten auch auf bildhauerische und fotografische Techniken zurückgreift. Sie kommentiert in ihrem Werk Identität und die damit verbundenen Erinnerungen, die Auflösung und Zerstörung von Nationalismus und Staat, den Verlust des Zugehörigkeitsgefühls und der Isolation. Immer wieder ist in ihren Werken die Realität der heutigen Gesellschaft ein wichtiges Thema. Viele Arbeiten der Künstlerin werden von Mythen, religiösen Überlieferungen und historischen Anekdoten aus Indien und anderen Ländern inspiriert. Sie können als gesellschaftspolitische Anmerkungen gesehen werden, in denen sie Ereignisse aus dem täglichen Leben und ihre persönlichen Erlebnisse verarbeitet. Die höchst poetischen Geschichten, die aus der Verflechtung dieser unterschiedlichen Quellen entstehen, vermitteln in ihrer Vielschichtigkeit sowohl abgehobene Ruhe als auch ein Gefühl der Unruhe.

Die Ungewissheit bezüglich der künftigen Beziehungen zwischen Indien und Pakistan und die Erinnerungen jener, die in Indien soziale und politische Katastrophen miterlebt haben, waren in letzter Zeit immer wieder Gegenstand von Kallats Arbeiten. Ihr ortsbezogenes Werk „Colostrum" zeigt in Reihen angeordnete Hochglanzaufkleber – in dunklem Safrangelb, Weiß und Dunkelgrün, den drei Farben der indischen Flagge – die stellvertretend für die indisch-pakistanische Grenze den Boden des Ausstellungsraums in zwei Teile teilen. Jeder der 354 Aufkleber trägt den Namen eines der Unterzeichner einer Initiative, die sich für ein Friedensabkommen zwischen Indien und Pakistan einsetzt. In ihrer fotografischen Arbeit „Crease / Crevice / Contour" (2008), die aus zehn Aufnahmen besteht, hat Kallat mit Hilfe billiger Gummistempel und roter Tinte auf dem Rücken einer Frau eine mosaikartige Fläche geschaffen. Die ganze Serie stellt die verrinnende Zeit und die Wechselfälle des Territorialkonflikts zwischen Indien und Pakistan dar, der unter dem Schlagwort „Line of Control (LOC)" bekannt ist. „Synonym" (2007) ist eine Serie von skulpturalen Portraits, die aus Hunderten von Gummistempeln hergestellt wurden. Die gummierten Teile der Stempel sind farbig und so angeordnet, dass sie ein kunstvolles, mosaikähnliches Muster bilden. Das Porträt, das senkrecht

Kallat, who obtained a BFA (painting) from Sir J.J. School of Fine Arts, Mumbai in 1996, is a painter who also incorporates sculptural and photographic techniques into her work to comment on identity and the memories related to identity, the disintegration and destruction of nationalism and the state, the loss of a sense of belonging, and isolation. Often, however, these works represent a record of the reality of contemporary society. Many of Kallat's works are inspired by myths, religious stories, and historical anecdotes from India and other countries, and are social and political commentaries in which she employs events from everyday life together with her own personal experiences. The extremely poetic narrative that results from interweaving these diverse sources conveys a complexity of both an intimate quietude and a sense of disquiet.

The uncertain future of Indian and Pakistani relations and the memories of those who have experienced social and political disaster in India, have been the subjects of many of Kallat's recent works. Her site-specific work *Colostrum* features rows of high-gloss stickers – in the three colours of the Indian national flag, deep saffron, white and dark green – set out as a representation of the Indo-Pakistan border and splitting the gallery floor into two. There are 354 stickers, each bearing the name of one of the 354 signatories of a movement lobbying for a peace agreement between India and Pakistan. In the photographic work *Crease / Crevice / Contour* (2008) comprising ten photographs, Kallat used cheap rubber stamps and red ink to shape a mosaic-patterned field on a woman's back. The series altogether depicts the passing of time and the vicissitudes of the territorial dispute between India and Pakistan known as "Line of Control (LOC)." *Synonym* (2007) is a series of sculptural portraits created with several hundred rubber stamps. The rubber part of the stamps is coloured, and the rubber stamps themselves are arranged to create an elaborate mosaic-like pattern. The portrait that is revealed by standing it up between two acrylic panels evokes the memories of men and women, both young and old, who remain missing as a result of disaster.

Major exhibitions include "The International Incheon Women Artists' Biennale (IWAB)" (South Korea, 2007),

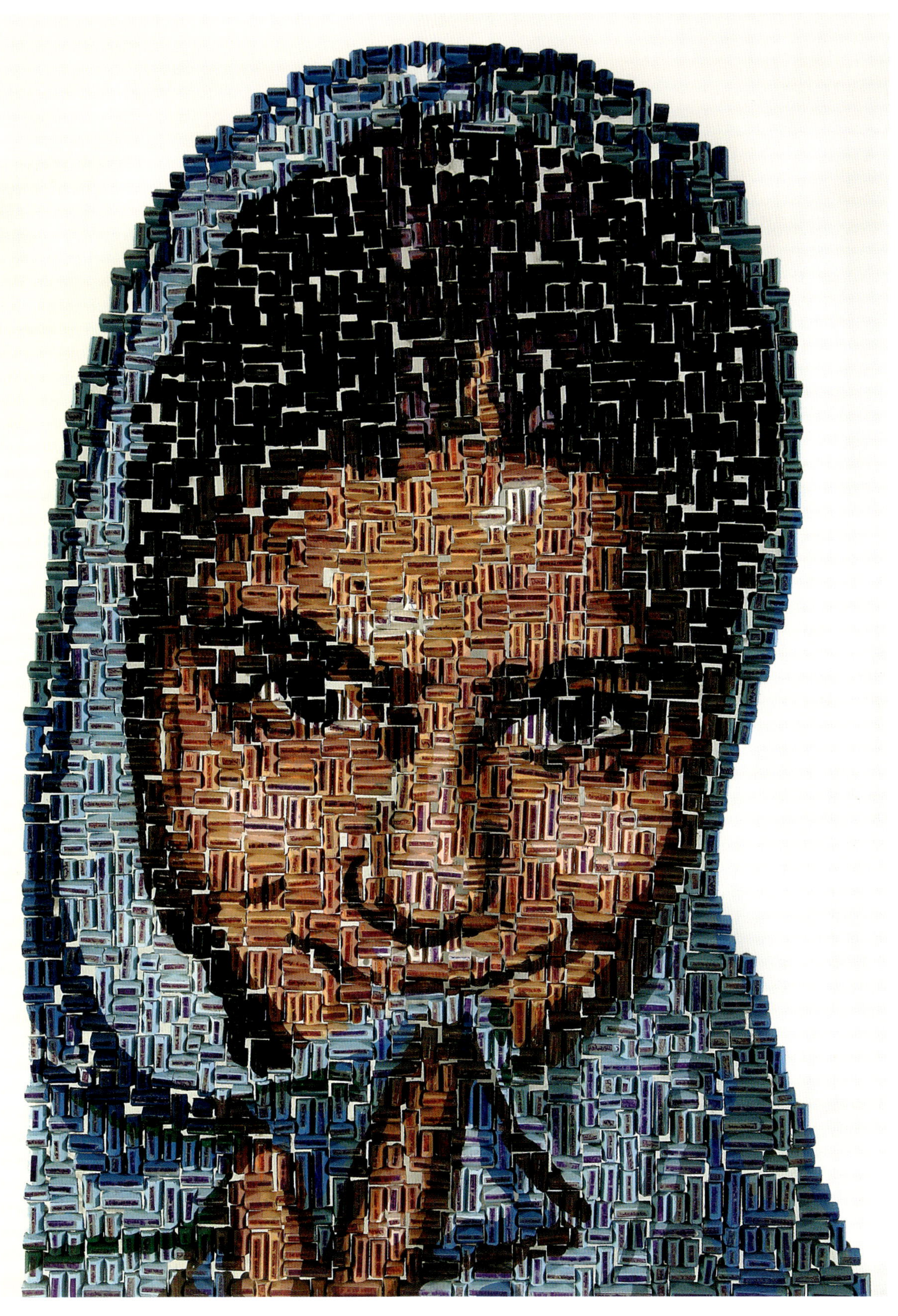

zwischen zwei Acrylplatten montiert, sichtbar wird, erinnert an Männer und Frauen unterschiedlichen Alters, die nach Katastrophen immer noch vermisst werden.

Wichtige Ausstellungen: „The International Incheon Women Artists' Biennale (IWAB)" (South Korea, 2007), „Thermocline of Art. New Asian Waves" (ZKM Center for Art and Media, Karlsruhe, 2007) und „Soft Power: Asian Attitude" (Shanghai Zendai Museum of Modern Art, 2007). (KM)

"Thermocline of Art. New Asian Waves" (ZKM Center for Art and Media, Karlsruhe, 2007), and "Soft Power: Asian Attitude" (Shanghai Zendai Museum of Modern Art, 2007). (KM)

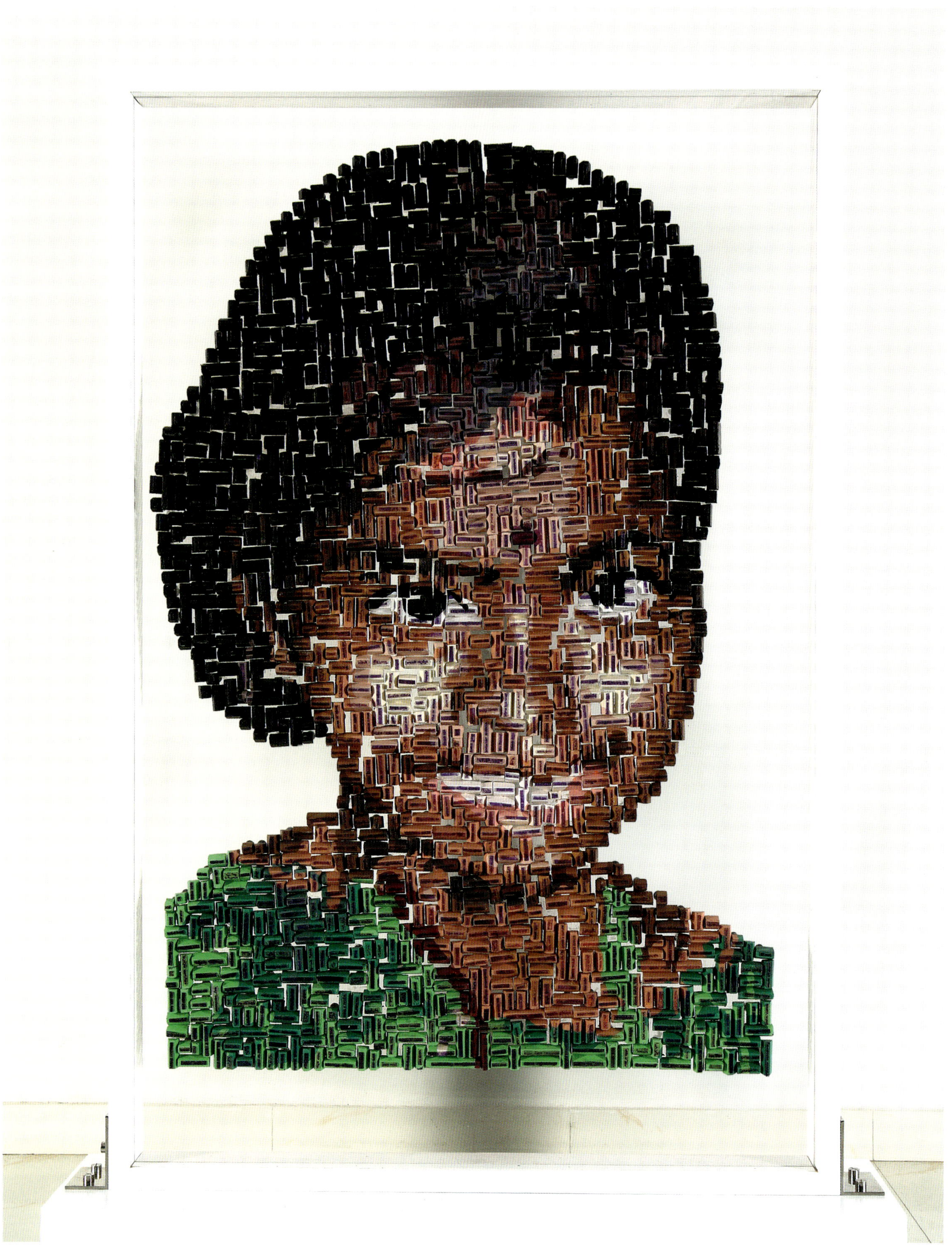

REENA SAINI KALLAT
Synonym, 2007 (S./p. 125)
Synonym, 2007

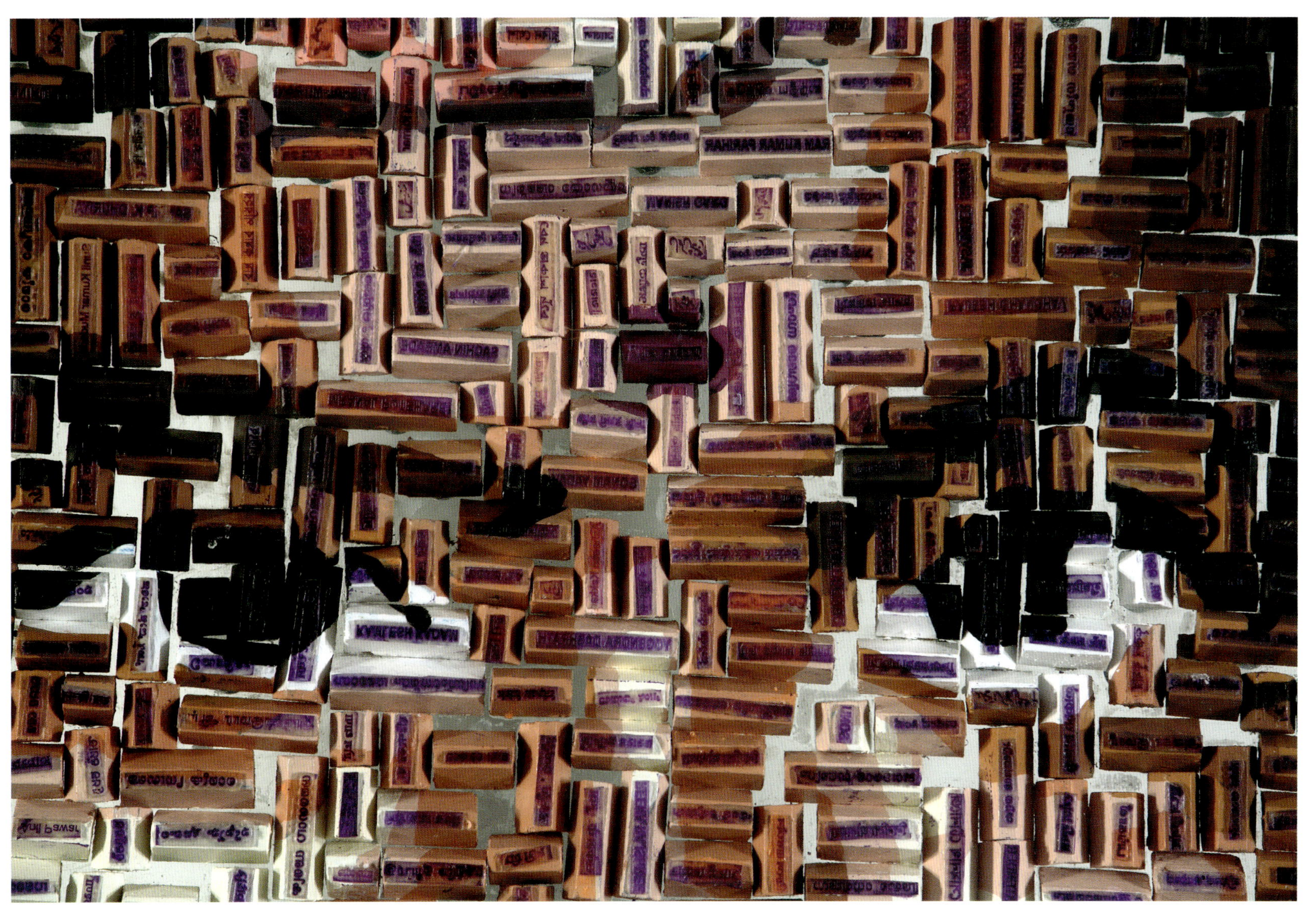

REENA SAINI KALLAT
Synonym, 2007 (Detail)

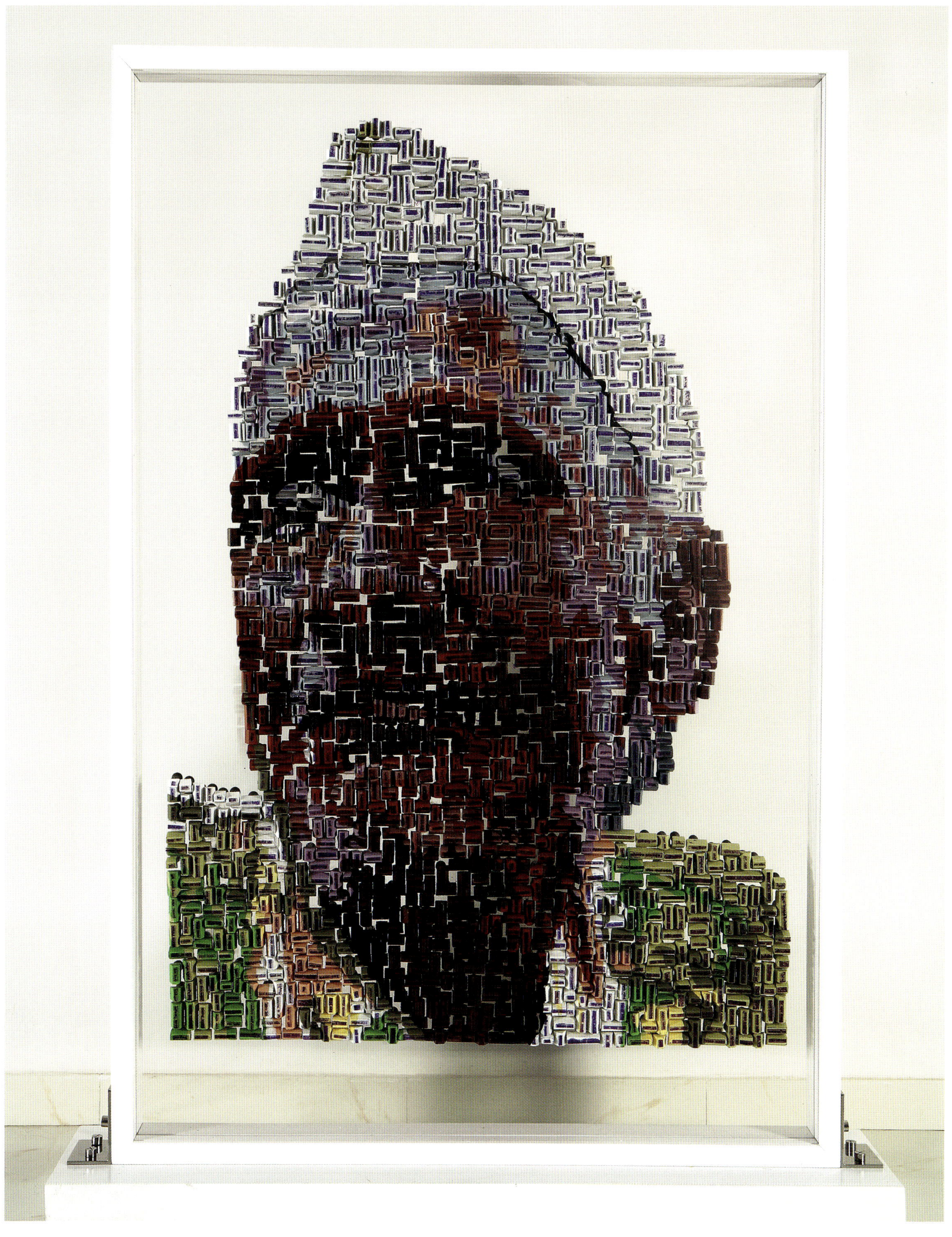

REENA SAINI KALLAT
Synonym, 2007

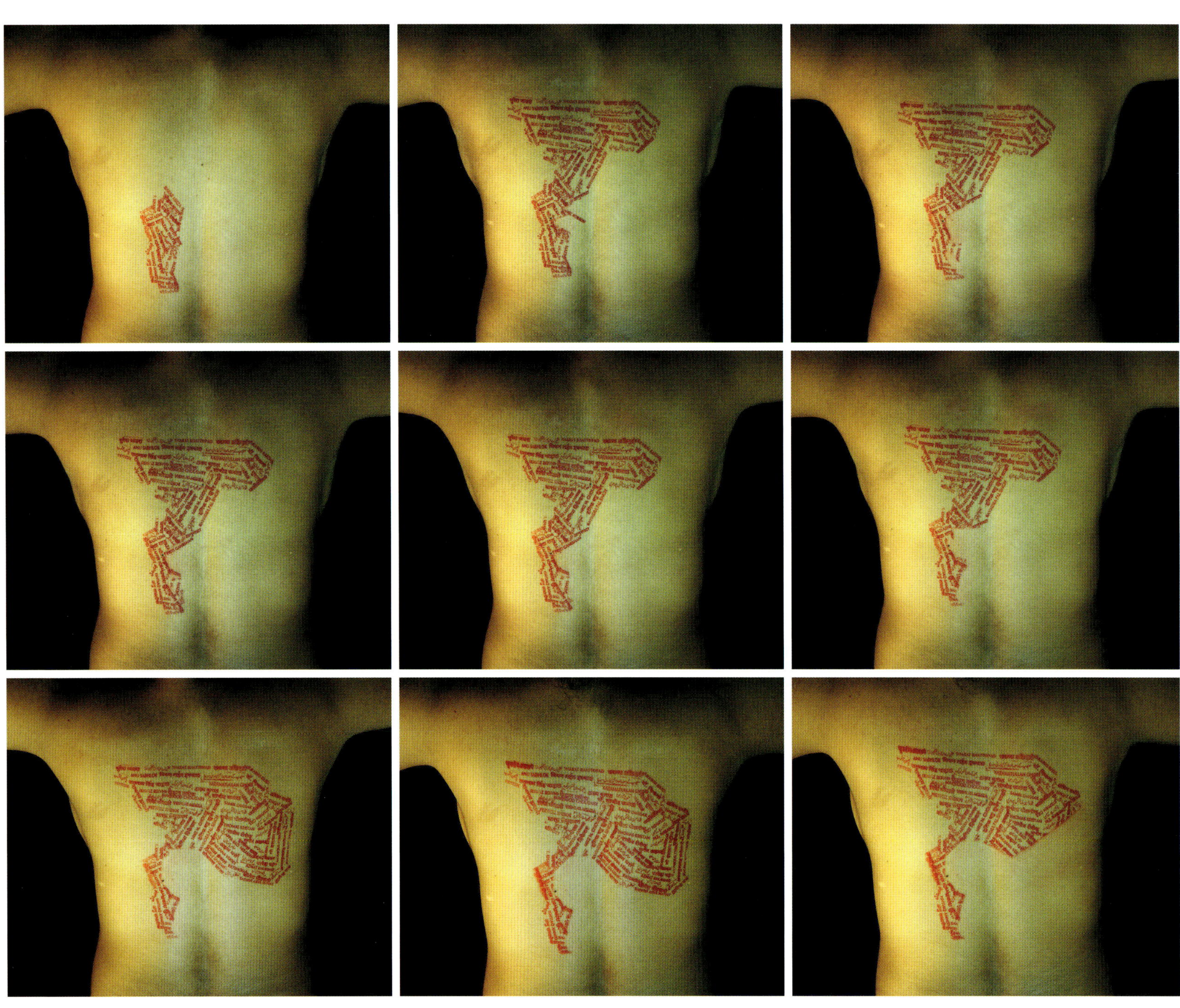

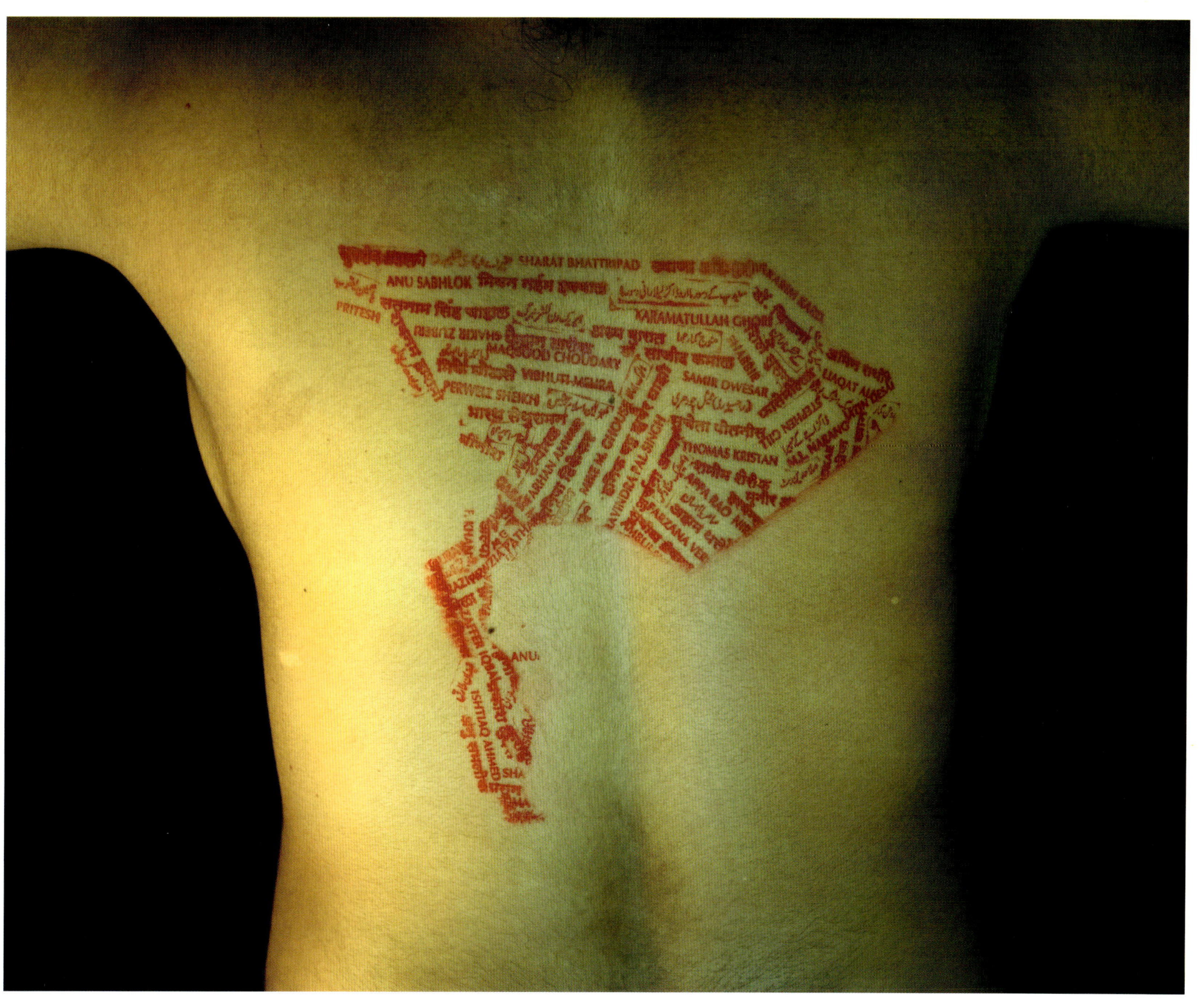

REENA SAINI KALLAT
Crease / Crevice / Contour, 2008

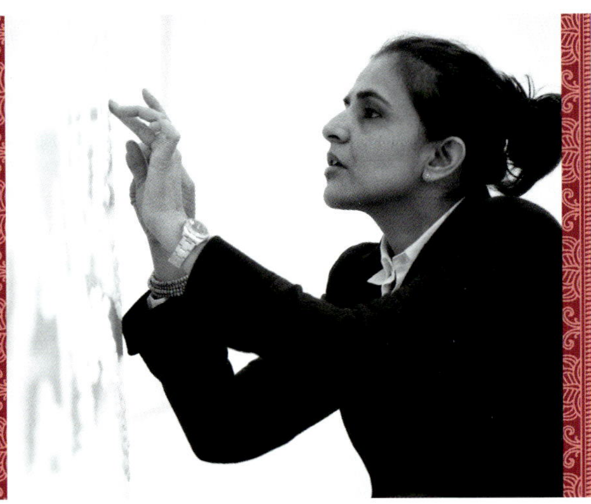

bharti kher

BHARTI KHER Geboren 1969 in London / Lebt in Gurgaon, Haryana
Born 1969 in London / Lives in Gurgaon, Haryana

1991 erwarb Kher ein BFA am Newcastle Polytechnic (jetzt Northumbria University) in Nordengland. In England geboren und aufgewachsen, ging Kher 1993 nach Delhi und verlegte sich vom Malen auf bildhauerische Arbeiten und Installationen. Unter dem Eindruck ihrer persönlichen Erfahrung thematisiert sie in diesen Arbeiten Fragen wie Identität, Mangel an Zugehörigkeitsgefühl und kulturelles Unbehagen, während die Wahl ihrer künstlerischen Mittel wohl das Ergebnis ihrer sorgfältigen Suche nach der optimalen Ausdrucksform dieser Themen ist.

Kher verleiht Erscheinungen, die sie in großer Zahl dem täglichen Leben und ihrer Umwelt entnimmt, bildlichen Ausdruck und kommentiert so Rassen- und Klassenfragen, die Konsumgesellschaft, den Feminismus und das Verhältnis zwischen Tradition und modernem Leben. Ihr Werk ist gekennzeichnet durch die massenhafte Verwendung von Bindis – ursprünglich die auf der Stirn getragenen Zeichen verheirateter Hindufrauen. Bindis sind wegen ihrer metaphorischen und paradoxen Bedeutung interessant. Wurden sie früher aufgrund ihres religiösen Sinngehalts getragen, sind sie heute in erster Linie ein profanes Mode Statement. Neben den „üblichen" kreisrunden, verwendet sie unzählige andere Ausprägungen der Bindis. Kreise, Pfeile oder Spermien fügen sich zu abstrakten organischen Formen, die an Sexualität, Schriften, Landkarten und Bewegungen von Menschen denken lassen. Kher ist auch für ihre lebensgroßen Skulpturen von Hyänen, Giraffen, Hirschen, Rehen und Hunden bekannt, die sie aus Glasfaser- oder Harzmaterialien formt. „The Skin Speaks a Language Not Its Own" (2006), einer ihrer Beiträge zur aktuellen Ausstellung, ist wohl das ehrgeizigste ihrer Werke. Ein weiblicher, halb liegender, halb sterbender Elefant, dessen Haut mit weißen, spermienförmigen Bindis übersät ist, versinnbildlicht für die Künstlerin eine Ansammlung von Erfahrungen, Zeit, Vergänglichkeit und Kultur, die ewig gleichen Themen der westlichen und östlichen Philosophie und Mythologie. Für die aktuelle Ausstellung hat Kher auch ein zweidimensionales Werk als Teil einer Serie geschaffen, an der sie in den letzten Jahren gearbeitet hat. Es besteht aus Bindis, die unter dem Titel „Psychogenic Fugue" (2008) an der Wand des Ausstellungsraums angebracht sind. Eine Vielzahl glitzernder, spiralförmig angeordneter

Kher obtained a BFA in 1991 from Newcastle Polytechnic (currently Northumbria University) in Northern England. Born and raised in England, Kher relocated to Delhi in 1993, since when she moved away from painting and began producing sculpture and installations. These works address issues such as that of identity, informed by her personal experience, the absence of a sense of belonging, and cultural discomfort, while her choice of media is arguably the result of her careful search for the optimum avenue of expression to convey these issues.

Kher depicts images that she has amassed from everyday life or surrounding environments that she uses to comment on racial and class issues, consumer society, feminism, and the relationship between tradition and modern life. The work is characterized by prolific use of the bindis, the decoration originally worn on the forehead of Hindu women. The bindi is interesting for its metaphorical and paradoxical significance. Once applied for its religious meaning, today the bindi is predominantly secular and a fashion statement. In addition to the "conventional" circular bindis, she uses a myriad of forms of the bindi. Predominantly circles, arrows or spermatozoa shapes that build up abstract organic forms that suggest place sexuality, texts, maps and movements of people. Kher is also known for her full-scale sculptures of hyena, giraffes, deer, and dogs molded from fibreglass and other materials. Kher's work in this exhibition, The Skin Speaks a Language Not Its Own (2006), is arguably the most ambitious example from her body of work. A female elephant, with its hide covered in white sperm shaped bindis half lying, half dying communicates itself for the artist as a record of experience, time, metabolism and culture. The perennial trope in Western and Eastern philosophies and mythology. For this exhibition, Kher has also created a new two-dimensional work as a part of the series that she has been producing in recent years. Entitled Psychogenic Fugue (2008), it features bindis applied to the wall in the exhibition space. The large number of glittering bindis has been arranged in a spiral pattern to create an enormous circle around 4 meters in diameter. This work which initially appears to be an abstract painting has great visual impact, both mystic and modernist.

Bindis bilden einen riesigen Kreis mit einem Durchmesser von 4 Metern. Das Werk, das auf den ersten Blick einem abstrakten Gemälde gleicht, hat eine starke Ausstrahlung, mystisch und modern zugleich.

Wichtige Ausstellungen, u.a. Gruppenausstellungen, wie „Under Construction: New Dimension of Asian Art“ (Tokyo Opera City Art Gallery and The Japan Foundation Asia Center, 2002) und „The 5th Asia–Pacific Triennale of Contemporary Art“ (Queensland Art Museum, Brisbane, 2006), und ihre Einzelausstellung „Virus“ (BALTIC Centre for Contemporary Art, Newcastle, U.K., 2008), „Sing to Them that will Listen“ (Emmanuel Perrotin, Paris, 2008). (KM)

Major exhibitions include such groups shows as "Under Construction: New Dimension of Asian Art" (Tokyo Opera City Art Gallery and The Japan Foundation Asia Center, 2002) and "The 5th Asia–Pacific Triennale of Contemporary Art" (Queensland Art Museum, Brisbane, 2006), her solo exhibition "Virus" (BALTIC Centre for Contemporary Art, Newcastle, U.K., 2008), Sing to Them that will Listen" (Emmanuel Perrotin, Paris, 2008). (KM)

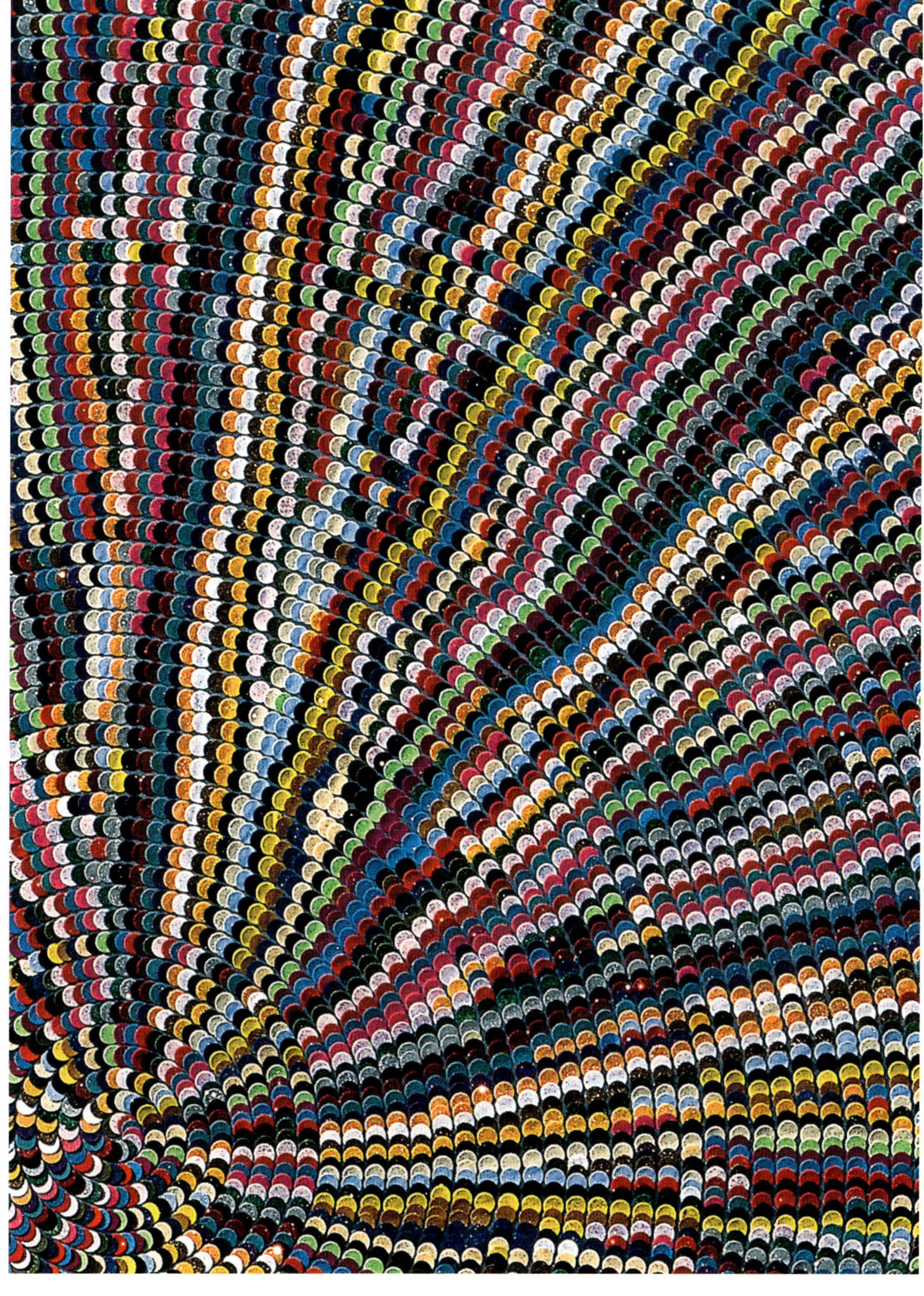

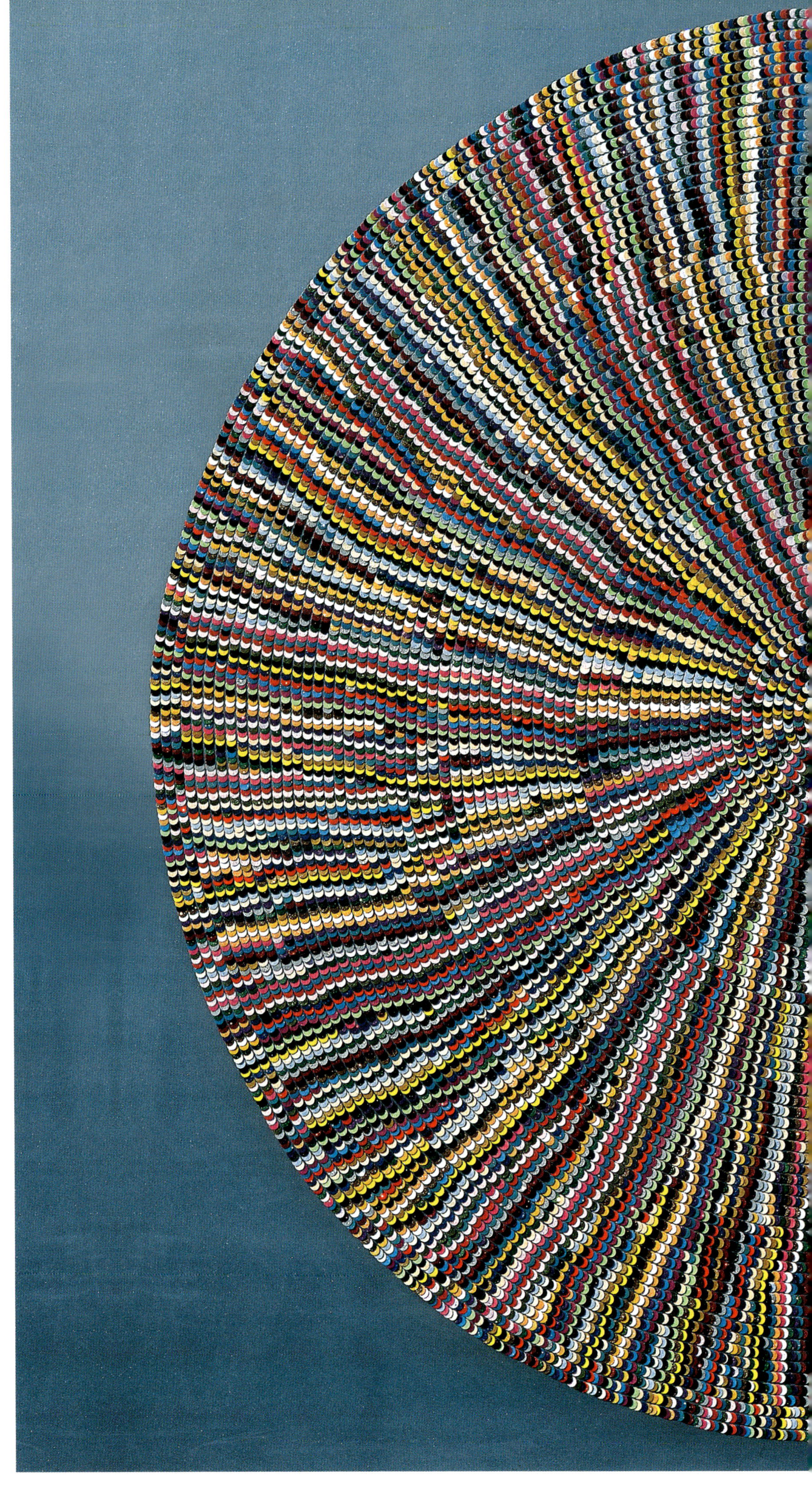

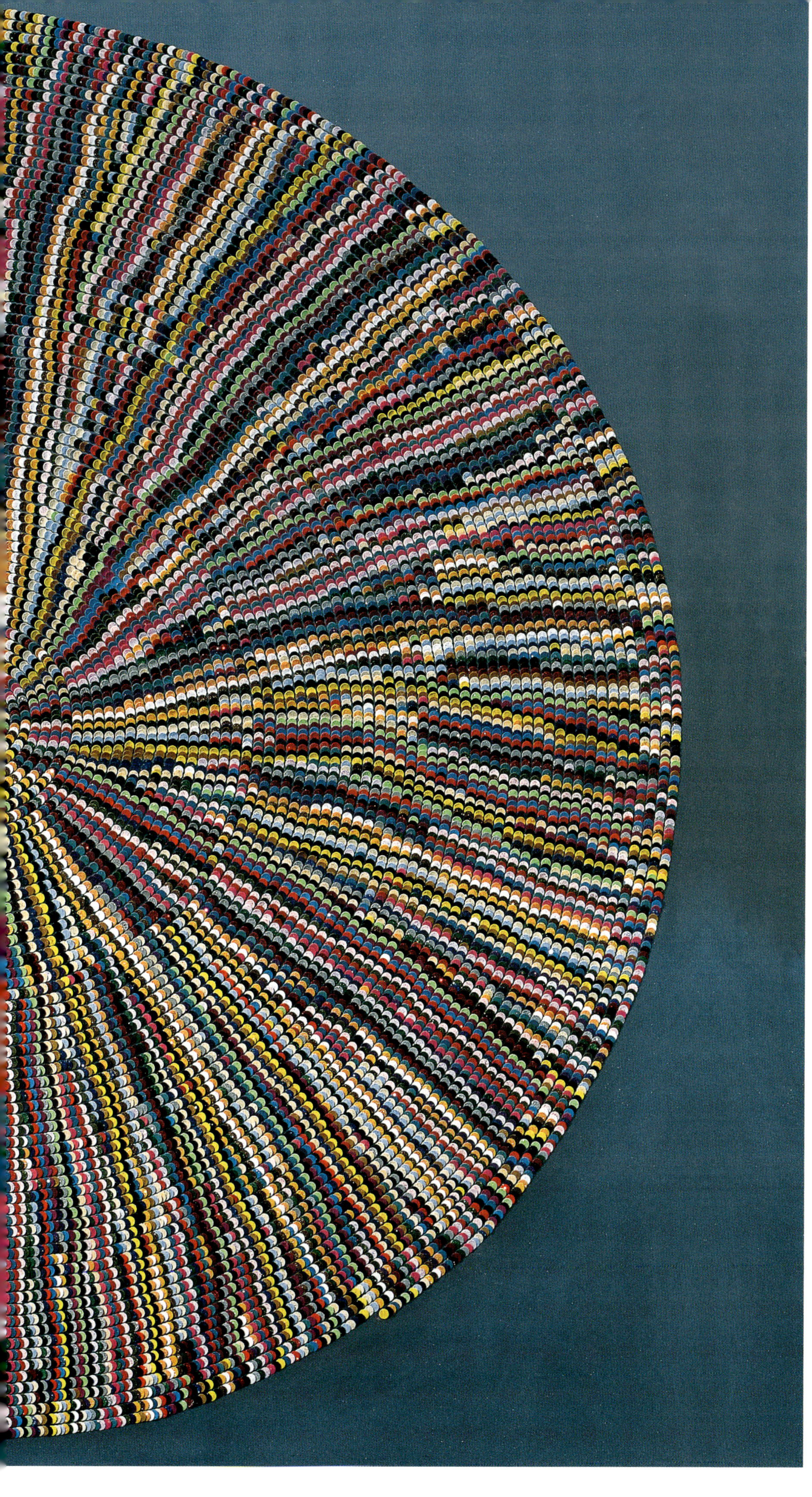

BHARTI KHER
Supernova, 2007
(Detail S./p. 133)

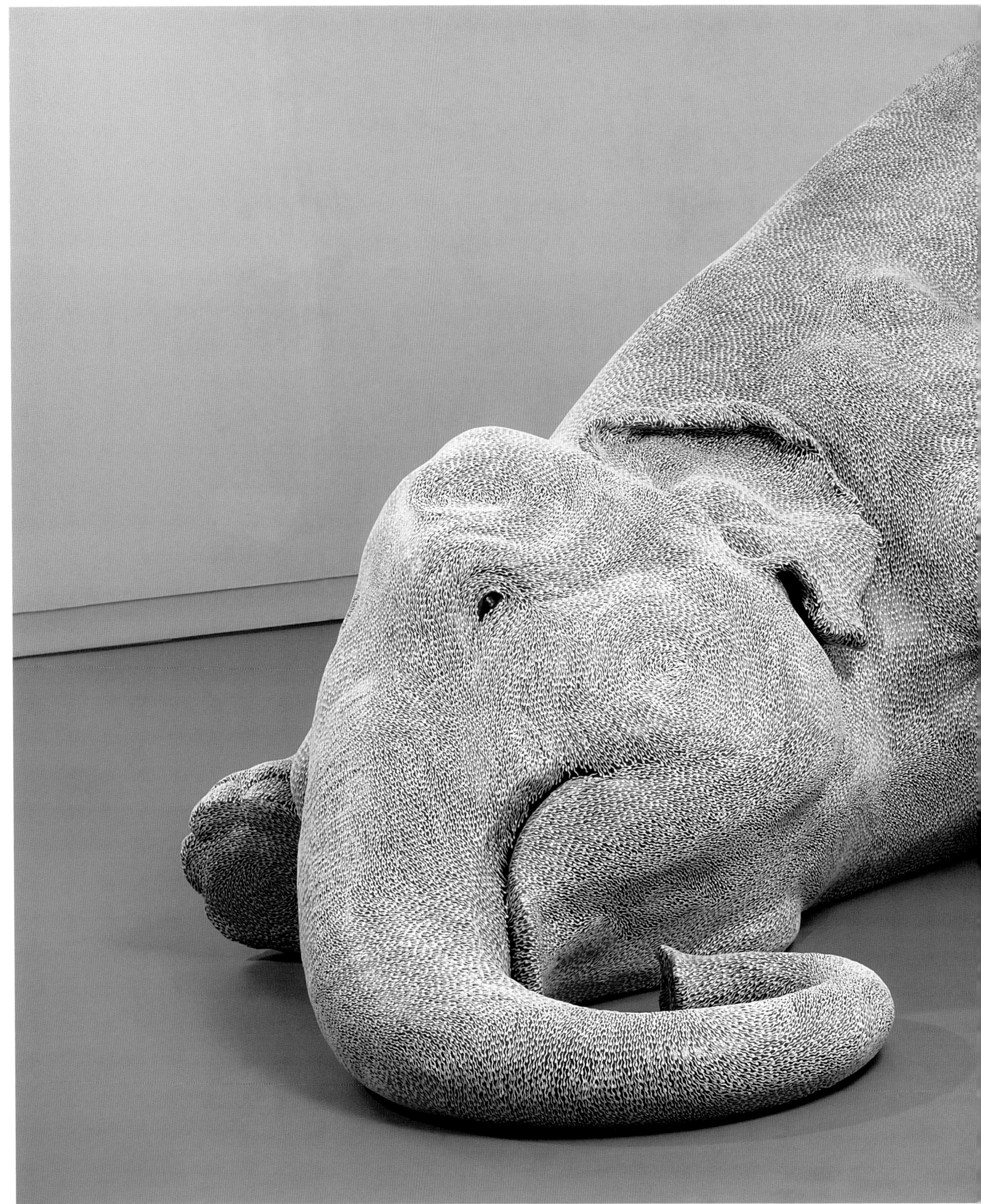

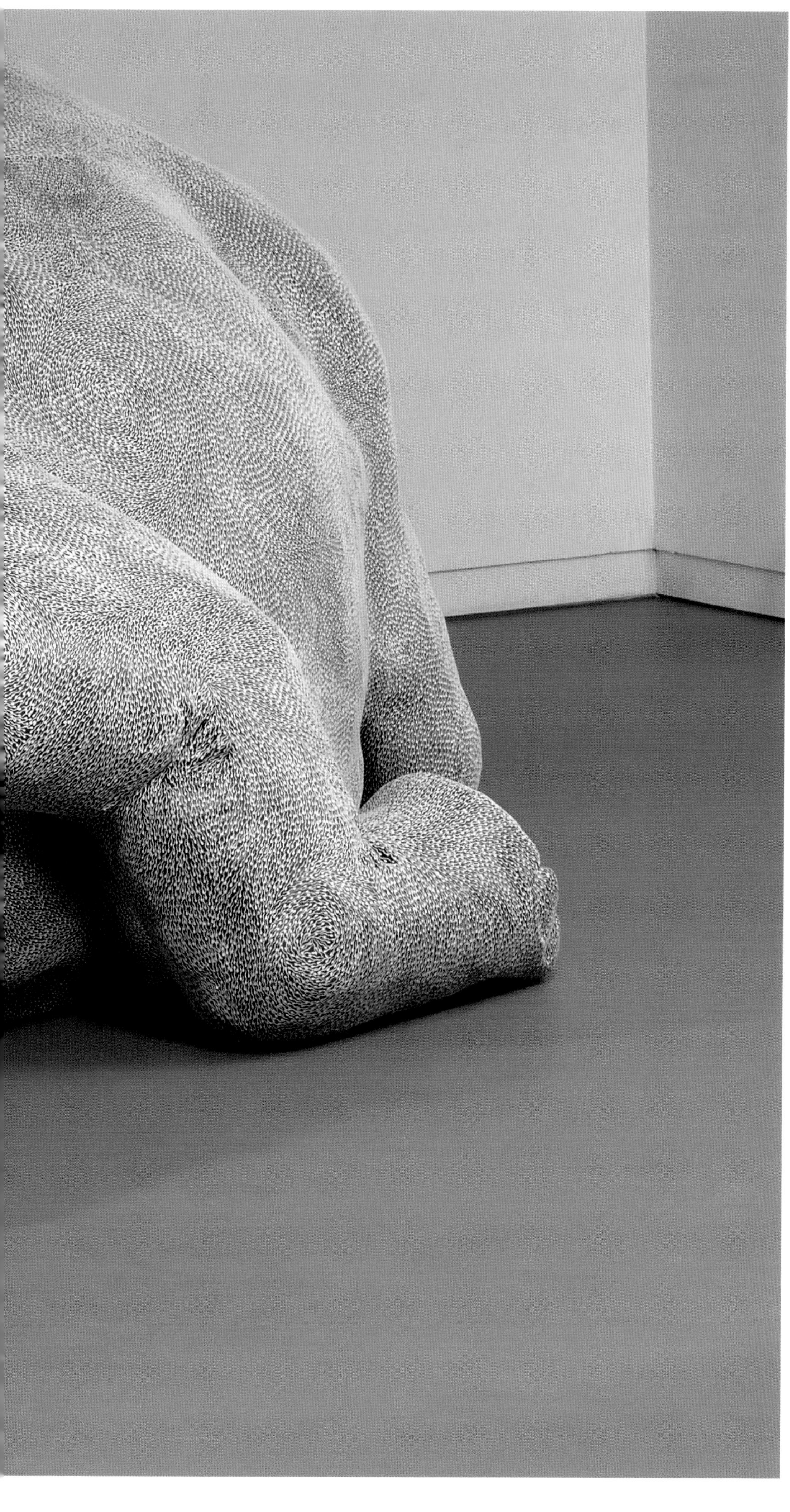

BHARTI KHER
The Skin Speaks a Language
Not its Own, 2006

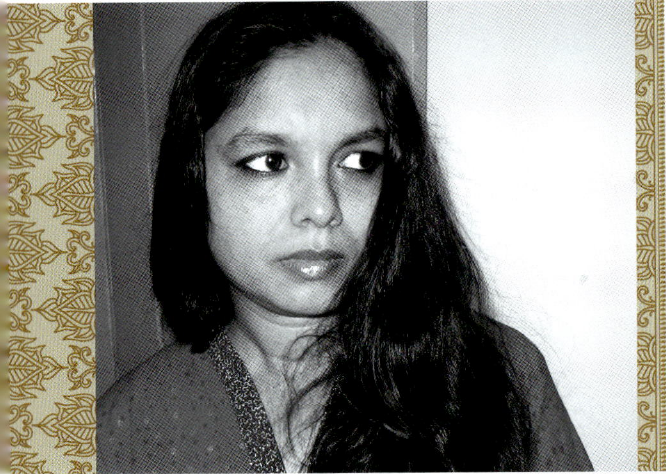

prabhavathi meppayil

PRABHAVATHI MEPPAYIL Geboren 1965 in Bangalore / Lebt in Bangalore
Born 1965 in Bangalore / Lives in Bangalore

Meppayil, die 1992 an der Ken School of Art, Bangalore, ein Diplom in Fine Arts erwarb, wuchs in Bangalore als Tochter eines traditionellen Goldschmieds auf. Hin und wieder setzt sie für ihre künstlerische Arbeit die Werkzeuge ihres Vaters ein, oder sie verwendet die klassische Temperatechnik, um handwerkliche Arbeitsmethoden und traditionelle Elemente der südindischen Miniaturmalerei in die zeitgenössische Kunst einzubringen. Meppayil ist bekannt als Minimalistin mit einem äußerst filigranen Malstil.

Auf den ersten Blick erscheint Meppayils Arbeit wie eine einfache, auf einer weißen Fläche angefertigte Zeichnung. Bei näherem Hinsehen entpuppt sich das Bild als Ergebnis der kunstvollen Verbindung winziger Punkte und feiner Linien mit Blattgold und Farbe, geschaffen durch die Überlagerung mehrerer Goldschichten unterschiedlicher Leuchtkraft, wodurch der Eindruck entsteht, dass diese aus der Leinwand hervortreten und über ihr schweben. Der Hintergrund entsteht durch ein Gemisch aus Kalkpulver und Klebstoff auf Sperrholzplatten. Durch sorgfältiges Polieren mit Sandpapier erzielt die Künstlerin eine keramikähnliche Oberflächenstruktur. Auf diese reinweiße Platte setzt sie mit feinen Linien fließende Darstellungen männlicher und weiblicher Silhouetten, Gliedmaßen, Tiere, Pflanzen und gelegentlich Fragmente abstrakter Formen. Das Zusammenspiel der subtilen Farbgebung, ähnlich einer Schattierung, mit dem gedämpften Goldglanz ergibt den Eindruck einer zugleich geisterhaften und lyrischen Welt. Eine andere Technik, die Meppayil in den letzten Jahren eingesetzt hat, besteht darin, das Sperrholz mit den bunten Stoffen abzudecken, die es auf dem Markt zu kaufen gibt, und diese dann mit Gesso (spezielles Grundierweiß) zu beschichten, um die Farbe „auszulöschen". Meppayil meint, dass „Kunst schaffen" nicht einfach Abbilden meint, sondern auch den Schaffensprozess, aus dem ein Objekt entsteht.

Dem Gold haftet von alters her eine symbolische Macht an, verbunden mit dem Image von Reinheit, Universalität und Erhabenheit. Meppayil integriert die sakrale, visuelle und mentale Wesenheit des Goldes in ihre Arbeit und schafft damit eine Aura der Ruhe, die die gesamte Fläche beherrscht. Obwohl sie nur natürliche Pigmente wie

Meppayil, who gained a Diploma in Fine Arts from the Ken School of Art, Bangalore in 1992, was raised in Bangalore as the daughter of a traditional goldsmith. At times she uses her father's tools in creating her work, or uses the classical tempera technique to incorporate techniques used in craft and in the traditional elements of Southern Indian miniature paintings into contemporary art. Meppayil is known as a minimalist with an extremely delicate painterly technique.

At first glance, Meppayil's work appears like a painting with a simple drawing executed on the flat white surface. A closer look reveals that the image has been depicted by a skilful use of small dots, fine lines and gold foil and paint, created by superimposing layers of gold of different luminosity so that they appear to emerge and float above the canvas. She mixes powdered chalk with glue and applies it to plywood to form the background, while sandpaper is used to carefully polish the surface to achieve a ceramic-like texture. Subtle lines are drawn on the pure white panel in supple depictions of the silhouettes of men and women, limbs, animals, plants, and at times fragments of abstract shapes. The coloration is subtle and almost like a tint, and this, combined with the understated gleam of the gold, has the effect of creating a world that appears both ghostly and lyrical. In recent years, Meppayil has also been using a technique in which she covers plywood with the sort of colourful fabric sold at markets, over which she layers gesso to "erase" the colour. According to Meppayil, creating art is not simply about depicting, but also represents the process of creating an object.

Since ancient times, gold has had symbolic power, with an image of purity, universality, and the sublime. Meppayil incorporates the sacred visual and psychological effects of gold into her work to create a quiet aura that dominates the entire surface. Although she only uses natural pigments such as lapis lazuli or malachite, the understated image created by the fine use of colour in conjunction with gold is sublimated into a mellifluous art. It is the texture of the surface and the materials themselves that arguably determine the essence of this artist's work. Meppayil's work conveys hazy memories and fleeting emotions, al-

Lapislazuli oder Malachit verwendet wird die durch den feinfühligen Einsatz von Farbe und Gold geschaffene, „verhaltene" Darstellung zu zauberhafter Kunst sublimiert. Man könnte sagen, dass die inhärente Struktur der Oberfläche und des Materials das Wesen ihrer künstlerischen Arbeit ausmacht. Meppayils Werk vermittelt undeutliche Erinnerungen und flüchtige Gefühle, fast so als wären ihre persönlichen Vorstellungen in das Bild übertragen worden. Der schwer fassbare Gegenstand, die erlesene bildliche Darstellung und die traditionellen Techniken verbinden sich zu einem einmaligen Ergebnis.

Meppayil wurde vor allem in indischen Galerien gezeigt, sie hat sich aber auch an einem Residency Program beteiligt und Workshops in der Schweiz abgehalten. Außerdem war sie bei „Horn Please: Narratives in Contemporary Indian Art" (Kunstmuseum Bern, 2007) vertreten. (MT)

most as though her personal ideas have been transferred into the painting. The coexistence of elusive subject matter, visual exquisiteness, and traditional techniques combine to make her work unique.

Meppayil has mainly been shown in domestic galleries, but has participated in a residency program and held some workshops in Switzerland. She also participated in "Horn Please: Narratives in Contemporary Indian Art" (Kunstmuseum Bern, 2007). (MT)

PRABHAVATHI MEPPAYIL
Untitled, 2007

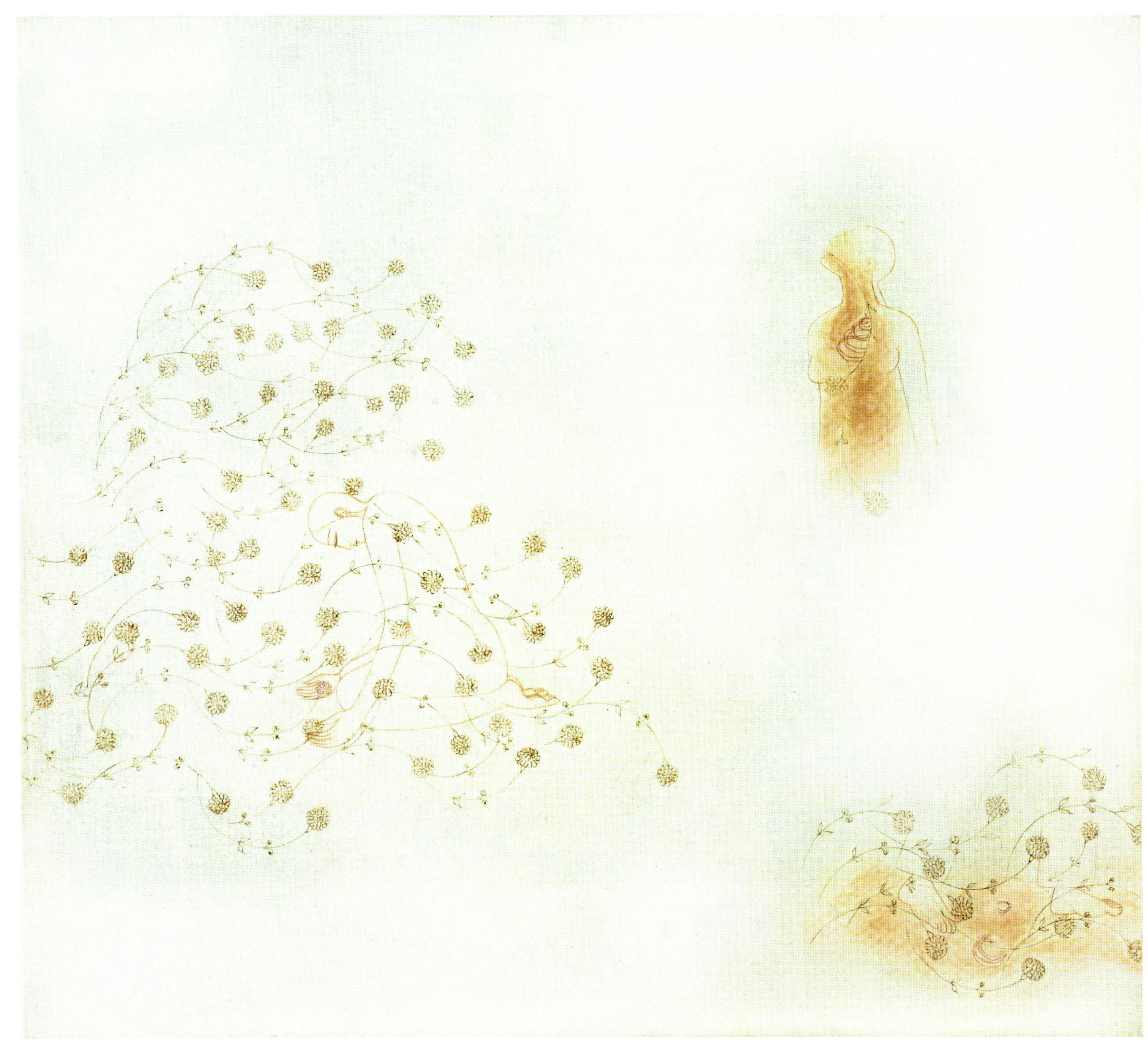

PRABHAVATHI MEPPAYIL
Untitled, 2007

PRABHAVATHI MEPPAYIL
Untitled, 2007

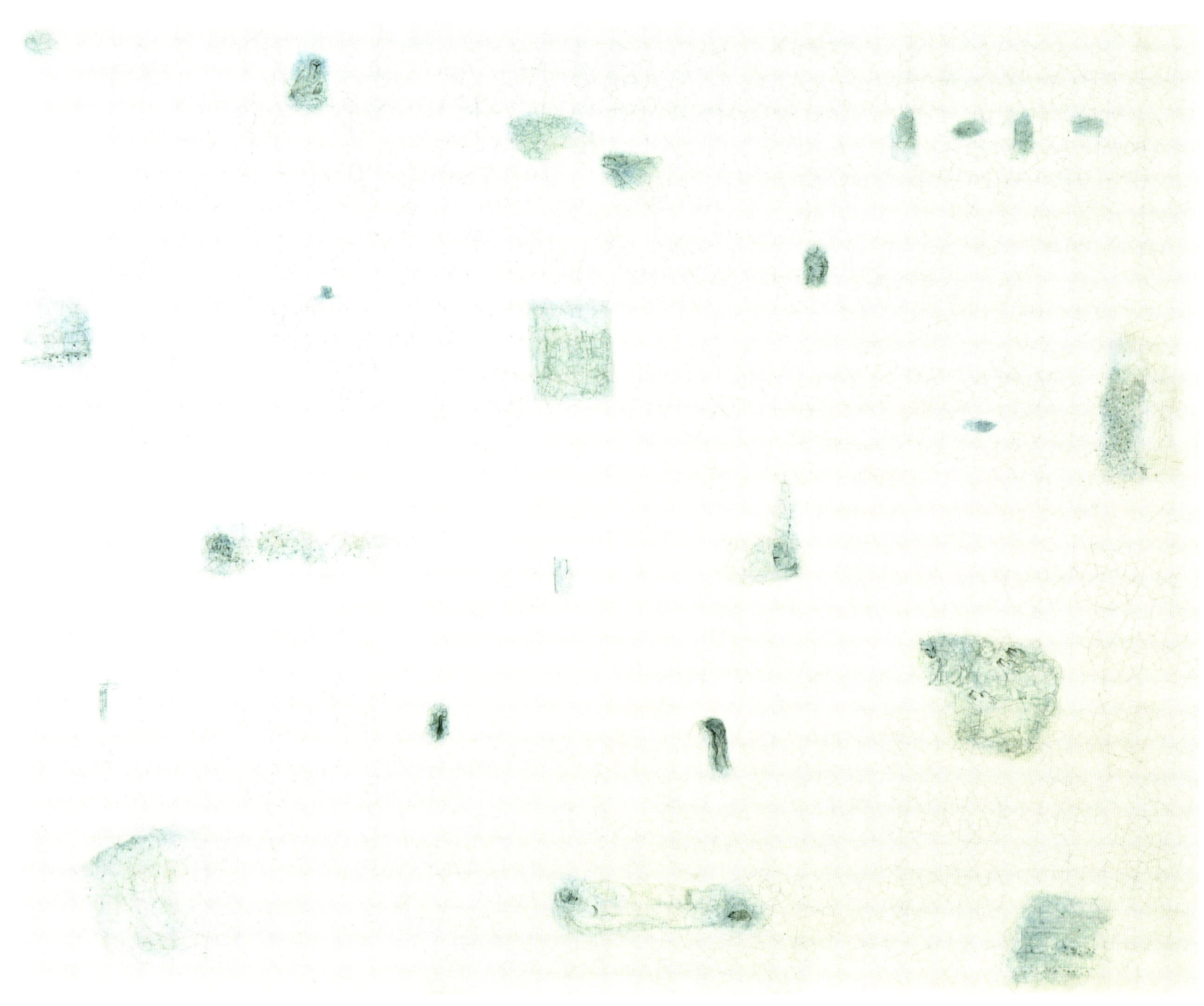

PRABHAVATHI MEPPAYIL
Untitled, 2007

PRABHAVATHI MEPPAYIL
Untitled, 2007

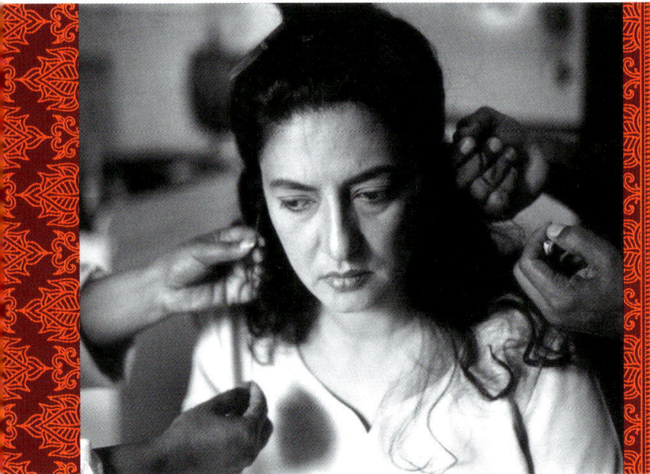

pushpamala n.

PUSHPAMALA N. Geboren 1956 in Bangalore / Lebt in Bangalore
Born 1956 in Bangalore / Lives in Bangalore

Pushpamala N. studierte Kunst (Bildhauerei) und erwarb 1985 ein MA an der Maharaja Sayajirao University of Baroda (Vadodara). 1986 wurde sie mit der 6th New Delhi Triennale Gold Medaille ausgezeichnet. Danach wandte sich Pushpamala N. von der Bildhauerei ab und verlegte sich Mitte der 1990er Jahre auf die Dokumentation ihrer eigenen Performances auf Fotos und Videos. Sie agierte gleichzeitig als Modell, Schauspielerin und Regisseurin und schaffte Arbeiten, die Schlaglichter auf soziale Probleme vor einem konfusen Hintergrund aus Gender und Geschichte werfen.

Das Projekt „Native Women of South India – Manners and Customs" (2000-04) setzte sie gemeinsam mit Clare Arni*, einer in Südindien ansässigen britischen Fotografin um. In „The Native Types", präsentiert sich Pushpamala N. als Frau unterschiedlicher Herkunft, unter anderen von Lakshmi, der Göttin von Fülle und Reichtum und der Verkörperung von Schönheit, von einer Filmheldin und von einem Kriminellen, der in einem Zeitungsartikel beschrieben wird. Indem sie diese aus Büchern, Gemälden, Katalogen und von Postkarten stammenden Bilder unterschiedlicher Frauen rekonstruiert, betont Pushpamala deren Scheinexistenz und zeigt auf, dass das indische Frauenklischee seinen Ursprung in einer von Männern dominierten Gesellschaft hat. Die Serie „The Ethnographic Types" wurde von Fotos inspiriert, die während der Kolonialzeit von Briten „für Forschungszwecke" von Indern gemacht wurden. Die „indigenen Stereotypen" wurden zusammen mit Vorrichtungen zur Vermessung der menschlichen Form auf Schwarzweißfotos festgehalten. Die Serie „The Ethnographic Types" prangert eindrucksvoll jene Briten an, die ethnische Gruppen wie Objekte behandelt hatten. Dennoch wirkt die Arbeit dank Pushpamala N.s scharfem Intellekt und ihrer Beobachtungsgabe auch immer wieder einnehmend und humorvoll. Nach Meinung der Künstlerin werden durch Fotografien und Gemälde nicht nur die klischeehaften Vorstellungen von indischen Frauen, sondern von der indischen Kultur an sich verstärkt, und es würden Versuche unternommen, diese Vorstellungen zur Basis einer nationalen indischen Identität zu machen. Obwohl Pushpamala N. häufig in einem Atemzug mit den feministischen Künstlerinnen Cindy Sherman

Pushpamala N. studied Fine Arts (Sculpture) and obtained MA at the Maharaja Sayajirao University of Baroda (Vadodara) in 1985, after which she embarked on a career as a sculptor in the early 80s, and was awarded the 6th New Delhi Triennale Gold Medal in 1986. Pushpamala N. then moved away from sculpture, and in the mid 90s began creating photographic and video records of her own performances. She is simultaneously the model, actress, and director, producing work that highlights social problems against a tangled background of gender and history.

The project "Native Women of South India – Manners and Customs" (2000-04) is a joint work with Clare Arni*, a British photographer based in South India. In "The Native Types," Pushpamala N. presents herself as women from diverse backgrounds, including Lakshmi, the goddess of abundance and the embodiment of beauty, a movie heroine, and a criminal described in a newspaper article. By reconstructing these images of various women derived from books, catalogues, postcards, and paintings, Pushpamala emphasizes their fictitiousness and reveals how the stereotype of Indian women was formed in a male-dominant society. "The Ethnographic Types" Series was inspired by photographs of Indians taken "for research purposes" by the British during the colonialist era. The "indigenous stereotypes" are captured, together with equipment to measure the human form, in black and white photographs. "The Ethnographic Types" Series conveys a powerful message denouncing the British who treated ethnic groups as objects, and yet the work is at times both delightful and humorous. This is due to Pushpamala N.'s incisive thinking and powers of observation. According to the artist, photographs and paintings not only enhance stereotypical images of women, but of Indian culture as a whole, and that there were attempts to establish India's national identity by using these images. Although Pushpamala N. is often grouped together with feminist artist Cindy Sherman and Eleanor Anti, she asserts that she was strongly influenced by Indian artists such as K.G. Subramanyan and Bhupen Khakhar whose works are rich in cynicism and wit.**

Major exhibitions include "Public Places / Private Spaces: Contemporary Photography and Video Art in India" (The

und Eleanor Anti genannt wird, betont sie den starken Einfluss, den indische Künstler wie K.G. Subramanyan und Bhupen Khakhar auf sie ausgeübt haben, deren Arbeiten reich an Zynismus und Witz sind.**

Wichtige Ausstellungen: „Public Places / Private Spaces: Contemporary Photography and Video Art in India" (The Newark Museum, USA, 2007), „Horn Please: Narratives in Contemporary Indian Art" (Kunstmuseum Bern, 2007) und „My India: Sonia Khurana, Pushpamala N., Tejal Shah" (Three female artists' exhibition, Centre Pompidou, Paris, 2008). (MT)

* CLARE ARNI, Geboren in Großbritanien / Lebt in Bangalore
** „Portrait of an Artist as an Actress", „The Hindu", 28. März 2004.

Newark Museum, USA, 2007), "Horn Please: Narratives in Contemporary Indian Art" (Kunstmuseum Bern, 2007), and "My India: Sonia Khurana, Pushpamala N., Tejal Shah" (Three female artists' exhibition, Centre Pompidou, Paris, 2008). (MT)

* CLARE ARNI Born in Great Britain / Lives in Bangalore
** "Portrait of an Artist as an Actress," *The Hindu,* 28 March 2004.

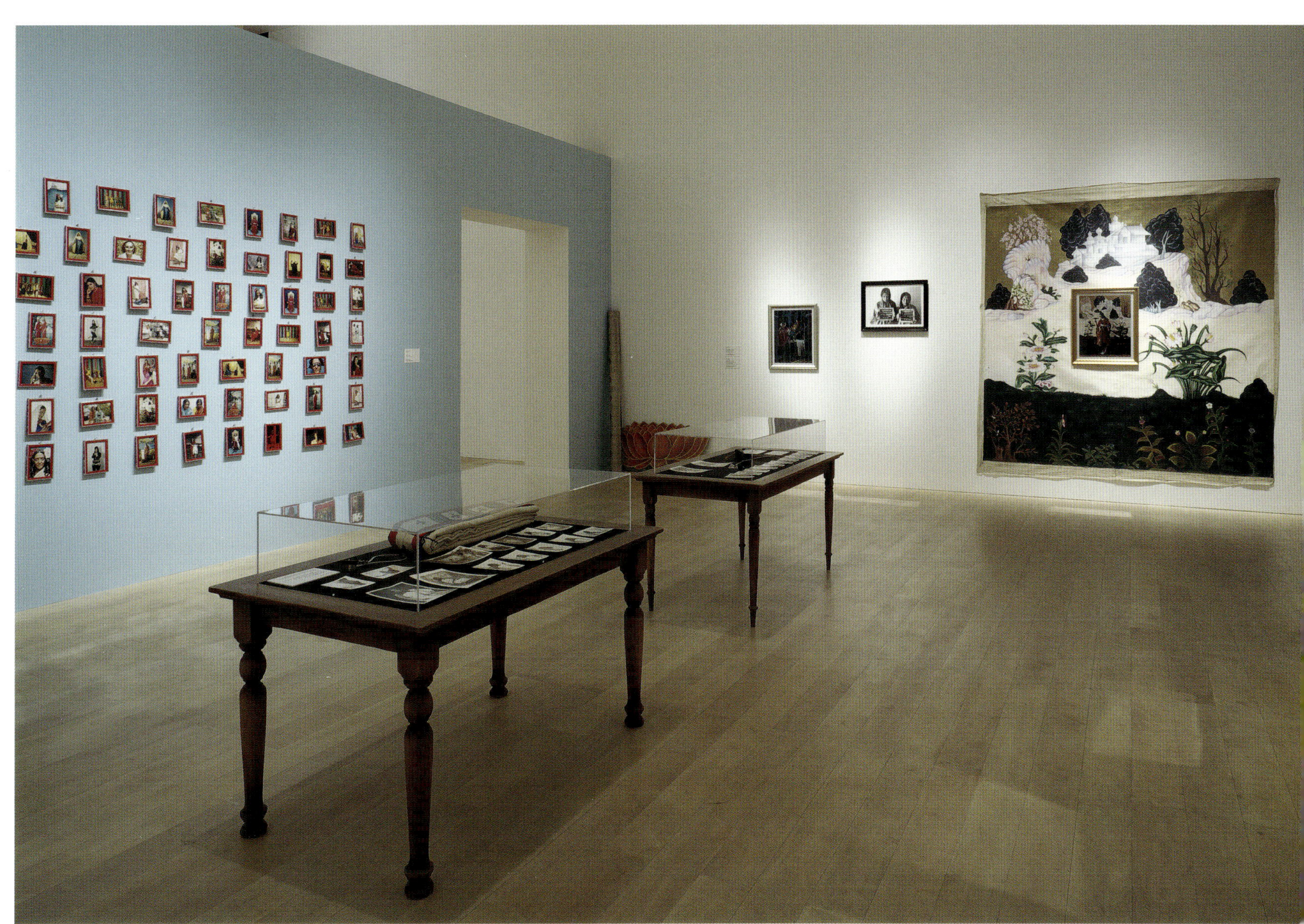

PUSHPAMALA N. and CLARE ARNI
Installation view

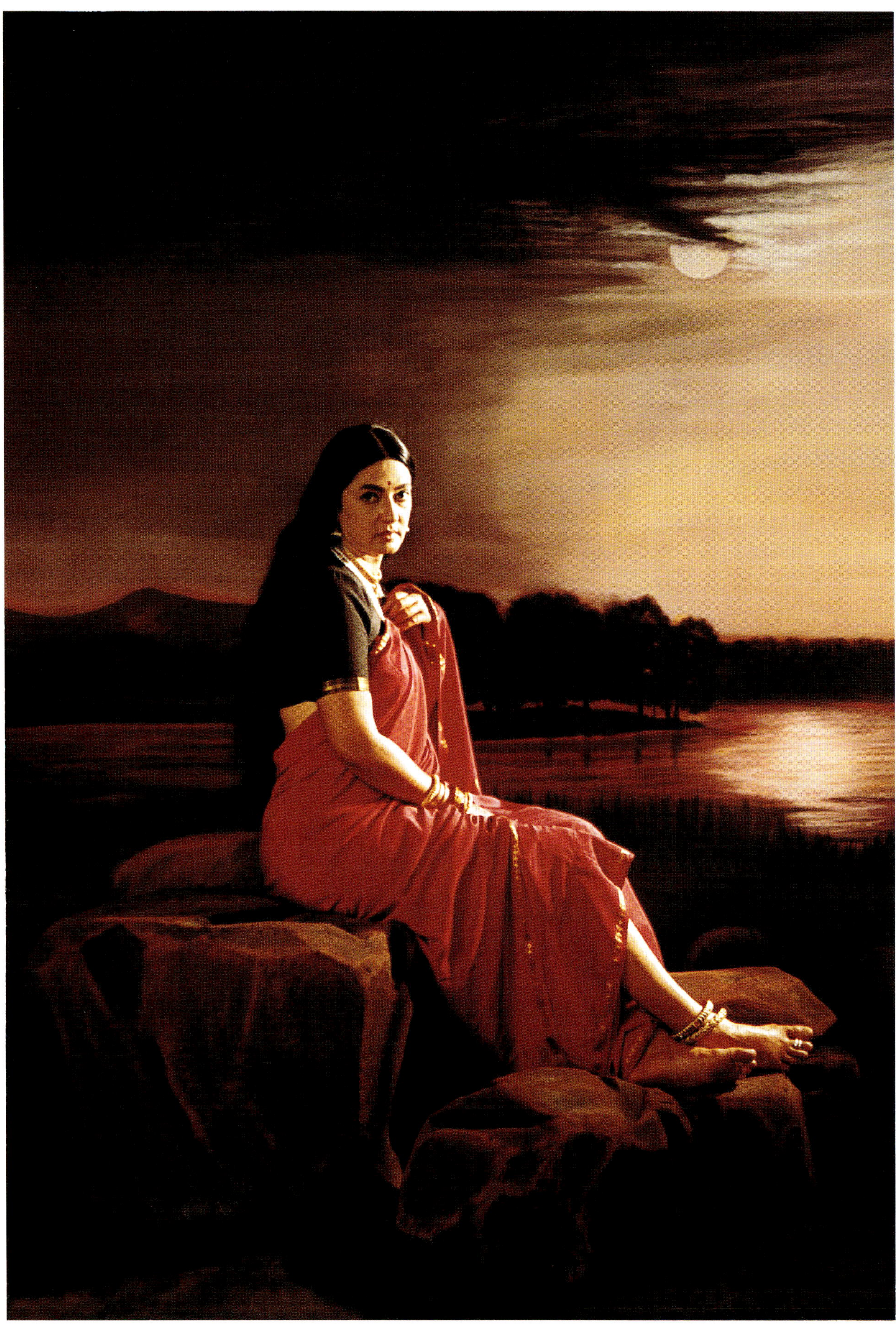

PUSHPAMALA N. and CLARE ARNI
The Native Types – Lady in Moonlight (After Raja Varma Oil Painting), Bangalore 2000–04
The Native Types – Lakshmi (After Oleograph from Ravi Varma Press, Early 20th Century), Bangalore 2000–04

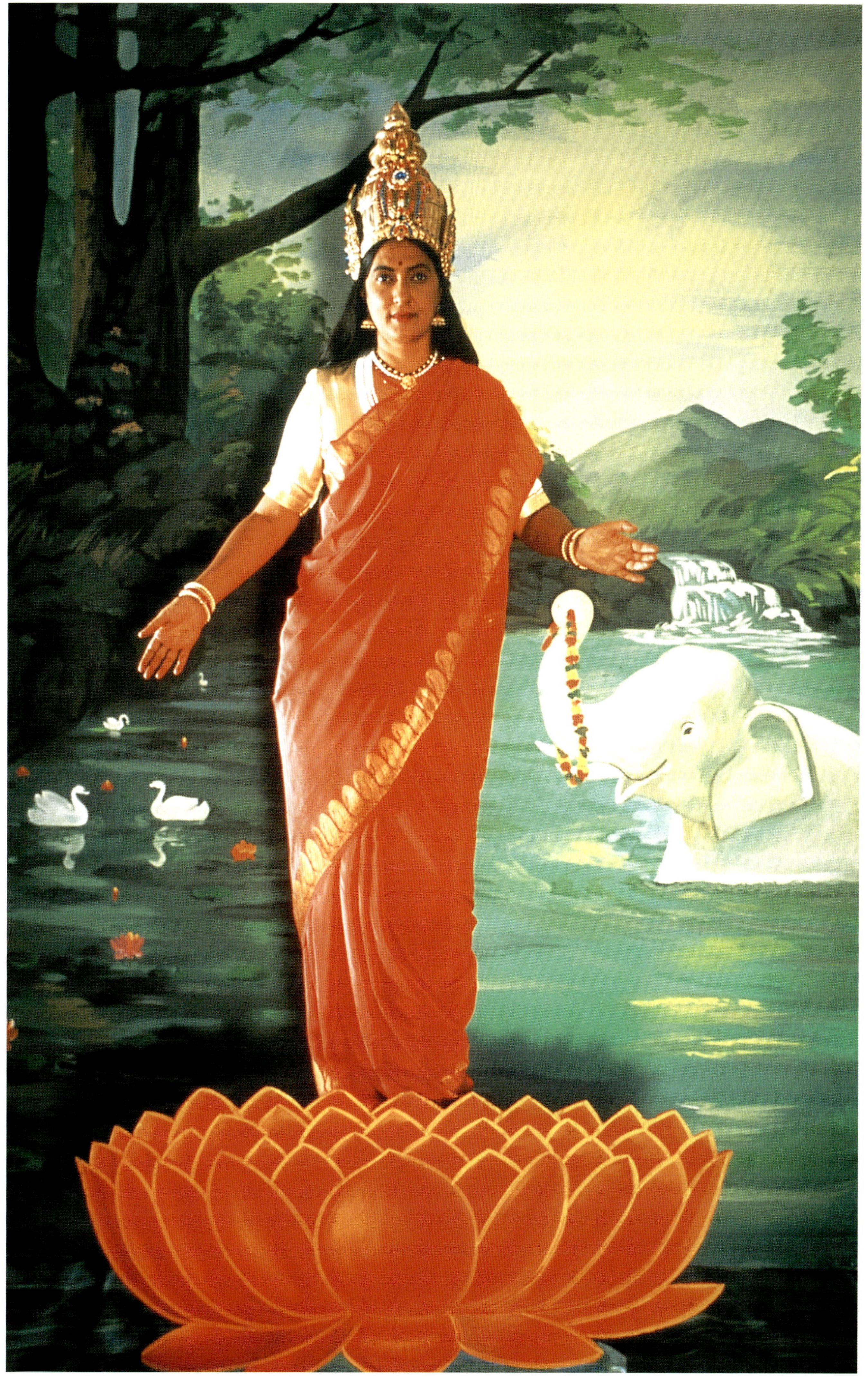

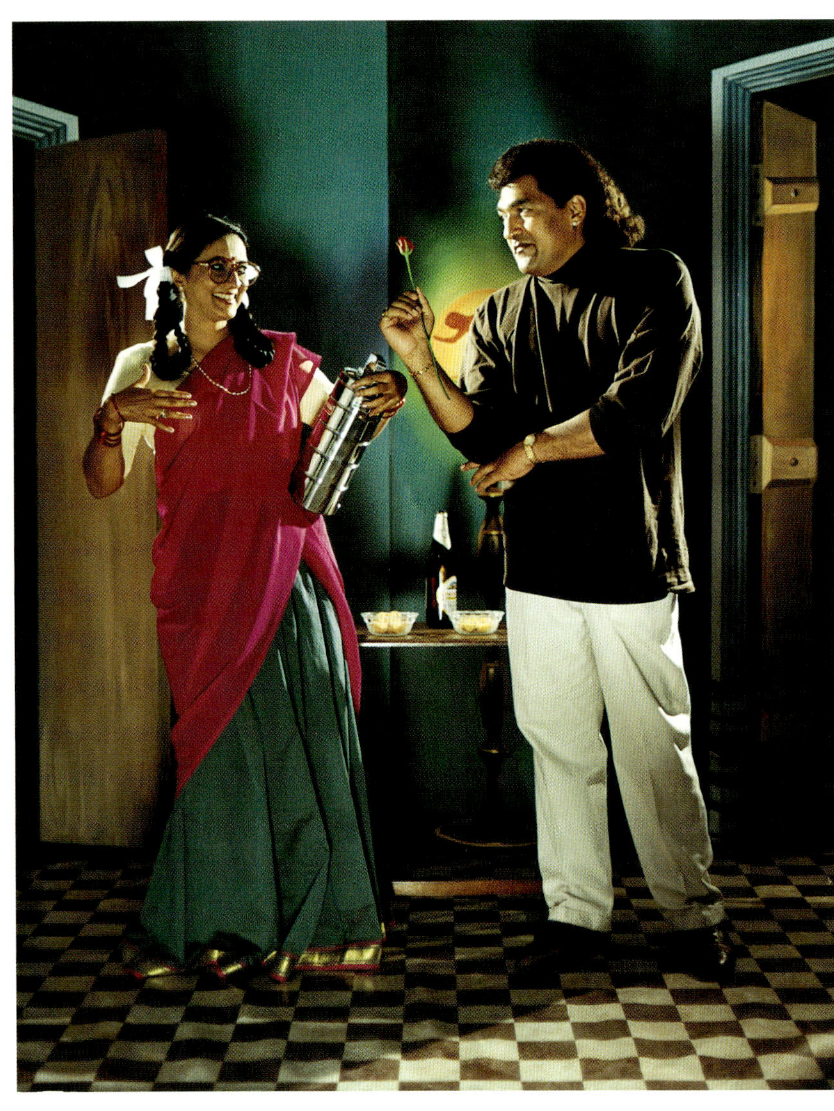

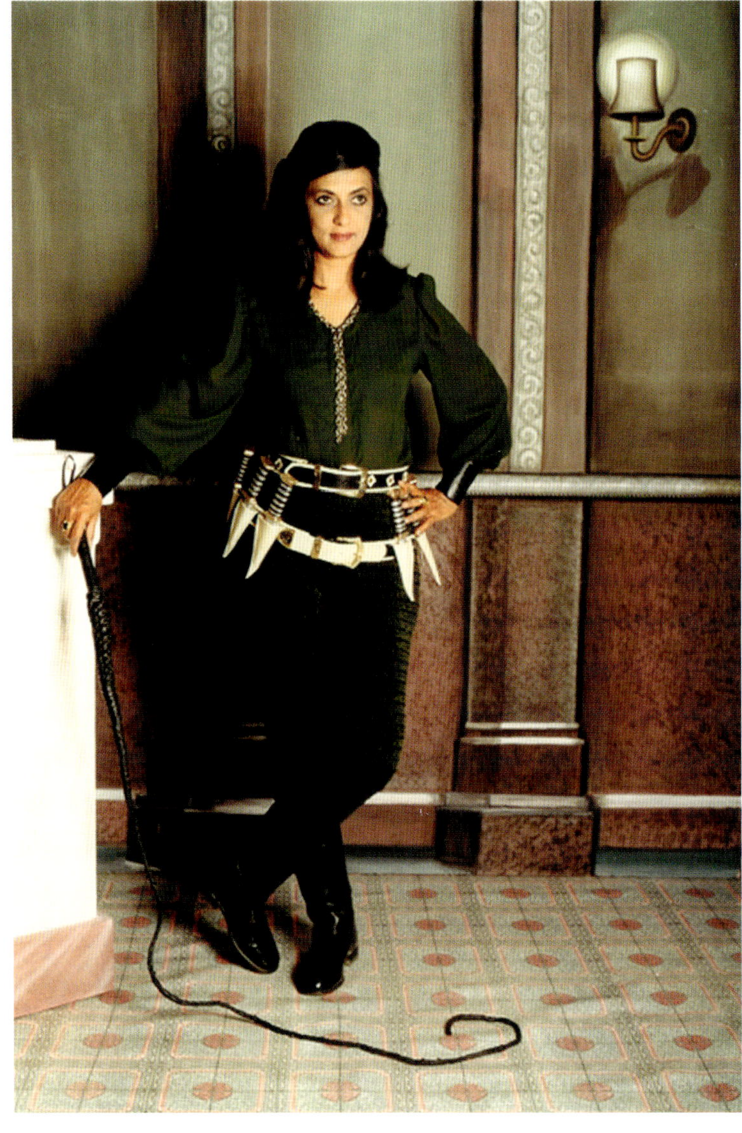

PUSHPAMALA N. and CLARE ARNI
The Native Types – Flirting (After 1990's Kannada Film Still), Bangalore 2000–04
The Native Types – Cracking the Wip (After 1970s Tamil Film Still), Bangalore 2000–04

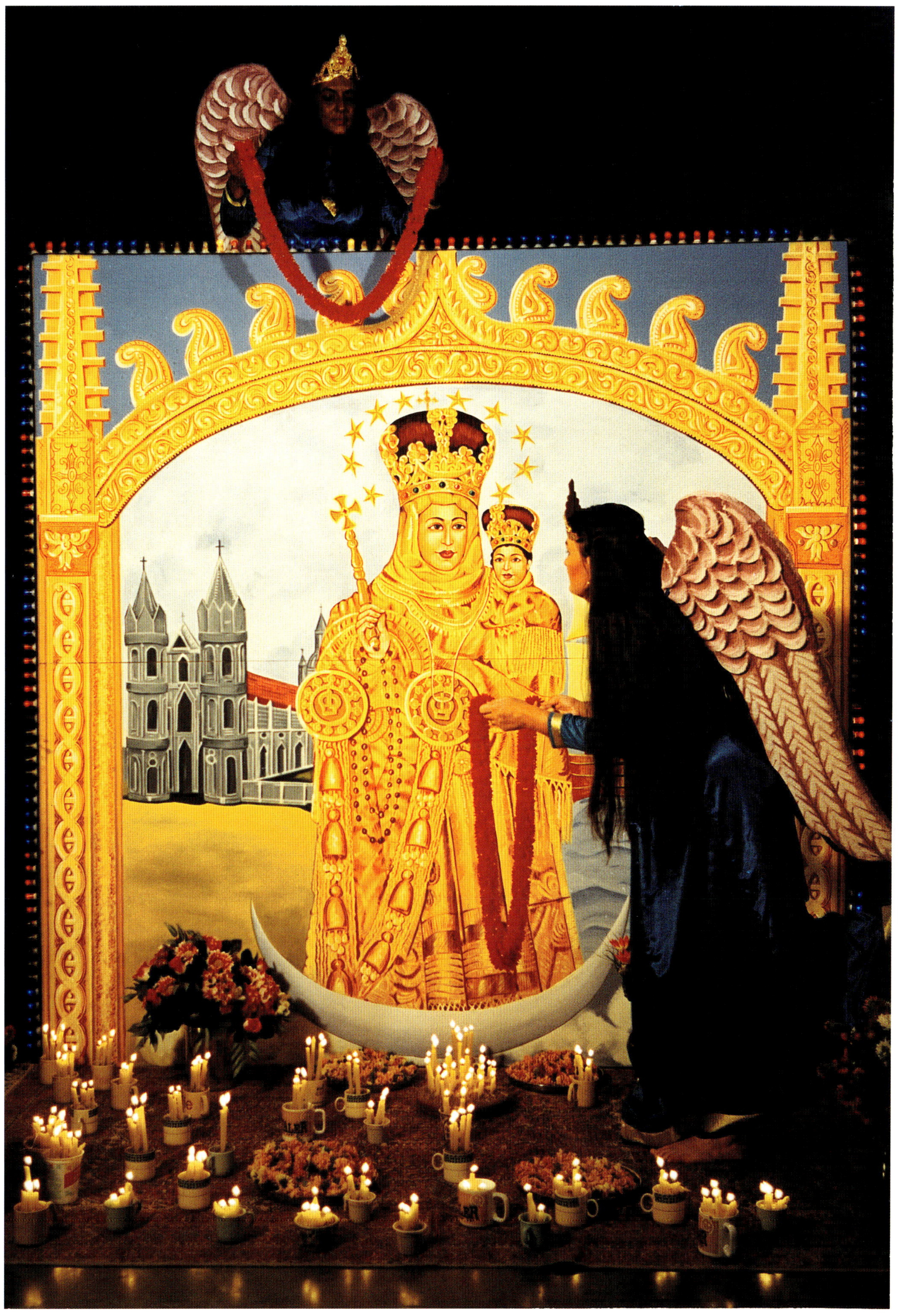

PUSHPAMALA N. and CLARE ARNI
The Native Types – Our Lady of Velankanni (After Contemporary Votive Image), Bangalore 2000–04

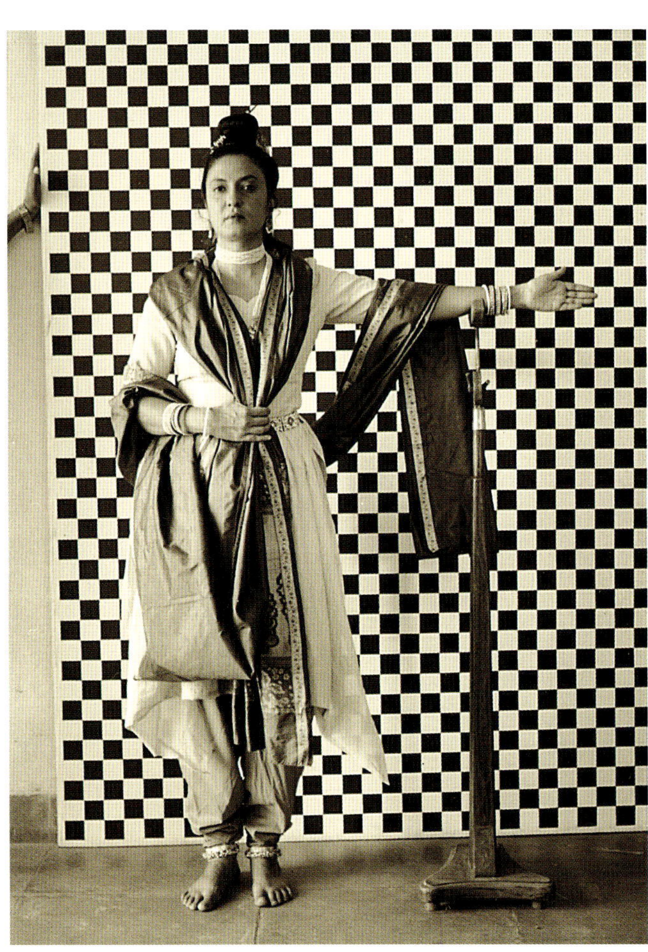

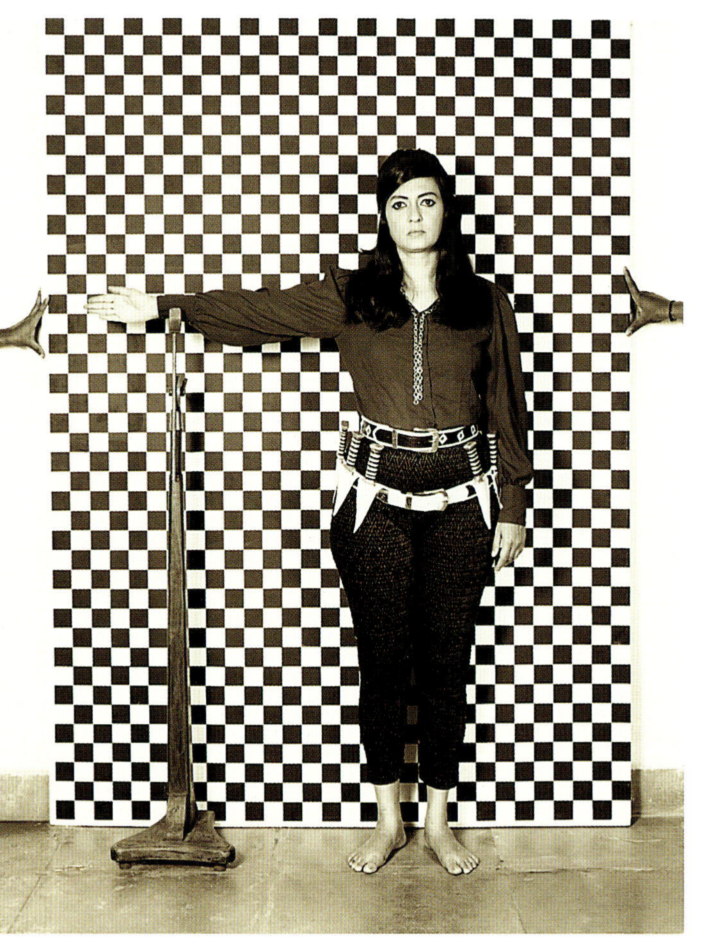

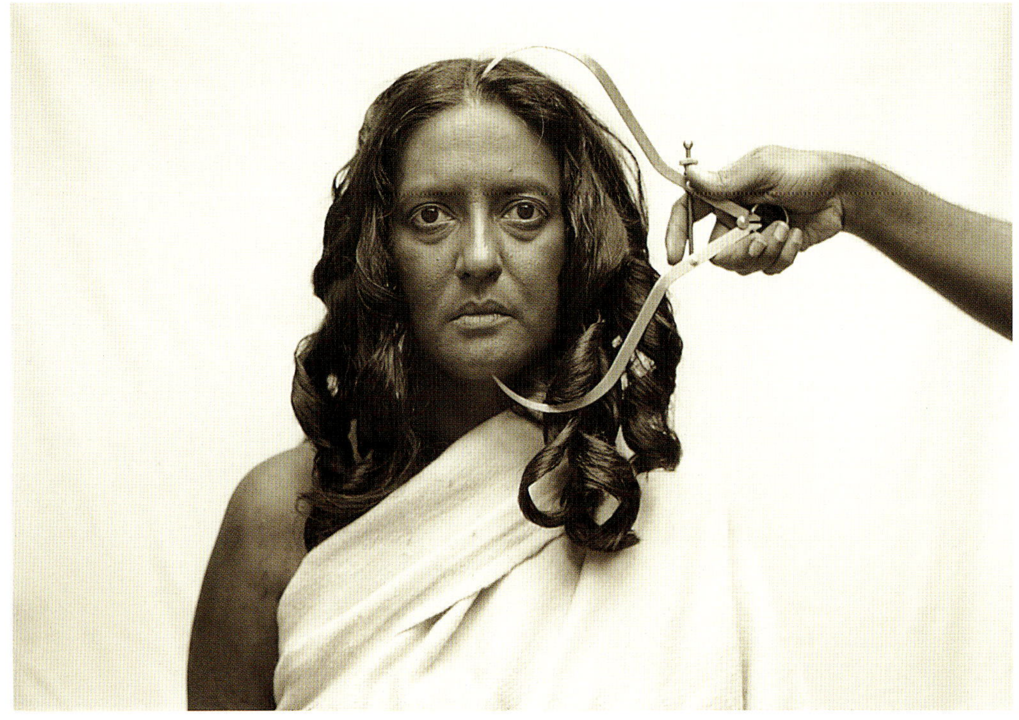

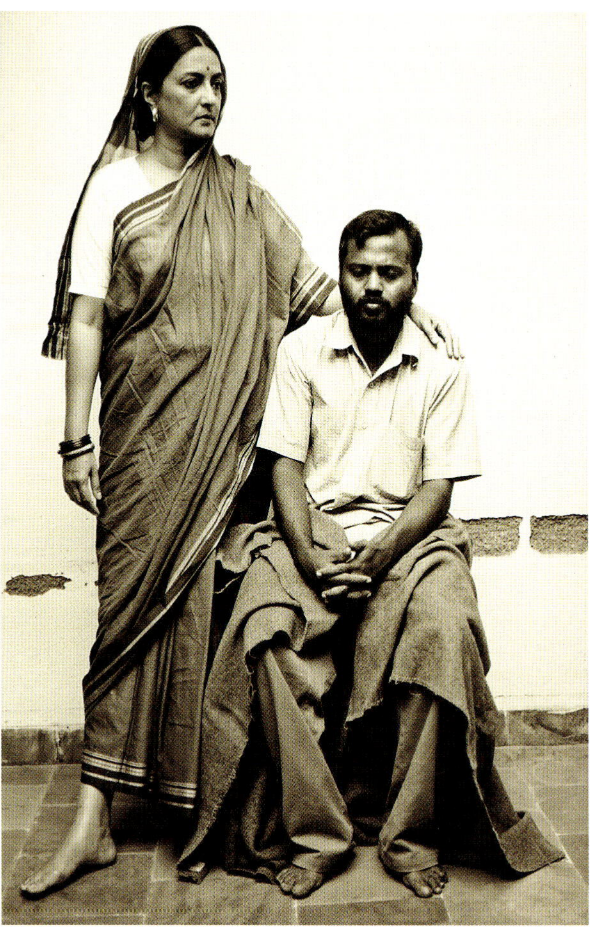

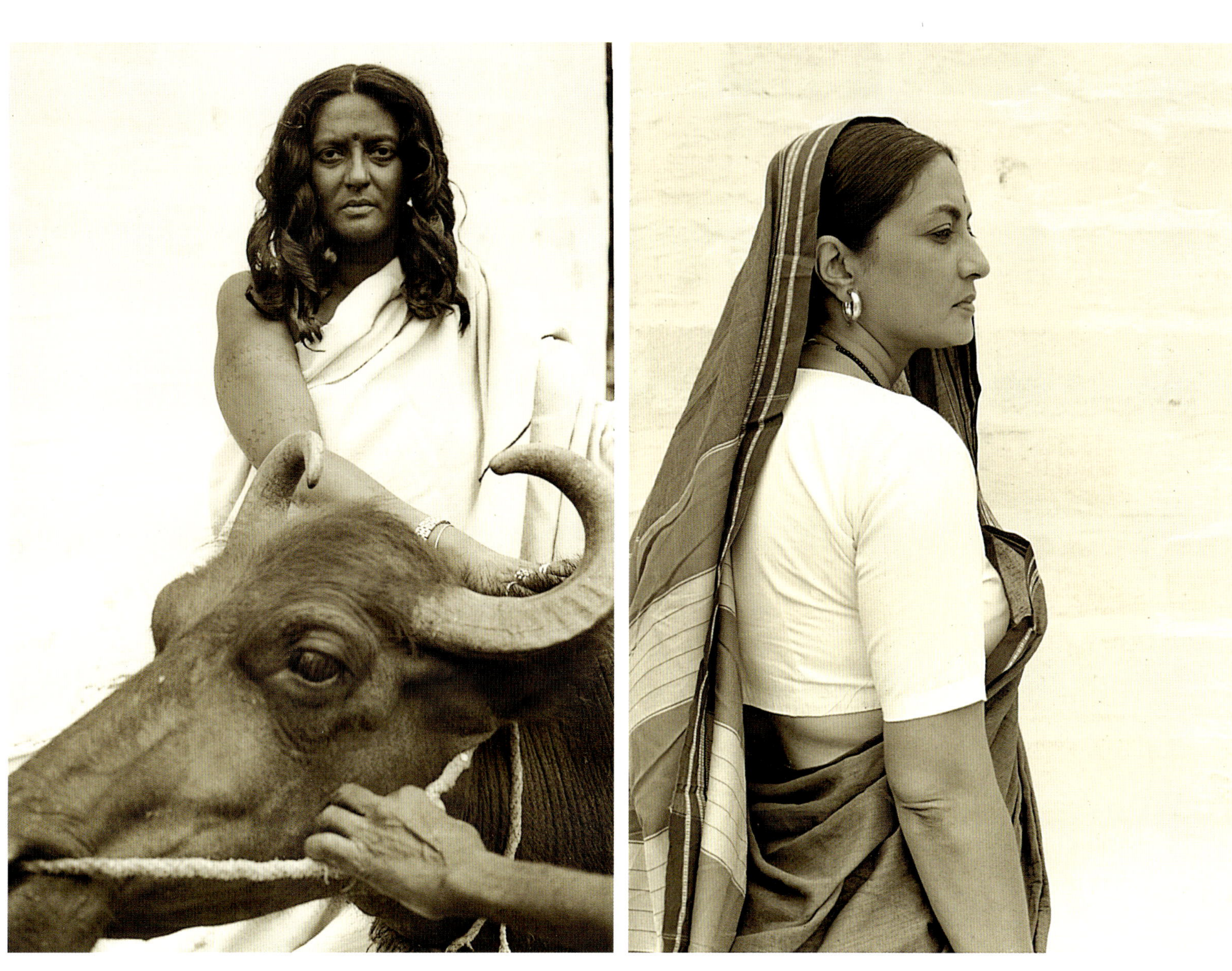

PUSHPAMALA N. and CLARE ARNI
From the photo-performance project
Native Women of South India: Manners and Customs, Bangalore 2000–04
The Ethnographic Types

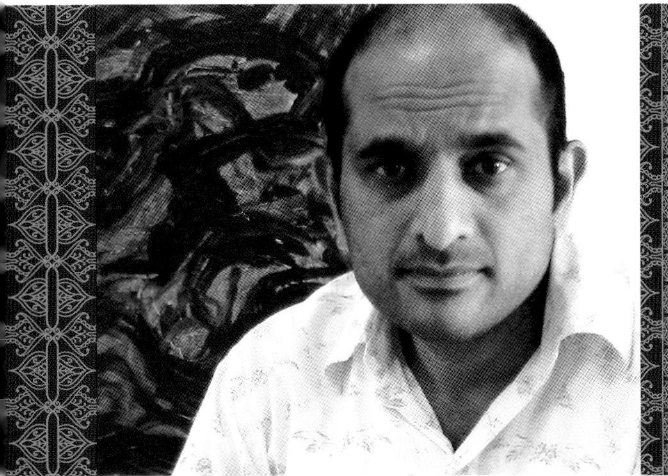

n.s. harsha

N.S. HARSHA Geboren 1969 in Mysore, Karnataka / Lebt in Mysore
Born 1969 in Mysore, Karnataka / Lives in Mysore

Nach Abschluss der School of Painting, Chamarajendra Academy of Visual Arts (CAVA), Mysore, im Jahr 1992, erwarb N. S. Harsha 1995 sein Magisterdiplom an der Maharaja Sayajirao University of Baroda (Vadodara). Entgegen dem unter den Künstlern seiner Generation herrschenden Trend, in die Städte abzuwandern, kehrte er in seinen Geburtsort zurück und ließ sich dort nieder. Die Werke, die angeregt von der Naturlandschaft Südindiens und dem einförmigen Tagesablauf ihrer Bevölkerung entstanden, lassen sich in vier Gruppen einteilen: die von der indischen Miniaturmalerei geprägte narrative Kunst, die Serie von Gemälden zum Thema Suburbanisation, Gemeinschaftsprojekte und site-specific Installationen. N. S. Harsha wurde 2008 bei der Artes Mundi 3, in Cardiff, Großbritannien, mit dem Artes Mundi Prize ausgezeichnet und hat einen Markenschal entworfen.

„Please Come Give Us A Speech“, ein Werk jüngeren Datums, ist eine Installation, in der sechs Leinwände in einem Halbkreis an der Wand angebracht sind, sodass dem vor dem Werk stehenden Betrachter zwangsläufig die Rolle des Redners zukommt. Mehrere hundert Personen sitzen auf Reihen grellbunter Plastikstühle, ähnlich wie am Beginn irgendeines Empfangs oder einer Versammlung. Manche plaudern mit ihren Sitznachbarn, andere sitzen mit verschränkten Armen. Ab und zu stellen sie sich neben eine Skulptur im Ausstellungsraum und erwecken den Eindruck gespannter Erwartung. Aus der Entfernung erscheinen die Personen in der Menge wie eine Serie immer gleicher Bilder. Bei näherem Hinsehen wird allerdings klar, dass jede einzelne Person samt ihrer Kleidung bis ins kleinste Detail abgebildet wurde. Das Wort „Us“ im Titel verweist darauf, dass auch der Künstler Teil der Gruppe ist. Bei der aktuellen Ausstellung hat er die Stühle für das Aufsichtspersonal der Galerie entworfen. Jeder Stuhl ist anders, aber die Schlagworte oder Satzteile, die jedem einzelnen zugeordnet sind – Mutter und Kind, Wissen, Erinnerungen an die eigene Kindheit – stehen alle für „Schutz und Sicherheit“. Auf einem der Stühle liegen zum Beispiel ein Schleier und Burkhas – wie sie von muslimischen Frauen getragen werden – die den Stuhl mit der dahinterliegenden Wand zu einem geometrischen Muster verknüpfen. Neben einem der Stühle steht ein Sack mit

After graduating from the School of Painting, the Chamarajendra Academy of Visual Arts (CAVA), Mysore in 1992, N. S. Harsha obtained his MA at Maharaja Sayajirao University of Baroda (Vadodara) in 1995. Although many artists of his generation relocate to cities, he returned to live in his birthplace. The effortless works inspired by the natural surrounds of Southern India and the simple everyday lives of its people can be largely divided into four categories: the narrative art informed by India's miniature paintings and the series of paintings depicting suburbanization, collaborative projects and site-specific installations. N. S. Harsha was awarded the Artes Mundi Prize at Artes Mundi 3, held in Cardiff, U.K. this year, and has designed a brand-name scarf.

N. S. Harsha's recent work, *Please Come Give Us A Speech,* is an installation in which six canvases are hung on the wall in a semi-circular shape, effectively turning the observer standing in front of the work into a speaker. Hundreds of people are sitting on brightly coloured plastic chairs arranged in rows, as though some sort of reception or a political or religious gathering is about to begin. The people, perhaps bored, are chatting to those sitting next to them. Others sit, their arms crossed. At times they pose by a sculpture in the exhibition space, and look as though they are waiting in anticipation. From a distance the individuals in the crowd appear to be a series of repeated images. On closer inspection, however, each individual, including what he or she is wearing, is depicted in painstaking detail. By the inclusion of the word "Us" in the title, the artist indicates that he is also one of the group. In this exhibition, he has designed the chairs for the attendants who function as security guards in the galleries. Each chair is different, but the key words or phrases associated with each chair – mother and child, knowledge, the memories of one's own early childhood – all represent "protection." For instance, there is a chair with a veil and burkhas, as worn by Muslim women, connecting the chair to the wall behind it to create a geometric pattern. There is also a chair with a bag of rice placed beside it "to protect" against hunger. The attendants who sit on these chairs are the ones who being "observed," and through this, the artist has engineered a new exchange of gazes between the gal-

Reis als „Schutz“ vor Hunger. Im gegebenen Fall ist es das auf den Stühlen sitzende Aufsichtspersonal, das „unter Beobachtung steht“, womit der Künstler neue Sichtkontakte zwischen den Besuchern der Galerie, den ausgestellten Werken und dem Aufsichtspersonal, das üblicherweise die Ausstellungsstücke „beschützt“, herstellt.

Wichtige Ausstellungen: „The 3rd Asia-Pacific Triennial of Contemporary Art“ (Queensland Art Gallery, Brisbane, 1999), „The 2nd Fukuoka Asian Art Triennale“ (Fukuoka Asian Art Museum, 2002) und „Artes Mundi 3“ (National Museum, Cardiff, U.K., 2008). (TK)

lery visitors, the works on exhibit, and the attendants, who normally "protect" the exhibits.

Major exhibitions include "The 3rd Asia-Pacific Triennial of Contemporary Art" (Queensland Art Gallery, Brisbane, 1999), "The 2nd Fukuoka Asian Art Triennale" (Fukuoka Asian Art Museum, 2002), and "Artes Mundi 3" (National Museum, Cardiff, U.K., 2008). (TK)

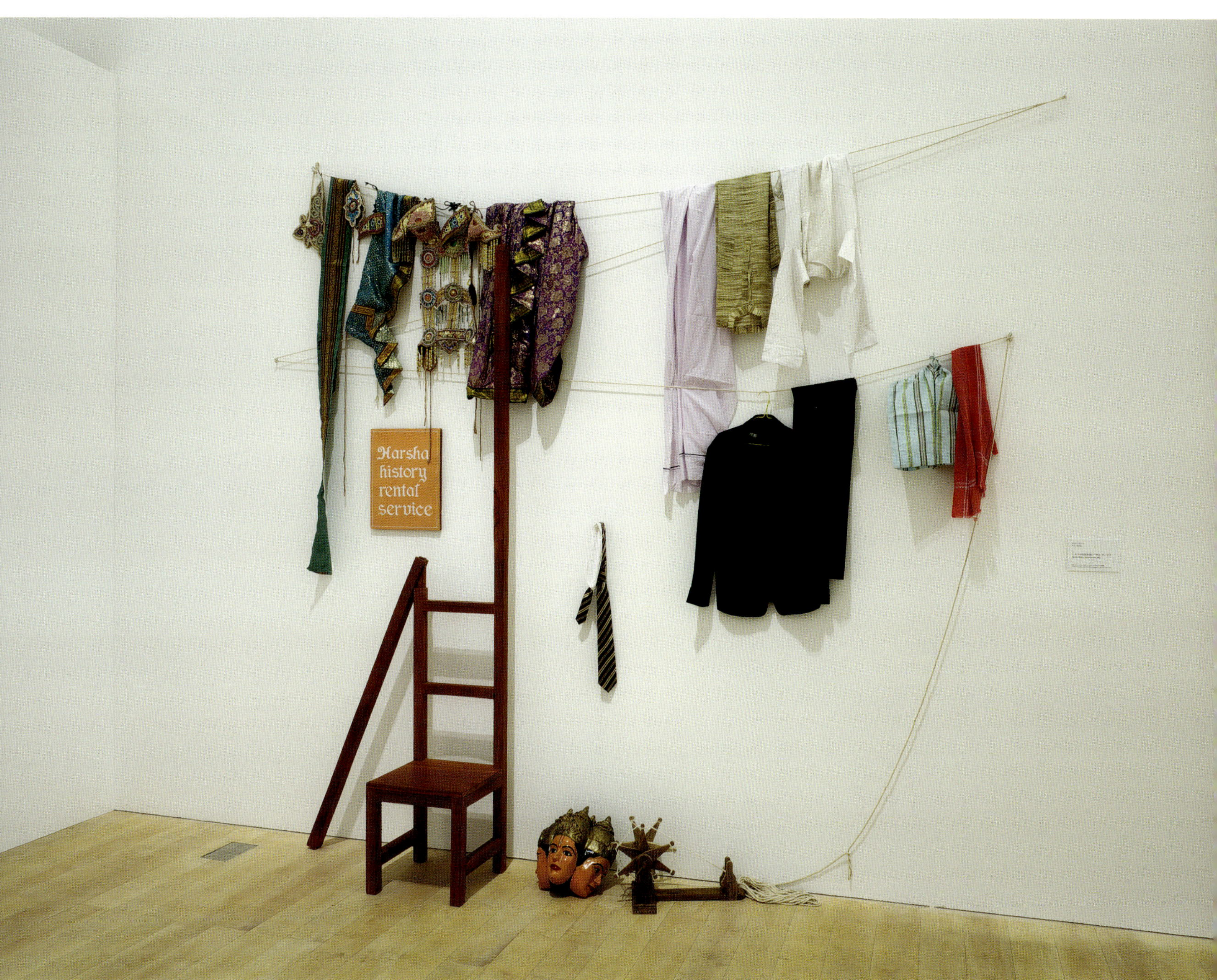

N. S. HARSHA
History Rental Service, 2008

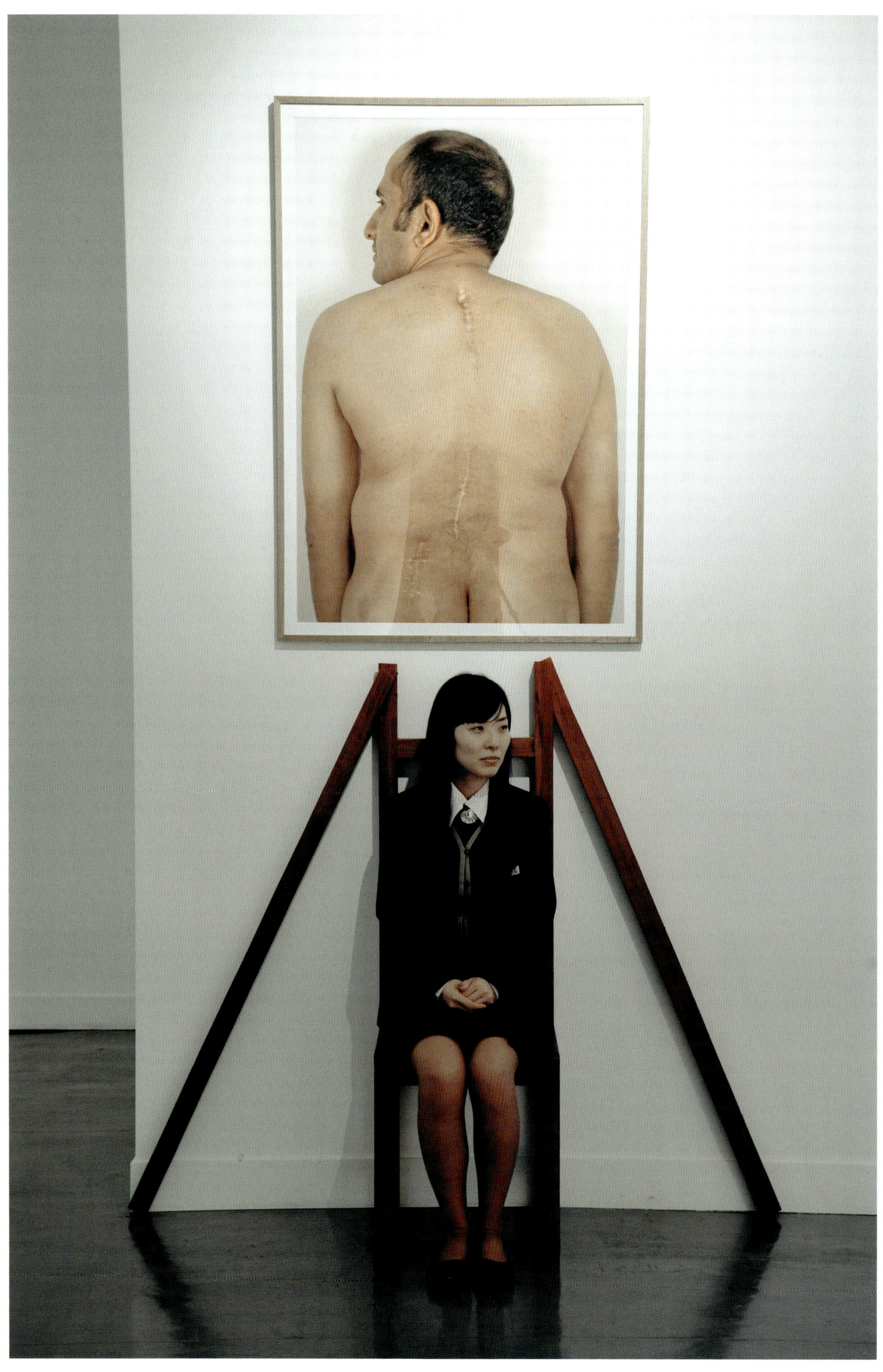

N. S. HARSHA
Disclosing Cultural Discomfort, 2008

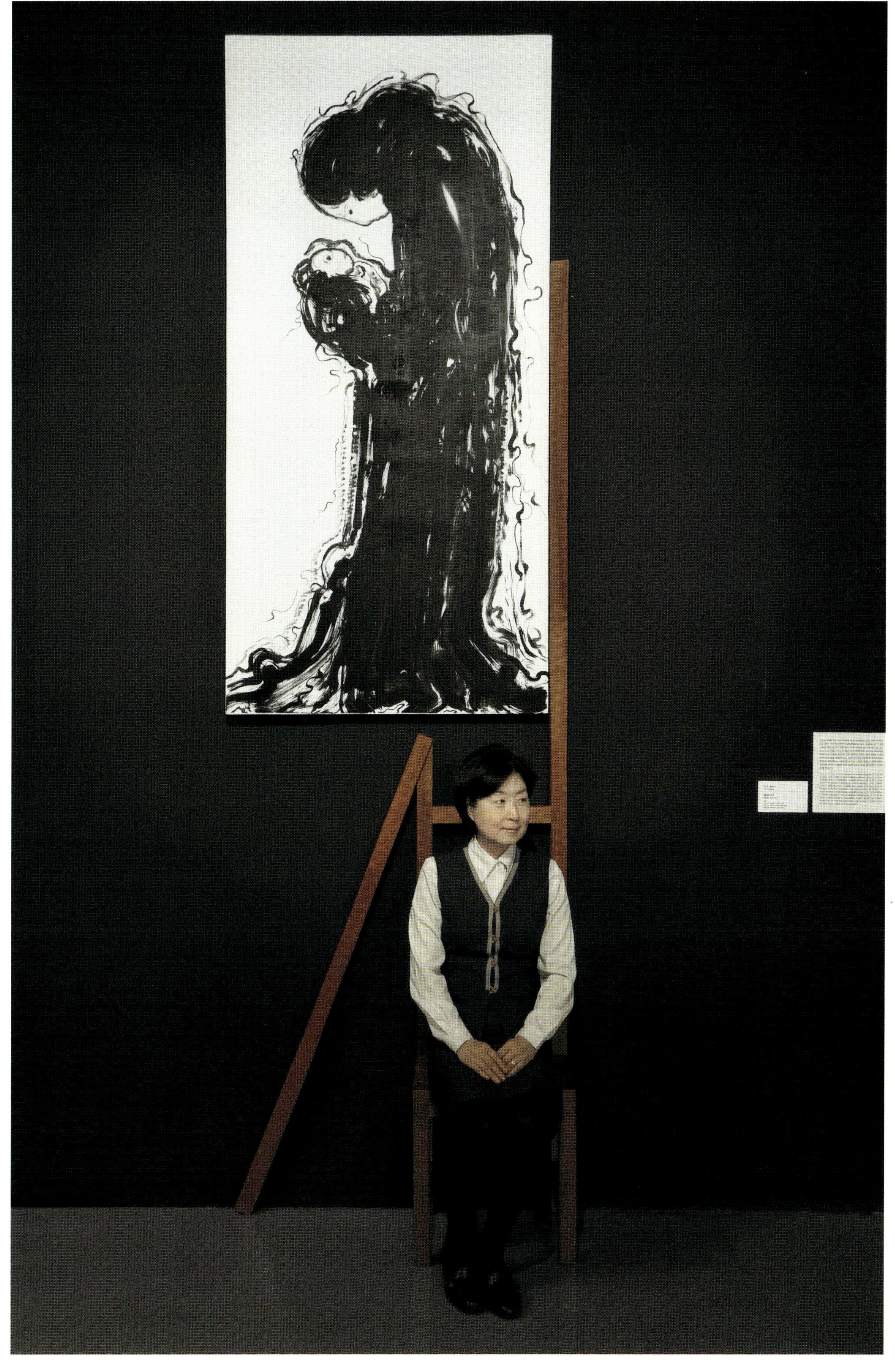

N. S. HARSHA
Mother and Child, 2008

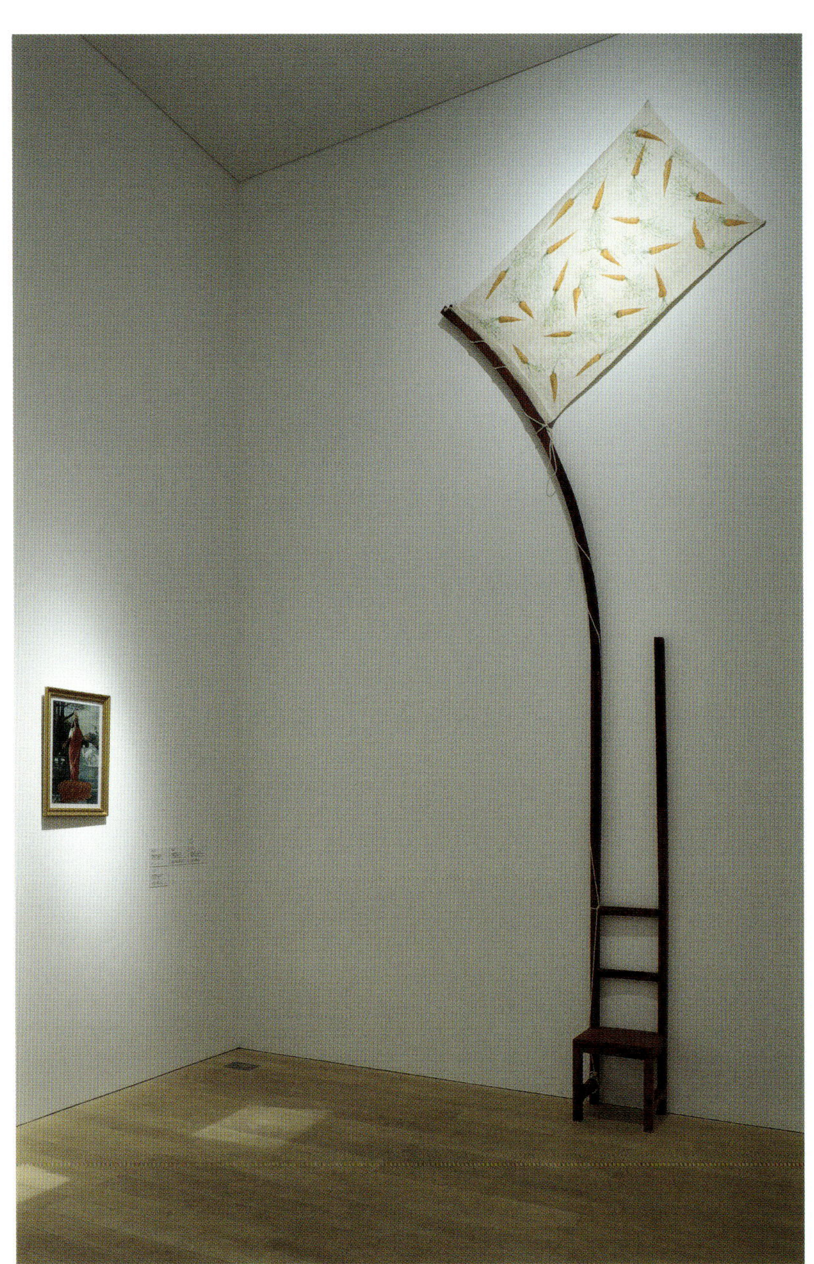

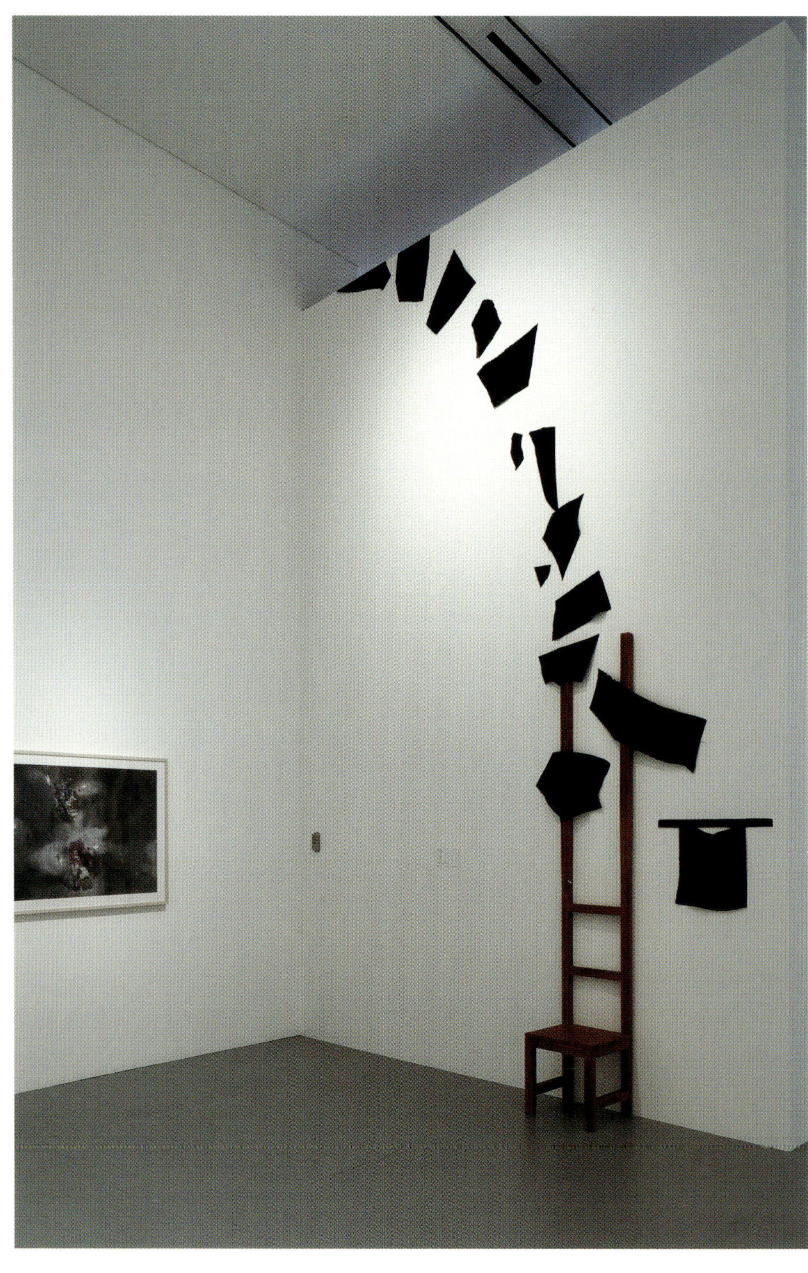

N. S. HARSHA
Guarding the 24 Carrot Country, 2008
Burka, 2008
Guarded Knowledge, 2008

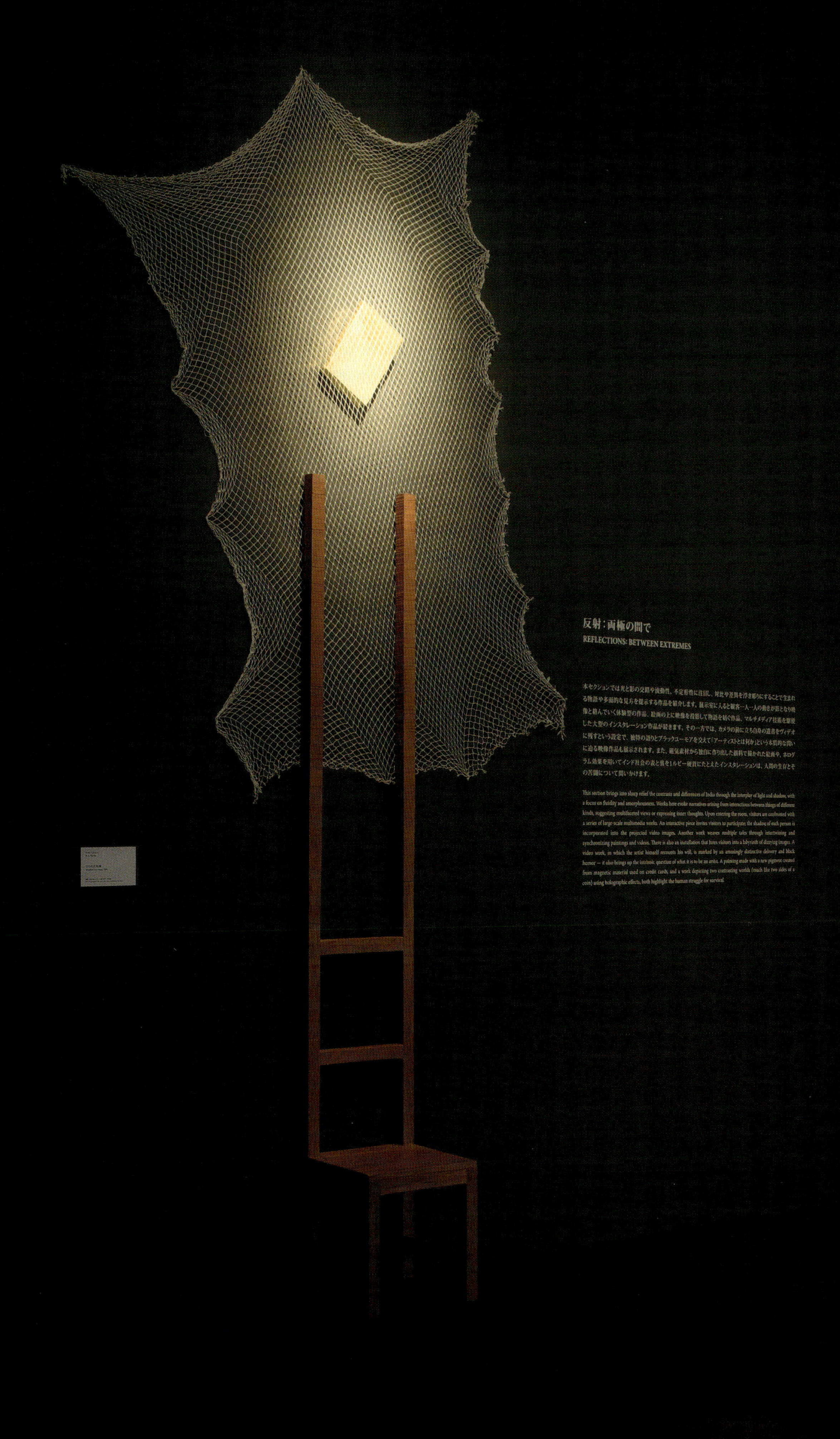
反射：両極の間で
REFLECTIONS: BETWEEN EXTREMES
本セクションでは光と影の交錯や流動性、不定形性に注目し、対比や差異を浮き彫りにすることで生まれる物語や多面的な見方を提示する作品を紹介します。展示室に入ると観客一人一人の動きが影となり映像と絡んでいく体験型の作品、絵画の上に映像を投影して物語を紡ぐ作品、マルチメディア技術を駆使した大型のインスタレーション作品が続きます。その一方では、カメラの前に立ち自身の遺書をヴィデオに残すという設定で、独特の語りとブラックユーモアを交えて「アーティストとは何か」という本質的な問いに迫る映像作品も展示されます。また、磁気素材から独自に作り出した顔料で描かれた絵画や、ホログラム効果を用いてインド社会の表と裏を1ルピー硬貨にたとえたインスタレーションは、人間の生存とその苦闘について問いかけます。
This section brings into sharp relief the contrasts and differences of India through the interplay of light and shadow, with a focus on fluidity and amorphousness. Works here evoke narratives arising from interactions between things of different kinds, suggesting multifaceted views or expressing inner thoughts. Upon entering the room, visitors are confronted with a series of large-scale multimedia works. An interactive piece invites visitors to participate: the shadow of each person is incorporated into the projected video images. Another work weaves multiple tales through intertwining and synchronizing paintings and videos. There is also an installation that lures visitors into a labyrinth of dizzying images. A video work, in which the artist himself recounts his will, is marked by an amusingly distinctive delivery and black humor — it also brings up the intrinsic question of what it is to be an artist. A painting made with a new pigment created from magnetic material used on credit cards, and a work depicting two contrasting worlds (much like two sides of a coin) using holographic effects, both highlight the human struggle for survival.

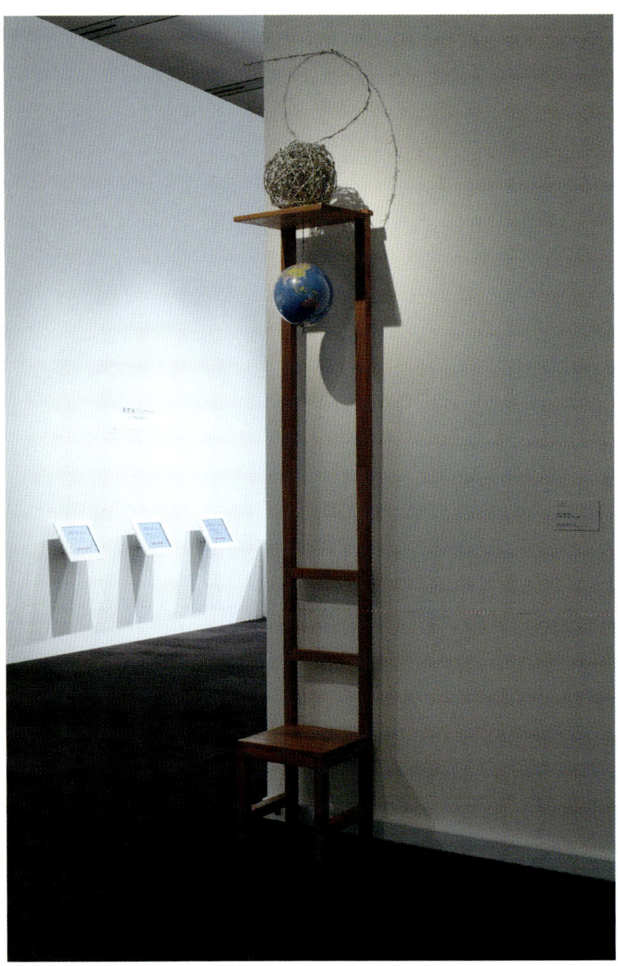
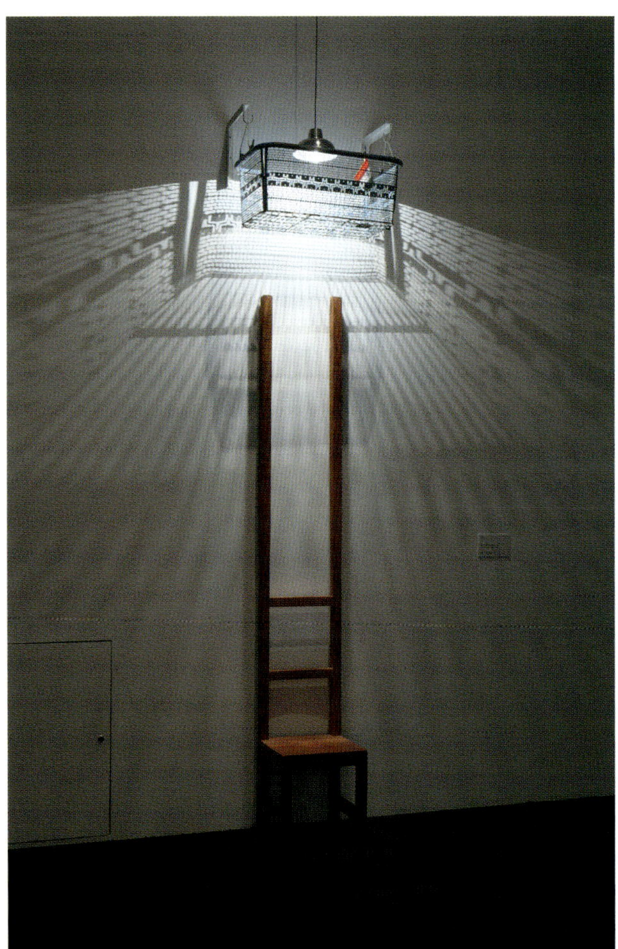
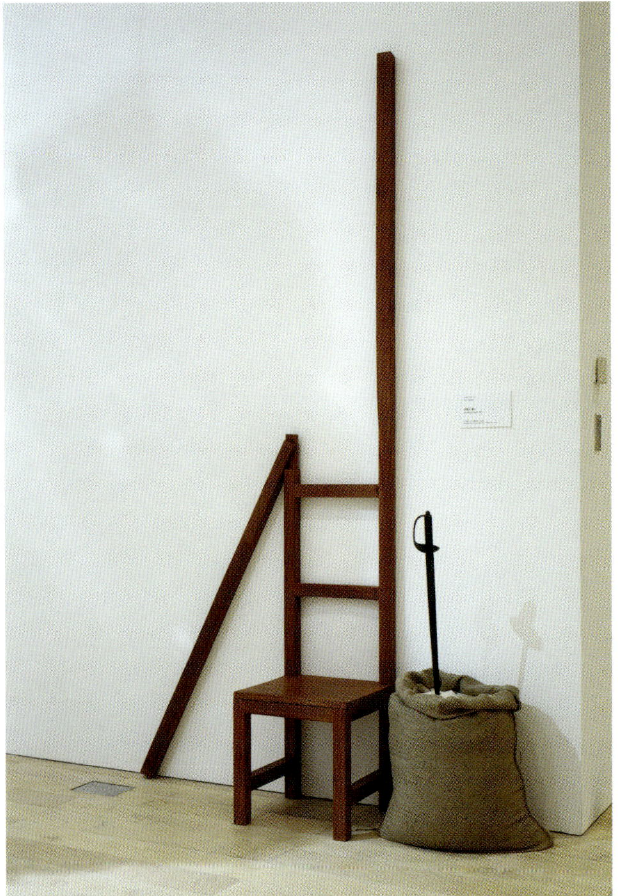
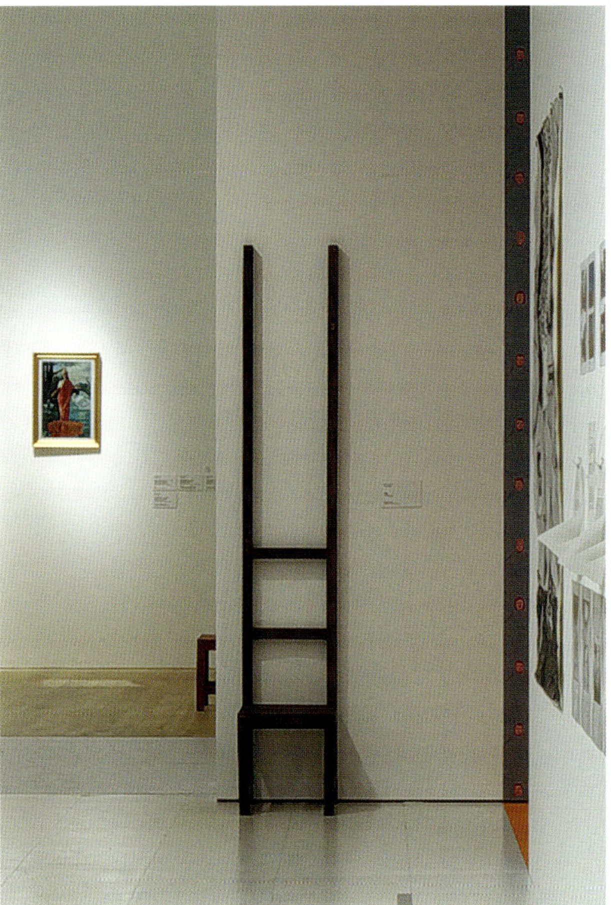

N. S. HARSHA
Guarding the Thorn Throne, 2008
My Childhood Was Very Bright, 2008
Guarding Hunger, 2008
Untitled, 2008

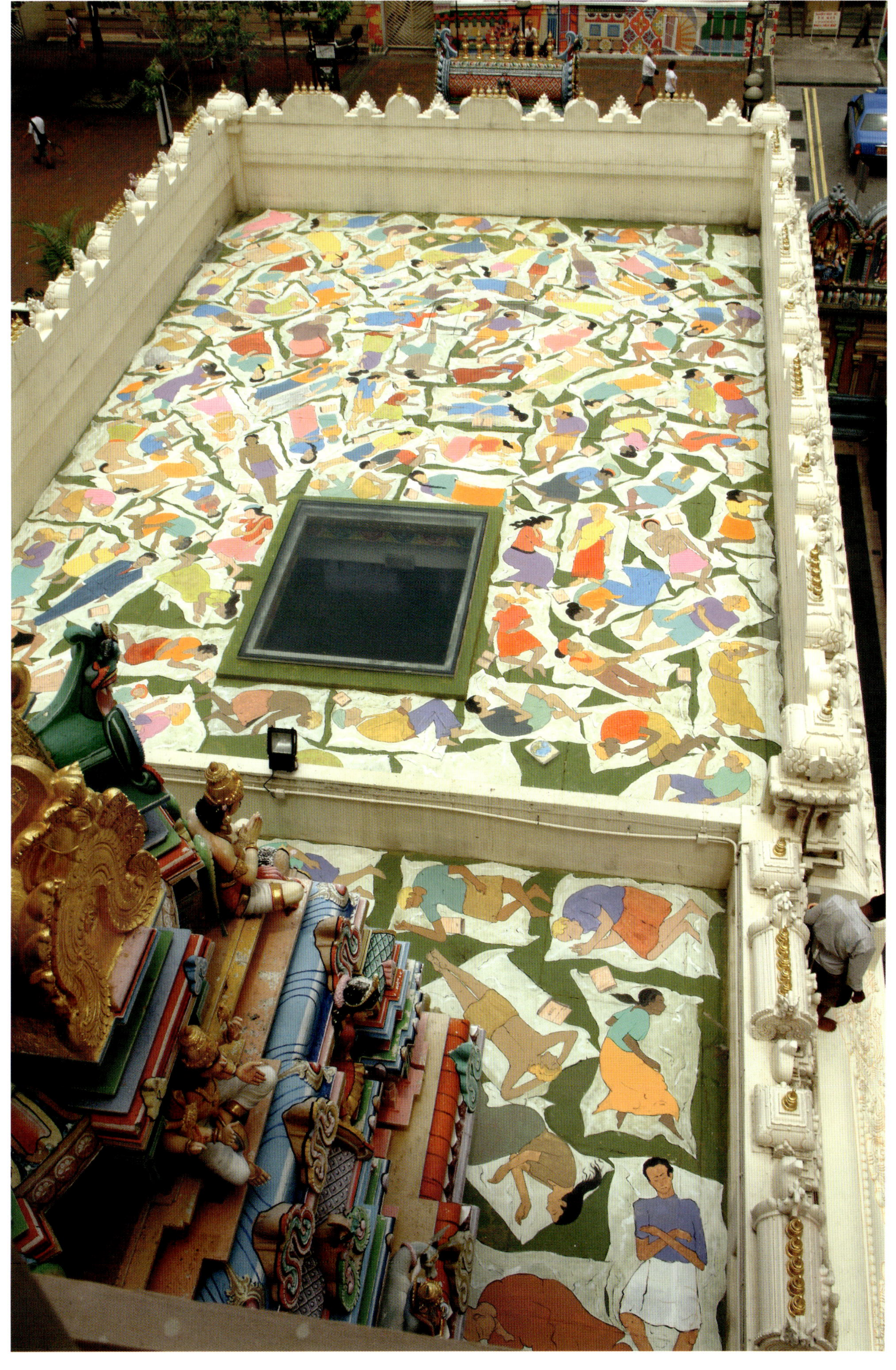

N. S. HARSHA
Cosmic Orphans, 2006

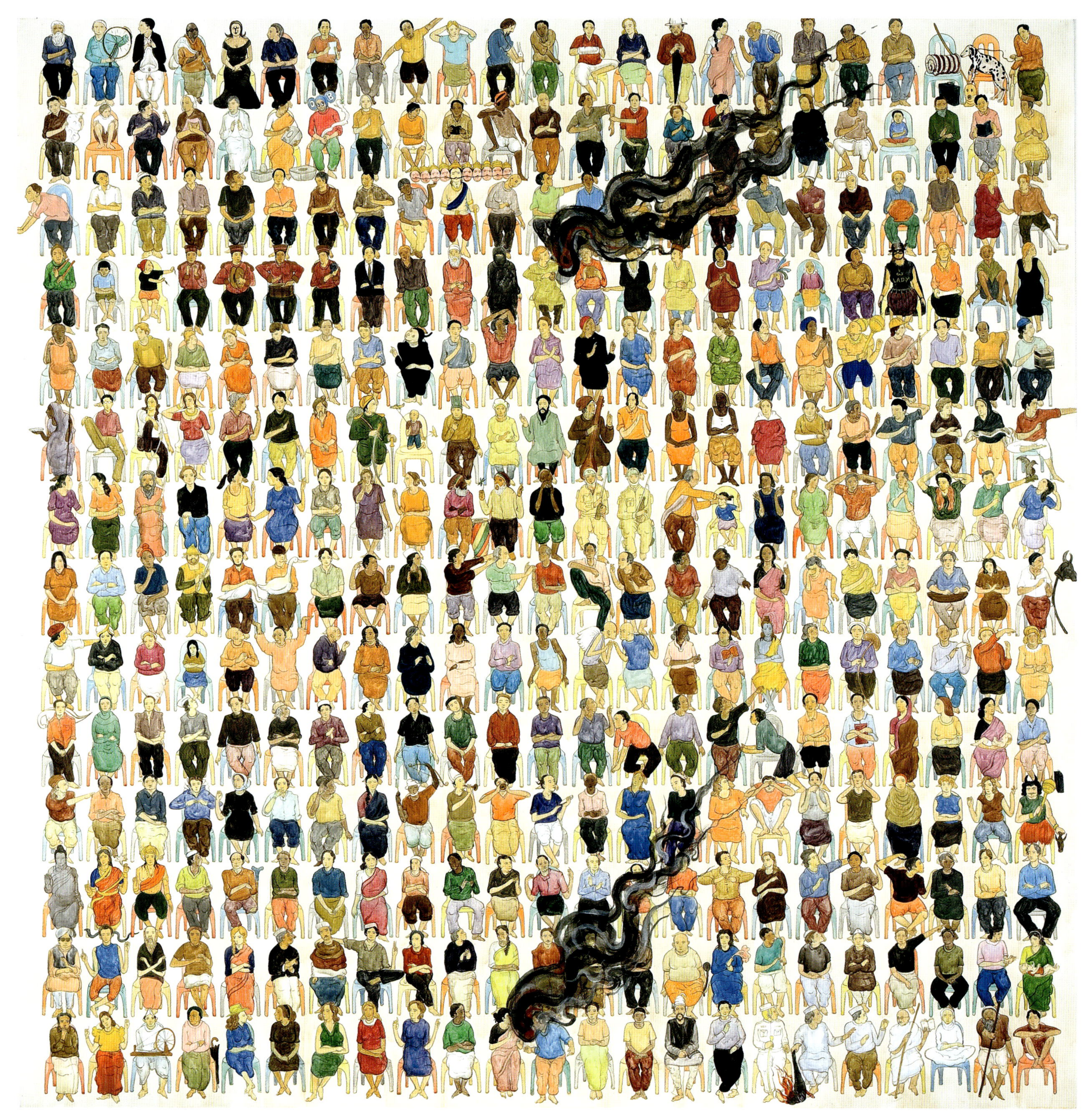

N. S. HARSHA
Please Come Give Us a Speech, 2008

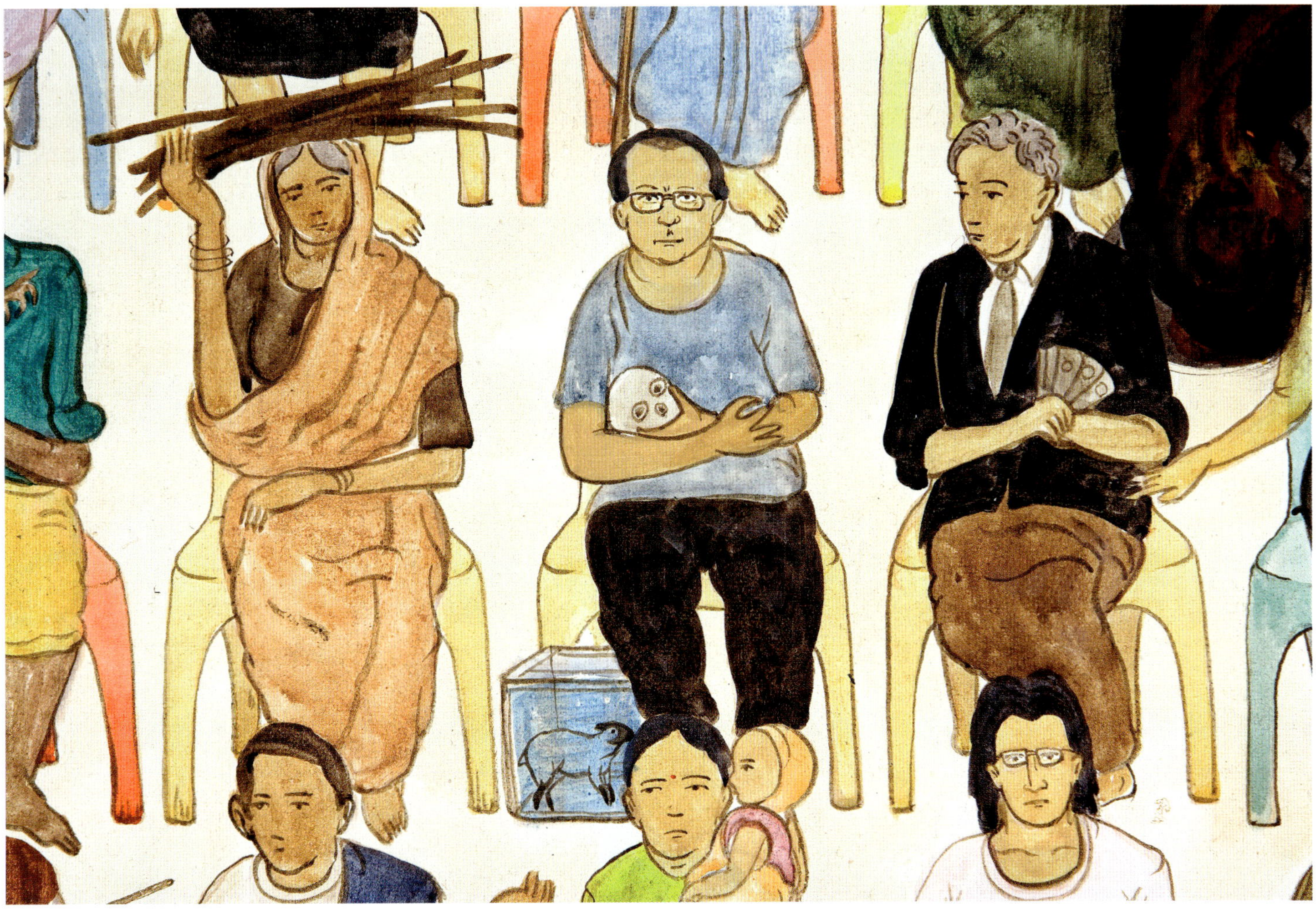

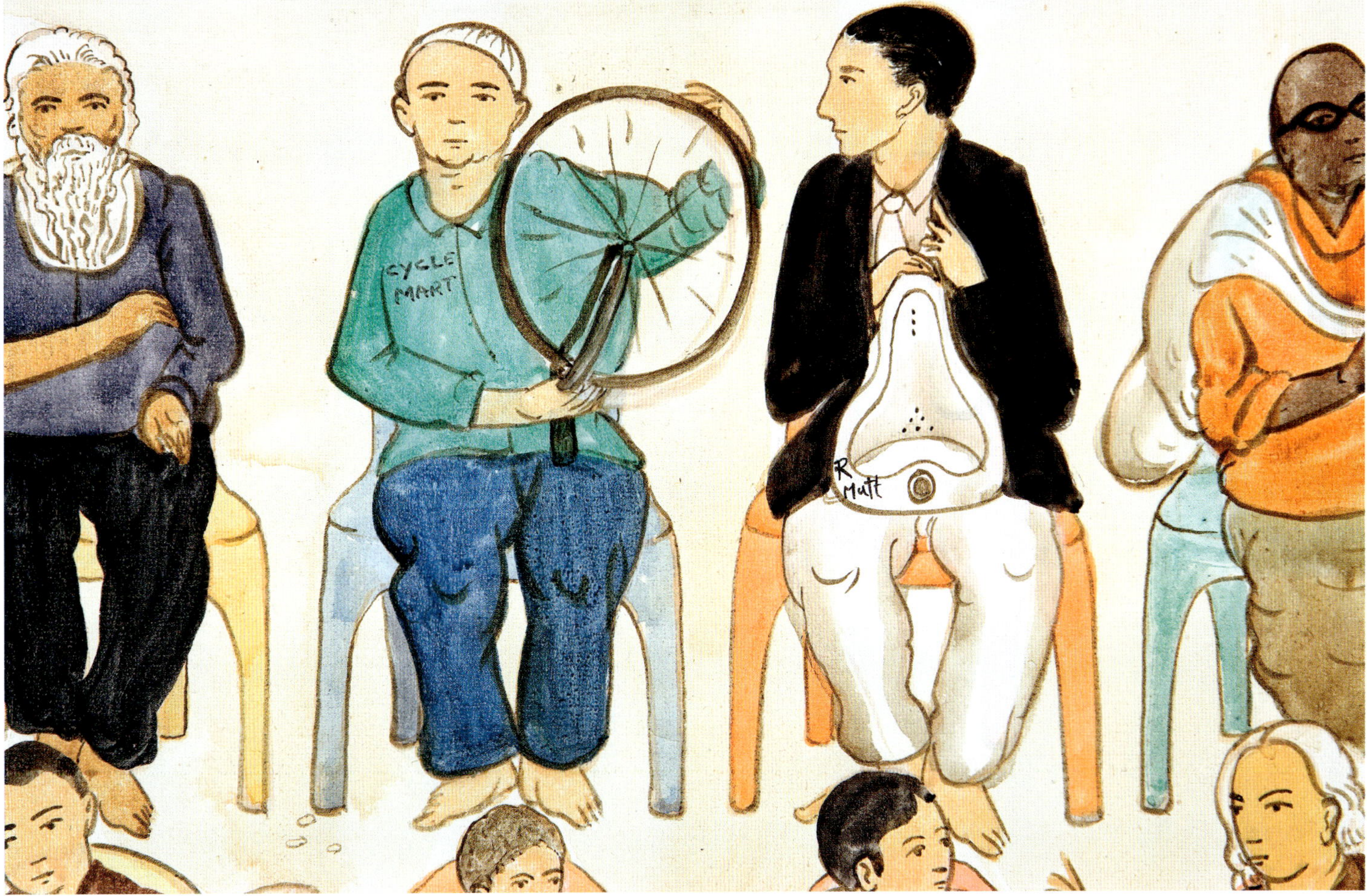

N. S. HARSHA
Please Come Give Us a Speech, 2008 (Detail)

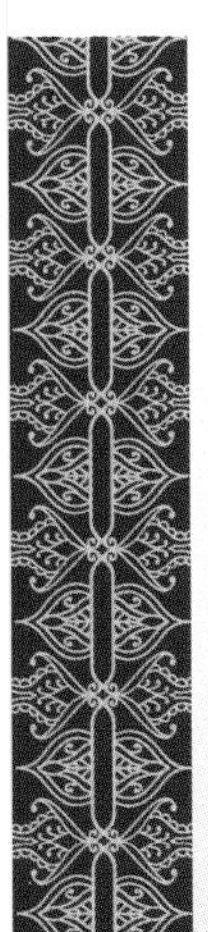
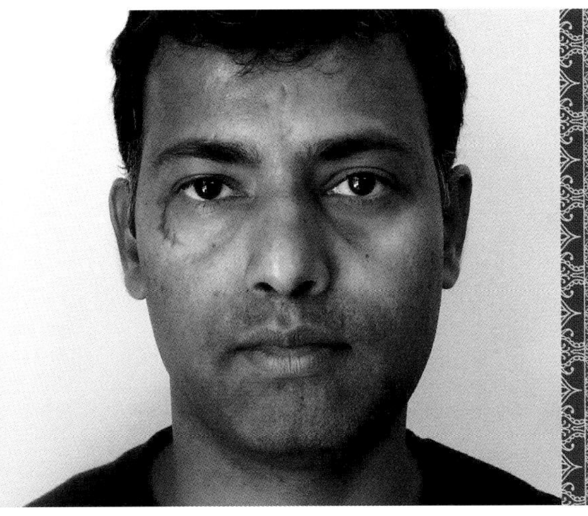

jagannath panda

JAGANNATH PANDA Geboren 1970 in Bhubaneswar, Orissa / Lebt in Haryana, Gurgaon
Born 1970 in Bhubaneswar, Orissa / Lives in Haryana, Gurgaon

Pandas Hauptfach am BK College of Arts and Crafts und an der Graduate School der Maharaja Sayajirao University of Baroda (Vadodara) war Bildhauerei. Er wuchs in einer Umgebung auf, die durchdrungen war von der singulären, traditionellen Kultur dieser Region. Aus seinem Familiennamen geht hervor, dass er einem Priestergeschlecht entstammt; als Vornamen erhielt er den Namen einer Schutzgottheit des Heiligtums von Orissa. Von 1997 bis 1998 lebte er in Japan, wo er mit einem Stipendium der Japan Foundation an der Fukuoka University of Education studierte; 2002 erwarb er ein Masterdiplom in Bildhauerei am Royal College of Art in London. In Pandas Frühwerk finden sich zwei- und dreidimensionale Arbeiten, in denen er mit seinem Geburtsort verbundene Themen und Gegenstände wie Hausrat, aber auch Naturphänomene wie Mond oder Sonne, traditionelle Kunstformen und mythologische Götter als Symbole nutzt. Nach dem Studium in England machte Panda die zeitgenössische Gesellschaft zum Gegenstand seiner künstlerischen Arbeit.

In den letzten Jahren legte Panda den Schwerpunkt seiner Arbeit auf die aktuelle Situation in Gurgaon – eine Vorstadt von Delhi und sein gegenwärtiger Wohnort. In „Water–05" (2005) zeigt Panda Menschen, die sich zur Wasserausgabe um einen Wasserwagen versammeln, der an der Mauer eines palastartigen, herrschaftlichen Wohnsitzes mit Swimmingpool abgestellt ist und weist damit auf die Diskrepanz zwischen dem Ideal und der Realität der Verstädterung hin. In „Ravana" (2005) stürzt der König der Rakshasas, eine Figur aus dem indischen Ramayana-Epos, von einem Hochhaus. Panda weist damit auf den Verfall der Tradition hin, wobei er die Vergangenheit und die Gegenwart, das Leben in der Stadt und auf dem Land, Mythos und Realität in einem sich wandelnden Indien offen legt und dazu Götter und Tiere wie Vögel und Insekten als Erzähler einsetzt. In der aktuellen Ausstellung zeigt Panda neue Gemälde und Skulpturen. In „The Being" (2008) wird im Vordergrund das vom Haus gefallene Blechdach gezeigt und am unteren Rand eine Ziegelreihe als Hinweis auf die Modernisierung der Architektur. Das Nashorn, das im Hintergrund schönen Erinnerungen an die Vergangenheit nachzuhängen scheint, hinterlässt beim Betrachter einen nachhaltigen Eindruck. In „The

Panda, who majored in sculpture at the BK College of Arts and Crafts and at Maharaja Sayajirao University of Baroda's Graduate School in Vadodara, grew up in an environment steeped in the traditional culture unique to the region. His family name indicates that he comes from a family of priests, while his first name is that of the guardian deity of the sacred site of Orissa. From 1997 to 1998 he was resident in Japan, studying at Fukuoka University of Education on a Japan Foundation scholarship, and in 2002 graduated MA in sculpture at the Royal College of Art in London. Panda's early work included two-dimensional and three-dimensional works in which symbolic use was made of subjects related to his birthplace, such as household goods, natural phenomena such as the moon or sun, traditional arts and mythological gods. After studying in England, contemporary society became one of the themes of Panda's art.

In recent years, Panda has been producing work focusing on the current situation in Gurgaon, in the suburbs of Delhi, where he now lives. In *Water–05* (2005), where people gather to receive water from a water truck parked outside the walls of a palatial mansion with a swimming pool, Panda has conveyed the discrepancy between the ideal and the reality of urbanization. *Ravana* (2005), in which the King of the Rakshasas from the Indian epic tale The Ramayana is falling past a high-rise building, hints at the decline of tradition, with Panda revealing the past and present, urban and rural life, mythology and truth in the changing India via the gods, animals, birds, and insects that he uses as his storytellers. Panda is showing new paintings and sculptures in this exhibition. In *The Being* (2008), the tin roof that has fallen off the house is depicted in the foreground, and bricks are lined up at the bottom to convey the modernization of architecture. A rhinoceros lingers in the background, as though cherishing the days gone past, and leaving a deep impression on the viewer. Meanwhile, in *The Epic II* (2008), which is reminiscent of the various Indian epic poems *The Mahabharata,* Panda has spun a new story, which features a tree spreading its branches at night, and also incorporates fabrics and gods unique to the Orissa region. In these works the surface of the canvas is made more distinctive by using a

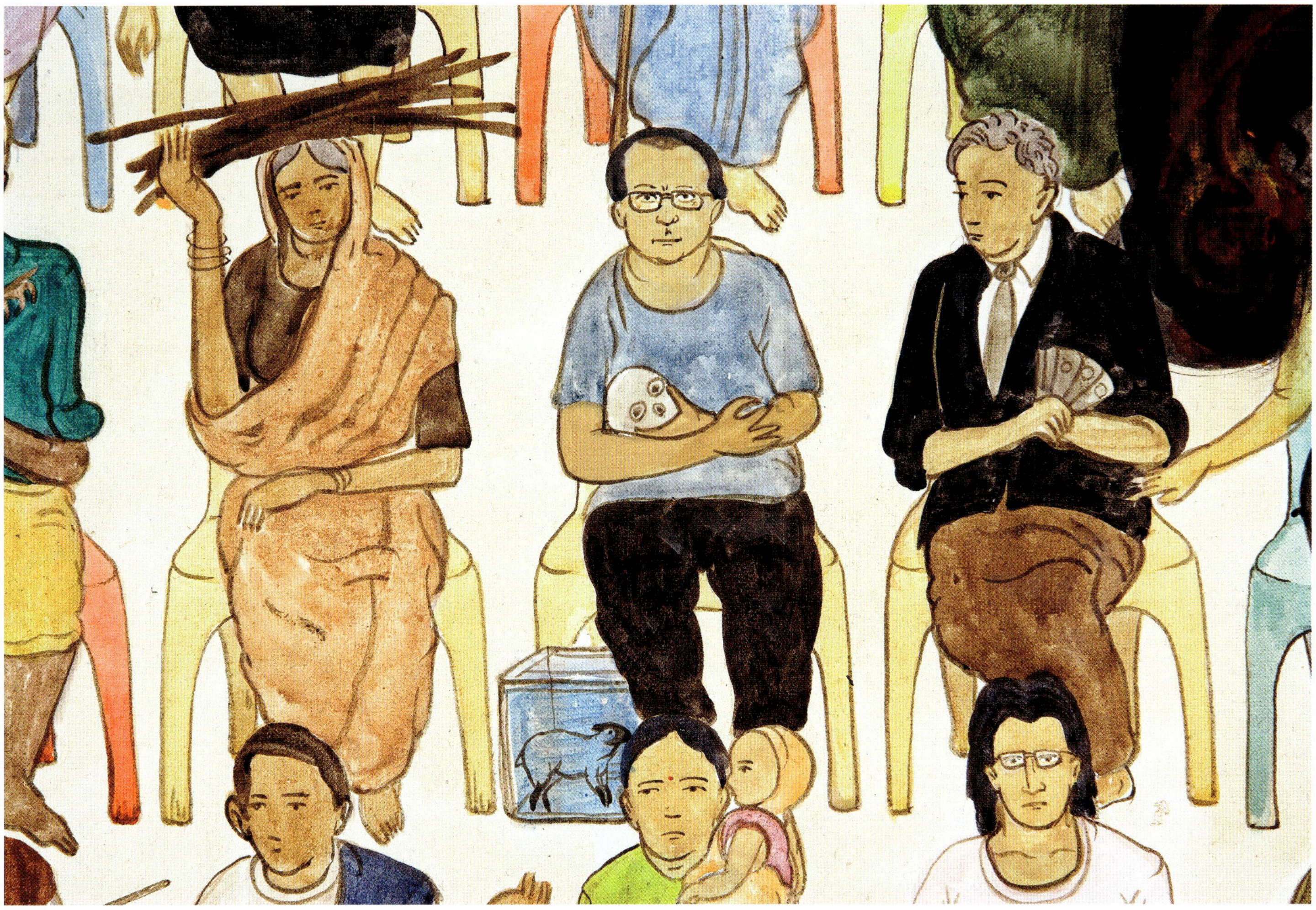

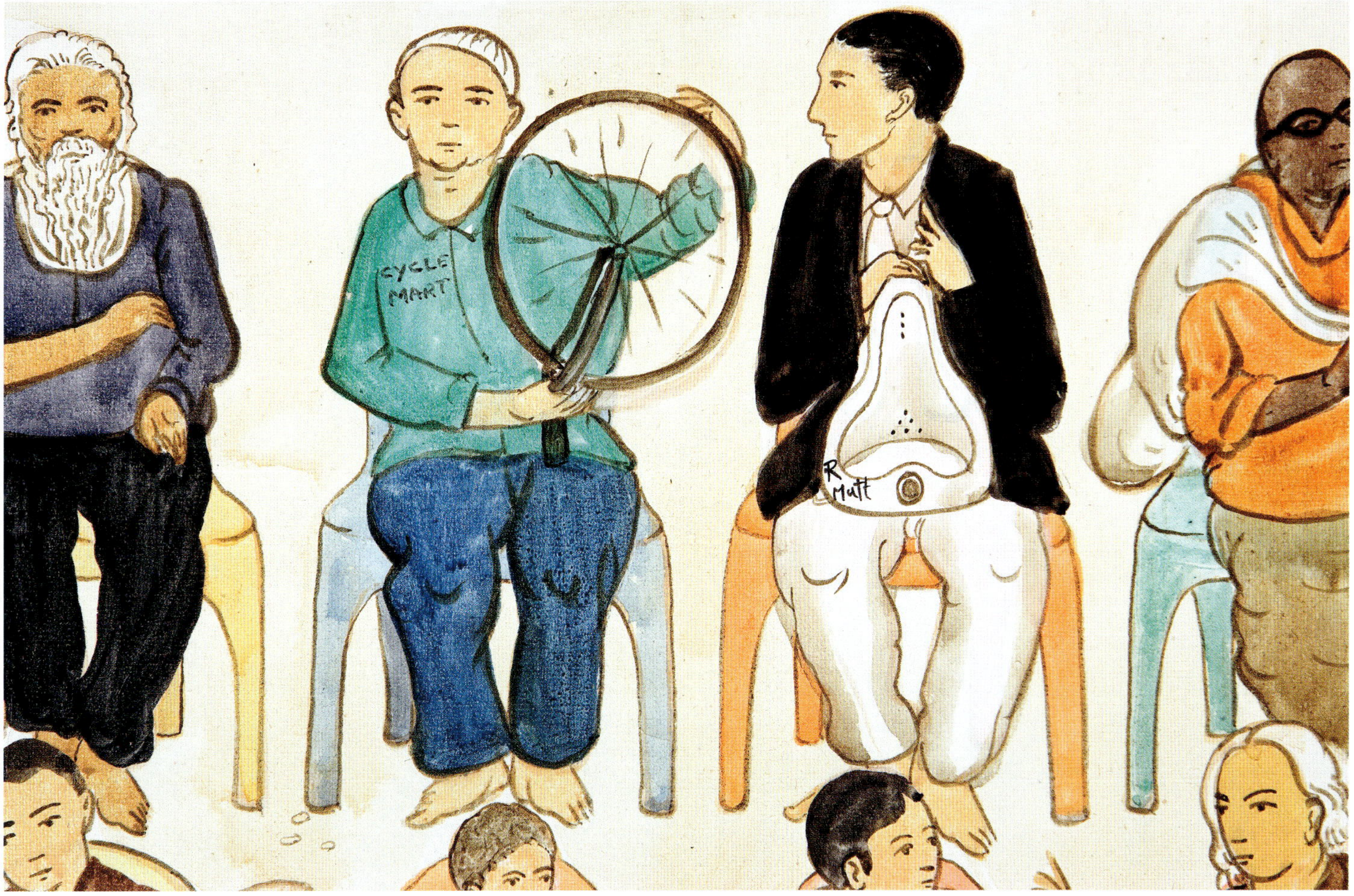

N. S. HARSHA
Please Come Give Us a Speech, 2008 (Detail)

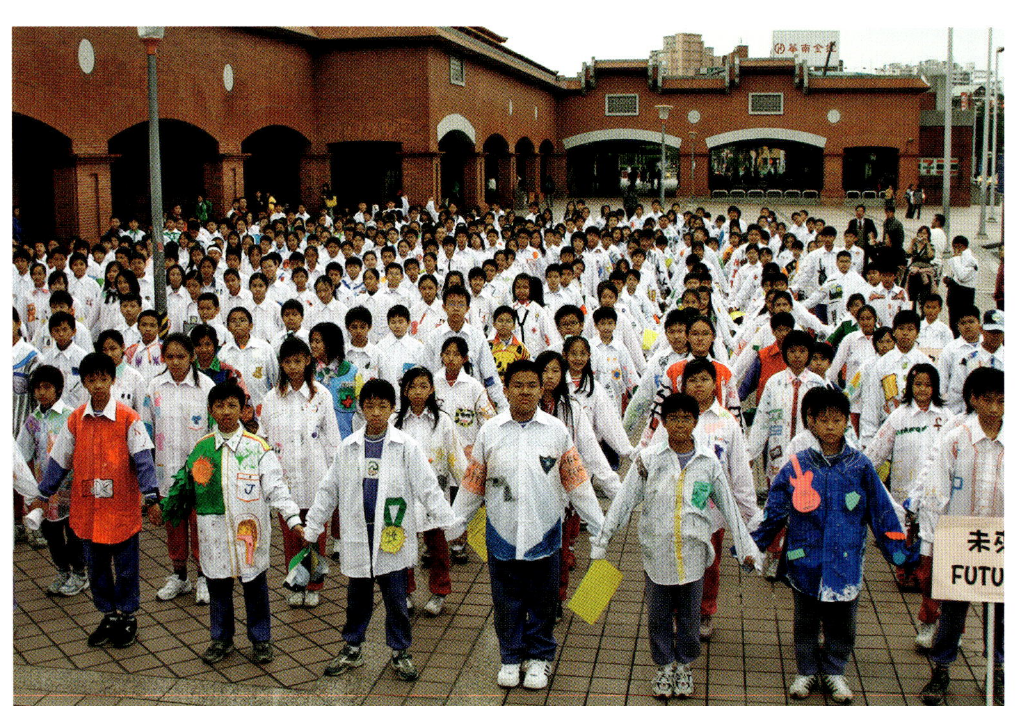

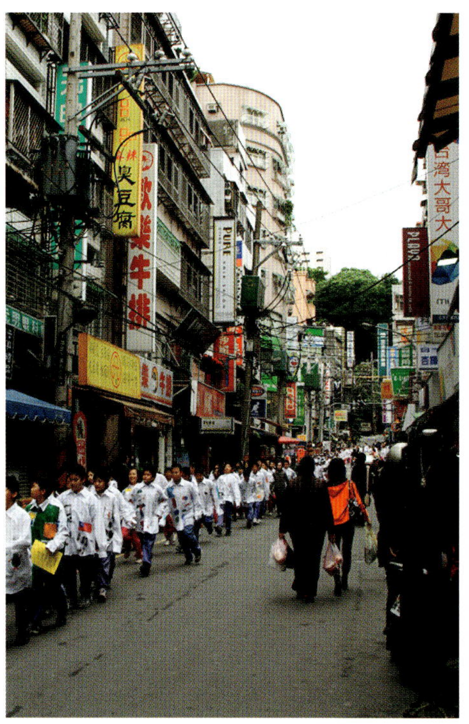

N. S. HARSHA
Future, 2007
Ambition and Dreams, project designed for TVS School, Tumkur, 2005

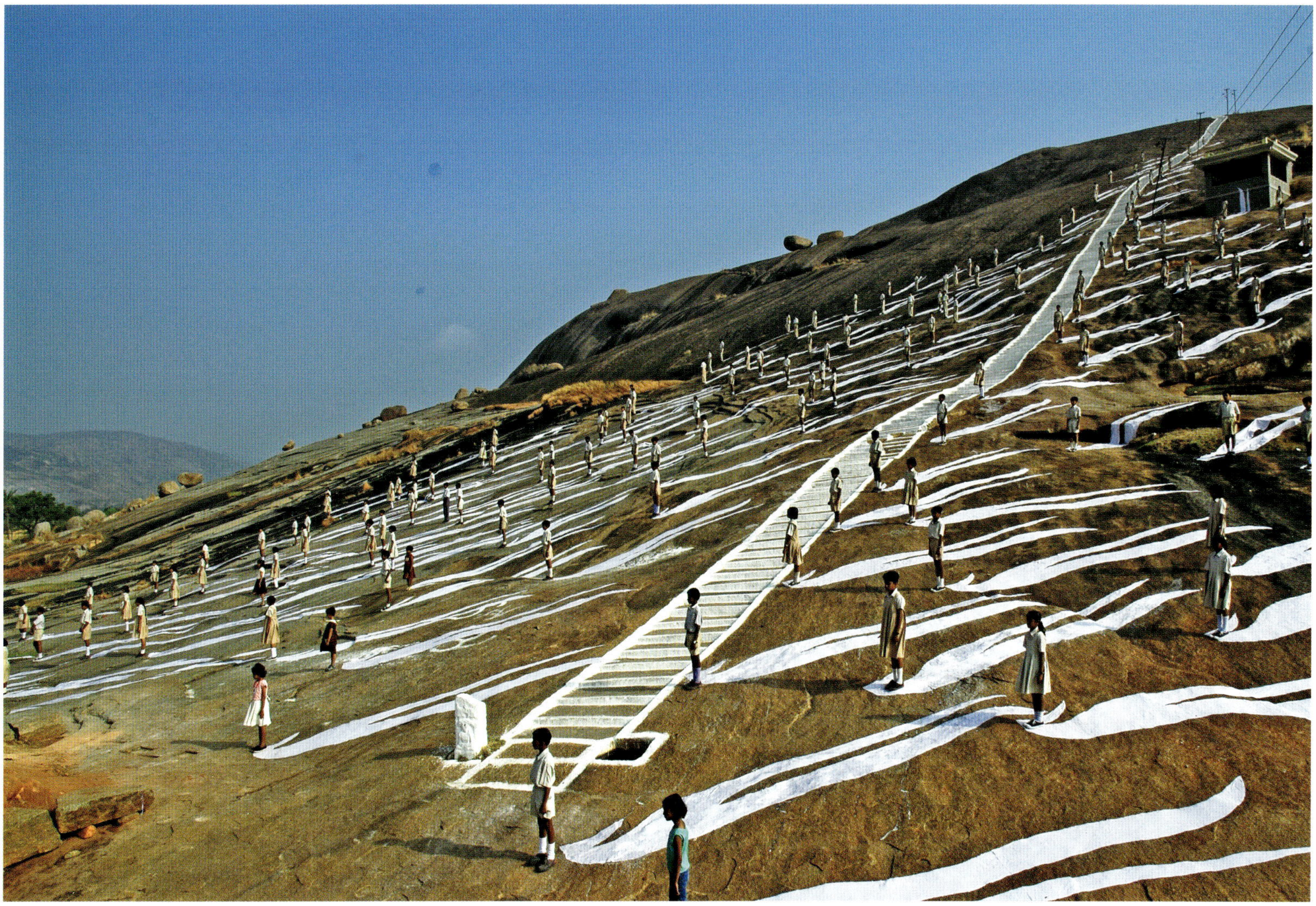

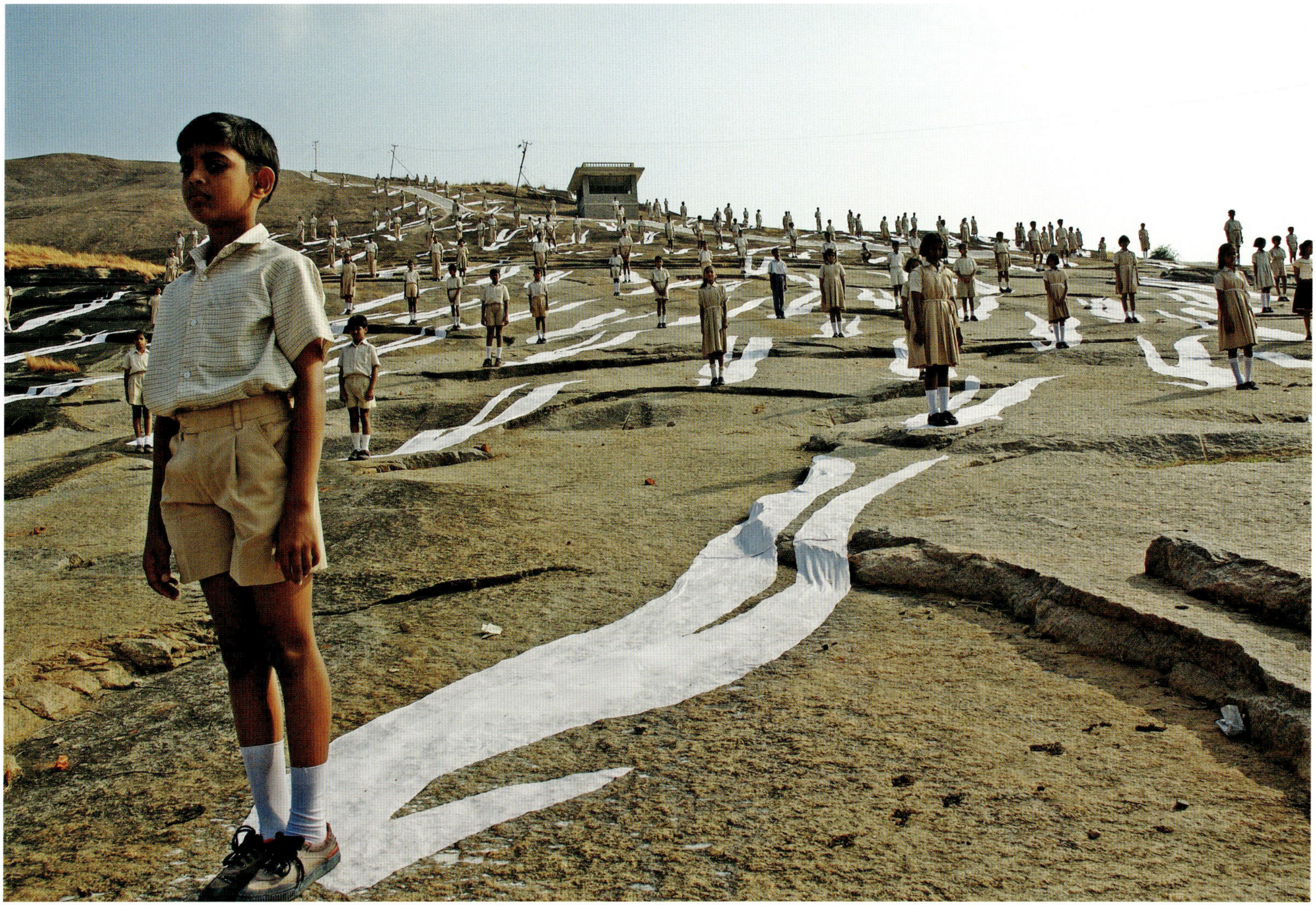

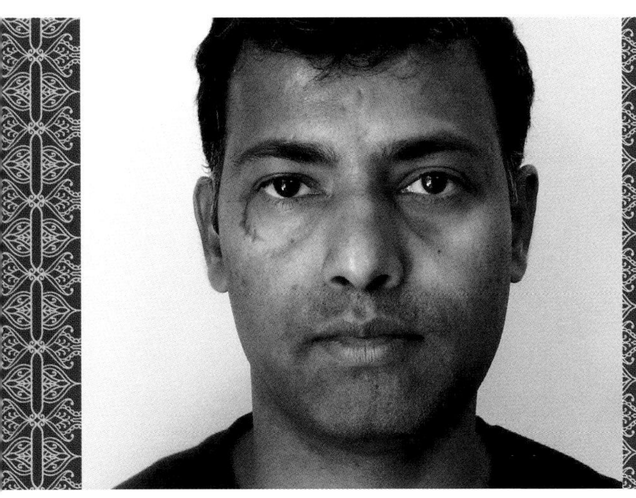

jagannath panda

JAGANNATH PANDA Geboren 1970 in Bhubaneswar, Orissa / Lebt in Haryana, Gurgaon
Born 1970 in Bhubaneswar, Orissa / Lives in Haryana, Gurgaon

Pandas Hauptfach am BK College of Arts and Crafts und an der Graduate School der Maharaja Sayajirao University of Baroda (Vadodara) war Bildhauerei. Er wuchs in einer Umgebung auf, die durchdrungen war von der singulären, traditionellen Kultur dieser Region. Aus seinem Familiennamen geht hervor, dass er einem Priestergeschlecht entstammt; als Vornamen erhielt er den Namen einer Schutzgottheit des Heiligtums von Orissa. Von 1997 bis 1998 lebte er in Japan, wo er mit einem Stipendium der Japan Foundation an der Fukuoka University of Education studierte; 2002 erwarb er ein Masterdiplom in Bildhauerei am Royal College of Art in London. In Pandas Frühwerk finden sich zwei- und dreidimensionale Arbeiten, in denen er mit seinem Geburtsort verbundene Themen und Gegenstände wie Hausrat, aber auch Naturphänomene wie Mond oder Sonne, traditionelle Kunstformen und mythologische Götter als Symbole nutzt. Nach dem Studium in England machte Panda die zeitgenössische Gesellschaft zum Gegenstand seiner künstlerischen Arbeit.

In den letzten Jahren legte Panda den Schwerpunkt seiner Arbeit auf die aktuelle Situation in Gurgaon – eine Vorstadt von Delhi und sein gegenwärtiger Wohnort. In „Water–05" (2005) zeigt Panda Menschen, die sich zur Wasserausgabe um einen Wasserwagen versammeln, der an der Mauer eines palastartigen, herrschaftlichen Wohnsitzes mit Swimmingpool abgestellt ist und weist damit auf die Diskrepanz zwischen dem Ideal und der Realität der Verstädterung hin. In „Ravana" (2005) stürzt der König der Rakshasas, eine Figur aus dem indischen Ramayana-Epos, von einem Hochhaus. Panda weist damit auf den Verfall der Tradition hin, wobei er die Vergangenheit und die Gegenwart, das Leben in der Stadt und auf dem Land, Mythos und Realität in einem sich wandelnden Indien offen legt und dazu Götter und Tiere wie Vögel und Insekten als Erzähler einsetzt. In der aktuellen Ausstellung zeigt Panda neue Gemälde und Skulpturen. In „The Being" (2008) wird im Vordergrund das vom Haus gefallene Blechdach gezeigt und am unteren Rand eine Ziegelreihe als Hinweis auf die Modernisierung der Architektur. Das Nashorn, das im Hintergrund schönen Erinnerungen an die Vergangenheit nachzuhängen scheint, hinterlässt beim Betrachter einen nachhaltigen Eindruck. In „The

Panda, who majored in sculpture at the BK College of Arts and Crafts and at Maharaja Sayajirao University of Baroda's Graduate School in Vadodara, grew up in an environment steeped in the traditional culture unique to the region. His family name indicates that he comes from a family of priests, while his first name is that of the guardian deity of the sacred site of Orissa. From 1997 to 1998 he was resident in Japan, studying at Fukuoka University of Education on a Japan Foundation scholarship, and in 2002 graduated MA in sculpture at the Royal College of Art in London. Panda's early work included two-dimensional and three-dimensional works in which symbolic use was made of subjects related to his birthplace, such as household goods, natural phenomena such as the moon or sun, traditional arts and mythological gods. After studying in England, contemporary society became one of the themes of Panda's art.

In recent years, Panda has been producing work focusing on the current situation in Gurgaon, in the suburbs of Delhi, where he now lives. In *Water–05* (2005), where people gather to receive water from a water truck parked outside the walls of a palatial mansion with a swimming pool, Panda has conveyed the discrepancy between the ideal and the reality of urbanization. *Ravana* (2005), in which the King of the Rakshasas from the Indian epic tale The Ramayana is falling past a high-rise building, hints at the decline of tradition, with Panda revealing the past and present, urban and rural life, mythology and truth in the changing India via the gods, animals, birds, and insects that he uses as his storytellers. Panda is showing new paintings and sculptures in this exhibition. In *The Being* (2008), the tin roof that has fallen off the house is depicted in the foreground, and bricks are lined up at the bottom to convey the modernization of architecture. A rhinoceros lingers in the background, as though cherishing the days gone past, and leaving a deep impression on the viewer. Meanwhile, in *The Epic II* (2008), which is reminiscent of the various Indian epic poems *The Mahabharata,* Panda has spun a new story, which features a tree spreading its branches at night, and also incorporates fabrics and gods unique to the Orissa region. In these works the surface of the canvas is made more distinctive by using a

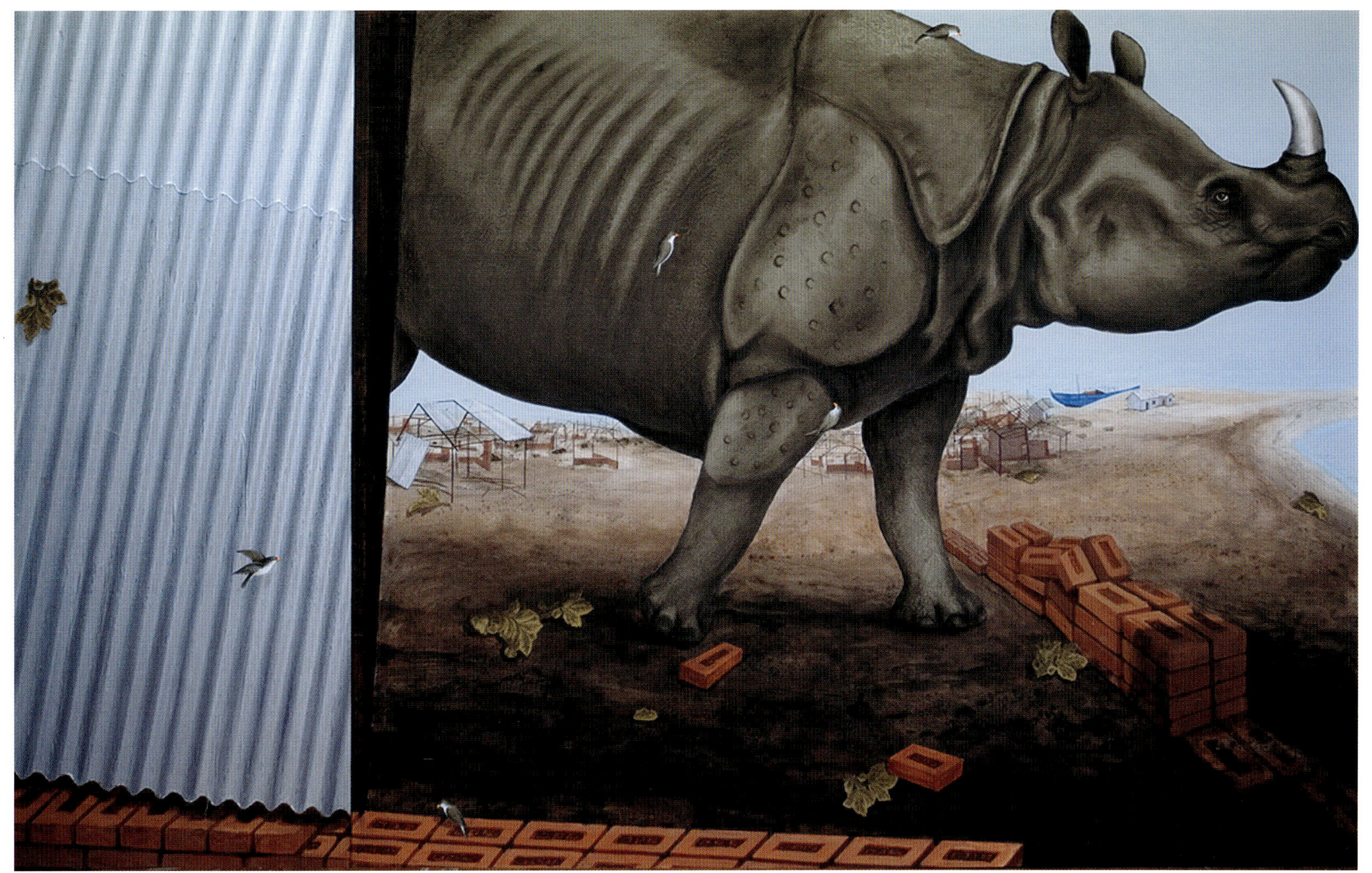

JAGANNATH PANDA
The Being, 2008

Epic II“ (2008), das an die vielen indischen Volksepen wie beispielsweise das Mahabharata erinnert, lässt Panda einen Baum nachts seine Äste ausbreiten und für die Region Orissa typische Stoffe und Götter vorkommen. In diesen Arbeiten setzt der Künstler eine in Orissa traditionelle Technik ein: die Farbe wird auf eine mit gemustertem Seidenstoff überzogene Leinwand aufgetragen, die dadurch einen unverwechselbaren Charakter erhält und so das beschauliche Bild im Hintergrund mit einem Gefühl der Entfremdung kontrastiert. „An Ancestor–I“ (2006) bezeichnet die aus bunt besticktem Stoff geschaffene Skulptur eines Pfaus, des indischen Nationalvogels. Auch diese Arbeit, in der vom Rumpf des Vogels ausgehend Blumen- und Blattmuster im Raum verstreut werden, repräsentiert zwei Dimensionen – die Zweidimensionalität des Gewebes und die Dreidimensionalität der Skulptur.

Wichtige Ausstellungen: die Einzelausstellung „Nothing Is Solid“ (Chemould Prescott Road, Mumbai, 2007), „Private / Corporate IV“ (Daimler Chrysler Contemporary, Berlin, 2007) und „Still Moving Image“ (Devi Art Foundation, Gurgaon, 2008). (TK)

traditional Orissa technique of applying paint onto patterned, silk fabric that has been stuck to the canvas, depicting a contrasting sense of alienation against the quiet background image. In *An Ancestor–II* (2006), brightly coloured embroidered fabric has been used to create a sculpture of a peacock, the national bird of India. This work, in which flower and leaf patterns have come from the torso and scattered in the space, also represents two dimensions – the two-dimensionality of the fabric and the three-dimensionality of the sculpture.

Major exhibitions include the solo exhibition "Nothing Is Solid" (Chemould Prescott Road, Mumbai, 2007), "Private / Corporate IV" (Daimler Chrysler Contemporary, Berlin, 2007), and "Still Moving Image" (Devi Art Foundation, Gurgaon, 2008). (TK)

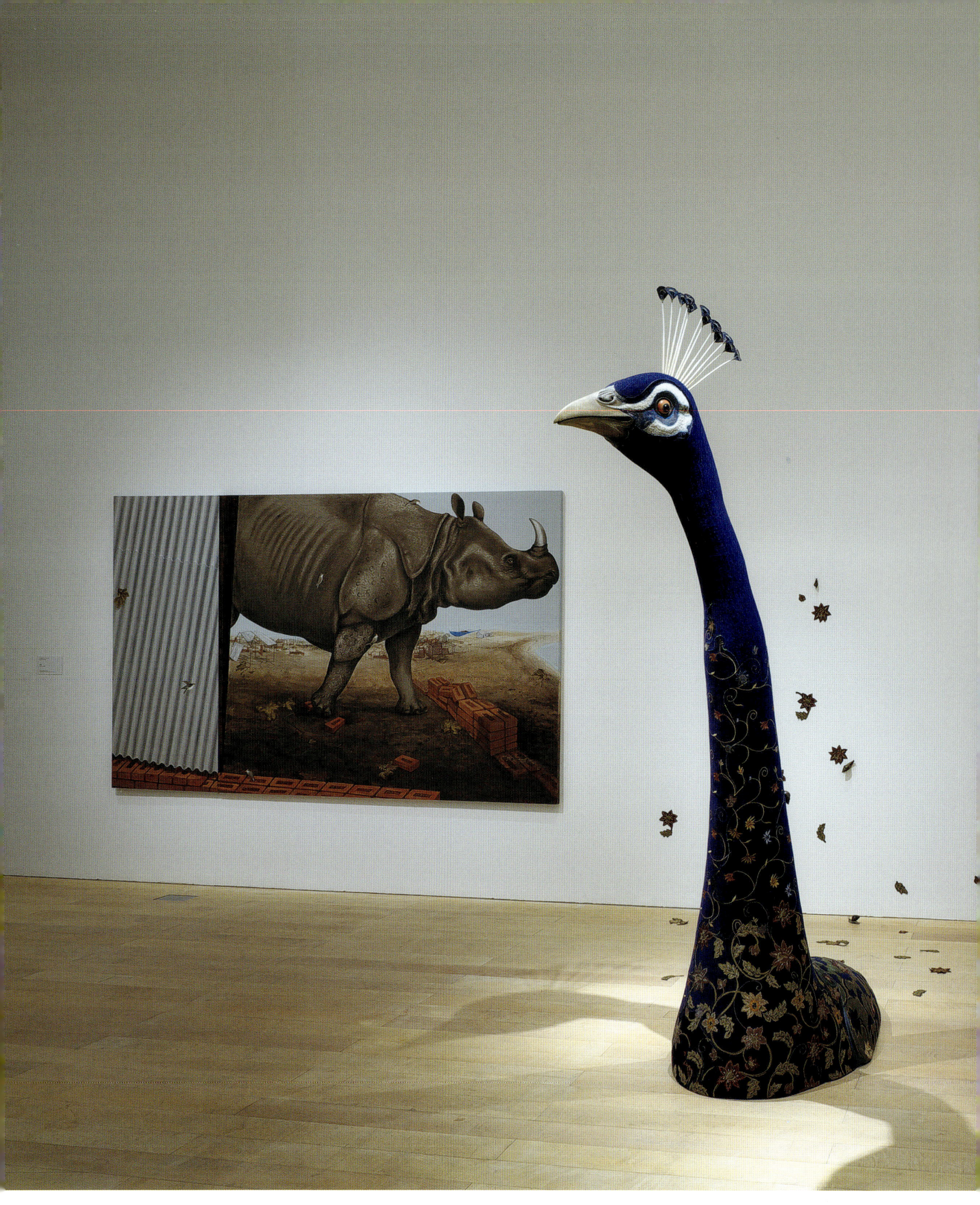

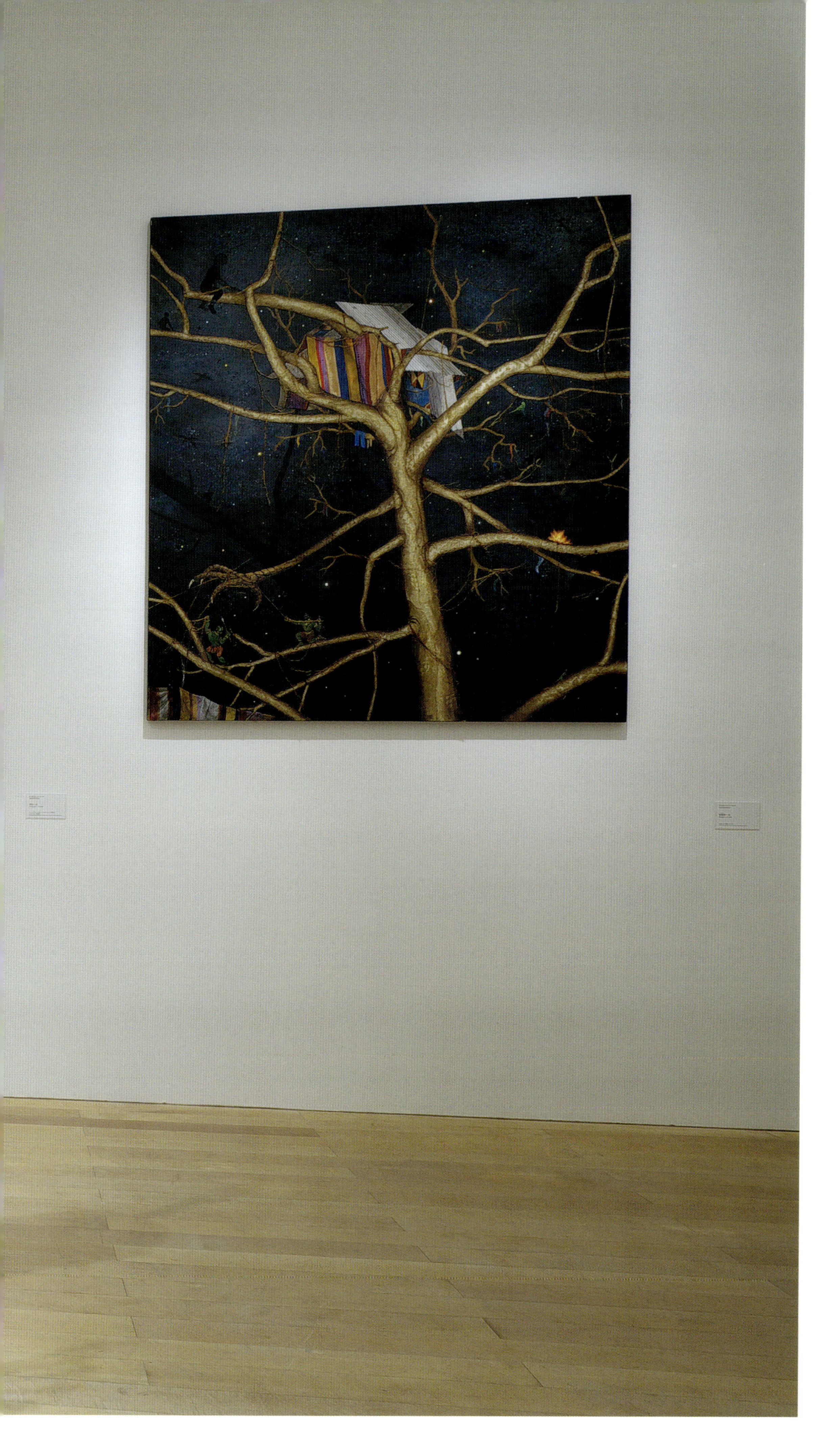

JAGANNATH PANDA
An Ancestor – II, 2006

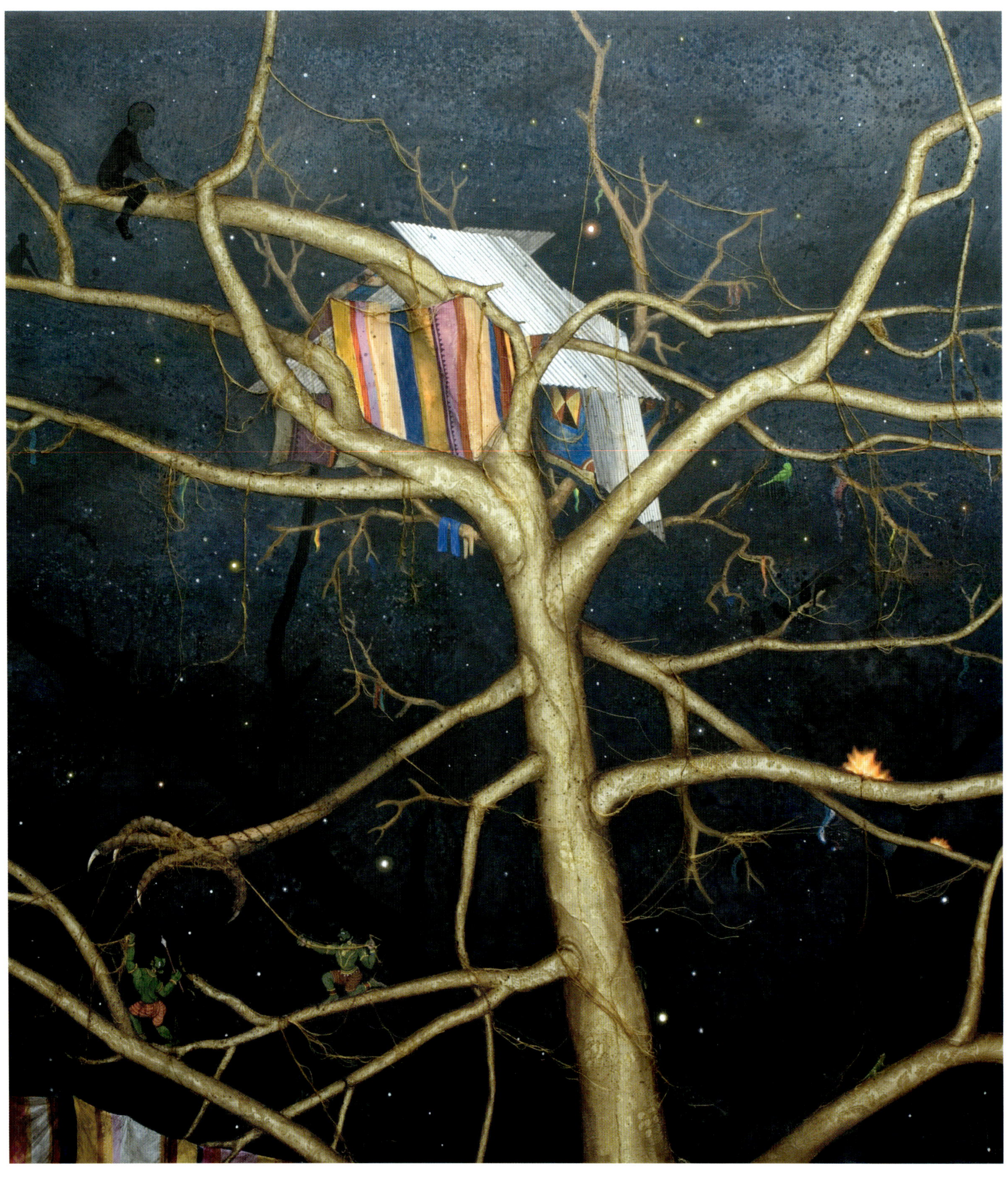

JAGANNATH PANDA
The Epic – II, 2008

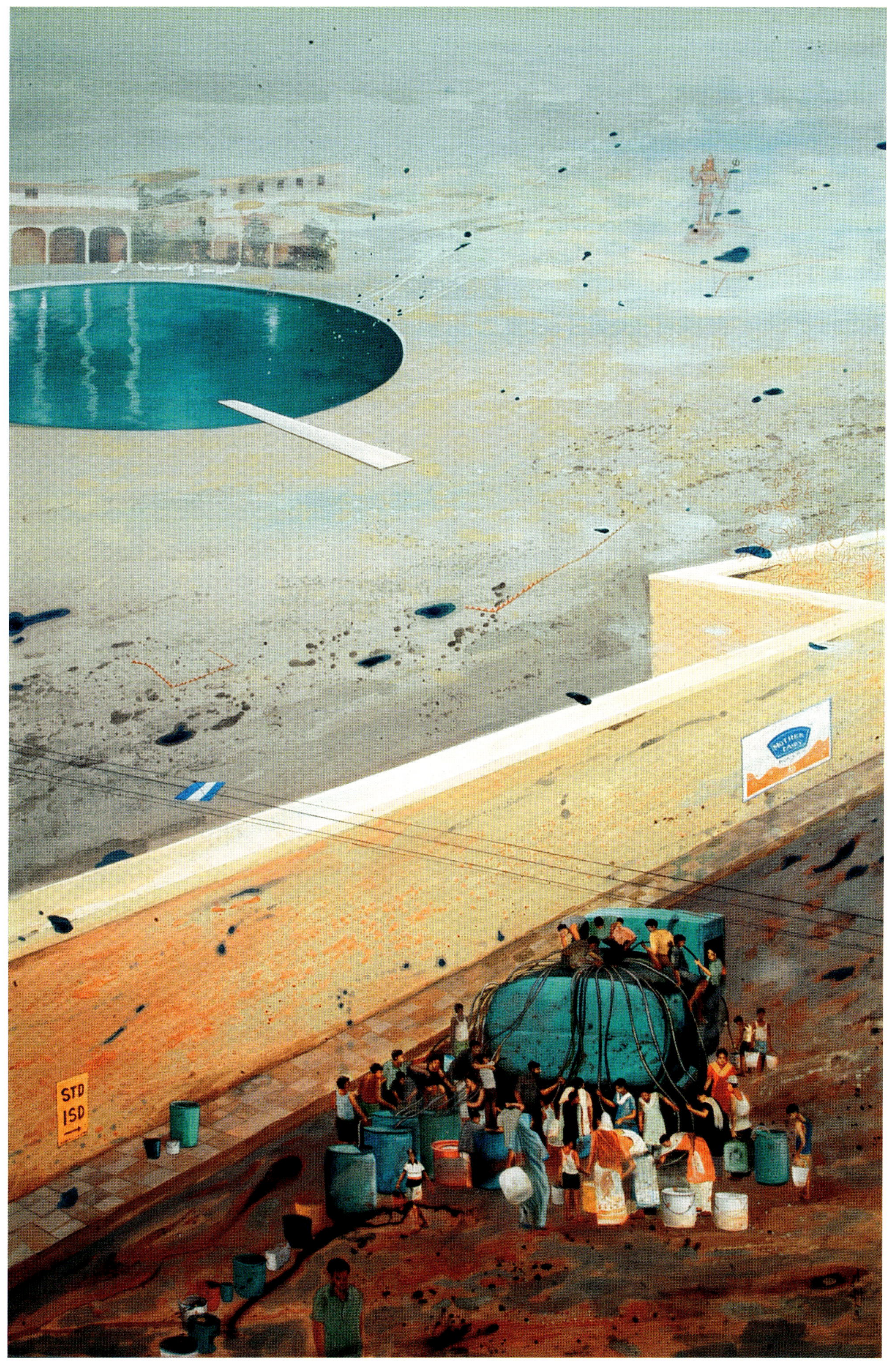

JAGANNATH PANDA
Water – 05, 2005

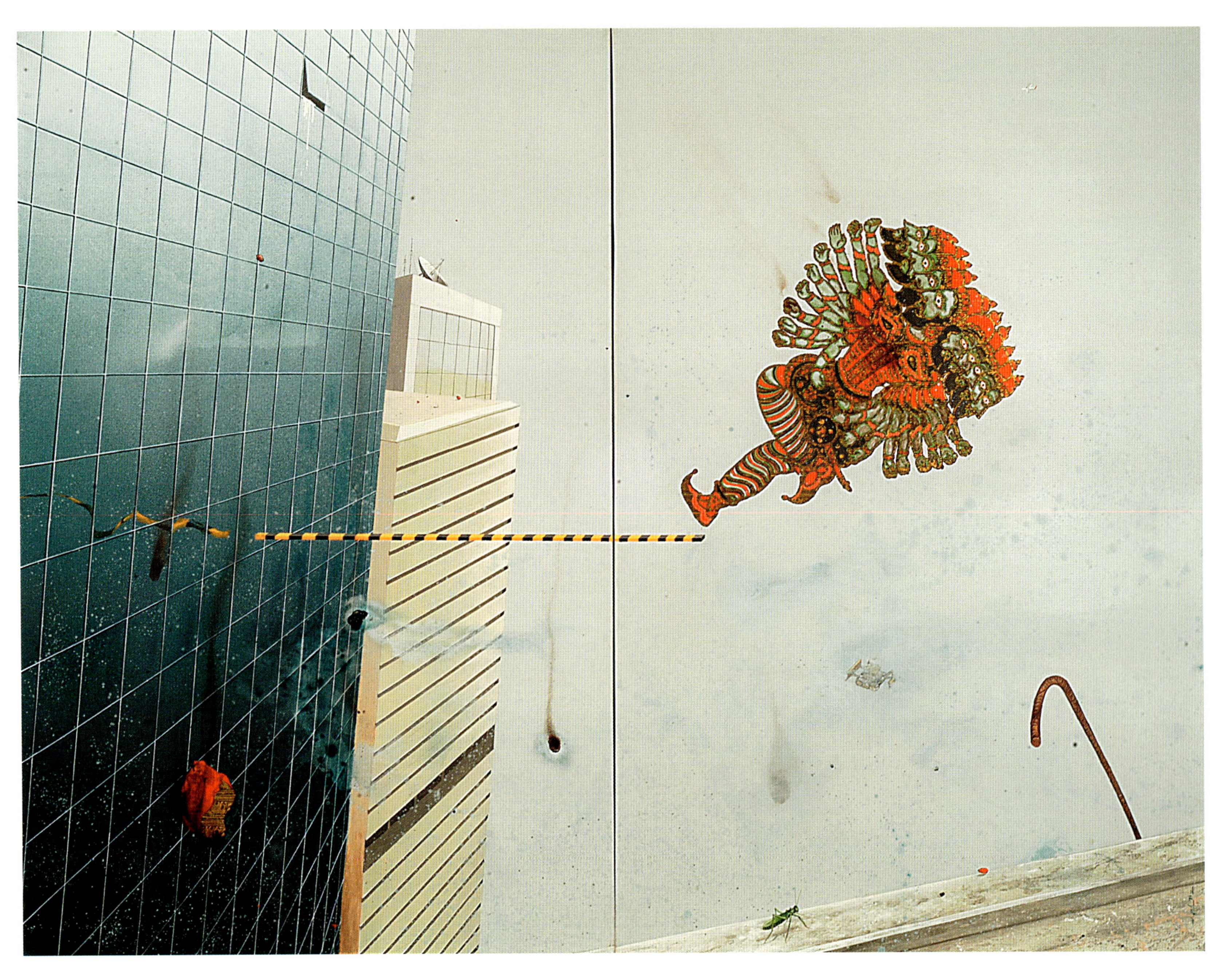

JAGANNATH PANDA
Ravana, 2005

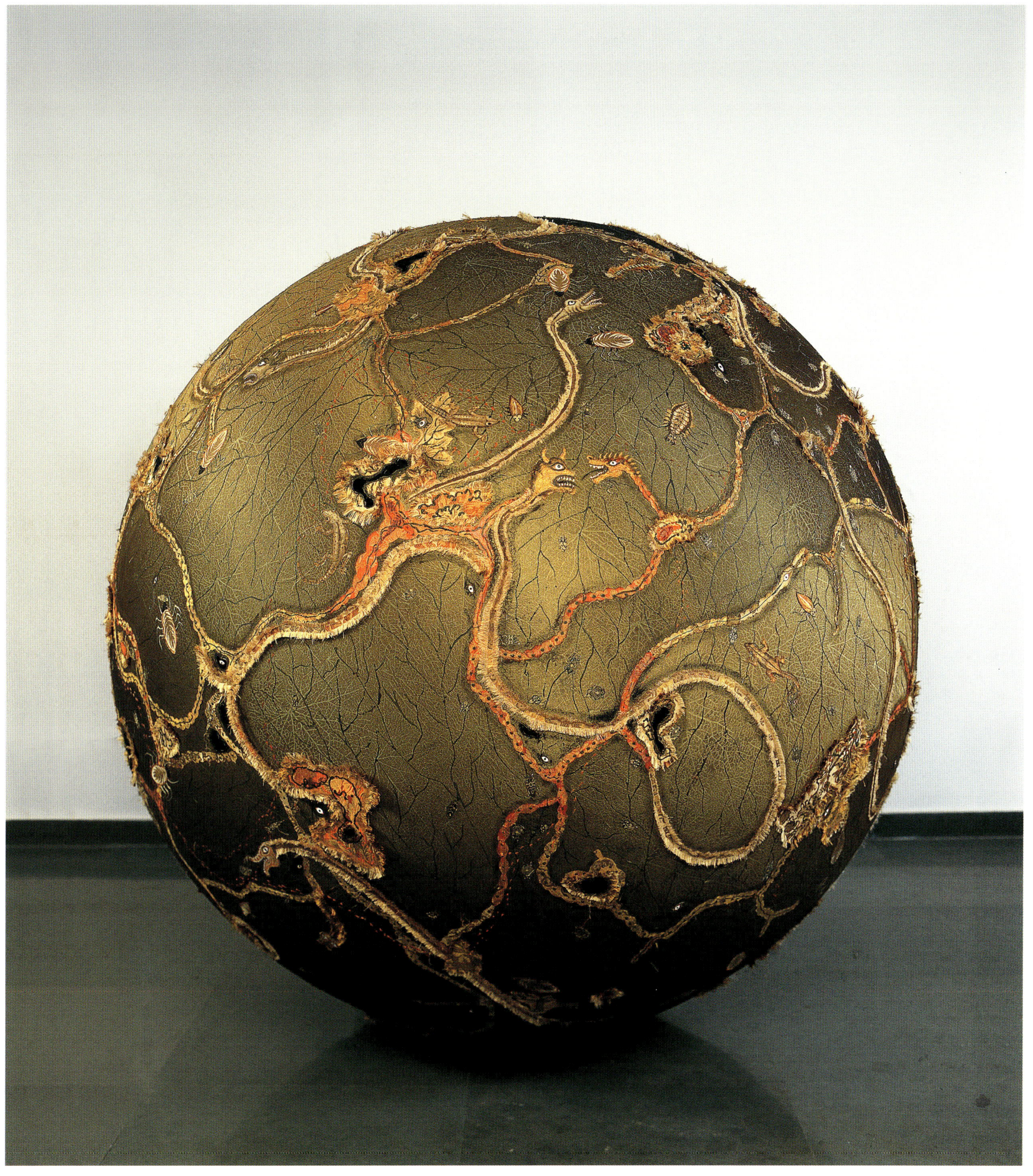

JAGANNATH PANDA
The Feral Sphere, 2007

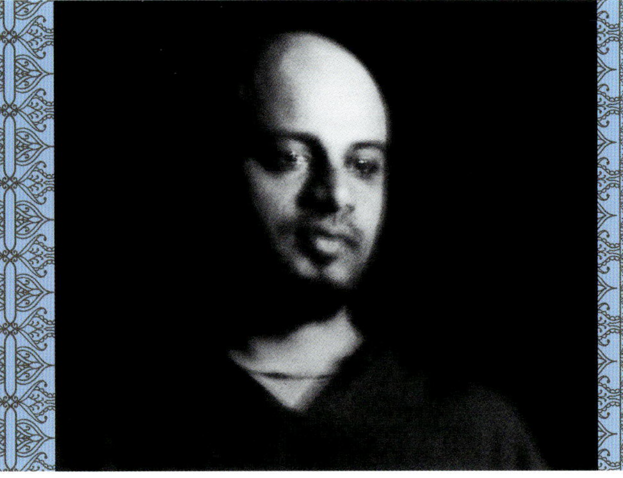

justin ponmany

JUSTIN PONMANY Geboren 1974 in Kerala / Lebt in Mumbai
Born 1974 in Kerala / Lives in Mumbai

Ponmany ist Absolvent der School of Painting, Sir J.J. School of Art, Mumbai. Er verwendet Acrylfarben, Hologramme und Salz, um neue visuelle Effekte in der zweidimensionalen Kunst auszuloten. In den letzten Jahren verfolgte er mit seinen Arbeiten einen eher konzeptuellen Kurs und schuf schwerpunktmäßig Installationen, Videos und Skulpturen, die sich mit der rasanten Verstädterung und dem Leben der Menschen in einer von der Technik dominierten Gesellschaft auseinandersetzen.

Ponmany lässt sich von der gigantischen, in dynamischem Wandel stehenden Stadt Mumbai und ihren Bewohnern inspirieren. In „Room No.12, Zehra Chawl, Achanak Nagar, Near Shankar Mandir" (2007) stellt Ponmany einen Arbeiter dar, dessen Kopf sich fast wie eine Tierhaut oder eine Weltkarte horizontal ausdehnt. Ponmany stellt innerhalb eines Rahmens sowohl den Gegenstand als auch seine Umgebung dar und nennt diese Arbeiten erweiterte Porträts („expanded portraits"). Die hochauflösende Abbildung, die von allen Seiten eingefangen wird, scheint nicht nur jene anzuprangern, die sich von Äußerlichkeiten und Informationen manipulieren lassen, sondern auch die Gesellschaft, die ihre Bürger kontrolliert. Die in die Landkarte eingearbeitete Portraitaufnahme wirft außerdem die Frage nach den Grenzen der eigenen Identität auf. „Fear of Destiny" (2006) sieht auf den ersten Blick wie eine Fotografie in schwarz/silber aus. Tatsächlich wurde für die Darstellung ein Pigment mit holografischen Eigenschaften verwendet, sodass sich die Leinwand je nach dem Standpunkt des Betrachters verfärbt. In dieser Serie spielt das glänzende, leuchtende Hologramm auf technischen Fortschritt und Massenkonsumkultur an. Die im Hintergrund abgebildeten Bibelzitate und Aphorismen über den Kapitalismus legen allerdings nahe, dass der Künstler versucht, die Diskrepanz zwischen diesen Zitaten und der Realität bzw. die von der Globalisierung ausgelösten sozialen Widersprüche zu vermitteln. Ponmany verwendet in seinen Arbeiten immer wieder Hakenkreuze. Die Verwendung einer uralten indischen Ikonographie im westlichen Kontext unterwirft dieses Symbol einem Bedeutungswandel, den der Künstler benutzt, um die Begriffe von Universalität und Randlage in unserer Welt in Frage zu stellen.

Ponmany, who graduated from the School of Painting, Sir J.J. School of Art, Mumbai, explores new visual effects in two-dimensional art through the use of materials such as acrylic paint, holograms and salt. In recent years, his work is taking a more conceptual direction, creating installations, videos and sculptures that focus on rapid urban development and the lives of people in a society dominated by technology.

Ponmany's source of inspiration is the enormous and dynamically transforming city of Mumbai and its residents. Ponmany has depicted a labourer in *Room No.12, Zehra Chawl, Achanak Nagar, Near Shankar Mandir* (2007). The image is a close up of the man's head that spreads horizontally, almost like an animal hide or world map. Ponmany calls these works "expanded portraits," and depicts, within a single frame, both the subject and the world surrounding him. The high-resolution image that has been captured from all directions seems to denounce both the individuals who are manipulated by external appearances and information, and the society that monitors others. The head shot, incorporated into the map, also prompts one to question where one's identity boundary lies. *Fear of Destiny* (2006) initially appears to be a black and silver photograph. In fact, the image has been depicted using a pigment with holographic properties, so that the canvas reveals different colours depending on the viewpoint of the observer. In this series, the shining, glowing hologram hints at technological progress and mass consumption culture. However, the depiction in the background of the image of quotes from the Bible or aphorisms about capitalism makes it evident that the artist is attempting to convey the disparity between these words / phrases and reality, and the social contradictions triggered by globalism. Ponmany also frequently uses swastikas in his work. By featuring, within a Western context, iconography that has been used since ancient times in India, these symbols take on a different meaning, and through this, the artist is questioning what exactly is universality and peripherality in this world.

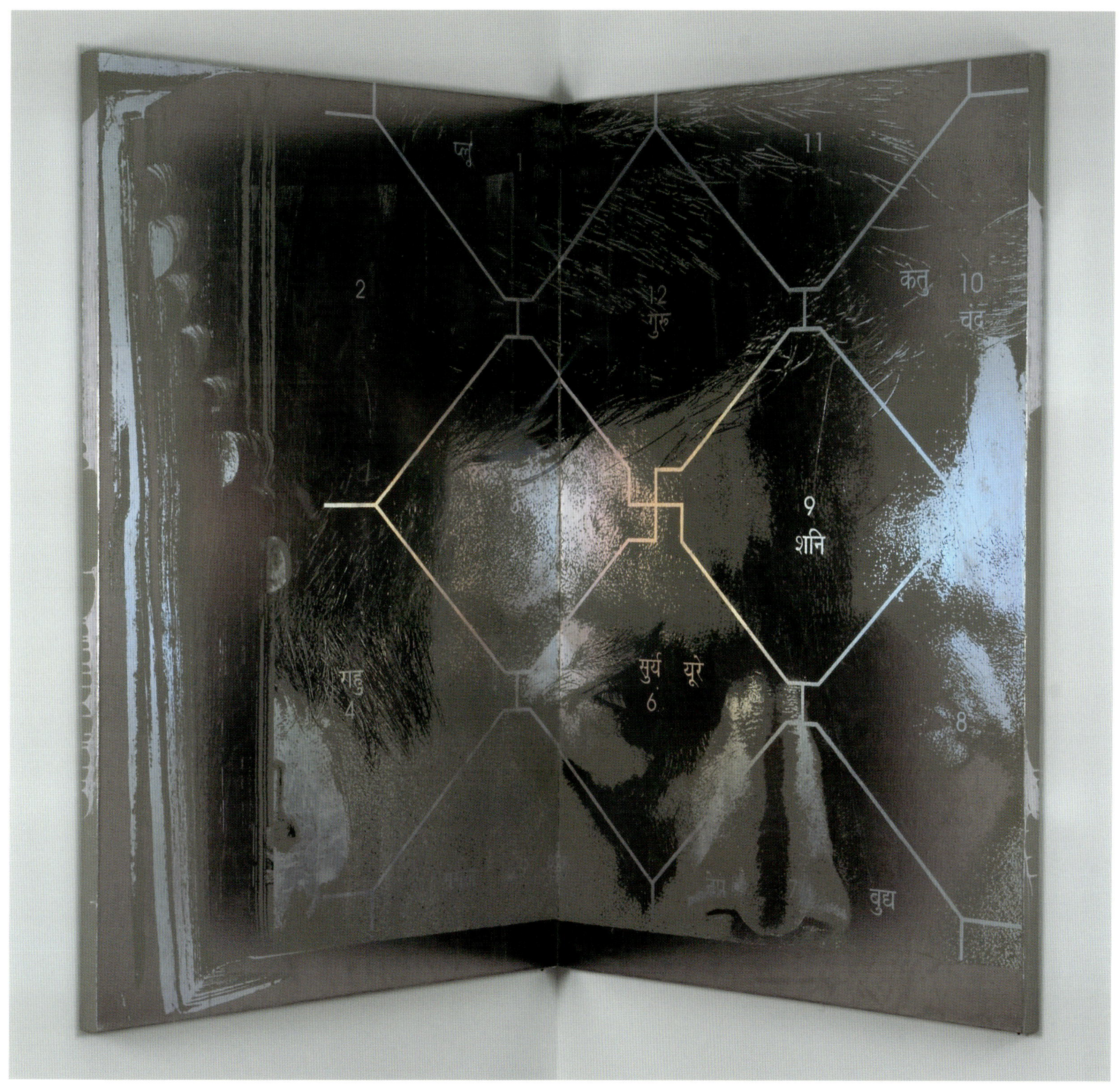

JUSTIN PONMANY
Fear of Destiny, 2007

Wichtige Ausstellungen: „Horn Please: Narratives in Contemporary Indian Art“ (Kunstmuseum Bern, 2007), „Thermocline of Art. New Asian Waves“ (ZKM Center for Art and Media, Karlsruhe, 2007), und „Hybrid Trend: Con-temporary Art of India and Korea“ (Seoul Arts Center, 2007). (MT)

Major exhibitions include "Horn Please: Narratives in Contemporary Indian Art" (Kunstmuseum Bern, 2007), "Thermocline of Art. New Asian Waves" (ZKM Center for Art and Media, Karlsruhe, 2007), and "Hybrid Trend: Con-temporary Art of India and Korea" (Seoul Arts Center, 2007). (MT)

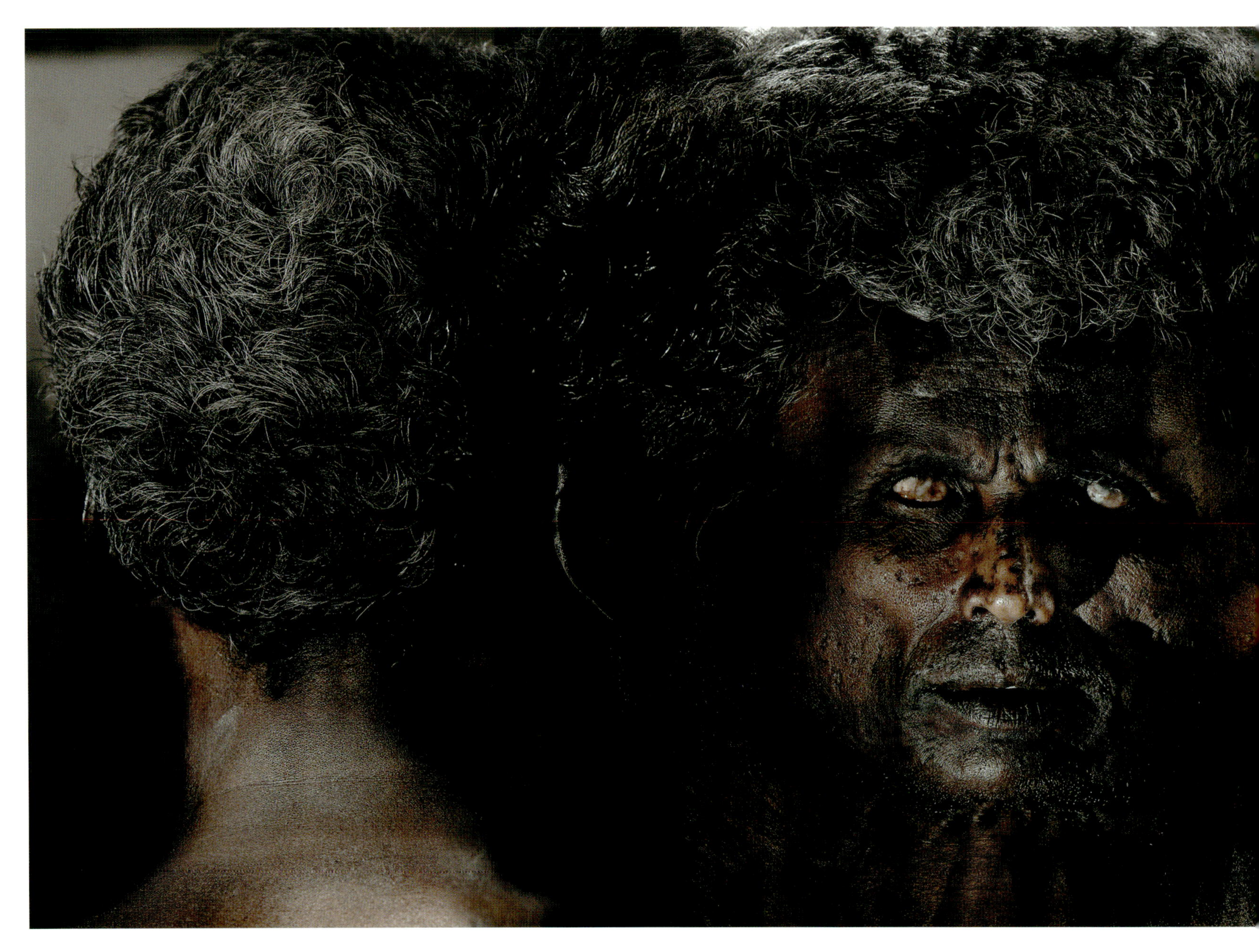

JUSTIN PONMANY
Room No.12, Zehra Chawl, Achanak Nagar, Near Shankar Mandir, 2007
3 Ranjana c.h.s Ahimsa Marg, 2006

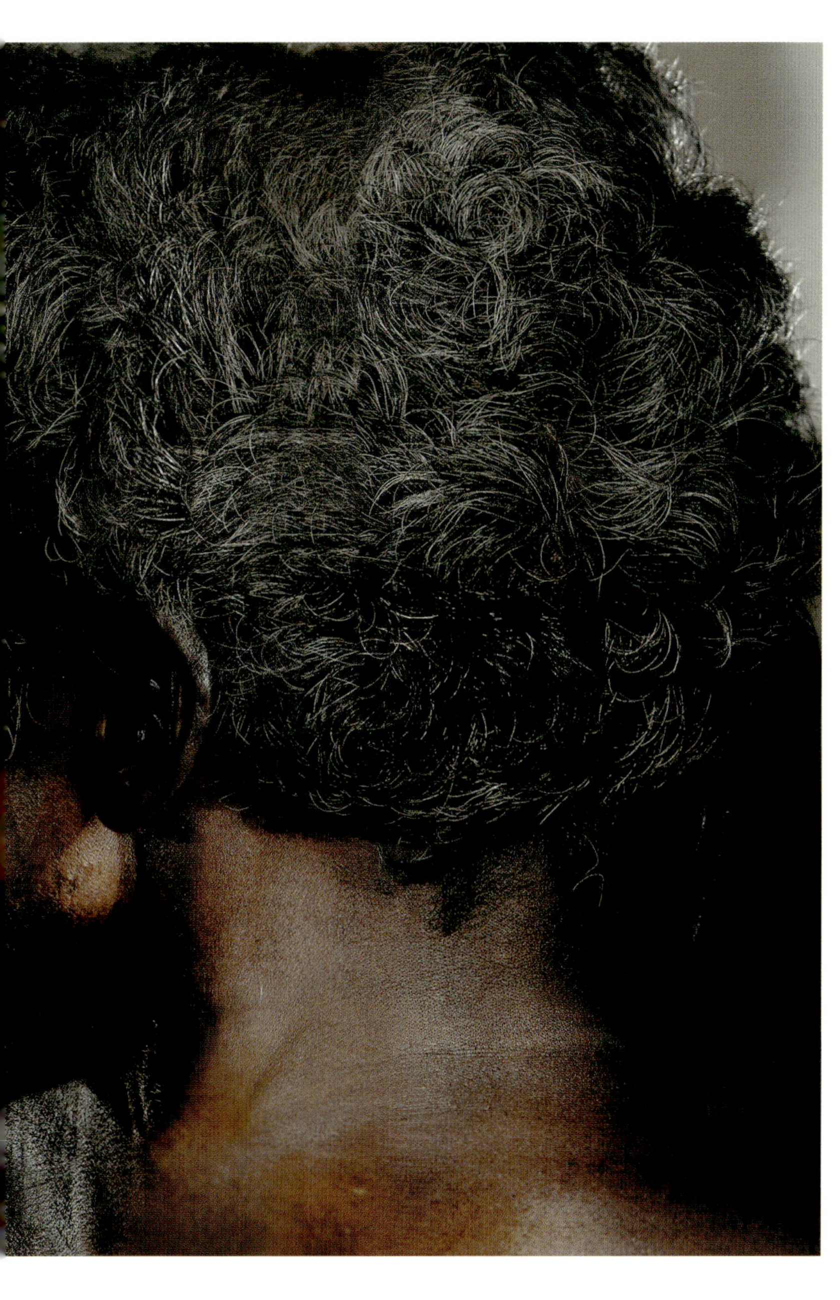

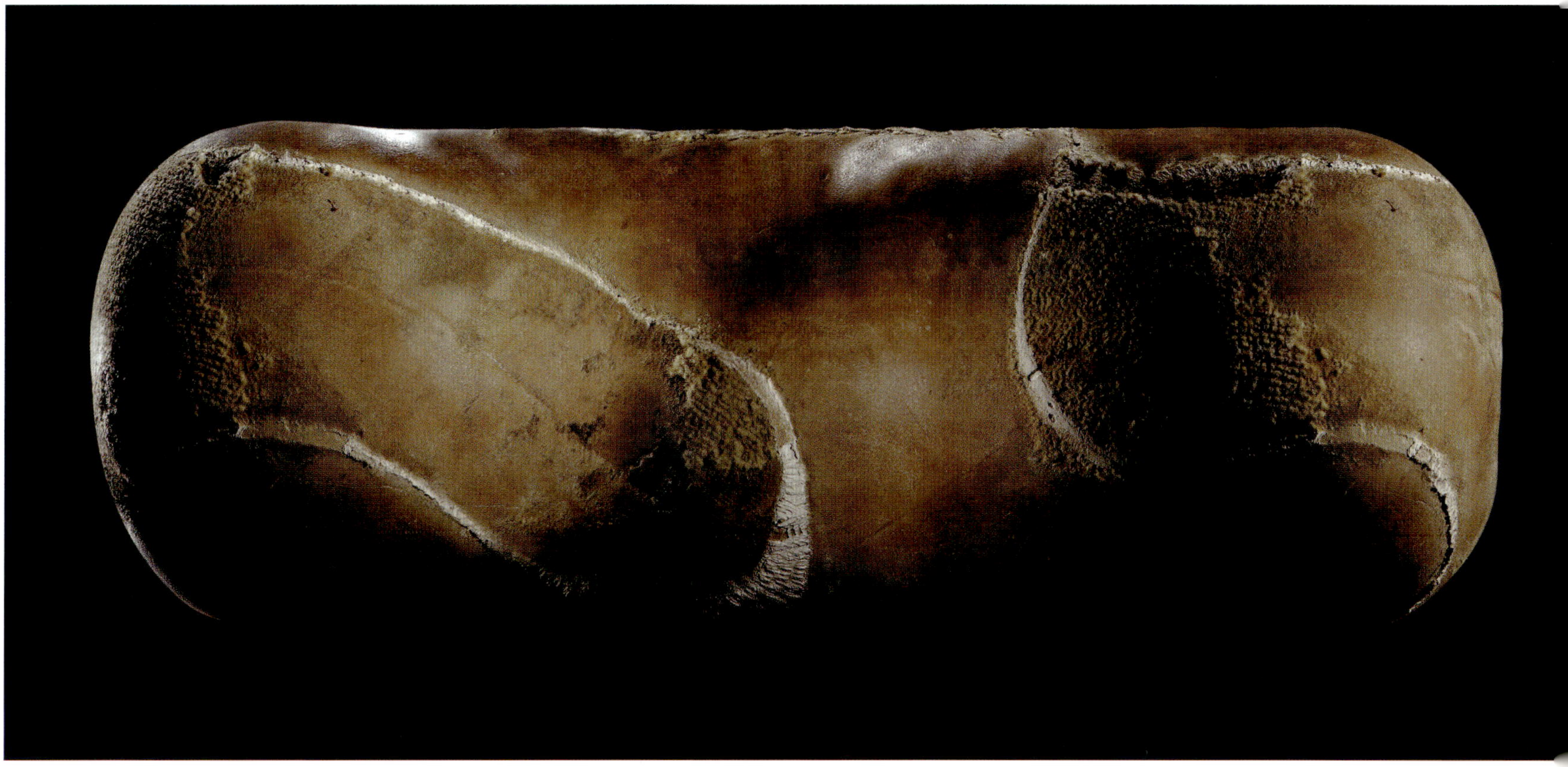

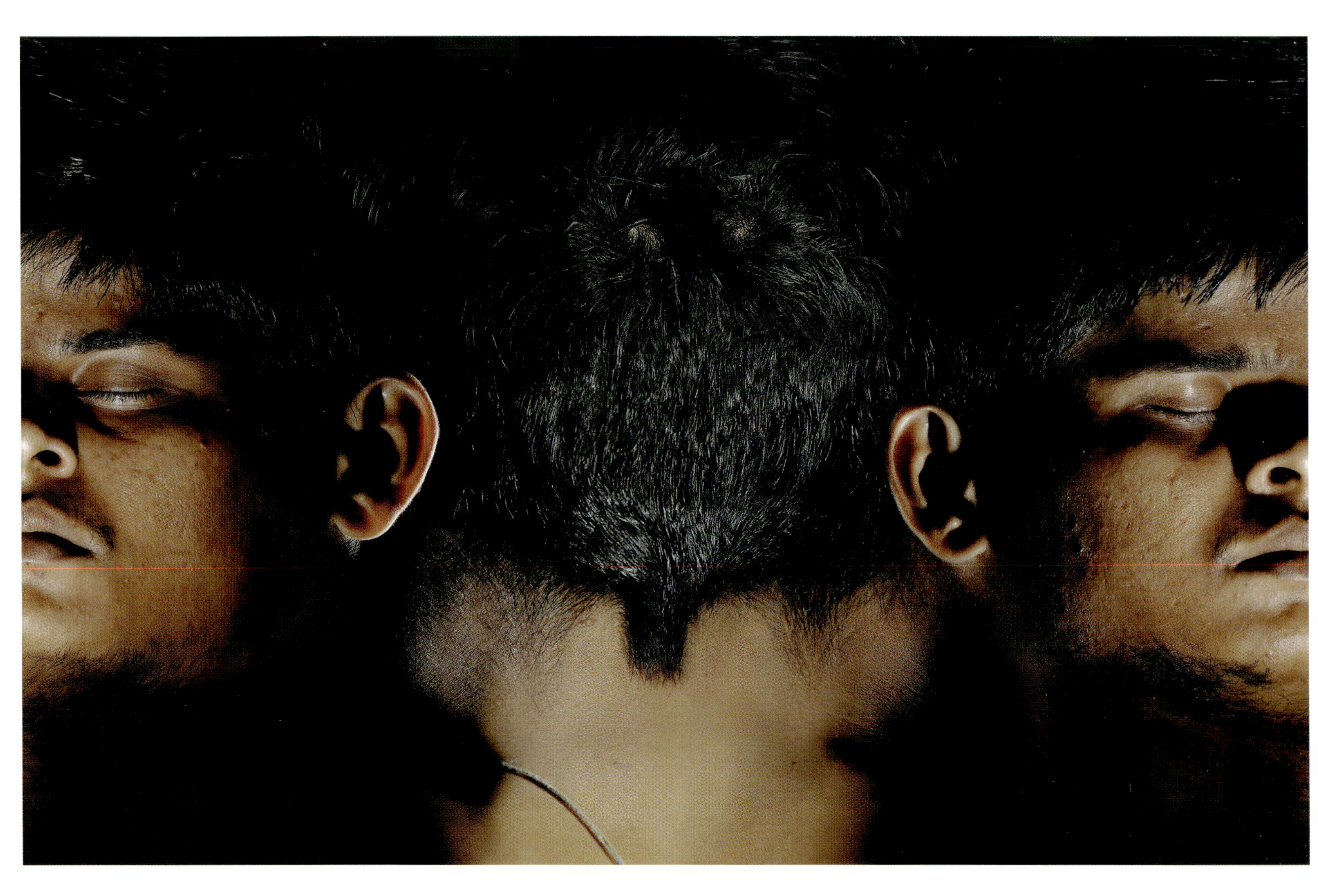

JUSTIN PONMANY
Kolkani Baugh, Room No.2, Selma Manzil, Doodj Naka, 2007

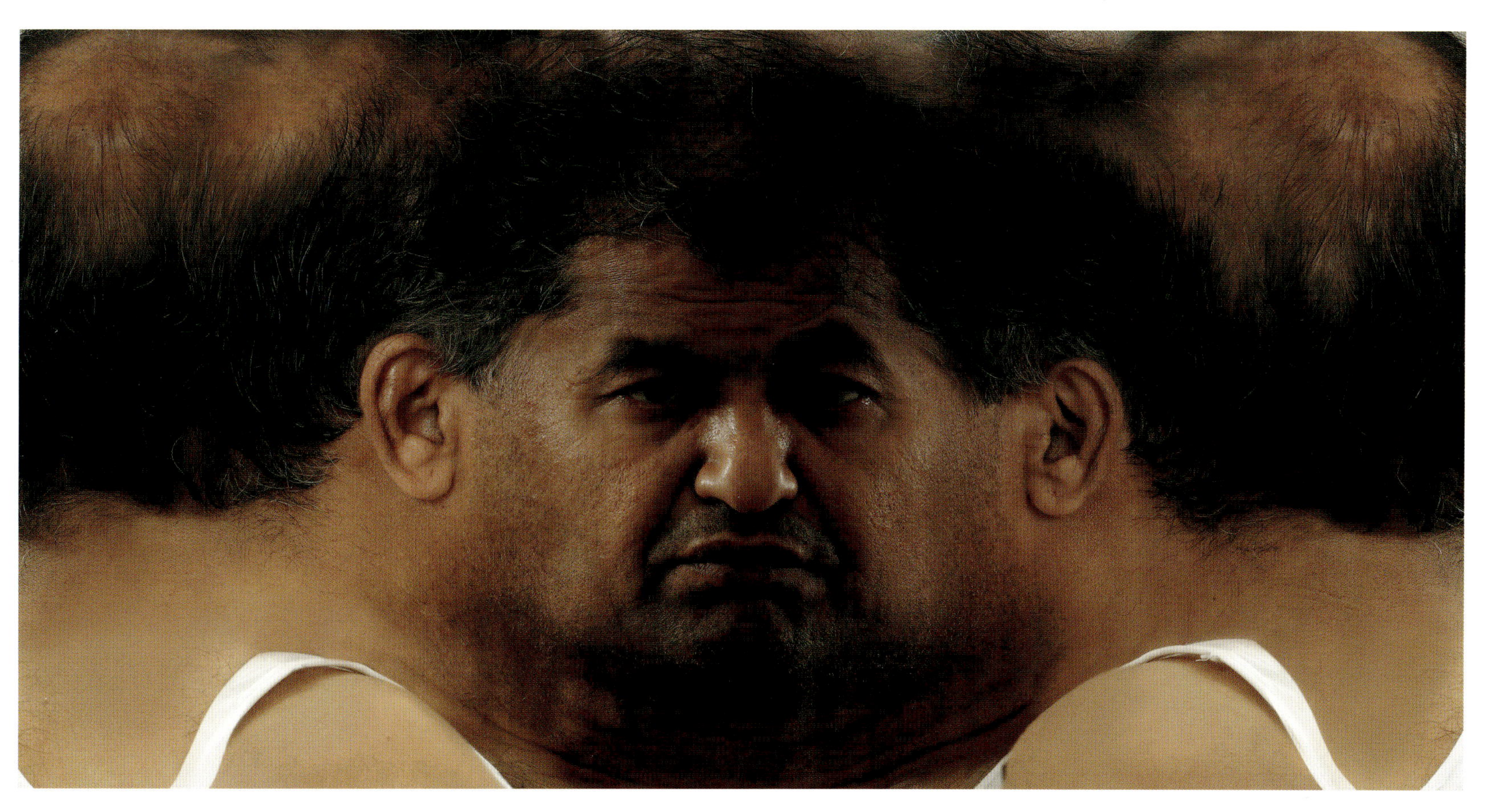

JUSTIN PONMANY
1-b Indraneel Bldg, rdp 1/338, sector 2, Charkop, 2007

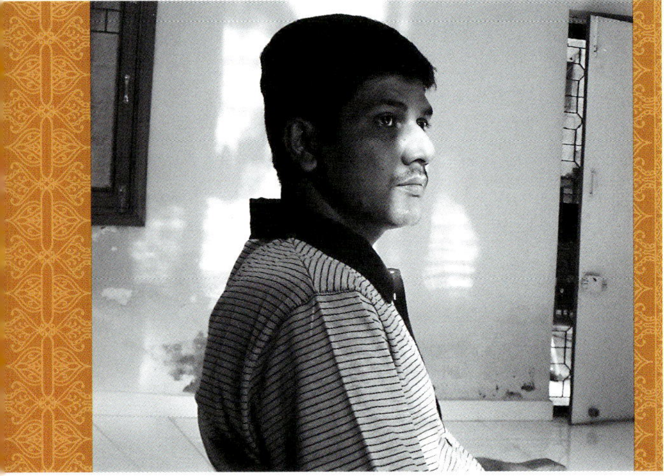

ashim purkayastha

ASHIM PURKAYASTHA Geboren 1967 in Pengagree Tea Estate, Assam / Lebt in Delhi
Born 1967 in Pengagree Tea Estate, Assam / Lives in Delhi

Purkayastha erwarb am Kala Bhavana (Institute of Fine Arts) der Visva-Bharati University in Santiniketan, Westbengalen, sein Bachelordiplom als auch 1994 ein Masterdiplom. Purkayastha stammt aus Sylhet, das ursprünglich zu Assam gehörte und dann Ostpakistan (dem heutigen Bangladesch) unterstellt wurde. Er wuchs im Grenzgebiet Nordost-Indiens auf. Seine persönlichen Einblicke in das Leben in geographischen und gesellschaftlichen Randgebieten haben ihn motiviert, die Definitionen von Nation und Landesgrenzen immer wieder in Gemälden, Fotografien und Installationen auszuloten.

Die Serie „Gandhi Man without Specs" ist ein laufendes Projekt, das im Jahr 2002 in Angriff genommen wurde. Das Thema ist Mahatma Gandhi, der so genannte „Vater der Republik Indien". Darstellungen von Gandhi als Hindu und Moslem, als schwarzer Mann oder „Harijan" („Geschöpf Gottes" oder „Unberührbarer") werden auf Bilder von Gandhi auf einem Briefmarkenbogen oder auf das „Ashoka Chakra" (Rad des Dharma) gezeichnet, das auf Stempelmarken das Universum und die gesellschaftliche Ordnung repräsentiert. Purkayasthas Technik belässt das ursprüngliche Bild im Zentrum des Werks. Die modifizierten Bilder werden rund um das Original angeordnet und stellen Inder und ihre Umwelt dar. Seine minutiöse Arbeit an diesen winzigen „amtlichen" Dokumenten in Form von Brief- und Stempelmarken vermittelt die Beharrlichkeit und die Unnachgiebigkeit, von der Gandhis Unabhängigkeitsbewegung getragen wurde. „Speak, See, Hear – No Evil" (2006), benannt nach der Lehre der drei weisen Affen, die während der Unabhängigkeitsbewegung mit Gandhi assoziiert wurde, ist eine Warnung davor, die Realität, der man sich stellen sollte, zu leugnen. In „Found Object Object/s" (2003–08) hat der Künstler Gandhis Porträt mit der Feder auf eine 1-Rupien-Note skizziert. Purkayasthas provokante Art, seinen Werken einen ironischen Anstrich zu geben und gleichzeitig eine Warnung an die indische Gesellschaft zu richten, ist nicht als persönlicher Angriff auf Gandhi zu werten. Indem er das vergöttlichte Bild des „Vaters der indischen Nation" umformt, bringt Purkayastha äußerst eloquent zum Ausdruck, dass Menschen und Ideen grundverschieden sind und sich nicht in eine Religion, Ethnie oder Sprachgruppe einordnen lassen und dass es

After obtaining a Bachelor Degree from the Kala Bhavana (Institute of Fine Arts) of the Visva-Bharati University, Santiniketan, in West Bengal, Purkayastha went on to obtain an MA from the same University in 1994. Purkayastha's roots are in Sylhet, which was forced to be divided into East Pakistan (now Bangladesh) and India, and he grew up in North East India near the border in an area under the State of Assam. It is because of his personal experience of living on both the geographical and social fringe that he continues to explore, through painting, photography, and installations, the definitions of Nation and state boundaries.

The "Gandhi Man without Specs" series is an ongoing work that began in 2002. The subject is Mahatma Gandhi, the founding father of the Indian Republic. Images of Gandhi representing a Hindu, Muslim, a black man or *Harijan* ("son of God" or "untouchable") are drawn over images of Gandhi on a single sheet of postage stamps, or over the *Ashoka Chakra* (Wheel of Dharma) that represents the universe and social order on revenue stamps. Purkayastha uses a technique in which the original image is retained in the centre of the work. The other, modified images are arranged so that they surround the original, representing Indians and their surroundings. His technique of meticulously working on these small "official" documents, such as postage stamps and revenue stamps, conveys the tenacious and relentless spirit behind Gandhi's independence movement. *Speak, See, Hear – No Evil* (2006) named after the lesson of the three wise monkeys, associated with Gandhi during the time of the movement for independence, warns that such an attitude could lead to one ignoring the reality that one ought to confront. In *Found Object Object/s* (2003–08), the artist has touched in the portrait of Gandhi on a rupee note with a pen. Purkayastha's confrontational approach of incorporating a sense of satire as well as a warning to the Indian society into his work is not meant for a personal attack on Gandhi. By transforming the deified image of the Father of India, Purkayastha eloquently conveys that people and ideas are diverse and cannot be categorized into a single religion, ethnic or linguistic group, and that it is this diversity that represents India, Purkayastha's motherland. His message through

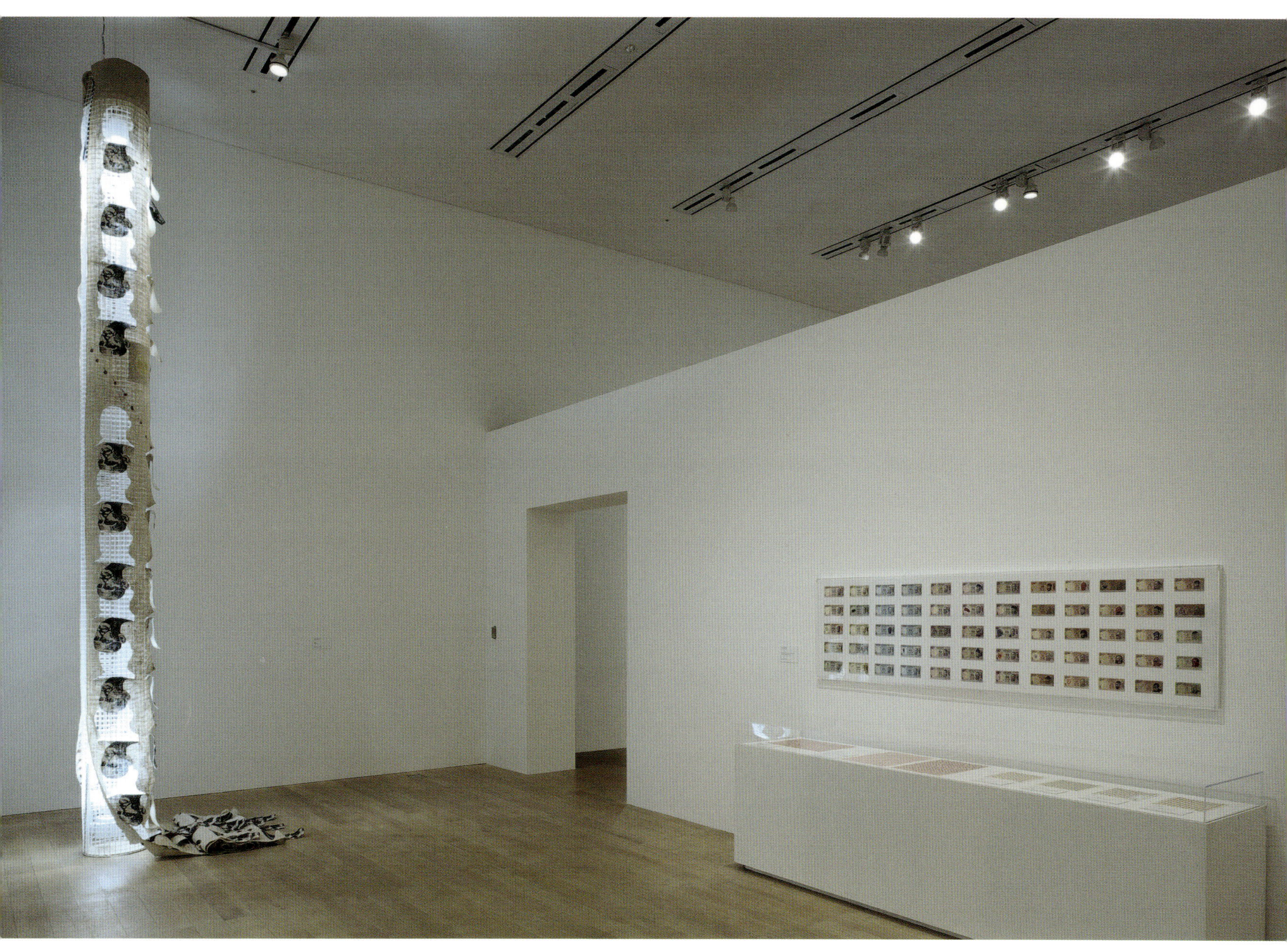

ASHIM PURKAYASTHA
Installation view

diese Vielfalt ist, für die Purkayasthas Heimat Indien steht. Die Botschaft, die durch die Abbildung Gandhis, der in Indien über jeder Kritik steht, vermittelt wird, soll einer Lobhudelei durch andere Künstler zuvor kommen.

Wichtige Ausstellungen: „Borderline“ (Rabindra Bhavan, LKA, New Delhi and Anant Art Gallery, Kolkota, 2006), „SUBCONTINGENT: The Indian Subcontinent in Contemporary Art / Il Subcontinente Indiano nell'Arte Contemporanea“ (Fondazione Sandretto Re Rebaudengo, Turin, Italia, 2006) und „SANTHAL FAMILY: Positions around an Indian Sculpture“ (Museum voor Hedendaagse Kunst Antwerpen, Antwerp, 2008). (TK)

the image of Gandhi who is above criticism in India is so sharp that it deters other artists' adulation.

Major exhibitions include "Borderline" (Rabindra Bhavan, LKA, New Delhi and Anant Art Gallery, Kolkota, 2006), "SUBCONTINGENT: The Indian Subcontinent in Contemporary Art / Il Subcontinente Indiano nell'Arte Contemporanea" (Fondazione Sandretto Re Rebaudengo, Turin, Italia, 2006), and "SANTHAL FAMILY: Positions around an Indian Sculpture" (Museum voor Hedendaagse Kunst Antwerpen, Antwerp, 2008). (TK)

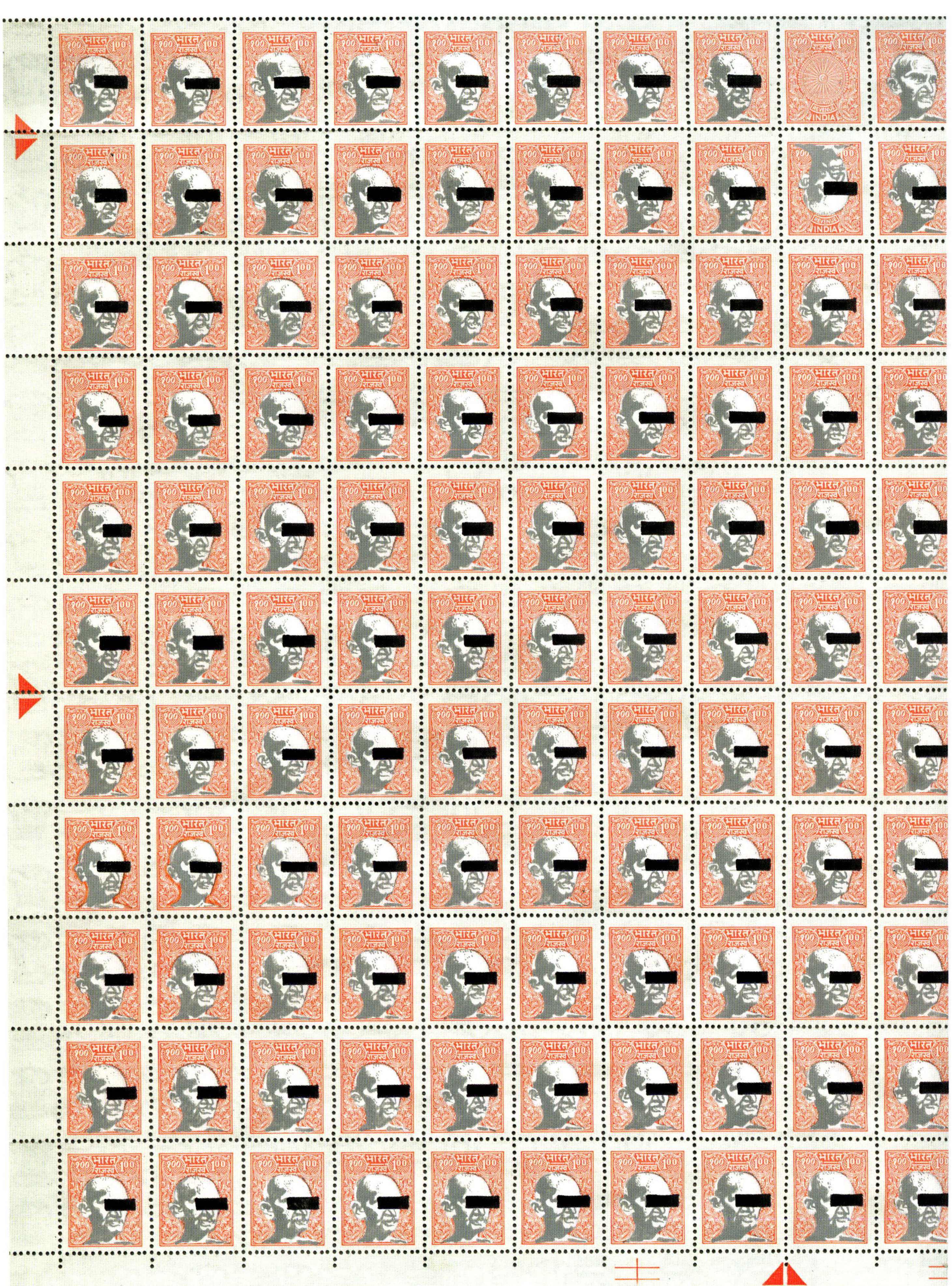

ASHIM PURKAYASTHA
Gandhi Man without Specs XV, 2006

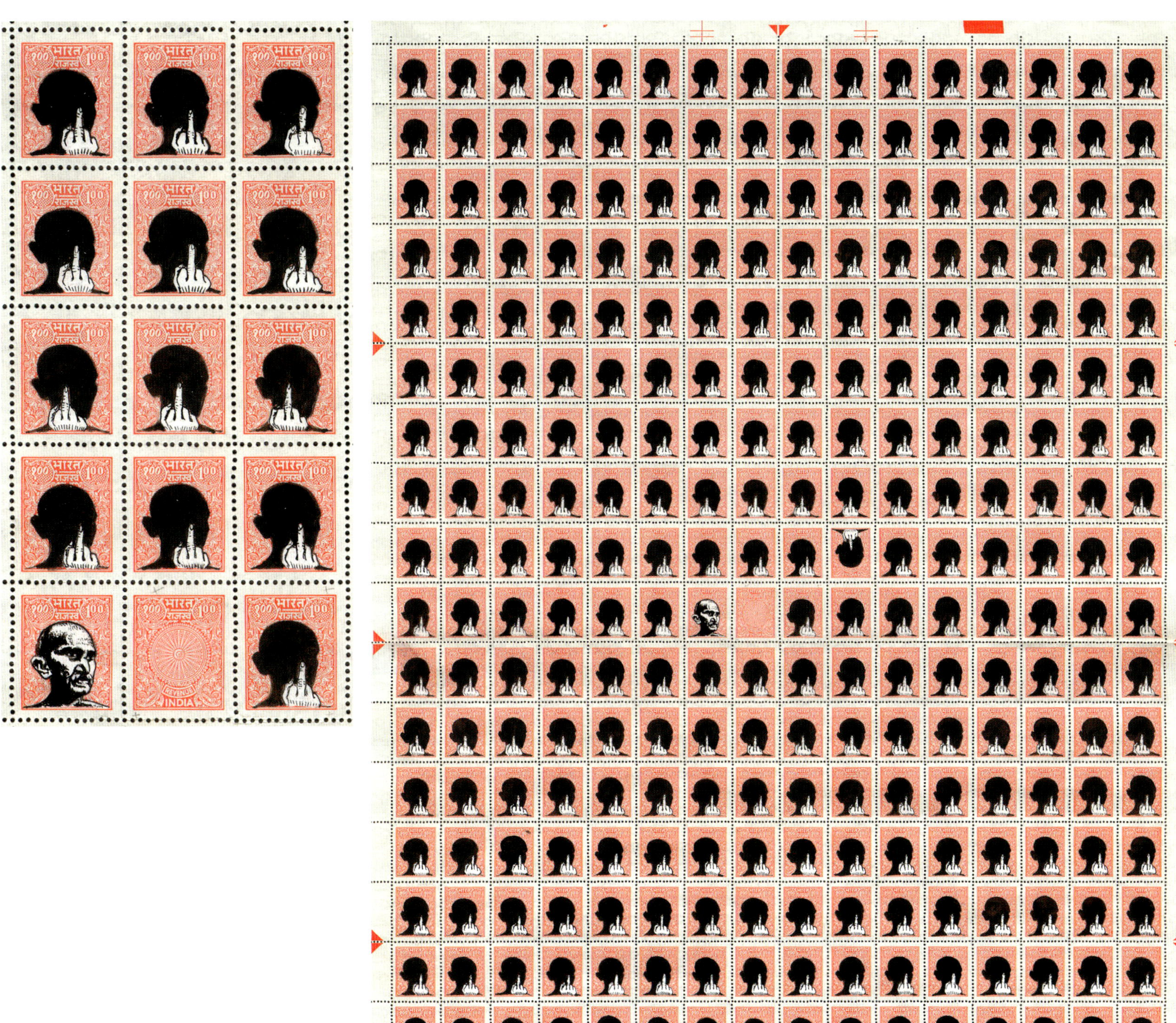

ASHIM PURKAYASTHA
Speak, See, Hear – No Evil, 2006

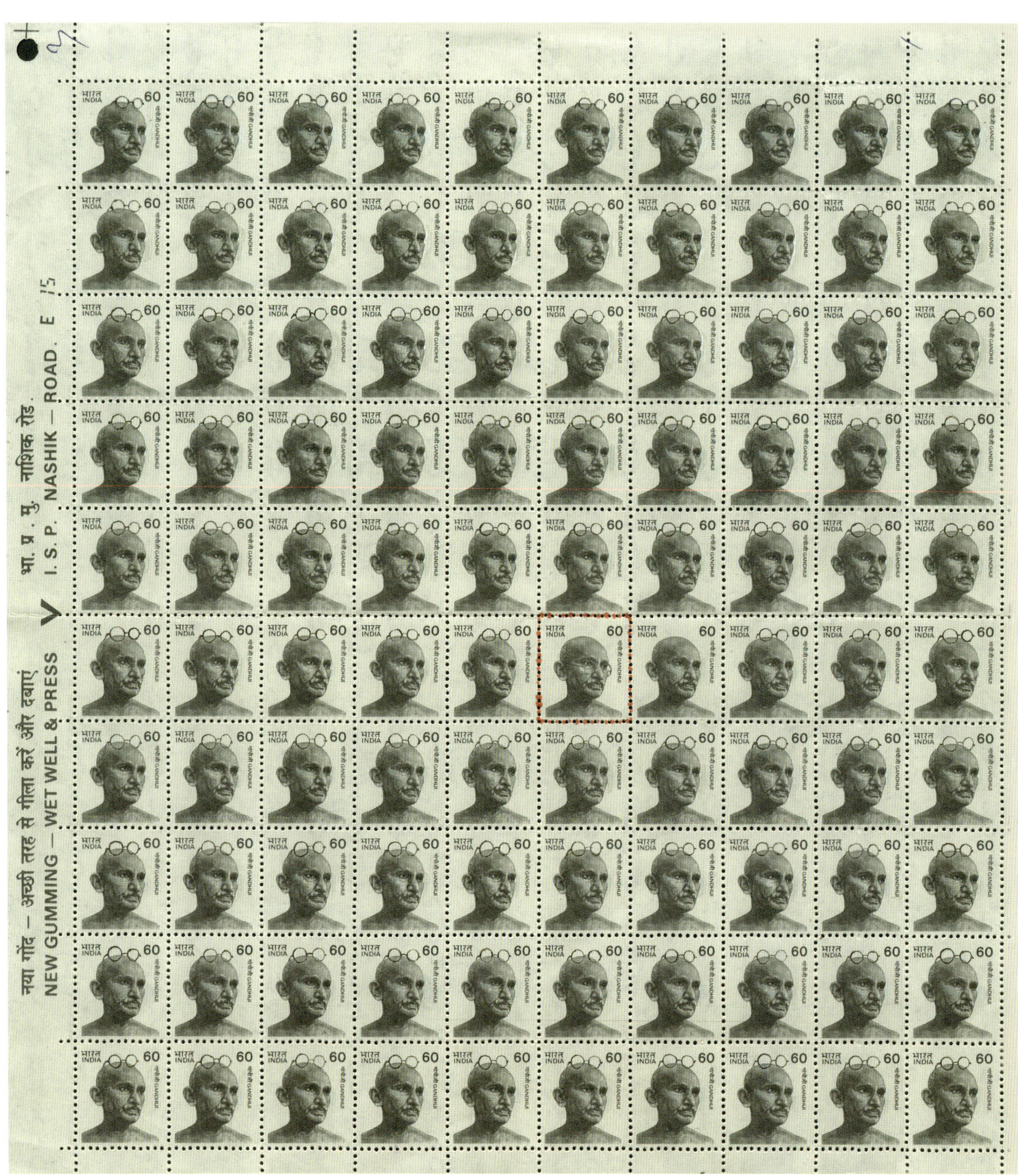

ASHIM PURKAYASTHA
Gandhi Man without Specs XIV, 2005

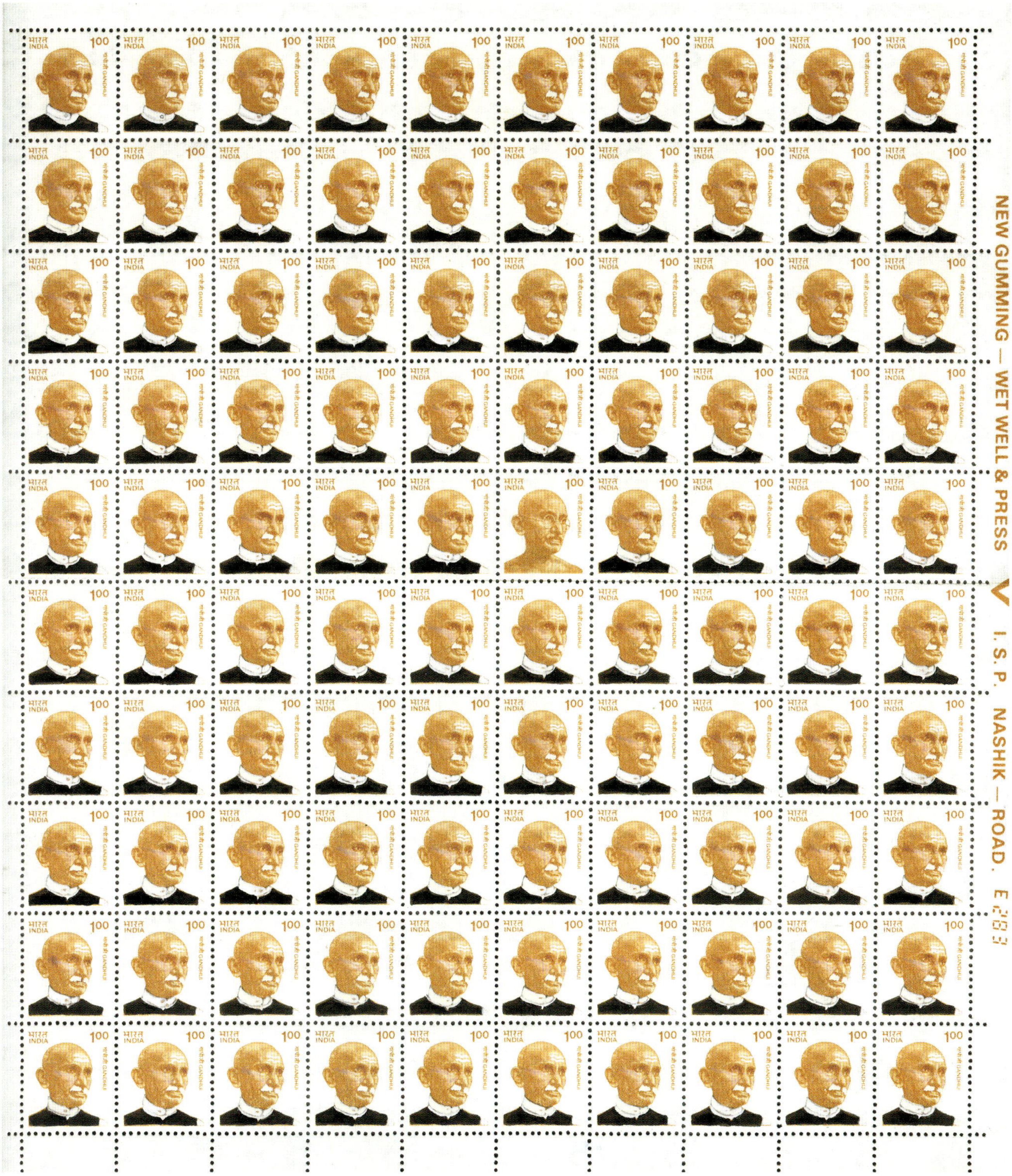

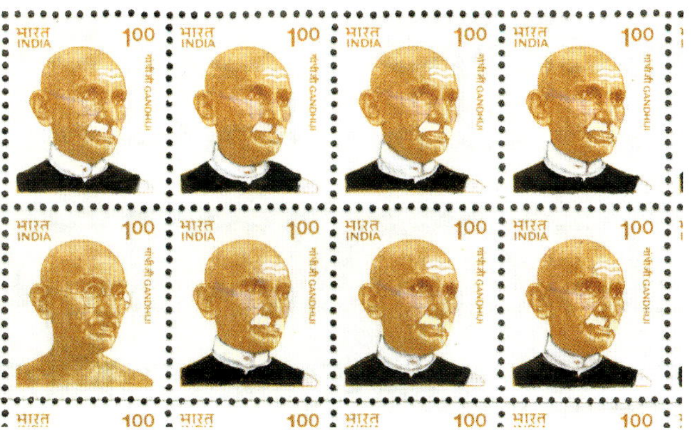

ASHIM PURKAYASTHA
Gandhi Man without Specs XII, 2006

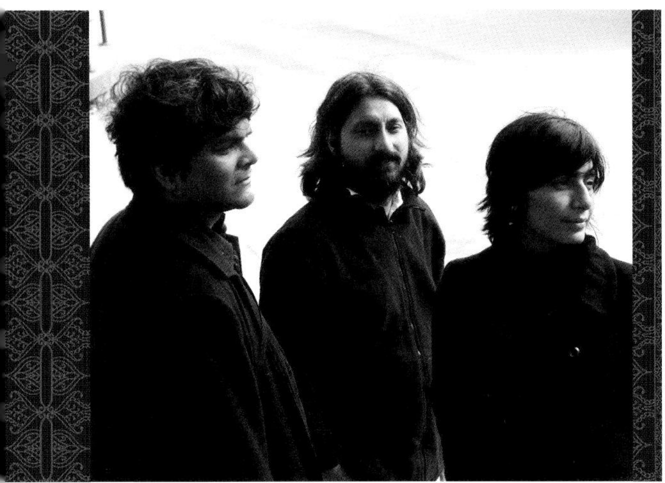

raqs media collective

RAQS MEDIA COLLECTIVE 1992 gegründet; mit Sitz in Delhi | Formed in 1992 in Delhi, where it continues to be based.
JEEBESH BAGCHI geboren 1965 in Delhi | Born 1965 in Delhi
MONICA NARULA geboren 1969 in Delhi | Born 1969 in Delhi
SHUDDHABRATA SENGUPTA geboren 1968 in Delhi | Born 1968 in Delhi

Raqs Media Collective wurde von drei Studenten ins Leben gerufen, die 1991 die Jamia Millia Islamia University mit Masterdiplom absolvierten. Unter den bei dieser Ausstellung vertretenen Künstlern handelt es sich wohl um die ungewöhnlichste Gruppe der neuen Künstlergeneration. Alle drei haben eine Affinität zum Dokumentarfilm, was im Namen der Gruppe und in ihrem Schaffen auch klar zum Ausdruck kommt. In ihrer Analyse der zeitgenössischen Gesellschaft, der Stadtentwicklung und der Globalisierung bedienen sich die Mitglieder des Raqs Media Collective sämtlicher Genres. Sie verwenden Software, Druckmedien, Text, Video und Performance und veranstalten Workshops, Vorträge und Kurse für Kuratoren. Für die Auseinandersetzung mit den Problemen, die die heutige Gesellschaft aufwirft, holen sie sich ihre Inspirationen von einem Expertennetzwerk, das im Lauf der Jahre im Hinblick auf einen umweltorientierten, vielseitigen Ansatz aufgebaut wurde. Im Jahr 2001 richtete die Gruppe mit Unterstützung und als Mitglied des Centre for the Study of Developing Societies (CSDS) in Delhi das „Sarai Media Lab" ein. Delhi ist nicht nur der Sitz von Raqs Media Collective, sondern auch der Geburtsort der drei Mitglieder, die sich einem konzeptuellen Stil verschrieben haben. Als Einwohner von Delhi kommentieren sie mit Einfühlungsvermögen das Leben der Menschen und die indische Gesellschaft.

Bei der aktuellen Ausstellung zeigt das Raqs Media Collective eine von Grund auf aktualisierte Version von „The Euphoria Machine: Preliminary Reverse Engineering Field Laboratory". Hier wird versucht, die Vorgänge und Methoden, die der Vermögensbildung und dem raschen und intensiven Wirtschaftswachstum zugrunde liegen, zu analysieren und sie eindrucksvoll und symbolisch in Form einer Maschine darzustellen. So gesehen ist „The Euphoria Machine" ein „Metagerät", in dem das rastlose menschliche Streben nach Glück und Zufriedenheit bis zur Raserei getrieben wird. Dem Ganzen liegt die Theorie zugrunde, dass diese Maschine von den ewig unbefriedigten menschlichen Wünschen und von Materialismus angetrieben wird; in der Tat ist es das menschliche Begehren, das hinter der globalen Verbreitung der Konsumkultur steht. Der zweite Weltkrieg wurde mit dem Argument gerechtfertigt,

Raqs Media Collective, formed by three students who graduated in 1991 with Master of Arts degrees in Mass Communications at Jamia Millia Islamia University, is arguably the most unusual of the new generation of artists, even amongst the artists participating in this exhibition. All three have a background in documentary film making, which is clearly reflected in their creative process and in their group's name. Raqs Media Collective analyzes contemporary society, urban development, and globalization by transcending genre. The Collective utilizes software, print media, text, video and performance, as well as holding workshops and lectures and organizing exhibitions and curatorial programs. To address issues generated by society today, the Collective frequently makes creative use of the network of specialists that has been developed over the years to pursue its environmental and multi-perspective approach. In 2001, the Collective established Sarai Media Lab in conjunction with, and as an affiliate of Delhi's Centre for the Study of Developing Societies (CSDS). Based in Delhi, the birthplace of all three members, Raqs Media Collective uses a conceptual style to comment, with a unique Delhiite sensibility, on Indian society and the lives of its people.

For this exhibition, Raqs Media Collective is showing a completely updated version, from concept through to end result, of *The Euphoria Machine: Preliminary Reverse Engineering Field Laboratory*. The aim of this work is to analyze the process and method behind the creation of wealth and rapid, intense economic growth, and to identify what kind of powerful and symbolic form should take, and to manifest this (as a machine/device). In other words, *The Euphoria Machine* is a "meta device," in which people's relentless search for happiness, satisfaction, and energy is becoming frenzied. The underlying hypothesis is that it is people's never-satisfied desire and materialism that fuels this device; indeed, it is human desire that is behind the consumption culture that continues to grow on a global scale. World War II has been justified as a war to uphold the tenets of people's right to pursue happiness, prosperity, freedom, and peace. This work, however, insightfully hints that it is actually the endless greed for beauty, health, happiness, love, joy and satisfaction that drives capitalism.

dass das Recht der Menschen auf das Streben nach Glück, Wohlstand, Freiheit und Frieden garantiert werden müsse. Die hier gezeigte Arbeit deutet allerdings darauf hin, dass es eigentlich die nie endende Gier nach Schönheit, Gesundheit, Glück, Liebe, Freude und Bedürfnisbefriedigung ist, die den Kapitalismus antreibt.

Wichtige Ausstellungen: „Documenta 11" (Kassel, 2002), „Taipei Biennale" (2004) und „iCon: India Contemporary" (The 51st Venice Biennale, 2005). Letztes Jahr war Raqs Media Collective an der Organisation und Kuratierung einer internationalen Ausstellung unter dem Titel „Manifesta 7: The European Biennial of Contemporary Art" (Trentino-Südtirol, Italia, 2008) beteiligt. (KM)

Major exhibitions include "Documenta 11" (Kassel, 2002), "Taipei Biennale" (2004), and "iCon: India Contemporary" (The 51st Venice Biennale, 2005). This year, Raqs Media Collective was involved in organizing an international exhibition "Manifesta 7: The European Biennial of Contemporary Art" (Trentino-Südtirol, Italia, 2008) as a co-curator. (KM)

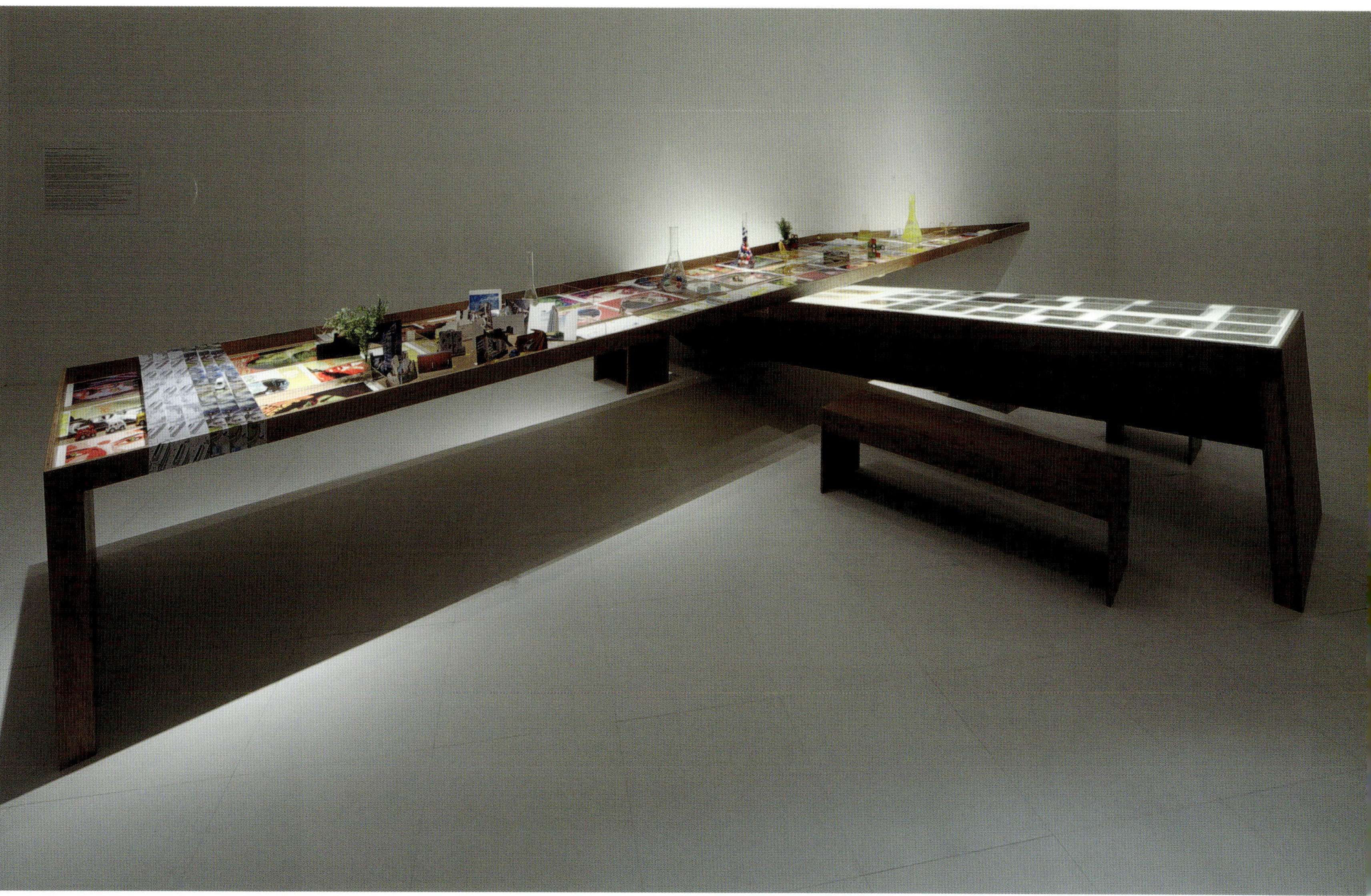

RAQS MEDIA COLLECTIVE
The Euphoria Machine: Preliminary Reverse Engineering Field Laboratory, 2008
Installation view

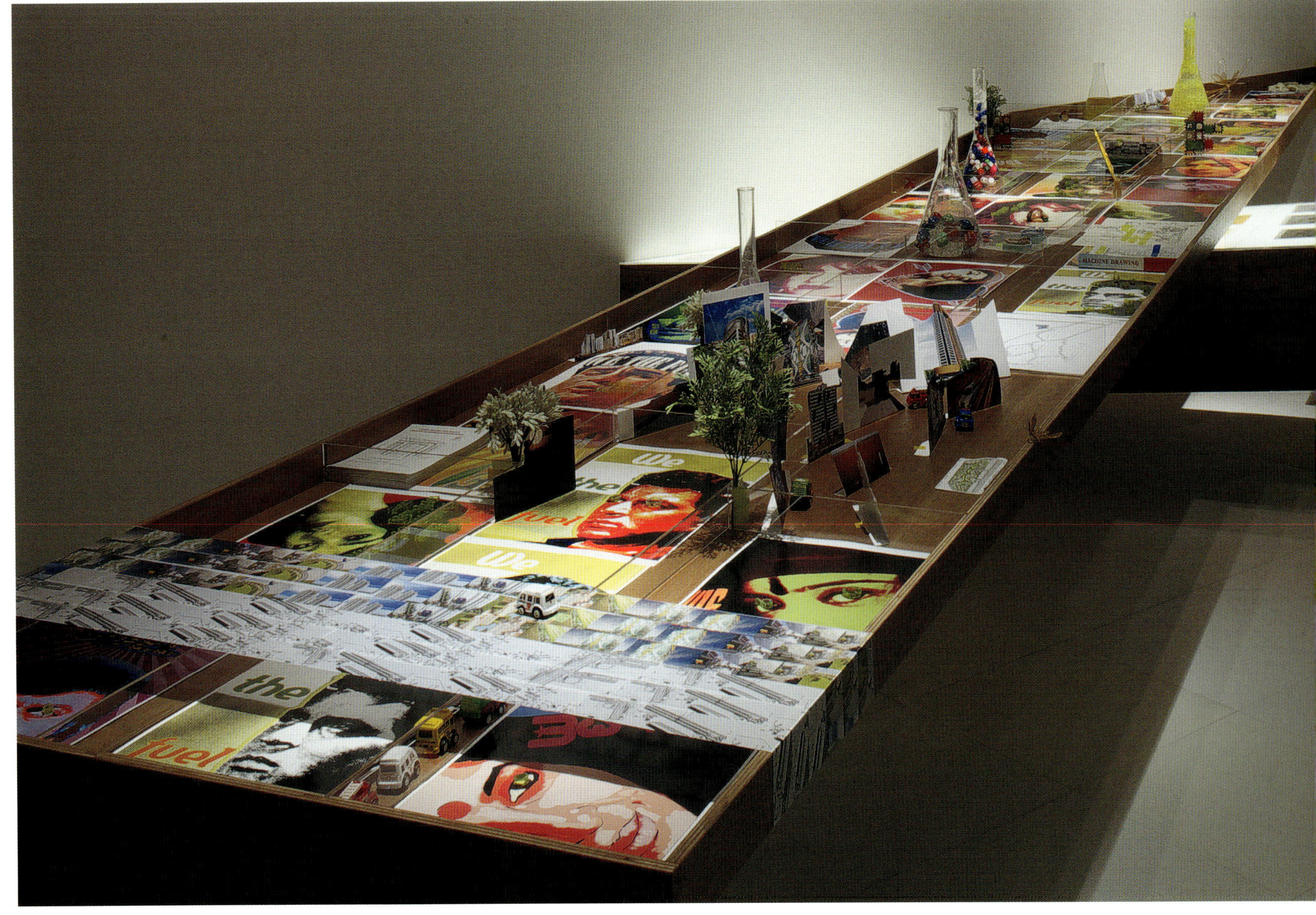

RAQS MEDIA COLLECTIVE
The Euphoria Machine: Preliminary Reverse Engineering Field Laboratory, 2008
Installation view

**The Euphoria Machine:
Preliminary Reverse Engineering Field Laboratory**

Was ist die „Euphorie-Maschine?"

„Die Euphorie-Maschine ist ein Raq-Projekt, das kürzlich als potentielles Langzeitprojekt mit dem Ziel gestartet wurde, die Art, wie sich der Wirtschaftswachstums- und Wohlstandsschöpfungsrausch machtvollen symbolischen und kulturellen Ausdruck verschafft, einer künstlerischen und kritischen Untersuchung zu unterwerfen.

‚Euphorie-Maschine' ist unsere Bezeichnung für die Wunsch- und Erkenntnis-Apparatur, mit der versucht wird, die Gesellschaft auf grenzenlose Energie und ebensolchen Wohlstand einzuschwören und gleichzeitig sämtliche Zweifel und abweichende Meinungen bezüglich der Methoden zur Gewinnung dieser Energie und dieses Wohlstands auszuräumen.

Angesichts der von einer Stimmungskrise und dem Gegenteil von Euphorie angeheizten verbreiteten Auffassung, dass sich das globale Finanzsystem in einer tiefen Krise befindet, erscheint ein ‚Reverse-Engineering-Experiment' mit Hilfe einer Maschine, die nicht wirklich so funktioniert wie sie sollte, an der Zeit.

Irgendwann nach dem Zweiten Weltkrieg besann sich Edward Louis Bernays – ein Neffe Sigmund Freuds und einer der Hauptstrategen der Kriegspropagandafeldzüge sowie der intellektuelle Pate der Werbe- und PR-Industrie – auf eine im Zuge seiner Kriegspropagandaarbeit gemachte entscheidende Entdeckung, die er nun für den künftigen Erfolg des Kapitalismus einzusetzen gedachte. Er hatte festgestellt, dass nie zuvor in der menschlichen Geschichte ein Krieg im Namen von Demokratie, Frieden und Wohlstand geführt worden war. Man hatte um Land gekämpft, um den Machtgewinn von Dynastien oder herrschenden Grup-

**The Euphoria Machine:
Preliminary Reverse Engineering Field Laboratory**

What is the Euphoria Machine?

"The Euphoria Machine Project is a recently instigated but potentially long term Raqs project aimed at an artistic and critical investigation of the way in which the frenzy of economic growth and wealth-creation acquires potent symbolic and cultural forms.

Euphoria Machine is the name we give to the apparatus of desire and cognition that seeks to create a consensus within society for boundless energy and wealth, and effaces all doubts and dissent about the ways in which this energy and wealth must be acquired.

Today, when there is a general perception of a systemic crisis of the global financial apparatus, fuelled by a crisis of sentiment and the inverse of euphoria, a 'reverse engineering experiment' on a machine that doesn't quite seem to be working as well it is supposed to, seems to be timely.

Sometime after the Second World War, Edward Louis Bernays, a nephew of Sigmund Freud, a key strategist of war-time propaganda campaigns and the intellectual god-father of the advertising and public relations industry, applied a key discovery he had made during the fashioning of war propaganda to the future success of Capitalism. The discovery was this – in no other war in Human History, had wars been fought in the name of democracy, peace and prosperity. They had been fought for land, for the expansion of a particular dynasty or ruling groups power, for religious zeal and for other concretely political purposes. The propaganda campaigns of the Second World War however, successfully named a different kind of motivation for war – the desire for happiness, peace, prosperi-

pen, für andere konkrete politische Ziele und aus Glaubenseifer. Die Propagandafeldzüge im Zweiten Weltkrieg beriefen sich auf ein anderes Kriegsmotiv – nämlich auf den Wunsch nach Glück, Frieden, Wohlstand und Freiheit. Das Gleichsetzen allgemein anerkannter Tugenden mit der Kriegsmaschine erwies sich als wirksame Antriebskraft.

Als der Krieg vorbei war, stellte Bernays fest, dass sich dasselbe Verfahren auch in ‚Friedenszeiten' anwenden ließ. Man musste den Menschen nur klar machen, dass der Einsatz ihrer Arbeitskraft im Interesse des Kapitals oder für den Erwerb von Dingen, die sie eigentlich nicht benötigten (mit dem alleinigen Ziel, die Kapitalmaschine am Laufen zu halten), gleich zu setzen sei mit dem grundlegenden menschlichen Streben nach Schönheit, Gesundheit, Glück, Liebe, Freude und Zufriedenheit. Man brachte den Menschen also bei, dass ihnen der Kauf von Schuhen oder die Arbeit in einem Call Center ein tief empfundenes Glücksgefühl vermitteln würde. Durch diesen raffinierten und gleichzeitig bedeutsamen Schachzug wurde die Trennung der Ware von ihrer Funktion vollzogen. Schuhe waren nicht mehr dazu da, Füße zu bekleiden und zu schützen; sie wurden statt dessen zu Auslösern persönlichen Wohlbefindens. Ein Job diente nicht mehr dazu, sich den Lebensunterhalt zu verdienen, sondern wurde zum Kennzeichen einer besonderen menschlichen Identität. Die Bausteine des Kapitals wurden als persönliche Antriebskräfte verinnerlicht.

In unseren Augen ist diese Verbindung zwischen tief verankerten inneren Antriebskräften und dem Betrieb des riesigen, unpersönlichen, globalen Wirtschaftsnetzes das Geheimnis der ‚Euphorie- Maschine'. Es ist auch der Stoff, der die Maschine antreibt. Die Gewinnung dieses Stoffes erfordert und bewirkt, dass die vielschichtigen menschlichen Lebenserfahrungen den Erfordernissen des Kapitalismus dienstbar gemacht werden.

Es ist nur ein kleiner Schritt von dem Wunsch, etwas zu besitzen, um das Gefühl hervorzurufen, das sein Besitz vorgeblich in uns auslöst, zum Ankauf von Anteilen an Dingen, die es noch gar nicht gibt – einfach weil man uns sagt, dass das Wohlstandskalkül vom Erwerb und vom Handel mit virtuellen Vermögenswerten abhängt. Die gegenwärtige Finanzkrise ist aus dem Antrieb entstanden, begriffliche anstatt reale Dinge zu erwerben und mit ihnen Handel zu treiben. Das Ergebnis sind imaginäre Vermögenswerte und imaginäre Schulden – allerdings besichert durch äußerst reale Transaktionskosten, die aus dem Transfer und Austausch dieser imaginären Vermögenswerte und Schulden entstehen. Wenn die realen Kosten die imaginären Einkünfte überschreiten, verwandelt sich die Euphorie in ihr Gegenteil. Gegenwärtig verbreiten die Abgase der ‚Euphorie-Maschine' pure Verzweiflung.

Diese Apparatur namens ‚Euphorie-Maschine' nimmt (in unseren Augen) die Form einer imaginären Meta-Maschine an, welche die Funktionen einer begrifflichen Maschine zur Fertigung des Wunsches nach immerwährender Energie und grenzenlosem wirtschaftlichem Wachstum erfüllt.

Der in Indien und auch anderswo herrschende Rummel um die sogenannte ‚indische Wirtschaft ist (trotz gewisser Andeutungen bezüglich einer ‚Apokalypse' der Weltwirtschaft) ein Beispiel für das Funktionieren der Euphorie-Maschine.

Auch die weiter zurückliegende Aufregung um den Wirtschaftsaufschwung Japans nach dem Krieg oder über den Aufstieg der asiatischen ‚Tiger'-Wirtschaften in den 1980er Jahren, aber auch die gegenwärtige Manie die chinesische Wirtschaft betreffend (sowie frühere Perioden der Hochkonjunktur in transatlantischen und westeuropäischen Volkswirtschaften) sind ausnahmslos Beispiele für das Wirken der ‚Euphorie-Maschine'.

Das Hauptprodukt der ‚Euphorie-Maschine' ist verarbeitete Wahrnehmung. Die Wahrnehmung, dass ‚Wachstum' an sich großartig ist, dass das BIP das Maß allen Glücks ist, dass es etwas wie eine ‚indische' Wirtschaft gibt und dass dieses als ‚indische Wirtschaft' bekannte Etwas floriert; selbst der Gedanke, dass es etwas gibt, das sich ‚indische' Kunst nennt und dass ‚indische' Kunst – als kleines, aber symbolisch bedeutsames Rädchen im Getriebe des indischen Marktes für hochwertige Nischenprodukte – floriert. Es handelt sich dabei ausnahmslos um Produkte und Nebenprodukte des Wirkens der Euphorie-Maschine.

Die Iteration dieses Projekts am Mori Art Museum im Rahmen der ‚Chalo! India' Ausstellung erfolgt in Form einer prozessualen Bearbeitung des durch das Laufen der Euphorie-Maschine bewirkten ‚Reverse Engineering'. Wir gehen von der Annahme aus, dass es diese Maschine gibt. Das Projekt verfolgt nicht den Zweck, ihre Existenz zu beweisen oder zu demonstrieren. Die Beweise sind mitten unter uns in Form von Plänen, Vorhersagen, Werbung, Grundsatzerklärungen, Blaupausen, Bilanzen, Berichten.

Das Projekt möchte vielmehr die Bestandteile der Maschine, deren Wirkungsweise und Ineinandergreifen so analysieren, dass offenkundig wird, wie der ‚Treibstoff' (menschliche Triebe und Wünsche) verbrannt wird, und wie die gewonnene Energie die beweglichen Teile der Maschine in Richtung auf das gewünschte Ergebnis antreibt."

Raqs Media Collective, Tokyo, November 2008

ty and liberty. The identification of common virtues with the war machine proved to be a very successful motivator.

Once the war ended, Bernays realized that the same process could be replicated in 'peacetime' only this time, people must be made to realize that contributing their labour to capital, or buying goods that they did not necessarily need (in order to keep the machine of capital running) could also be done by identifying these acts with basic human drives for beauty, health, happiness, love, joy and contentment. So, people were told that they could feel a profound happiness, if they bought a shoe, or went to work in a call centre. This was a subtle but significant shift, in that it divorced a good from its function. A shoe, for instance was no longer something that covered and protected your feet, instead, it became a key to your personal well being. A job was no longer something you did to earn a living, it became a mark of your special identity as a human being. The building blocks of Capital were internalized as personal drives.

To us, this marriage between deep seated internal drives and the running of the vast impersonal network of a global economy is the secret of the 'Euphoria Machine.' It is also the material that fuels the machine. The extraction of this material both requires as well as results in the subordination of the complexity of human life-experiences to the needs of capital.

It is a short distance from desiring a thing for the feeling we are told its possession will induce to acquiring stakes in things that do not yet exist simply because we are told that the calculus of prosperity depends on the acquisition and transaction of virtual assets. The current financial crisis emerges from a drive to acquire and transact things that are notional rather than real. Thus we have notional assets, notional debts underwritten by some very real transaction costs involved in the transfer and exchange of notional assets and debts. It is when the real costs overwhelm notional returns that we experience the opposite of euphoria. Currently, the euphoria machine's exhaust only produces despair.

This apparatus – the Euphoria Machine – takes (for us) the form of an imaginary machine – a meta-machine that works as the conceptual engine of the desire for perpetual energy and limitless economic growth.

The current hype around the so-called 'Indian' economy, both within India, and elsewhere in the world, (despite the easy gestures towards 'doomsday' in the global economy) is an instance of the working of the Euphoria Machine.

At earlier times, the excitement around the post-war economic boom in Japan, or the rise of the 'Asian Tiger' economies in the Nineteen Eighties, or the current mania around the Chinese economy, (as well as earlier 'boom' periods in trans-atlantic and western European eocnomies are all instances of the 'Euphoria Machine' at work).

The key product of the Euphoria Machine is processed perception. The perception that all 'growth' is wonderful, that happiness can be indexed by GDP, that there is such a thing as an 'Indian' Economy, and that this thing known as the 'Indian Economy' is booming. Even the idea that there is such a thing known as 'indian' Art, and that 'indian' Art, a small but symbolically significant cog in the machine of the Indian Market in niche high value goods is booming. All these are products, and by-products of the working of the Euphoria Machine.

The iteration of this project at the Mori Art Museum for the 'Chalo! India' exhibition takes the form of the processual elaboration of the 'reverse engineering' of the Euphoria Machine at work. We start with the assumption that we know the machine exists. The project's intent is not to prove or demonstrate its existence. Its proofs are all around us, in plans, projections, advertisements, policy statements, blueprints, balance sheets, reports.

Instead, the project aims to analyse its constituent parts, their operations and their interconnections in such a manner as to show how the 'fuel' (human drives and desires) is combusted and how that energy runs the moving parts of the machine so as to achieve the desired end."

Raqs Media Collective, Tokyo, November 2008

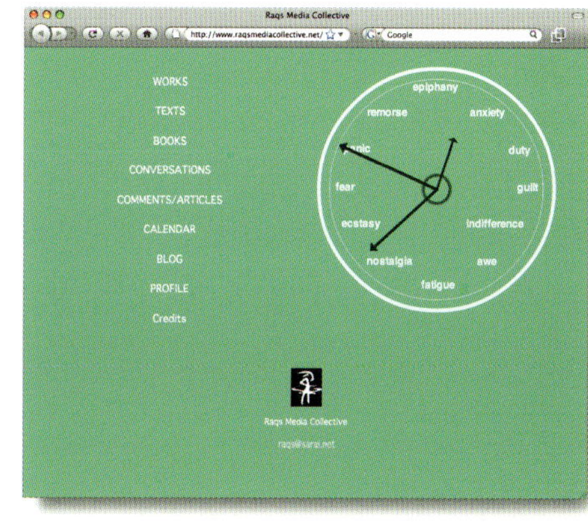

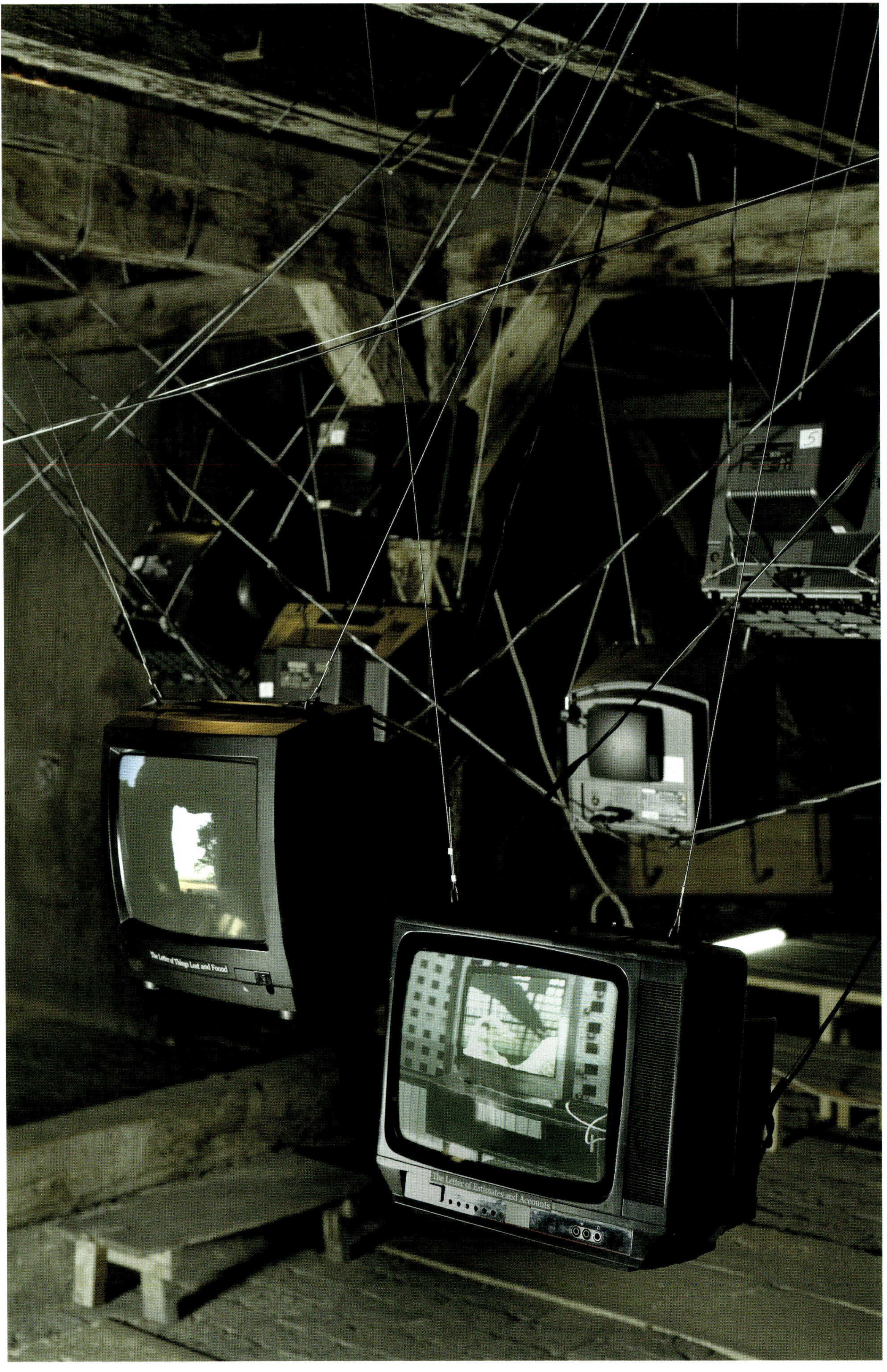
5
The Letter of Things Lost and Found
The Letter of Estimates and Accounts

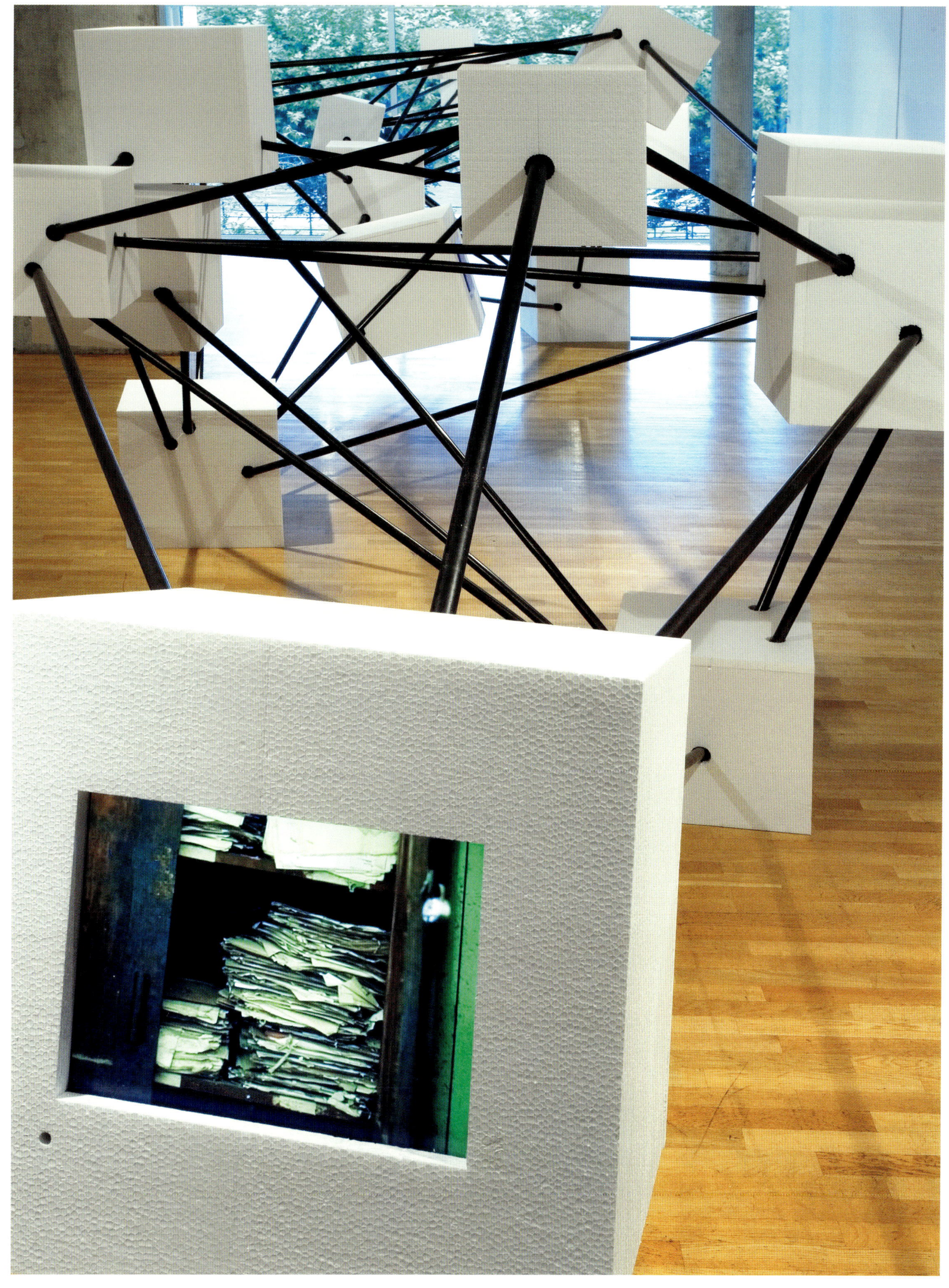

RAQS MEDIA COLLECTIVE
The K.D. Vyas Correspondence Vol.1, 2006 (S./p. 188–189)

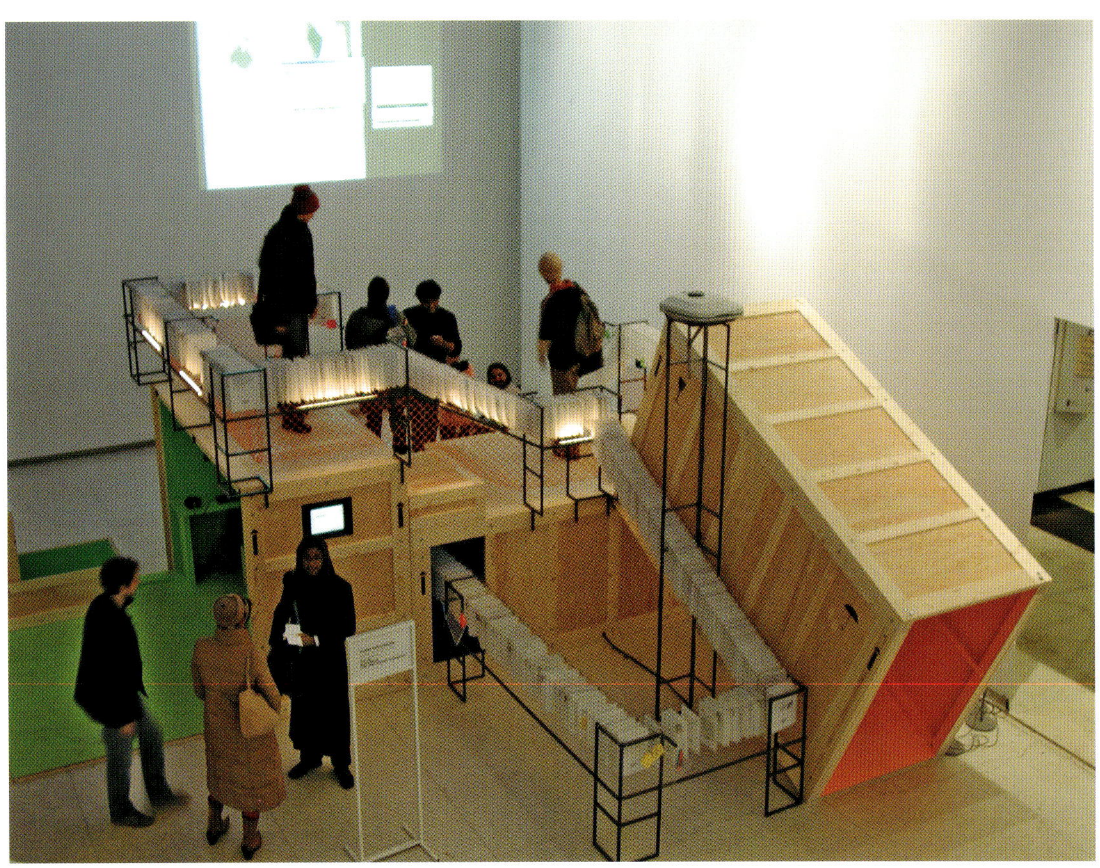

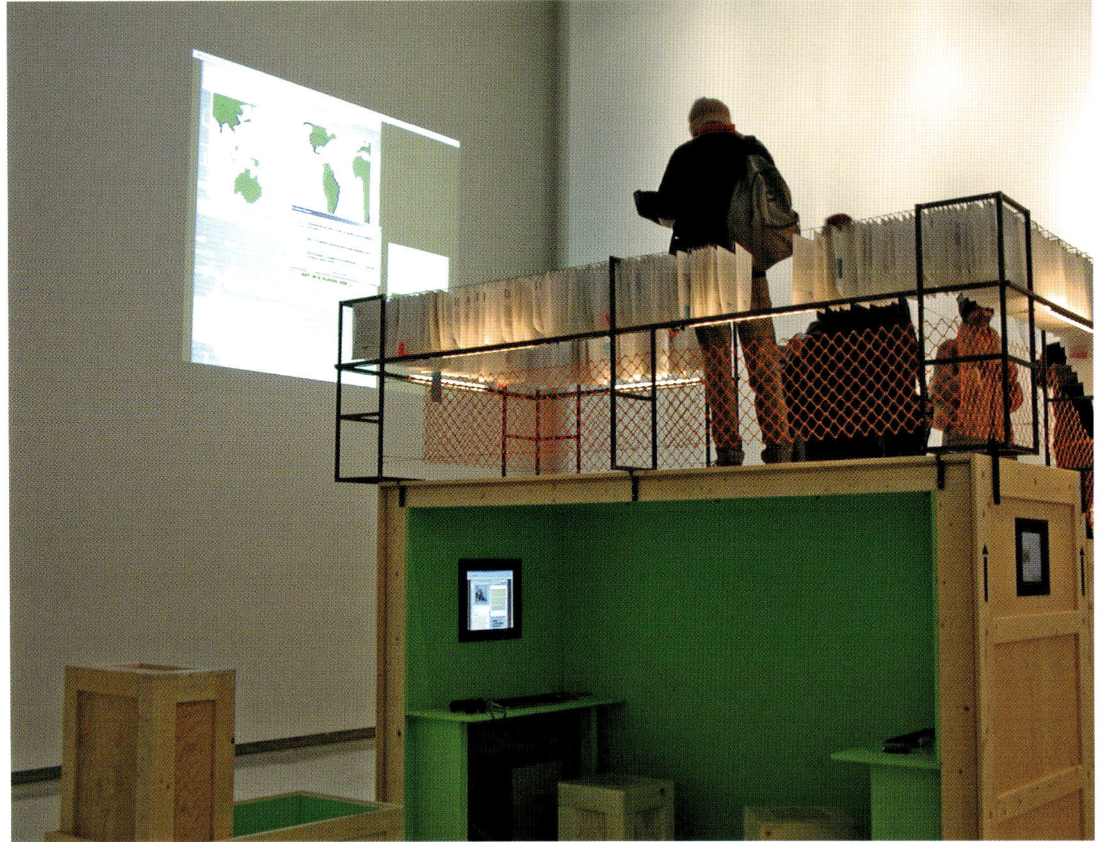

RAQS MEDIA COLLECTIVE + ATELIER BOW-WOW
Temporary Autonomous Sarai (TAS), 2003

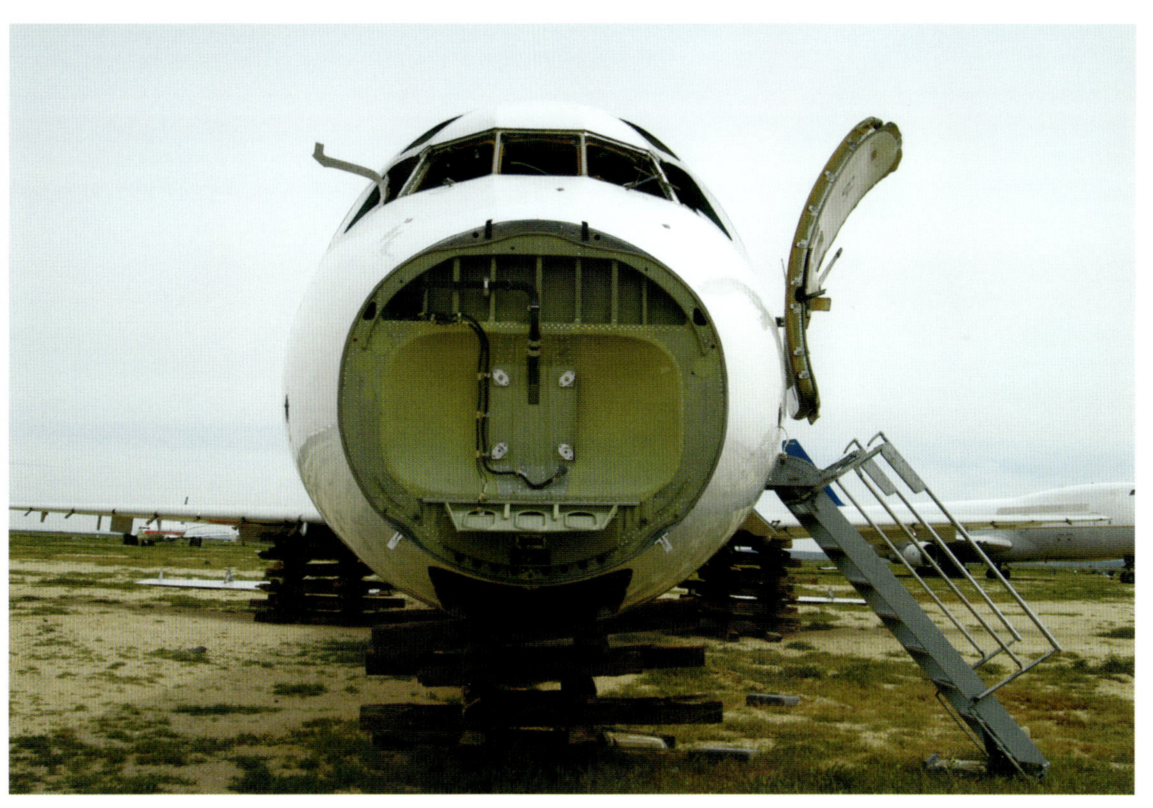

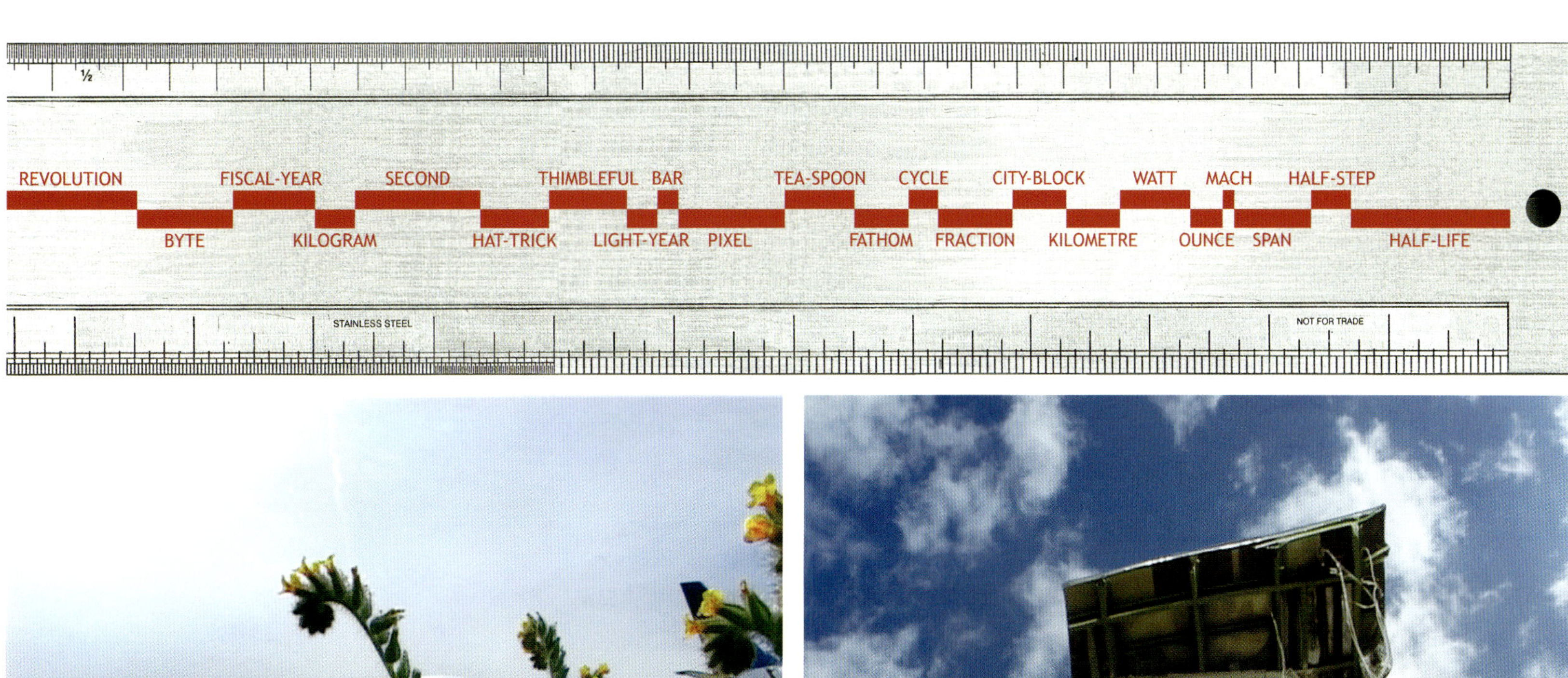

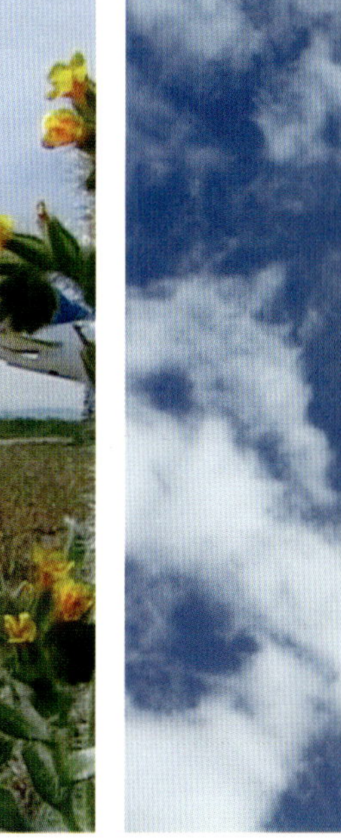

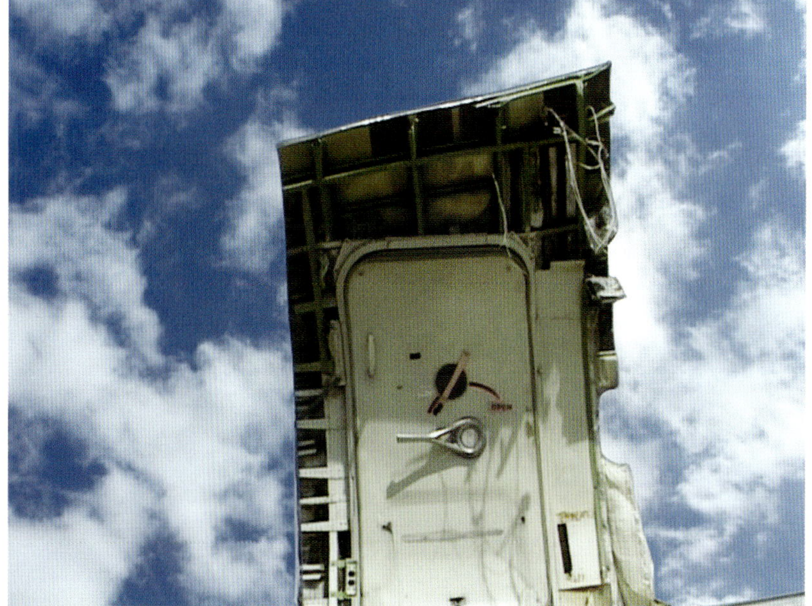

RAQS MEDIA COLLECTIVE
There Has Been a Change of Plan, 2006
A Measure of Anacoustic Reason, 2005

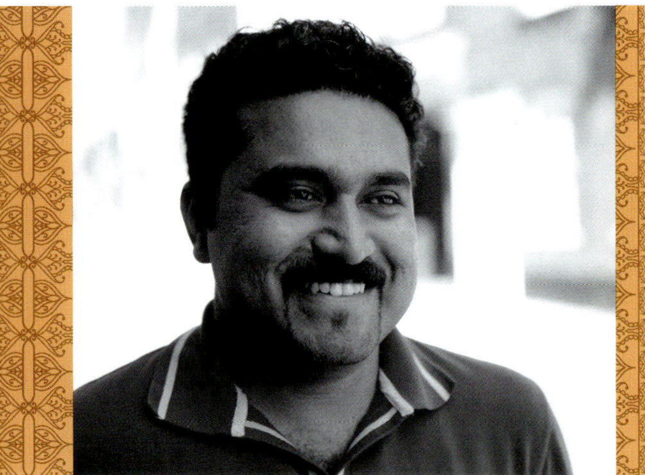

gigi scaria

GIGI SCARIA Geboren 1973 in Kothanalloor, Kerala / Lebt in Delhi
Born 1973 in Kothanalloor, Kerala / Lives in Delhi

Scaria studierte am College of Fine Arts, Thiruvananthapuram, Kerala. Er belegte als Hauptfach Malerei und schloss sein Studium 1995 ab. Anschließend ging er nach Dehli, das zum Standort seiner künstlerischen Karriere wurde. Er war zunächst als Schulbuchillustrator tätig und erwarb anschließend ein Masterdiplom in Malerei an der Jamia Millia Islamia University, New Delhi. Seine persönlichen Erfahrungen mit der harten Realität eines Migrantenlebens während seiner Zeit als Student im Aufbaustudium weckten sein soziales Bewusstsein. Scaria widmet sich in seinem Studio und Heim in Old Delhi – dem ursprünglichen Teil der Stadt, in dem sich noch immer Spuren des Mogulreiches finden – der Darstellung dieser Metropole als Migranten- und Arbeiterstadt mit den Mitteln von Malerei, Video und Fotografie.

Das vorherrschende Thema in der Serie „Option of Alternate Master Plan", die Scaria 2006 in Angriff nahm, sind die Probleme dieser Stadt, mit denen die Regierung von Delhi zu kämpfen hat. In seinen ihm eigenen humorvollen Lösungen zeigt Scaria reale Probleme auf. Beispiele dafür sind die Werke: „Court" (2006) dessen Hintergrund in der Farbe des roten Sandsteins von Lal Qila (ein Fort, das in der Mogulzeit errichtet wurde und von den Mogulherrschern bewohnt wurde) gehalten ist; „Keep Delhi Clean" (2006), in dem sämtliche Gebäude der Stadt – die von Menschen überquellenden Wohnhäuser, die illegalen Bauten und selbst der dichte Verkehr – weggefegt werden; „City Within" (2006), in dem der Künstler Werbung für die Urbanisierung der Dächer, anstatt für ihre Begrünung macht; und „City Centre" (2006), in dem er dafür eintritt, die Verkehrsstaus zu mindern, indem man die Gebäude durch Straßenüberführungen miteinander verbindet. „Panic City" (2007) ist ein Video, auf dem Scaria zunächst den Rundumblick vom Minarett der Jama Masjid Moschee – der größten Moschee Indiens – filmte und dann digital bearbeitete. Zum Rhythmus klassischer Musik dehnen sich die Gebäude aus und ziehen sich wieder zusammen – möglicherweise als Hinweis darauf, dass die schadhaften Gebäude der Altstadt letztlich der rasant fortschreitenden Vertikalisierung zum Opfer fallen werden. In „A Day with Sohail and Mariyan" (2004) hat Scaria Kinder gefilmt, die in den Slums leben und in der Nacht die Stra-

Scaria majored in painting at the College of Fine Arts, Thiruvananthapuram, Kerala, graduating in 1995, after which he moved to Delhi where his career is now based. After working as a textbook illustrator, Scaria went on to obtain an MA in painting at Jamia Millia Islamia University, New Delhi. While a post-graduate student, Scaria's experiences of the harsh reality of life as a migrant to the city triggered his social awareness. He continues to depict Delhi as a city of migrants and labourers through the media of painting, video, and photography, from his studio and home in Old Delhi, the original part of the city that still retains vestiges of the Mughal Empire.

The urban issues of Delhi that the government has struggled to address form the theme informing the series Option of Alternate Master Plan which Scaria embarked on in 2006. Real problems are revealed by Scaria's typically humorous solutions through works such as *Court* (2006) – the background colour of which is similar to the red sandstone of Lal Qila – a fort built during the Mughal era and in which the entire city of Delhi is surrounded by a spiral rampart and in the centre of which is a judicial court, *Keep Delhi Clean* (2006), in which all the city's buildings – the overcrowded housing, the illegal buildings and even the heavy traffic – have been swept away, *City Within* (2006), in which the artist promotes not rooftop greening but rooftop urbanization, and *City Centre* (2006), in which the artist suggests that buildings linked by overpasses and overhead crossings will alleviate traffic congestion. *Panic City* (2007) is a video in which Scaria filmed and then digitally edited the 360-degree view from the minaret of India's largest mosque, Jama Masjid. The buildings rhythmically expand and contract to classical music, as though suggesting that the ageing buildings of the old city will eventually become victims of rapid verticalization. In *A Day with Sohail and Mariyan* (2004), Scaria has filmed children who live in the slums and who patrol the streets of Delhi in the middle of the night in search of rubbish. The video captures the flash of a cigarette as it is lit in the darkness and the prematurely grown-up face of a young boy exhaling smoke, with the camera recording the children until dawn, covering the night they spend collecting rubbish. The work reveals their child-like qualities when

ßen Delhis auf der Suche nach Abfällen durchstreifen. Das Video zeigt das Aufglimmen einer Zigarette, die im Dunkeln angezündet wird und einen Buben mit den Zügen eines Erwachsenen, der den inhalierten Rauch ausstößt. Die Kamera folgt den Kindern bis zur Morgendämmerung und dokumentiert damit eine ganze Nacht, die sie damit verbracht haben, Abfälle zu sammeln und zu sortieren. Die Arbeit zeigt auch, wie kindlich sie eigentlich noch sind, wenn sie auf ihrer Suche auf Landkarten und Spielzeug stoßen und damit zu spielen beginnen. Gleichzeitig wird durch die dokumentarische Darstellung eines Tages im Leben dieser Teenager deutlich, dass sie zähe und harte Arbeiter sind, die sich durch die nächtelange Plackerei am Leben erhalten.

Wichtige Ausstellungen: „Public Places / Private Spaces: Contemporary Photography and Video Art in India" (The Newark Museum, USA, 2007), „Horn Please: Narratives in Contemporary Indian Art" (Kunstmuseum Bern, 2007) und „Triviality of Our Everyday Existence: Recent Photographs and Video" (The Changdong National Art Studio, Seoul, and Palette Art Gallery, New Delhi, 2008). (TK)

they come across maps or toys in their search and start playing with them. However, by depicting a day in the lives of these teenagers in a documentary style, the work also reveals the tenacity and toughness of these workers as they support themselves by spending all night collecting and sorting rubbish.

Major exhibitions include "Public Places / Private Spaces: Contemporary Photography and Video Art in India" (The Newark Museum, USA, 2007), "Horn Please: Narratives in Contemporary Indian Art" (Kunstmuseum Bern, 2007), and "Triviality of Our Everyday Existence: Recent Photographs and Video" (The Changdong National Art Studio, Seoul, and Palette Art Gallery, New Delhi, 2008). (TK)

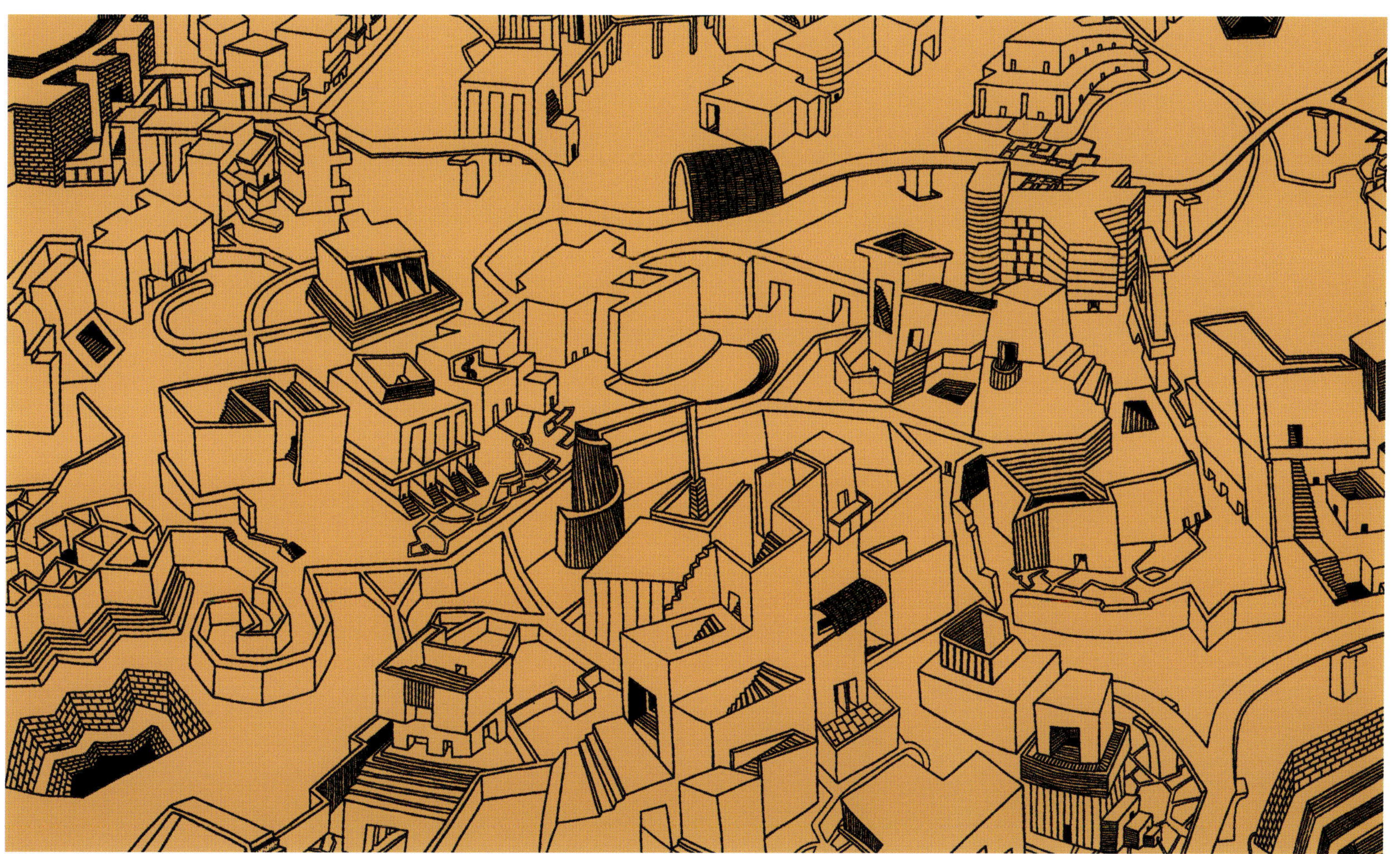

GIGI SCARIA
Option of Alternate Master Plan / City Centre, 2006 (Detail)

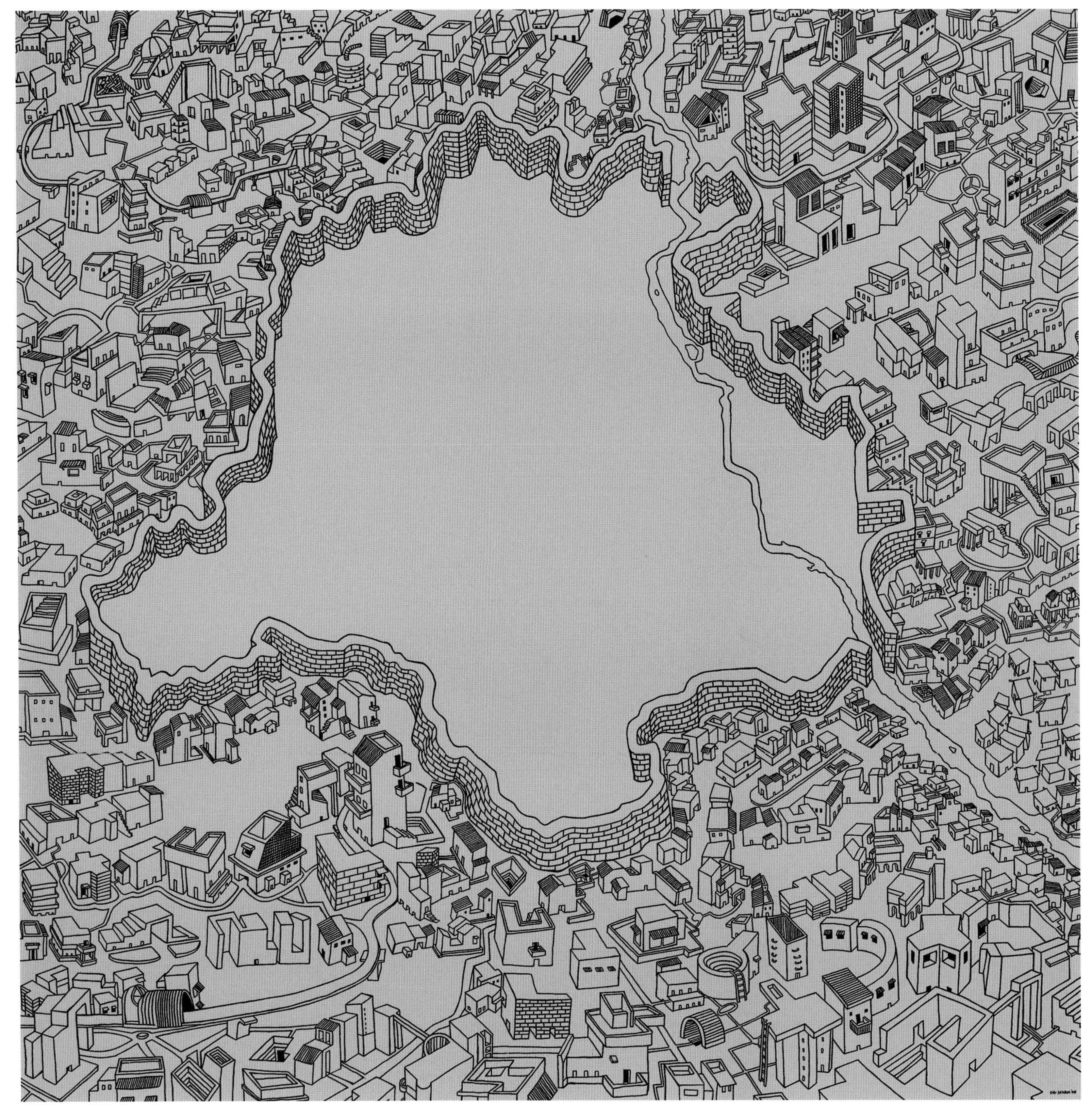

GIGI SCARIA
Keep Delhi Clean, 2006

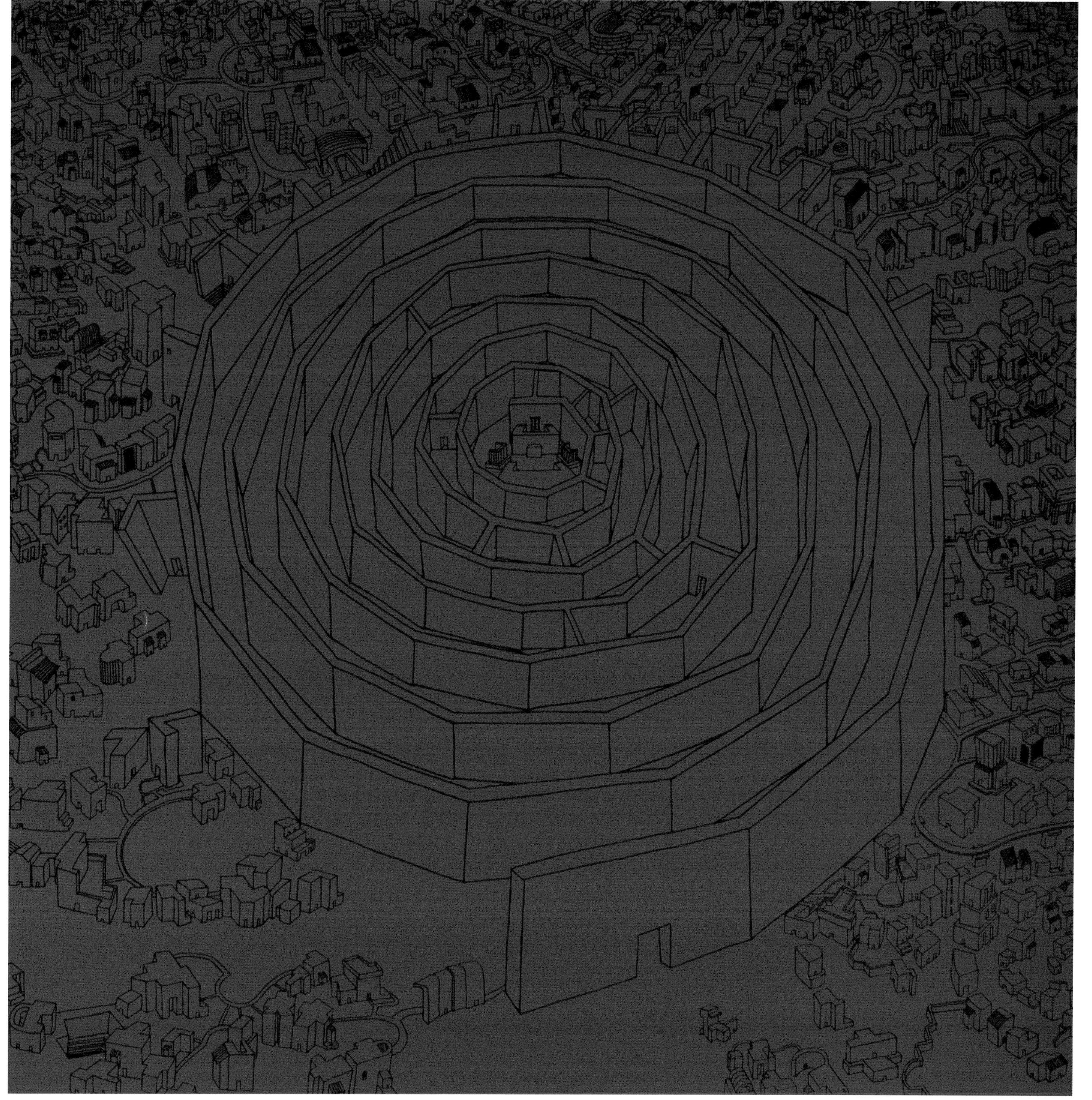

GIGI SCARIA
Option of Alternate Master Plan / Court, 2006

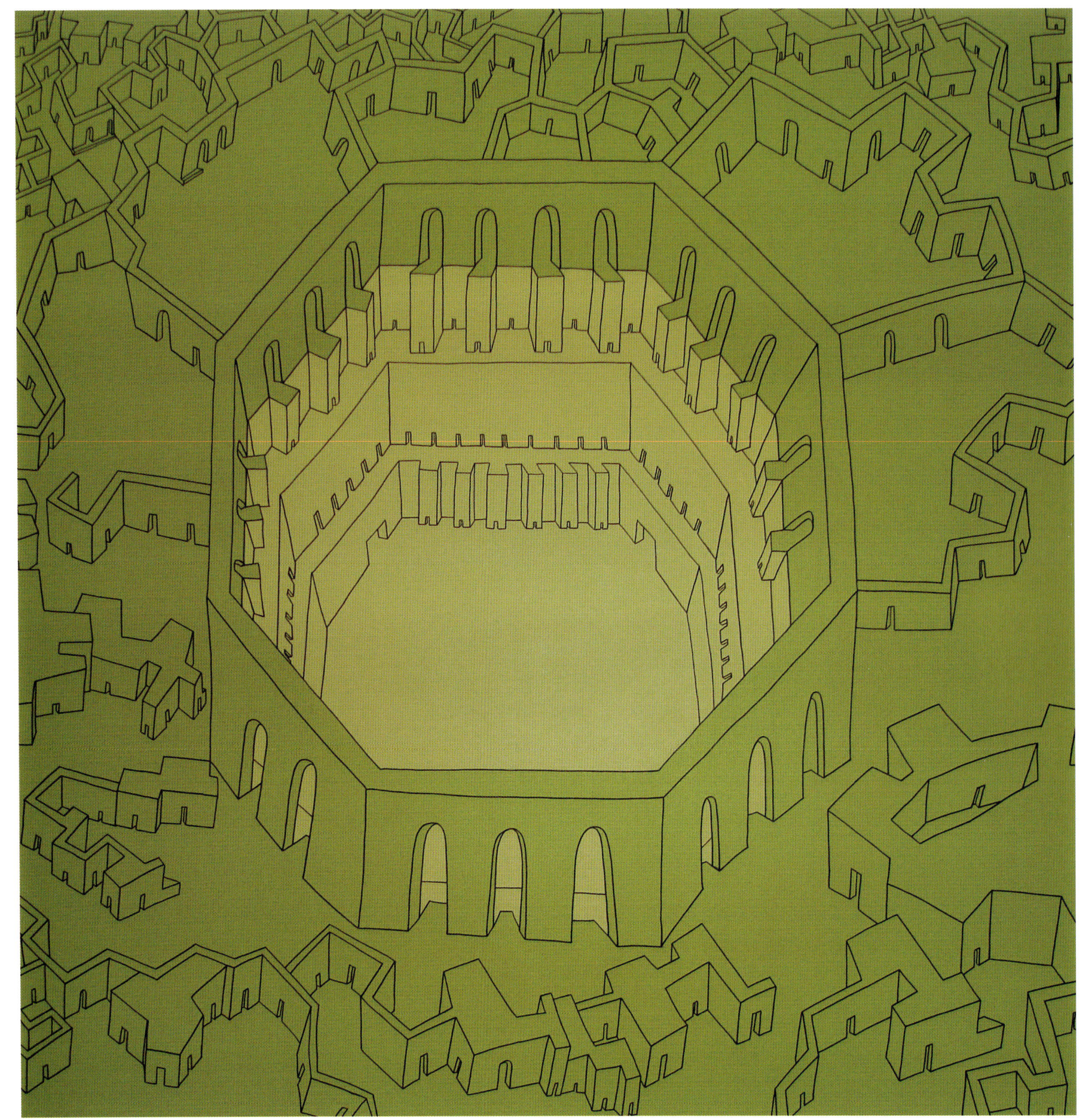

GIGI SCARIA
Site Under Excavation, 2008

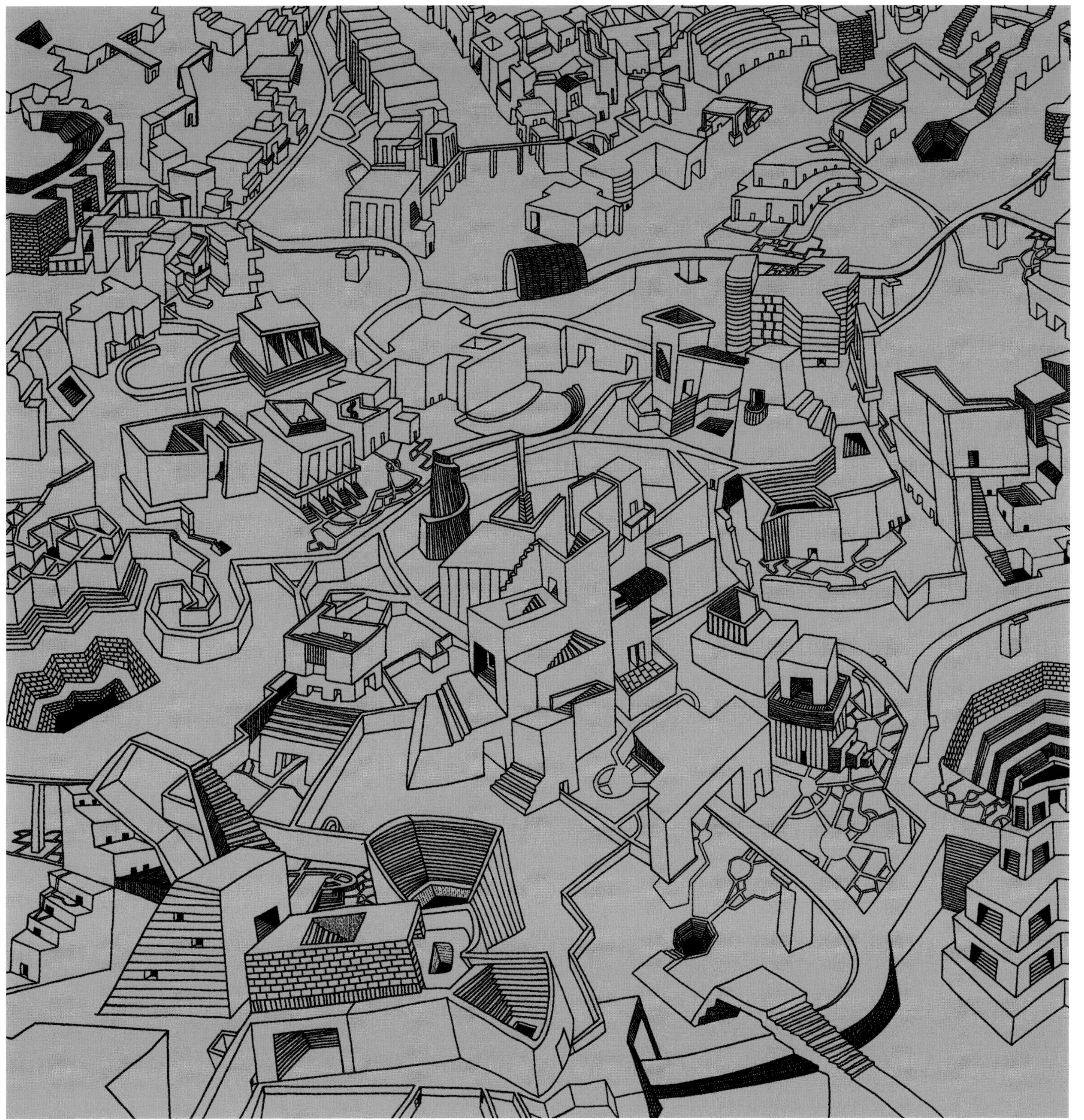

GIGI SCARIA
Option of Alternate Master Plan / City Centre, 2006

GIGI SCARIA
A Day with Sohail and Mariyan, 2004

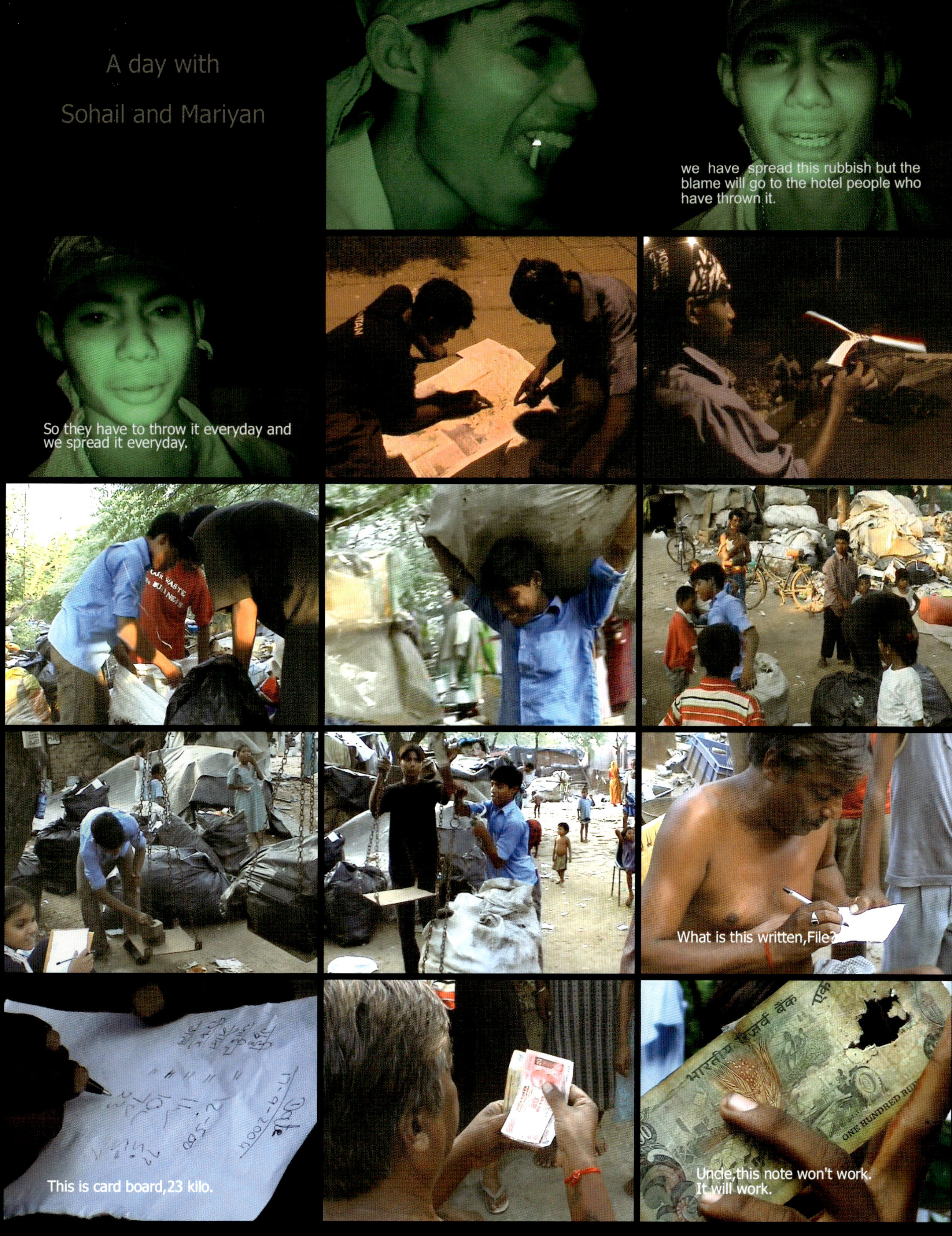
A day with
Sohail and Mariyan
we have spread this rubbish but the blame will go to the hotel people who have thrown it.
So they have to throw it everyday and we spread it everyday.
What is this written,File?
This is card board,23 kilo.
Uncle,this note won't work.
It will work.

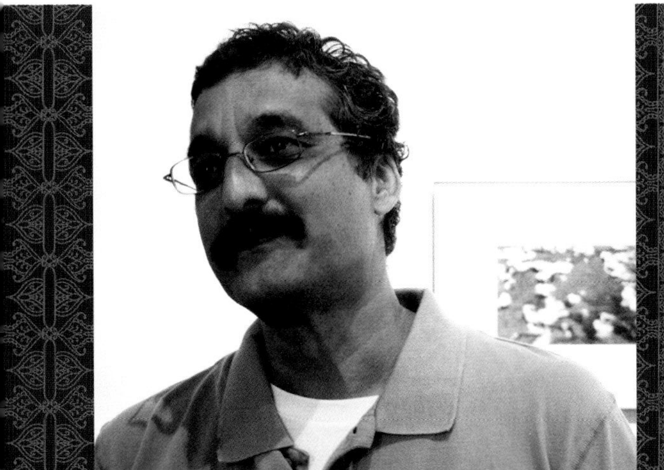

nataraj sharma

NATARAJ SHARMA Geboren 1958 in Mysore, Karnataka / Lebt in Vadodara
Born 1958 in Mysore, Karnataka / Lives in Vadodara

Nataraj Sharma studierte zunächst Design. Nachdem er einige Jahre in der Werbebranche tätig war, kehrte er 1988 an die Maharaja Sayajirao University von Baroda (Vadodara) zurück, um sein Studium mit einem Masterdiplom (in Malerei) abzuschließen. Anfänglich galt sein Interesse der Pop-Art, dem Kitsch sowie fotografischen bzw. Werbemotiven, wobei er seinen Schwerpunkt auf die figurative Malerei legte. Seit etwa 1990 wurde seine Arbeit zunehmend von der Auseinandersetzung mit der Industrialisierung und der Mechanisierung geprägt. Was er bildlich beschreibt, sind die Auswirkungen der stürmischen Industrialisierung im heutigen Indien mit ihrer rasant wachsenden Zahl an Fabriken und Maschinen auf die ursprüngliche Landschaft und das Leben der Menschen in den immer größer werdenden Städten.

„Air Show", seine hier gezeigte Arbeit, ist ein typisches Beispiel für die Werke, die Sharma in den letzten Jahren geschaffen hat. 2003 war er bei einer Flugschau Zeuge einer Vorführung des Surya Kiran Aerobatic Teams (SKAT) der Indian Air Force. Er war von der fantastischen Darbietung fasziniert, in der Schönheit, Aggressivität und spielerische Elemente zusammen wirken. Nach der Fertigstellung des Gemäldes erkannte er das Potential für seine Umsetzung in die dritte Dimension. Für die skulpturale Version von „Air Show" schuf der Künstler eine Art Rastergitter, um einerseits die physisch-räumliche Dimension auszudrücken und andererseits als praktische Vorrichtung, auf der die Flugzeugformationen angebracht werden. Sharma setzt das Gitter immer wieder ein, um den Eindruck von Ordnung, Klarheit und Logik zu erwecken. Zunächst fertigte er kubische Metallrahmen an, die er anschließend zu einer riesigen 3-D-Gitterstruktur mit variablen Dimensionen zusammenfügte. In diese Struktur schweißte er Formationen grob gegossener Flugzeuge in formvollendetem Flug ein, die immer wieder die Gesetze der Schwerkraft zu überwinden scheinen, während das Gitter gleichzeitig ihre Bewegung zu zügeln vorgibt, woraus ein dynamischer Kontrast entsteht. Sharma ist außerdem stets daran interessiert, Malerei und Skulptur miteinander zu verbinden und hat als Kontrapunkt zur hier gezeigten skulpturalen Installation „Air Show" zwei Arbeiten mit unterschiedlichen Medien geschaffen: „Measure (Air)" (2008) und „Measure (Water)" (2008).

Nataraj Sharma initially studied design. After a few years of working in advertising he returned, in 1988, to the Maharaja Sayajirao University of Baroda (Vadodara) to complete his MA (painting). He was initially interested in pop art, kitsch, photographic and advertising motifs, with a particular emphasis on figurative painting. From around 1990, however, a growing concern with industrialization and mechanization has informed his work. He depicts how the dramatic industrialization of contemporary India, the mushrooming factories and the machines that are the tools of this industrialization have impacted on the original landscape and the lives of the people living in the ever-expanding cities.

Air Show, his oeuvre shown in this exhibition, is one of Sharma's representative works in recent years. In 2003 he witnessed a display by the Indian Air Force's Surya Kiran Aerobatic Team (SKAT), and was not only enthralled by the brilliance of the performance, but was also drawn to the way that a number of elements such as violence and beauty, aggression and play were integrated into the experience. Naturally, this experience became the source of inspiration for the painting *Air Show.* As soon as he completed the painting, however, Sharma realized that there was potential for converting the work into the third dimension. He created a gridded structure in the sculptural version of the *Air Show* to express the physical dimensions of space as well as a practical device to hold the formations of planes – as he has used the grid often in his work to create a sense of order, clarity and logic. To begin with, he made a series of metal cube shaped frames, which he then assembled to create an enormous 3-D grid structure of variable dimensions. And, within this structure, he welded formations of roughly cast planes in lyrical flight that seem, at times, to be in defiance of gravity. The grid system also appears to be restraining their movement which results in an effect of dynamic contrast. In addition, Sharma has always had an interest in placing painting with sculpture; and as a counterpoint to the sculptural installation *Air Show* for this exhibition, there are two mixed media works; *Measure (Air)* (2008) and *Measure (Water)* (2008).

2001 erhielt Sharma „The Sotheby Award for the Best Emerging Indian Artist". Wichtige Ausstellungen: „Edge of Desire: Recent Art in India" (Art Gallery of Western Australia, Perth, 2004), „iCon: India Contemporary" (The 51st Venice Biennale, 2005) und „India Crossing" (Studio la Città, Verona, 2008). (KM)

Sharma won "The Sotheby Award for the Best Emerging Indian Artist" in 2001. Major exhibitions include "Edge of Desire: Recent Art in India" (Art Gallery of Western Australia, Perth, 2004), "iCon: India Contemporary" (The 51st Venice Biennale, 2005), and "India Crossing" (Studio la Città, Verona, 2008). (KM)

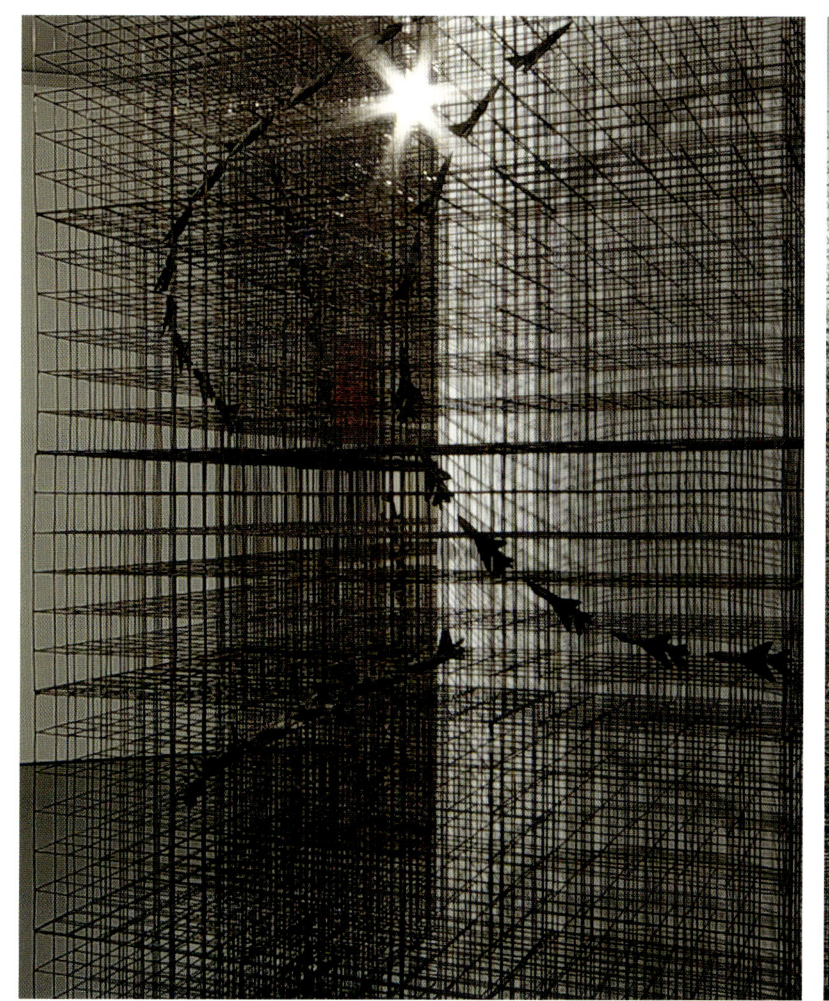

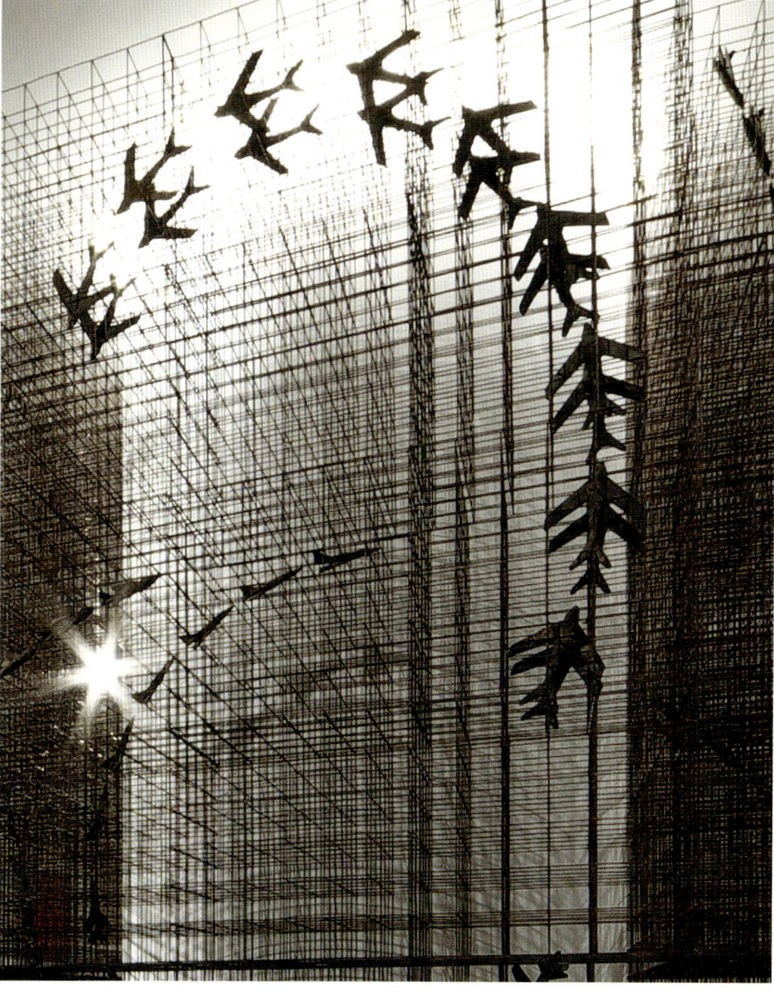

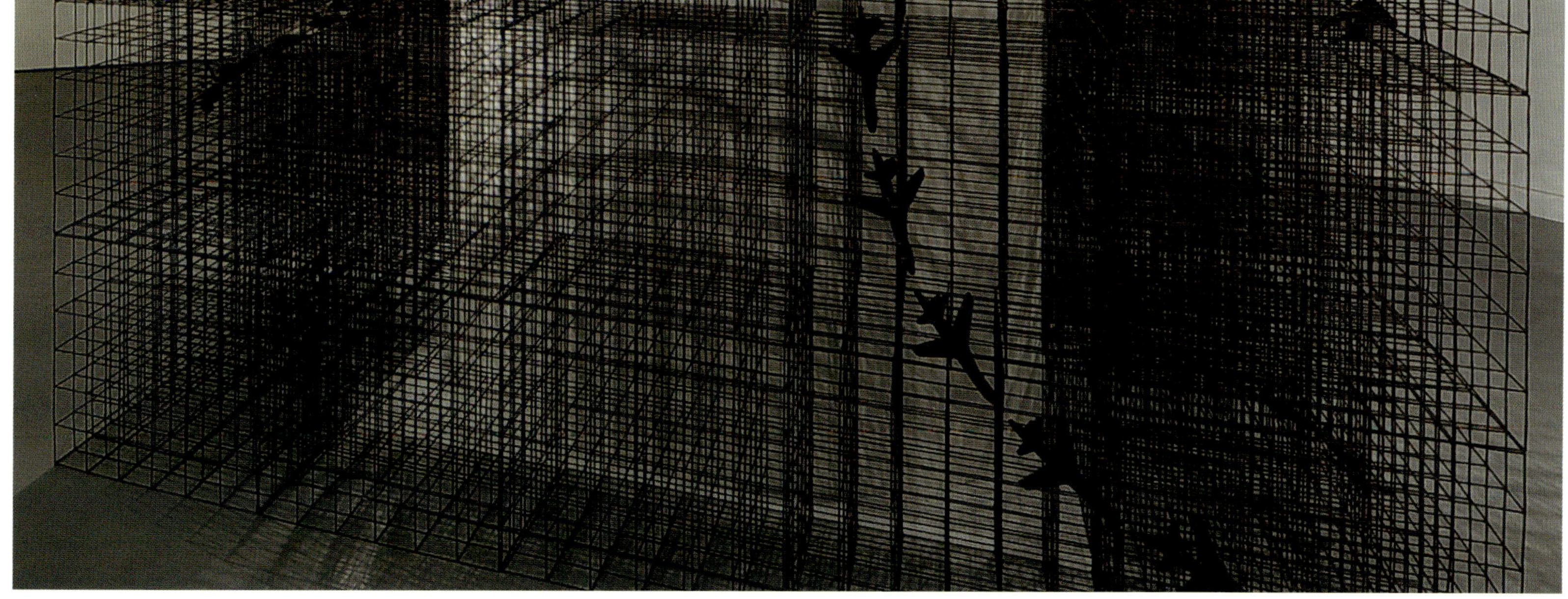

NATARAJ SHARMA
Air Show, 2008 (Detail)

NATARAJ SHARMA
Air Show, 2008

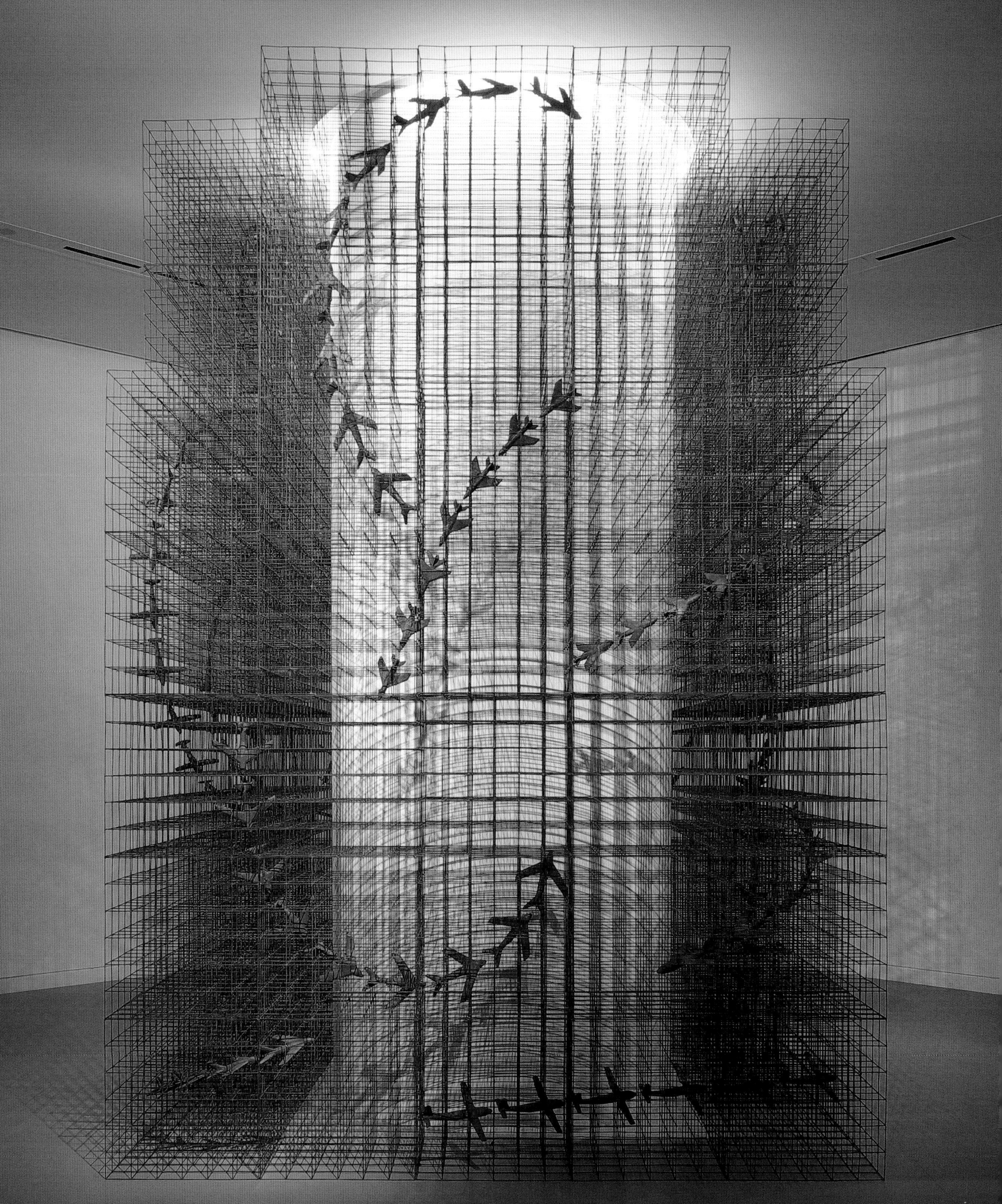

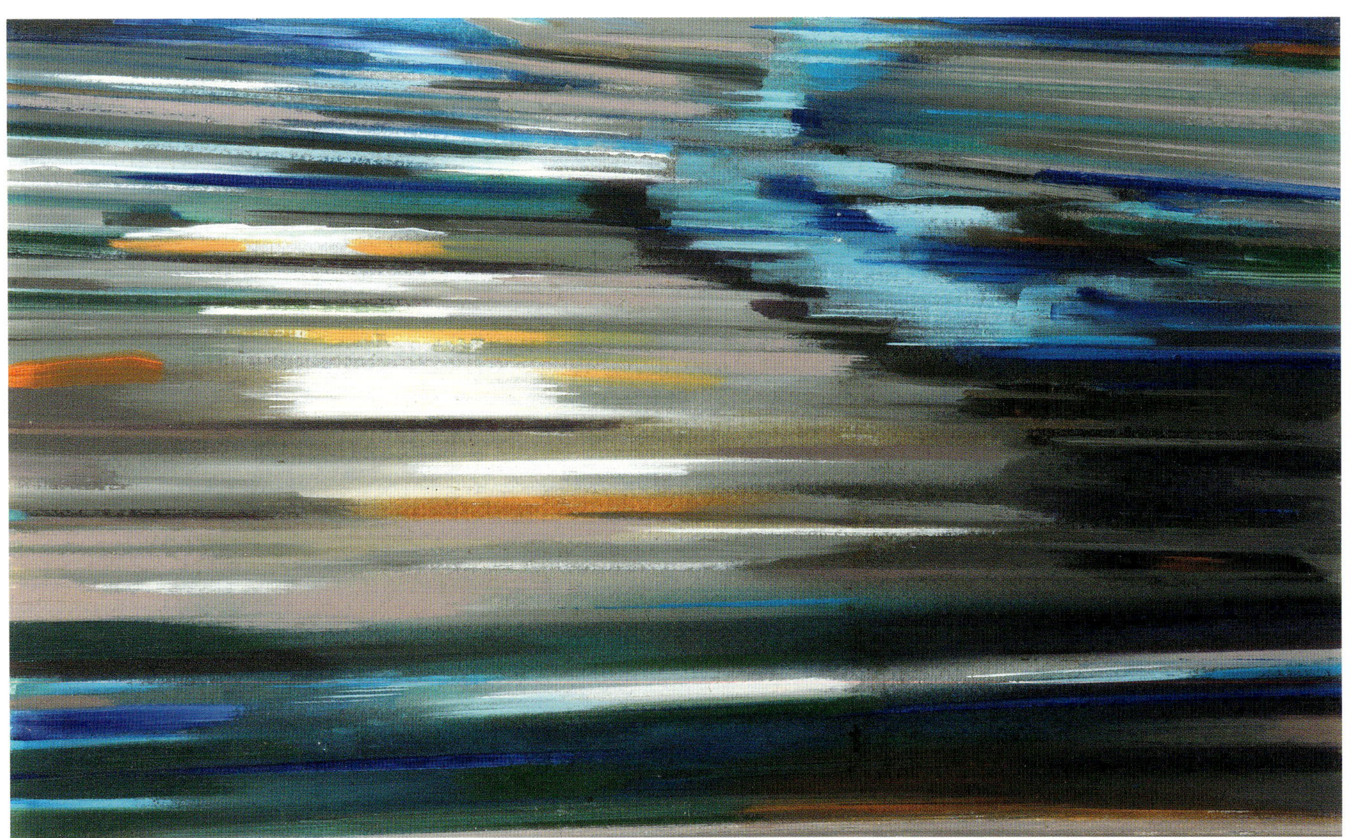

NATARAJ SHARMA
Arrival (Baroda), 2007
Arrival (Mumbai), 2007

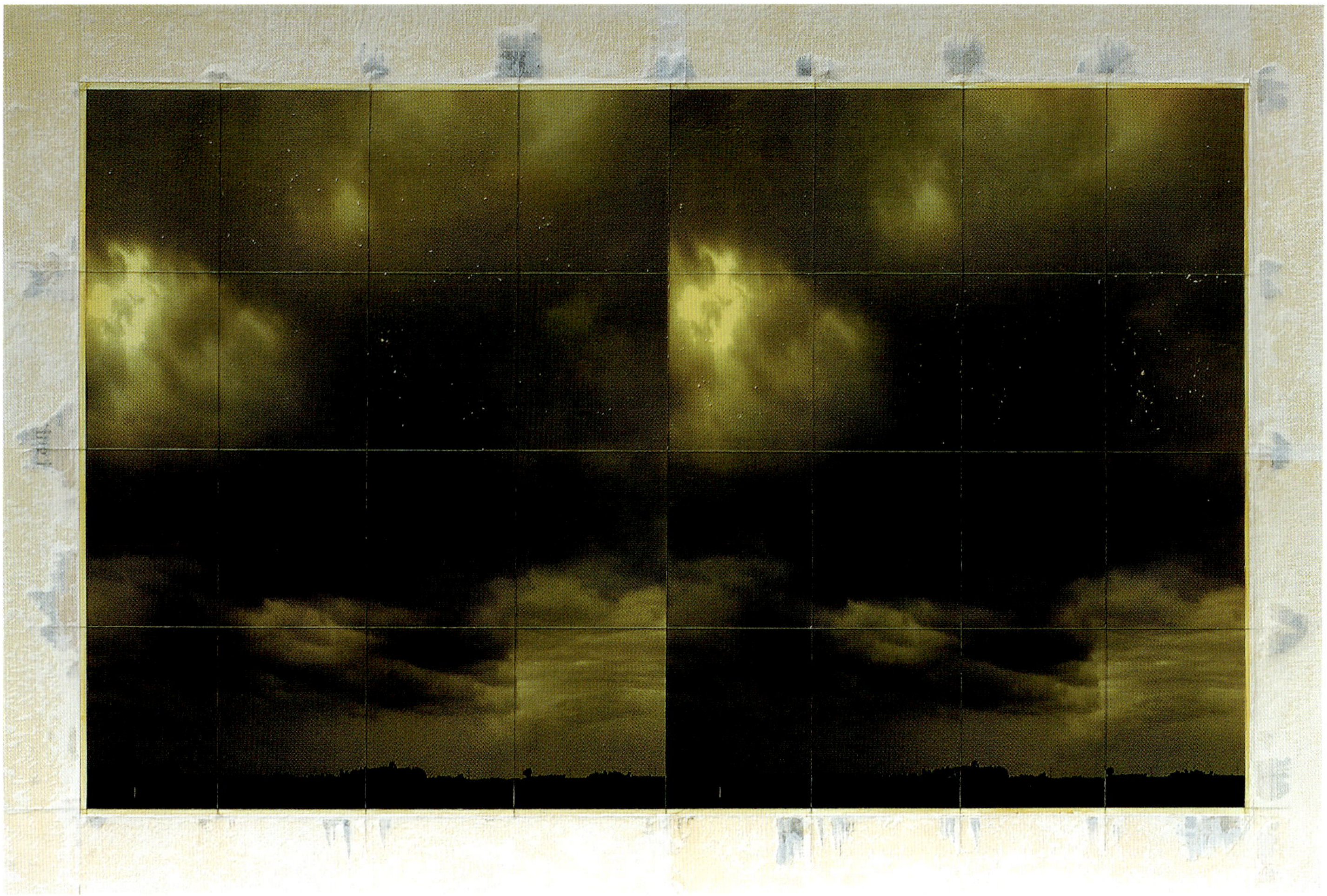

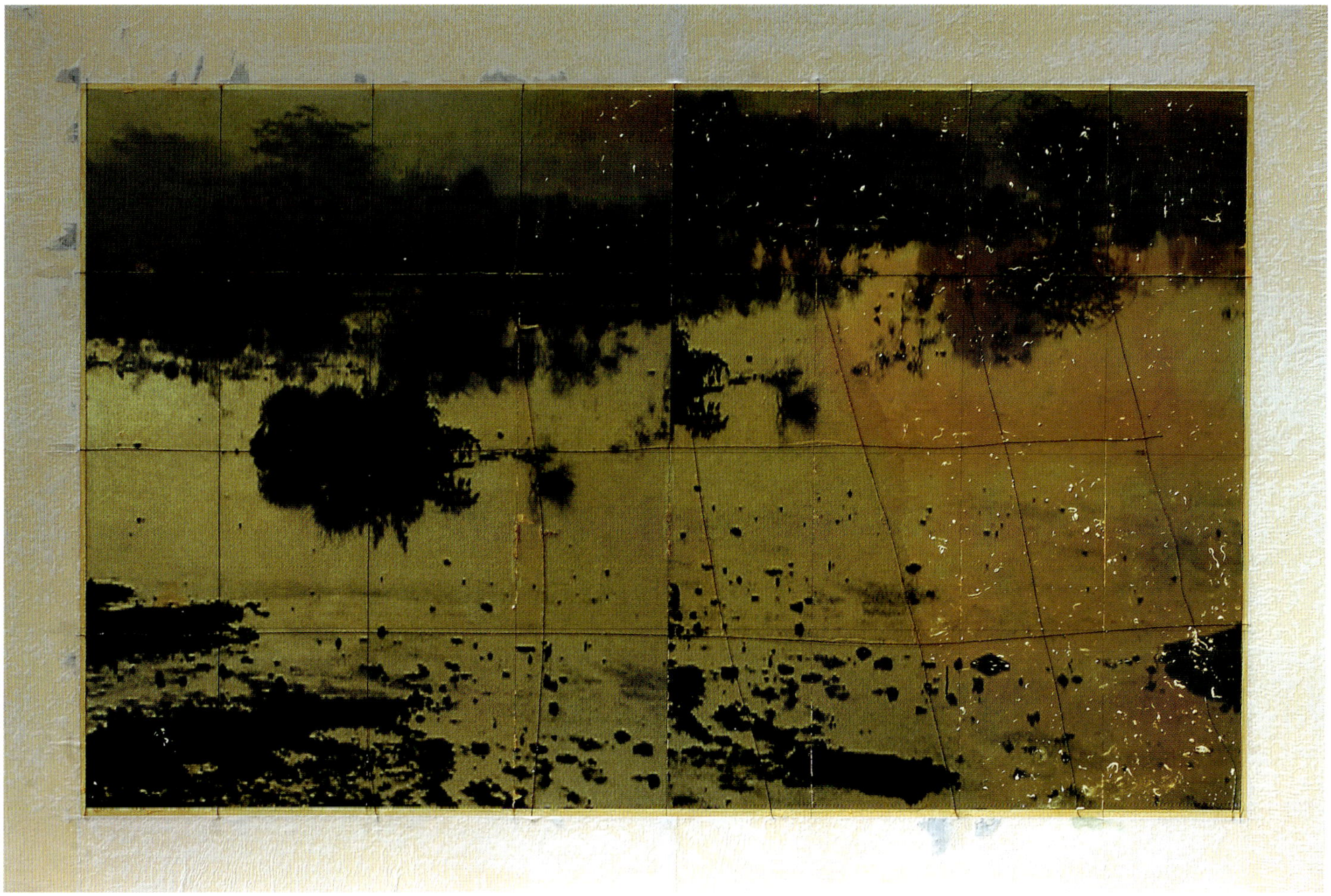

NATARAJ SHARMA
Measure (Air), 2008
Measure (Water), 2008

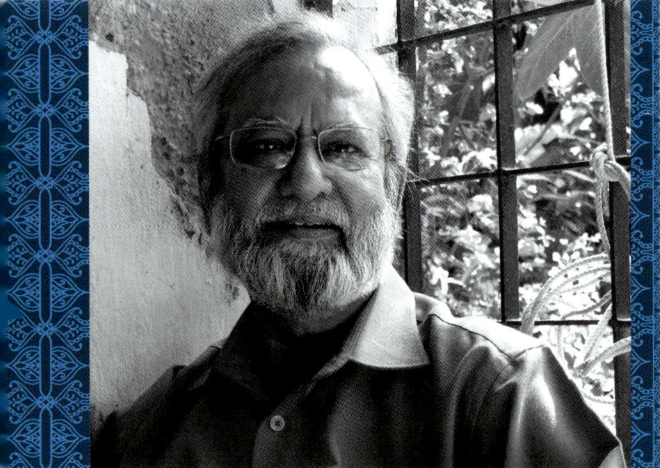

gulammohammed sheikh

GULAMMOHAMMED SHEIKH Geboren 1937 in Surendranagar, Gujarat / Lebt in Vadodara
Born 1937 in Surendranagar, Gujarat / Lives in Vadodara

1961 erwarb Sheikh ein Masterdiplom in Malerei an der Kunstfakultät der Maharaja Sayajirao University of Baroda (Vadodara). (Später unterrichtete er an der Universität und 1982 wurde er zum Leiter der Kunstfakultät ernannt.) 1963 schloss sich Sheikh der „Group 1890" an, die sich gegen den westlich orientierten Trend in der zeitgenössischen Kunst richtete. Während seines Studiums am Royal College of Art in London entdeckte er den Reiz der indischen Miniaturmalerei und der Wandmalereien im italienischen Siena – eine Erfahrung, die ihm die Augen für die klassische Kunst des Ostens und des Westens öffnete. Nach seiner Rückkehr nach Indien suchte Sheikh nach Möglichkeiten, die beiden Kunststile miteinander zu verbinden. 1969 bis 1970 war er Mitherausgeber des Kunstmagazins „Vrishchik" und in den späten 1970er Jahren spielte er eine zentrale Rolle in der Baroda School, die die Krisenanfälligkeit der indischen Gesellschaft mit den Mitteln der Malerei darstellte. Sheikhs Sicht der Dinge wurde u. a. von Bhupen Khakhar, Vivan Sundaram sowie dem Kunstkritiker Geeta Kapur geteilt. 1981 organisierten sie die „Place for People" - Ausstellung mit betont narrativen Gemälden, in denen soziale Themen im Mittelpunkt standen. Diese Einbindung einer modernen Perspektive übte einen nachhaltigen Einfluss auf die indische Kunst aus.

Inspiriert von den „mappae mundi" – den kreisförmigen Weltkarten, die im Mittelalter in den christlichen Ländern entstanden – hat Sheikh in den letzten Jahren Gemälde, dreidimensionale Arbeiten und Videos geschaffen. Angeregt von der Ebstorfer mappa mundi, die im Zweiten Weltkrieg ein Raub der Flammen wurde, schuf Sheikh seine ganz eigene Welt, indem er Mythologien aller Kulturen, historische Persönlichkeiten und zeitgenössische Phänomene in einer Darstellung verband. Der Beitrag zur aktuellen Ausstellung ist „Mappamundi beyond Border", eine Videoarbeit, bestehend aus Sheikhs mappa mundi-Malereien, die auf drei im Stil eines Tryptichons aufgestellte Leinwände projiziert werden. Die projizierten Bilder sind das Ergebnis einer „digitalen Collage", entstanden durch das Bemalen digital gedruckter mappae mundi. Das Video beginnt mit der Frage „Whose World?" und zeigt Karten, die kulturelle und philosophische Einsicht und menschliches Miteinander bekunden. Für „Kaavad: Travelling Shrine:

Sheikh obtained an MA in Painting from the Faculty of Art at Maharaja Sayajirao University of Baroda (Vadodara) in 1961, after which he taught at the University, and was appointed Head of the Faculty of Art in 1982. In 1963, Sheikh joined "Group 1890," which rejected the Western-centric tendency of contemporary art. While studying at the Royal College of Art in London, he discovered the attraction of both Indian miniature paintings and the murals of Siena, Italy, an experience that opened his eyes to Eastern and Western classical art. On his return to India, Sheikh explored ways of combining the two artistic styles. An associate editor of art magazine *Vrishchik* from 1969 to 1970, Sheikh became a central figure, during the late 70s, of the Baroda School that depicted the instability of Indian society through the medium of painting. Sheikh's vision was shared by Bhupen Khakhar, Vivan Sundaram, and art critic Geeta Kapur and others. In 1981 they organized the "Place for People" exhibition, featuring highly narrative paintings depicting social issues. The incorporation of a modern perspective had a major influence on subsequent Indian art.

In recent years, Sheikh has been creating paintings, three-dimensional works, and videos inspired by *mappa mundi,* the circular world maps produced in Christian countries during medieval times. Inspired by the Ebstorf *mappa mundi* which was destroyed by fire during World War II, Sheikh creates his own unique world by integrating mythologies from all cultures, historical figures, and contemporary phenomena into the image. In this exhibition, *mappa mundi* beyond Border, a video piece consisting of Sheikh's *mappa mundi* painting images, projects onto three screens set up like a triptych. These projected images are created out of "digital collage," in which he paints onto digitally printed *mappa mundi*. The video begins with the question "Whose World?" and features maps that suggest cultural and philosophical understanding and coexistence. In *Kaavad: Travelling Shrine: Home* (2008), Sheikh has created a rectangular solid representing a *kaavad* (shrine), used in Rajasthan. Sheikh attached a double door to the side of the shrine, with a mechanism such that opening and closing the doors reveals a different door painting. This is not a small work, like *Kaavad: Travelling*

Home" (2008), hat Sheikh einen rechteckigen Festkörper geschaffen, der einen für Rajasthan typischen Schrein (kaavad) darstellt. An einer Seite des Schreins hat Sheikh eine Doppeltür mit einem Mechanismus angebracht, der beim Öffnen und Schließen der Türen unterschiedliche Bemalungen sichtbar werden lässt. Anders als bei „Kaavad: Travelling Shrine: Journeys" (2002–04) handelt es sich hier um ein groß dimensioniertes Werk, das die Besucher begehen können. Die Darstellungen auf den Türen zeigen den Dichter Kabir (der über das Zusammenleben von Hindus und Muslimen geschrieben hat), Menschen, die Yoga betreiben und Mahatma Gandhi, und sie laden die Betrachter ein, den Schrein zu betreten. Auf einer Weltkarte werden in einer Zusammenschau Majnun, die Hauptfigur in einem persischen Liebesgedicht, Maria Magdalena, Kabir und muslimische Tänze dargestellt. Die verschiedenen Erzählungen entwickeln sich simultan und überlagern gelegentlich Darstellungen von Sheikh, der eine Kunst auslotet, die die Grenzen zwischen Religion, Politik und Zeitaltern überwindet.

Wichtige Ausstellungen: „Returning Home, a retrospecitve selection from 1968 to 1985" (Centre Georges Pompidou, Musée National d' Art Moderne, Paris, 1985), „Cinema India: The Art of Bollywood" (Victoria and Albert Museum, London, 2002), „The Edge of Desire: Recent Art in India" (The Art Gallery of Western Australia, Perth, 2004) und „Horn Please: Narratives in Contemporary Indian Art" (Kunstmuseum Bern, 2007). (TK)

Shrine: Journeys (2002–04), but a large work that the visitors can walk through. The doors feature the poet Kabir, who wrote about coexistence between Hindus and Muslims, yoga practitioners, and Mahatma Gandhi, and they invite the observer to enter the shrine. Meanwhile, Majnun, the main character from a Persian love poem, Mary Magdalene, Kabir, and Muslim dancing are all depicted on a single map of the world. The various stories unfold simultaneously, and at times are superimposed over images of Sheikh, who has continued to explore art that transcends the boundaries of religion, politics, and the times.

Major exhibitions include "Returning Home, a retrospecitve selection from 1968 to 1985" (Centre Georges Pompidou, Musée National d' Art Moderne, Paris, 1985), "Cinema India: The Art of Bollywood" (Victoria and Albert Museum, London, 2002), "The Edge of Desire: Recent Art in India" (The Art Gallery of Western Australia, Perth, 2004), and "Horn Please: Narratives in Contemporary Indian Art" (Kunstmuseum Bern, 2007). (TK)

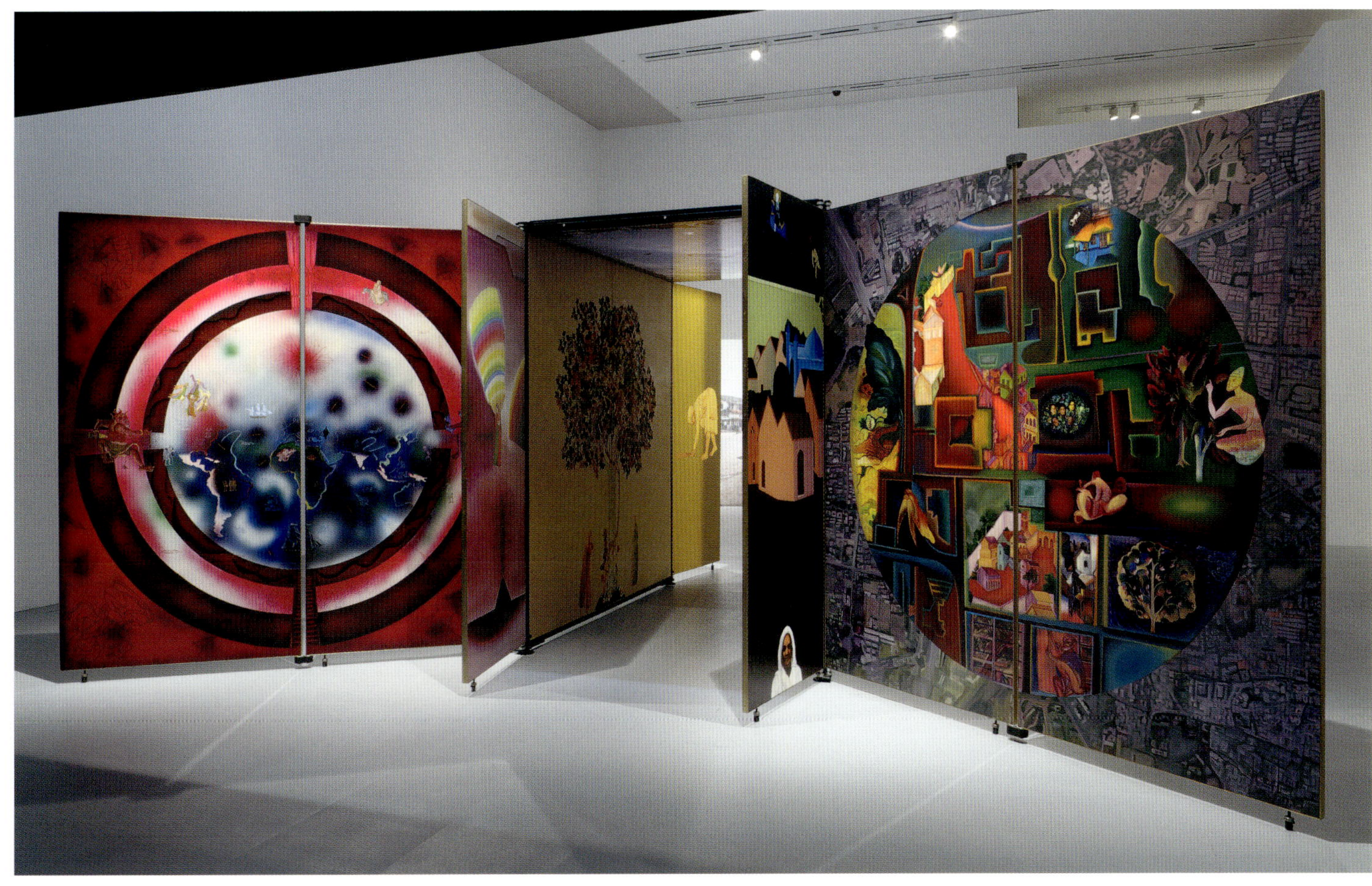

GULAMMOHAMMED SHEIKH
Kaavad: Travelling Shrine: Home, 2008

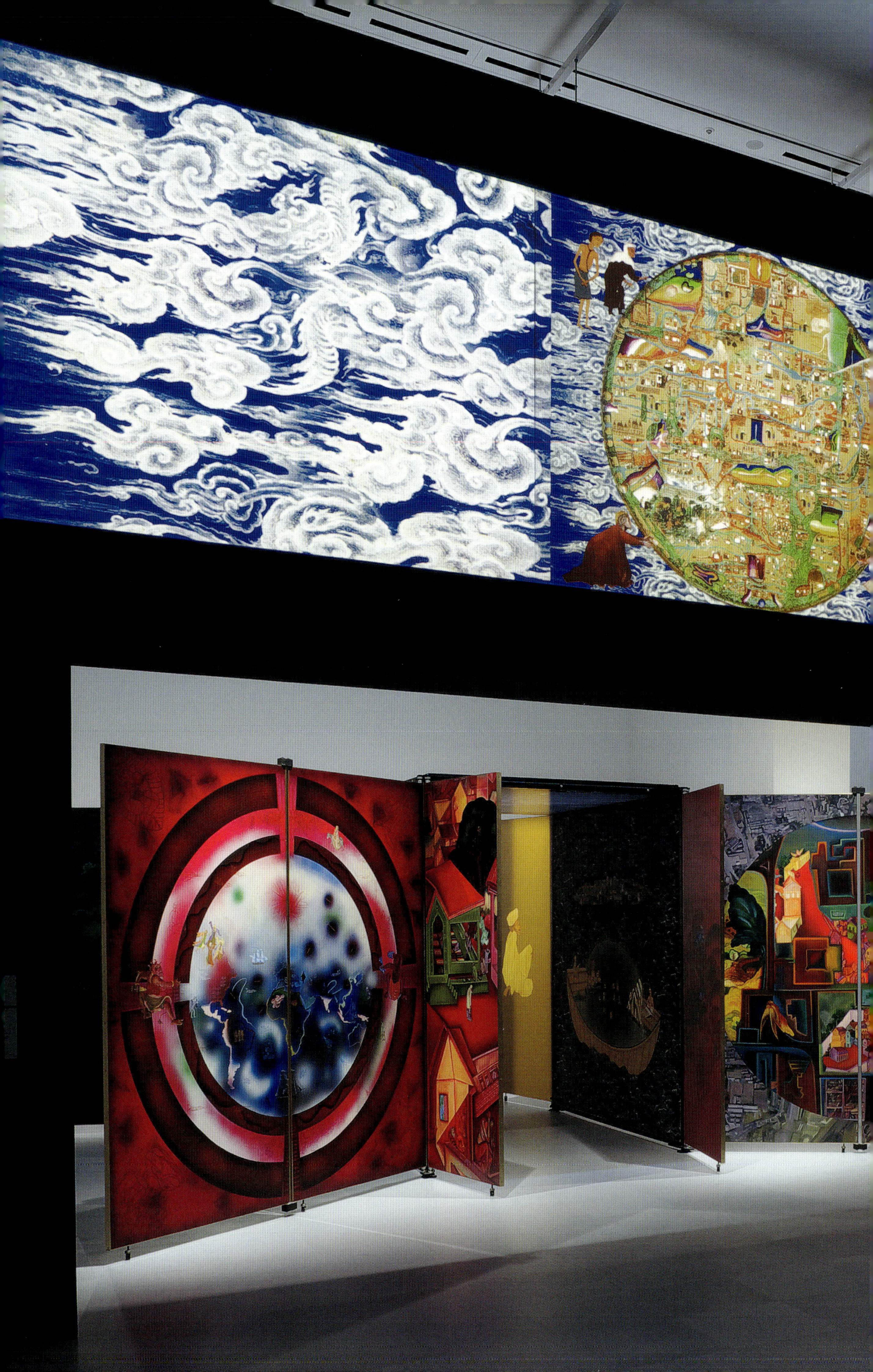

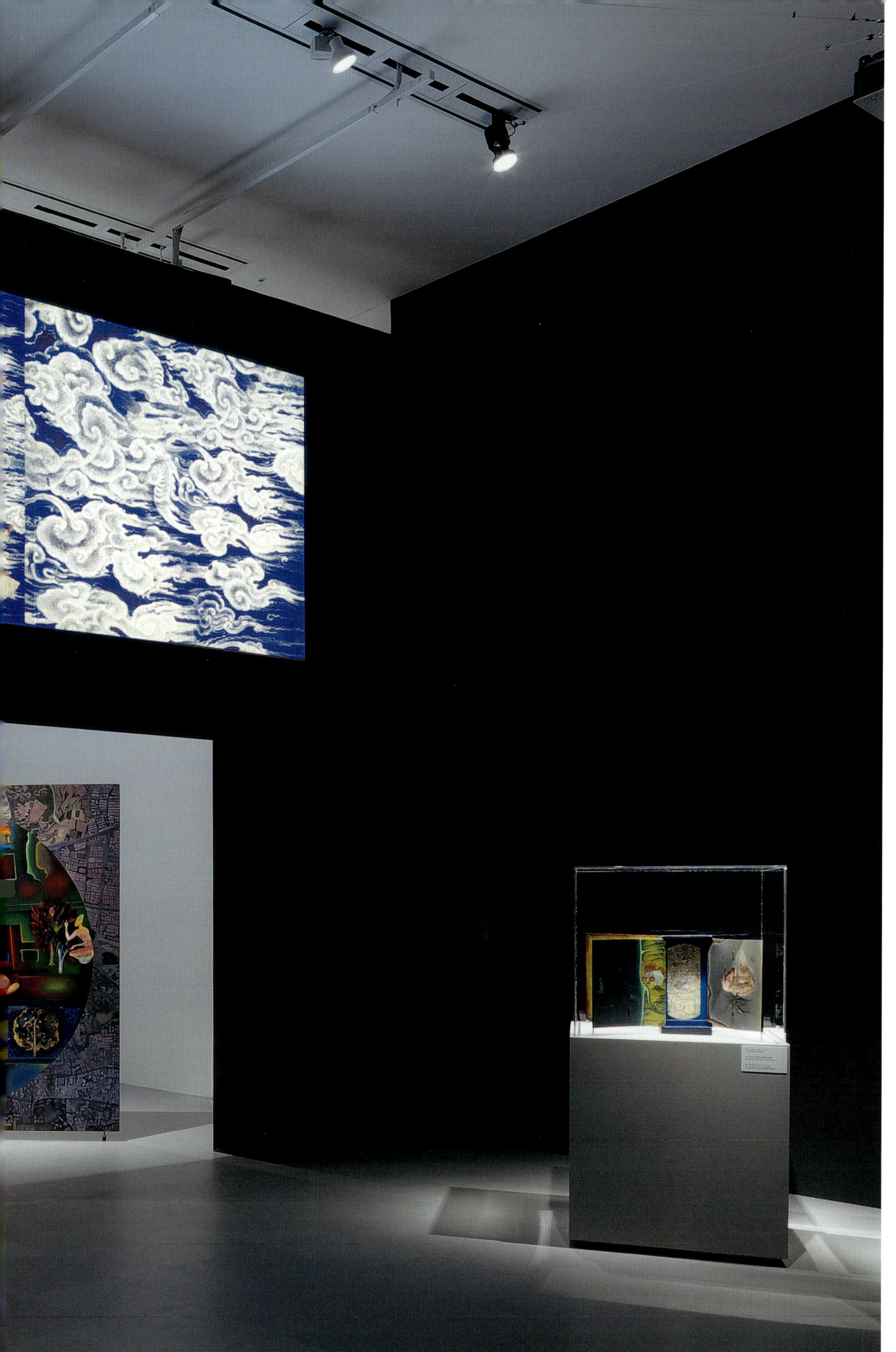

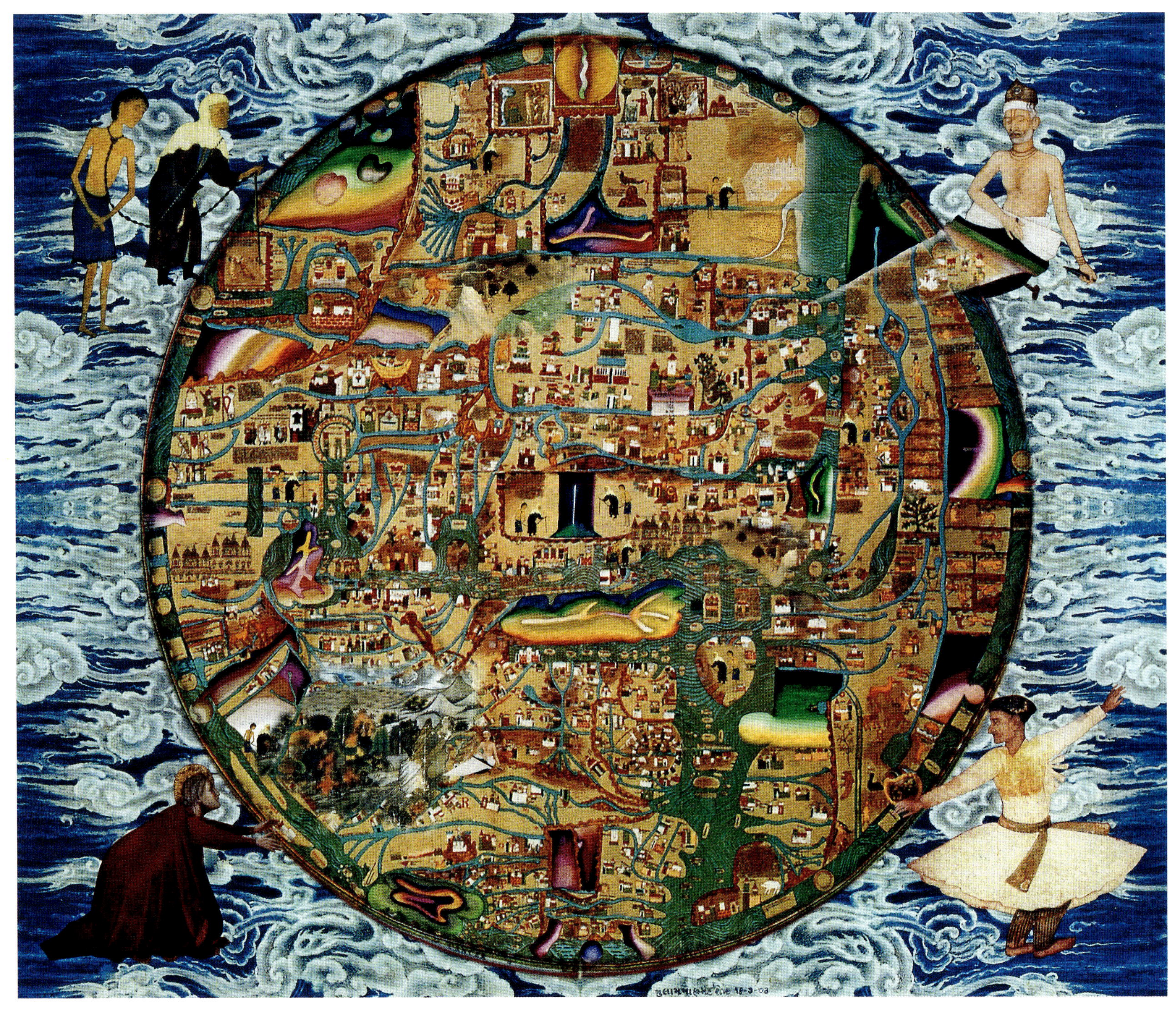

GULAMMOHAMMED SHEIKH
Installation view (S./p. 208/209):
Kaavad: Travelling Shrine: Home, 2008
Kaavad: Travelling Shrine: Journeys, 2002–04 (links / left)

Looking for Layla from: Mappamundi suite, 2003

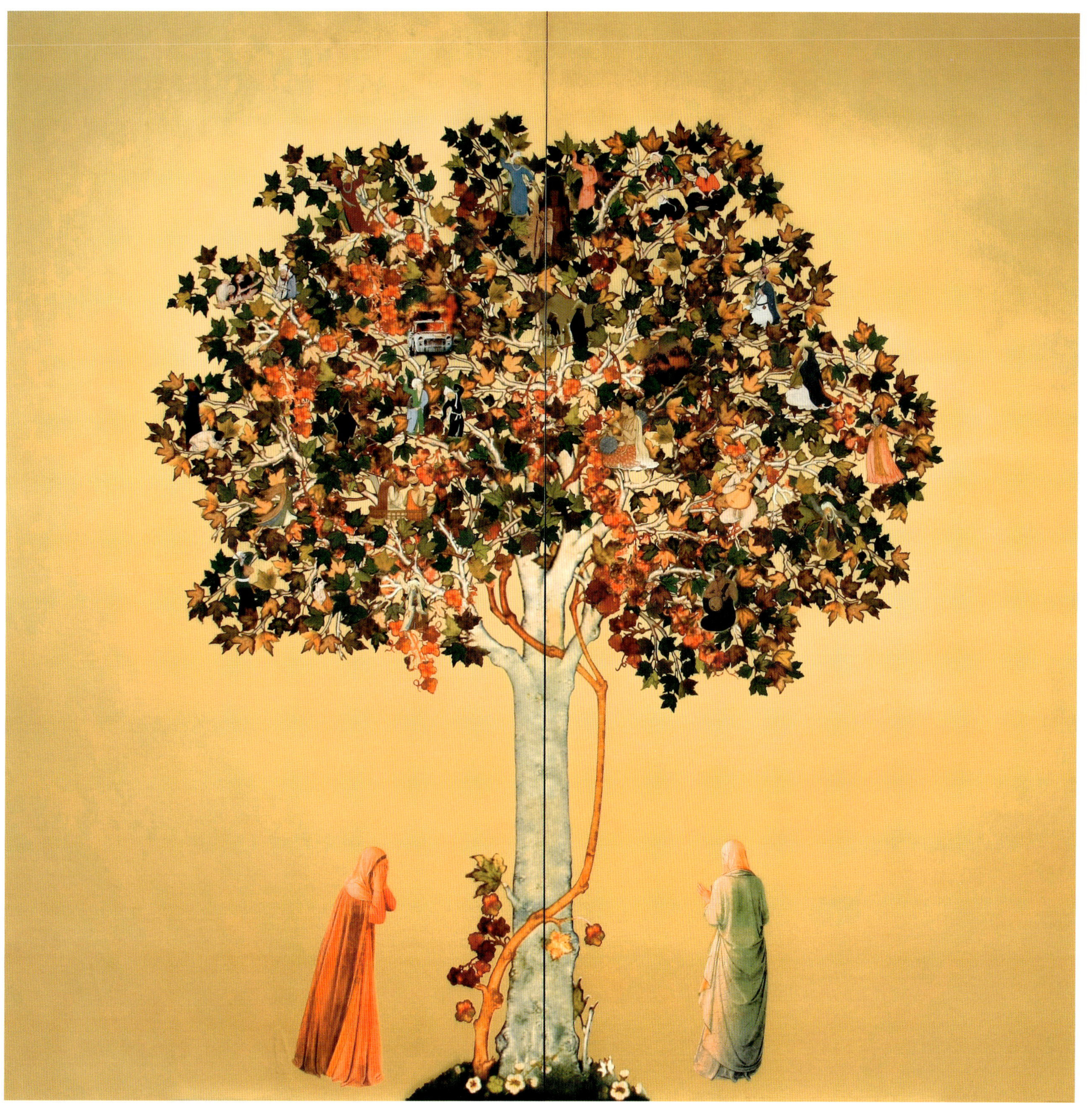

GULAMMOHAMMED SHEIKH
Speaking Tree from: Kaavad: Travelling Shrine: Home, 2008

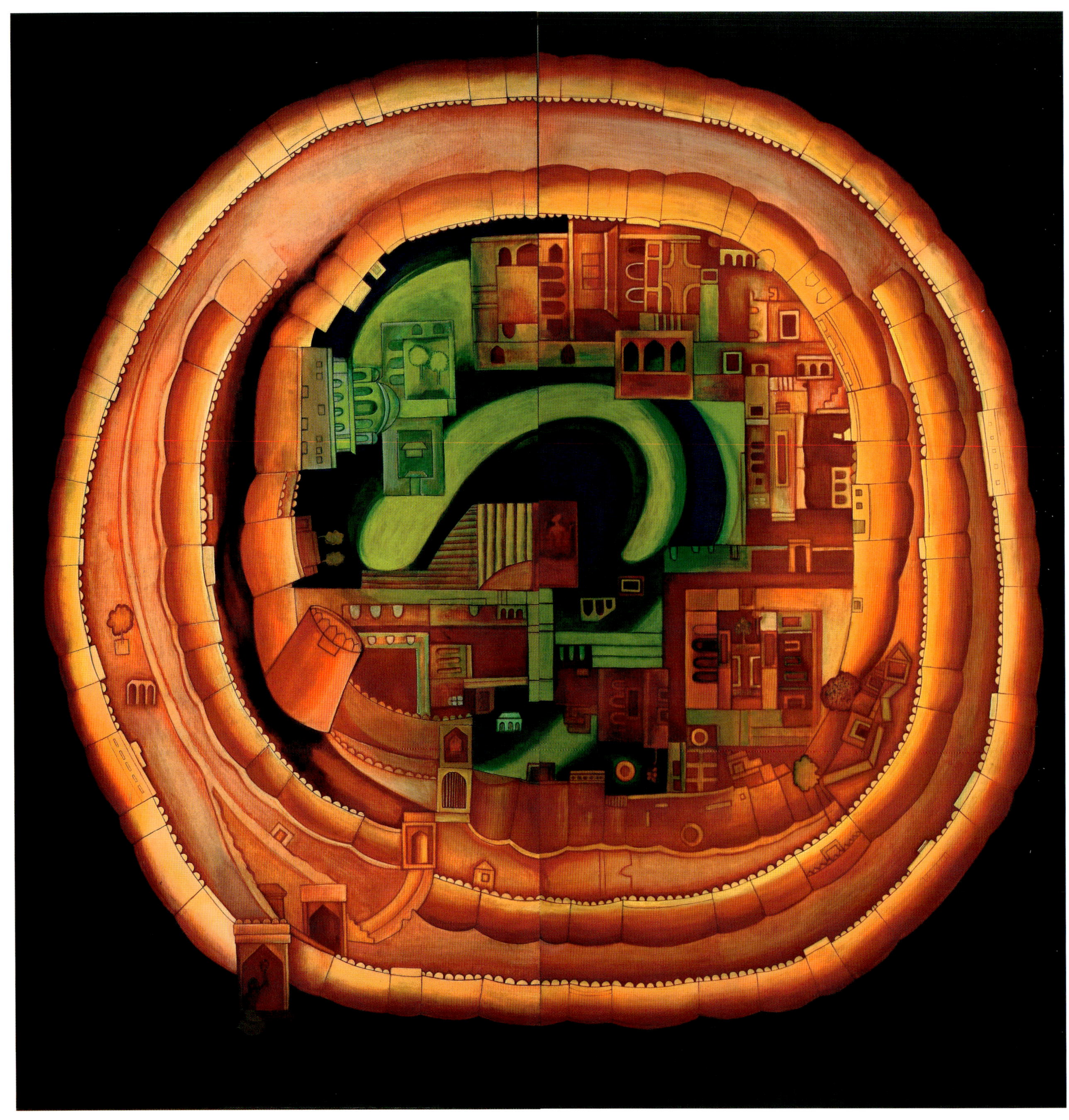

GULAMMOHAMMED SHEIKH
Mute City from: Kaavad: Travelling Shrine: Home, 2008
Shoriken Crossing the Sea on Sword from: Kaavad: Travelling Shrine: Home, 2008

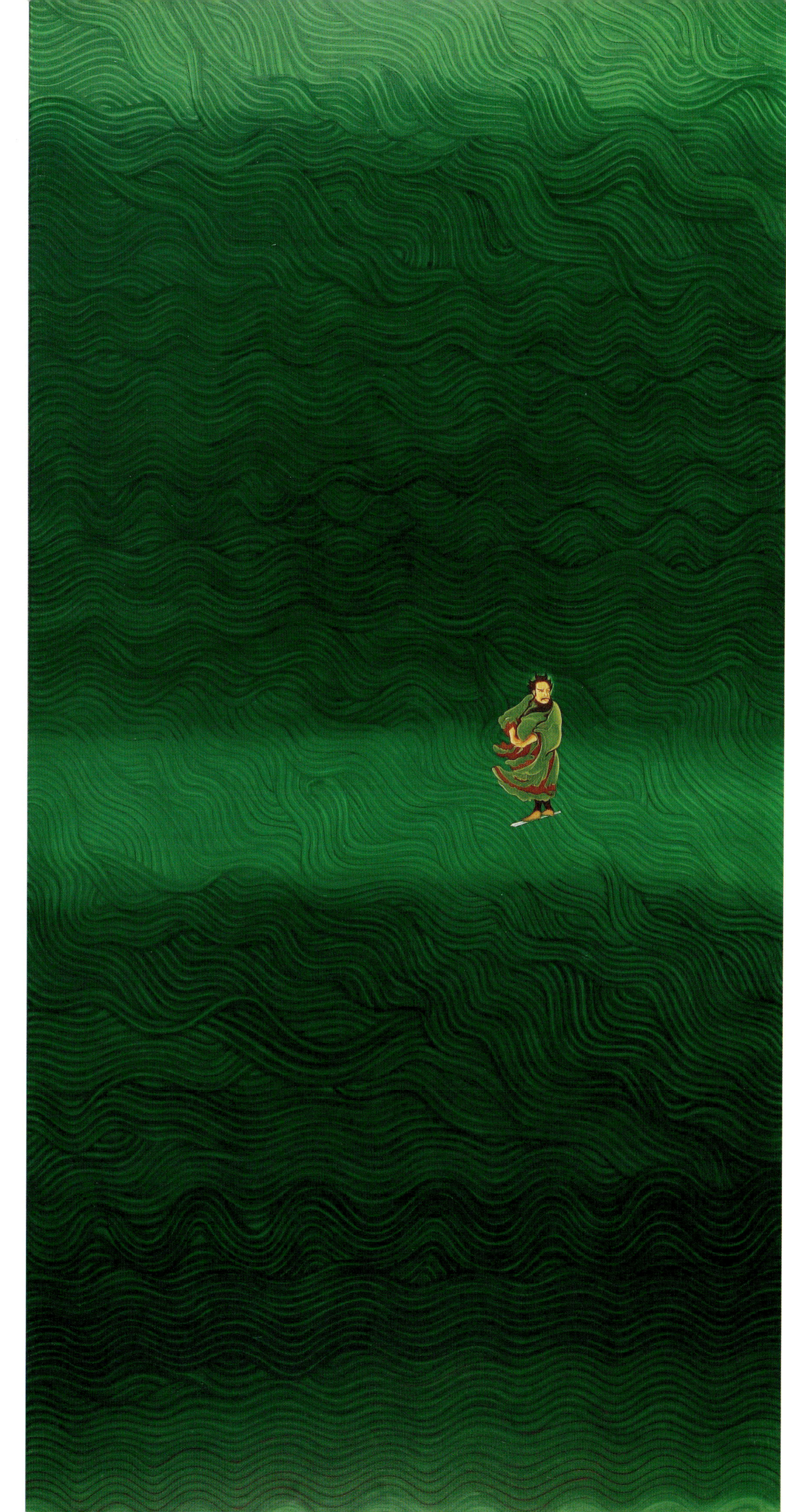

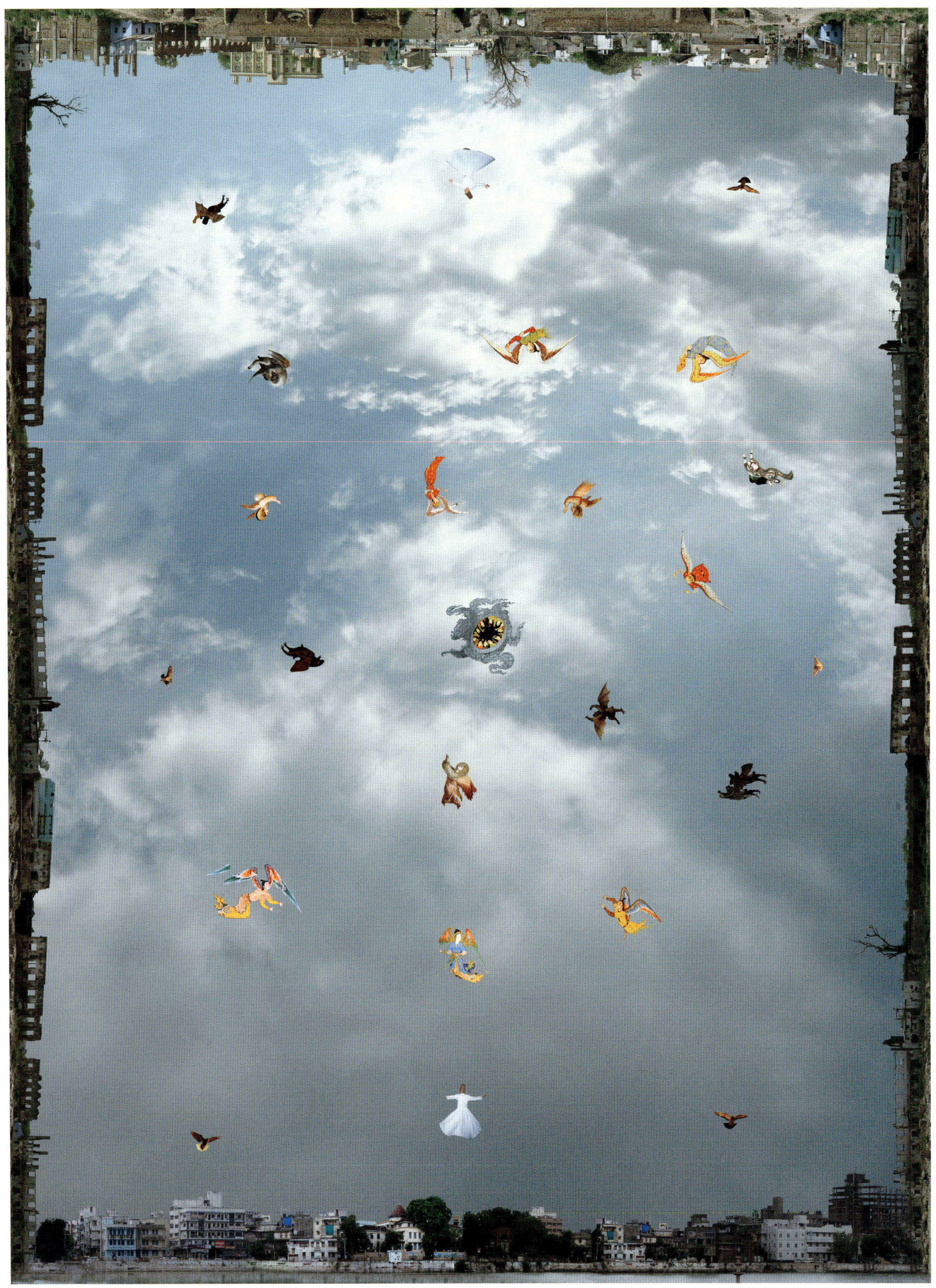

GULAMMOHAMMED SHEIKH
Visitors of the Sky from: Kaavad: Travelling Shrine: Home, 2008

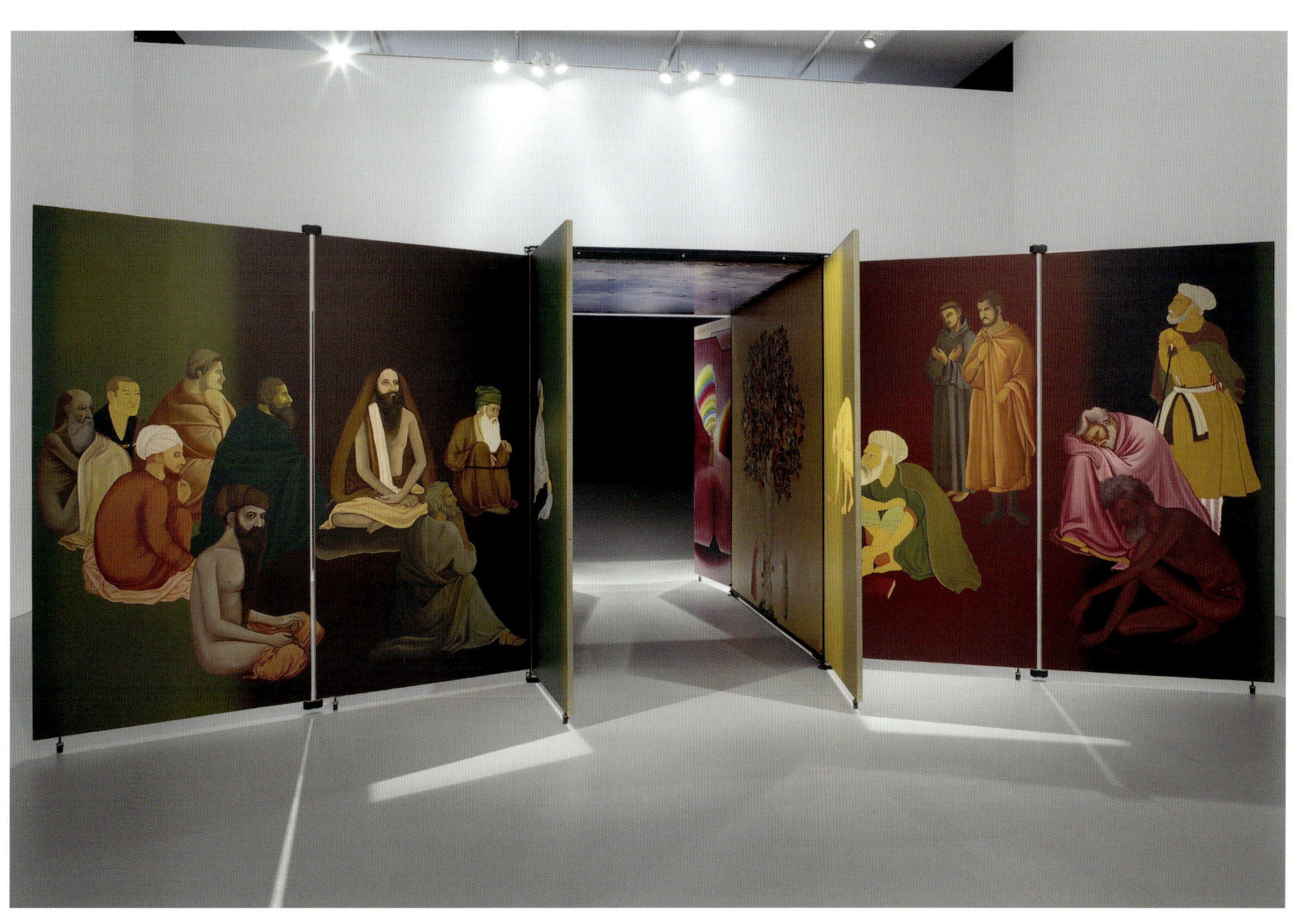

GULAMMOHAMMED SHEIKH
L: Sadhus, Sufis & Saints
R: Seekers & Sceptics
von / from: Kaavad: Travelling Shrine: Home, 2008

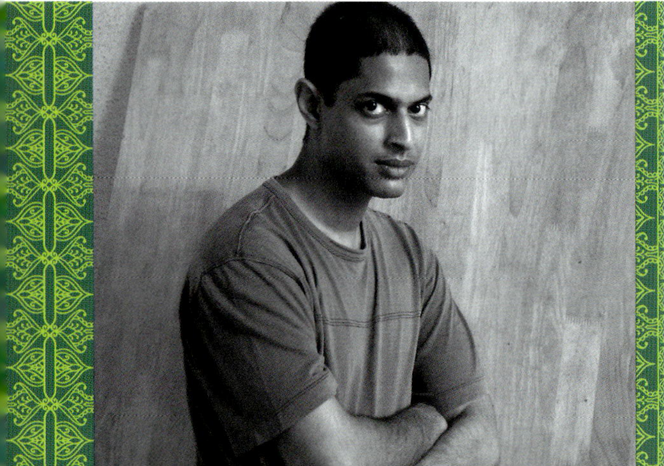

kiran subbaiah

KIRAN SUBBAIAH Geboren 1971 in Siddapur, Karnataka / Lebt in Bangalore
Born 1971 in Siddapur, Karnataka / Lives in Bangalore

1992 schloss Subbaiah sein Studium der Malerei am Kala Bhavan Visual Arts Department der Visva-Bharati University in Santiniketan, Westbengalen, mit einem Bachelordiplom ab und erwarb anschließend Masterdiplome in Bildhauerei an der Maharaja Sayajirao University von Baroda (Vadodara) und am Royal College of Art, London. In den letzten Jahren erweiterte Subbaiah seinen Schwerpunkt von Skulpturen und Assemblagen auf eine ganze Reihe von Medien – darunter Video, Text, Ton und Internet – die er gekonnt in seinen Arbeiten einsetzt. Subbaiah ist einer der wenigen Vertreter der konzeptuellen Kunst in Indien. Im Gegensatz zur Mehrzahl der indischen Künstler, die sich mit gesellschaftspolitischen Fragen auseinandersetzen, vertritt Subbaiah die Meinung, dass die Kunst in der Gesellschaft weder eine besondere Rolle zu spielen noch etwas beizutragen hat. Die Website http://www.geocities.com/antikiran/ von „Antikiran", seinem Alter Ego, gibt einen Überblick über seine Arbeiten, die einerseits durch einen trockenen bis tiefgründigen Sinn für Humor gekennzeichnet sind und andererseits durch eine Ichbezogenheit, die sich in der Auseinandersetzung mit seinem Alter Ego äußert.

„Suicide Note", eine hier gezeigte Arbeit, ist ein Beispiel für Subbaiahs ichbezogene Werke. Nachdem der Künstler zu Beginn des Videos ankündigt, dass das Geschehen „keinerlei Aufmerksamkeit verdiene" (weil das Ganze nicht ernst zu nehmen sei), beschließt er Selbstmord zu begehen und offenbart in seinem „Abschiedsbrief" seine respektlosen, spöttischen und gelegentlich mahnenden Gedanken zum eigenen Tod. Man erhält einen flüchtigen Eindruck von Subbaiahs hochgradiger Sensibilität – eine Konfrontation der beiden Subbaiahs –, übergangslos gefolgt von einem Paradigmenwechsel hin zu einem Monolog und einer geschickten Manipulation von Raum und Zeit. Darin wird der Augenblick des Selbstmords eingebaut. In diesem Werk fällt die Unterscheidung zwischen Ernst und Spaß schwer; man könnte es auch als schlechten Scherz auffassen, mit dem der Künstler die Betrachter zu verwirren sucht.

After obtaining a Bachelor of Arts (in Painting) in 1992 from the Visual Arts Department of Kala Bhavan of the Visva-Bharati University in Santiniketan, West Bengal, Subbaiah went on to obtain MAs (in Sculpture) from both the Maharaja Sayajirao University of Baroda (Vadodara), and the Royal College of Art, London. In recent years Subbaiah's focus on sculpture and assemblage has broadened, and he has also been creating work skilfully utilizing a range of different media including video, text, sound, and the Internet. One of the few conceptual artists in India, Subbaiah represents a new direction in Indian art. While much of Indian art is concerned with socio-political commentary, Subbaiah pursues a unique path, believing that there is no need for art to play a specific role in, or to contribute towards society. The website *http://www.geocities.com/antikiran/* run by "Antikiran", his alter ego, outlines his oeuvres, much of which shares a dry or dark sense of humour, while there are also many self-referential works in which the artist confronts his alter ego.

Suicide Note, a video work in this exhibition, is one example of Subbaiah's self-referential work. After the artist makes a statement at the beginning of the video that "There's no need to pay attention to it (as the story is nothing serious)." he then decides to commit suicide and expresses, through his "suicide note", his own thoughts about his death in an irreverent or contumely manner, and also at times in an admonishing tone. There are glimpses of Subbaiah's sharp sensibility – a confrontation between the two Subbaiahs which is quickly followed by a paradigm shift into a monologue and a skilful manipulation of space and time into which is incorporated the moment of suicide. A curious tale, it is difficult to distinguish whether the artist is serious or joking, and could also be seen as a bad joke, an attempt by the artist to confound the viewer.

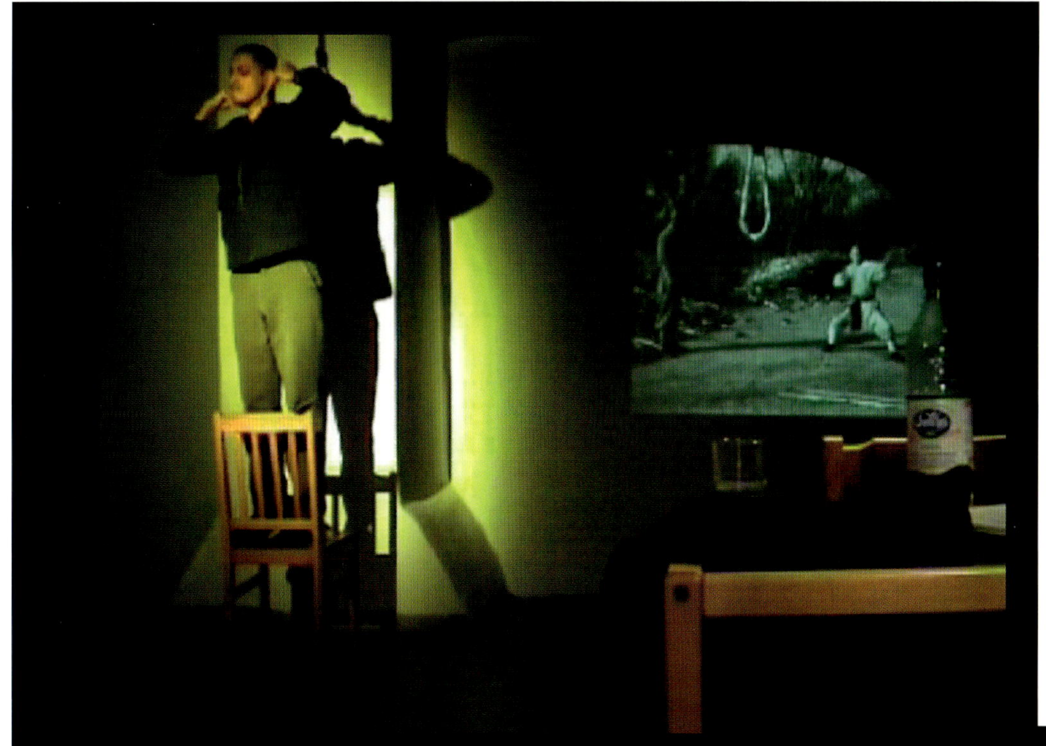

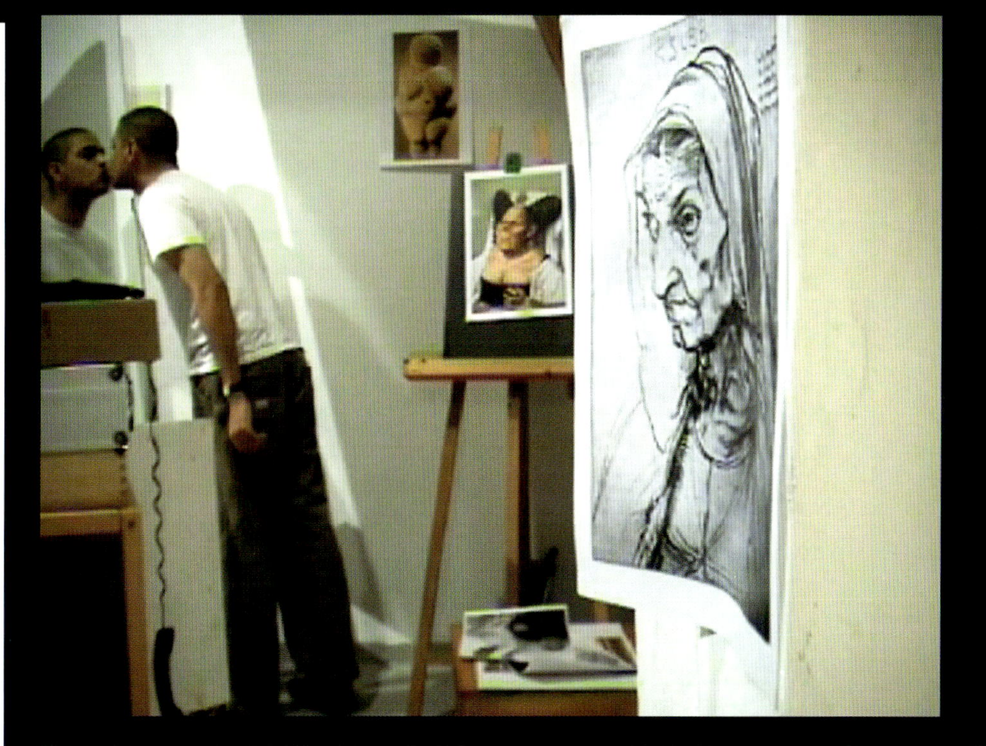

KIRAN SUBBAIAH
Suicide Note, 2006

Wichtige Ausstellungen: „Have We Met?“ (The Japan Foundation, Tokyo, 2004), „Mirror Worlds“ (Australian Center for Photography, Sydney, 2004), „SUBCONTINGENT: The Indian Subcontinent in Contemporary Art / Il Subcontinente Indiano nell'Arte Contemporanea“ (Fondazione Sandretto Re Rebaudengo, Turin, Italia, 2006) und „The 2nd Singapore Biennale: Wonder“ (2008). (KM)

Major exhibitions include "Have We Met?" (The Japan Foundation, Tokyo, 2004), "Mirror Worlds" (Australian Center for Photography, Sydney, 2004), "SUBCONTINGENT: The Indian Sub-continent in Contemporary Art / Il Subcontinente Indiano nell'Arte Contemporanea" (Fondazione Sandretto Re Rebaudengo, Turin, Italia, 2006), and "The 2nd Singapore Biennale: Wonder" (2008). (KM)

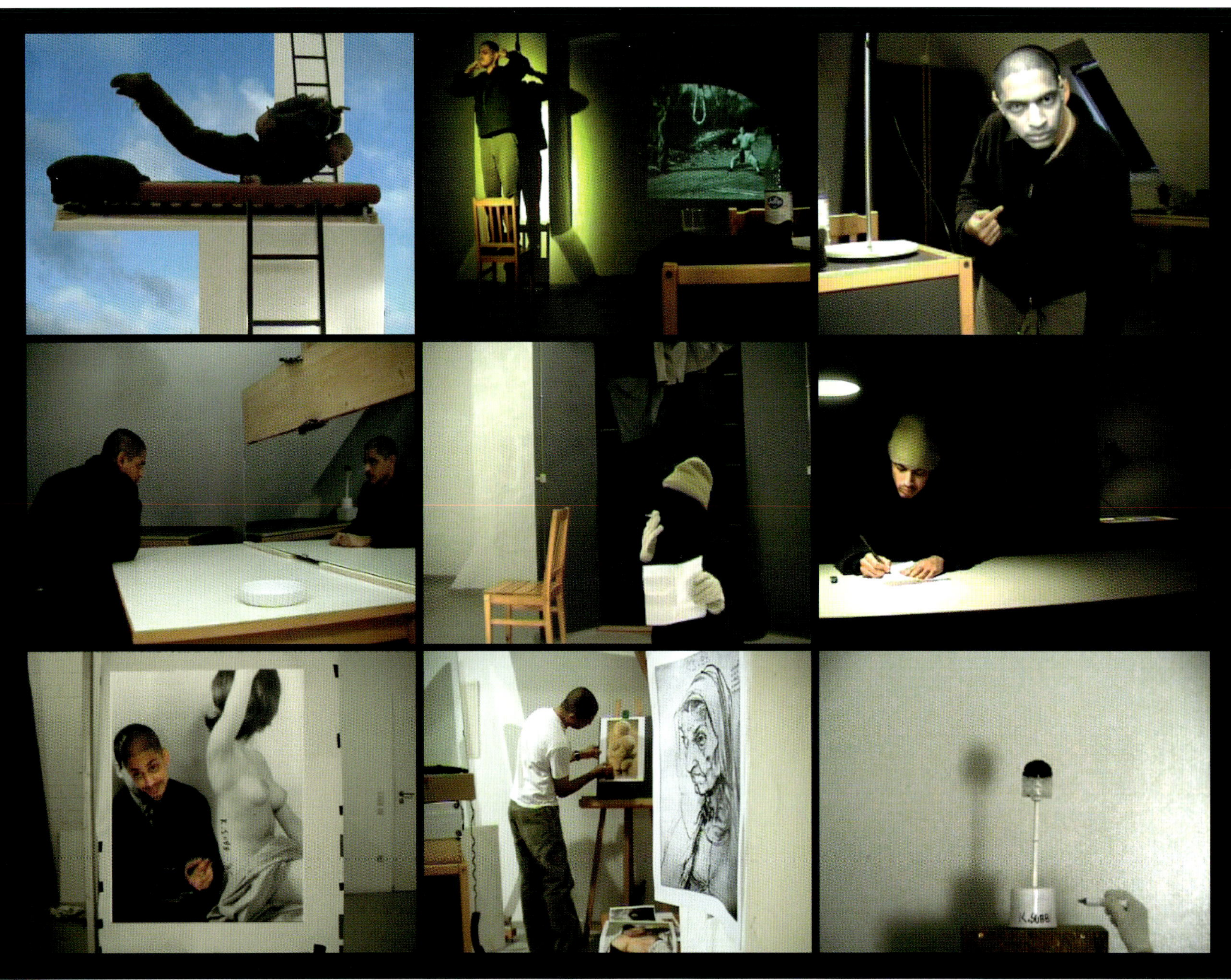

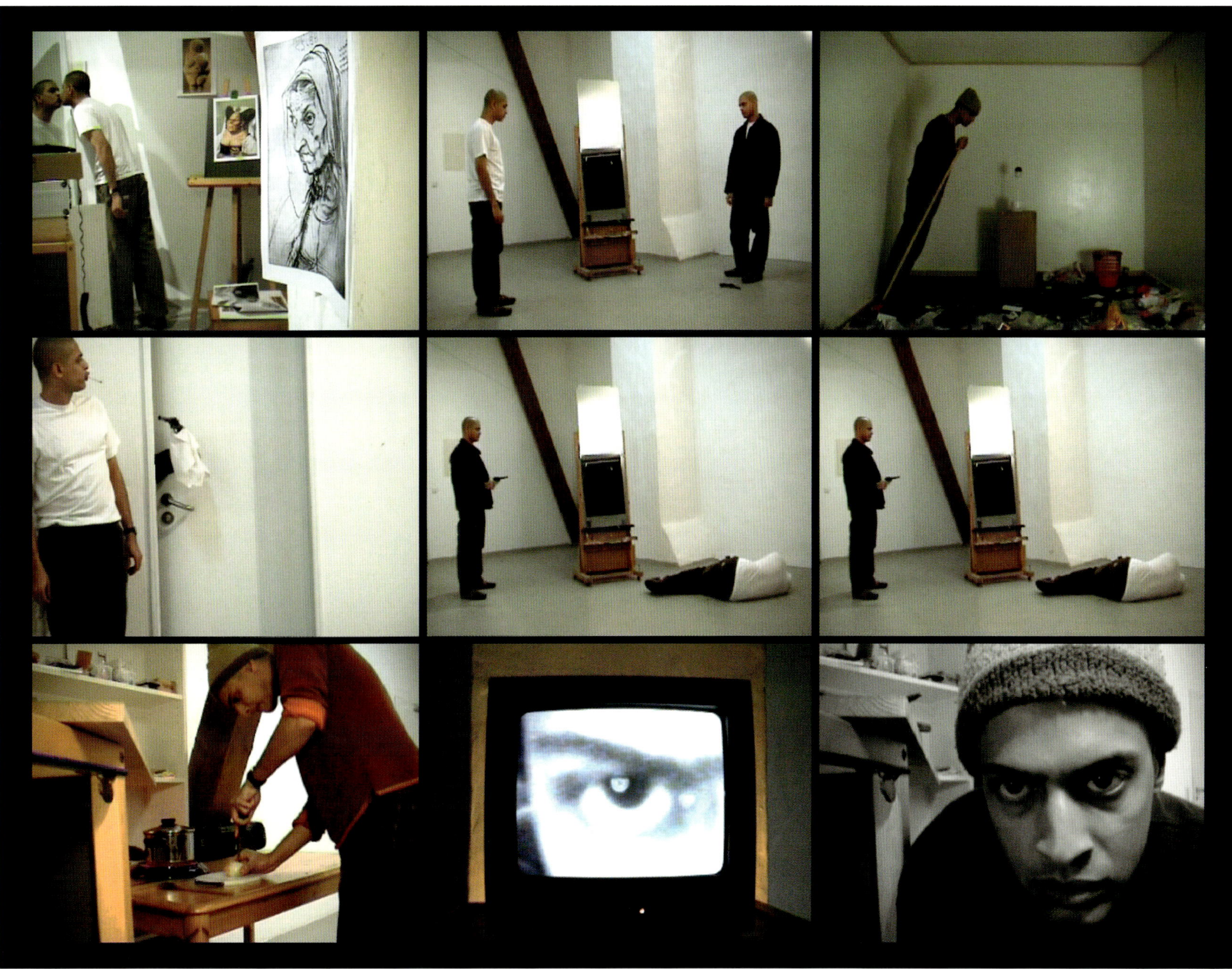

KIRAN SUBBAIAH
Suicide Note, 2006

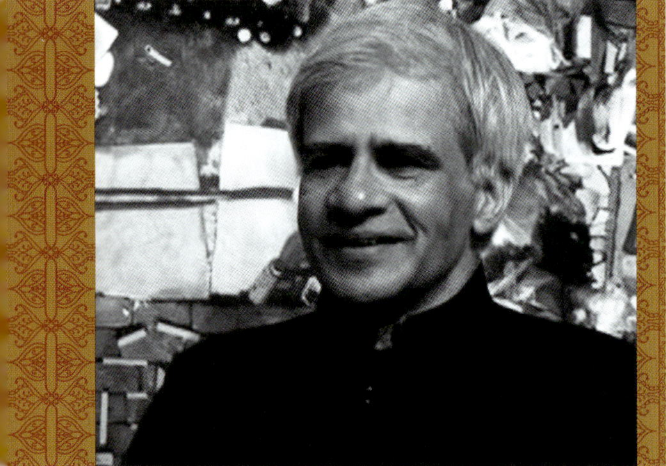

vivan sundaram

VIVAN SUNDARAM Geboren 1943 in Shimla, Himachal Pradesh / Lebt in Delhi
Born 1943 in Shimla, Himachal Pradesh / Lives in Delhi

Sundaram absolvierte die Maharaja Sayajirao University of Baroda (Vadodara) und studierte anschließend bei R. B. Kitaj an der Slade School of Fine Art, London. Seine Karriere begann in den späten 1960er Jahren. Von den 1970er bis zu den 1980er Jahren war Sundaram Mitglied der Baroda School, die die zweite Generation der indischen Künstler nach der Unabhängigkeit repräsentiert und sich der Darstellung der gesellschaftlichen Realität mit den Mitteln eines betont narrativen Malstils widmet. Anfang der 1990er Jahre schuf Sundaram Arbeiten, die von der Liberalisierung der indischen Wirtschaft, der Globalisierung und dem aufkommenden religiösen Fundamentalismus geprägt waren. Auch seine Technik hat sich gewandelt und er konzentriert sich gegenwärtig auf Fotografie, Video und Installationen mit Readymades und Objets trouvés.

In den letzten Jahren kam es zu einer Zusammenarbeit zwischen Sundaram und „Chintan", einer NGO, die in Indien als „unrein" geltende Reinigungskräfte unterstützt. Aus Abfall und Müll, der von Reinigungskräften in Delhi gesammelt wurde, kreierte Sundaram ein Diorama der Stadt und fertigte davon eine Fotoserie an. „Master Plan" (2008) bietet eine Rundsicht auf das Diorama. Bei näherem Hinsehen erkennt der Betrachter, dass diese geplante Stadt im Wesentlichen aus Zahnbürsten, Kartons und bunten Plastikgegenständen besteht, die auf den Straßen weggeworfen wurden. Die Miniaturautos, welche die fliesengepflasterten Straßen entlang fahren, die aus Karton angefertigten Wohnsiedlungen, der rote Balken, der eine Hochstraße darstellt, die Türme aus durchsichtigen Plastikflaschen und die Gebäude aus leeren Dosen ergeben eine Vision der idealen Stadt, die Delhi durch den fortgesetzten Ausbau des U-Bahnsystems, der Straßen und anderer Infrastrukturanlagen gerne werden möchte. Inzwischen hat Sundaram mit „Metal Box" (2008), in dem die Wasserverschmutzung angesprochen wird, und mit „Barricade (with Two Drains)" (2008) die nachteiligen Auswirkungen der Verstädterung aus mikroskopischer Sicht durch die digitale Bearbeitung von Nahaufnahmen des Dioramas dargestellt. In „A Brief Ascension of Marian Hussain" (2005) zeigt er den Buben Marian, der zu Beginn des Videos begraben unter einem Abfallberg auf dem

After graduating from Maharaja Sayajirao University of Baroda (Vadodara), Sundaram studied under R. B. Kitaj at the Slade School of Fine Art, London, and embarked on his career in the late 60s. From the 70s to the 80s, Sundaram was a member of the Baroda School, which is recognized as representing the second generation of post-Independence Indian artists, and depicted the realities of society through narrative-rich representative painting. At the beginning of the 90s, Sundaram produced work informed by the deregulation of the Indian economy, globalism, and the rise of religious fundamentalism. His technique also underwent a transformation, and he now creates photography, video and installations featuring ready-made and found objects.

In recent years, Sundaram has been collaborating with "Chintan", an NGO providing support to those who work as cleaners, who are regarded as "unclean" in India. He created a diorama of the city using rubbish and refuse collected by cleaners in Delhi, and then took a series of photographs of the diorama. *Master Plan* (2008) is a panoramic view of this diorama. On closer inspection, the observer realizes that the key components making up this planned city are toothbrushes, cardboard boxes and colourful plastic products found discarded on the roads. The miniature cars moving along the tiled road, the collective housing made of cardboard, the red beam representing an elevated road, the towers made of clear plastic bottles and the buildings built from empty cans combine to create a vision of the ideal city that Delhi is aiming to become, as its subway system, roads and other infrastructure are progressively improved. Meanwhile, in *Metal Box* (2008), that evokes water pollution, and *Barricade (with Two Drains)* (2008), Sundaram depicts the adverse effects of urbanization from a microscopic perspective through close ups of the diorama and digital processing. In *A Brief Ascension of Marian Hussain* (2005), Sundaram features the young boy cleaner Marian from the opening of the video, in which the boy is initially lying down, almost buried under a mountain of rubbish, until he climbs the top of the mountain, and then starts to float upwards until he disappears, as though being drawn up into the heavens. The video depicts Marian's harsh environment in a fantastical

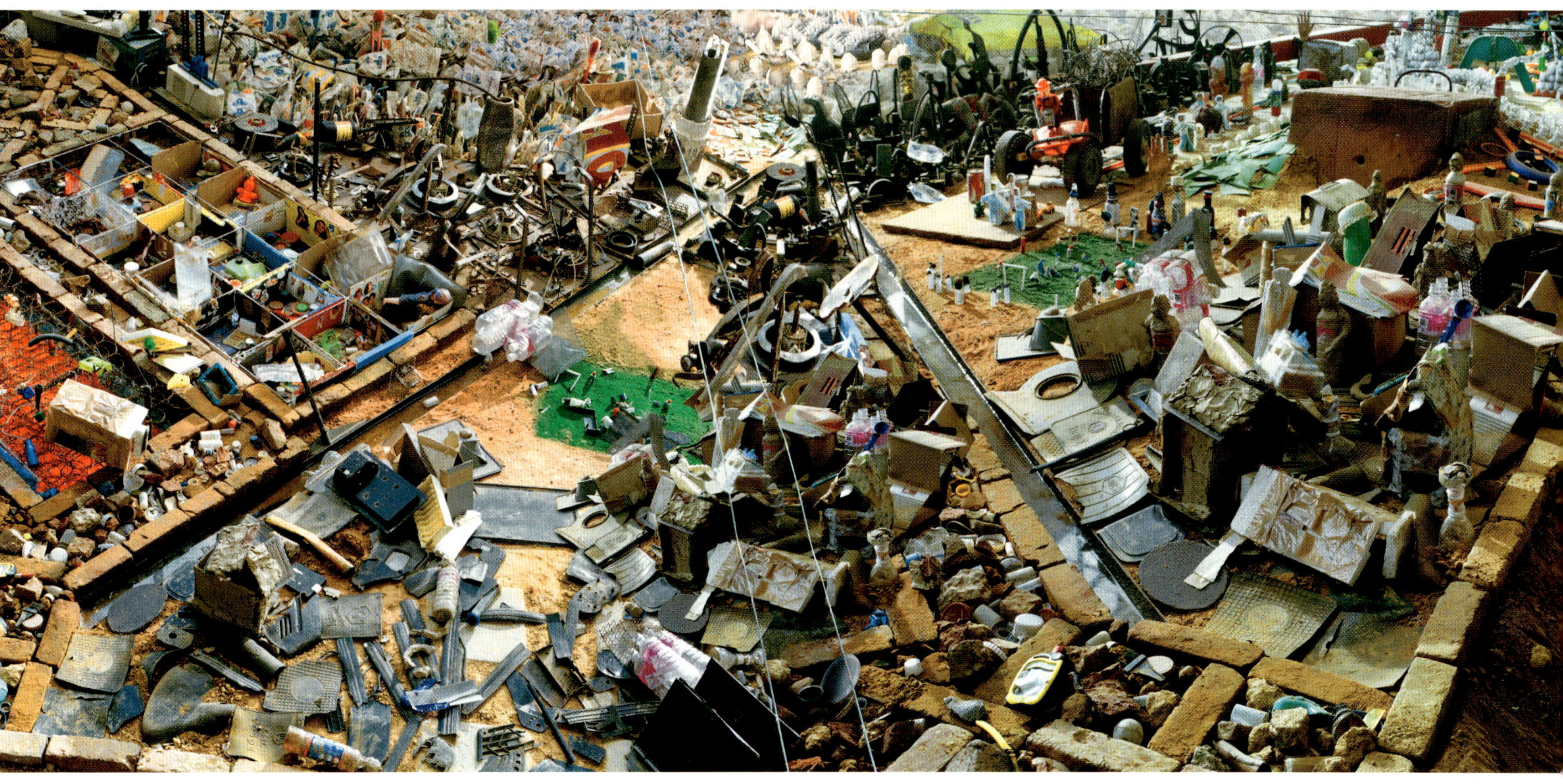

VIVAN SUNDARAM
Barricade (with two drains), 2008

Boden liegt, diesen Berg dann erklettert, um letztlich nach oben zu entschweben, so als würde er in den Himmel aufsteigen. Der fantastische Stil, in dem das Video Marians unwirtliches Umfeld schildert, soll Sundarams Frage, ob das gegenwärtige Wirtschaftswachstum eine Zukunft schaffen kann, die für in Armut lebende Kinder erstrebenswert ist, zum Ausdruck bringen.

Wichtige Ausstellungen: „Indian Video Art: History in Motion" (Fukuoka Asian Art Museum, 2004) sowie die Einzelausstellungen „Amrita Sher-Gil" (Tate Modern, 2007) und „Trash" (Chemould Prescott Road, Project 88, Mumbai, 2008). (TK)

style to convey Sundaram's question – can the current economic growth deliver a future that children in poverty can aspire to?

Major exhibitions include "Indian Video Art: History in Motion" (Fukuoka Asian Art Museum, 2004) and solo exhibitions "Amrita Sher-Gil" (Tate Modern, 2007) and "Trash" (Chemould Prescott Road, Project 88, Mumbai, 2008). (TK)

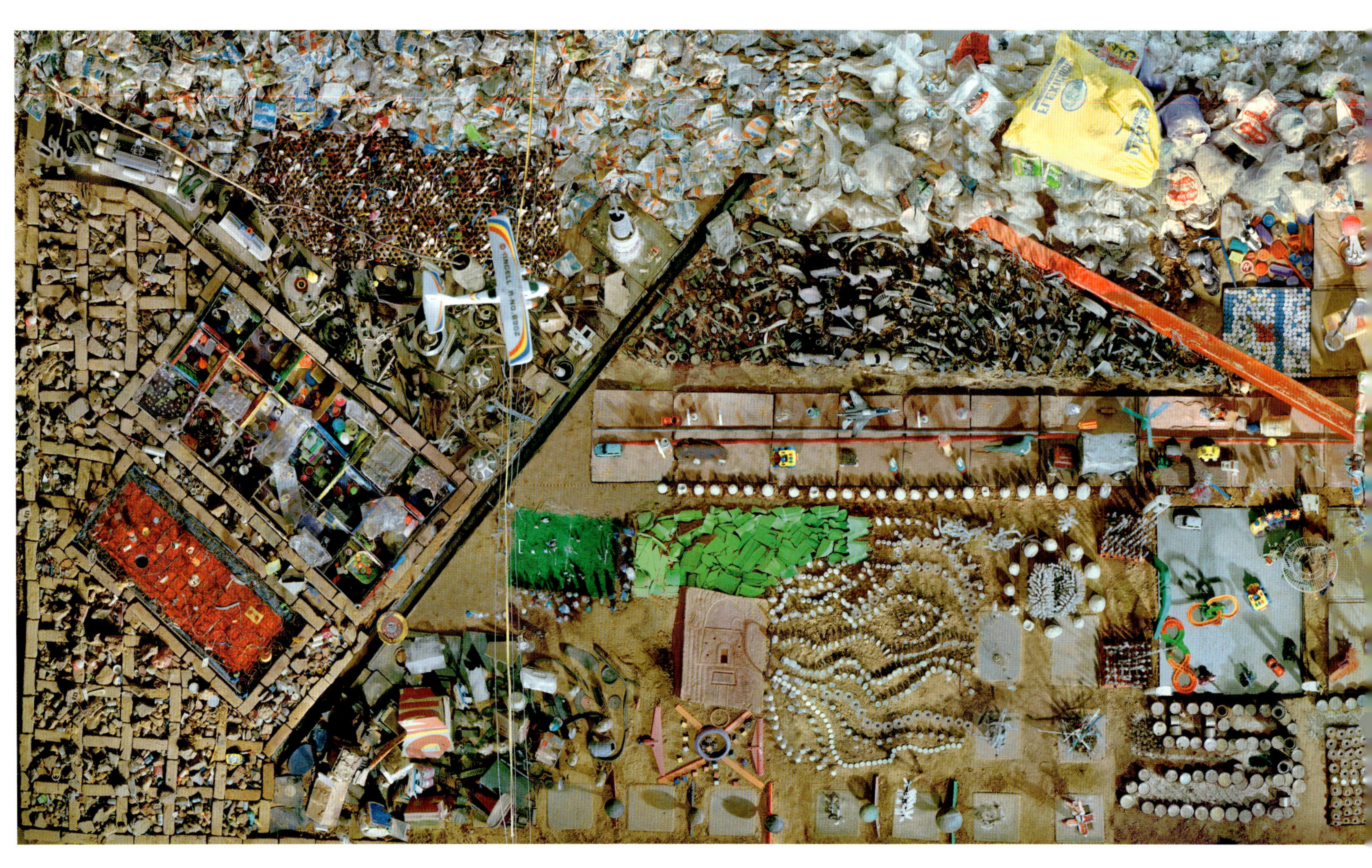

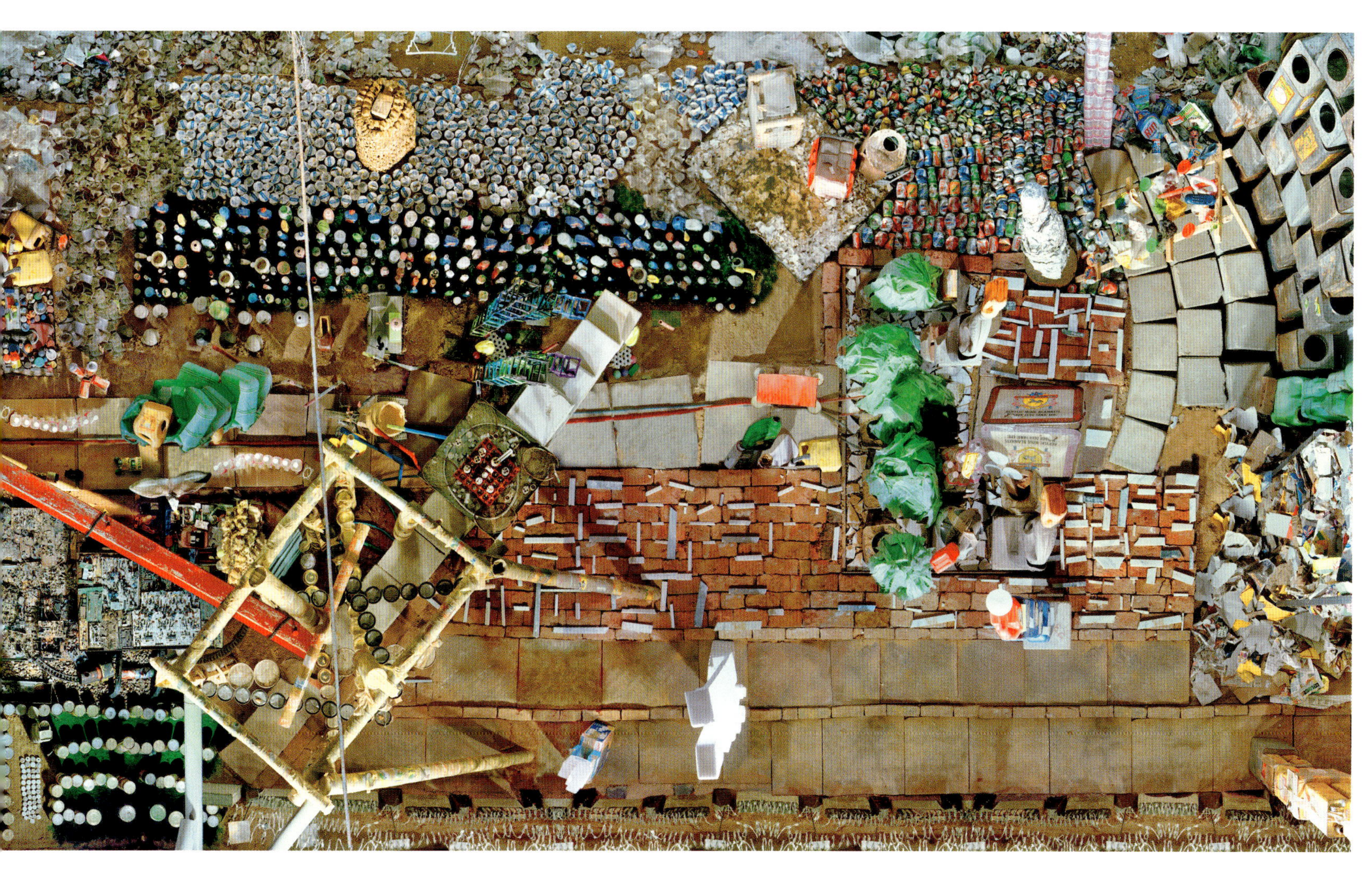

VIVAN SUNDARAM
Master Plan, 2008

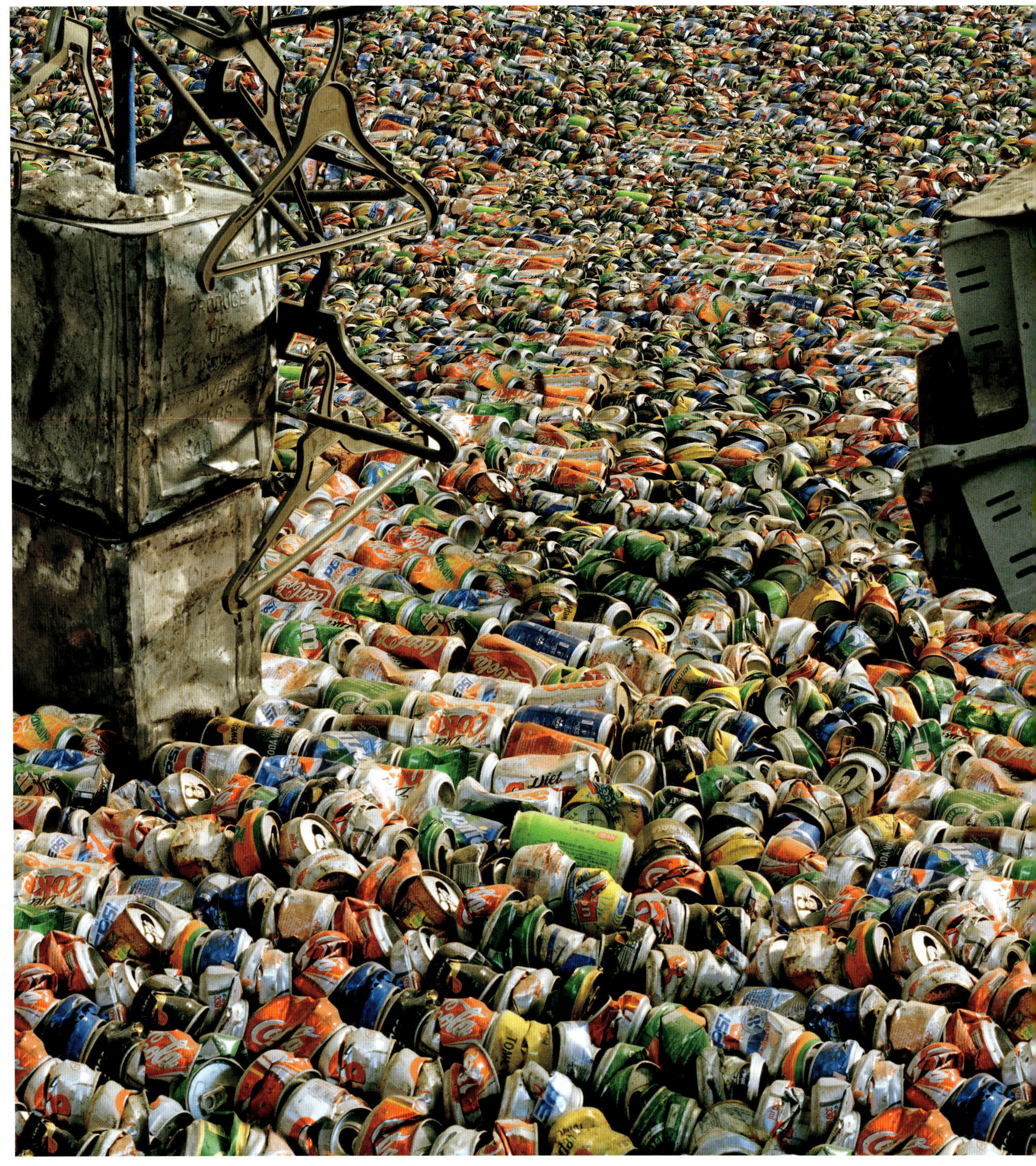

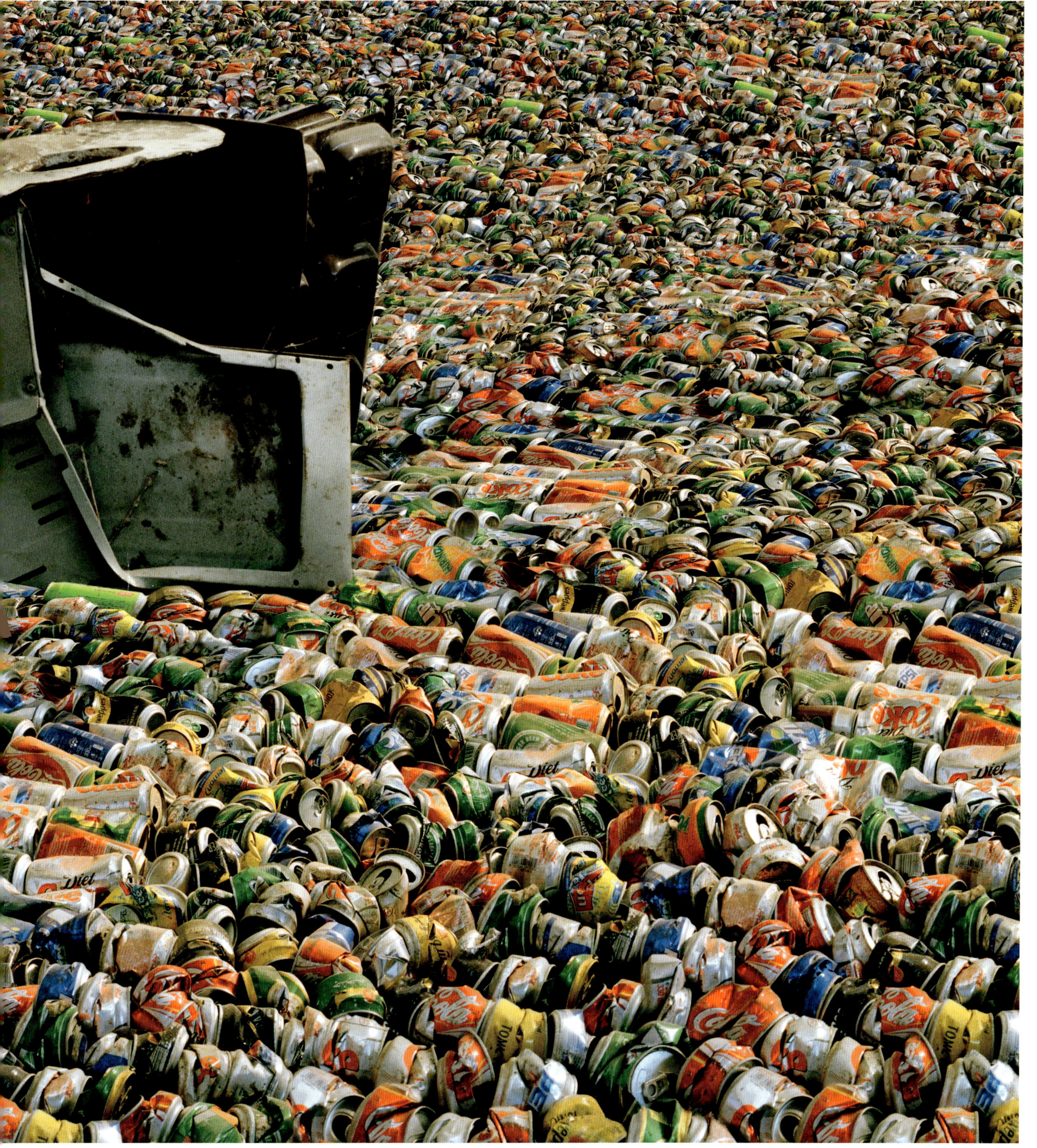

VIVAN SUNDARAM
Metal Box, 2008

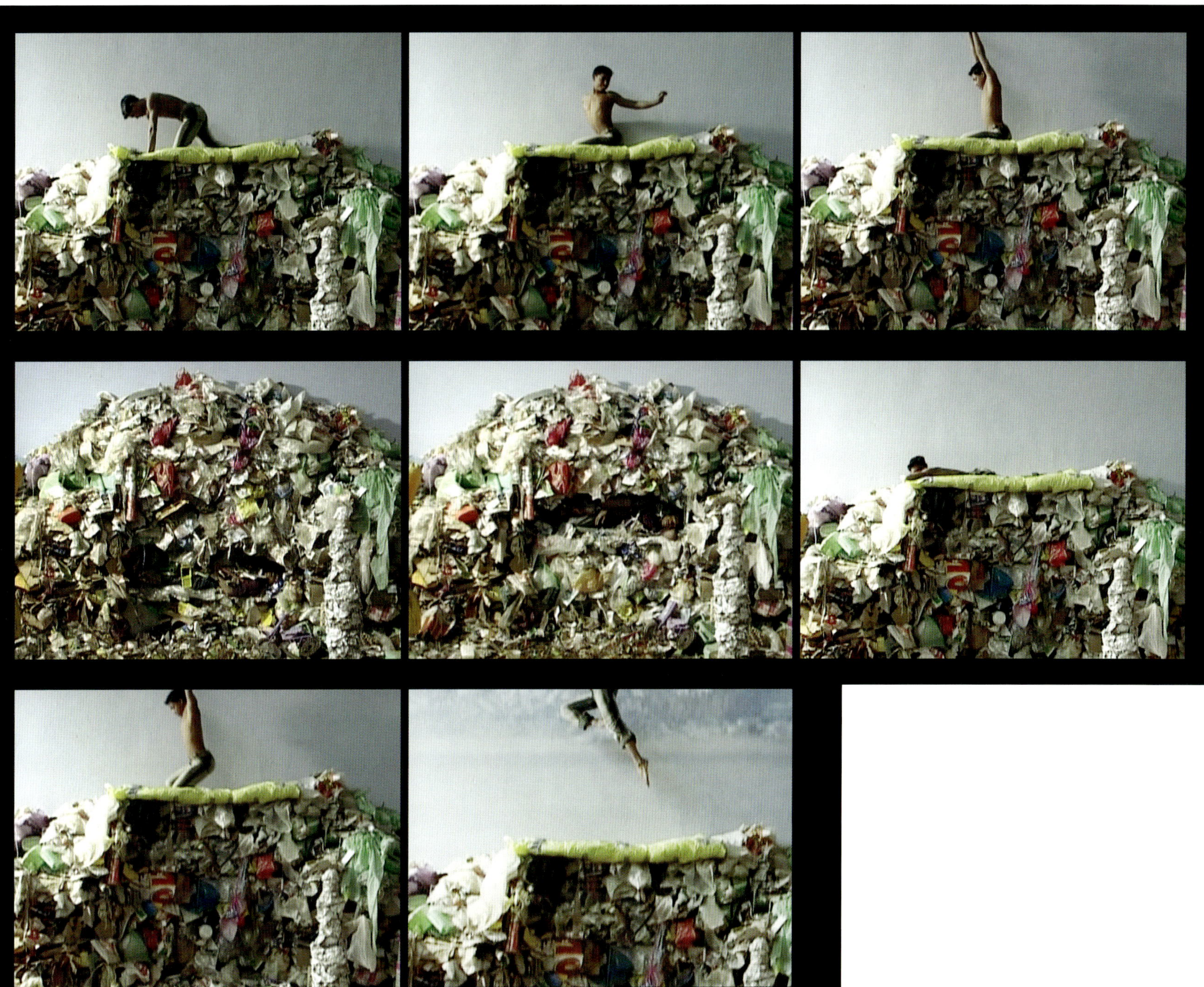

VIVAN SUNDARAM
The Brief Ascension of Marian Hussain, 2005

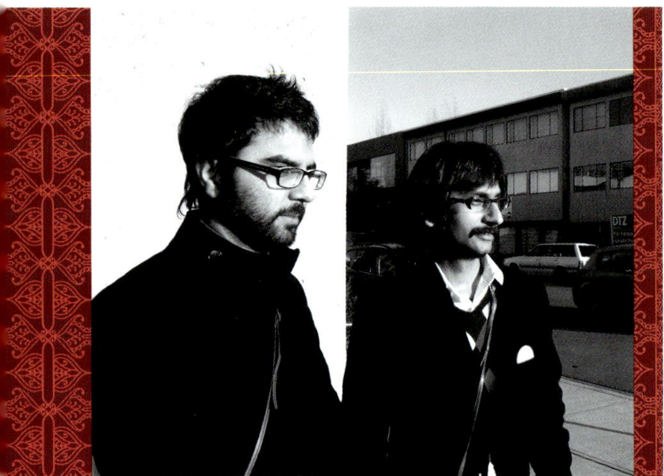

thukral & tagra

JITEN THUKRAL geboren 1976 in Jalandhar, Punjab | Born 1976 in Jalandhar, Punjab
SUMIR TAGRA geboren 1979 in Delhi | Born 1979 in Delhi
Thukral und Tagra leben in Gurgaon, Haryana | Thukral and Tagra live in Gurgaon, Haryana

Nach Abschluss des Kunststudiums am Chandigarh Art College erwarb Thukral sein Masterdiplom am New Delhi College of Art. Tagra absolvierte nach Abschluss seines Studiums am New Delhi College of Art 2006 ein höheres Fachsemester in Kommunikations-Design am National Institute of Design, Ahmedabad. Thukral und Tagra gehören zur neuen Generation von Künstlern, die ihre Volljährigkeit in den ersten Jahren der Globalisierung erlangten, als Information und Güter aus Übersee aufgrund der Liberalisierung der indischen Wirtschaft im Jahr 1991 allgemein verfügbar wurden. Die beiden Künstler lernten sich während ihres Studiums am New Delhi College of Art kennen und begannen gemeinsam zu arbeiten. 2003 gründeten sie Bosedk Design, eine Firma, die in den Bereichen Werbung, Büro-Innenausstattung und Produktdesign tätig war. Ab 2005 begann das Duo unter dem Namen Thukral & Tagra Gemälde, Skulpturen und Installationen zu schaffen. Die beiden Künstler werden für ihre unverbrauchte neue Sensibilität gefeiert, die gekennzeichnet ist durch eine gekonnte Einbindung von Ort und Zeit – so bringen sie indische Tradition und japanische Subkulturen in äußerst ausgefeilte Kompositionen ein.

Die „Bosedk“-Serie war bei einer ihrer jüngsten Ausstellungen zu sehen: Es handelt sich dabei um verschieden geformte Behälter, mit Etiketten versehen, die von den beiden Künstlern entworfen wurden. Die Behälter sind in Reihen auf Regalen angeordnet, in der Absicht, die Gleichwertigkeit von Kunst und Alltagsgütern zu demonstrieren. In anderen Arbeiten haben sich die beiden durch die stilvolle Präsentation von Original-Designer-Kondomen, Unterwäsche und Sandalen sowie ihrer eigenen Gemälde, mit HIV auseinandergesetzt. Thukral & Tagra beweisen die Vielseitigkeit ihrer Kunst auch mit Arbeiten, in denen Jugendliche in Erscheinung treten, die wie die beiden Künstler aus Punjab stammen. Für die aktuelle Ausstellung haben Thukral & Tagra ein neues Werk für die "Punjab Boys"-Serie geschaffen. Der Eingang zur aktuellen Ausstellung wird durch Transparente und Aufkleber der beiden Künstler markiert. Die Installation „Effugio“ thematisiert junge Leute, die vom Erfolg in Europa oder Amerika träumen, während sie sich – von Thukral & Tagra wie üblich stilvoll gestaltet – in der Stadtlandschaft von Gurgaon

After graduating in Fine Arts from Chandigarh Art College, Thukral obtained his MA at New Delhi College of Art. Tagra completed a course in Communications Design at the graduate school of the National Institute of Design, Ahmedabad in 2006 after graduating from New Delhi College of Art. Both Thukral and Tagra belong to the new generation of artists who came of age during the early years of globalization when information and products from overseas became widely available as a result of the deregulation of the Indian economy in 1991. The two artists met and began collaborating while studying at New Delhi College of Art. In 2003 they established Bosedk Design, a company that undertakes advertising, office interior design and product design. From 2005 the duo began to create paintings, sculpture and installations under the name Thukral & Tagra. They are acclaimed for their fresh new sensibility marked by a skilful integration of locality and contemporaneity by blending Indian traditions and Japanese subcultures into work that is marked by highly sophisticated composition.

Recent exhibitions include the "Bosedk" series, in which various shaped containers with labels designed by the duo are arranged in rows and on shelves, like a supermarket, to demonstrate the equivalence of art and everyday products. In other works, the duo has addressed the issue of HIV by stylishly presenting original design condoms, underwear, and sandals as well as their paintings. Thukral & Tagra has also produced works featuring youths who, like these artists, are also from the Punjab, and in these ways, continue to show work informed by multiple themes. In this exhibition, Thukral & Tagra has created a new work in the "Punjab Boys" series. In this exhibition, banners and stickers – designed by the duo – marks the entrance to the exhibition. Inside, the installation entitled *Effugio* is themed on the youths who dream of success in Europe and the United States as they gather in the megapolis of Gurgaon and are depicted in a refined way, typical of these two artists. The wall is covered with computer designed wallpaper and that could be described as a contemporary miniature painting – placed are the busts with its surface patterned with Punjab boy along with over-decorated furniture. Meanwhile, bottles of American chocolate syrup

versammeln. Die Wand ist mit einer Computertapete überzogen, die man als zeitgenössische Miniaturmalerei bezeichnen könnte – auf diese sind gemusterte Punjab Boys-Büsten montiert, ergänzt durch schwülstig dekorierte Möbel. Auf den Glasregalen sind Flaschen mit amerikanischem Schokoladensirup aufgereiht, deren Etiketten mit Bildern junger Inder beklebt sind. In „Dominus Aeris – Elegance" (2008), wurden digitale Bearbeitungstechniken eingesetzt, um die im westlichen „Punjub Barockstil" errichteten Bauten – die vom Haus der Künstler aus zu sehen sind – in ein Hochhaus umzuwandeln. Das Ergebnis wurde auf Leinwand gemalt – das farbenfrohe, kitschige Gebäude steht stellvertretend für die benachbarte Stadtlandschaft, die sich immer noch im Entwicklungsstadium befindet.

Wichtige Ausstellungen: „Everyday Bosedk" (Gallery Nature Morte, New Delhi, 2007), „Put it On" (Bose Pacia Gallery, New York, 2007) und „Adolescere-Domus" (Art Basel 38, Schweiz, 2007). (TK)

with images of young Indians stuck onto the labels line the glass shelves. In *Dominus Aeris – Elegance* (2008), digital processing has been used to transform the Indian-Western style housing called 'Punjab Baroque,' that can be seen from their house, into a high-rise building. The result has then been painted on to canvas, the colourful and kitsch building representing the neighbouring urban landscape that continues to undergo development.

Major exhibitions include "Everyday Bosedk" (Gallery Nature Morte, New Delhi, 2007), "Put it On" (Bose Pacia Gallery, New York, 2007), and "Adolescere-Domus" (Art Basel 38, Schweiz, 2007). (TK)

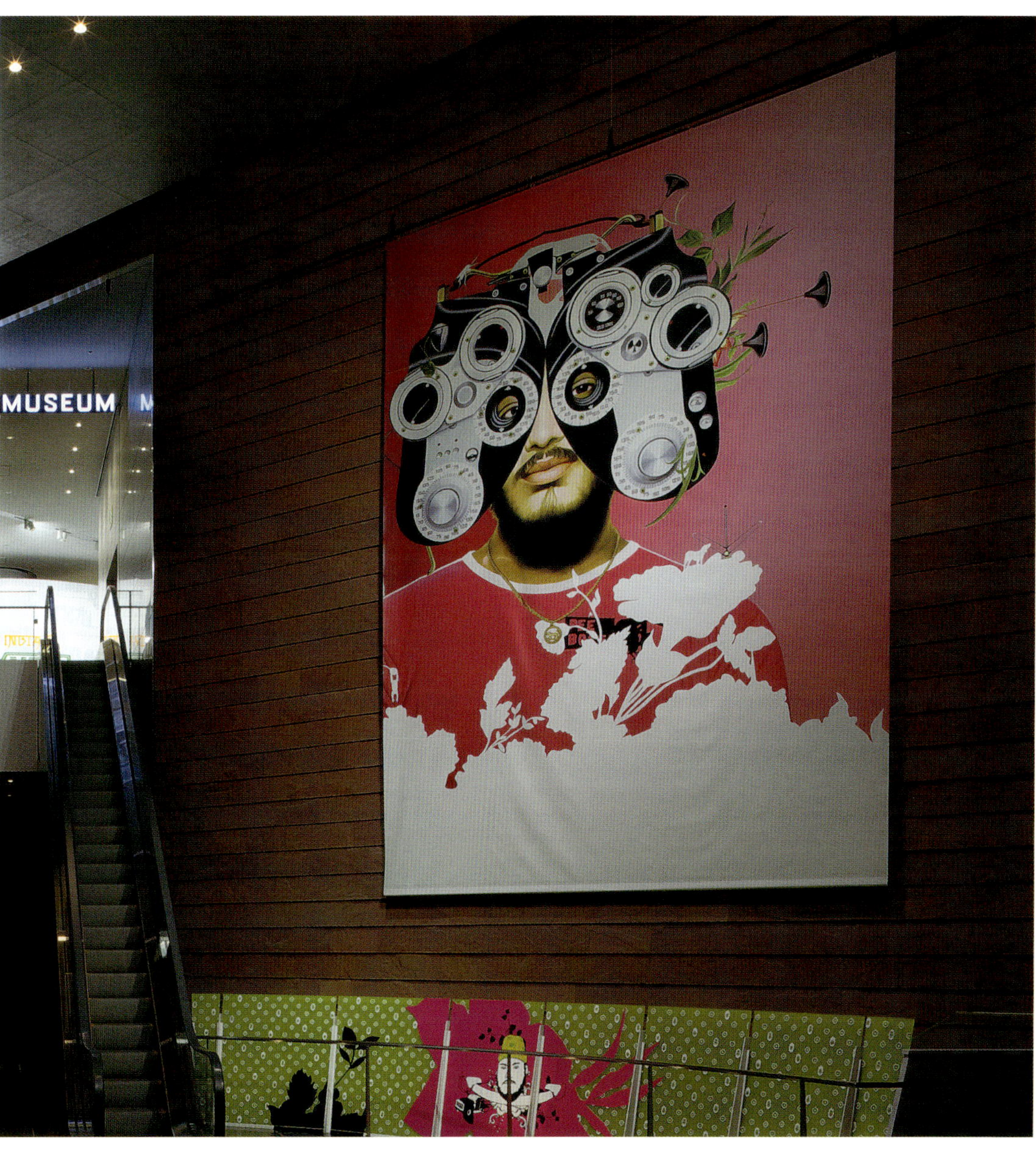

THUKRAL & TAGRA
Installation view

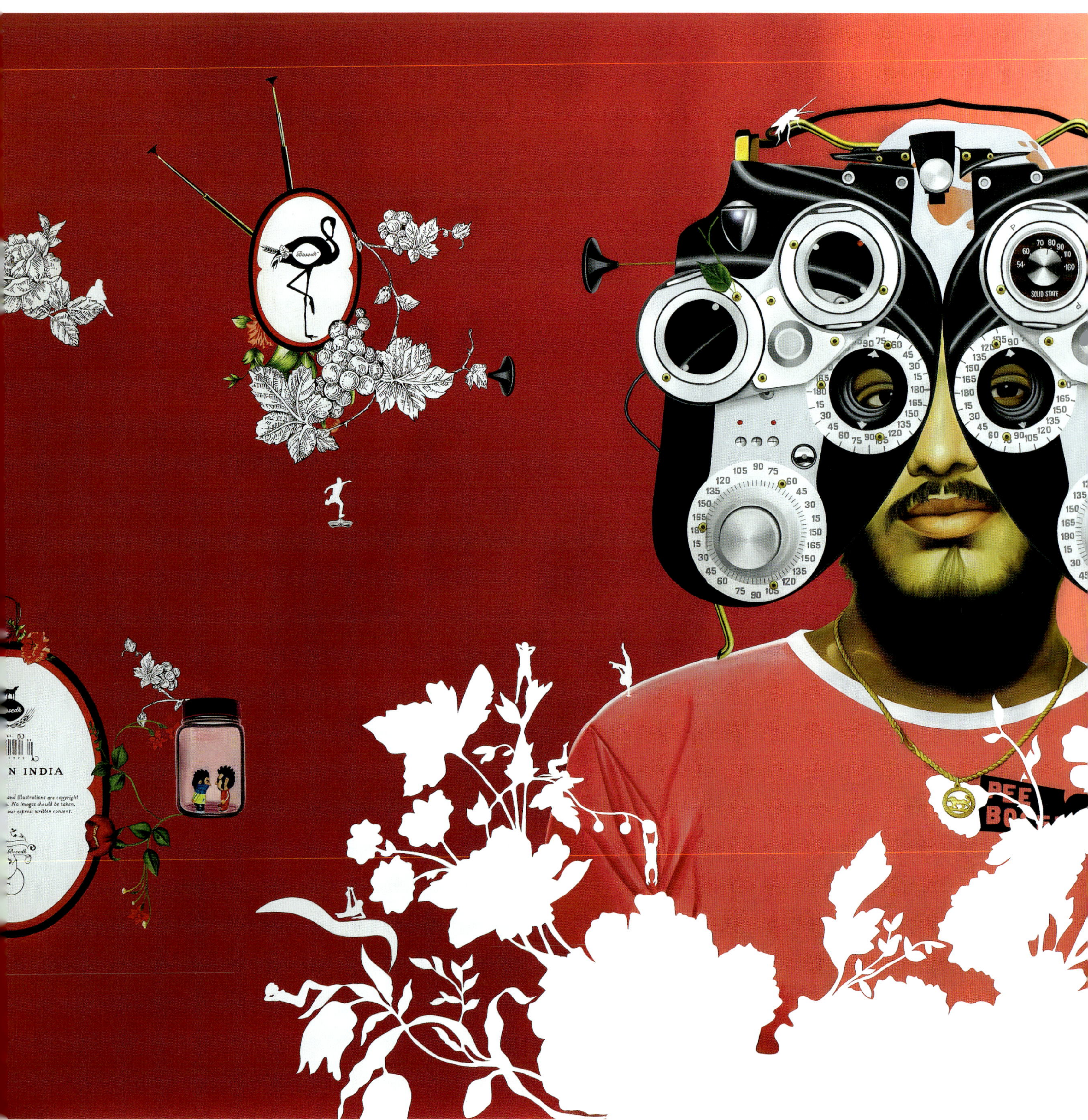

THUKRAL & TAGRA
Phantom IX-B, 2007

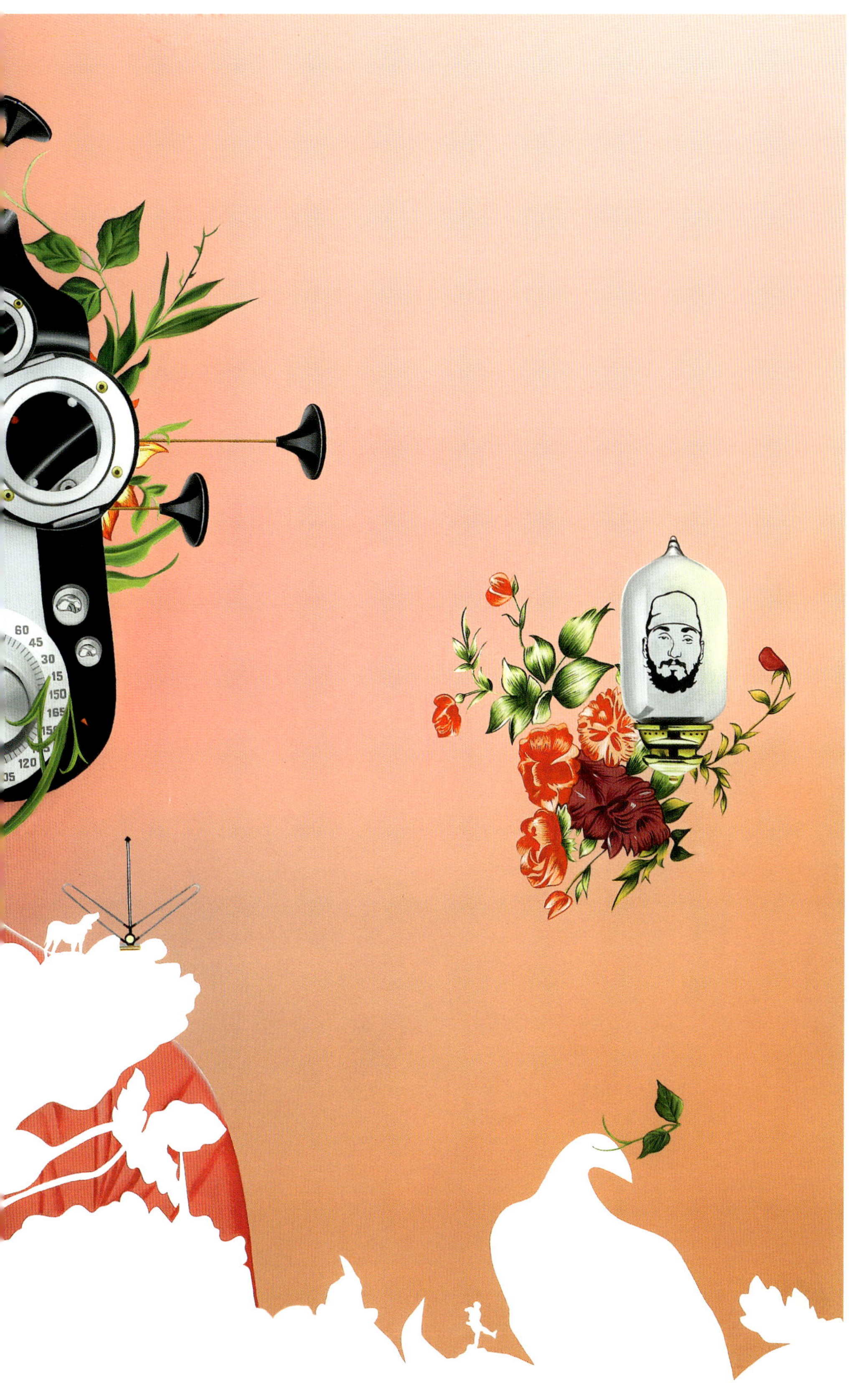

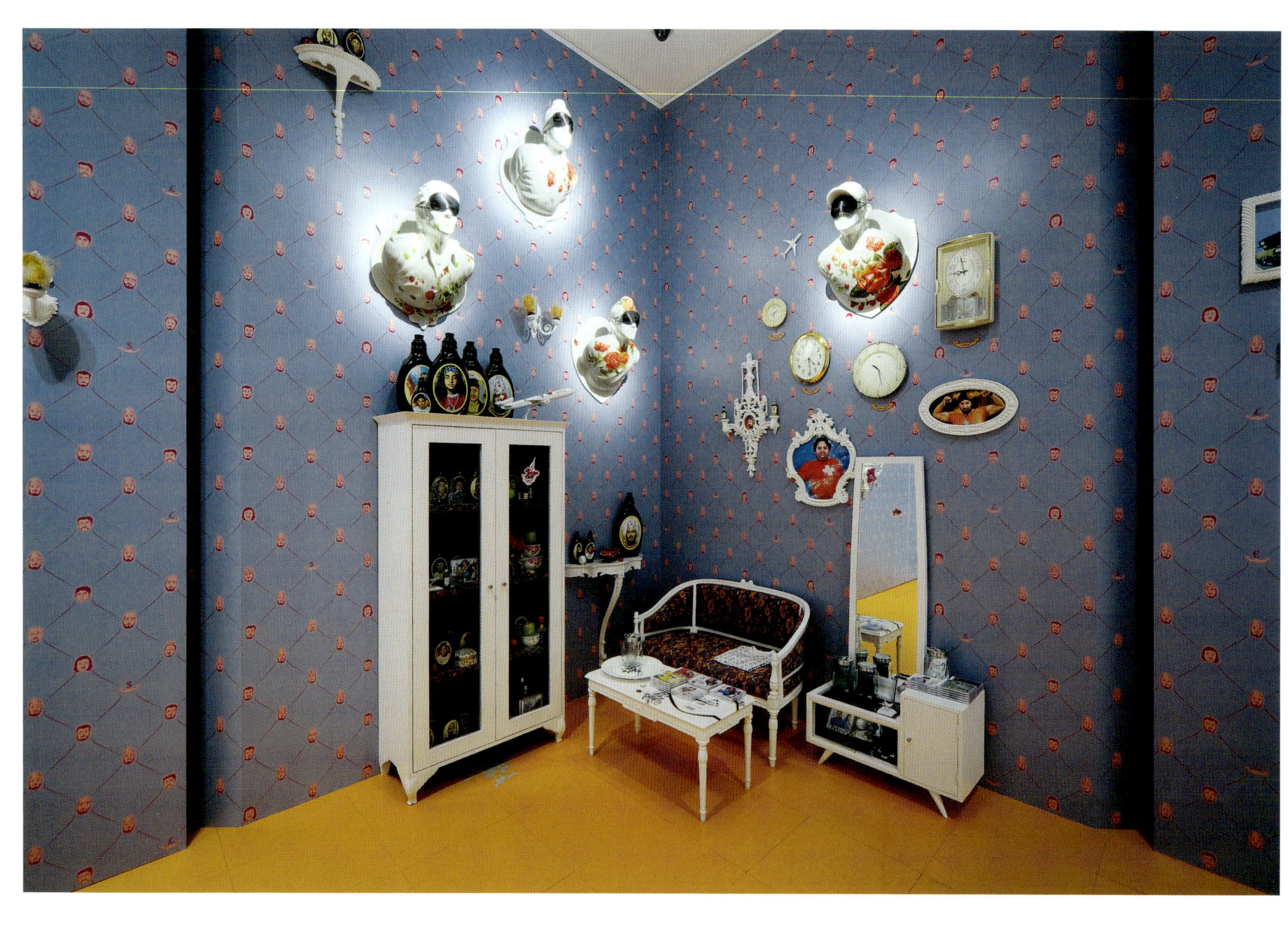

THUKRAL & TAGRA
Effugio, 2008

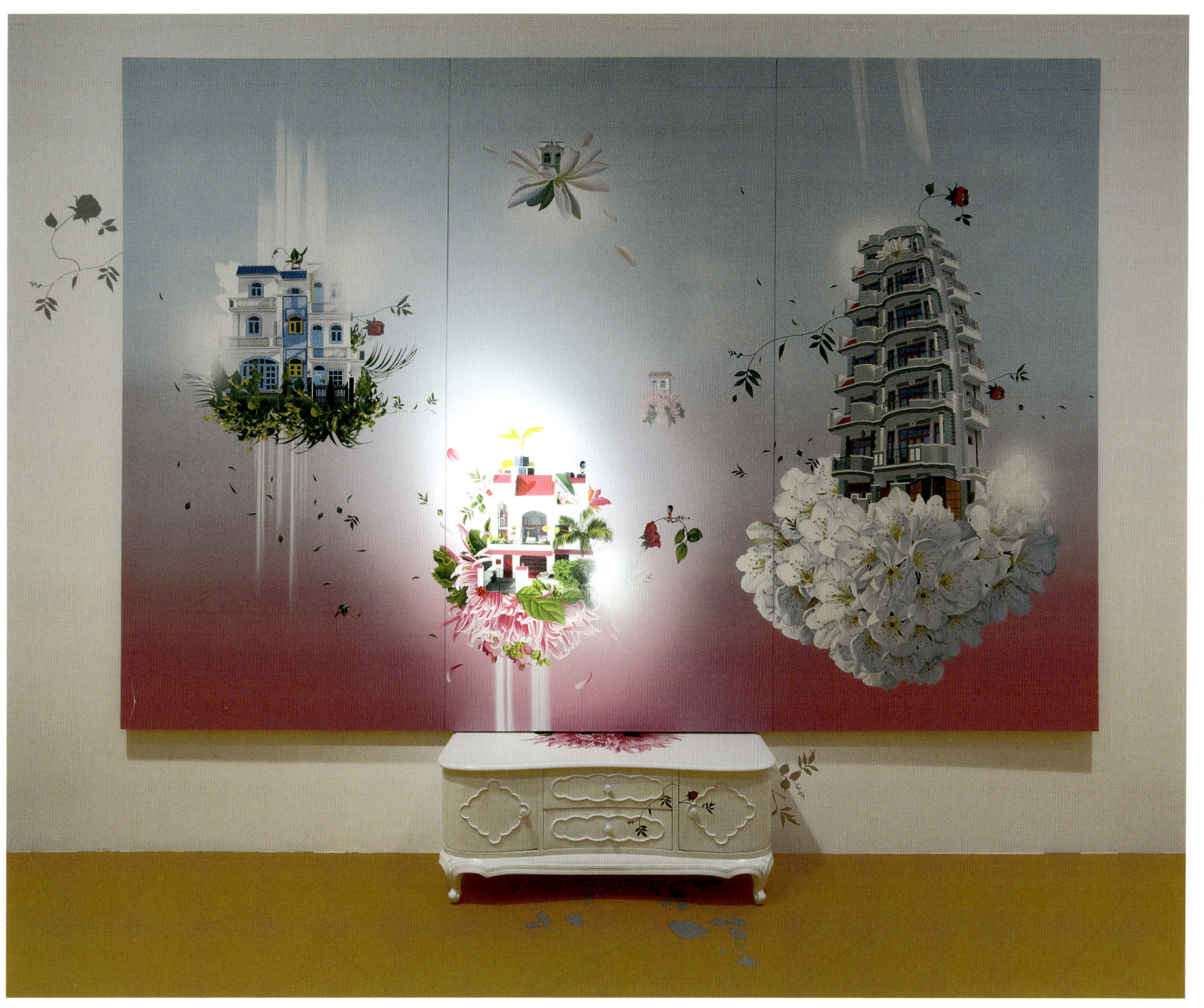

THUKRAL & TAGRA
Dominus Aerius-Elegance, 2008 (S./p. 234/235)

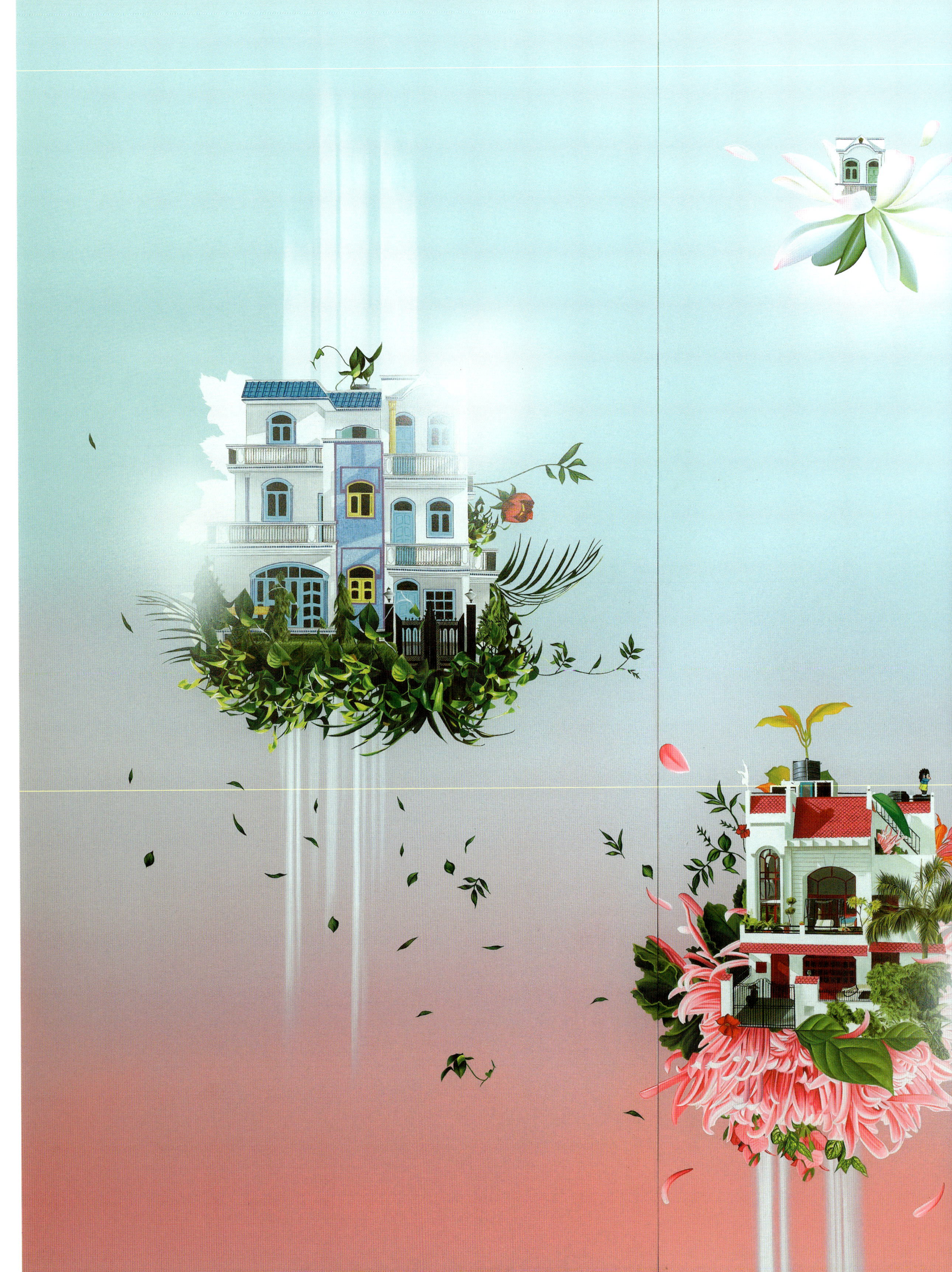

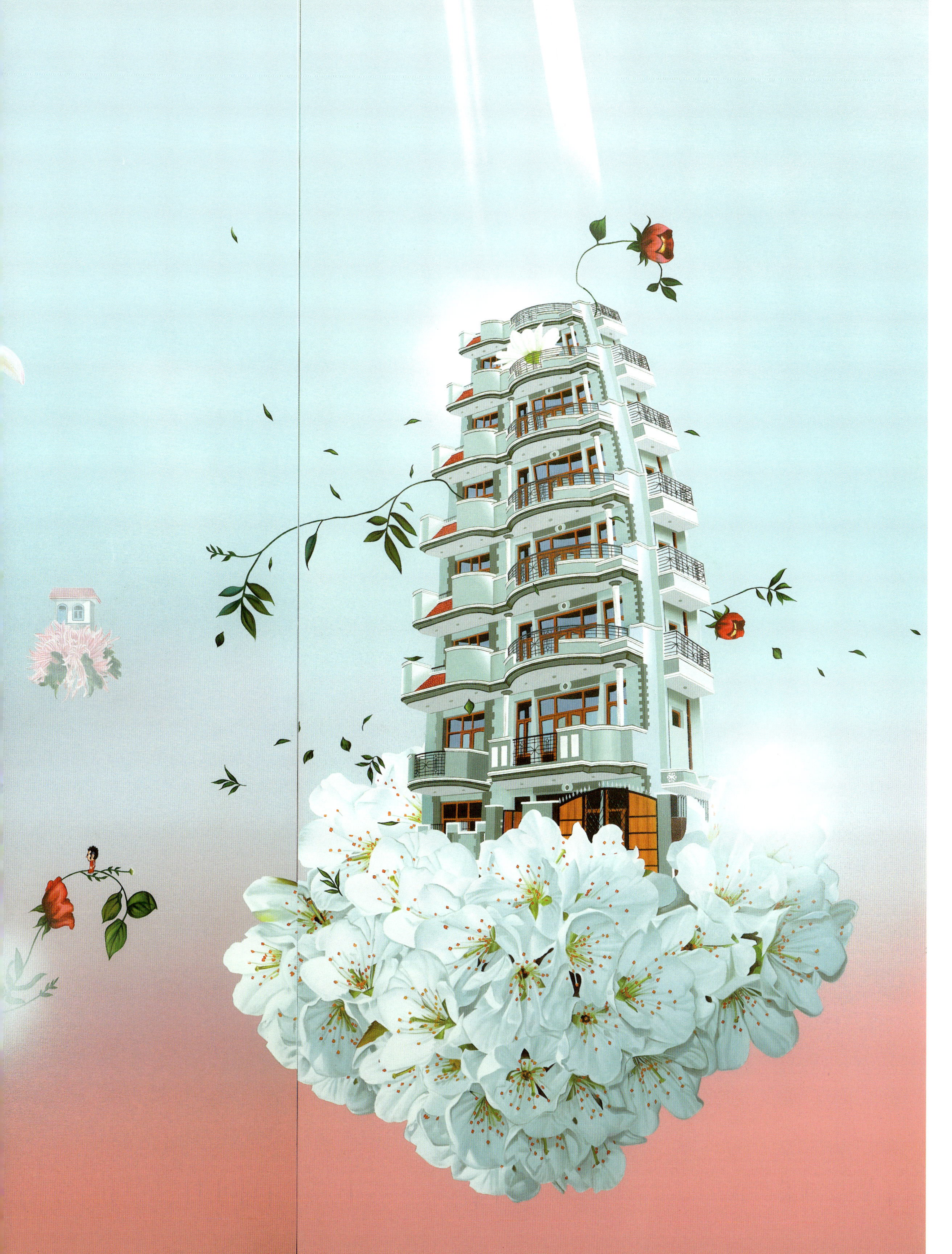

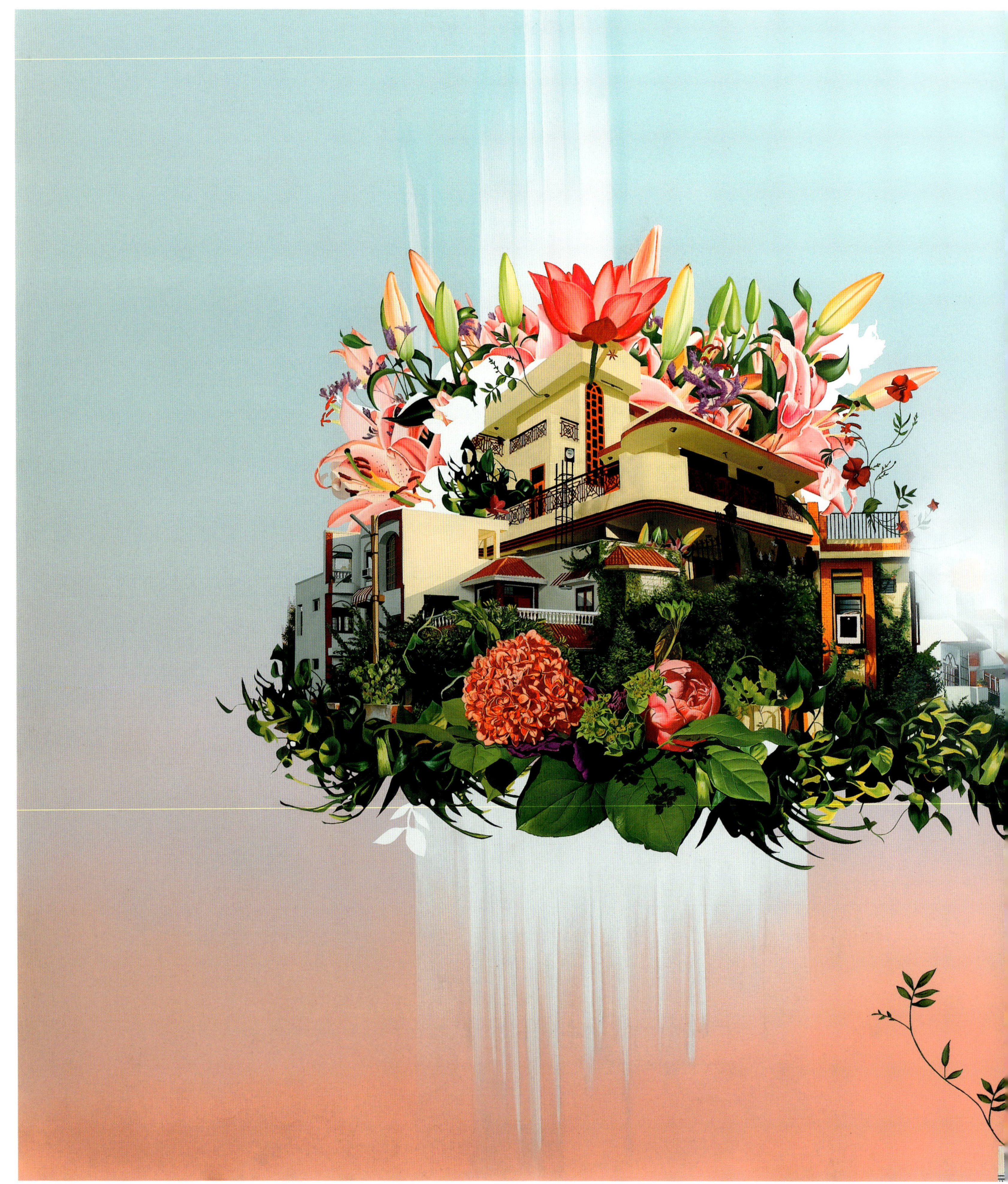

THUKRAL & TAGRA
Dominus Aerius #4, 2008

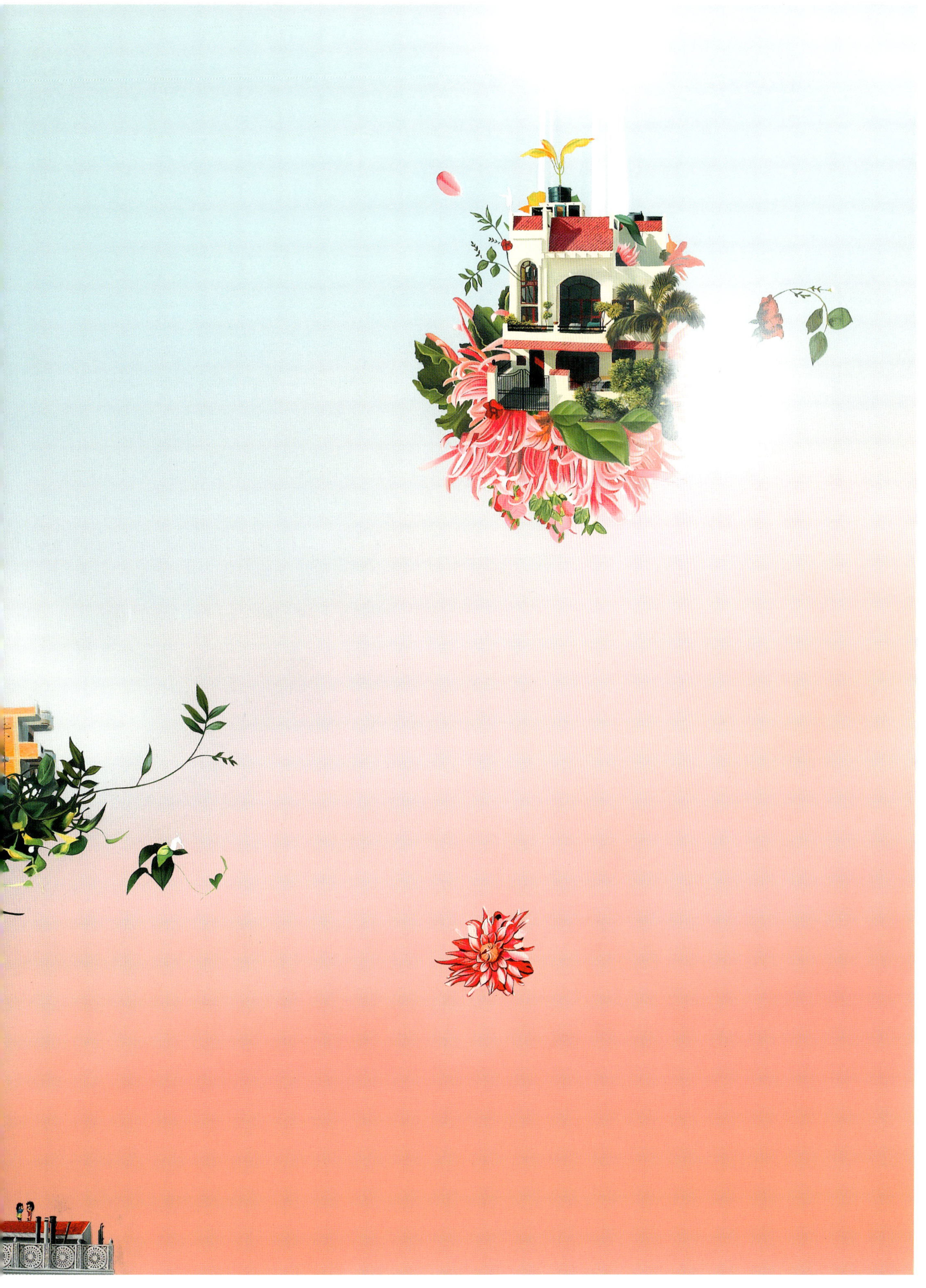

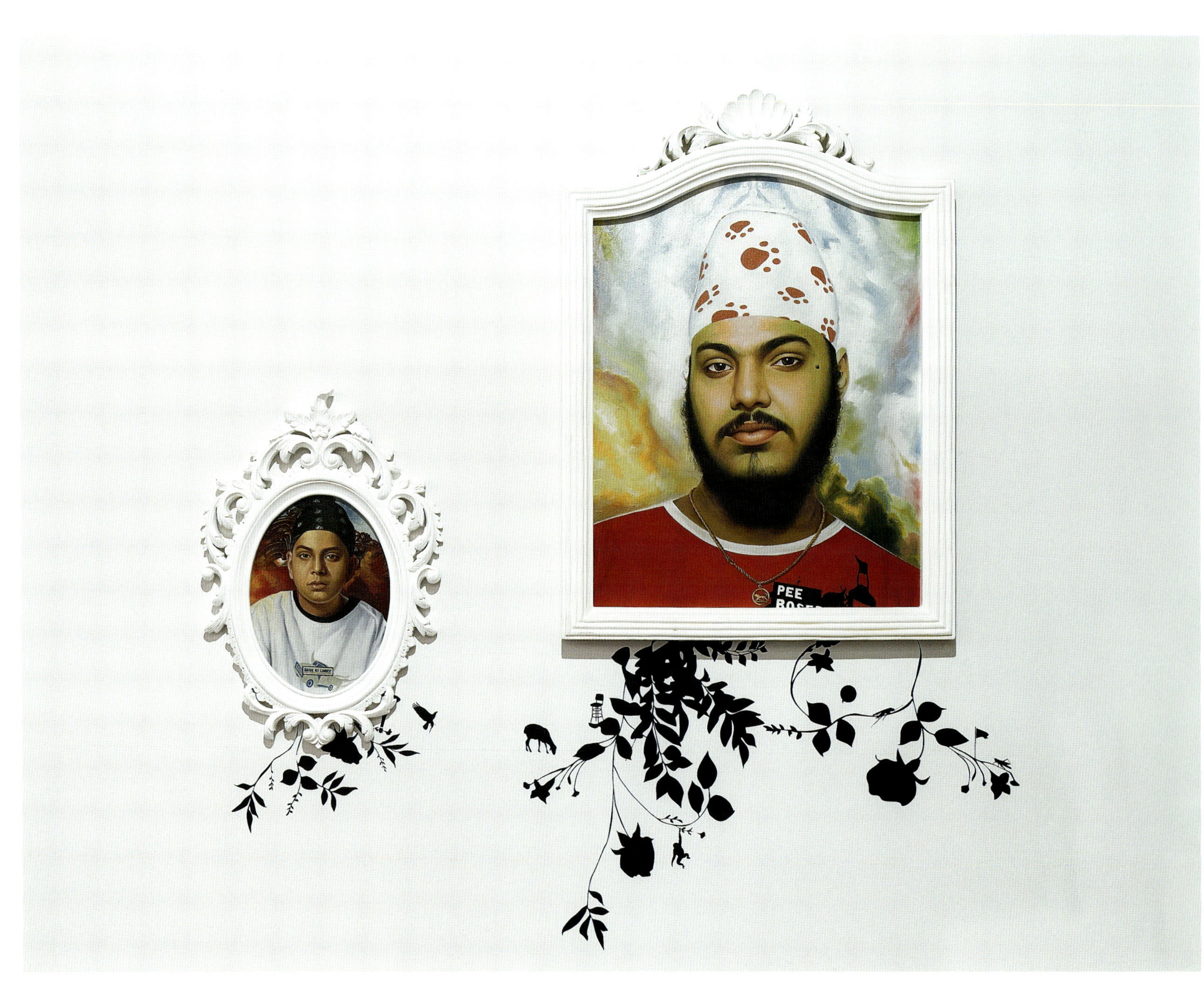

THUKRAL & TAGRA
Morpheus – 2, Morpheus – 3, 2007

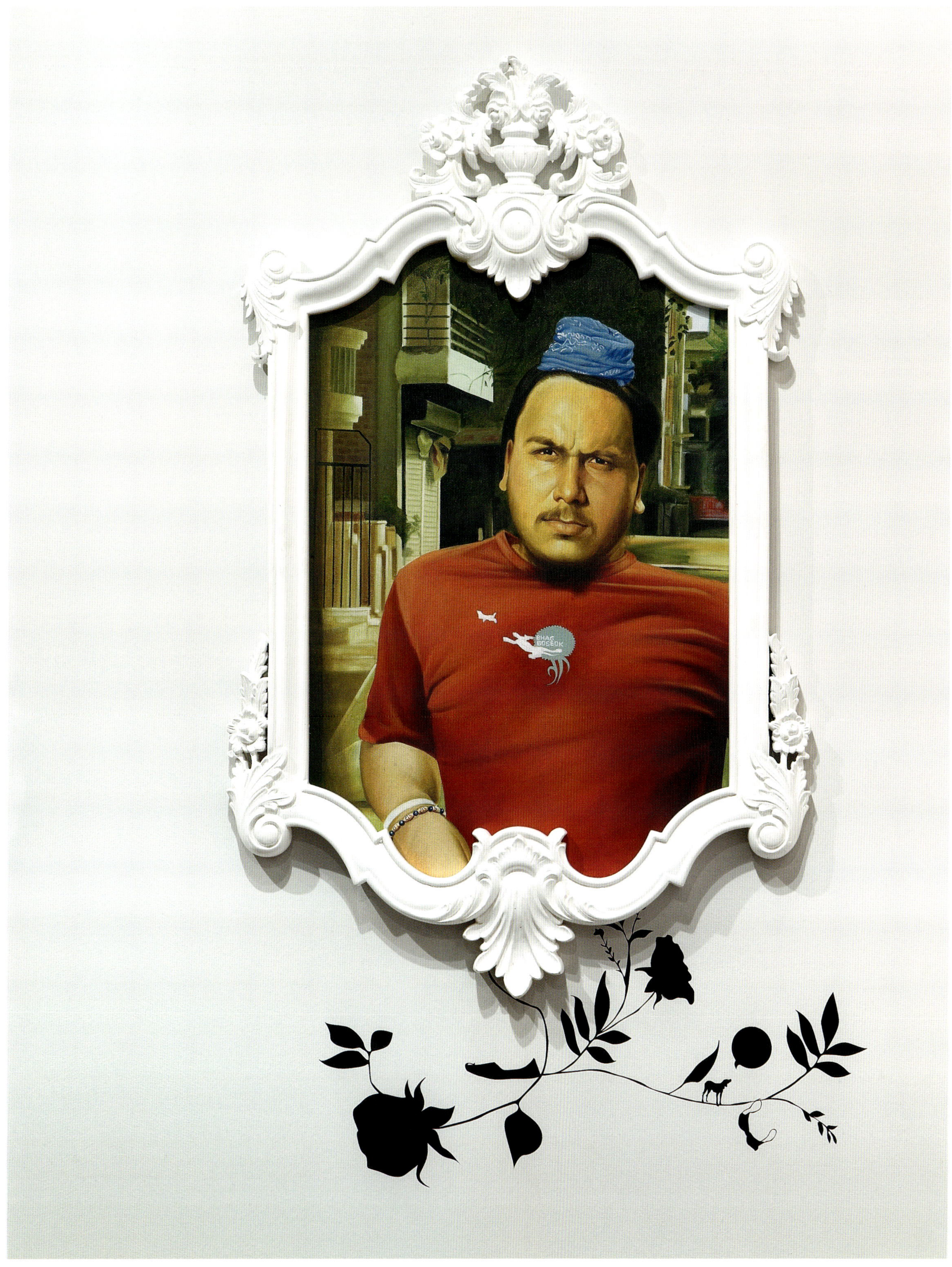

THUKRAL & TAGRA
Morpheus 1, 2007

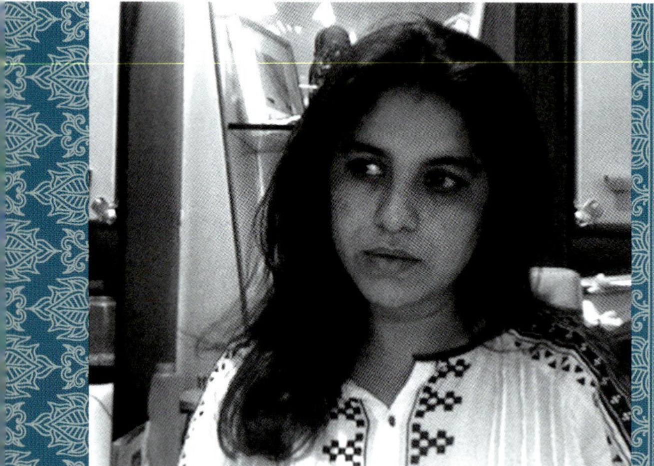

hema upadhyay

HEMA UPADHYAY Geboren 1972 in Vadodara / Lebt in Mumbai
Born 1972 in Vadodara / Lives in Mumbai

Upadhyay studierte Malerei an der Maharaja Sayajirao University of Baroda (Vadodara), wo sie 1997 ein Masterdiplom erwarb. Seither ist sie in Mumbai ansässig, was auch in ihren Arbeiten zum Ausdruck kommt. Seit dem Jahr 2000 malt Upadhyay Aquarelle, auf die sie aus Fotos ausgeschnittene Aufnahmen von sich selbst bei der Verrichtung unterschiedlicher Tätigkeiten klebt. Die Verknüpfung von Malerei und Fotografie macht diese winzigen „Porträts" inmitten einer Stadtlandschaft gleichzeitig zu sehr persönlichen Darstellungen von Ambitionen und Ängsten. Mit dieser Technik schuf Upadhyay 2005 eine Reihe von Arbeiten, deren Thema die immer wieder aufeinanderprallenden politischen und religiösen Auffassungen sind. In einem älteren Werk hat Upadhyay als Kommentar zu der Auseinandersetzung zwischen den Atommächten Indien und Pakistan 2000 Kakerlaken aus Aluminium geformt. In einer anderen Arbeit stellt sie ihren freiwilligen Umzug nach Mumbai dem durch deren Trennung erzwungenen Umzug ihrer Eltern gegenüber: Ausgedrückt wurde dies durch Buchstaben, die die Künstlerin nach der gezielten Aussaat von Fingerhirsesamen auf einem Hang gepflanzt hat. In den letzten Jahren hat Upadhyay eine neue Richtung eingeschlagen und konzentriert sich auf „Dharavi" – einen Stadtteil von Mumbai, der gleichzeitig als größter Slum ganz Asiens gilt.

In der Arbeit „Ladki Number One" (2001) glaubt man unzählige winzige Upadhyays zu sehen, wie sie eine Leiter erklettern, die schräg von einem Gebäudedach in den Himmel ragt. Einige Figuren scheinen immer wieder in Gefahr zu sein, ihren Halt zu verlieren, während andere, die beim Klettern Hilfe bekommen, fast wie spielende Kinder wirken. Die Arbeit ist auch ein Hinweis auf die Bemühungen der Mädchen, Erste zu sein, und sie überwinden Hindernisse, die ihnen durch die Zugehörigkeit einer Kaste, ihr Geschlecht und ihre Identität im äußerst konkurrenzbetonten Mumbai entgegengestellt werden. „Visitors 1972–98" (2001) zeigt eine Reihe von Bildern Upadhyays, wie sie auf einer Wolke liegt, zwischen Wolken nach unten auf die sich rasant entwickelnde Welt späht, oder einfach ihren Tagträumen hingegeben ist. Der Titel des Werks ist ein Hinweis auf den Entwicklungsprozess der Künstlerin von ihrer Geburt bis zu ihrem Studienabschluss,

Upadhyay studied painting at Maharaja Sayajirao University of Baroda (Vadodara), where she went on to obtain an MA in 1997. She has since been based in Mumbai, which also informs her work. Since 2000, Upadhyay has produced watercolours, onto which she pastes cut-outs from photographs of herself engaged in various activities. These tiny 'portraits' placed inside an urban landscape also represent personal landscapes of both aspiration and anxiety, depicted through the relationship between painting and photography. In 2005, Upadhyay created a series of works using this technique, the theme of which is the frequent confrontation between political and religious views. In one of her less recent works, Upadhyay used aluminium to meticulously create 2000 cockroaches as a comment on the struggle between the nuclear powers of India and Pakistan. Another work contrasts her voluntary move to Mumbai with the move forced onto her parents as a result of partition, expressed through words formed by planting ragi seeds on a slope so that they would grow in the shape of letters. In recent years, Upadhyay's work has taken a new direction and is focusing on "Dharavi" in Mumbai, the largest slum in Asia.

In *Ladki Number One* (2001), numerous tiny Upadhyays are climbing a ladder that rises up into the sky at an angle from the roof of a building. At times some of the figures almost lose their footing, while others are assisted in their climb and almost appear like children playing. The work also suggests the efforts of the girls to be Number One by overcoming issues of caste, gender, and identity in heavily competitive Mumbai. *Visitors 1972–98* (2001) features a series of images of Upadhyay – lying on a cloud and peering down, between the clouds, at the rapidly developing world below, or simply facing up or down, daydreaming. The title of the work suggests the process from the artist's birth through to her graduation, but the many Upadhyays could also be remembering their lives before their move to Mumbai. *Mute Migration* (2008) is Upadhyay's latest work in her ongoing slum series that she embarked on in 2004, and features materials that are the same as the garbage collected at Dharavi. The work consists of five panels filled with images of numerous aluminium houses in bright colours. High-rise buildings

aber die vielen Upadhyays könnten sich ebenso gut auf ihr Leben vor dem Umzug nach Mumbai beziehen. „Mute Migration“ (2008) ist Upadhyays jüngste Arbeit in ihrer laufenden Slum-Serie, die sie 2004 in Angriff nahm und in der sie mit Materialien arbeitet, die in Dharavi als Abfall gesammelt werden. Die Arbeit besteht aus fünf Platten, bedeckt mit den Abbildungen zahlreicher grellbunter Aluminiumhäuser. Dazwischen verstreut sind Hochhäuser, quasi als greifbarer Beweis, dass die Entwicklung selbst an diesen Ort, der das Symbol städtischer Armut schlechthin ist, vordringt.

Wichtige Ausstellungen: „The 3rd Fukuoka Asian Art Triennale“ (Fukuoka Asian Art Museum, 2005, „Mumbai: Maximum City“ (Lille 3000) (Le Tri Postal, Lille, France 2006) und „Eurasia“ (Museo di Arte Moderna e Contemporanea di Trento e Rovereto [MART], Rovereto, Italia, 2008) (TK)

are scattered among the houses as if to demonstrate the reality that development is even encroaching on this place, the symbol of urban poverty.

Major exhibitions include “The 3rd Fukuoka Asian Art Triennale” (Fukuoka Asian Art Museum, 2005), and “Mumbai: Maximum City (Lille 3000)” (Le Tri Postal, Lille, France 2006), and “Eurasia” (Museo di Arte Moderna e Contemporanea di Trento e Rovereto [MART], Rovereto, Italia, 2008) (TK)

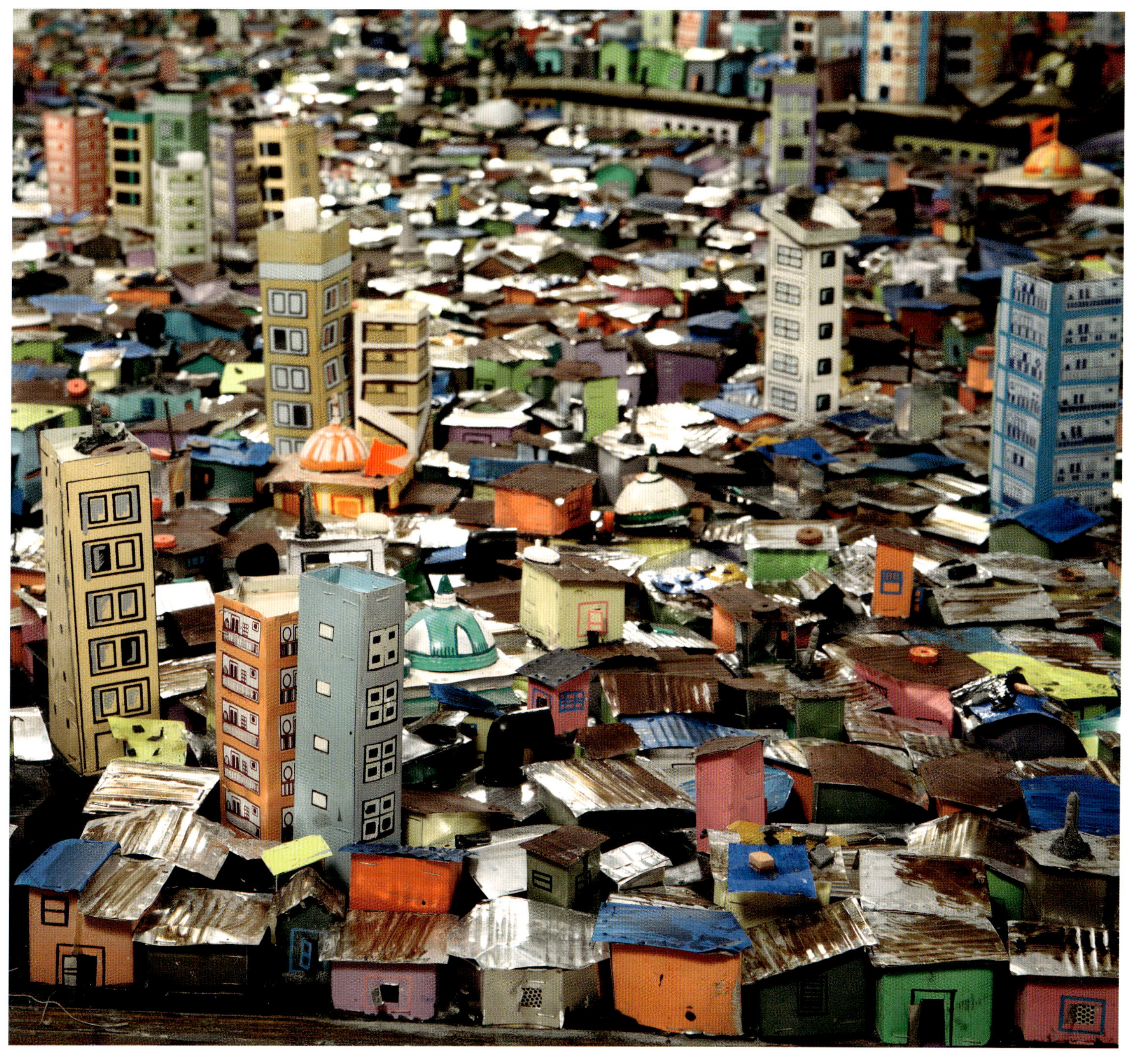

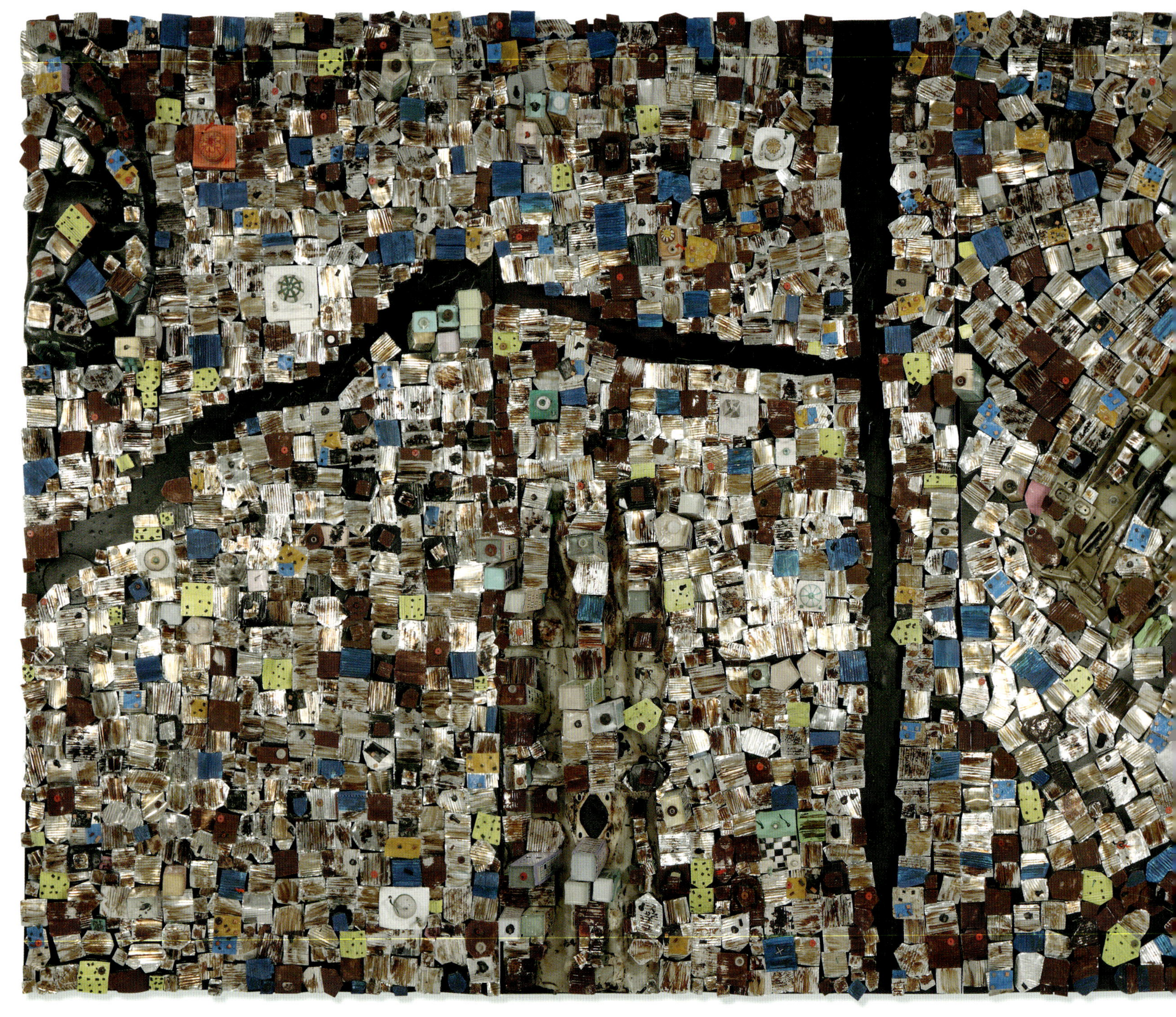

HEMA UPADHYAY
Mute Migration, 2008 (Detail S./p. 241)

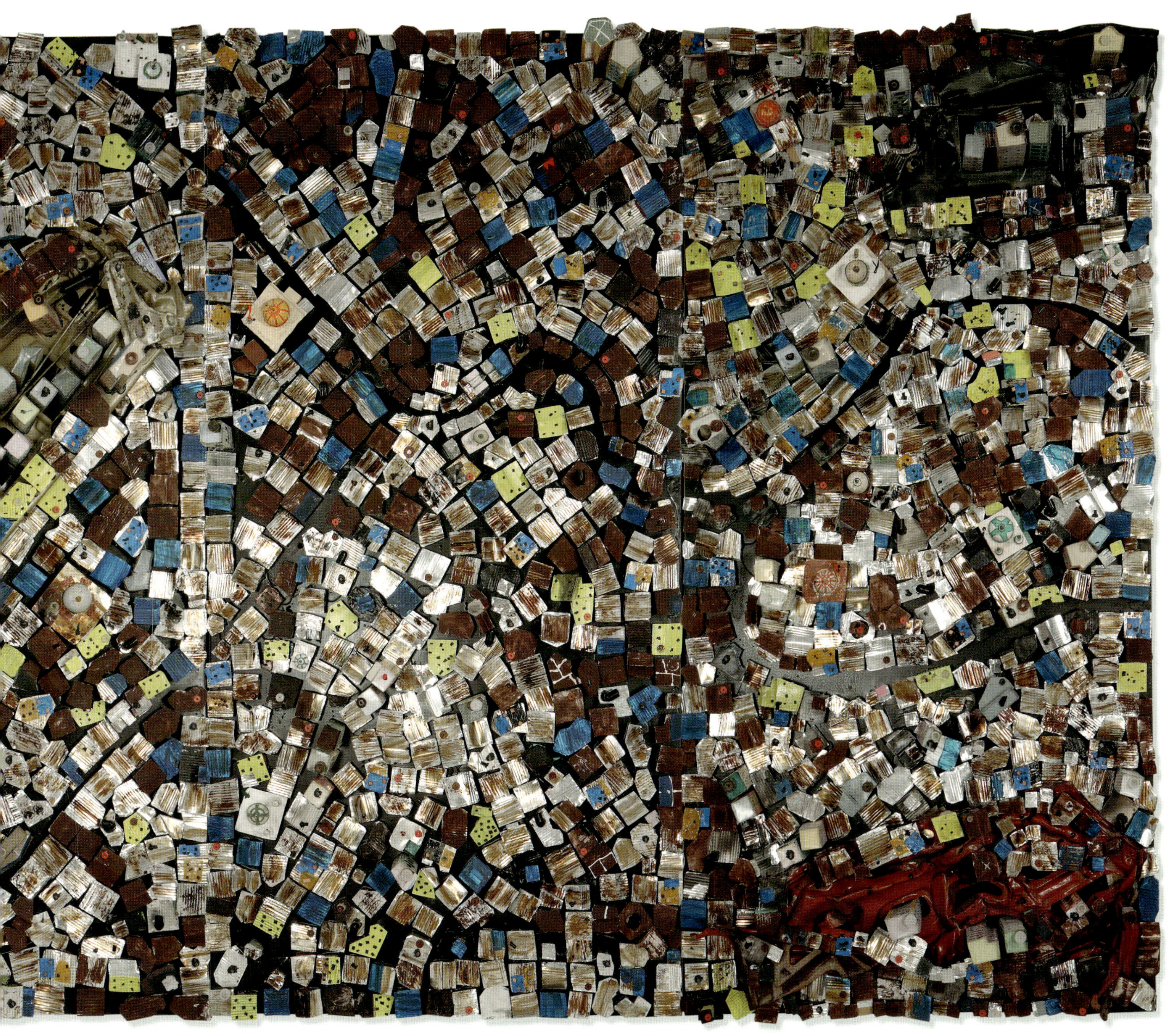

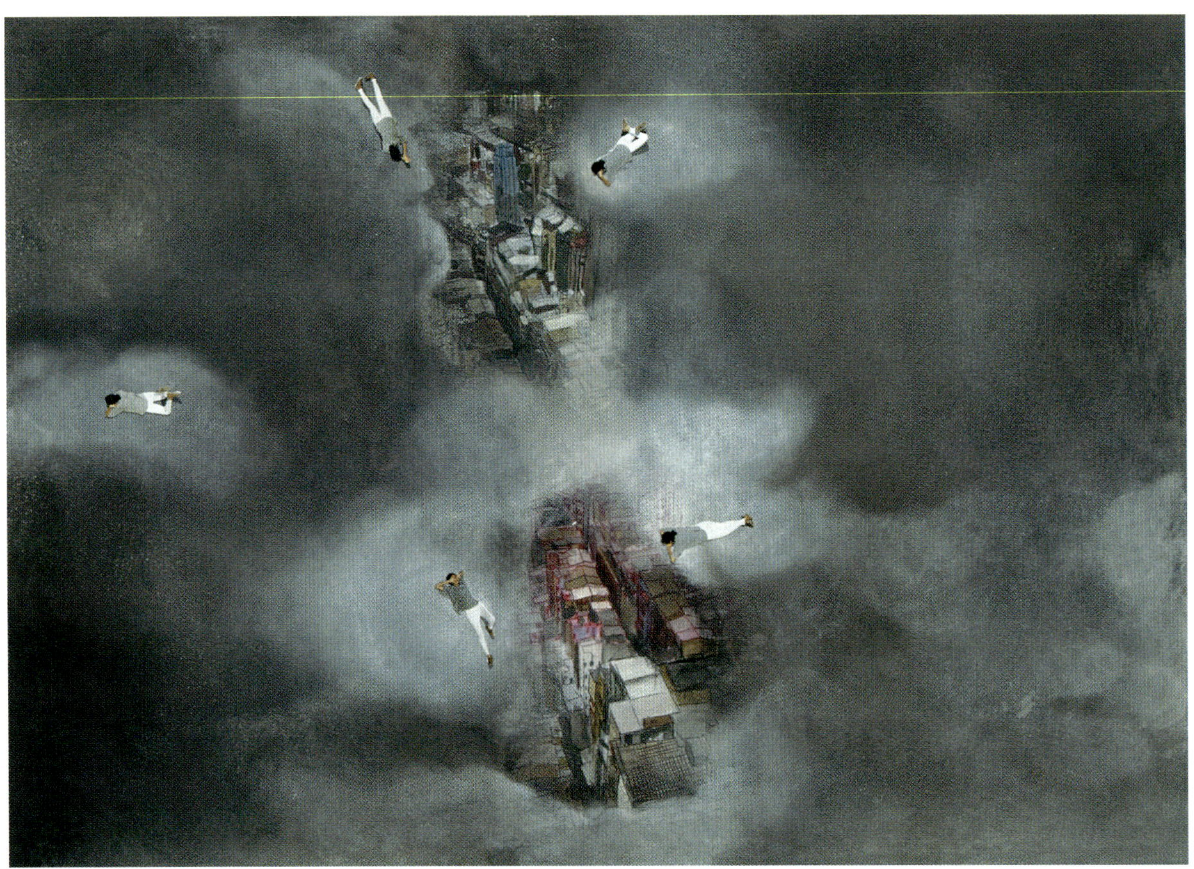

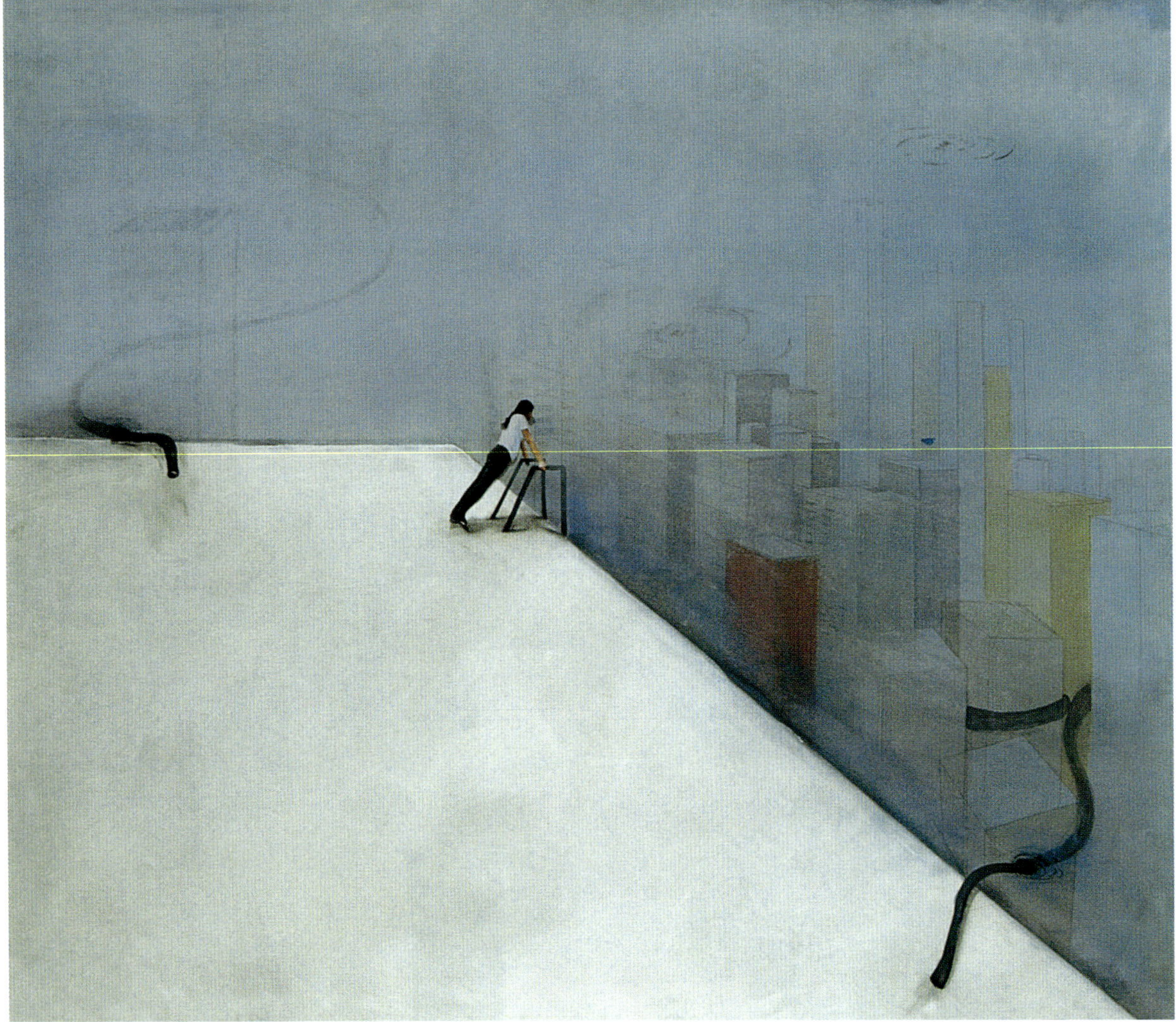

HEMA UPADHYAY
Visitors, 1972 Until 1998, 2001
I Have a Feeling That I Belong, 2000

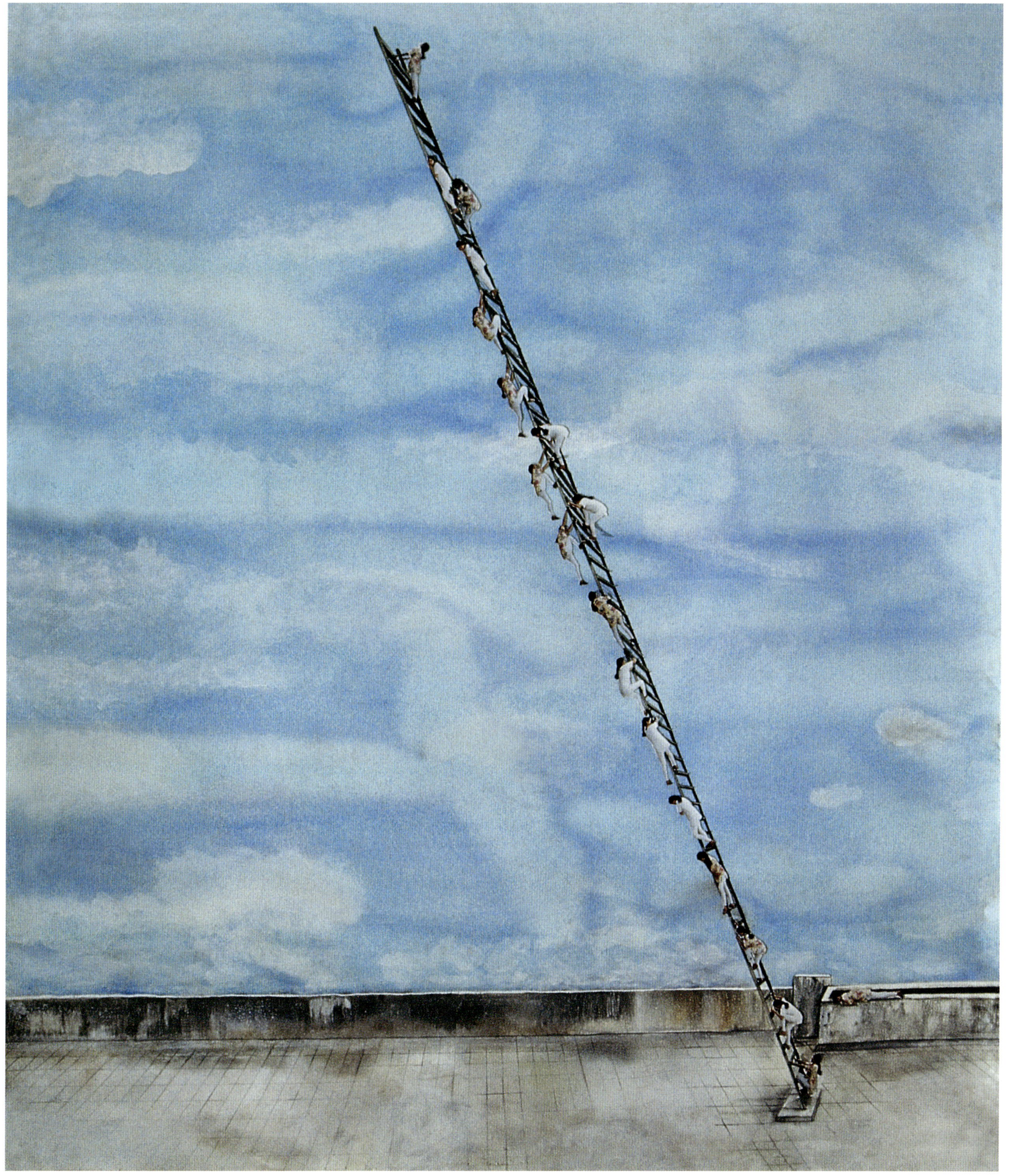

HEMA UPADHYAY
Ladki Number One, 2001

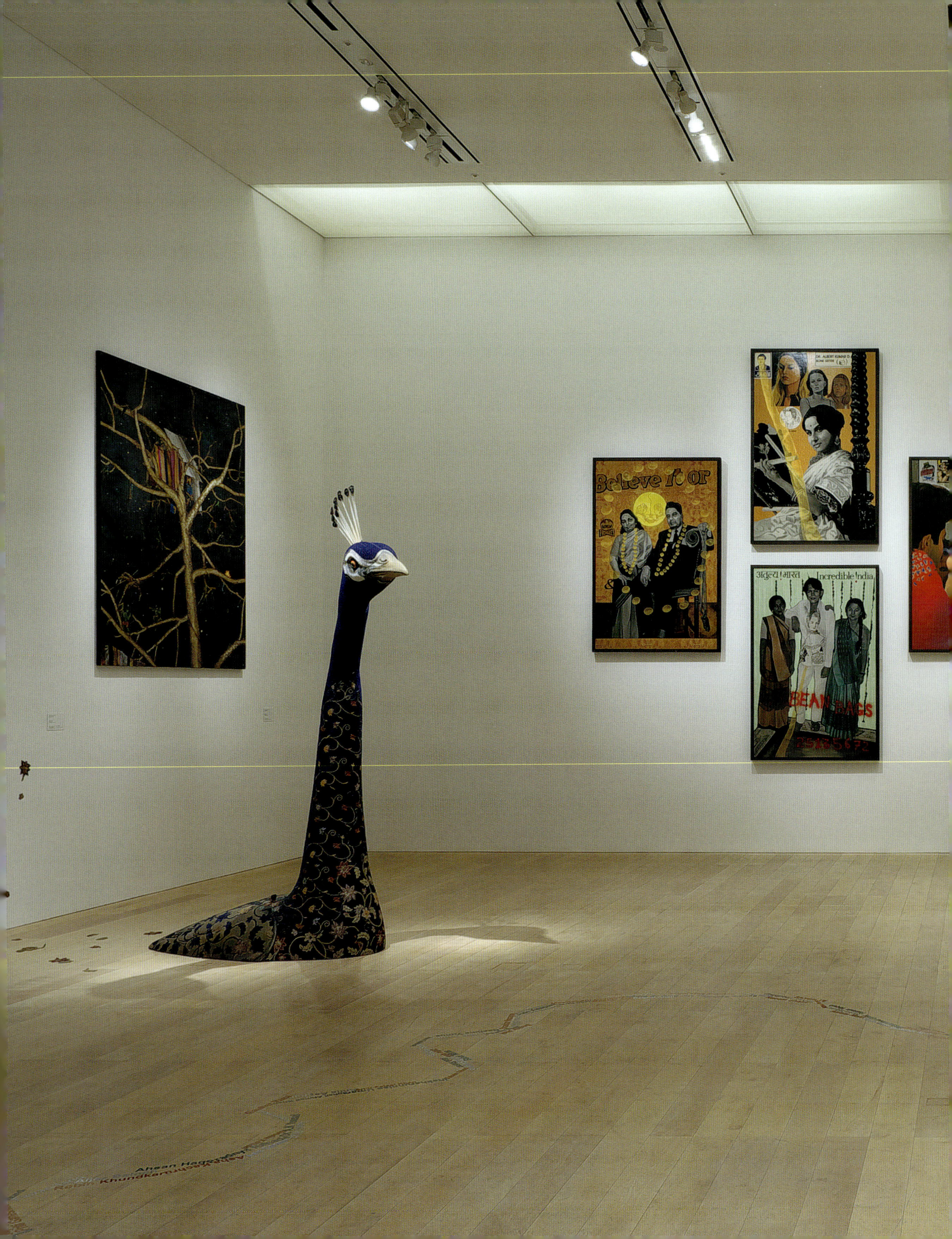
Believe it or
Incredible India
BEAN BAGS

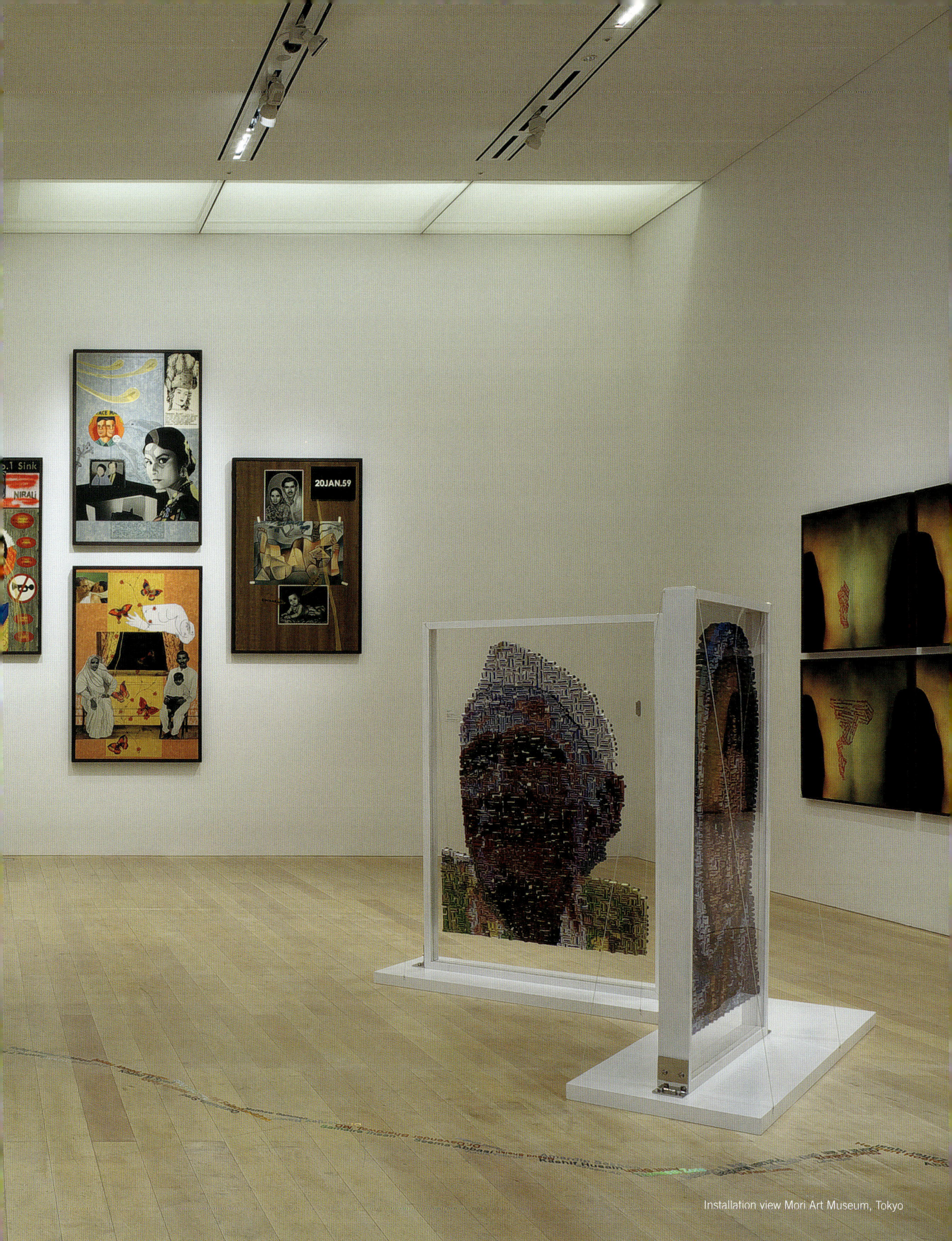

Installation view Mori Art Museum, Tokyo

CHRONOLOGISCHER ÜBERBLICK I CHRONOLOGY

ANMERKUNGEN

- Diese Chronologie versteht sich als Zusatzinformation für ein besseres Verständnis der zeitgenössischen indischen Kunst. Es handelt sich um eine Zusammenfassung der indischen Geschichte seit der Unabhängigkeit. In kunstgeschichtlicher Hinsicht liegt der Schwerpunkt auf Strömungen seit den 1990er Jahren.
- In der folgenden Aufstellung sind nur internationale Ausstellungen erwähnt, wie beispielsweise Biennalen oder große Einzelausstellungen und Projekte von großer historischer Bedeutung für die indische Kunstgeschichte.
- Der Abschnitt über die indische Kunstgeschichte enthält teilweise auch Angaben über Literatur und Film.

Redaktionelle Verantwortung: Ashizawa Issei (allgemeine Geschichte Indiens) und Nancy Adajania (indische Kunstgeschichte)

[NOTES]

- This timeline is meant to serve as reference material for analyzing the current state of Indian art. It is a summary of India's history since independence. With regard to art history, it places particular emphasis on movements from the 1990s and onward.
- The exhibitions noted in this timeline are limited to international exhibitions like the Biennale, large-scale solo shows, and projects that have major historical significance within the scope of India's art history.
- The section on India's art history partially includes items relating to literature and film.

Editorial Supervision: Ashizawa Issei (India's General History) and Nancy Adajania (Indian Art History)

	ZUSAMMENFASSUNG DER ALLGEMEINEN GESCHICHTE INDIENS	AN OUTLINE OF INDIAN GENERAL HISTORY	KURZER ABRISS DER INDISCHEN KUNSTGESCHICHTE	AN OUTLINE OF INDIAN ART HISTORY
1947	Indien und Pakistan werden in zwei unabhängige Länder aufgeteilt. Jawaharlal Nehru von der Kongress-Partei wird Indiens erster Premierminister und hat dieses Amt bis 1964 inne. Pakistans Invasion in Kaschmir löst den ersten Konflikt zwischen Indien und Pakistan aus (1947–49).	India and Pakistan are partitioned into two independent countries. Jawaharlal Nehru of the Congress Party becomes India's first Prime Minister; to serve until 1964. Pakistan invades Kashmir, beginning the 1st Indo-Pakistani conflict (1947–49).	Binode Behari Mukherjee vollendet sein 30 Meter langes Fresko „Hindi-Heilige im Mittelalter" an den Wänden des Hindi Bhavan in der Tagore Vishwa Bharti Universität in Santiniketan, Bengal. Die Progressive Artists Group (PAG) entsteht in Mumbai und übt großen Einfluss auf die Entwicklung der modernen Kunst aus (Mitglieder: F. N. Souza, M. F. Husain, S. H. Raza, K. H. Ara, H. A. Gade, S. K. Bakre).	A hundred-foot-long fresco 'Medieval Hindi Saints' is completed by Binode Behari Mukherjee in Hindi Bhavan, in Tagore's Vishwa Bharti University, at Santiniketan, Bengal. Progressive Artists Group (PAG) is formed in Mumbai, becoming influential in the formation of modernist art (Members: F. N. Souza, M. F. Husain, S. H. Raza, K. H. Ara, H. A. Gade, S. K. Bakre).
1948	Mahatma Gandhi wird ermordet. Chakravarthi Rajagopalachari folgt Lord Mountbatten als Generalgouverneur von Indien nach.	Mahatma Gandhi is assassinated. Chakravarthi Rajagopalachari succeeds Lord Mountbatten as Governor-General of India.		
1949	Die Vermittlung der Vereinten Nationen führt zu einem Waffenstillstand zwischen Indien und Pakistan. Aufnahme der diplomatischen Beziehungen zwischen Österreich und Indien.	The United Nations' mediation led to a ceasefire between India and Pakistan. Begin of Diplomatic Relations between India and Austria.	Die ursprünglichen Mitglieder der PAG – Souza und Raza – reisen nach London und Paris. Ram Kumar besucht im Jahr 1949 Paris, Akbar Padamsee im Jahr 1951. Gründung der Fakultät für bildende Künste an der Maharaja Sayajirao Universität in Baroda. Eröffnung des Indischen Rates für Kulturelle Beziehungen (Indian Council for Cultural Relations (ICCR).	The original members of the PAG – Souza and Raza – travel to London and Paris. Ram Kumar also travels to Paris in 1949 and Akbar Padamsee in 1951. Constitution of Faculty of Fine Arts at the Maharaja Sayajirao University of Baroda. Inauguration of the Indian Council for Cultural Relations (ICCR).
1950	Indiens Verfassung wird verabschiedet. Rajendra Prasad wird erster Präsident Indiens. All India Radio (AIR) nimmt den Sendebetrieb auf.	The Constitution of India is promulgated. Rajendra Prasad becomes the first President of India. All India Radio (AIR) transmits its first broadcast.	Die Jehangir Art Gallery (JAG) eröffnet in Mumbai.	Jehangir Art Gallery (JAG) opens in Mumbai.
1951	Indien stellt mit Verabschiedung eines ersten Fünfjahresplanes auf Planwirtschaft um. Das Indian Institute of Technology wird in Kharagpur errichtet.	India transitions to a planned economy with the launch of its 1st Five-Year Plan. The Indian Institute of Technology is established in Kharagpur.		
1952	Japan und Indien nehmen diplomatische Beziehungen auf. Die Kongress-Partei feiert einen überwältigenden Sieg bei Indiens ersten allgemeinen Wahlen, die 1951–52 abgehalten werden.	Japan and India establish diplomatic relations. The Congress Party wins an overwhelming victory in India's 1st general election, held 1951–52.		

1954	Premierminister Nehru und der chinesische Premier Tschu Enlai treffen zu Gesprächen zusammen und beschließen die fünf Prinzipien der friedlichen Koexistenz (Pancha Sila). Frankreich übergibt die Verwaltung von Puducherry (früher Pondicherry) an Indien.	Prime Minister Nehru and Chinese Premier Zhou Enlai hold talks and announce the Five Principles of Peaceful Co-existence (Pancha Sila). France restores administration of Puducherry (Pondicherry) to India.	Die indische Regierung richtet die Nationalgalerie für Moderne Kunst (National Gallery of Modern Art, (NGMA), in Delhi ein. Die Lalit Kala Akademi (LKA), ein zentralisierter Arts Council, wird auf persönliche Initiative Nehrus ins Leben gerufen.	The Government of India establishes the National Gallery of Modern Art, (NGMA), Delhi. Lalit Kala Akademi (LKA), a centralized arts council, is also instituted on the personal initiative of Nehru.
1955	Premierminister Nehru, der chinesische Premier Tschu, Präsident Sukarno von Indonesien und der ägyptische Präsident Gamal Abdel Nasser spielen eine zentrale Rolle bei der Abhaltung der ersten asiatisch-afrikanischen Konferenz in Bandung, mit der die „Bewegung der Blockfreien Staaten" vorbereitet wird.	Prime Minister Nehru, Chinese Premier Zhou, President Sukarno of Indonesia, and President Gamal Abdel Nasser of Egypt play central roles in holding the first Asian-African Conference in Bandung, initiating the Non-Aligned Movement.	Erste „nationale Kunstausstellung" an der LKA, Delhi.	"First National Exhibition of Art," LKA, Delhi.
1956	Mit der Resolution zur Industriepolitik betritt Indien den Weg zum Sozialismus. Unter der Führung von B. R. Ambedkar konvertieren 300.000 unberührbare Hindus in einer Massenzeremonie zum Buddhismus. Der States Reorganization Act verfügt eine Neuordnung der indischen Bundesstaaten auf Grundlage von Sprachgrenzen.	The Industrial Policy Resolution puts India on a path towards socialism. Led by B. R. Ambedkar, 300,000 Hindu untouchables undergo mass conversion to Buddhism. The States Reorganization Act reorganizes India's states based on linguistic boundaries.	Satyajit Rays erster Spielfilm „Pather Panchali" (1955) gewinnt beim Filmfestival in Cannes 1956 einen Preis als „bestes menschliches Dokument".	Satyajit Ray's debut feature *Pather Panchali* (1955) wins the Best Human Document Award, at the 1956 Cannes Film Festival.
1957	Japan und Indien beschließen ein Kulturabkommen.	Japan and India conclude their Cultural Agreement.	Satyajit Rays nächster Film (der zweite Teil der „Apu Trilogy") „Aparajito" (1956) gewinnt den goldenen Löwen beim Filmfestival von Venedig.	Satyajit Ray's following film (the second of *Apu Trilogy),* Aparajito (1956) wins the Golden Lion at Venice Film Festival.
1959	Ein Aufstand in Tibet veranlasst den 14. Dalai Lama nach Indien zu flüchten. 14.000 tibetanische Flüchtlinge folgen ihm ins Exil.	An uprising in Tibet prompts the 14th Dalai Lama to seek refuge in India. 14,000 Tibetan refugees follow him into exile.		
1960			Das Nationalmuseum in Delhi wird eröffnet. Von den 1960ern bis in die 1970er Jahre erhalten viele indische Künstler (V. S. Gaitonde, Akbar Padamsee, Krishen Khanna, K. G. Subramanyan, u.v.a.) Stipendien aus dem Rockefeller Fund.	National Museum opens in Delhi. From the 1960s to the 1970s, many Indian artists (V. S. Gaitonde, Akbar Padamsee, Krishen Khanna, K. G. Subramanyan, among others) receive the Rockefeller Fund Fellowship.
1961	Indien erhebt mit Militärgewalt Anspruch auf die portugiesisch kontrollierten Territorien Goa, Daman und Diu.	India reclaims the Portuguese-held territories of Goa, Daman, and Diu by military force.		
1963	Gründung des ersten Österreich-Indien Vereins.	Founding of the first Austrian-Indian Association	Die „Group 1890", eine Künstlergruppe zu der u. a. J. Swaminathan, Jeram Patel, Ambadas, Himmat Shah, Gulammohammed Sheikh und Jyoti Bhatt gehören, gibt ihr anarchistisches Manifest bekannt.	Group 1890, a formation that included J. Swaminathan, Jeram Patel, Ambadas, Himmat Shah, Gulammohammed Sheikh, Jyoti Bhatt and others, announced its anarchist manifesto.
1964	Tod von Premierminister Nehru.	Prime Minister Nehru dies.		
1965	Grenzstreitigkeiten in Kaschmir lösen den zweiten Konflikt zwischen Indien und Pakistan aus (1965–66).	A dispute over the Kashmir border sets off the 2nd Indo-Pakistani conflict (1965–66).		
1966	Die Erklärung von Taschkent beendet den indisch-pakistanischen Krieg von 1965. Indira Priyadarshini Gandhi, die Tochter von Jawaharlal Nehru, wird Premierministerin.	The Tashkent Declaration concludes the Indo-Pakistani War of 1965. Indira Priyadarshini Gandhi, daughter of Jawaharlal Nehru, becomes Prime Minister.	Der Künstler und Lehrer K. C. S. Paniker eröffnet ein Künstlerdorf in Cholamandal, in der Nähe von Chennai.	Artist-teacher K. C. S. Paniker establishes an artists' village complex in Cholamandal, near Chennai.
1968	Die Beatles besuchen Indien und treffen mit Maharishi Mahesh Yogi zusammen.	The Beatles visit India and meet with Maharishi Mahesh Yogi.	Die LKA eröffnet die „Triennale-India", eine der frühesten internationalen Kunstinitiativen eines asiatischen Landes.	The LKA inaugurates "Triennale-India," one of the earliest Asian art initiatives in international art.
1969	Die Kongress-Partei spaltet sich in zwei Gruppen.	The Congress Party splits into two factions.	Die Künstler Gulammohammed Sheikh und Bhupen Khakhar geben das Magazin „Vrishchik" heraus.	The artists Gulammohammed Sheikh and Bhupen Khakhar begin to edit the magazine *Vrishchik.*
1970	Ein Zyklon in Ostpakistan (jetzt Bangladesh) fordert hunderttausende Menschenleben.	A cyclone in East Pakistan (now Bangladesh) results in hundreds of thousands of deaths.		
1971	Der Abschluss des indisch-sowjetischen Vertrags für Freundschaft, Zusammenarbeit und Frieden bereitet den Weg zu freundlichen bilateralen Beziehungen mit der Sowjetunion. Indien interveniert in einer Unabhängigkeitsbewegung in Ostpakistan und löst damit den dritten Konflikt zwischen Indien und Pakistan aus (1971–72). Ostpakistan wird zum unabhängigen Bangladesh.	The Indo-Soviet Treaty of Friendship, Cooperation, and Peace is concluded, clarifying a path for friendly bilateral relations with the Soviet Union. India intervenes in an independence movement in East Pakistan, igniting the 3rd Indo-Pakistani conflict (1971–72). East Pakistan becomes independent Bangladesh.	Die 2. „Triennale-India", LKA, Delhi V. S. Naipaul gewinnt als erster gebürtiger Inder den Booker-Preis für sein Buch „In a Free State" (dt. „Sag mir, wer mein Feind ist").	"The 2nd Triennale-India," LKA, Delhi V. S. Naipaul, as the first person of Indian origin, wins a Booker Prize for his book *In a Free State.*
1972	Der dritte indisch-pakistanische Konflikt wird beendet; Indien und Pakistan unterzeichnen das Abkommen von Simla.	The 3rd Indo-Pakistani conflict comes to an end, and India and Pakistan sign the Simla Agreement.	„25 Jahre indische Kunst", LKA, Delhi	"25 years of Indian Art," LKA, Delhi

1973			Satyajit Rays Film „Ashani Sanket“ (1955) gewinnt den „Goldenen Bären“ bei den Internationalen Filmfestspielen Berlin.	Satyajit Ray's *Ashani Sanket* (1955) wins Golden Bear at the Berlin International Film Festival.
1974	Indien führt erfolgreiche unterirdische Atomtests durch und wird damit zur sechsten Nuklearmacht der Welt.	India successfully carries out an underground nuclear test, making it the world's 6th nuclear power.		
1975	Indien startet seinen ersten Satellit. Indira Gandhi beginnt ein autoritäres Regime, das bis 1977 dauern sollte.	India launches its first satellite. Indira Gandhi begins a period of authoritarian rule that is to last until 1977.	3. „Triennale-India“	"The 3rd Triennale-India"
1976	Indien und Pakistan nehmen erneut diplomatische Beziehungen auf, und die Zugverbindung zwischen den beiden Ländern wird wiederhergestellt.	India and Pakistan re-establish diplomatic relations, and a train between the two countries resumes running.	Die Jehangir Nicholson Gallery of Modern Art am NCPA in Mumbai zeigt ihre erste Ausstellung. Vivan Sundaram gründet das Kasauli Art Centre für internationale Kunstworkshops und Seminare.	Jehangir Nicholson Gallery of Modern Art at NCPA, Mumbai, inaugurates its first exhibition. Vivan Sundaram founds the Kasauli Art Centre for international artists' workshops and seminars to be held.
1977	Die herrschende Kongress-Partei erleidet bei den allgemeinen Wahlen eine schwere Niederlage. Die Janata-Partei, eine Koalition von Oppositionsparteien, errichtet eine neue Regierung, die bis 1980 im Amt bleibt.	The ruling Congress Party suffers a resounding defeat in general elections. The Janata Party, a coalition of opposition parties, establishes a new government to last until 1980.		
1978			4. „Triennale-India“ Geeta Kapur veröffentlicht die Publikation „Contemporary Indian Artists: M. F. Husain, Bhupen Khakhar, Akbar Padamsee, F. N. Souza, Ram Kumar and J. Swaminathan“.	"The 4th Triennale-India" Publication of *Contemporary Indian Artists: M. F. Husain, Bhupen Khakhar, Akbar Padamsee, F. N. Souza, Ram Kumar and J. Swaminathan* by Geeta Kapur.
1979	Die Börse in Mumbai (jetzt unter dem Namen Bombay Stock Exchange Limited bekannt) führt am 1. April 1979 den Sensex Index mit einem Basiswert von 100 ein. Mutter Teresa erhält den Friedensnobelpreis.	The Stock Exchange, Mumbai (now the Bombay Stock Exchange Limited) starts using Sensex index with a base value of 100 on April 1, 1979. Mother Teresa receives the Nobel Peace Prize.	Die Ausstellung „Modern Asian Art: India, China and Japan“, findet im Fukuoka Art Museum in Japan statt (als erste einer Serie mit dem Namen „Asian Art Show“, dem Vorläufer der „Fukuoka Asian Art Triennale“).	The exhibition "Modern Asian Art: India, China and Japan," takes place at Fukuoka Art Museum, Japan (as a part of the first of its series called "Asian Art Show" which is the precursor of "Fukuoka Asian Art Triennale").
1980	Die Kongress-Partei kehrt an die Macht zurück, und Indira Gandhi wird noch einmal Premierministerin.	The Congress Party returns to power, and Indira Gandhi once again becomes the Prime Minister.		
1981	Eine Devisenkrise zwingt Indien, einen Kredit über 5 Milliarden Sonderziehungsrechte (SDR) vom Internationalen Währungsfonds aufzunehmen.	A foreign currency crisis compels India to borrow 5 billion SDRs from the International Monetary Fund (IMF).	Eine Gruppe von sechs Künstlern (Bhupen Khakhar, Vivan Sundaram, Gulammohammed Sheikh, Jogen Chowdhury, Nalini Malani und Sudhir Patwardhan) organisiert zusammen mit der Kritikerin Geeta Kapur die figurativ-narrative Ausstellung „Place for People“ mit einem Schwerpunkt auf lokalen und regionalen Aspekten am JAG in Mumbai. Salman Rushdie gewinnt den Booker-Preis für seinen zweiten Roman „Mitternachtskinder“.	A group of six artists (Bhupen Khakhar, Vivan Sundaram, Gulammohammed Sheikh, Jogen Chowdhury, Nalini Malani and Sudhir Patwardhan) along with the critic Geeta Kapur organize the figurative-narrative exhibition "Place for People," which emphasizes the politics of the local and the regional, at the JAG, Mumbai. Salman Rushdie wins a Booker Prize for his second novel, *Midnight's Children.*
1982	Beginn der Ausstrahlung von Farbfernsehen. Die 9. Asian Games werden in Delhi abgehalten. Indien ist zum zweiten Mal seit 1951 Gastgeber der Spiele.	Color television broadcast begins. The 9th Asian Games are held in Delhi. It is the second time since 1951 for India to host the Games.	5. „Triennale-India“ Bharat Bhavan (eine autonome, vom Staat geförderte Institution) wird von J. Swaminathan in Bhopal eröffnet. Zeitgenössische städtische Kunst und Tribal Art werden Seite an Seite ausgestellt. „Festivals of India“ organisiert eine Reihe von Kulturveranstaltungen in London, Paris und Moskau (–1986).	"The 5th Triennale-India" Bharat Bhavan (an autonomous state-sponsored institution) is inaugurated by J. Swaminathan in Bhopal, where contemporary metropolitan art and tribal art is exhibited side by side. A number of cultural events organized through "Festivals of India," in London, Paris, and Moscow (–1986).
1983	Der Bundesstaat Punjab, in dem sich Autonomiebestrebungen intensivieren, wird unter die Kontrolle der Zentralregierung gestellt. Subramanyan Chandrasekhar gewinnt den Nobelpreis für Physik. Die „Banditenkönigin“ Phoolan Devi ergibt sich den Behörden.	The state of Punjab, where a movement for autonomy had been intensifying, is placed under the control of the central government. Subramanyan Chandrasekhar wins the Nobel Prize in Physics. The female bandit Phoolan Devi surrenders.		
1984	Die Zentralregierung bringt mit Militärgewalt einen Sikh-Tempel unter Kontrolle, von dem aus die Autonomiebewegung von Punjab gelenkt wird. Premierministerin Indira Gandhi wird von einem ihrer Sikh-Leibwächter ermordet. Gandhis Sohn, Rajiv Ratna Gandhi, wird Premierminister. Indiens erste U-Bahn nimmt den Fahrbetrieb in Calcutta auf.	The central government uses military force to bring a Sikh temple, the strongpoint of the Punjab autonomous movement, under its control. Prime Minister Indira Gandhi is assassinated by one of her Sikh bodyguards. Gandhi's son, Rajiv Ratna Gandhi, becomes Prime Minister. India's first subway begins service in Calcutta.		

1985	Es kommt zu einem Kompromiss zwischen dem Bundesstaat Punjab und der Zentralregierung. Die Explosion einer Bombe an Bord des Air-India Fluges 182 (vermutlich platziert von radikalen Sikh) tötet alle 329 Passagiere. Es handelt sich um den folgenschwersten Terroranschlag in der zivilen Luftfahrt vor dem 11. September 2001.	A compromise is reached between the state of Punjab and the central government. A bomb aboard Air India Flight 182 kills all 329 passengers on board. This is the single deadliest terrorist incident prior to the events of September 11 in 2001.	Eine Ausstellung von jungen Avantgarde-Künstlern mit dem Titel „Seven Young Sculptors" (darunter N. N. Rimzon und Pushpamala N.) wird von Vivan Sundaram kuratiert. „The 2nd Asian Art Show"	An exhibition of young avant-garde artists, "Seven Young Sculptors" (N. N. Rimzon, Pushpamala N., among others) curated by Vivan Sundaram. "The 2nd Asian Art Show"
1986			6. „Triennale-India" „1st Bharat Bhavan Biennale of Contemporary Art" in Bhopal.	"The 6th Triennale-India" "The 1st Bharat Bhavan Biennale of Contemporary Art," Bhopal.
1987	Indien entsendet Truppen als Reaktion auf einen ethnischen Konflikt in Sri Lanka.	India dispatches troops in response to ethnic conflict in Sri Lanka.	Die erste Auktion von Christie's findet in Mumbai statt.	The first Christie's auction was held in Mumbai.
1988	Premierminister Rajiv Gandhi besucht China. Es ist dies der erste Besuch eines indischen Premierministers seit der Chinareise von Gandhis Großvater, Premierminister Nehru, 34 Jahre zuvor. Indien und Pakistan halten ein hochrangiges Gipfeltreffen ab und unterzeichnen ein Abkommen, das gegenseitige Angriffe auf Nuklearanlagen verbietet.	Prime Minister Rajiv Gandhi visits China. It is the first time for a prime minister to visit the country since Gandhi's grandfather, Prime Minister Nehru, did so 34 years earlier. India and Pakistan hold a high-level summit and sign an agreement prohibiting attacks on one another's nuclear facilities.	„Festival of India" in Japan (der damalige Premierminister Rajiv Gandhi wohnt den Eröffnungsfeierlichkeiten bei)	"Festival of India" in Japan (then Prime Minister Rajiv Gandhi attends the opening ceremony)
1989	Premierminister Rajiv Gandhi stattet Pakistan einen offiziellen Besuch ab. Es ist der erste Besuch eines indischen Premierministers seit 26 Jahren. Die Kongress-Partei verliert bei den neunten allgemeinen Wahlen. Die Janata Dal-Partei errichtet eine Regierung und bleibt bis 1991 an der Macht. Der 14. Dalai Lama erhält den Friedensnobelpreis.	Prime Minister Rajiv Gandhi makes an official visit to Pakistan, the first visit by an Indian prime minister in 26 years. The Congress Party loses power in the 9th general elections. The Janata Dal Party establishes a government and stays in power until 1991. The 14th Dalai Lama receives the Nobel Peace Prize.	„The 1st Bharat Bhavan International Biennale of Prints" in Bhopal Die erste Auktion von Sotheby's findet in Mumbai in Zusammenarbeit mit The Times of India statt. „3. Asian Art Show"	"The 1st Bharat Bhavan International Biennale of Prints," Bhopal The 1st Sotheby's auction was held in Mumbai in collaboration with The Times of India. "The 3rd Asian Art Show"
1990	Der Sensex-Index der Börse von Mumbai überschreitet die 1.000-Punkte Marke.	The Mumbai Stock Exchange *Sensex* index tops 1,000 points.		
1991	Rajiv Gandhi wird während des Wahlkampfs für die zehnten allgemeinen Wahlen ermordet. P.V. Narasimha Rao von der Kongress-Partei wird Premierminister. Angesichts einer Devisenkrise akzeptiert Indien einen Notkredit vom internationalen Währungsfonds. Eine neue Resolution zur Industriepolitik führt Indien auf den Weg der wirtschaftlichen Liberalisierung.	Rajiv Gandhi is assassinated while campaigning for the 10th general elections. P.V. Narasimha Rao of the Congress Party becomes Prime Minister. Faced with a foreign currency crisis, India accepts an emergency loan from the International Monetary Fund (IMF). A new resolution on industrial policy steers India toward economic liberalization.	7. „Triennale-India" „National Exposition of Contemporary Art", NGMA	"The 7th Triennale-India" "National Exposition of Contemporary Art," NGMA
1992	Ausstrahlung des ersten kommerziellen Satellitenfernsehprogramms. Hindus zerstören eine Moschee in Ayodhya, was zu religiös motivierten Gewaltausschreitungen mit zahlreichen Toten führt.	The first commercial satellite television broadcast begins transmission. Hindus destroy a mosque in Ayodhya, igniting religious violence that results in numerous deaths.	Das Medienkollektiv Raqs wird gegründet. Das Glenbarra Art Museum mit einer umfangreichen Sammlung zeitgenössischer indischer Kunst eröffnet in Hyogo, Japan.	Raqs Media Collective founded. Glenbarra Art Museum with the extensive collection of Indian contemporary art opens in Hyogo, Japan.
1993	Eine Reihe von Bomben explodiert an zwölf Plätzen in Mumbai und fordert zahlreiche Todesopfer.	A series of bombs hits 12 major facilities in Mumbai, causing a large number of casualties.	„1. Asia-Pacific Triennial of Contemporary Art", Queensland Art Gallery, Brisbane	"The 1st Asia-Pacific Triennial of Contemporary Art," Queensland Art Gallery, Brisbane
1994	Aishwarya Rai wird Indiens zweite Siegerin bei einer Wahl zur Miss World seit 1966. Im Jahr 2008 zieht Indien mit fünf Siegerinnen bei Miss World Konkurrenzen im Rennen um das Land mit den meisten Gewinnerinnen mit Venezuela gleich.	Aishwarya Rai becomes India's second winner of the Miss World beauty pageant since 1966. India will have produced a total of five recipients of the Miss World title by 2008, tying with Venezuela to produce the most winners of any country in the world.	8. „Triennale-India" „The 4th Asian Art Show" Die Ausstellung „100 Jahre indische Kunst" an der NGMA aus den eigenen Sammlungsbeständen eröffnet den Blick auf alternative Aspekte der indischen Moderne.	"The 8th Triennale-India" "The 4th Asian Art Show" An exhibition "One Hundred Years of Indian Art," NGMA, based on the NGMA Collection, adds alternative views to the ideas of Indian modernism.
1995	Bombay ändert seinen offiziellen Namen in Mumbai, was der örtlichen Aussprache besser entspricht. Aufgrund ähnlicher Bestrebungen wird Madras im selben Jahr in Chennai umbenannt, Kalkutta wird 2001 zu Calcutta, und das Prince of Wales Museum wird in Chhatrapati Shivaji Maharaj Museum umbenannt.	Bombay changes its official name to Mumbai, which more accurately reflects the local pronunciation. In similar moves, Madras is renamed Chennai in the same year, Calcutta becomes Calcutta in 2001, and the Prince of Wales Museum is renamed the Chhatrapati Shivaji Maharaj Museum.		

1996	Die Janata Dal-Partei stellt noch einmal die Regierung, die bis 1998 im Amt bleibt. Die frühere „Banditenkönigin" Phoolan Devi wird in das Parlament gewählt. Der chinesische Präsident Jiang Zemin stattet Indien einen offiziellen Besuch ab.	The Janata Dal party once again establishes a government, which is to last until 1998. The former bandit Phoolan Devi is elected to parliament. Chinese President Jiang Zemin makes an official visit to India.	M. F. Husains Aktbild einer hinduistischen Göttin wird von einer militanten rechtsgerichteten Hindu-Gruppe zerstört. Das Auktionshaus Christie's eröffnet ein Büro in Mumbai. Die erste Ausgabe des Kunstmagazins „Art India" erscheint. „2. Asia-Pacific Triennial of Contemporary Art" Die Ausstellung „Traditions/Tensions: Contemporary Art in Asia" findet bei der Asia Society in New York statt. Unter den teilnehmenden Künstlern sind: Sheela Gowda, Bhupen Khakhar, Nalini Malani, Ravinder G. Reddy und Arpita Singh. Eine neue Zweigstelle der NGMA wird in Mumbai eröffnet	M. F. Husain's nude painting of the Goddess is vandalized by a militant Hindu right-wing group. Auction house Christie's opens its Mumbai office. The first issue of *Art India* magazine is published. "The 2nd Asia-Pacific Triennial of Contemporary Art" "Traditions/Tensions: Contemporary Art in Asia," held at the Asia Society in New York. Participating artists from India includes Sheela Gowda, Bhupen Khakhar, Nalini Malani, Ravinder G. Reddy and Arpita Singh. A new branch of the NGMA opens in Mumbai.
1997	Mutter Teresa stirbt. K. R. Narayanan (1997–2002) ist der erste Präsident aus der früheren Kaste der Unberührbaren.	Mother Teresa dies. K. R. Narayanan (1997–02) becomes the first member of the former untouchable caste to become President.	Der Khoj Workshop für internationale Künstler wird in Delhi eingerichtet. Eine Ausstellung aus Beständen des Glenbarra Art Museum beginnt an der NGMA in Delhi und reist von dort nach Calcutta, Bangalore und Mumbai. Suzanna Arundhati Roy gewinnt 1997 den Booker-Preis für ihren Roman „Der Gott der kleinen Dinge".	Khoj International Artists' Workshop established in Delhi. The exhibition highlighting the collection of Glenbarra Art Museum starts from NGMA in Delhi, travelling to Calcutta, Bangalore and Mumbai. Suzanna Arundhati Roy wins the Booker Prize in 1997 for her novel, *The God of Small Things.*
1998	Die Bharatiya Janata Partei errichtet eine Koalitionsregierung. Atal Behari Vajpayee (1998–2004) wird Premierminister. Amartya Sen erhält den Nobelpreis für Wirtschaft. Nach der Durchführung eines unterirdischen Atomversuchs im Bundesstaat Rajastan deklariert sich Indien als Atommacht. Pakistan führt daraufhin ebenfalls einen eigenen Atomversuch durch.	The Bharatiya Janata Party establishes a coalition government. Atal Behari Vajpayee (1998–04) becomes Prime Minister. Amartya Sen wins the Nobel Prize in Economics. India declares itself a nuclear power after conducting an underground nuclear test in the state of Rajasthan. Pakistan subsequently conducts its own nuclear test.	Das Mohile Parikh Centre for Visual Art in Mumbai wir zum Angelpunkt internationaler Seminare über Kunstpraxis und Theorie. Die Künstlerinitiative „Open Circle" wird von Tushar Joag und Sharmila Samant (später auch Archana Hande und Shilpa Gupta) in Mumbai gegründet. Sie existiert heute nicht mehr, hat aber zahlreiche Straßenaktionen, Workshops, Seminare und Kunstfestivals organisiert.	Mohile Parikh Centre for Visual Art in Mumbai becomes pivotal in international seminars on art practice and theory. An artists' initiative, Open Circle, was founded by Tushar Joag and Sharmila Samant (later joined by Archana Hande and Shilpa Gupta), in Mumbai. It is defunct today, but it has organized street actions, workshops, seminars and art festivals.
1999	Sonia Gandhi, die Witwe des verstorbenen Rajiv Gandhi, steht an der Spitze der Kongress-Partei. Premierminister Vajpayee stattet Pakistan einen Staatsbesuch ab. Zusammen mit Premierminister Nawaz Sharif erfolgt eine gemeinsame Erklärung, die sich für eine friedliche Lösung für den Streit um Kaschmir ausspricht. Bewaffnete pakistanische Gruppen dringen in den Bezirk Kargil im von Indien kontrollierten Kaschmir ein und lösen damit einen Konflikt aus, der die beiden Länder an den Rand eines Atomkriegs bringt.	Sonia Gandhi, widow of the late Rajiv Gandhi, becomes president of the Congress Party. Prime Minister Vajpayee makes an official visit to Pakistan. He and Prime Minister Nawaz Sharif issue a joint statement pledging to work for a peaceful resolution to the dispute over Kashmir. Armed Pakistani groups advance into the Kargil district in Indian-controlled Kashmir, sparking conflict and bringing the two countries to the verge of nuclear war.	„The 1st Fukuoka Asian Art Triennale", Fukuoka Asian Art Museum, Fukuoka „The 3rd Asia-Pacific Triennial of Contemporary Art" Das Kala Ghoda Arts Festival beginnt im gleichnamigen Kunstdistrikt von Mumbai.	"The 1st Fukuoka Asian Art Triennale," Fukuoka Asian Art Museum, Fukuoka "The 3rd Asia-Pacific Triennial of Contemporary Art" Kala Ghoda Arts Festival begins in the eponymous arts quarter of Mumbai.
2000	Anlässlich des ersten Staatsbesuchs durch einen Präsidenten der Vereinigten Staaten seit 22 Jahren besucht Bill Clinton Indien.	Bill Clinton visits India in the first official visit by a United States President in 22 years.	Jhumpa Lahiris „Interpreter of Maladies" (1999, dt. „Melancholie der Ankunft") gewinnt den „Pulitzer Prize for Fiction" 2000.	Jhumpa Lahiri's *Interpreter of Maladies* (1999) wins the 2000 Pulitzer Prize for Fiction.
2001	Bei einer Volkszählung stellt sich heraus, dass die Bevölkerungszahl Indiens eine Milliarde Menschen übersteigt. Phoolan Devi, die Kriminelle die zur Politikerin wurde, wird ermordet. Mehr als 200 Inder sterben bei den Terroranschlägen des 11. September. Islamistische Extremisten aus Pakistan infiltrieren das indische Parlamentsgebäude und wenden Waffengewalt an. Indien und Pakistan beenden die diplomatischen Beziehungen, rufen ihre Botschafter zurück und unterbrechen die Luft-, Bahn- und Busverbindungen zwischen den beiden Ländern.	A national census indicates India's population has surpassed 1 billion. Phoolan Devi the former-bandit-turned-politician, is assassinated. Over 200 Indians perish in the terrorist attacks of September 11. Islamic extremists from Pakistan infiltrate the Indian parliament building and attack with firearms. India and Pakistan sever diplomatic relations, withdrawing their ambassadors and suspending air, rail, and bus service between the two countries.	Die Apeejay Media Gallery wird in Delhi eröffnet. Die erste temporäre Ausstellung der Tate Modern mit dem Titel „Century City: Art and Culture in the Modern Metropolis" gibt einen umfassenden Überblick über die zeitgenössische Kunstszene in Indien. Das Japan Foundation Asia Center organisiert Atul Dodiyas Einzelausstellung „Bombay: Labyrinth/Laboratory" in Tokyo. V. S. Naipaul erhält den Literaturnobelpreis.	Apeejay Media Gallery opens in Delhi. Tate Modern's first temporary exhibition "Century City: Art and Culture in the Modern Metropolis" covers Indian contemporary art scene extensively. The Japan Foundation Asia Center organizes Atul Dodiya's solo show *Bombay: Labyrinth/ Laboratory* in Tokyo. V. S. Naipaul receives the Nobel Prize in Literature.

2002	Ein muslimischer Mob setzt einen Zug mit Hindupilgern im Bundesstaat Gujarat in Brand. Die Hindus reagieren mit Angriffen auf Moslems, was weitere Aufstände nach sich zieht. Die indische Regierung hebt die Beschränkungen für pakistanische Flugzeuge im indischen Luftraum auf, und die beiden Länder reduzieren die Anzahl ihrer an der gemeinsamen Grenze stationierten Truppen. Madhu Sudan erhält den Rolf Nevanlinna Preis für Errungenschaften in der Computerwissenschaft. Die U-Bahn von Delhi nimmt den Betrieb auf.	A Muslim mob sets fire to a train carrying Hindu pilgrims in the state of Gujarat. Hindus retaliate by attacking Muslims, sparking riots. The Indian government lifts restrictions on Pakistani planes entering Indian airspace, and the two countries reduce the size of their forces stationed along their mutual border. Madhu Sudan receives the Rolf Nevanlinna Prize for contributions to computer science. The Delhi subway commences operation.	Beteiligung des Medienkollektivs Raqs sowie von Amar Kanwar und Ravi Agarwal an der „Documenta 11" Kassel. „The 2nd Fukuoka Asian Art Triennale", Fukuoka Asian Art Museum, Fukuoka „Asia-Pacific Triennial of Contemporary Art 2002 (Fourth)", Queensland Art Gallery, Brisbane	Raqs Media Collective, Amar Kanwar and Ravi Agarwal participate in "Documenta 11," Kassel. "The 2nd Fukuoka Asian Art Triennale," Fukuoka Asian Art Museum, Fukuoka "Asia-Pacific Triennial of Contemporary Art 2002 (Fourth)," Queensland Art Gallery, Brisbane
2003	Indien und Pakistan einigen sich auf einen Waffenstillstand in Kaschmir. Die diplomatischen Beziehungen werden wieder aufgenommen, Botschafter werden ausgetauscht, und die Bus- und Flugverbindungen zwischen den beiden Ländern werden wiederhergestellt. Der Sensex Index der Börse in Mumbai überschreitet die 5.000-Punkte Marke.	India and Pakistan agree to a ceasefire in Kashmir. Diplomatic relations are resumed, ambassadors exchanged, and bus and air service between the two countries is restored. The Mumbai Stock Exchange *Sensex* tops 5,000 points.	Anlässlich des Todes von Bhupen Khakar findet eine Retrospektive über den Künstler an der NGMA in Mumbai statt. Die Chemould Galerie feiert ihren 40. Jahrestag mit einer Ausstellung „Crossing Generations: diVERGE" an der NGMA in Mumbai.	Bhupen Khakar's retrospective at the NGMA in Mumbai upon his death. Gallery Chemould celebrates its 40-year anniversary with an exhibition "Crossing Generations: diVERGE" at the NGMA in Mumbai.
2004	Die Kongress-Partei bildet eine Koalitionsregierung und Manmohan Singh wird Premierminister.	The Congress Party forms a coalition government, with Manmohan Singh becoming Prime Minister.		
2005	Ein schweres Erdbeben ereignet sich in der Region Kaschmir, dem Zentrum der Grenzstreitigkeiten zwischen Indien und Pakistan. Mehr als 70.000 Menschen werden getötet. Premierminister Manmohan Singh besucht die Vereinigten Staaten von Amerika und hält Gespräche mit dem amerikanischen Präsidenten George W. Bush. Die beiden Staatsmänner unterzeichnen im Jahr 2006 ein Abkommen zur zivilen Atomzusammenarbeit. Der Chinesische Premier Wen Jiabao stattet Indien einen offiziellen Besuch ab. Ein Erdbeben in Sumatra fordert viele Tausende Menschenleben und Vermisste in Indien. Premierminister Manmohan Singh besucht China. Die beiden Länder unterzeichnen umfangreiche Abkommen.	The Great Pakistan Earthquake strikes the Kashmir region, center of a border dispute between India and Pakistan. Over 70,000 people are killed. Prime Minister Manmohan Singh visits the United States and holds talks with the American President George W. Bush, and the two leaders sign the Civilian Nuclear Cooperation Agreement in 2006. Chinese Premier Wen Jiabao makes an official visit to India. An earthquake strikes Sumatra, resulting in many thousands of dead and missing in India. Prime Minister Manmohan Singh visits China. The two countries issue comprehensive declarations of agreement.	„iCon: India Contemporary" wird von Bose Pacia in Zusammenarbeit mit Peter Nagy bei der 51. Biennale von Venedig organisiert. „The 3rd Fukuoka Asian Art Triennale"	"iCon: India Contemporary," organized by Bose Pacia in collaboration with Peter Nagy at the "51st Venice Biennale." "The 3rd Fukuoka Asian Art Triennale"
2006	Präsident Bush besucht Indien, und die beiden Länder einigen sich auf eine Trennung zwischen Indiens zivilen und militärischen Atomprogrammen. Es gibt mehr als 100 Millionen Mobiltelefonbesitzer in Indien. Der Nathu La Pass zwischen Indien und China wird nach 44 Jahren wieder eröffnet. Synchronisierte terroristische Bombenanschläge treffen sieben Züge in der Stadt Mumbai und fordern zahlreiche Todesopfer. Der Sensex Index der Börse in Mumbai überschreitet die 10.000-Punkte Marke.	President Bush visits India, and the two countries reach agreement on separating India's civilian and military nuclear programs. The number of mobile phone users in India tops 100 million. The Nathu La Pass connecting India and China is reopened after 44 years. Synchronized terrorist bombs strike seven trains in the city of Mumbai, resulting in numerous deaths. The Mumbai Stock Exchange Sensex tops 10,000 points.	„The 5th Asia-Pacific Triennial of Contemporary Art"	"The 5th Asia-Pacific Triennial of Contemporary Art"

2007	Indien verzeichnet für das Finanzjahr 2006 einen Überschuss in der Zahlungsbilanz in Höhe von 36,6 Milliarden Dollar. S. R. Srinivasa Varadhan erhält den Abel-Preis für Mathematik. Pratibha Devisingh Patil wird Indiens erste Präsidentin. Der Sensex Index der Börse in Mumbai überschreitet die 20.000-Punkte Marke. Indiens Bruttoinlandsprodukt 2007 beträgt etwa 1,99 Billionen Dollar, was das Land weltweit an die zwölfte Stelle setzt. Indiens BIP pro Kopf beträgt allerdings nur etwa 991 Dollar, was den 130. Rang bedeutet. (Quelle: Daten des IWF)	India records a $36.6 billion balance of payments surplus for fiscal 2006. S. R. Srinivasa Varadhan receives the Abel Prize for mathematics. Pratibha Devisingh Patil becomes India's first female President. The Mumbai Stock Exchange Sensex hits 20,000 points. India's gross domestic product for 2007 is approximately $1.99 trillion, the 12th highest in the whole world. However, India's per capita GDP is approximately $991, ranking 130th. (Source: IMF data)	Beteiligung von Nalini Malani und Riyas Komu an der 52. Biennale von Venedig. Die indische Regierung richtet trotz offizieller Einladung von den Veranstaltern keinen offiziellen nationalen Pavillon im „Arsenale" ein. Zur gleichen Zeit wird im Zuge der Pinault Foundation Collection Exhibition eine riesige Skulptur von Subodh Gupta am Canale Grande aufgestellt. Beteiligung von Atul Dodiya, Sheela Gowda, Amar Kanwar, Nasreen Mohammedi und C. K. Rajan an der „Documenta 12". Die Ausstellung „Thermocline of Art: New Asian Waves", mit der eine Reihe von indischen Künstlern vertreten sind, findet in Deutschland statt. Das Calcutta Museum of Modern Art (KMOMA) wird gegründet und soll 2012 eröffnet werden. Chandramohan, ein Kunststudent im letzten Jahr an der Kunstfakultät der M. S. Universität, wird wegen Erregung öffentlichen Ärgernisses verhaftet, weil die von ihm ausgestellten Malereien bei einer Universitätsausstellung angeblich die religiösen Gefühle der Hindu verletzen. Aktivisten von VHP (Vishwa Hindu Parishad) unter der Führung eines Mitglieds der BJP dringen in die Universität ein und schlagen den Künstler zusammen. Der Dekan der Kunstfakultät, Prof. Shivji Panikkar, wird von seinem Amt suspendiert, weil er sich weigert, die Universitätsausstellung zu schließen. Das „Komitee zur Befreiung von Chandramohan", in dem Anwälte, Kritiker, Galeristen, Künstler und Aktivisten vertreten sind, konstituiert sich in Mumbai. Es koordiniert einen landesweiten Protest in Mumbai, Delhi und Vadodara gegen die Verhaftung von Chandramohan.	Nalini Malani and Riyas Komu participate in the "52nd Venice Biennale." The Indian government did not set up an official national pavilion in the Arsenale despite the official invitation by the Venice Biennale. Meanwhile, The Pinault Foundation Collection Exhibition is organized featuring an enormous sculptural work by Subodh Gupta alongside the Grand Canal. Atul Dodiya, Sheela Gowda, Amar Kanwar, Nasreen Mohammedi and C. K. Rajan participate in "Documenta 12." "Thermocline of Art: New Asian Waves" featuring a number of Indian artists is organized in Germany. Calcutta Museum of Modern Art (KMOMA), is founded. The museum is expected to open in 2012. Chandramohan, a final year art student at the Faculty of Fine Arts, M. S. University, was arrested on grounds of public obscenity for presenting paintings at a University exhibition that allegedly offended Hindu religious sentiment. VHP (Vishwa Hindu Parishad) activists led by a BJP leader entered the university and beat up the artist. The dean of the Fine Arts faculty, Prof. Shivji Panikkar, was suspended because he refused to close down the university exhibition. The Free Chandramohan Committee comprising lawyers, critics, gallerists, artists and activists, was set up in Mumbai. It coordinated a nationwide protest in Mumbai, Delhi and Vadodara to protest against Chandramohan's arrest.
2008	Für das Steuerjahr 2008 wird ein nationales Budget von 7,5 Billionen Rupien vorgestellt. Es kommt zu einer Serie von nicht miteinander in Zusammenhang stehenden terroristischen Anschlägen in Jaipur im Bundesstaat Rajasthan, in Ahmedabad im Bundesstaat Gujarat und in Bangalore im Bundesstaat Karnataka. Die Anzahl von Mobiltelefonbenutzern übersteigt 200 Millionen. Am 26. November 2008 starben 173 Menschen, als moslemische Terroristen mehrere Ziele in Mumbai, darunter einen Bahnhof, das jüdische Zentrum und das berühmte Taj-Hotel, angriffen. Im Hotel nahmen sie Geiseln und lieferten sich bis 29. November Kämpfe mit Militär und Polizei.	A national budget of 7.5 trillion rupees is proposed for fiscal 2008. In separate incidents, terrorists set off a series of bombs in Jaipur in Rajasthan State, Ahmedabad in Gujarat State, and Bangalore in Karnataka State. The number of mobile phone users tops 200 million. 172 people died on November 26 2008 after terrorists attacked several destinations, a train station, the Jewish Centre and the famous Taj Hotel in Mumbai. The Indian military and police were fighting until November 29 against the terrorists after they had taken hostages in the Taj Hotel.	N. S. Harsha erhält den Artes Mundi Award. Das Medienkollektiv Raqs ist Mitkurator der „Manifesta 7: Die europäische Biennale für zeitgenössische Kunst", und der Kunstkritiker Ranjit Hoskote ist einer der Kuratoren der „Gwangju Biennale 2008". Lekha und Anupam Poddar errichten die Devi Art Foundation in Delhi. Das Privatmuseum besitzt eine topaktuelle Sammlung zeitgenössischer indischer Kunst. Nalini Malani und andere indische Künstler werden nach New Orleans zur Eröffnungsausstellung von „Prospect 1", der größten Biennale internationaler zeitgenössischer Kunst in den USA, eingeladen. Ausstellung „Chalo! India. Eine neue Ära indischer Kunst" im Mori Art Museum, Tokyo.	N. S. Harsha receives Artes Mundi Award. Raqs Media Collective co-curates "Manifesta 7: The European Biennial of Contemporary Art" and an art critic Ranjit Hoskote co-curates "Gwangju Biennale 2008." Lekha and Anupam Poddar set up Devi Art Foundation, in Delhi. A private museum, it has a cutting edge collection of contemporary Indian art. Nalini Malani and other Indian artists are invited to the inaugural show of "Prospect 1," in New Orleans, the largest biennial of international contemporary art in the USA. Exhibition "Chalo! India. A New Era of Indian Art" at the Mori Art Museum, Tokyo.
2009			Ausstellung „Chalo! India. Eine neue Ära indischer Kunst" im National Museum of Contemporary Art, Korea. Ausstellung „Chalo! India. Eine neue Ära indischer Kunst" im Essl Museum, Klosterneuburg / Wien.	Exhibition "Chalo! India. A New Era of Indian Art" at the National Museum of Contemporary Art, Korea. Exhibition "Chalo! India. A New Era of Indian Art" at the Essl Museum, Klosterneuburg / Vienna.

ANNÄHERUNG AN INDIEN
APPROACHING INDIA

Deepak Ananth

„A certain idea of India“ (Eine gewisse Vorstellung von Indien) wird sich den Besuchern dieser Ausstellung wahrscheinlich aufdrängen. Das ist nicht nur der Titel von Alberto Moravias Erzählung über seine Reise in den Subkontinent im Jahr 1961 in Begleitung von Elsa Morante und Pier Paolo Pasolini, sondern es ließe sich damit wahrscheinlich auch der große Textkorpus an ausländischen Diskursen über Indien in den nunmehr einigen Jahrzehnten seit seiner Unabhängigkeit überschreiben.

Die nuancierte, elegante Analyse der Dinge, die Moravia während seines Aufenthaltes sah und erlebte, könnte in keinem größerem Kontrast zu den erregten, rastlosen Impressionen stehen, die Pasolini in seinem Buch verewigte: Schon der Titel – „Der Atem Indiens“ (1962) – zeigt die Empfindsamkeit seiner Reaktionen auf die von den drei Freunden besuchten Städte und Landschaften. Hier waren zwei sehr unterschiedliche Temperamente unterwegs, und die Wahrnehmungen des Schriftstellers und des Poeten und zukünftigen Filmemachers („Accatone“ entstand in diesem Jahr) jener Aspekte Indiens, die Ausländern unweigerlich auffallen – die Armut, das Kastensystem, die Menschenmengen, das koloniale Erbe, die Qualität des Lichtes, die Tempel, der religiöse Eifer – waren unvermeidlich von den Sensibilitäten und Sympathien ihrer jeweiligen Weltsichten geprägt. Moravias melancholischer Humanismus kontrastierte hier mit Pasolinis idiosynkratischer Mischung aus leidenschaftlichem Marxismus, mystischer Begeisterung und ambivalenter Einstellung zum modernen Fortschritt.

Die Abgeklärtheit und Klarheit des Autors von „Die Verachtung“, „La Noia“ and „Der Konformist“ und die sinnliche Lyrik des großen italienischen „Zivilpoeten“, wie Moravia Pasolini einst beschrieb, ließe sich noch von einem dritten Aspekt zu Indien aus diesen Jahren ergänzen, nämlich die von Roberto Rossellini 1957-59 für das italienische Fernsehen produzierte Serie (in zehn Folgen) „L'India vista da Rossellini“ (Indien aus der Sicht von Rossellini). Es handelte sich hier um unverknüpfte Beobachtungen, die als vorbereitende Notizen für den Film „India, Matri Bhumi“ („Indien, Mutter Erde“) gelten können, der 1959 beim Filmfestival von Cannes Premiere hatte. Dieser Film, ein merkwürdiges Hybrid aus Dokumentation und Fiktion, gewissermaßen eine poetische Ethnologie, lag Rossellini besonders am Herzen, weil er darin einen neuen Weg sah, nicht nur Wissen und Information sondern auch die Gefühle und Verhaltensweisen der gezeigten Menschen zu vermitteln. Obwohl der Film mit Straßenszenen in Bombay beginnt, spielt er im Wesentlichen im ländlichen Indien, in den Dörfern, in dem was Nehru, der kosmopolitischste aller indischen Staatsmänner, als das „wahre Indien“ bezeichnete (auch Moravia und Pasolini beschreiben ausführlich ihr Erleben der ländlichen Gebiete). Aber der berühmteste Lobgesang auf das Indien der Dörfer ist natürlich Satyajit Rays „Pather Panchali“ (dt.: Apus Weg ins Leben: Auf der Straße), und es ist nicht ohne Ironie, dass ein stark vom Neorealismus geprägter indischer Autor just dann sein internationales Debüt feierte (der Film gewann 1956 in Cannes einen Preis als „bestes menschliches Dokument“), als Rossellini, der Übervater des Neorealismus, in seinem Indienfilm begann, mit einer neuen filmischen Erzählweise zu experimentieren (Ray begann seine Karriere als Filmemacher als Assistent von Jean Renoir während des Drehs zu „Der Fluss“, 1951). Rossellini war von Nehru eingeladen worden, seinen Film zu machen,

"A certain idea of India" is probably what will come to mind to viewers visiting this exhibition. It happens to be the title of Alberto Moravia's account of his trip to the subcontinent in 1961, undertaken in the company of Elsa Morante and Pier Paolo Pasolini, and it is how one might also qualify the large corpus of texts that makes up the foreign discourse on India in the several decades since independence.

The nuanced, elegant analysis of what Moravia saw and encountered during his sojourn couldn't offer a greater contrast with the excited, restless impressions that Pasolini gathered in his book, its very title – The Scent of India (1962) – an indication of the sentient nature of his responses to the cities and landscapes through which the three friends had travelled. Two distinct temperaments were on tour, and the perceptions of the writer and of the poet and would-be film maker (Accatone was made in that year) of those aspects of India that inevitably strike foreigners – the poverty, the caste system, the crowds, the colonial heritage, the quality of the light, the temples, the religious fervour – were perforce tinged by the sensibilities and sympathies informing their respective "world-views," Moravia's melancholy humanism contrasting with Pasolini's idiosyncratic amalgam of impassioned Marxism and mystic exaltation and ambivalence about modern progress.

The detachment and lucidity of the author of Contempt and Boredom and The Conformist, and the sensuous lyricism of modern Italy's great "civil poet," as Moravia once described Pasolini, could be complemented by a third frame through which India was approached in these years. This was the series (in ten episodes) that Roberto Rossellini made for Italian television in 1957–59, L'India vista da Rossellini, freewheeling observations that were in the nature of preparatory visual note-taking for the film called India, Matri Bhumi ("India, Motherland"), which premiered at the Cannes film festival in 1959. A curious hybrid of documentary and fiction, a poetic ethnology, as it were, Rossellini was particularly attached to this film for what he saw as its novel approach to conveying knowledge and information as well as the feelings and behaviour of the individuals featured in it. Although the film opens with street scenes in Bombay, its heart is in rural India, in the villages, in what Nehru, most cosmopolitan of Indian statesman, described as the "real India" (Moravia and Pasolini, too, dwell at length on their experience of the countryside). But the most famous paean to village India is, of course, Satyajit Ray's Pather Panchali, and it is ironic that an Indian auteur, deeply marked by neorealism, should make his international début (the film won an award at Cannes in 1956 for "best human document") just when Rossellini, the tutelary figure of neorealism, begins to experiment with a new form of cinematic narration in his India film (Ray began his career as a film maker as an assistant to Jean Renoir during the making of The River, 1951). Rossellini had been invited by Nehru to make his film, and it was Nehru, too, who authorized the screening of Pather Panchali in Cannes in the face of reservations voiced by Indian diplomats that the film projected an image of India that was far from being optimistic.

Official vigilance (on the part of the Indian Censor Board) about films that failed to project a "positive" image of the country ensured that Louis Malle's unblinkered vision of India – in his documentary Calcutta, and in the seven films he made for French television called l'Inde fantôme in 1968 – was (and

und es war auch Nehru, der die Vorführung von „Pather Panchali" in Cannes erlaubte, trotz der von indischen Diplomaten vorgebrachten Bedenken, der Film zeige ein gar nicht optimistisches Bild von Indien.
Offizielle Wachsamkeit (von Seiten der indischen Zensurbehörde) bei Filmen, die kein „positives" Bild des Landes entwarfen, führte dazu, dass Louis Malles ungeschönte Vision von Indien – in seinem Dokumentarfilm „Calcutta" und in seinen sieben Filmen für das französische Fernsehen unter dem Namen „L'Inde fantôme" (dt. etwa: geisterhaftes Indien) – damals wie heute nicht öffentlich in indischen Kinos gezeigt werden darf. Aus mehr als dreißig Stunden (über einen Zeitraum von sechs Monaten gedrehtem) Material machte Malle mehr als acht Stunden Film. Man hat den Eindruck, dass der Film endlos weitergehen könnte, so fesselnd ist dieses Abtauchen in eine Realität, die ohne Tricks oder Inszenierung gezeigt wird. Diese Straßensicht von Indien scheut auch nicht davor zurück, die überwältigende Armut und das Elend zu zeigen, dem Malle begegnete. Es gibt lange Sequenzen ohne Kommentar, und wo ein Kommentar aus dem Off existiert, ist er nüchtern, sachlich und in Ichform gehalten. Diese fehlende Emphase ist schon ein Zeichen dafür, wie entschlossen der Regisseur war, sich nicht von Empfindlichkeiten leiten zu lassen. Dennoch deutet das häufig eingestandene Unverständnis angesichts der vom Auge der Kamera bzw. vom Kommentar-Ich erfassten Szenen darauf hin, dass es bei den Filmen von Malle letztendlich um Askese geht – seine eigene, insofern die Filme von der Unmöglichkeit der Objektivität zeugen. Bei den Dokumentarfilmen geht es genauso um die Begegnung mit einer schmerzlichen Realität wie um die Anstrengungen des Filmemachers, dieser Aufgabe filmisch gerecht zu werden. Kein Wunder, dass der erste Film den Titel „Die unmögliche Kamera" trägt und der Untertitel der gesamten Sequenz „Reflektionen über eine Reise" lautet. Die Tatsache, dass die Filme vielleicht Grenzfall einer Denkweise sind, die sich aufmacht „die Gegenwart zu leben ohne zu versuchen sie zu verstehen" war Malle durchaus bewusst. Warum sonst hätte er den Titel „geisterhaftes Indien" für den gesamten Zyklus gewählt, der das Ergebnis generischer Objektivität ist, des Willens zur Nicht-Betroffenheit, der seiner Haltung als Dokumentarfilmer zugrunde liegt?
Ein Beleg dafür, dass Indien ein reines Fantasieobjekt sein könnte, eine imaginäre Projektion, eine Abstraktion oder Einbildung, findet sich in dem Film „India Song", den Marguerite Duras 1975 nach ihrem eigenen Roman produzierte. Obwohl der Film im Jahr 1937 im französischen Konsulat in Kalkutta spielt, ist das Indien im Titel nur eine begriffliche Anspielung auf „Les Indes", die französische Bezeichnung der Kolonialzeit für die Region, die sich vom indischen Subkontinent bis zum französischen Indochina aus Duras' Kindheit erstreckt. Das ist das Gebiet, das Duras zu einem Kammerspiel um die enigmatische Figur der Frau des französischen Botschafters und ihre Liebhaber kondensiert: die Monologe (als Off-Stimmen) dieser einsamen Subjekte betten den Film in eine sich auf Zurückliegendes beziehende Struktur ein, wie sie für Duras typisch ist. Die unaussprechliche Vergangenheit, die als Last auf dem Bewusstsein liegt, ist ihr Lieblingsthema, während der repetitive, beschwörende Stil, die Nicht-Synchronisation von Bildern und Ton, ihr bevorzugtes formales Ausdrucksmittel ist. Aber als das Klagelied der Bettlerin, die durch den Park des Konsulats geistert, aus dem Off ertönt, trennen sich „India" und „Song". Diese unsichtbare Alterität bildet den Rahmen für Duras' unbeirrt europäische Romanze, ihr stilisiertes, geistreiches Spiel von erotischem Getändel und Tod. Im Konsulat steht die Zeit zur Cocktail-Stunde still: träge Gesten, verschleierte Motive, bedeutungsvolle Blicke, Schweigen, langsame Walzer und ein wiederkehrendes musikalisches Leitmotiv. Draußen herrscht eine Abstraktion namens Indien, eine spezifische Andersartigkeit: die schwüle Hitze des Monsun, Erstarrung, der Ganges, üppige Vegetation, Hungersnot, Lepra ... – der Kontrast zu Louis Malles unbeirrbaren Blick auf die Leprakranken in den Straßen Kalkuttas ist deutlich, aber „L'Inde fantôme" ist auch ein Dokumentarfilm und „India Song" eine Fantasie.
Man sollte den Film von Duras besser mit dem 25 Jahre früher entstandenen Film „Der Fluß" (1951) von Jean Renoir vergleichen – sein erster Farbfilm

still is) publicly banned from Indian screens. From over thirty hours of footage (shot over a period of six months), Malle retained more than eight hours, and one does have the impression that the films could go on indefinitely, so riveting is his immersion in a reality framed without artifice or a prior mise-en-scène. The street-level view of India doesn't flinch from the overwhelming poverty and squalor that Malle encountered. There are long sequences without commentary, and when there is a voice-over, it is sober and matter of fact and speaks in the first person, the very understatement an indication of the degree of self-control in the film maker's determination to be undeterred by squeamishness. And yet the frequent avowals of incomprehension in the face of what the camera eye/I was recording suggests that Malle's films are finally about an ascesis – his own, inasmuch as they evince the near-impossibility of vanquishing the subjective. The documentaries are as much about the encounter with a painful reality as they are about their maker's efforts to be equal to the task of filming it. No wonder that the first film is titled "The Impossible Camera" and that the subtitle of the sequence as a whole is "Reflections on a Voyage." That the films are perhaps a limit-case of an attitude that sets out "to live things in the present without trying to understand them" must not have escaped Malle, for why else would he have chosen "Phantom India" as the overall title for a cycle that is the outcome of the generic objectivity, the will to equanimity underlying his documentary stance?
That India could be a purely phantasmal object, an imaginary projection, an abstraction or a conceit, is borne out by India Song, the film, based on her own play/novel, that Marguerite Duras made in 1975. Although the setting is the French consulate in Calcutta in 1937, the India of the title is no more than a notional allusion to Les Indes, the French colonial designation for the region extending from the Indian subcontinent to the French Indo-China of Duras's childhood. This is the territory that Duras contracts to a huis clos, a chamber drama centred on the enigmatic figure of the French Ambassador's wife, and her lovers: the (voice-over) soliloquies of these monadic subjects structure the film's narrative in a recursive framework that is a quintessentially Durassian mannerism. The ineffable past, and the burden this represents for consciousness, is her subject of predilection, the repetitive, incantatory style, the non-synchronisation of the visual and the aural, her preferred formal means. But somewhere along the way, "India" and "Song" become out of sync, literally, in that the dirge of the beggar woman who haunts the gardens of the consulate is heard off-screen, and it is this invisible alterity that frames Duras' resolutely European romance, her stylized jeux d'esprit of erotic dalliance and death. Within the consulate, time stands still at the cocktail hour: languid gestures, undeclared motives, meaningful looks and silences, slow waltzes and a recurring musical leitmotif. Beyond it, an abstraction called India, a generic otherness: the inferred presence of the monsoon, heat, torpor, the Ganges, luxuriant vegetation, famine, leprosy... The contrast with Louis Malle's unwavering look at the lepers on the streets of Calcutta is eloquent, but then l'Inde fantôme is a documentary whereas India Song is a fantasy.
Duras's film could be more usefully contrasted with a work made twenty-five years earlier, Jean Renoir's The River (1951) – his first film in colour – based on the novel by Rumer Godden and shot entirely on location near Calcutta. For all the differences in style, temperament and world-view that separate the maker of The Rules of the Game and the author of the screenplay for Hiroshima, Mon Amour, their "India" films can nevertheless be juxtaposed in terms of the narratives that are voiced, specifically, the nature of the voice-overs deployed. The mesmerizing repetition of words (and the ponderous silences which punctuate them) is a Durassian device or tic for creating an atmospherics – a species of mantras for translating the inertia and languor of an erotic endgame in a supposedly tropical setting; the world outside, "an overpopulated city on the banks of the Ganges", exists only as a spectral, inchoate sound – the morose wail of the errant beggar woman. The voice-over in The River, in contrast, belongs to another narrative regime; it speaks from the pages of the

nach der Romanvorlage von Rumer Godden und gänzlich an Originalschauplätzen in der Nähe von Kalkutta gedreht. Trotz aller Unterschiede in Stil, Temperament und in der Weltsicht zwischen dem Regisseur von „Die Spielregel" und der Autorin des Drehbuchs für „Hiroshima, Mon Amour", lassen ihre Indien-Filme dennoch einen Vergleich in Bezug auf die erzählten Narrative zu, besonders was die Technik der Off-Stimme betrifft. Die hypnotisierende Wiederholung von Wörtern (und das bedeutungsvolle Schweigen, von dem sie immer wieder unterbrochen werden) ist ein Kunstgriff oder Tick, mit dem Duras Atmosphäre schafft – eine Art Mantra, mit dem die Trägheit und Mattigkeit eines erotischen Endspiels an einem angeblich tropischen Schauplatz verdeutlicht werden sollen. Die Welt draußen, „eine überbevölkerte Stadt an den Ufern des Ganges", existiert nur als geisterhaftes, undefiniertes Geräusch – die Klagerufe der herum irrenden Bettlerin. Der Off-Ton in „Der Fluß", andererseits, folgt einer anderen narrativen Strategie. Er erzählt aus dem Tagebuch eines der Protagonisten und gibt in der Tradition der romanhaften Beschreibung von Ereignissen die Geschichte einer englischen Familie, die in Bengal lebt, wieder: „Die Geschichte handelt von meiner ersten Liebe, vom Heranwachsen an den Ufern eines weiten Flusses", hören wir in der Eröffnungssequenz, und weiter: „die erste Liebe mag überall gleich sein, egal ob man sie in Amerika, England, Neuseeland oder Timbuktu erlebt ... aber die Atmosphäre meiner Geschichte wäre in jedem Fall anders gewesen, und auch die Menschen, die an dem Fluss leben, wären anders gewesen". Die Funktion der Off-Stimme ist es, die Besonderheit des indischen Schauplatzes anzudeuten – der Schauplatz des Erwachsenwerdens des Erzählers und des Dramas von Tod und Erneuerung. Indien ist offensichtlich eine exzellente Metapher für diesen Kreislauf des Lebens, wie auch für den leisen Humanismus von Renoirs filmischem Geniestreich. Filmtechnisch und poetisch gibt er das Land präzise wieder (und man kann sehen, was Satyajit Ray vom Talent des französischen Meisters für das Einfangen eines zivilisatorischen Ethos gelernt hat; eine Gabe, die auch Renoirs jüngerer Zeitgenosse, der große Henri Cartier-Bresson hatte). Immer wieder tauchen Untiefen in Rumer Goddens Drehbuch auf – nicht nur im gewollt literarischen Tenor der Off-Stimme, sondern besonders in den Worten eines der anglo-indischen Protagonisten. Aber vielleicht ist dieser Misston nur für indische Ohren zu hören.

Renoirs Film wurde, wie der von Rossellini, im gerade unabhängig gewordenen Indien gedreht, in Jawaharlal Nehrus Indien, das seinem Konzept der Moderne verpflichtet war. Er war es, der den berühmtesten Architekten der Welt beauftragte, nach der Teilung des Landes durch die Briten die Hauptstadt des indischen Teils der Provinzen Punjab zu entwerfen und zu bauen. So erhielt also Le Corbusier freie Hand bei der Planung der Stadt Chandigarh: „Zu diesem Zeitpunkt in der Evolution der modernen Zivilisation repräsentiert Indien eine besonders attraktive geistige Qualität", bemerkte er im Jahr 1950. „Unsere Aufgabe ist es, die Architektur zu finden, die in diese mächtige und tiefgründige Zivilisation eintaucht und mit Hilfe von modernen Werkzeugen einen Platz in der Gegenwart für sie findet." Chandigarh sollte eine Stadt der Zukunft sein: schlicht, rational, utilitaristisch, ein radikaler Bruch mit der traditionellen Architektur Indiens und dem Erbe der Kolonialzeit. Trotz seines Anspruchs auf einen völligen Neubeginn konnte es Le Corbusier kaum vermeiden, von der Großartigkeit der imperialen Mughal-Architektur oder dem prunkvollen Palast von Lutyens für den Vizekönig in New Delhi (fertiggestellt im Jahr 1931) beeinflusst zu werden, wie nur allzu deutlich an den palastartigen Dimensionen des Kapitolkomplexes zu sehen ist, den er für Chandigarh entwarf. Der Weg zur Moderne war mit guten Absichten und Stahlbeton gepflastert (ganz zu schweigen von geradlinigen Straßenzügen und Sektoren), aber die Ambivalenz in den Reaktionen auf Le Corbusiers indisches Magnum Opus erklärt sich sicherlich mit der absichtlichen Abgrenzung seiner Architektur vom Rest des Stadtgefüges. Ihre Neuheit war nicht nur in formaler Hinsicht befremdlich – man nehme beispielsweise die monumentale Leere des zentralen Platzes, ganz das Gegenteil der Agora, die dem Architekten

journal of one of the protagonists, and, in the tradition of the novelistic recounting of events, tells the story of an English family living in Bengal: "It is the story of my first love, about growing up on the banks of a wide river", is what we hear in the opening section. "First love might be the same in any place. It might have been in America, in England, in New Zealand, or in Timbucktu... But the flavour of my story would have been different in each, and the flavour of the people who live by the river would have been different." The function of the voice-over is precisely to signal the specificity of the Indian setting – the backdrop to both the narrator's coming of age and the drama of death and regeneration. The river is evidently the metaphor par excellence for this lifecycle, as it is for the unobtrusive humanism of Renoir's filmic genius. Cinematically, poetically, he gets India right (and one can see what Satyajit Ray learnt from the French master's gift for capturing a civilizational ethos, a gift shared by Renoir's younger contemporary, the great Cartier-Bresson); the reefs, such as they are, emerge periodically in Rumer Godden's screenplay – not only in the self-consciously literary tenor of the voice-over but especially in the speech of the one Anglo-Indian protagonist in the scenario. But perhaps this is jarring only to an Indian ear.

Renoir's film, like Rossellini's, was made in newly independent India, Nehru's India, committed to an idea of the modern, as envisioned by him. It was he who commissioned the most famous architect in the world to conceive and build the capital of the Indian part of the province of Punjab in the wake of the partition of the country by the British. So Le Corbusier was given carte blanche to plan the city of Chandigarh: "At this moment in the evolution of modern civilization India represents a quality of spirit, particularly attractive", he observed in 1950. "Our task is to discover the architecture to be immersed in the sieve of this powerful and profound civilization and the endowment of favourable modern tools to find it a place in present time." Chandigarh was to be a city of the future: spare, rational, utilitarian, marking a radical break from both the vernacular of traditional Indian architecture and the colonial legacy. However, for all his claims of building upon a clean slate, Le Corbusier was hardly oblivious to the grandeur of imperial Mughal architecture or to the grandiosity of Lutyens' palace for the Viceroy in New Delhi (completed in 1931), as is amply borne out by the palatial scale of the Capitol complex designed by him in Chandigarh. The path to modernity was paved with good intentions and reinforced concrete (not to mention grids and sectors), but some of the ambivalence in the reactions to Le Corbusier's Indian magnum opus surely lies in the architecture's willed separateness from the rest of the city fabric. Its newness was estranging, and not only formally – witness the monumental emptiness of the central square, the very opposite of the agora that the architect originally intended it to be (Alain Tanner's film, "Une ville â Chandigarh – Le Corbusier en Inde", made in 1965, the year of the architect's death, contains valuable footage of the building work that was still in progress, while John Berger's accompanying commentary dwells on the social vicissitudes of an undertaking of this magnitude. In the fifty years since its completion, the city has been reclaimed for its use-value by succeeding generations of citizens, in the idiosyncratic Indian way in such matters).

Modernist spatiality as a civilizational blueprint was part of the architectural hyperbole or working illusion of Le Corbusier's master plan, but, for all the rough concrete out of which it is made, Chandigarh remains something of an abstraction, a concept or an idea. It photographs beautifully in black and white, notably through the lens of Lucien Hervé, whose images dramatically underscore the sculptural and graphic qualities of Corbusian architectonics (Hervé's modernist eye was not less captivated by the abstract, archetypal forms of the jantar mantars, the eighteenth century observatories in Delhi and Jaipur). While the sharply defined geometries created by the play of light and shade make for aesthetically pleasing surface designs in the photographs, the architecture – abstracted in the images – had, in reality, to perforce reckon with the harsher fact of blazing sun, not to mention dust storms and rain

ursprünglich vorgeschwebt war (Alain Tanners Film, „Une ville â Chandigarh – Le Corbusier en Inde“, 1965 im Todesjahr des Architekten gedreht, enthält wertvolle Aufnahmen über die Bauarbeiten, die noch vor sich gingen, während John Bergers begleitender Kommentar sich über die sozialen Unwägbarkeiten eines zu groß angelegten Unternehmens auslässt. In den fünfzig Jahren seit ihrer Fertigstellung haben aufeinander folgende Generationen von Einwohnern sich die Stadt auf typisch indische Weise wieder zu Eigen gemacht.)

Das Raumkonzept der Moderne als zivilisatorischer Entwurf war Teil der architektonischen Anmaßung oder Arbeitsillusion von Le Corbusier, aber trotz der Massen von Sichtbeton, die für ihren Bau verwendet wurden, bleibt die Stadt Chandigarh eine Art Abstraktion, ein Konzept oder eine Idee. Sie lässt sich wunderschön in schwarz-weiß fotografieren, besonders durch die Linse von Lucien Hervé, dessen Bilder die skulpturalen und grafischen Qualitäten der Architektur von Corbusier wunderbar einfangen (Hervés modernistischer Blick war genauso begeistert von den abstrakten archetypischen Formen der „Jantar Mantars“, der astronomischen Sternwarten aus dem 18. Jahrhundert in Delhi and Jaipur). Während die scharf definierte Geometrie im Spiel von Licht und Schatten auf den Fotografien wunderbar ästhetische Eindrücke schafft, musste sich die auf den Bildern abstrahierte Architektur in der Realität gegen harte Tatsachen wie gleißendes Sonnenlicht, Staubstürme und Regen während des Monsuns behaupten. Mit diesen klimatischen Faktoren, die einen direkten Einfluss auf das existenzielle Ethos des Alltagslebens in Indien hatten, wurde Le Corbusier in Chandigarh nicht wirklich fertig.

Bei der Suche nach einem Gebäudekomplex, der die Extreme des indischen Klimas erfolgreich meistert und in formal-architektonischer Hinsicht richtungweisend ist, stößt man auf das Meisterwerk des Indian Institute of Management (1954) in Ahmedabad, das Le Corbusiers großer amerikanischer Zeitgenosse Louis Kahn baute. Ein weiteres Beispiel für eine leider nie realisierte Architektur ist der Tempelbau, mit dem Constantin Brancusi in den 1930er Jahren vom Herrscher von Indore beauftragt wurde. Er sollte am Ufer des Flusses Narmada in Maheshwar liegen, und zu seinen hervorstechenden Merkmalen gehörten eine unterirdische Passage und ein von Skulpturen – „Birds in Space“ – umgebenes Wasserbecken. Brancusi war von den Brunnen, Wassertanks, unterirdischen Gängen und Treppen des Forts im nahen Mandu sehr beeindruckt gewesen, das er 1937 als Gast des Maharadschas besucht hatte. Ein Beispiel für einen großen Bildhauer, der sich zwar sehr für indische Kunst interessierte – er besaß viele Hindu-Holzschnitzereien und Miniaturmalereien und schrieb eine Reihe von sehr poetischen Reflektionen über Shiva-Statuen – aber Indien selbst nie besuchte, ist Brancusis berühmter älterer Zeitgenosse Auguste Rodin.

Le Corbusier erhielt auch Aufträge für Häuser von Privatkunden in Ahmedabad (von ihm stammt auch das großartige Haus des Baumwollspinnereiverbandes aus dem Jahr 1956), besonders für die Familie Sarabhai – führende Industriemagnaten und Förderer der Kunst – die auch die Initiative ergriff, ausländische Künstler einzuladen, mit dem von ihnen produzierten Papier zu arbeiten. Robert Rauschenberg war der erste, der diese Gelegenheit 1974 nützte, gefolgt von James Rosenquist, Keith Sonnier, Frank Stella, Howard Hodgkin und vielen anderen. Ahmedabad ist ein wichtiges Textilzentrum, und Rauschenbergs Faszination für die Farben und Stoffe, die er dort vorfand (wie sein Sohn bestätigt, der ihn nach Indien begleitete), fand Niederschlag in den Arbeiten, die er bald nach seiner Rückkehr in die Vereinigten Staaten fertig stellte, besonders in der Serie „Jammer“ aus dem Jahr 1975, in der er große monochrome Rechtecke aus Seide oder Satin an Stangen oder der Wand befestigte, wobei ihr Faltenwurf an Segel oder Flaggen erinnerten. Diese Assoziationen sind sicherlich angemessen für den Erfinder einer „Bildfläche, die die Welt wieder herein lässt“, wie Leo Steinberg es so anschaulich ausdrückte. Das Paradigma dieser Bildfläche beschrieb Steinberg als „Flachbett-Bildebene – ein Untergrund so hart und unnachgiebig wie eine Werkbank“, mit der „Ebenflächigkeit eines unordentlichen Schreibtisches oder eines nicht

during the monsoon. These were climatic factors with a direct bearing on the existential ethos of daily life in India that Le Corbusier wasn't quite able to dominate in Chandigarh.

For a complex of buildings that succeeded in mastering the vagaries of the Indian climate and being a major formal architectural statement, we must look to the masterpiece that is The Indian Institute of Management (1954) in Ahmedabad, built by Le Corbusier's great American contemporary, Louis Kahn. An example of an architecture that was, alas, never realized is the temple that Brancusi was commissioned to design by the ruler of Indore during the 1930s. It was envisaged on the banks of the Narmada River in Maheshwar, and its notable features included a subterranean passage and a water basin, with sculptures – the Birds in Space – placed around it. Brancusi had been greatly impressed by the fountains, water tanks, underground corridors and staircases at the fort in nearby Mandu which he visited while a guest of the maharaja in 1937. An example of a great sculptor who was deeply interested in Indian art – he owned many Hindu wood carvings as well as miniature paintings, and wrote, with poetic insight, a suite of reflection on statues of Shiva – but who never visited India is Brancusi's illustrious older contemporary, Rodin.

It was in Ahmedabad, too, that Le Corbusier was commissioned to build houses for private clients (he was also the author of the superb Millowners' Association Building of 1956 in that city), notably for the Sarabhai family – leading industrial magnates and patrons of the arts – and it is they who took the initiative to invite artists from abroad to work with the paper produced by their mills. Robert Rauschenberg was the first to avail himself of this opportunity in 1974, followed, subsequently, by James Rosenquist, Keith Sonnier, Frank Stella, Howard Hodgkin, among others. Ahmedabad is an important centre for textiles, and Rauschenberg's fascination for the colours and fabrics he encountered there (as attested by his son who accompanied him to India) is registered in the works he made soon after his return to the United States, particularly in the "Jammer" series of 1975 that deploy large monochromatic rectangles of silk or satin attached to a pole or pinned to the wall, their folds evocative of the rippling of sails or flags – associations that are surely appropriate for the inventor of "a pictorial surface that let the world in again", in Leo Steinberg's memorable phrase. The paradigm of that pictorial surface was what Steinberg famously called "the flatbed picture plane" – "a bedrock as hard and resistant as a workbench", "the flatness of a disordered desk or an unswept floor..." In other words, a horizontal working surface whose ingenious Indian version could well be the mud floors of village homes. This telluric substance (used for a variety of construction purposes) mixed with paper pulp produced "rag mud", a compound out of which Rauschenberg made some of the works in the "Bones and Unions" series (1975) during his Indian sojourn (A major precedent for a work made of mud and mold is Rauschenberg's own extraordinary Dirt Painting (for John Cage) of 1953).

The exposure to indigenous handcrafted materials brought out the artisanal strain in Rauschenberg's working methods, as it did in Frank Stella's maquettes for his metal reliefs: the "Indian Birds" series, made in 1977, during his stay at the Sarabhai residence. But unlike the restless scavenging impulse that lay at the heart of Rauschenberg's openness to experiment with whatever came his way, Stella's preoccupations in Ahmedabad appear to have been more narrowly focused on the problems internal to the evolution of his art practice, based as these were on certain formal tenets elaborated prior to his arrival in India. The tasks preoccupying him at the time hinged on the question of how far he could go in the affirmation of the sculptural and architectural dimensions of an art whose matrix was resolutely pictorial and abstract. The "Indian" component of the maquettes were the sheets of tin alloy used for making cans for soft drinks, "a serendipitous choice of materials", according to William Rubin, in that "the fragments of commercial logos and other print and design elements on the tin enriched the irregular curves cut from them

gefegten Fußbodens …". Mit anderen Worten: eine horizontale Arbeitsfläche, deren raffiniertes indisches Äquivalent durchaus die Lehmböden der ländlichen Behausungen sein könnten. Wenn man dieses Erdmaterial (das für eine Reihe von Bauzwecken Verwendung findet) mit Papierzellstoff mischt, entsteht daraus sogenannter „rag mud", ein Stoff, aus dem Rauschenberg während seines Aufenthaltes in Indien einige der Arbeiten in der Serie „Bones and Unions" (1975) herstellte (ein Präzedenzfall für eine Arbeit aus Schlamm und Humus ist Rauschenbergs eigenes außergewöhnliches Werk „Dirt Painting (for John Cage)" aus dem Jahr 1953).

Die Begegnung mit indigenen handgefertigten Materialien inspirierte Rauschenberg zu einem kunsthandwerklichen Anstrich in seinen Arbeitsmethoden, ähnlich wie es auch Frank Stella mit seinen Maquettes (Metallreliefs) ging: die Serie „Indian Birds" entstand 1977 während seines Aufenthaltes im Heim der Familie Sarabhai. Im Unterschied zu dem rastlosen Aneignungsimpuls, der Rauschenbergs Experimentierfreudigkeit mit allem was ihm unter die Augen kam zugrunde lag, schien es Stella in Ahmedabad mehr um die inneren Probleme seiner eigenen Kunstpraxis und deren Entwicklung zu gehen, die sich auf gewisse formale Grundsätze stützten, die er schon vor seiner Ankunft in Indien entwickelt hatte. Alles konzentrierte sich bei ihm damals auf die Frage, inwieweit er in der Betonung der skulpturalen und architektonischen Dimensionen einer Kunst gehen konnte, deren Matrix ganz entschieden bildhaft und abstrakt war. Die „indische" Komponente der Maquettes war das Weißblech von Getränkedosen. „Eine glückliche Materialwahl" nannte William Rubin es, weil „die Fragmente von kommerziellen Logos und anderen Druck- und Designelementen auf dem Blech die unregelmäßig ausgeschnittenen geschwungenen Kurven mit einem fast malerischen Licht- und Schattenspiel erhöhten, das deutliche Anklänge an Pop Art trug." Und Rubin spekuliert weiter: „der Glitzer, das Gold, die ‚geschmacklosen' Farbtöne, die auf den ‚Indian Birds, gemalt, gebeizt oder eingewaschen waren, reflektieren seine Erfahrung der indischen Stadtszenerie – die Pailletten und Kosmetika, … die exotischen Farben der Textilien, die Farbigkeit des Straßenlebens." Und was den Titel betrifft, so „erinnerten die fertigen Maquettes Stella an Vögel in Käfigen, daher suchte er sich ein Buch über die indische Vogelwelt, aus dem er die Titel bezog".

Also könnte man die Arbeiten aus Stellas indischer „Erfahrung" – laut, strahlend, barock, verführerisch und wunderschön – mit einem bunten Gefieder vergleichen, mit dessen Hilfe er sich eine weitere Feder an den Hut steckte. Der Aufenthalt in Indien war ein Arbeitsaufenthalt. Er hatte zahlreiche Assistenten zur Verfügung, wohnte angenehm und war nicht gefordert, über den fremden Kontext nachzudenken. „Weder vor noch während seiner Indienreise zeigte Stella besonderes Interesse an der indischen Kunst", schreibt Rubin in seiner maßgeblichen Monographie über den Künstler. Das lässt sich von Howard Hodgkin nicht sagen, der nicht nur ein alter Hase in Bezug auf Reisen auf dem Subkontinent war, sondern auch Künstler, Ästhet und Kunstkenner gleichermaßen. Schon lange vor seinem Aufenthalt in der Sarabhai-Stiftung im Jahr 1978 liebte er indische Miniaturmalerei (die er passioniert sammelt) und besuchte das Land häufig. Damals hatte er bereits eine eigene Bildsprache entwickelt, ein begrenztes Repertoire von einfachen Formen, das er bemerkenswert flexibel für den Ausdruck einer breiten Gefühlspalette einsetzte: die Farben waren leuchtend, die Nuancen hinreißend, das Spiel der Pinselstriche zwischen Verbergen und Enthüllen angemessen für die privaten Einblicke, die Strukturen eines Gefühls oder einer Erinnerung, die in den Bildern angesprochen werden. Während der Entstehungsprozess von Ölbildern auf Holzgrund normalerweise langwierig und zäh war und endlosen Korrekturen unterlag, musste Hodgkin seine Arbeitsmethode in Ahmedabad modifizieren: „Ich entschloss mich, Textilfarben auf ungeleimtem Papier zu verwenden. Viele dieser Farben waren für Indien typisch und sehr außergewöhnlich. Zweimal am Tag, in der Früh und am Nachmittag, wurden vier oder sechs Blatt Papier auf Zinkblech geliefert, abgedeckt mit Musselin. Man hatte ein-

with a quasi-painterly, all-over flicker of light and dark that had legible 'pop' associations". "The glitter, the gold, the 'bad taste' hues that were painted, stained, or washed into the Indian Birds", Rubin goes on to speculate, "reflect his experience of India's urban scene—the sequins and cosmetics, … the exotic dyes of the textiles, the colourism of street life". And as for the title, "the finished maquettes reminded Stella of birds in cages, so he found a book on birds in India, from which the titles are taken".

So the works – brash, brilliant, baroque, beguiling and beautiful – arising from Stella's Indian "experience" could be likened to a multi-coloured plumage, providing him with another feather in his cap. The stint in India was a working assignment, numerous assistants were at his disposal, the living conditions agreeable, considerations about the foreign context uncalled for. "Neither before nor during his trip to India did Stella show a particular interest in that country's art", writes Rubin in his authoritative monograph on the artist. This could hardly be said of Howard Hodgkin, an old "India hand" in the tradition of the traveller to the subcontinent who is also an artist and aesthete and art connoisseur. His love for Indian miniature painting (of which he's an avid collector) and his frequent visits to the country long predated his stay at the Sarabhai foundation in 1978. By that time his pictorial language had come into its own, a limited repertory of simplified forms remarkably versatile for the range of feelings it could be made to suggest: the paint was luscious, the hues ravishing, the play of concealment and disclosure enacted by the brush strokes finely tuned to the private epiphanies, the textures of a sensation or a memory, commemorated in the pictures. While the gestation of the oil paintings on wood was usually long and drawn out, subject as they were to endless revisions, in Ahmedabad Hodgkin had to modify his working methods: "I decided to use textile dyes on unsized paper. Many of these were colours indigenous to India, and all quite extraordinary. Twice a day, in the morning and afternoon, four or six pieces of paper were delivered on zinc plates, covered with muslin. It was an hour and a half from the time they were delivered wet, until they dried… Using brushes and rags I worked very quickly… The dye would spread inside the paper while I was working, and would continue to change and modify even after I'd stopped… It was a great strain as I was remembering images from all my previous trips to India… Many of the pictures were vignettes of things I'd seen, like a concrete wall with garlands of flowers hanging from it; vistas of the sky and the horizon; a train crossing the distant landscape, and so on. They are a kind of anthology of Indian images, and also a sampler of all the different kinds of language I use in my paintings, but used in an almost simplistic way." But it is perhaps precisely the simplified pictorial vocabulary of the "Indian Leaves" (the title of this set of works) that also allows one to see them as a late modernist (and therefore characteristically left-handed) encomium to certain aspects of Indian miniature painting, notably in the choice of colours and the omnipresence of framing borders.

Other artists, less bound to a medium, have made their independent way to India. Wolfgang Laib has been visiting the country since the mid-nineteen seventies (soon after finishing his medical studies in Tubingen). The poetic archaism of the substances to which he is drawn (pollen, wax, honey, milk, rice), the ritualistic aspect of the preparation and presentation of his installations, his monkish aloofness, the sense of the work as a votive offering – all these features suggest certain elective affinities between his "world-view" and the renunciatory protocol of Indian ascetics or sanyasins. But the contemplativeness that he wishes his work to instil in the minds of those who encounter it is unclouded by religious considerations, however much he might take the life of St Francis of Assisi as a moral exemplum. The notion of spiritual healing that his art aspires to belongs rather to a line of thinking associated with that post-minimalist shaman, Joseph Beuys.

The mythopoetic conceits of Francesco Clemente's drawings and pastels seem to have been bolstered by his numerous trips to India, his dandyish exploration of Indian folkloric esoterica becoming more pronounced once he

undeinhalb Stunden von der Zeit zu der sie angeliefert wurden, bis sie getrocknet waren ... Ich verwendete Pinsel und Lappen und arbeitete sehr rasch ... Die Farbe breitete sich während meiner Arbeit immer mehr im Papier aus, und das Bild änderte sich sogar noch nachdem ich aufgehört hatte ... Es war eine große Belastung, da ich mich an die Bilder all meiner früheren Indienreisen erinnerte ... Viele der Bilder waren Vignetten von Dingen, die ich gesehen hatte, etwa eine Betonwand mit Blumengirlanden, Eindrücke von Himmel und Horizont, ein Zug, der durch eine weit entfernte Landschaft fährt, etc. Eine Art von Anthologie von Indienbildern und auch ein Musterbuch für all die unterschiedlichen Sprachen, die ich in meiner Malerei verwende, aber auf fast simplistische Weise." Vielleicht ist es ja gerade das vereinfachte Vokabular der „Indian Leaves" (so der Titel dieser Blätterserie), das es dem Betrachter erlaubt, sie als spätmodernistisches (und daher charakteristisch ungeschlachtes) Loblied auf gewisse Aspekte der indischen Miniaturmalerei anzusehen, besonders die Farbwahl und die Allgegenwärtigkeit von Umrandungen.

Andere Künstler, die nicht so sehr einem Medium verpflichtet waren, haben Indien auf eigene Faust bereist. Wolfgang Laib besucht das Land seit Mitte der 1970er Jahre (kurz nachdem er sein Medizinstudium in Tübingen abgeschlossen hatte). Die poetisch-archaische Natur der von ihm präferierten Substanzen (Pollen, Wachs, Honig, Milch, Reis), der ritualistische Aspekt der Vorbereitung und Präsentation seiner Installationen, seine mönchische Unnahbarkeit, der Anklang von Opfergaben in seinem Werk – all diese Elemente deuten eine gewisse Wahlverwandtschaft zwischen seiner „Weltsicht" und dem genügsamen Leben der indischen Asketen oder „Sanyasins" an. Die Besinnlichkeit, die sein Werk im Geist der Betrachter erwecken soll, ist aber nicht von religiösen Überlegungen überschattet, wie sehr er sich auch das Leben des Franz von Assisi zum moralischen Vorbild nehmen mag. Das Konzept der geistigen Heilung, die seine Kunst anstrebt, verbindet man eher mit der Gesinnung des post-minimalistischen Schamanen Joseph Beuys.

Die mythopoetischen Dünkel der Zeichnungen und Pastellmalerei von Francesco Clemente scheinen durch seine zahlreichen Indienreisen gestärkt worden zu sein. Seine dandyhafte Auseinandersetzung mit indischer Folkloreesoterik wurde ausgeprägter, sobald er auf den Zug der italienischen „Trans-Avantgarde" aufsprang. Dem Aufruf dieser Bewegung (wenn man sie so nennen kann) zur Figuration zurückzukehren folgend und im Einklang mit ihrer Vorliebe für die Einbindung geographisch weit auseinander liegender Kunstpraktiken, hat Clemente mit indischen Kunsthandwerkern zusammengearbeitet, besonders mit Künstlern aus Orissa, die für ihn in ihrem charakteristischen Pat-Stil (friesartige Aneinanderreihungen von Figuren) großformatige Gemälde anfertigen, deren Ikonographie aber vom Maler festgelegt wird.

Eine komplexere Herangehensweise an eine transkulturelle Begegnung stellt Richard Longs Bearbeitung von tribalem Gebiet dar. Das Gebiet war jenes der Warlis, das Long als Gast des Warli-Künstlers Jivya Mashe Soma besuchte. Sein Adivasi-Gastgeber (dieses indische Wort für „indigene Einwohner" bezeichnet Menschen, die zu tribalen Gemeinschaften gehören) schien etwas befremdet von Longs üblicher Arbeitsweise, den Boden mit Kreisen und Pfaden zu markieren, die sich so sehr von den Details des Lebenszyklus unterschied, die Mashe mit stilisierten Figuren auf den aus Kuhdung hergestellten Wänden der Dorfbehausungen darstellt. Der „horror vacui" des Adivasi-Künstlers steht in deutlichem Gegensatz zu den ephemeren Schlamm- und Aschemustern, mit denen der Land Artist Richard Long leere Räume versieht. Man könnte diesen Gegensatz auch als Lehrstunde in den unterschiedlichen kulturellen Valenzen von „Primitivismus" ansehen.

Kulturelle „Zusammenarbeit" ganz anderer Art findet sich in Luigi Ontanis Fotografien von sich selbst in Gesellschaft von gutaussehenden indischen Jugendlichen in Posen aus dem ikonographischen Repertoire der Hindu-Gottheiten, wie sie auf kitschigen Kalendern und Drucken dargestellt sind. (Ein berühmter Präzedenzfall für solche Rollenspiele: Wilhelm von Gloedens

joined the bandwagon of the Italian "Trans-avant-garde". In keeping with that movement's (if it can be so designated) call to a return to figuration and its embrace of geographically far-flung art practices, Clemente has collaborated with Indian artisans, notably folk artists from Orissa, who have realised large-scale paintings for him in their characteristic pat style – frieze-like alignments of figures – but whose iconography is dictated by the painter.

A rather more complex attempt at a transcultural encounter is Richard Long's passage on tribal land, that of the Warlis, as a guest of the Warli artist Jivya Mashe Soma. His Adivasi host (the Indian word for "first inhabitants", designating people belonging to tribal communities) seems to have looked somewhat askance at Long's characteristic way of marking the ground with circles and paths, so different from the minutiae of the life-cycle depicted by Mashe's stick figures on the cow dung walls of village dwellings. The Adivasi artist's horror of the void is in marked contrast to the Land artist's ephemeral mud and ash patterns in empty spaces, a contrast that can also be taken as an object lesson in the different cultural valences of "primitivism".

Cultural "collaboration" of another kind is enacted in Luigi Ontani's photographs of himself in the company of comely Indian youths, assuming poses mined from the iconographic repertory of the Hindu gods as incarnated in the kitsch bazaar realism of calendars and prints. (A famous precedent for such role playing: Wilhelm von Gloeden's photographs of nubile Sicilian peasant boys parading as Antique ephebes). The vernacular look of these images is not inadvertent, given that the artful tableaux composed by Ontani (replete with props and costumes) are photographed in the studios of small-town commercial Indian photographers. These playful Indian avatars of himself (often assuming the guise of figures on society's margins but who remain the stock-in-trade of quaint stereotypes about exotic India: the snake charmer, the monkey or bear trainer...) are amusing in the way of Camp mannerisms, at once narcissistic and archly parodic, their faux-naïf oneirism and mixture of cultural codes a witty antidote to the solemn pieties about the self and the other.

The theatricalization of personal identity as a form of cultural alterity finds its consummate expression in the personae assumed by Pierre Loti, adept as he was in having himself photographed in a variety of oriental disguises (Ontani's masquerades belong to this streak of flamboyance in the affirmation of selfhood). Loti made an extended trip to India in 1900, taking photographs of the places he visited (notably the temple towns of the south and Benares) and detailed notes that he elaborated into a book after his return to France. Its perverse title, L'Inde (sans les Anglais), registers Loti's decision to turn a blind eye on the colonial presence, as if the otherness that he wished to experience at first hand would lose its exotic appeal were he to countenance his fellow Europeans on Indian soil, who were English to boot! He was curious to learn about Hinduism, and prone to nostalgia as he was, saw it as a continuum of immemorial rites and beliefs. But his narrative is full of vivid descriptions of landscapes and people and everyday life: many of his Indian acquaintances seem to have affably assumed the role of native informants, and so the literary style of his travelogue is leavened with telling ethnographic aperçus.

For an example of the writer as a roving consciousness abroad – as irreverential about himself and where he comes from as he is about the "elsewhere" to which he has elected to travel – we must look to Henri Michaux and the barbed, bemused account of his stay in India, written in the 1930s and first published in 1945. Given his heightened sense of the absurd, Michaux could well have called his idiosyncratic text "Impressions of India" in the spirit of Raymond Roussel's novel Impressions of Africa: both books put a spoke in the wheel of Western rationalism and logical causality. Michaux's scepticism about the Western logos and its civilizational certitudes was surely spurred by the impending catastrophe of the Second World War; his essay, for all its witticisms and wayward, quirky reflections on diverse aspects of Indian life and culture, is titled A Barbarian in Asia. "Knowledge does not progress with time.

Fotografien von sizilianischen Bauernknaben, die als antike Epheben posieren). Der volkstümliche Look dieser Bilder ist wenig überraschend angesichts der Tatsache, dass die von Ontani kunstvoll arrangierten Tableaux (inklusive Requisiten und Kostüme) in den Studios von Kleinstadtfotografen angefertigt werden. Diese spielerischen indischen Avatare seiner Selbst (oft als gesellschaftliche Randfiguren verkleidet, aber immer im Rahmen der altbekannten, exotischen Indien-Stereotype: Schlangenbeschwörer, Dompteur mit Affen oder Bären ...) sind auf manieriert-affektierte Weise amüsant, gleichzeitig narzisstisch und überaus parodistisch. Ihre vorgetäuschte naive Verträumtheit und die bunte Mischung aus kulturellen Kodes stellen ein witziges Gegengewicht für die pathetischen Anmutungen über das Selbst und den Anderen dar.

Die Theatralisierung der persönlichen Identität als Form der kulturellen Alterität findet ihren höchsten Ausdruck in den Figuren, in die Pierre Loti hineinschlüpft, der sich selbst geschickt in einer Vielzahl von orientalischen Kostümierungen fotografieren ließ (auch Ontanis Maskeraden besitzen diesen flamboyanten Anstrich in ihrer dargestellten Selbstbestätigung). Loti machte im Jahr 1900 eine lange Reise nach Indien, wo er die besuchten Orte fotografierte (besonders die Tempelstädte des Südens und Benares) und detaillierte Notizen machte, die er nach seiner Rückkehr nach Frankreich zu einem Buch ausarbeitete. Dessen perverser Titel, „L'Inde (sans les Anglais)" (Indien ohne die Engländer), zeugt von Lotis Entschluss, die Präsenz der Kolonialmacht zu ignorieren, so als ob die Andersartigkeit, die er aus erster Hand zu erleben wünschte, ihre exotische Anziehungskraft verlöre, wenn er auf indischem Boden anderen Europäern, und noch dazu Engländern, begegnete. Er interessierte sich für den Hinduismus, den er als alter Nostalgiker als Kontinuum von undenklich alten Riten und Überzeugungen ansah. Aber seine Erzählung strotzt auch von lebendigen Beschreibungen von Landschaften, Menschen und des Alltagslebens: viele seiner indischen Bekanntschaften scheinen ihm als freundliche Informanten gedient zu haben, und der literarische Stil seines Reisebuches ist mit markanten ethnographischen Apercus gewürzt.

Ein Beispiel für den Schriftsteller als in der Fremde umherstreifendes Bewusstsein – ebenso respektlos sich selbst und seiner Herkunft gegenüber wie dem „Anderswo", das zu bereisen er entschlossen ist – finden wir in Henri Michaux und dem spitzzüngigen, etwas konsternierten Bericht über seinen Indienaufenthalt, der in den 1930ern geschrieben und 1945 erstmals veröffentlicht wurde. Angesichts seines scharfen Blicks für das Absurde hätte Michaux seinen idiosynkratischen Text ruhig „Eindrücke aus Indien" betiteln können, ganz im Geiste von Raymond Roussels Roman „Eindrücke aus Afrika": beide Bücher streuen Sand in das Getriebe von westlichem Rationalismus und logischer Kausalität. Michauxs Skepsis über den westlichen Logos und seine zivilisatorischen Gewissheiten wurde zweifellos von der nahenden Katastrophe des zweiten Weltkriegs genährt. Trotz all seiner Witzeleien und schrägen Reflektionen über diverse Aspekte indischen Lebens und indischer Kultur trägt das Buch den Titel „Ein Barbar in Asien". „Wissen vermehrt sich nicht im Laufe der Zeit. Unterschiede werden übersehen. Man schließt Kompromisse. Man verständigt sich. Und man hört auf, Schlussfolgerungen zu ziehen. Dieses fatale Gesetz funktioniert so, dass die ständigen Einwohner Asiens und die Personen, die am meisten mit ihnen zu tun haben, sich nicht an dem Punkt befinden, wo ein fokussierter Blick aufrecht erhalten werden kann, während ein Passant mit seinem unschuldigen Blick manchmal den Finger auf das Wesentliche legen kann." Da ist nichts „Barbarisches" an diesen Gedanken, obwohl es Michaux ist, der sie äußert: der scherzende Ton des Buches ist wahrscheinlich seine Methode, in einer Welt Zeit zu schinden, die noch nicht begriffen hat, was er in seinem Vorwort hellsichtig als die „planetare Zivilisation der Zukunft" beschreibt.

Die englische Version eines Aufenthalts in fremden Gefilden, die gleichzeitig ein Porträt der ausländischen Befindlichkeiten darstellt, ist oft von einer ge-

Differences are overlooked. You compromise. You come to an understanding. And you cease to come to conclusions. This fatal law acts in such a way that the permanent residents of Asia and the persons who are most thrown together with the Asiatics are not at the exact point where a focused vision can be retained, whereas a passerby, with his innocent eye, is able sometimes to lay his finger on the centre." Nothing "barbarian" about these thoughts, although it is Michaux who voices them: the jocular tone of his book is probably a way of temporizing with a world that hasn't yet taken the measure of what he presciently announces in his preface as "the coming planetary civilization."

The English version of a sojourn in foreign climes that is also a portrait of a sensibility abroad is often tinged with the irony that is a staple of English letters in the interwar period. E.M. Forster's The Hill of Devi (1953) recounts his experience of living in the tiny principality of Dewas Senior where he was employed as secretary to the ruler in 1921. His Highness was a fantasist, with pronounced mystical yearnings, a character at once colourful and complex, clueless about affairs of state, and not less exasperating for being "lovable and brilliant and witty and charming". The irony sheathing Forster's perplexed equanimity when faced by his seigneurial employer's whims and caprices was what probably allowed him to fulfil his notional duties and to write the letters describing the mad goings-on within this microcosm of princely India. Some of this material, transposed and shorn of all quaintness, formed the basis of Forster's A Passage to India (1924), his great novel about the colonial encounter that ends on an enigmatic note of deferral, keeping in abeyance the possibility of friendship between its Indian and English protagonists. (A novel that draws on experiences comparable to those described by Forster in his memoir of the ruler of Dewas Senior but in a tone that is unrelentingly effervescent in its wit and whimsicality is his friend J.R. Ackerley's Hindoo Holiday (1932), a narrative in the form of a journal of Ackerley's tenure as companion to the Maharaja of Chhokrapur during the 1920s that is a masterpiece of comic observation).

Forster's brief account of his first visit to the country in 1912-1913 was titled "Adrift in India", and drifting might indeed be the word to describe the peregrinations (from the 1940s onwards) of writers in the subcontinent seeking a dépaysement or escape route from settled habits of mind, and willing to accept temporarily the material discomforts of an alien land in exchange for what the experience of being there might bring in terms of an enlargement of their mental horizons. Paul Bowles was one such promeneur solitaire in the tradition of the American expatriate choosing to live off-shore of the American imperium. He had settled in Tangier in 1947, and although India never assumed the importance that North Africa had as a setting for his novels, he did write about his journeys "on the road" in India (with eighteen suitcases of clothing in tow!) and the adventures that befell him as a form of first-person reportage, with a sharp eye for the contrasts – of class and religion – that made up the shifting mosaic of a society in transition (His travelogue Their Heads Are Green and Their Hands Are Blue was published in 1963). But more typically, India has long been the destination of those keen to shed the baggage of the cultures to which they were born, fellow travelers on the path to alternative forms of enlightenment promised by Eastern systems of thought. The most famous writer to have made common cause with Hindu philosophy is Christopher Isherwood, who became a zealous advocate of a world-view based on the doctrine of Vedanta as imparted to him by his spiritual mentor Swami Prabhavananda, himself a follower of Ramakrishna. (My Guru and his Disciple, a book written late in his life is a record of his spiritual apprenticeship). Isherwood's "conversion" happened in California, where he had settled soon after his move to the United States in 1939; the "self-realization" that is the goal of Vedanta philosophy would not have been out of place in a culture that saw itself as a haven of alternative forms of self-affirmation. Isherwood's pre-war career in (homo) sexual hedonism could accommodate itself to an ethics that did not insist on self-abnegation, which is not to suggest that there

wissen Ironie gefärbt, die ein Markenzeichen der englischen Literatur in der Zwischenkriegszeit ist. E.M. Forsters „The Hill of Devi" (1953) erzählt von seinen Erlebnissen im winzigen Fürstenstaat Dewas Senior, wo er 1921 einen Posten als Sekretär des Herrschers inne hatte. Seine Hoheit der Fürst war ein Fantast mit ausgeprägten mystischen Neigungen, eine schillernde und komplexe Figur, ahnungslos was Staatsgeschäfte betraf, und, obwohl „liebenswürdig und brillant und witzig und charmant", ziemlich anstrengend. Es war wahrscheinlich der Schutzschild der Ironie, mit dem Forster in perplexer Gleichmütigkeit den Launen und Kapricen seines Arbeitgebers gegenübertrat, das es ihm erlaubte, seine offiziellen Pflichten zu erfüllen und Briefe zu schreiben, in denen er die verrückten Vorkommnisse in diesem Mikrokosmos des fürstlichen Indien beschrieb. Teile dieses Materials bildeten, transponiert und von aller Exzentrik befreit, die Grundlage für „A Passage to India" (1924, dt. Auf der Suche nach Indien), Forsters großen Roman über die koloniale Begegnung, die in einem enigmatischen Schwebezustand endet und die Möglichkeit einer Freundschaft zwischen den indischen und britischen Protagonisten offen lässt. (Ein Roman, der auf ähnlichen Erfahrungen beruht wie jenen, die Forster in seinen Memoiren über den Herrscher von Dewas Senior beschreibt, ist das in einem gnadenlos spritzigen Ton voller Witz und Wunderlichkeiten erzählte „Hindoo Holiday". Die von Forsters Freund J.R. Ackerley (1932) verfasste Erzählung in Tagebuchform über Ackerleys Anstellung als Begleiter des Maharadscha von Chhokrapur in den 1920ern ist ein Meisterwerk an komischer Beobachtungsgabe.)

Forsters kurze Erzählung über seinen ersten Besuch in Indien in den Jahren 1912-1913 trug den Titel „Adrift in India" (dt. etwa: ziellos unterwegs in Indien), und das wäre wahrscheinlich eine gute Beschreibung für die (ab den 1940ern) auf dem Subkontinent herumziehenden Schriftsteller. Sie suchten einen Umgebungswechsel oder einen Fluchtweg aus allzu festgelegten Denkgewohnheiten und waren bereit, als Preis für die Erweiterung ihres geistigen Horizontes zeitweilig die physischen Unbequemlichkeiten eines fremden Landes auf sich zu nehmen. Paul Bowles war einer dieser einsamen Wanderer in der Tradition der Amerikaner, die es vorzogen, fern des amerikanischen Imperiums zu leben. Er hatte sich 1947 in Tanger niedergelassen, und obwohl Indien in seinen Romanen nie denselben Stellenwert einnahm wie Nordafrika, schrieb er über seine Reisen „on the road" in Indien (mit achtzehn Koffern voll Kleidung im Schlepptau!) und die Abenteuer, die er dabei erlebte. Seine Reportage in Ichform zeugt von einem scharfen Blick für die Kontraste – in Bezug auf Klasse und Religion —, die das changierende Mosaik einer Gesellschaft im Wandel ausmachten. (Sein Reisebuch „Their Heads Are Green and Their Hands Are Blue" wurde 1963 veröffentlicht).

Typischerweise ist Indien seit langem das Reiseziel jener, die den Ballast der Kulturen, in die sie hineingeboren wurden, abwerfen wollen. Reisende auf dem Weg zu alternativen Formen der Erleuchtung, wie sie in asiatischen Weltanschauungen versprochen werden. Der berühmteste Schriftsteller, der sich der Hinduphilosophie anschloss, war Christopher Isherwood, der zum eifrigen Verkünder einer Weltanschauung wurde, die auf der Doktrin von Vedanta basiert, wie sie ihm von seinem geistigen Mentor Swami Prabhavananda, selbst ein Anhänger von Ramakrishna, nahegebracht wurde. („My Guru and his Disciple", das er gegen Ende seines Lebens schrieb, erzählt von seiner spirituellen Lehrzeit). Isherwoods „Konvertierung" ereignete sich in Kalifornien, wo er sich bald nach seinem Umzug in die Vereinigten Staaten im Jahr 1939 niedergelassen hatte. Die „Selbstverwirklichung", die das Ziel der Vedanta-Philosophie darstellt, hätte in einer Kultur, die sich selbst als Zufluchtsort für alternative Formen der Selbsterkenntnis ansah, nicht befremdet. Isherwoods Vorkriegskarriere als (homo)sexueller Hedonist passte ganz gut zu einer Ethik, die nicht auf Selbstverleugnung bestand, womit aber nicht angedeutet werden soll, dass er diesem besonders abstrusen Zweig der Hindulehre aus Opportunismus nähertrat.

„Die Hinwendung nach Fernost", die sich in Isherwoods Schriften nachvollziehen lässt, ist kaum identisch mit dem für die Gegenkultur der 1960er typischen

was anything opportunistic about his understanding of a particularly abstruse branch of Hindu doctrine.

"The turn to the East" elaborated in Isherwood's writings is hardly identical with the escapism that often characterized the counterculture of the sixties, although there were genuine, if somewhat naïve seekers, too, among those who had decided to "drop out" from the rat race, their backpacks carrying well thumbed copies of The Tibetan Book of the Dead or Hermann Hesse's Siddhartha, not to mention the hidden stash of grass. The psychedelic "highs" that set the mood-tone of the decade also translated as a visual style of vivid colours and complex patterns in painting, design and fabric. (The formal confluence of mass produced commercial logos and the abstract configuration of mandalas – the visual diagrams of Tibetan tantric esoterica aimed at inducing meditation – is instanced in the Californian artist John McCracken's paintings of the early seventies). Hesse's revival as a cult author of the counterculture is, of course, linked to the oriental wisdom that informed the contemplative tenor of some of his books; his family had long been steeped in Indian philosophy, his grandparents and his parents having lived in India for many years as Protestant missionaries, and one of his cousins, who had settled in Japan, was an acknowledged authority on Zen Buddhism. Hesse travelled to the East in 1911, visiting Malaysia, Singapore, Sumatra and Ceylon, but despite the title Aus India ("From India") that he gave to the journal he kept during this voyage, Hesse didn't actually set foot in the country, as if in his mind's eye the very idea of India englobed the spiritual Orient as such.

A writer who did travel to India, incorporating his experiences of some of the major Buddhist and Hindu sites in the complex architecture of his novel, The Temple of Dawn (1970), the third in the Sea of Fertility tetralogy, is Mishima Yukio. The elaborate plot, whose time-span ranges from 1939 to 1967, revolves around the motif of reincarnation, and includes within its orbit reflections on pre-and post-war Japanese society, long disquisitions on the Hindu and Buddhist versions of samsara, bombing raids on Japan, and the main protagonist's erotic obsession. The story is an allegorical quest, and the detour through the arcana of philosophic concepts of rebirth is surely linked to questions of Japan's spiritual regeneration.

The search for meaning – a phrase that is itself redolent of the counterculture – led Allen Ginsberg, the druggy poet "guru" of the Beats, to India in 1961: the story of his wanderings – that took him to Rishikesh and Benares and Calcutta – and during which he encountered an array of characters, some louche, others lofty-minded (brilliantly recounted by Deborah Baker in her book A Blue Hand), reads as a cross between a pilgrim's and a rake's progress. As for Günter Grass, he was hardly in search of spiritual succour when he sojourned in Calcutta twenty-five years later, a visit occasioned by the staging, in Bengali translation, of his play "The Plebeians Rehearse the Uprising" (This was Grass's reimagining of "Coriolanus" as Bertolt Brecht might have directed it at the time of the workers' rebellion in East Germany in 1953). His Calcutta journal, accompanied by graphic, expressionistic drawings of slums and their dispossessed inhabitants, is an impassioned and often virulent response to the social injustice at the root of the poverty and destitution he encountered. The title of his book, Show Your Tongue, a colloquial expression of shame indigenous to India, also refers to the fearsome goddess of annihilation, Kali, venerated in Bengal, and usually represented with her tongue hanging out. As it happens, it was this avenging deity that Allen Ginsberg chose as the motif for one of the first poems that he attempted to write in India, "depict(ing) her as the Statue of Liberty, her neck adorned with the martyred heads of the Rosenbergs, her foot crushing the body of Uncle Sam, while her breasts spurted jazz." ("The goddess of dread and destruction, of night and chaos", as Georges Bataille described her, had an emblematic presence in the dissident surrealist's radically anti-idealist writings of the late 1920s).

"When I discovered India what I was saying started to change", wrote John Cage. And when I discovered China and Japan I changed the very fact of

Eskapismus. Allerdings gab es auch dort echte, wenn auch vielleicht naive, Suchende unter jenen, die sich entschieden hatten, aus der Tretmühle zu fliehen, ihre Rucksäcke mit zerlesenen Exemplaren des Tibetanischen Totenbuches oder Hermann Hesses „Siddharta“ und natürlich einem Vorrat an Haschisch gefüllt. Die psychedelischen „Highs“ die die Stimmung jener Dekade bestimmten, kamen auch optisch in lebhaften Farben und komplexen Mustern in Malerei, Design und Stoffen zum Ausdruck. (Das formale Zusammentreffen von massenproduzierten kommerziellen Logos und der abstrakten Konfiguration von Mandalas – den meditationsfördernden Diagrammen der tibetanisch-tantrischen Esoterik – erlebt man in den Bildern des kalifornischen Künstlers John McCracken aus den frühen 1970ern). Das Revival von Hesse als Kultautor der Gegenkultur hängt natürlich mit den östlichen Weisheiten zusammen, die den kontemplativen Tenor seiner Bücher bestimmten. Seiner Familie war die indische Philosophie wohl vertraut, da seine Großeltern und Eltern viele Jahre als protestantische Missionare in Indien gelebt hatten, und einer seiner Cousins, der in Japan lebte, eine anerkannte Autorität auf dem Gebiet des Zen-Buddhismus war. Hesse reiste 1911 in den fernen Osten, besuchte Malaysia, Singapur, Sumatra und Ceylon, setzte aber trotz des Titels „Aus Indien“, den er seinem Reisetagebuch gab, nie einen Fuß in das Land, so als stünde schon die bloße Idee von Indien in seinem Kopf stellvertretend für den gesamten spirituellen Orient.

Ein Schriftsteller der Indien tatsächlich bereiste und seine Erlebnisse an einigen großen Stätten des Buddhismus und Hinduismus in die komplexe Architektur seines Romans „Der Tempel der Morgendämmerung“ (1970, dritter Teil der Tetralogie „Das Meer der Fruchtbarkeit) einbaute, war Mishima Yukio. Die umfangreiche Handlung, die sich über die Jahre 1939 bis 1967 erstreckt, dreht sich um das Motiv der Reinkarnation und beinhaltet neben den Reflektionen über die japanische Gesellschaft vor und nach dem Krieg lange Abhandlungen über hinduistische und buddhistische Versionen von „Samsara“, Bombenangriffe auf Japan und die erotischen Obsessionen der Hauptfigur. Das Buch beschreibt eine allegorische Sinnsuche, und der Umweg über die Mysterien der philosophischen Konzepte der Wiedergeburt muss sicherlich in Zusammenhang mit Fragen der spirituellen Erneuerung Japans gesehen werden.

Die Suche nach dem Sinn – ein Ausdruck, der selbst eng mit der Gegenkultur verbunden ist – führte auch Allen Ginsberg, den drogensüchtigen Dichter und Guru der Beat Generation, 1961 nach Indien. Die Geschichte seiner Reise – die ihn nach Rishikesh, Benares and Calcutta führte – und auf der er einer Reihe von Figuren begegnete, manche zwielichtig, andere von nobler Gesinnung (brillant erzählt von Deborah Baker in ihrem Buch „A Blue Hand“), liest sich wie eine Kreuzung zwischen Pilgerfahrt und lebemännischer Lustreise. Günter Grass wiederum war wohl kaum auf der Suche nach spirituellem Beistand, als er 25 Jahre später Calcutta besuchte. Anlass seiner Reise war die Inszenierung seines Stückes „Die Plebejer proben den Aufstand“ in bengalischer Sprache (die Grasssche Version von „Koriolanus“ wie Bertolt Brecht es vielleicht zur Zeit des Arbeiteraufstands in Ostdeutschland 1953 inszeniert hätte). Sein Kalkutta-Tagebuch, das auch drastische, expressionistische Zeichnungen der Slums und ihrer notleidenden Bewohner enthält, ist eine leidenschaftliche und oft heftige Reaktion auf die soziale Ungerechtigkeit, die an der Wurzel all der Armut und des Elends liegt. Der Titel seines Buches „Zunge zeigen“, ein umgangssprachlicher Ausdruck für „Schande“ in Indien, verweist auch auf die furchteinflößende Göttin der Vernichtung, Kali, die in Bengal verehrt wird und meist mit heraushängender Zunge dargestellt ist. Es war übrigens auch diese Rachegöttin, die Allen Ginsberg als Motiv für eines der ersten in Indien geschriebenen Gedichte wählte, „dargestellt als Freiheitsstatue, ihr Hals mit den Märtyrerköpfen der Rosenbergs geschmückt, ihr Fuß den Körper von Uncle Sam zertretend, während Jazz aus ihren Brüsten fließt“. („Die Göttin der Angst und Zerstörung, der Nacht und des Chaos“, wie Georges Bataille sie beschrieb, spielte eine emblematische Rolle in den radikal anti-idealistischen Schriften des dissidenten Surrealisten in den späten 1920ern).

saying anything: I said nothing anymore. Silence, since everything already communicates, why wish to communicate?

The aesthetics of silence, the ethics of speech: India is the sounding-board for both these approaches, and for countless others, including some that are decidedly unflattering. A case in point is V.S. Naipaul's career in acerbic commentary on most things Indian, bristling with an irritability that has, over the years, long ceased to be merely epidermic. The path taken by him has led to a point of no return : from India as An Area of Darkness (1964) to India : A Wounded Civilization (1977). The "grudging affection" for the country expressed in the last of his travel books, India : A Million Mutinies Now (1990) is something most secular-minded Indians might want to do without, given that it extends to an alarmingly sectarian idea of nationhood based on hindutva or the "Hindu essence" (sic). (This is where the greatness of Naipaul as a novelist parts company with the less than magnanimous observer and analyst of the Indian scene). The antidote to Naipaulian glumness and grumpiness about India would be the gleeful narrative excess, the irrepressible exuberance, of Salman Rushdie's increasingly tireless tall tales. All these "documents" form part of a "museum-without-walls", to borrow André Malraux's famous idea of an archive henceforth accessible to everyone because based on technologies of mass reproduction – the musée imaginaire that succeeds the Ajaib Gher or "the Wonder House as the natives call the Lahore Museum," with which Kipling begins Kim (1901), that landmark of the literature of imperialism. The deterritorialized archive or museum would include Malraux's own hectic, rhetorical flourishes that characterize the reminiscences of his passage to the subcontinent in the late 1950s, as recorded in his Anti-Memoirs (1968), as they would the learned writings of Heinrich Zimmer, Alain Danielou, Mircea Eliade, Octavio Paz, and the luminous pages devoted to India in that great masterpiece of autobiography as anti-travelogue, Claude Levi-Strauss's Tristes Tropiques, unsurpassed as a lament for lost civilizations.

Deepak Ananth
Art historian, critic and independent curator based in Paris
Ananth studied at The Courtauld Institute of Art, University of London. He currently teaches at École régionale des Beaux-Arts in Caen. Curatorial projects include exhibitions of contemporary French art ("Thresholds", 1995), nineteenth century French painting ("Histoires Parallèles", 1995–96), Surrealism ("Surrealismo", 2001), contemporary Indian art ("Indian Summer", 2005; "L'Inde dans Tous les Sens", 2006; "Passages", 2006; "Prospects", 2007; "The Home and the World", 2008). He has written on a range of modern and contemporary European and Indian artists, mostly for museum publications. These include essays on Matisse, Picasso, Bonnard, Vuillard, Howard Hodgkin, Sarkis, Anish Kapoor, Amrita Sher-Gil, Vivan Sundaram, Mrinalini Mukherjee, Jitish Kallat, Dayanita Singh, Raghubir Singh and N. S. Harsha. He was a selector for the Artes Mundi Prize in 2006.

„Als ich Indien entdeckte, veränderte sich allmählich das was ich sagte", schrieb John Cage. „Und als ich China and Japan entdeckte, änderte ich die Tatsache des Sprechens an sich: ich sagte gar nichts mehr. Schweigen. Warum sollte man, nachdem alles bereits kommuniziert ist, noch den Wunsch nach Kommunikation haben?"
Die Ästhetik des Schweigens, die Ethik des Sprechens: Indien ist ein Resonanzboden für beide Ansätze, sowie für zahllose andere. Einige davon wurden in diesem Aufsatz angesprochen. Ein breiter gefasstes Panorama würde V.S. Naipauls Karriere der herben Kommentare über so gut wie alles, was Indien betrifft, einschließen, die von einer schon lange nicht mehr oberflächlich zu nennenden Reizbarkeit gekennzeichnet sind. Der von ihm beschrittene Weg führte zu einem Punkt ohne Wiederkehr: von Indien als „Land der Finsternis" (1964, dt.) zu „Indien – eine verwundete Kultur" (1977). Die „mürrische Zuneigung" zu diesem Land im letzten seiner Reisebücher „Indien – Land des Aufruhrs" (1990) ist etwas, auf das die meisten säkular eingestellten Inder wohl gut verzichten könnten, erstreckt sie sich doch auch auf eine gefährlich sektiererische Vorstellung von nationaler Identität, die auf „Hindutva" oder der „Essenz des Hinduismus" (sic) basiert. (Hier trennen sich die Wege zwischen Naipaul dem großen Romancier und Naipaul dem nicht sehr großmütigen Beobachter und Analytiker der indischen Szene.) Als Gegengift für Naipauls mürrisch-düstere Einstellung zu Indien können das fröhlich überbordende Narrativ und der unbeirrbare Überschwang von Salman Rushdies immer mehr legendengeschwängerten Geschichten gelten. All diese „Dokumente" bilden Teil eines „Museums ohne Mauern", um André Malrauxs berühmte Idee eines für jedermann zugänglichen Archivs zu bemühen, das auf den Technologien der Massenproduktion basiert. Das „musée imaginaire" als Nachfolger des „Ajaib Gher" oder „Wunderhaus, wie Eingeborene das Museum von Lahore Museum nennen", so der Anfang von Rudyard Kiplings Buch „Kim" (1901), das Wahrzeichen der Literatur des Imperialismus. Das entterritorialisierte Archiv oder Museum würde auch Malrauxs eigene hektische rhetorische Schnörkel enthalten, die seine Erinnerungen an seinen Besuch des Subkontinents in den späten 1950ern prägen, aufgezeichnet in seinen „Anti-Memoirs" (1968). Ebenso enthielten sie die gelehrten Schriften von Heinrich Zimmer, Alain Danielou, Mircea Eliade, Octavio Paz und die lichterfüllten Seiten, die Claude Levi-Strauss in „Tristes Tropiques" Indien widmet, seinem Meisterwerk der Autobiographie als Anti-Reisebuch, das als unübertreffliche Klage um verlorene Zivilisationen angesehen werden muss.

Deepak Ananth
Kunsthistoriker, Kritiker, freiberuflicher Kurator mit Sitz in Paris
Ananth studierte am Courtauld Institute of Art, University of London. Momentan unterrichtet er an der École régionale des Beaux-Arts in Caen. Zu den von ihm kuratierten Projekten zählen Ausstellungen zeitgenössischer französischer Kunst („Thresholds", 1995), französischer Malerei des 19. Jahrhunderts („Histoires Parallèles", 1995–96), surrealistischer Kunst („Surrealismo", 2001) und zeitgenössischer indischer Kunst („Indian Summer", 2005; „L'Inde dans Tous les Sens" 2006; „Passages", 2006; „Prospects", 2007; „The Home and the World", 2008). Er hat Beiträge über eine Reihe moderner und zeitgenössischer europäischer und indischer Künstler vor allem für Museumspublikationen geschrieben. Darunter Essays über Matisse, Picasso, Bonnard, Vuillard, Howard Hodgkin, Sarkis, Anish Kapoor, Amrita Sher-Gil, Vivan Sundaram, Mrinalini Mukherjee, Jitish Kallat, Dayanita Singh, Raghubir Singh und N. S. Harsha. Er war Auswahljuror für den Artes Mundi Prize 2006.

WERKVERZEICHINS I LIST OF WORKS

WERKE IN DER AUSSTELLUNG I EXHIBITED WORKS

A. BALASUBRAMANIAM

Shell As Body, 2007
Fiberglass, Holz und Acryl / fibreglass, wood and acrylic
45.7 x 53.3 x 20.3 cm
Courtesy Talwar Gallery, New York / New Delhi
S. / p. 41, 43

Hidden Sight, 2007
Fiberglass, Holz und Acryl / fibreglass, wood and acrylic
57.9 x 52.1 x 7.6 cm
Courtesy Talwar Gallery, New York / New Delhi
S. / p. 42

Kaayam, 2008
Fiberglassguss / fibreglass cast
Dimensionen varbiabel / dimensions variable
Courtesy Talwar Gallery, New York / New Delhi
S. / p. 44/45

SARNATH BANERJEE

NANO, 2008
Conté auf Papier /conté on paper
Je / each 70 x 50 cm
Collection of the Artist
S. / p. 53

Tito Years, 2008
Stift, Bleistift, Wasserfarbe und Foto auf Papier, Inkjet Print, Farbe auf Gewebeschuhe und zwei Monitore / pen, pencil, watercolour and photograph on paper, inkjet print, paint on canvas shoes and two monitors
Dimensionen variable / dimension variable
Sarnath Banerjee, personal collection
S. / p. 50, 51

Colonel's Brain, 2008
Aquarelle und Bleistift auf Papier / watercolour and pencil on paper
Je / each 21 x 15 cm
Collection of the Artist
S. / p. 48, 49

KRISHNARAJ CHONAT

The Coracle, 2008
Stahl, Fiberglass, Kunstharzguss, Holz / steel, fibreglass, acrylic casting resin, wood
Top: 154 x 154 x 183 cm, Basin:183 cm, 80 x ø,
Courtesy Collection of the artist
S. / p. 55, 56

NIKHIL CHOPRA

Yog Raj Chitrakar and Tokyo, 2008
Opening Perfomance at Mori Art Museum, Tokyo
Diashow / slide show
S. / p. 63–65

ATUL DODIYA

Pringle Mala from Saptapadi: Scenes from Marriage (Regardless), 2003–06
Email und Kunstlack auf Laminat / enamel and synthetic varnish on laminate
183 x 122 cm
Courtesy Bodhi Art, Mumbai
S. / p. 75

Shri Jivan Chaya of Gandhi Nagar from Saptapadi: Scenes from Marriage (Regardless), 2003–06
Email und Kunstlack auf Laminat /
enamel and synthetic varnish on laminate
183 x 122 cm
Courtesy Collection of Preethi Krishna
S. / p. 77

Charu from Saptapadi: Scenes from Marriage (Regardless), 2004–06
Email und Kunstlack auf Laminat /
enamel and synthetic varnish on laminate
183 x 122 cm
Courtesy Vadehra Art Gallery, New Delhi
S. / p. 71

Karuna from Saptapadi: Scenes from Marriage (Regardless), 2004–06
Email und Kunstlack auf Laminat /
enamel and synthetic varnish on laminate
183 x 122 cm
Courtesy Vadehra Art Gallery, New Delhi

Bloodline from Saptapadi: Scenes from Marriage (Regardless), 2004–06
Email und Kunstlack auf Laminat /
enamel and synthetic varnish on laminate
183 x 122 cm
Courtesy Vadehra Art Gallery, New Delhi
S. / p. 72

Devi and the Sink from Saptapadi: Scenes from Marriage (Regardless), 2004–06
Email, Kunstlack und Acryl-Epoxid auf Laminat /
enamel, synthetic varnish and acrylic epoxy on laminate
183 x 122 cm
Courtesy Mr. & Mrs. Drake-Brockman
S. / p. 73

Family Tree from Saptapadi: Scenes from Marriage (Regardless), 2006
Email und Kunstlack auf Laminat /
enamel and synthetic varnish on laminate
183 x 122 cm
Courtesy Vadehra Art Gallery, New Delhi
S. / p. 76

SHILPA GUPTA

Untitled (Shadow #3), 2007
Interaktive Video Installation /
interactive video installation
Dimensionen variable / dimensions variable
Courtesy the artist
S. / p. 80, 81

100 Hand Drawn Maps of India, 2007–08
Video Projektion / single-channel video projection, 3'45"
Courtesy the artist
S. / p. 82

Tryst with Destiny, 2007–08
Mikrophon, Mikrophonständer mit eingebauten Lautsprächern / microphone, microphone stand with built-in speaker
Courtesy the artist
S. / p. 82, 83

Memory, 2007–09
Standortspezifische, temporäre Installation /
temporary wall with the word "MEMORY" cut out, site-specific installation
S. / p. 82, 83

SUBODH GUPTA

OK Mili, 2005
Edelstahl Utensilien, Armartur, CD-Rom /
stainless steel utensils, armature, CD-ROM
Dimensions variable
Edition von / of 2
Courtesy Ranbir Singh collection
S. / p. 88

Bullet, 2007
Lebensgroße Royal Enfiled, Bullet: Messing, Chrome /
life-sized Royal Enfield, bullet: brass, chrome
110 x 225 x 75 cm
Courtesy collection of the Artist
S. / p. 89

Door, 2007
Messing / brass
205.7 x 88.9 x 12.7 cm
Courtesy collection of the Artist
S. / p. 87

Still Steal Steel #11, 2008
Öl und Email auf Leinwand / oil and enamel on canvas
198 x 366 cm
Courtesy collection of the Artist

TUSHAR JOAG

Chronicles of UNICELL (Triptych), 2008
Verschiedene Materialien auf Papier /
mixed media on paper
Je / each 183 x 112 cm
S. / p. 96, 97

Explanatory Drawings of UNICELL Projects Introduced at Chalo! India Exhibition, 2008
Verschiedene Materialien auf Papier /
Mixed media on paper
Je / each 183 x 112 cm

UNICELL: Locomotion Course, 2008
Stickers on the floor
Dimensionen variabel / dimensions variable
S. / p. 101

C.A.S. (Commuter Attachment Systems)
Exploded View – 1
from UNICELL: C. A. S. (Commuter Attachment Systems) for Local Trains series, 2005
Fiberglass, Harz, Flusseisen / fibreglass, resin, mild steel
152.4 x 88.9 x 45.7 cm
Courtesy of the Artist and Artist Pension Trust (APT Mumbai)
S. / p. 98–100

Mumbai to Shanghai Post Box – 1
from UNICELL: Street Vendors Mimetic Scheme (S.V.M.S.) series, 2007
Fiberglass, Harz, Holz / fibreglass, resin, wood
137 x 51 x 46 cm
Vadehra Art Gallery, New Delhi
S. / p. 102

Looking for Flora (Chowpatty, Goregaon, Haji Ali, Shivaji Park)
from UNICELL: Monuments and Edifices series, 2006
Fotografie / photograph
72.4 x 96.5 cm (x4)
Collection of the Artist

UNICELL: Venice of the East, 2005/08
Karte, Briefe, Statistic / map, letters, statistics
Dimensionen variabel / dimensions variable

UNICELL: Floating Devices for the Narmada Dam Affected People, 2005–08
Ziechnungen und Fotografien in Postkartenformat / drawings and postcard-sized photographs
Dimensionen variabel / dimensions variable
S. / p. 103

ANANT JOSHI

Navel One and the Many, 2007
Multimedia Installation, Plastik Spielzeug, Edelstahl, Rasierklingen / multimedia installation, plastic toys, stainless steel, razor blades, 2 OHPs, motor, acrylic sheet, regulator
Courtesy of the Artist and Chemould Prescott Road, Mumbai
S. / p. 105–107

RANBIR KALEKA

Crossings, 2005
4 –Kanal- Videoprojektion auf Leinwand / 4-channel video projection on canvas-based screen, 15'
Shumita and Arani Bose Collection, New York
Courtesy of Bose Pacia, New York
S. / p. 111–115

JITISH KALLAT

Artist Making Local Call, 2005
Digitaldruck auf Netzvinyl / digital print on vinyl mesh
241 x 1040 cm
Courtesy collection of the Artist
S. / p. 117–119

Death of Distance, 2006
Graphit auf Fiberglass, Linsenrasterdruck / black lead on fiberglass, lenticular print,
Skulptur / sculpture: ø 161 x 10 cm
Photos: je / each 46 x 59 cm
Courtesy collection of the Artist
S. / p. 122/123

Autosaurus Tripous, 2007
Kunstharz, Farbe, Stahl, Messing / Resin, paint, steel, brass
168 x 259 x 135 cm
Collection of the Artist
S. / p. 120/121

REENA SAINI KALLAT

Synonym, 2007
Mit Acryl bemalter Gummistempel / with acrylic painted rubberstamps
Je / each 180 x 120 cm
Collection of the Artist
S. / p. 125–129

Crease / Crevice / Contour, 2008
Fotografie / photograph
Je / each 116 x 127 cm
Collection of the Artist
S. / p. 130, 131

Colostrum, 2008
Dreifärbige Aufkleber auf dem Boden / Stickers in three colours on the floor
Dimensionen variabel / dimensions variable
Courtesy collection of the artist

BHARTI KHER

The Skin Speaks a Language Not Its Own, 2006
Fiberglass und Vynil Bindis / fibreglass and vynil bindis
183 x 153 x 457 cm
Courtesy private collection, Switzerland
Cover hinten / back, S. / p. 136/137

Psychogenic Fugue, 2009
Verschieden färbige Bindis auf der Wand / Multi-colour bindis on the wall
ø 4 m
Courtesy the artist and Gallery Hauser and Wirth , London, Zurich

PRABHAVATHI MEPPAYIL

Untitled, 2007
Naturfarben und Goldblatt auf Kalkkreidenpaneel / natural pigments and gold leaf on lime gesso panel
61.8 x 61.4 x 3 cm
courtesy Mori Art Museum, Tokyo
S. / p. 139

Untitled, 2007
Naturfarben auf Kalkkreidenpaneel / natural pigments on lime gesso panel
61 x 61.5 x 2.8 cm
courtesy Mori Art Museum, Tokyo
S. / p. 141

Untitled, 2007
Naturfarben auf Kalkkreidenpaneel / natural pigments on lime gesso panel
40.9 x 45.8 x 2 cm
courtesy Mori Art Museum, Tokyo
S. / p. 140

Untitled, 2007
Naturfarben und Goldblatt auf Kalkkreidenpaneel / natural pigments and gold leaf on lime gesso panel
40.7 x 45.7 x 2 cm
courtesy Mori Art Museum, Tokyo

Untitled, 2007
Naturfarben auf Kalkkreidenpaneel / natural pigments on lime gesso panel
35.6 x 30.7 x 2 cm
courtesy Mori Art Museum, Tokyo

Untitled, 2007
Naturfarben auf Kalkkreidenpaneel / natural pigments and gold leaf on lime gesso panel
30.5 x 35.6 x 2 cm
courtesy Mori Art Museum, Tokyo

Untitled, 2007
Naturfarben auf Kalkkreidenpaneel / natural pigments and gold leaf on lime gesso panel
40 x 47.9 x 2 cm

Untitled, 2007
Naturfarben auf Kalkkreidenpaneel / natural pigments on lime gesso panel
40 x 48.2 x 2 cm
S. / p. 143

Untitled, 2008
Naturfarben und Gold auf Kalkkreidenpaneel / natural pigment and gold point on lime gesso panel
122.5 x 152.5 x 3.8 cm
S. / p. 142

Untitled, 2008
Naturfarben, und Gold auf Kalkkreidenpaneel / natural pigment, gold point and gold leaf on lime gesso panel
122.5 x 153 x 3.8 cm

PUSHPAMALA N. AND CLARE ARNI

The Native Types – Cracking the Whip (After 1970s Tamil Film Still), Bangalore 2000–04
C-Print auf Metallic-Papier / on metallic paper
70 x 57.5 cm
Courtesy of Nature Morte, New Delhi and Bose Pacia, NY
S. / p. 148

The Native Types – Returning from the Tank (After Raja Ravi Varma Oil Painting), Bangalore 2000–04
C-Print auf Metallic-Papier / on metallic paper
70 x 57.5 cm
Courtesy of Nature Morte, New Delhi and Bose Pacia, NY

The Native Types – Lakshmi (After Oleograph from Ravi Varma Press, Early 20th Century), Bangalore 2000–04
C-Print auf Metallic-Papier / on metallic paper
70 x 57.5 cm
Courtesy of Nature Morte, New Delhi and Bose Pacia, NY
Cover vorne / front, S. / p. 147

Backdrop (The Native Types – Lakshmi [After Oleograph from Ravi Varma Press, Early 20th Century]) Bangalore 2000–04
Farbe auf Stoff / paint on fabric
239.4 x 239.4 cm
Courtesy of Bose Pacia, NY

The Native Types – Flirting (After 1990's Kannada Film Still), Bangalore 2000–04
C-Print auf Metallic-Papier / on metallic paper
70 x 57.5 cm
Courtesy of Nature Morte, New Delhi and Bose Pacia, NY
S. / p. 148

The Native Types – Toda (After 19th Century British Anthropometric Photograph), Bangalore 2000–04
Gelatine Silver Print auf grobfaserigem Papier / on fiber paper
70 x 57.5 cm
Courtesy of Nature Morte, New Delhi and Bose Pacia, NY

The Native Types – Criminals (After Police Photograph, Times of India), Bangalore 2000–04
Gelatine Silver Print, harzbeschichtet / on resin coated paper
57.5 x 70 cm
Courtesy of Nature Morte, New Delhi and Bose Pacia, NY

The Native Types – Lady in Moonlight (After Raja Varma Oil Painting), Bangalore 2000–04
C-Print auf Metallic-Papier / on metallic paper
70 x 57.5 cm
Courtesy of Nature Morte, New Delhi and Bose Pacia, NY
S. / p. 146

Backdrop (The Native Types – Lady in Moonlight [After Raja Varma Oil Painting]), Bangalore 2000–04
Farbe auf Stoff / paint on fabric
239.4 x 239.4 cm
Courtesy of Bose Pacia, NY

The Native Types – Yogini (After 16th Century Deccani Miniature Painting), Bangalore 2000–04
C-Print auf Metallic-Papier / on metallic paper
70 x 57.5 cm
Courtesy of Nature Morte, New Delhi and Bose Pacia, NY

Backdrop (The Native Types – Yogini [After 16th Century Deccani Miniature Painting]), Bangalore 2000–04
Farbe auf Stoff / paint on fabric
239.4 x 239.4 cm
Courtesy of Bose Pacia, New York

The Native Types –Circus (After Famous Circus B&W Photo by Mary Ellen Mark), Bangalore 2000–04
C-Print auf Metallic-Papier / on metallic paper
57.5 x 70 cm
Courtesy of Nature Morte, New Delhi and Bose Pacia, NY

The Native Types – Our Lady of Velankanni (After Contemporary Votive Image), Bangalore 2000–04
C-Print auf Metallic-Papier / on metallic paper
70 x 57.5 cm
Courtesy of Nature Morte, New Delhi and Bose Pacia, NY
S. / p. 149

Native Women of South India: Manners and Customs, The Ethnographic Types, Bangalore 2000–04
Gelatine Silver Print, sepiafarben auf grobfaserigem Papier / sepia-toned on fiber paper
Je / each 10.2 x 15.2 cm – 22.9 x 30.5 cm
Courtesy of Nature Morte, New Delhi and Bose Pacia, NY
S. / p. 150–151

The Ethnographic Series – Props, 2002–03
Holz, Metall und Stoff / wood, metal and fabric
Courtesy of Bose Pacia, NY

Props from "The Native Types", 2002–03
Holzpaneele, Linoleum / wood panels, linoleum
Courtesy of Bose Pacia, NY

The Popular Series, 2002–03
Fotografien / photographs
Je / each 19.7 x 14 cm (~ 100 Prints)
Courtesy of Nature Morte, New Delhi and Bose Pacia, NY

N. S. HARSHA

Mother and Child, 2008
Acryl auf Leinwand und Holzstuhl / acrylic on canvas and wooden chair
Dimensionen variable / dimensions variable
Courtesy collection of the Artist
S. / p. 155

Burka, 2008
Stoff und Holzstuhl / cloth and wooden chair
Dimensionen variable / dimensions variable
Courtesy collection of the Artist
S. / p. 156

Guarded Knowledge, 2008
Fischernetz, vergoldetes Buch und Holzstuhl / Fish net, gold gilded book and wooden chair
Dimensionen variable / dimensions variable
Courtesy collection of the Artist
S. / p. 157

Guarding Hunger, 2008
Reis Sackleinen, Schwert und Holzstuhl / rice, hessian bag, sword and wooden chair
Dimensionen variable / dimensions variable
Courtesy collection of the Artist
S. / p. 158

Guarding the 24 Carrot Country, 2008
Acryl auf Leinwand, Faden und Holzstuhl / acrylic on canvas, thread and wooden chair
Dimensionen variable / dimensions variable
Courtesy collection of the Artist
S. / p. 156

Harsha History Rental Service, 2008
Holzstuhl, Kleidungsstücke, Maske, diverse gefundene Objekte / wooden chair, used cloth, costumes, mask, found objects
Dimensionen variable / dimensions variable
Courtesy collection of the Artist
S. / p. 153

My Childhood Was Very Bright, 2008
Bündeltasche, ind. Nationalflage, Metalstange und Licht / used cradle, national flag (India), metal holder and light
Dimensionen variabel / dimensions variable
Courtesy collection of the Artist
S. / p. 158

Guarding the Thorn Throne, 2008
Plastik Weltkugel, Stacheldraht und Holzstuhl / plastic globe, barbed wire and wooden chair
Dimensionen variable / dimensions variable
Courtesy collection of the Artist
S. / p. 158

Disclosing Cultural Discomfort, 2008
Holzstuhl und Fotografie / lamda print and wooden chair
Dimensionen variable / dimensions variable
Courtesy collection of the Artist
S. / p. 154

Untitled, 2008
Holzstuhl / wooden chair
248.9 x 43.2 x 40.6 cm
Courtesy collection of the Artist
S. / p. 158

JAGANNATH PANDA

An Ancestor – II, 2006
Fiberglass, Sperrholz, Stoff, Acryl, Keramikplatte, Kleber / fibreglass, plywood, fabric, acrylic, tile, glue
366 x 244 x 244 cm
Courtesy Chisel Art Pvt Ltd.
S. / p. 166/167

The Being, 2008
Acryl, Stoff, Kleber auf Leinwand / acrylic, fabric, glue on canvas
213 x 304 cm
Courtesy of Nature Morte, New Delhi
S. / p. 165

The Epic – II, 2008
Acryl, Stoff, Kleber auf Leinwand / acrylic, fabric, glue on canvas
228 x 213 cm
Courtesy of Bose Pacia, New York
S. / p. 168

JUSTIN PONMANY

3 Ranjana c.h.s Ahimsa Marg, 2006
C-Print
139.7 x 303.5 cm
Courtesy of the Artist and Bose Pacia Gallery, NY
S. / p. 175

Fear of Destiny, 2007
C-Print
Je / each 190.5 x 132 cm
Courtesy collection of the Artist
S. / p. 173

Room No.12, Zehra Chawl, Achanak Nagar, Near Shankar Mandir, 2007
C-Print
136.5 x 295.9 cm
Courtesy Arvind Vijaymohan Collection
S. / p. 174/175

ASHIM PURKAYASTHA

Found Object Object/s, 2003–08
Tinte auf Währung / Ink on currency
Courtesy collection of the Artist

Gandhi Man without Specs IX, 2003
Acryl und Tinte auf Briefmarke / acrylic and ink on postage stamps (Set von / of 100)
45.7 x 25.4 cm
Courtesy collection of the Artist

Black Gandhi / Man Without Specs XIV, 2005
Acryl und Tinte auf Briefmarke / acrylic and ink on postage stamps (Set von / of 100)
25.4 x 45.7 cm
Courtesy collection of the Artist
S. / p. 182

Gandhi Man without Specs XII, 2006
Acryl und Tinte auf Briefmarke / acrylic on postage stamps (Set von / of 100)
22.9 x 25.4 cm
Courtesy collection of the Artist
S. / p. 183

Gandhi Man without Specs XV, 2006
Acryl und Tinte auf Briefmarke / acrylic and ink on revenue stamps (Set von / of 320)
41.1 x 34.3 cm
Courtesy collection of the Artist
S. / p. 180

Speak, See, Hear – No Evil, 2006
Acryl und Tinte auf Stempelmarke / acrylic and ink on revenue stamps (Set von / of 320)
41.1 x 34.3 cm
Courtesy collection of the Artist
S. / p. 181

You Call Him Father of the Nation I Can Call Him Man without Specs, 2006
Acrylic and ink on revenue stamps (Set von / of 180)
41.1 x 34.3 cm
Collection of the Artist

Untitled, 2006
Mixed media on jute, iron and wire mesh
Installation
Courtesy collection of the Artist
S. / p. 179

RAQS MEDIA COLLECTIVE

The Euphoria Machine: Preliminary Reverse Engineering Field Laboratory, 2008
Installation
Courtesy Raqs Media Collective
S. / p. 185–187

GIGI SCARIA

Keep Delhi Clean, 2006
Acryl auf Leinwand / acrylic on canvas
183 x 183 cm
Courtesy private Collection
S. / p. 194

Option of Alternate Master Plan / City Centre, 2006
Acryl auf Leinwand / acrylic on canvas
183 x 183 cm
Courtesy collection of Siddarth and Parul Gupta, Delhi
S. / p. 193, 197

A Day with Sohail and Mariyan, 2004
Video, 17'
Courtesy of the artist
S. / p. 199

NATARAJ SHARMA

Air Show, 2008
Kupfer / copper
366 x 366 x 427 cm
Courtesy collection of the Artist
S. / p. 201–203

Measure (Air), 2008
Verschiedene Materialien / mixed media
115 x 175 cm
Courtesy collection of the Artist
S. / p. 205

Measure (Water), 2008
Verschiedene Materialien / mixed media
115 x 175 cm
Courtesy collection of the Artist
S. / p. 205

GULAMMOHAMMED SHEIKH

Kaavad: Travelling Shrine: Journeys, 2002-04
Holzkiste, faltbare Türen mit Schutz, Gouache, Kasein, Eitempera, Wasserfarbe, Inkjet Print / wooden box, folding doors with protective lamination, gouache, casein, egg tempera, watercolour, inkjet print
48 x 106 x 40 cm
Courtesy collection of the Artist
S. / p. 209

Kaavad: Travelling Shrine: Home, 2008
Raum mit faltbaren Türen und Wänden, bemalt mit Acryl, Öl und teilweise Guache, Melanin Lamination, Messingstreifen, Digitaldruck auf Papier und Vinyl / room with folding doors and 'walls' (made of boards mounted on steel structure enclosing an inner chamber) painted in acrylic, oil and partially in gouache with melamyne lamination, brass strips, digital print on paper and vinyl, electric lights and others
244 x 782 x 732 cm
Collection of the Artist

Overall coordination with technical and digital facilitation: Sukhdev Rathod
Consultation on structure: B. V. Suresh
Team of painters: Jaldip Chauhan, Nimesh Patel, Sukhdev Rathod, Harish C. H., Sidharth Pansari, Kushal Bhattacharjee, M. Siva Kumar, Chandan Kashyap, Vishal Parmar and Gulammohammed Sheikh
Fabrication of metal frames and structure: Dilip Patel, Ravi Engineering, Vadodara
Digital print on paper and vinyl and backlit box: Ilesh Vyas, Lalita, Vadodara
Rahul Amin, CMD Jyoti Limited for studio facility at Abhilash Guest House, Vadodara
Photo credits for "Ark" and „Visitors of the Sky": Sukhdev Rathod, Jaldip Chauhan, Kabir Sheikh, Gulammohammed Sheikh
S. / p. 207, 208/209, 211–215

Mappamundi beyond Border, 2008
3-Kanal Video Projektion / 3-channel video projection on screen, 18'
Courtesy collection of the Artist
S. / p. 208/209

KIRAN SUBBAIAH

Suicide Note, 2006
Video, 26'
Copyleft: Kiran Subbaiah
S. / p. 217–219

VIVAN SUNDARAM

The Brief Ascension of Marian Hussain, 2005
Video Projektion / Single-channel video projection on screen, 2' 50"
Courtesy collection of the Artist
S. / p. 227

Barricade (with Two Drains), 2008
Digital Print
100 x 220 cm
Courtesy collection of the Artist
S. / p. 221

Metal Box, 2008
Digital Print
100 x 188.5 cm
Courtesy collection of the Artist
S. / p. 224/225

Master Plan, 2008
Digital Print
143.5 x 503 cm
Courtesy collection of the Artist
S. / p. 222/223

THUKRAL & TAGRA

Effugio, 2008
Verschiedene Materialien / mixed media
Dimensionen variabel / dimensions variable
Courtesy of Nature Morte, New Delhi
S. / p. 232

Dominus Aerius – Elegance, 2008
Acryl und Öl auf Leinwand / acrylic and oil on canvas
244 x 366 cm
Courtesy Taguchi Collection Tokyo
S. / p. 233, 234/235

HEMA UPADHYAY

Ladki Number One, 2001
Gouache, Arcryl, Pastell und Fotografien auf Papier / gouache, acrylic, dry pastels and photographs on paper
121.9 x 91.4 cm
Courtesy collection of Sree Goswami
S. / p. 245

Mute Migration, 2008
Altauto, Aluminium Blätter, Email, gefundene Objekte, Schiffssperrholz, Hardware / car scrap, aluminum sheets, enamel, found objects, marine ply and hardware
245 x 610 x 38.1 cm
Courtesy of Chemould Prescott Road
S. / p. 241, 242/243

ERGÄNZENDE WERKE I REFERENCE ONLY

KRISHNARAJ CHONAT

Milk and Skin, 2002
Leder, Fleece, unechte Perlen und Silicon / leather, fleece, fake pearls and silicon
110 x 85 x 55 cm
S. / p. 60

Milk and Skin, 2002
Leder, Fleece, unechte Perlen und Silicon / leather, fleece, fake pearls and silicon
110 cm x 85 x 55 cm
S. / p. 61

Private Sky, 2007
Steel, fiberglass, fake fur, plastic, automotive paint, mist machine and mirrors
203 x 127 x 156 cm
S. / p. 57

Untitled, 2007
Fake pearls and silicone on fiberglass
S. / p. 58, 59

NIKHIL CHOPRA

What Will I Do with All This Land?, 2005
S/W Fotografie, b/w photograph
58.4 x 39.3 cm
Courtesy of Chatterjee & Lal, Mumbai
S. / p. 66

The Death of Sir Raja III, 2005
Live performance at Kitab Mahal, Mumbai
S. / p. 67

Sir Raja III Visits Khowaja Press, 2007
Live performance at Khoj International Artists' Association, New Delhi
S. / p. 67

Yog Raj Chitrakar: Memory Drawing II, 2007
Live performance at Chatterjee & Lal Gallery, Mumbai
S. / p. 69

ATUL DODIYA

Adam and Eve from Saptapadi: Scenes from Marriage (Regardless), 2004–06
Email und Kunstlack auf Laminat / Email und Enamel and synthetic varnish on laminate
183 x 122 cm
Collection of Dinesh Vazirani
S. / p. 74

SHILPA GUPTA

There Is No Explosive in This – II, 2007
Interaktive Installation und Fotografien / interactive installation and photographs
S. / p. 84

There Is No Explosive in This – III, 2007
Interaktive Installation und Fotografien / interactive installation and photographs
S. / p. 84

100 Queues, 2007–08
Auf Fotografie basierende mechanische Installation / photo-based mechanical installation
15 x 335 x 10 cm
S. / p. 85

Half Windows, 2008
Fotografie, Diasec / Diasec mounted photograph
249 x 110 cm
S. / p. 79

SUBODH GUPTA

God Hungry, 2006
Edelstahl Utensilien / stainless steel utensils
Dimensions variable
S. / p. 93

Silk Road, 2007
Förderband, Edelstahl, rostfreie Utensilien / conveyor, stainless steel, rust-proof utensils
192 x 480 x 480 cm
Courtesy of In SITU Fabienne Leclerc, Paris
S. / p. 91

Dubai to Calcutta, 2006
Bronze, aluminum
105 x 68 x 85 cm
S. / p. 92

Kuwait to Delhi, 2006
Bronze, aluminum
93 x 79 x 85 cm
S. / p. 92

Still Steal Steel #2, 2008
Oil and enamel on canvas
198 x 366 cm
S. / p. 90

Still Steal Steel #3, 2008
Oil and enamel on canvas
198 x 366 cm
S. / p. 90

TUSHAR JOAG

C.A.S. (Commuter Attachment Systems) Trial-Run – a from UNICELL: C.A.S. (Commuter Attachment Systems) for Local Trains series, 2005
Acryl auf Leinwand / acrylic on canvas
232 x 152.4 cm
S. / p. 98

Locomotion Course Diagram RR
from UNICELL: Locomotion Course series, 2005
Acryl auf Leinwand / acrylic on canvas
232 x 152.4 cm
S. / p. 101

Locomotion Course Diagram LL
from UNICELL: Locomotion Course series, 2005
Acryl auf Leinwand / acrylic on canvas
232 x 152.4 cm
S. / p. 101

Shanghai Couch
from UNICELL: Street Vendors Mimetic Scheme (S.V.M.S.) Series, 2006
Verschiedene Materialien / mixed media
S. / p. 102

ANANT JOSHI

May Look Closer Than They Appear, 2008
Goldblatt, Zeitungspapier, ausgeschnittene Anzeigen / gold leaf, newspaper, advertisement cutting
120 x 720 cm
S. / p. 108–109

BHARTI KHER

Supernova, 2007
Bindis auf bemaltem Brett / bindis on painted board
S. / p. 133, 134/135

N. S. HARSHA

Cosmic Orphans, 2006
Wandmalerei / emulsion wall paint
Ortspeziefische Malerei / site specific painting at Sri Krishna Temple, Singapore Biennale 2006
S. / p. 159

Please Come Give Us a Speech, 2008
Acryl auf Leinwand / acrylic on canvas
182 x 1097cm
S. / p. 160, 161

Ambition and Dreams, 2005
project designed for TVS school Tumkur
S. / p. 163

Future, 2007
Workshop at Deng Kang Elementary School, Danshui, Taiwan
S. / p. 162

JAGANNATH PANDA

Water – 05, 2005
Acryl auf Leinwand / acrylic on canvas
183 x 122 cm
Courtesy of Nature Morte, New Delhi and Bose Pacia, New York
S. / p. 169

The Feral Sphere, 2007
Fiberglass, Stoff, Kleber, Acyrl / fibreglass, fabric, glue, acrylic
152.4 x 152.4 x 152.4 cm
Courtesy of Nature Morte, New Delhi and Bose Pacia, New York
S. / p. 171

Ravana, 2005
Acryl auf Leinwand / acrylic on canvas
183 x 244 cm
Courtesy of Nature Morte, New Delhi and Bose Pacia, NY
S. / p. 170

JUSTIN PONMANY

Kolkani Baugh, Room No. 2, Salma Manzil, Doodj Naka, 2007
C-print
139.7 x 224.8 cm
Courtesy of Bose Pacia Gallery, New York
S. / p. 176

1-b Indraneel Bldg, RDP 1/38, Sector 2, Charkop, 2007
C-print
140.3 x 276.9 cm
Courtesy of Bose Pacia Gallery, New York
S. / p. 177

RAQS MEDIA COLLECTIVE + ATELIER BOW-WOW

Temporary Autonomous Sarai (TAS), 2003
Installation view at Walker Art Center, Minneapolis, 2003
S. / p. 190

RAQS MEDIA COLLECTIVE

A Measure of Anacoustic Reason, 2005
Installation view at The 51st Venice Biennale, 2005
S. / p. 191

The KD Vyas Correspondence Vol. 1, 2006
18 screens, 9 soundscapes, metal architecture, theromocol casing
S. / p. 188, 189

There Has Been a Change of Plan, 2006
Fotografie / photograph
S. / p. 191

GIGI SCARIA

Option of Alternate Master Plan / Court, 2006
Acryl auf Leinwand / acrylic on canvas
183 x 183 cm
Courtesy private Collection
S. / p. 195

Site Under Excavation, 2008
Acryl auf Leinwand / acrylic on canvas
183 x 183 cm
Courtesy collection of Rohit Gandhi and Rahul Khanna
S. / p. 196

NATARAJ SHARMA

Arrival (Mumbai), 2007
Öl auf Papier / oil on paper
15.2 x 25.4 cm
S. / p. 204

Arrival (Baroda), 2007
Öl auf Papier / oil on paper
15.2 x 25.4 cm
S. / p. 204

THUKRAL & TAGRA

Morpheus – 1, 2007
Öl und Acryl auf Leinwand / oil and acrylic on canvas
Courtesy of Nature Morte, New Delhi
S. / p. 239

Morpheus – 2, Morpheus – 3, 2007
Öl und Acryl auf Leinwand / oil and acrylic on canvas
Courtesy of Nature Morte, New Delhi
S. / p. 238

Phantom IX-B, 2007
Öl und Acryl auf Leinwand / oil and aclyric on canvas
182 x 367cm
Courtesy of Nature Morte, New Delhi
S. / p. 230/231

Dominus Aerius #4, 2008
Öl und Acryl auf Leinwand / oil and aclyric on canvas
244 x 366 cm
Courtesy of Nature Morte, New Delhi
S. / p. 236/237

HEMA UPADHYAY

I Have a Feeling That I Belong, 2000
Gouache, Acryl, Trockenpastel und Fotografie auf Papier / Gouache, acrylic, dry pastels and photograph on paper
91.4 x 121.9 cm
Courtesy of Chemould Prescott Road, Mumbai
S. / p. 244

Visitors, 1972 Until 1998, 2001
Gouache, Acryl, Trockenpastel und Fotografie auf Papier / Gouache, acrylic, dry pastels and photographs on paper
91.4 x 121.9 cm
Collection of Mr. Jai Danani
S. / p. 244

COPYRIGHTS & PHOTO CREDITS

COPYRIGHTS DER ABGEBILDETEN WERKE | COPYRIGHTS OF THE ILLUSTRATED WORKS:

Please refer to list of works for courtesy information.

FOTONACHWEIS DER WERKE | PHOTO CREDITS OF THE WORKS:
Art & Public – Cabinet PH, Geneva: S. / p. 92
Bartholomew/Netphotograph.com: S. / p. 137, Cover back side
Iris Dreams: S. / p. 120, 125–129, 241, 242/243
Marc Domage: S. / p. 93
Rebecca Fanuele: S. / p. 91
Shivani Gupta: S. / p. 67
Shivani Gupta & Rohan Mukerjee: S. / p. 69
GallerySKE, Bangalore: S. / p. 55
Munir Kabani: S. / p. 66
Jitish Kallat: S. / p. 117–119
Khoj International Ariststs' Association: S. / p. 67 unten / bottom
Namin Kim and You Heeyun, courtesy National Museum of Contemporary Art, Korea: S. / p. 154, 155
Manish Mehta: S. / p.210–214
Archive Mori Art Museum, Toyko: S. / p. 11, 13–18, 20–22, 25, 63–65
Monica Narula: S. / p. 191 oben / up
Michaek Strasser / TB A-21, Vienna, 2007, courtesy: Thyssen-Bornemisza Art Contemporary, Vienna: S. / p. 188
Norbert Thigulety: S. / p. 189
Osamu Watanabe, courtesy Mori Art Museum, Tokyo: S. / p. 2/3, 38/39, 44/45, 47, 56, 80, 81, 82/83, 88, 95, 107, 114, 115, 122/123, 145, 153, 156, 157, 158, 166/167, 179, 185, 186/187, 201, 203, 207, 208/209, 215, 229, 232, 233, 246/247

FOTONACHWEIS DER KÜNSTLERPORTRAITS | PHOTO CREDITS OF ARTIST PORTRAITS
If not mentioned otherwise: courtesy the artist

Akshay Abhishek M.: S. / p. 138
Jason Alden; Subodh Gupta at the Serpentine Gallery, London, Exhbition : "Indian Highway"
10th Dec 2008 - 22nd February 2009: S. / p. 86
Rana Dasgupta: S. / p. 184
© Ajay Dodiya & Pankaj Liya, courtesy Atul Dodiya: S. / p. 70
Shrutti Garg: S. / p. 78
Shilpa Gupta: S. / p. 104
Tushar Joag: S. / p. 94
Jitish Kallat: S. / p. 124
Reena Saini Kallat: S. / p. 116
Dave Lewis: S. / p. 192
Courtesy Nature Morte Gallery, Mumbai: S. / p. 172
Barry Mowatt, Vancouver - March 09: S. / p. 228
Pranati Panda: S. / p. 164
Kabir Sheikh: S. / p. 206
Guillaume Ziccarelli, courtesy Galerie Emmanuel Perrotin: S. / p. 132

Yogini C-2 of "The Process Series" from "Native Women of South India: Manners and Customs"
by Pushpamala N. and Clare Arni, 2000–2004: S. / p. 144

IMPRESSUM I IMPRINT

CHALO! INDIA
EINE NEUE ÄRA INDISCHER KUNST
A NEW ERA OF INDIAN ART

ESSL MUSEUM
KUNST DER GEGENWART
AN DER DONAU-AU 1
A-3400 KLOSTERNEUBURG / WIEN

T:+43 (0)2243 37050-150
F:+43 (0)2243 37050-22
INFO@ESSL.MUSEUM
WWW.ESSL.MUSEUM

AUSSTELLUNG / EXHIBITION
Kurator / Curated by Akiko Miki **Ausstellungsorganisation / Exhibition organized by** Günther Oberhollenzer **Organisatorische Assistenz / Organizational assistance** Anna Szöke **Öffentlichkeitsarbeit / Public relations** Nina Auinger, Regina Holler-Strobl, Anna Fras **Marketing** Sonja Sagan, Lisa Grünwald, Katharina Unger, Nadine Giron **Ausstellungslogistik / Exhibition logistics** Leone Strizik, Bernhard Gollner **Aufbau-Technik / Exhibition installation** Ronald Gollner, Clemens Drabek, Andreas Rottenschlager, Budislav Ilic, Alexander Plenk, Stefan Schuster **Besonderer Dank an / special thanks to** DP-art, Brixen (Südtirol/Italien) **Restauratorische Betreuung / In charge of conservation** Ute Kannengießer, Magdalena Duftner, Melanie Nief, Anna Biber **Office Management** Andrea Wintoniak **Kunstvermittlung / Educational program** Karin Altmann, Lucie Binder-Sabha, Andreas Hoffer, Mela Maresch, Maria-Theresia Moritz, Adelheid Sonderegger, Anton Sutterlüty

MORI ART MUSEUM FÜR DIE AUSSTELLUNGSTOUR / FOR THE EXHIBITION TOUR
Ausstellungsdesign / Exhibition Design Naotake Maeda **Tour registrar** Miho Tagomori **Koordination / Coordination** Tomoko Kuroiwa, Kayo Machino, Sachiko Nishimaki, Takahide Tsuchiya, Mimi Nakajima, Hitomi Sasaki

KATALOG / CATALOGUE
Katalogredaktion / Editorial staff Günther Oberhollenzer, Anna Szöke **Archives & Copyrights** Ines Ratz, Eva Köhler, Renate Claudi, Andreas Bach, Sylvia Winkelmayer **Grafik / Graphic design** Elisabeth Hartmann **Druck / Printer** Stiepan Druck G.m.b.H, Leobersdorf **Autoren / Authors** Karlheinz Essl, Fumio Nanjo, Akiko Miki, Deepak Ananth, Peter Nagy, Sabine B. Vogel **Texte zu den Künstlern / texts about the artists** Tomoko Kuroiwa (TK), Akiko Miki (AM), Kayo Machino (KM), Sachiko Nishimaki (SN), Miho Tagomori (MT) **Lektorat / Proof reading** Anna Fras, Silvia Köpf, Pia Praska, Anna Szöke **Übersetzung / Translation** Susanne Watzek, Erika Obermayer

Prestel Verlag
Königinstraße 9
80539 München
Tel. +49 (0)89 24 29 08-300
Fax +49 (0)89 24 29 08-335
www.prestel.de

Prestel Publishing Ltd.
4 Bloomsbury Place
London WC1A 2QA
Tel. +44 (0)20 7323-5004
Fax +44 (0)20 7636-8004

Prestel Publishing
900 Broadway, Suite 603
New York, N.Y. 10003
Tel. +1 (212) 995-2720
Fax +1 (212) 995-2733
www.prestel.com

Prestel books are available worldwide. Please contact your nearest bookseller or one of the above addresses for information concerning your local distributor.

Die Deutsche Nationalbibliothek verzeichnet diese Publikation in der Deutschen Nationalbibliografie; detaillierte bibliografische Daten sind im Internet über http://dnb.ddb.de abrufbar.

ISBN 978-3-7913-4304-4

Dieser Katalog erscheint anlässlich der Ausstellung /
This catalogue is published on the occasion of the exhibition
CHALO! INDIA. Eine neue Ära indischer Kunst / A New Era of Indian Art
02.09.09 – 01.11.09

>CHALO! INDIA. Eine neue Ära indischer Kunst< wurde ursprünglich vom Mori Art Museum in Tokyo organisiert.
>CHALO! INDIA. A New Era of Indian Art< is originally organized by Mori Art Museum, Tokyo.

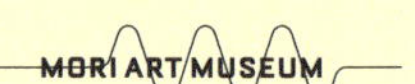

"Enter India, upstage, facing the audience, into

the age of 'opar di gurgur di aneksi di be-dhyana di mung di daal af di Pakistan aind Hindustan af di dar ftte munh...'"

Rehan Ansari, Journalist

Note: A quotation from Toba Tek Singh, a representative story by the Urdu short-story writer Saadat Hasan Manto. The title is the name of an actual town in Pakistan's Panjab Province. The work is considered a masterpiece of writing about the tragic partition of India and Pakistan in 1947. The story deals with Bishan Singh, a mentally ill man from Toba Tek Singh held in a concentration camp in Lahore, Pakistan, who is forcibly sent to India. The words quoted here are the words mumbled by Bishan Singh, driven temporarily mad on learning of his fate.

"Enter India, upstage, facing the audience, into

the age of options;
India is a creature of n-dimensional proportions, a character too large for this stage, and each member of the audience sees a different facet and wonders if they will ever know this behemoth, lumbering toddler-like with no apparent direction, but clearly going somewhere."

Samit Basu, Speculative Fiction Writer

"Enter India, upstage, facing the audience, into

the age of
plenty,
dearth,
surveillance,
disguise,
misrecognition."

Nivedita Menon, Political Philosopher

"Enter India, upstage, facing the audience, into

the age of a dreamy strangeness."

Veena Das, Anthropologist

"Enter India, upstage, facing the audience, into

the age of an 'encounter between modernity and tradition, between caste and capitalism."

Chandrabhan, Political Columnist

"Enter India, upstage, facing the audience, into

the age of despair.
India looks at the sea of male heads in front of her and thinks, we've been battling for millenia and the buggers still haven't learnt to respect us. She turns to her aide, Kali, and says, Sister, I think it's time to lop their heads off. Anyway, your necklace looks like it needs renewing."

Urvashi Butalia, Publisher / Writer

"Enter India, upstage, facing the audience, into

the age of belligerence, dementia and hedonism."

Aijaz Hussain, Journalist

"Enter India, upstage, facing the audience, into

the age of confluence where distinct and contradictory Times (histories, production modes and people) live out the ordinary, the everyday simultaneously in Space; and thus, perforce, etch out the contemporary either through selection and exclusion or in the imagination (memory and future)."

Gargi Sen, Documentary Filmmaker

"Enter India, upstage, facing the audience, into

the age of
feet-less fatigue,
to the sound of bodyless panting, panting..."

J. Devika, Historian

"Enter India, upstage, facing the audience, into

the age of air conditioned abnegation."

Mahmood Farooqui, Historian / Actor

"Enter India, upstage, facing the audience, into

the age of Kali™."

Rana Dasgupta, Writer

Note: According to Hindu teaching, the world goes through a cycle of four ages (yuga), endlessly repeated. The fourth of these ages, Kali-yuga, corresponds to what is called the last age in Buddhism. It is said that the present age is Kali-yuga, characterized by strife, suffering, social uncertainty, and mired in corruption. In the text here the word Kali has the Trade Mark symbol attached to it, suggesting property and ownership rights and symbolizing our capitalist society.

"Enter India, upstage, facing the audience, into

the age of new mythologies...
India has just awoken from a seemingly long sleep, and is still getting used to the bright lights and loud noise. There are flashes of a dream that it had of waking up after a seemingly long sleep, but it cant recall much else and smiles emptily..."

Lawrence Liang, Legal Scholar

"Enter India, upstage, facing the audience, into

the age of
uncertainty
as never seen before."

Inder Salim, Performance Artist